THE BIG BOOK OF CATHOLIC ANSWERS

VOLUME 1: **THE OBJECT OF OUR FAITH**

THE BIG BOOK OF CATHOLIC ANSWERS

VOLUME 1: **THE OBJECT OF OUR FAITH**

Published by Catholic Answers, Inc.
2020 Gillespie Way
El Cajon, California 92020
1-888-291-8000 orders
619-387-0042 fax
catholic.com

Printed in the United States of America

Cover and interior design by Maria L.T. Bowman

978-1-68357-365-4
978-1-68357-366-1 Kindle
978-1-68357-367-8 ePub

CONTENTS

PART 2—DIVINE REVELATION

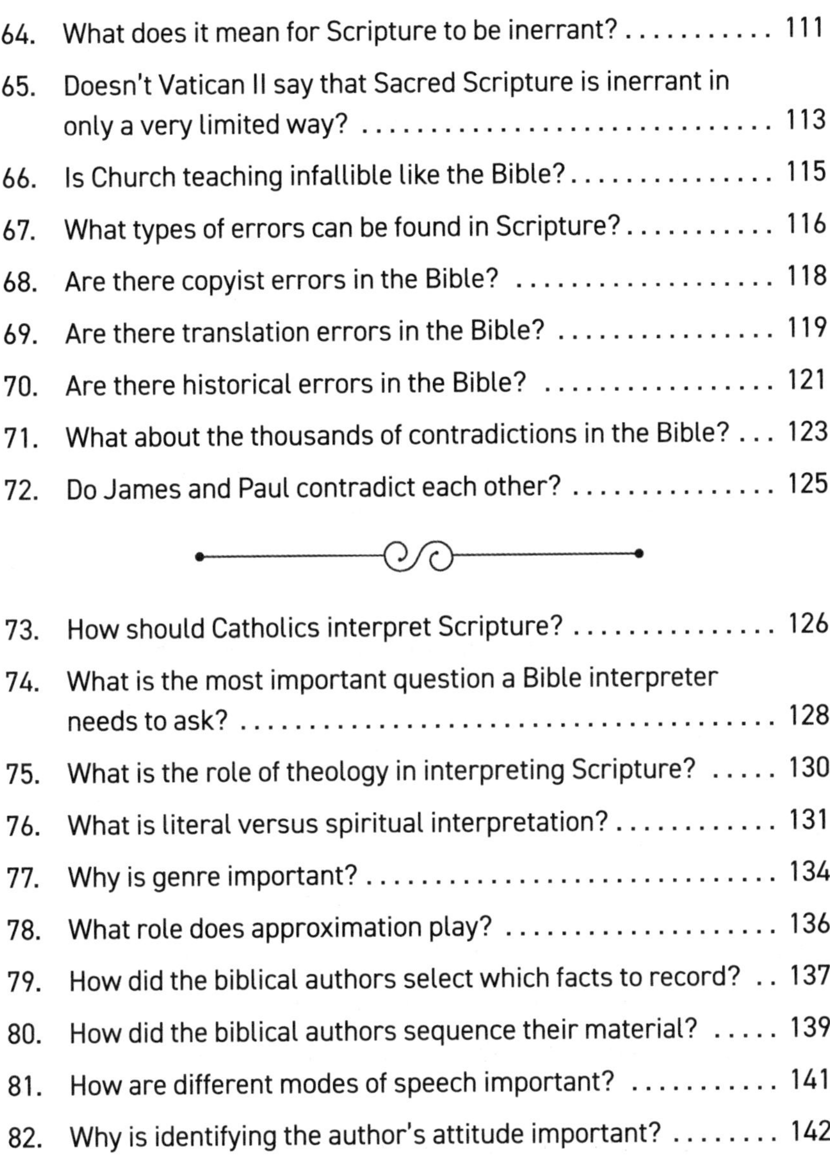

PART 3—THE BOOKS OF THE BIBLE

PART 4—THE CHRISTIAN MYSTERY

EDITOR'S INTRODUCTION

The parlor game "Twenty Questions" was already past its heyday when I was a child, so there was reason to doubt, when Catholic Answers kicked off its *20 Answers* booklet series a decade ago, whether many readers would note the reference. Either way, those booklets have been a success—with over a million copies read, shared, given away to doubters and seekers, translated and published abroad, and repeatedly re-thumbed for a needed refresher on some truth of the Faith.

Good philosophy tells us that by nature humans seek the truth. Our minds are inquisitive. And the questions to which we most ardently seek answers are those related to the highest, the deepest, the eternally consequential things.

In our age, though, giving such answers has become bad manners. If one answer is true, its contrary must be false; this annoys relativists. Answers that invoke metaphysics or theology can't be proven in a laboratory; empiricists find this intolerable. To say that our God is the one God and there are no other gods apart from him . . . well, that's just not *nice*.

To come bearing answers, then—to come bearing *Catholic* answers—puts us immediately under an eye of suspicion. And yet, be ready with answers we must; we are the light of the world.

It's because of this conundrum that I find the content of the *20 Answers* series, and this first of three omnibus volumes that draw from it, so extraordinary. Whatever kinds of pat or rote or angry or dimwitted or triumphalistic answers that skeptics might variously expect to find here, they will not find. Neither will they be bored or beaten down with academic doubletalk. Instead, each answer is a small, crisp, crystal-clear nugget of truth, held up with love for the reader to inspect and engage.

Taken individually, these answers correct, sharpen, and edify us on Catholic matters; taken together, they're an apologetical and catechetical gold mine. We hope this volume and the two to follow will be instruments of saving knowledge and occasions of grace for you, your loved ones, and anyone in the world toward whom you shine your light.

A Big Book needs a big team behind it, and this team deserves to be acknowledged. First, the *20 Answers* authors: Jimmy Akin, Fr. Hugh Barbour, Andrew Bieszad, Jim Blackburn, Karlo Broussard, Mark Brumley, Fr. Daniel Dozier, Fr. Mike Driscoll, Matt Fradd, Joe Heschmeyer. Trent Horn, Christopher Kaczor, Shaun McAfee. Tom Nash, Jason Negri, Matt Nelson, Michael O'Neill. Tim Staples, Stacy Trasancos, Kevin Vost †, Fr. Sebastian Walshe, Steve Weidenkopf, and yours truly.

Special thanks are also due to Laura Yanikoski, who handled with cool aplomb the massive task of dicing, organizing, and recombining almost a million words of text; to designer Maria Bowman; and to Catholic Answers production manager Erik Gustafson, the many-armed switchboard operator who keeps all the parties connected.

Todd Aglialoro
Director of Publishing
Catholic Answers Press

PART 1

FAITH AND REASON

INTRODUCTION

There is a modern myth that faith and reason are locked in a centuries-old and intractable battle. We must choose: either faith or reason. Either we embrace spirituality, revelation, and a life of loving God and neighbor, or we embrace reason, science, and a life based on reality.

This way of thinking about faith and reason is embraced by two groups of people that otherwise disagree about almost everything. The first group includes many Protestant Fundamentalists who embrace faith and reject reason. They are suspicious of science and hostile to philosophy, and think that faith alone and the Bible alone settle every significant issue. The second group is made up of the New Atheist types who claim that embracing reason, science, and logic means we must reject the existence of God, the trustworthiness of Jesus, and the work of God in the Church.

These two groups—quite loud in our society though not great in number—debate as if it were obvious and indisputable that faith and reason are old enemies. We must choose, they think, between the two, and never can faith and reason be reconciled.

But this is not the Catholic approach, as we will see in the following questions.

1. What is Christian faith?

In general, *faith* can be understood as the acceptance of something as true based on the trustworthiness of the one revealing it. Any kind of deep friendship requires a trust between friends. Otherwise, the relationship will remain superficial, without any deep intimacy and communication of what is most important to both. In true friendship, each person speaks from the heart, revealing what is of deep significance. To accept as true what a friend says involves having human faith in our friend's trustworthiness and honesty.

Christian faith is in some ways like human faith. If we have faith in Christ, we accept as true what he reveals about himself. If you had met Jesus while he was walking on the earth, you could have known for yourself certain truths about him, such as his height, his weight, and the sound of his voice. If you heard Jesus say to you, "The Father and I are one" or "Whoever has seen me has seen the Father," you would have the choice whether or not to accept what Jesus says as true. The person with Christian faith views Jesus as an honest and trustworthy person, and therefore accepts what Jesus says as true.

In a similar way, if you view your friend as an honest and trustworthy person, you would probably accept as true what your friend tells you about himself.

But Christian faith is unlike human faith in some respects. Since it is, according to the *Catechism of the Catholic Church* (CCC), "adherence to God and assent to his truth, Christian faith differs from our faith in any human person. It is right and just to entrust oneself wholly to God and to believe absolutely what he says. It would be futile and false to place such faith in a creature" (150). As Christ differs from the average human being, so Christian faith differs from human faith. An average man could be a liar trying to manipulate you or could be honestly mistaken about something that he tells you. Most human beings are not maximally trustworthy.

If the Christian God exists, then there is an all-knowing, all-good, all-loving, and all-powerful Creator. An all-knowing God cannot be ignorant or mistaken about anything past, present, or future. If God is perfectly good and loving, then all his actions reflect perfect goodness and infinite love. A perfectly loving and good God does not do evil actions such as lying and manipulating. So what such a God reveals deserves our *maximal* trust. This is Christian faith.

2. What is reason?

When we speak about *reason*, we mean uses of the human mind to seek and to understand the truth. We can use our reason in academic disciplines such as psychology, mathematics, and history. Reason is also exercised in producing various technologies and in living life wisely.

Two uses of human reason are especially important when considering the relationship between faith and reason. One is found in *science*, in which people use the method of empirical verification to determine whether or not some hypothesis is true. Another is found in *philosophy*, in which people seek wisdom by defining terms, assessing the truth of propositions, and making arguments to establish conclusions.

Some people think that the Church opposes reason, at least as used in science and philosophy. But when we look at what the Church teaches about both science and philosophy, we discover that just the opposite is true. The Church does not oppose science,[1] but for centuries has supported it. Every Catholic university in the world has departments of science. The Pontifical Academy of Science supports scientific research and gatherings of scientists each year within the walls of the Vatican. The Church proclaimed

St. Albert the Great—a medieval pioneer of natural science—the patron saint of scientists.

And Catholics have contributed some of the most significant scientific discoveries of all time. For example, a Catholic priest named Georges Lemaître is known as the father of the Big Bang theory because, using equations from Albert Einstein, he convinced the scientific world that the entire universe (all space, all time, and all matter) arose from a single point. Catholic Alexander Flemming invented penicillin. Gregor Mendel, an Augustinian priest, founded modern genetics. Another Catholic, Louis Pasteur, founded microbiology and created the first vaccine for rabies and anthrax. Nicolas Copernicus, another Catholic cleric, first proposed that the earth revolved around the sun. The list is long of Catholics, indeed many priests and especially Jesuits, who contributed to the development of science.

And what about philosophy? When some people think of philosophy, they think of a college course, the content of which may be pretty remote from the concerns of everyday life. But philosophy is for everyone, and one of the great gifts Pope St. John Paul II left the Church was a reminder of that. We may not be aware of it, but as reasoning human beings we engage in philosophy every day. For example, each of us has some standard by which we judge whether a statement is true or false—this is *epistemology*. Each of us has some standard by which we judge whether an action is right or wrong—this is *moral philosophy*. Each of us has some view about what really exists in reality—this is *philosophy of nature* and *metaphysics*.

Every human being is, in some sense, a philosopher. In his great encyclical on faith and reason, Pope St. John Paul II noted that everyone explicitly or implicitly asks,

> Who am I? Where did I come from and where am I going? Why is there evil? What is there after this life? . . . They are questions that have their common source in the quest for meaning that has always compelled the human heart. In fact, the answer given to these questions decides the direction that people seek to give to their lives (*Fides et Ratio* 1).

Does the Church oppose reason as it is used in philosophy? On the contrary, John Paul II, who was himself a professor of philosophy, continued, "The Church cannot but set great value upon reason's drive to attain goals that render people's lives ever more worthy. It sees in philosophy the way to come to know fundamental truths about human life. At the same time, the Church considers philosophy an indispensable help for a deeper understanding of faith and for communicating the truth of the gospel to those who do not yet know it" (*Fides et Ratio* 5).

For this reason, the Church has produced some of the most important philosophers of all time, including St. Augustine, St. Thomas Aquinas, and Descartes. In our own time, Catholic professors teach at some of the most prestigious universities in the world. Catholic universities require all their students to study philosophy. The Church does not oppose the use of reason in science or in philosophy or in any other realm, but rather encourages and celebrates it.

3. Is it irrational to believe without evidence?

A conflict between faith and reason arises only when people use incorrect definitions of these terms. It is true that reason involves the use of the mind to make sense of the world and justify the beliefs we think are true, whereas faith is belief in things unseen. As St. Paul wrote, "We walk by faith, not by sight" (2 Cor. 5:6).

However, faith is not "believing without evidence" or "belief in the absence of evidence" or "believing despite evidence." Rather, it is defined as "evidence of things not seen" (Heb. 11:1, NABRE). St. Thomas explains this unusual use of the word *evidence* in the following way:

> Evidence induces the intellect to adhere to a truth, wherefore the firm adhesion of the intellect to the non-apparent truth of faith is called *evidence* here.
>
> In this way faith is distinguished from all other things pertaining to the intellect. For when we describe it as *evidence*, we distinguish it from opinion, suspicion, and doubt, which do not make the intellect adhere to anything firmly; when we go on to say, *of things that appear not*, we distinguish it from science and understanding, the object of which is something apparent.[2]

Faith gives us "evidence" of what is not immediately apparent to our limited intellect, on the ground that it is *evident* to the one who reveals it to us.[3] The *Catechism* defines faith in this way:

> Faith is the theological virtue by which we believe in God and believe all that he has said and revealed to us (1814).

> What moves us to believe is not the fact that revealed truths appear as true and intelligible in the light of our natural reason: we believe "because of the authority of God himself who reveals them, who can neither deceive nor be deceived" (156).

This doesn't mean that theists have no rational ground to stand on. Reason alone is enough to show us God exists, without supernatural faith. Even the Bible reminds us that we can discern God's existence from the natural world, without any supernatural revelation: "For from the greatness and beauty of created things comes a corresponding perception of their Creator" (Wis. 13:4–5). St. Paul himself wrote that God's nature "has been clearly perceived in the things that have been made" (Rom. 1:19-20). Thus, the *Catechism* summarizes:

> The world, and man, attest that they contain within themselves neither their first principle nor their final end, but rather that they participate in Being itself, which alone is without origin or end. Thus, in different ways, man can come to know that there exists a reality which is the First Cause and final end of all things, a reality "that everyone calls God" (34).

So, although it is true that not everything that is an object of faith can be proved by the light of natural reason (that is why it is faith!), faith is not thereby unreasonable or irrational. It is not unreasonable or irrational to rely upon the informed opinion of a trustworthy and competent source, when our own knowledge does not suffice on any given matter. We do this daily in our human lives. Why should it be irrational to do so when it comes to matters of faith? It would be irrational only if we placed our confidence in any and every opinion, without any effort to verify that source's credibility.

For example, by reason you know that a plane is capable of flying, but you have "faith"—that is, belief that cannot be proven directly—that any particular plane is able to fly. You trust—but you don't *absolutely know*—that the plane is maintained properly and the pilot is actually a pilot. Now, with some diligence you could corroborate these beliefs, but there are other beliefs that we must simply accept with faith-like trust. These include the belief that the laws of physics will not change suddenly mid-flight, causing the plane to crash. Such a belief cannot be proven but must simply be assumed.

So when St. Paul writes that "we walk by faith, not by sight," he doesn't mean that we should blindly accept anything as true. He also doesn't mean that we can't have a natural, rational knowledge of God, or that this knowledge can't inform and ground the beliefs that we hold by faith. (The Catholic Church even teaches as dogma that God can be known with certainty of human reason.) What Paul means, rather, is that in this life we are called to walk in confident expectation of what God has promised us and that we are not to become discouraged by trials.

4. Do faith and reason contradict each other?

Both the truths of faith and truths of reason come ultimately from God, who is the truth. The *Catechism,* citing the first and second Vatican Councils, puts the point as follows:

> Though faith is above reason, there can never be any real discrepancy between faith and reason. Since the same God who reveals mysteries and infuses faith has bestowed the light of reason on the human mind, God cannot deny himself, nor can truth ever contradict truth.
>
> Consequently, methodical research in all branches of knowledge, provided it is carried out in a truly scientific manner and does not override moral laws, can never conflict with the faith, because the things of the world and the things of faith derive from the same God. The humble and persevering investigator of the secrets of nature is being led, as it were, by the hand of God in spite of himself, for it is God, the conserver of all things, who made them what they are (159).

Faith and reason are compatible because both faith and reason ultimately come from God. God is the author of two books—the book of creation and the book of revelation. Whatever is in creation, including chemistry, physics, biology, and sociology, arises ultimately from God, who is the First Cause. Whatever is in revelation—the identity of Jesus as true God and true man, the sacraments, and the nature of God as Father, Son, and Holy

Spirit—arises from God. God does not contradict himself, so what we can learn from creation does not contradict what we learn from revelation.

But why couldn't God contradict himself? God cannot contradict himself for the same reason God cannot commit suicide. God cannot commit suicide because he is eternal, having perfect possession of life without beginning and without end. God is not composed of body and soul, such that he could begin to decompose. That God cannot kill himself is part of divine perfection. Likewise, that God cannot contradict himself is part of divine perfection. God's knowledge is perfect, unerring, and utterly complete. Moreover, God is not composed of a mind having different parts that could be in contradiction. So God cannot be intellectually mistaken and self-contradictory. If God cannot contradict himself, then what God provides in revelation cannot contradict what God provides in creation.

Of course, there can be *apparent* contradictions between faith and reason. For example, maybe a theologian misinterprets Scripture, and on the basis of this misinterpretation it seems that science and faith are in conflict. A famous example of this is when some theologians misunderstood Scripture as asserting that the faithful must believe that the earth rather than the sun was at the center of our solar system.

We know very well that the earth revolves around the sun, and we are not denying this if we say, "The sun is setting tonight at 7:35 p.m." It would be both obnoxious and beside the point for someone to reply, "No, you should say, 'The earth is rotating, making it the case that at 7:35 from our location the sun will no longer be visible.'" Hundreds of years ago, some theologians mistakenly took colloquial manners of speech about the sun for statements of scientific precision.

So, one way an apparent but illusory conflict between faith and reason can arise is through a misunderstanding of faith. Another way is through a misunderstanding of what is rational.

For example, in his book *An Inquiry Concerning Human Understanding*, the philosopher David Hume said,

> All the objects of human reason or enquiry may naturally be divided into two kinds, to wit, *relations of ideas* and *matters of fact*. Of the first kind are the sciences of geometry, algebra, and arithmetic, [which are] discoverable by the mere operation of thought. . . . Matters of fact, which are the second object of human reason,

> are not ascertained in the same manner; nor is our evidence of their truth, however great, of a like nature with the foregoing.[4]

From this perspective, statements are meaningful only in two cases. Either the statement must be true by definition—"The whole is greater than its parts"—or the statement must be empirically verified: "This box of chocolate weighs six ounces." Hume's principle is that we should only accept what is true by definition (relation of ideas, like mathematics) or true by empirical verification (matters of fact, like experimental science). You'll note that the statement "God exists" does not fit into either category. God is not a material object, composed of parts, so God cannot be empirically verified like a box of chocolates. Nor is it true by definition that "God exists" simply by virtue of the meaning of the word *God*. According to Hume, then, belief in God is "nothing but sophistry and illusion."

> If we take in our hand any volume; of divinity or school metaphysics, for instance; let us ask, Does it contain any abstract reasoning concerning quantity or number? No. Does it contain any experimental reasoning concerning matter of fact and existence? No. Commit it then to the flames: for it can contain nothing but sophistry and illusion.[5]

However, it turns out that Hume's principle is self-contradictory, since it is not true by definition (relation of ideas) or by empirical verification (matters of fact). Is Hume's principle simply a matter of abstract reasoning concerning quantity or number? No. It is not true by definition of words, nor is it true like a mathematic formula. Does Hume's principle contain any experimental reasoning concerning matters of fact and existence? No. It was not shown to be the case through dissecting frogs, mixing chemicals, or using Bunsen burners. So if we take Hume's advice, we should commit Hume's principle to the flames, for it can contain nothing but sophistry and illusion.

As Peter Kreeft pointed out, "If all statements that are neither mathematical nor empirical are meaningless, then that very statement (that all statements that are neither mathematical nor empirical are meaningless) is meaningless, because it is neither mathematical nor empirical."[6] Faith and reason certainly can come into apparent contradiction if either someone misunderstands faith or someone misunderstands reason, or both. But faith and reason, properly understood, are harmonious.

5. Can reason cooperate with faith?

Many people in our day see reason and faith as competing, opposite principles, often expressed now in terms of *science* versus *religion*, with the implication that you must choose one. Yet not long ago, just before the dawn of our millennium, Pope St. John Paul II wrote that "faith and reason are like two wings on which the human spirit rises to the contemplation of truth" (*Fides et Ratio*, preamble). Twelve years later, in 2010, Pope Benedict XVI proclaimed that "there is friendship between science and faith and that through their vocation to the study of nature, scientists can take an authentic and fascinating path of holiness."[7]

Benedict was pointing specifically to lessons taught by St. Albert the Great, the patron saint of scientists. And John Paul II was echoing the wisdom of Albert's greatest pupil, St. Thomas Aquinas. Indeed, in his great encyclical *Fides et Ratio* (Faith and Reason), John Paul would examine in depth Thomas's role in the proper understanding of the relationship between the two, noting, for example,

> In an age when Christian thinkers were rediscovering the treasures of ancient philosophy, and more particularly of Aristotle, Thomas had the great merit of giving pride of place to the harmony which exists between faith and reason. Both the light of reason and the light of faith come from God, he argued; hence there can be no contradiction between them.
>
> More radically, Thomas recognized that nature, philosophy's proper concern, could contribute to the understanding of divine revelation. Faith therefore has no fear of reason, but seeks it out and has trust in it. Just as grace builds on nature and brings it to fulfillment, so faith builds upon and perfects reason (43).

Albert's and Thomas's championing of science and philosophy met no small resistance during their lifetimes. Some of Thomas's critics argued that he was diluting the wine of divine wisdom with the water of human wisdom. Thomas, however, knew that there is only one truth and that the truth of the Faith could never be contradicted by reason, but that reason could help draw some people to the Faith and help clarify theological principles for the faithful. He did not believe that the philosophy of noble men diluted the Faith; rather, "those who use philosophical doctrines in Sacred

Scripture in such a way as to subject them to the service of the Faith, do not mix water with wine, but change water into wine."[8]

In reality, faith and reason don't *compete* with each other; they *complete* each other. They are not contradictory but complementary. Whether God's existence is self-evident, how his existence can be proved through reason, and what his fundamental attributes are—these are matters that can be determined by the power of reason alone (though Thomas sometimes references verses from Scripture to show how reason and revelation point to the same conclusions). Such issues are sometimes called the *preambula fidei*, the preambles of faith, the highest truths we can reach about God through philosophy and natural (reason-based) theology, and which give a firm reasonable foundation to our faith.

All the same, the essential mysteries of our faith surpass the limits of the human intellect and must be revealed to us by God. "It was necessary for the salvation of man that certain truths which exceed human reason should be made known to him by divine revelation."[9] It is through such divine revelation that we can move beyond the "god of the philosophers," the great "I AM," to "the God of Abraham, Isaac, and Jacob," and from questions like "What is God?" to questions like "Who is God?" But even for questions such as these, faith calls upon reason to properly understand what God's revelation intends.

6. Why would God reveal a truth that we can know through reason?

We read in the *Catechism* that "our holy mother, the Church, holds and teaches that God, the first principle and last end of all things, can be known with certainty from the created world by the natural light of human reason. Without this capacity, man would not be able to welcome God's revelation. Man has this capacity because he is created 'in the image of God'" (CCC 36). This teaching is found also in the First Vatican Council, in Thomas Aquinas's *Summa Theologiae*, and in many other places.

And yet, the *Catechism* tells us, "In the historical conditions in which he finds himself, man experiences many difficulties in coming to know God by the light of reason alone" (37). For example, not everyone has the intelligence to grasp the philosophical arguments of Augustine, Aquinas, Descartes, Leibniz, or Plantinga. For most of human history, the majority of people could not read at all. But God's revelation is for everyone, literate and nonliterate alike.

Moreover, for much of human history, people were struggling simply to stay alive, lacking in sufficient food and basic necessities. They had to spend most of their time working from dawn to dusk simply to go on living. Obviously, such dire conditions would make it hard, if not impossible, for the average person to curl up at night with their copy of Aquinas's *Summa Theologiae* or Descartes's *Meditations on First Philosophy*. But God's revelation is not just for the rich, who have the leisure time for study of the greatest questions in life, but for everyone.

Consider, for example, the complicated philosophical proofs and negative theological analyses regarding God's existence and attributes that lead to the conclusion that God is self-subsistent being itself, the source and font of all existence, the single, eternal being whose essence and existence are one. All this is compressed into a few words in God's book of divine revelation. When Moses asks God's name, he tells him, "I AM WHO I AM." Further, God tells Moses, "Say this to the sons of Israel, 'I AM has sent me to you.'" And further, "Say this to the sons of Israel, 'The Lord, the God of your fathers, the God of Abraham, the God of Isaac, the God of Jacob, has sent you'" (Exod. 3:14, 15).

Even for those with sufficient education and leisure, problems still remain. As the *Catechism* notes,

> There are many obstacles which prevent reason from the effective and fruitful use of this inborn faculty. For the truths that concern the relations between God and man wholly transcend the visible order of things, and, if they are translated into human action and influence it, they call for self-surrender and abnegation. The human mind, in its turn, is hampered in the attaining of such truths, not only by the impact of the senses and the imagination, but also by disordered appetites which are the consequences of original sin. So it happens that men in such matters easily persuade themselves that what they would not like to be true is false or at least doubtful (37).

The philosopher Thomas Nagel exemplifies the way in which motivated thinking can happen:

> I want atheism to be true and am made uneasy by the fact that some of the most intelligent and well-informed people I know are religious believers. It isn't just that I don't believe in God and, naturally, hope that I'm right in my belief. It's that I hope there is no God! I don't want there to be a God; I don't want the universe to be like that.[10]

Why would it matter if God existed? Nagel doesn't say. But one possibility is that if God exists, then there is an ultimate standard for right and wrong, a divine being to whom we owe our existence and who can make moral claims upon us as our Creator. Someone who wishes to evade responsibility to God will almost certainly be motivated to reject arguments for his existence, no matter what the evidence. Some parents, wishing that their son did not commit murder, will remain convinced of his innocence even in the face of overwhelming evidence. So too, someone who wishes to avoid moral responsibility to God, might willfully reject sound, valid, and compelling arguments for God's existence.

Finally, God also reveals his existence and attributes because if all we had was human reason to rely upon, we might fall into theological errors. For example, many ancient peoples recognized a divine work in creation but attributed it to multiple gods. Others have thought of the ultimate principle of reality as a combination of good and evil, like the light and the dark sides of the Force. Looking at the mixture of good and evil that exists in the world, they mistakenly reasoned to the conclusion that God must be a combination of good and evil, light and darkness.

For all these reasons, in order to give us clarity and certainty, God reveals his existence and characteristics to us, even though we can learn about these things through the natural use of our reasoning abilities.

> Even as regards those truths about God which human reason could have discovered, it was necessary that man should be taught by a divine revelation; because the truth about God such as reason could discover, would only be known by a few, and that after a long time, and with the admixture of many errors. Whereas man's whole salvation, which is in God, depends upon the knowledge of this truth. Therefore, in order that the salvation of men might be brought about more fitly and more surely, it was necessary that they should be taught divine truths by divine revelation .[11]

7. Are there truths of faith that reason cannot discover?

Some truths of faith, like God's existence or the wrongfulness of murder, are truths that any person of good will properly could discover using reason. But other truths of faith—such as that God is Father, Son, and Holy Spirit—transcend what we can know by reason.

If we had been alive 2,000 years ago, we could have seen Jesus of Nazareth with our own eyes. We could have known various truths about him, such as his height, his hair color, or his voice. But this kind of knowledge is rather superficial. To really get to know someone, to really become deep friends, requires a mutual trust. Deep friendship requires a disclosure in which the heart of each friend is revealed and accepted by the other. Friendship is deepened through shared experiences and through sharing what is most significant but often not obvious at first glance. Jesus calls his disciples not servants but friends (John 15:15), so Jesus reveals to us what we could not know on our own. What are these truths?

Jesus teaches about God as Father, Son, and Holy Spirit. Jesus teaches us that whoever eats his body and drinks his blood has eternal life. Jesus tells us that the apostles have authority to teach in his name and that he will never abandon us, but will send the Holy Spirit to lead us into the fullness of truth. These truths—the Trinity, the sacraments, the Church—go beyond what we can know simply by using our reason. These truths do not contradict reason, but they transcend reason.

To believe these truths *is* reasonable, however, because it is reasonable to trust what Jesus teaches us. The *Catechism* puts the point as follows:

> So "that the submission of our faith might nevertheless be in accordance with reason, God willed that external proofs of his revelation should be joined to the internal helps of the Holy Spirit." Thus the miracles of Christ and the saints, prophecies, the Church's growth and holiness, and her fruitfulness and stability "are the most certain signs of divine revelation, adapted to the intelligence of all"; they are "motives of credibility" (*motiva credibilitatis*), which show that the assent of faith is "by no means a blind impulse of the mind" (156).

We do not believe with "blind faith," but rather we go beyond what reason alone can show, because Jesus himself is trustworthy and reasonably believed—a fact vindicated not only by his way of life and the many miracles he performed but also, and primarily, by his resurrection from the dead.

8. What is fideism?

The Catholic ideal is the harmony between faith and reason. But we can err by an overemphasis and exaggeration of either faith or reason. One way to go wrong is to focus on faith to the exclusion of reason. This is called *fideism*, which Pope St. John Paul II understood as a failure "to recognize the importance of rational knowledge and philosophical discourse for the understanding of faith, indeed for the very possibility of belief in God" (*Fides et Ratio* 55). Fideism mistakenly thinks that all that is needed is faith—faith alone suffices—and that reason is therefore at best superfluous and at worst an enemy.

Some Christians exhibit fideism. As John Paul II continued, "One currently widespread symptom of this fideistic tendency is a 'biblicism' which tends to make the reading and exegesis of Sacred Scripture the sole criterion of truth". The sixteenth-century idea that the Bible alone is the source of truth is an expression of fideism. (It's also self-contradictory, for there is no verse in the Bible that says, "the Bible alone is the source of truth.")

Yet the study of the Bible alone is not sufficient for all of theological reflection: "Those who devote themselves to the study of Sacred Scripture should always remember that the various hermeneutical approaches have their own philosophical underpinnings, which need to be carefully evaluated before they are applied to the sacred texts".

No text, not even the Bible, can interpret itself or provide its own theory and methodology of interpretation. Adjudicating among various theories and methodologies of interpretation belongs not to theology itself but rather to philosophy, with its study of the way language communicates and the way human beings come to know. Implicitly or explicitly, the study of Scripture—even by those who claim to be taught by Scripture alone—is informed by some interpretive method, a method that is brought to the text of Scripture and should be justified by good reasons: reasons philosophy can provide. Theology needs philosophy, even theology understood as scriptural exegesis.

Fideism is problematic because it is ultimately a denial of the unity of truth and the goodness of the created order. Reason helps to clarify faith and purify it from superstition. Reason makes more evident the unity and the plausibility of faith, as well as its claim to concern universally valid objective truth.

"Deprived of reason, faith has stressed feeling and experience and so runs the risk of no longer being a universal proposition" (*Fides et Ratio* 48). A theology of experience generally is not enough. If there is such a thing as revelation, then revelation, although always related to human experience, may reveal things that simply could not be known through normal human experience. Philosophical reason, and by extension theological reason, seeks to establish what is universally true rather than to examine the particular experience of a person or group of persons. We need faith and reason working in harmony to achieve maximal insight into revelation and the created order.

9. What is rationalism?

Just as fideism is a one-sided overemphasis on faith, *rationalism* is a one-sided overemphasis on reason. Fideism wants faith alone without reason. Rationalism wants reason alone without faith. What we cannot know by means of reason is unknowable, unimportant, and to be rejected.

Rationalism is problematic because it assumes that reason alone is sufficient for all useful knowledge and therefore denies any role for faith. For example, one form of rationalism is *scientism*—the claim that science is the only path for learning the truth. If scientism is true, everything that is not scientifically proven should be rejected. So, many matters of faith, such as God's existence or the resurrection of Jesus should be rejected.

But scientism itself is unreasonable. Indeed, scientism is self-contradictory. "Science is the only path for learning the truth" is not something proven in science. Biology does not show that science is the only path for learning the truth. Chemistry does not show that science is the only path for learning the truth. Physics does not show that science is the only path for learning the truth. Indeed, no scientific discipline shows that science is the only path for learning the truth. So, scientism is self-contradictory and should therefore be rejected.

Rationalism is unreasonable because it assumes that God cannot and would not reveal to us matters that go beyond what we can know by reason alone. But why should we think that is true? If God exists, then God transcends us massively in terms of power, goodness, and knowledge. It would not be surprising—indeed it would be expected—that God might reveal to us things that we could not understand through our own natural reasoning power. Just as a loving parent knows so much more than a small child and so "reveals" much about the world to the child, so a loving God reveals to us important truths, particularly about God as Father, Son, and Holy Spirit.

Unfortunately, some people overemphasize reason to the detriment of faith. John Paul II decried "a certain rationalism" that is manifested "particularly when theologians, through lack of philosophical competence, allow themselves to be swayed uncritically by assertions which have become part of current parlance and culture but which are poorly grounded in reason" (*Fides et Ratio* 55). For example, a theologian might assume that miracles do not happen, and then attempt to reinterpret all the miracles of Jesus in a non-miraculous way. An ethicist might assume that utilitarianism is true, and so revise ethical precepts to accord with the greatest happiness of the greatest number. In such cases, a mistaken view of reason leads to a mistaken reinterpretation of faith.

John Paul saw "a need to affirm the distinction between the mysteries of faith and the findings of philosophy, and the transcendence and precedence of the mysteries of faith over the findings of philosophy" (*Fides et Ratio* 51). What he means is that God's revelation transcends what we could learn simply through philosophy. Many philosophers from Aristotle to today have offered arguments that belief in God is reasonable. But what John Paul II calls "the mysteries of faith" go beyond what any philosopher can show making use of reason alone. To believe that the one God is Father, Son, and Holy Spirit is the result of the revelation of Jesus. Aristotle did not prove and could not prove the Trinity. The best he would do was to argue for an Unmoved Mover at the origin of the universe. So if we were to adopt rationalism we would limit ourselves and deprive ourselves of the help of revelation.

Consider, for example, how your friendships would be severely damaged if you adopted rationalism as the basis for your friendship and rejected trusting the revelations of your friends about their lives. Imagine saying to a friend, "Yes, I know you are asking me to believe you that you are really sad about losing your job. But can I take this on faith? Why should I trust you? Perhaps you're a great actor who is able to pretend to be sad, but in fact you aren't sad at all. I cannot, using my own reason, investigate and confirm your inner emotions, so until I have this confirmation I refuse to believe that you are sad." That friendship would end up being shallow or nonexistent. So too, if we are to have a deep, vibrant friendship with God, this requires a trust in God and treating God as trustworthy.

10. Does scientific progress make faith unreasonable?

The Christian faith is summarized in the Apostles' Creed. Not a sentence from this creed is disproven or even made implausible by scientific discoveries. Science does not prove that God does not exist. Does biology disprove the possibility of the divine? Does chemistry disprove God? Does physics show that no Creator exists? No. In fact, science as science is *not capable* of disproving God's existence. Science uses the empirical method of experimentation in order to test hypotheses. The empirical method limits itself to what can be derived from the senses—what we can see, hear, touch, taste, and smell. God is not something that we can directly see, hear, touch, taste, and smell. God transcends his creation.

Nor can science prove that Jesus is not God's son, didn't become incarnate, or didn't rise from the dead. Science does not show that the forgiveness of sins is not possible. Science teaches us many truths, very important truths, but science does not prove or disprove the Christian faith. Just as science does not prove or disprove the wrongfulness of murder or the goodness of loving your mother.

On the contrary, scientific progress has in some ways made faith *more* reasonable. As science progresses it becomes more and more obvious that nature has an order. If nature did not have an order to it, scientific investigation and discoveries would not be possible. So scientific discoveries provide more and more evidence that the universe has an order. But the fact of an ordered universe is itself important evidence pointing to a creator of the universe. Bishop Robert Barron makes the point this way:

> [The natural world] as we experience it, is marked, through and through, by intelligibility, that is to say, by a formal structure that makes it understandable to an inquiring mind. In point of fact, all of the sciences . . . rest on the assumption that at all levels, microscopic and macroscopic, being can be known. . . . Ratzinger argues that the only finally satisfying explanation for this universal objective intelligibility is a great Intelligence who has thought the universe into being. Our language provides an intriguing clue in this regard, for we speak of our acts of knowledge as moments of "recognition," literally a re-cognition, a thinking again what has already been thought. Ratzinger cites Einstein in support of this connection: "in

> the laws of nature, a mind so superior is revealed that in comparison, our minds are as something worthless."[12]

Given the intelligibility of the universe, it is easier to come to the conclusion that whatever gave rise to the universe is intelligent. Given the order of the universe, it becomes easier to conclude that the First Cause of the universe must exist.

Hence, it is no surprise that Catholic scientists see no contradiction between excellence in scientific study and their Catholic faith. One such award-winning scientist is Kenneth Miller, professor of biology at Brown University. He is the author of numerous books, including *Darwin's God: A Scientist's Search for Common Ground Between God and Evolution*, and a keen advocate for the compatibility of science with Catholic faith. At an address at the University of Notre Dame, he said, "Science is built upon two great elements of faith. The first is that the universe is rational, understandable and accessible to human thought. The second is that truth is to be preferred to ignorance." To be a great scientist and a person of Catholic faith is no more in tension than to be a great artist and a person of faith.

Skeptics may gloat that when reason and faith conflict—especially in the area of science—it is always faith that must accommodate the findings of science. But this is not always true.

For example, when science claims that the best way to study the spread of syphilis is to inject impoverished minorities with placebo vaccines and lie about the treatment these people were receiving (as occurred between 1932 and 1972 in the Tuskegee syphilis experiments), it is science that has erred. It must change and accommodate the truth that you should "love your neighbor as yourself" and not use people in the same way you would use laboratory guinea pigs.

Or consider another example. For hundreds of years scientists committed to naturalism believed that the universe was eternal, whereas the Bible and the Church taught that the universe had a beginning in time.[13] Instead of the Faith accommodating science, it turns out that science may have to accommodate the Faith, as new evidence from Big Bang cosmology points toward an ultimate beginning of the universe. As former NASA scientist Robert Jastrow writes, "For the scientist who has lived by his faith in the power of reason, the story ends like a bad dream. He has scaled the mountain of ignorance; he is about to conquer the highest peak; as he pulls himself over the final rock, he is greeted by a band of theologians who have been sitting there for centuries."[14]

11. How do you explain that the majority of scientists are atheists?

Ninety-three percent of the members of the National Academy of Sciences, one of the most elite scientific organizations in the United States, are reported to not believe in God.[15] Is it an argument against the truth of religious belief that so many of these intelligent people don't believe in God?

Let's take a closer look at what is behind these figures, drawn from a 1998 survey by Larson and Witham.[16] First, the National Academy of Sciences (NAS) represents a small number of scientists, counting about 2,400 members in 2024.[17] But the National Center for Science and Engineering Statistics of 2019 indicate that there are 28,627,000 persons in the United States with a Science & Engineering occupation or degree.[18] This means that the NAS membership represents only about one in twelve thousand scientists in the nation. And in reality, the Larson and Witham survey was limited only to a *subgroup* of the already limited NAS membership—only the biologists, mathematicians, physicists, and astronomers. And of the 517 members whose responses were solicited, only slightly over half responded to the survey. Clearly, using the 93 percent statistic to prove that scientists in general are overwhelmingly atheists would be inaccurate.

In addition, because the survey was intended as a comparison to the 1914 landmark survey by psychologist James H. Leuba, it used the same questions he had used, asking whether one believed in "a God in intellectual and effective communication with humankind, i.e., a God to whom one might pray in expectation of receiving an answer."[19] Doubting or dismissing the possibility of entering direct intellectual and effective communication with the Supreme Being is not the equivalent of affirming his non-existence!

In fact, a 1997 survey conducted by the same Larson and Witham on a random test group of a thousand individuals from *American Men and Women of Science* (1995) provided quite a different outcome. Using a more precisely formulated Gallup question, this survey showed that 40 percent of scientists affirmed belief in a God sufficiently personal and involved in human affairs to guide evolution.[20] A more recent survey conducted by Pew Research Center (2009) reports that 51 percent of scientists believe that God or some higher power exists.[21]

Whatever the case may be, we can't resolve the question of God's existence by relying on the personal opinions of scientists, because the existence of God is not a scientific question. Science restricts itself to searching for natural explanations of observed phenomena. Natural scientists (such as the biologists, chemists, and physicists that make up the Pew study) are no more equipped to make conclusions about God than they are equipped to make conclusions about economics, history, literature, or philosophy. Since the question of God is philosophical in nature, scientists who investigate it are no more qualified than any other educated laymen.

Finally, it may not be science that turns people into atheists but atheism that turns people into scientists. In Elaine Ecklund's book *Science vs. Religion: What Scientists Really Think*, she demonstrates through various interviews that many scientists reject religion for personal reasons prior to becoming scientists as opposed to rejecting religion on scientific grounds.

Another possible interpretation would be that the data represents a generational divide. According to the Pew Research Center, whereas fewer than half of the scientists over the age of sixty-five believe in God or a higher power, a full two thirds of scientists under the age of thirty-four believe in God or a higher power, with the majority of that group believing in God by an almost two-to-one margin.[22] Rather than retreat from science in order to protect the faith of our children, we should encourage our children to become scientists in order to protect the faith of other people!

12. How can I deepen my faith?

Just as we can grow more physically healthy by daily exercise, so too our faith can grow healthier by daily practice, increasing our capacity to know, love, and serve God.

The great moral philosopher Germain Grisez offers a number of suggestions for deepening faith. First, Grisez suggests, "One should remain receptive to *catechetical formation*. Having accepted the person of Jesus by faith and turned to him with conversion of heart, one receives catechetical formation to know him better, to fully understand the gospel's promises and requirements, and to know how to follow the way Jesus marked out for his disciples."[23] Fortunately, we have many resources today to help us to receive instruction. For example, you could read each day a little bit from Scripture, the *Catechism*, or the lives of the saints.

Second, Grisez notes, "One should respond to *challenges* to one's faith. Faith is often challenged, either by the objections of others or by one's own experiences."[24] Our questions, difficulties, and challenges of faith shift radically over the years, as old questions are answered and new ones arise. Our restlessness in asking questions and seeking answers is part of the goodness of the human mind, which is ever seeking the perfect truth of God. Each person is different, so people have various individual questions, difficulties, and challenges of faith. We are fortunate because we have an ancient, rich, and ongoing tradition of reflection about virtually every question that might arise. We can seek answers to our questions from the great teachers of the Catholic faith, whether old or new, whether online or in person. Everyone has questions, and these questions can be an aid to faith in helping it grow.

Third, Grisez notes that *prayer* is a great aid to faith, especially "conscious and active participation in the liturgy," which is practiced "not only in the Profession of Faith (the *Credo*) but also in the acceptance of the scriptural readings as the word of the Lord, the affirming *Amen* to the reality of the Eucharist as Jesus' body and blood, and so on."[25] We can make our own the prayer a father once said to Jesus: "I believe, help my unbelief!" (Mark 9:24).

Fourth, Grisez suggests that we build our faith in *community*, not merely as an individual and solitary endeavor. "All believers," he says, "should cooperate to sustain and build up one another's faith." When our faith is challenged, we "should communicate the problem accurately and confidently to someone capable of helping." In turn we take the "sound and satisfying responses to challenges" that we learn and not only incorporate them into our own faith, but share them with others, together building up the faith of the Church.[26] Since our faith can be built up in community, it is helpful to have small groups and circles of friends with whom we can share in the life of faith.

Fifth, it is a great idea to have a *spiritual director*, either a priest or a well-trained layperson, who can act as a coach in the life of faith, a guide in the journey of life. It is difficult for us to be good judges of our own situation. We can be too hard on ourselves or not hard enough. So it is incredibly helpful to have an experienced and trustworthy person to help us in our faith journey. When questions arise, a spiritual director can help us find the answers we need. Honestly and openly speaking to a person we trust is itself often enough to ease difficulties.

Finally, we can remember that some of the greatest minds in the history of humankind have accepted Christian belief. So if we cannot find answers to our questions at the moment, we should not conclude that no answers are to be found or that we are foolish for accepting Christian beliefs.

13. What if I feel that I have lost my faith?

Faith, in the Christian tradition, is a theological virtue that comes from God as a gift. So any baptized person has received this gift of faith. The gift of faith is a habit that is still present in us even when we are not using it. If I have the habit of playing the piano, I remain a piano player even when sleeping or swimming. So the gift of Christian faith remains in a person whether or not a person is at the moment using this gift or even sensing this gift.

Indeed, Christian faith is a bit like citizenship. To be born in the United States is to be a U.S. citizen, which remains so until a person explicitly renounces citizenship. A good citizen votes and does not break laws. But even a citizen who does not vote and does break laws remains a citizen. So too, Christian faith as a habit infused by God remains with us even in our ups and downs. This understanding of faith does not depend upon our passing feelings or any emotional sense of closeness with God.

Indeed, to *feel* faith and to *have* faith are two different matters. The hypochondriac feels sick but actually has good health. So too, a person might feel a lack of faith but actually have a very strong gift of faith. Indeed, even a great saint like Mother Teresa of Calcutta felt a lack of God's presence for around fifty years. In a way, this feeling that God does not exist, or that God is absent, can be evidence of a deep faith. Only a wife can feel the absence of her husband. So too, only a soul that is ordered to God by faith can feel the loss of the presence of God. Faith is not a matter of feeling this presence.

For those feeling a loss of faith, it would be helpful to engage in the practices that can help increase faith. And what if a person is not sure whether or not faith is present? Fr. Richard John Neuhaus once said, "If you would believe, act as though you believe, leaving it to God to know whether you believe, for such leaving it to God is faith."[27] Act as a person of faith acts, do what a person of faith does, and love as a person of faith loves. Rather than focus on feelings, make the choices and decisions of a person of faith, leaving it to God whether or not the feelings arise.

14. What are some resources for exploring the Catholic understanding of faith and reason?

There are many excellent resources for exploring the Catholic understanding of faith and reason, beginning with Pope St. John Paul II's *Fides et Ratio*. Over the centuries, many people have eloquently treated the topic, so this list of resources is not by any means definitive but is merely a beginning.

St. Augustine of Hippo, a pivotal figure in the long conversation about the harmony of faith and reason, died in the year 430 and wrote much about the relationship of faith and reason. Perhaps the best books for a beginner to explore Augustine's views would be *Confessions* and *On Christian Doctrine*. In the *Confessions*, Augustine presents his autobiography and explores different perspectives of faith (such as Christianity and Manicheanism) and different perspectives of reason (Platonism, skepticism, Aristotelianism). In *On Christian Doctrine*, Augustine argues in favor of secular learning as an indispensable aid to understanding the Bible. In his long writing career, Augustine produced a powerful synthesis of faith and reason that harmonized Platonic philosophy and Christianity in an incredibly influential and long-lasting way.

A second incredibly influential figure is St. Thomas Aquinas (1227–1274), who produced perhaps the greatest synthesis between faith and reason, fusing together the theology of Augustine and the philosophy of Aristotle. The Church does not impose any particular philosophy on its members. But it does propose Aquinas as a model for philosophical and theological insight, calling him the Universal Doctor of the Church. It was Pope Leo XIII in his encyclical *Aeterni Patris* who first underscored the value of Thomas's thought, making it the gold standard for Catholic philosophy and theology.

Pope Leo's encyclical paved the way for the Thomistic revival that brought the Church much fruit, including the work of Jacques Maritain, Etienne Gilson, Joseph Pieper, and Fr. Reginald Garrigou-Lagrange, John Paul II's dissertation director.

The Second Vatican Council, in its decree on priestly formation, noted, "By way of making the mysteries of salvation known as thoroughly as they can be, students should learn to penetrate them more deeply with the help of speculative reason as exercised under the tutelage of St. Thomas" (*Optatam Totius* 16).

Unfortunately, this recommendation was not widely adopted after the council. Instead, there was a large-scale rejection of Thomism in many

Catholic centers of higher education. John Paul II was not satisfied with this communal intellectual experiment:

> If it has been necessary from time to time to intervene on this question, to reiterate the value of [Aquinas's] insights and insist on the study of his thought, this has been because the Magisterium's directives have not always been followed with the readiness one would wish. In the years after the Second Vatican Council, many Catholic faculties were in some ways impoverished by a diminished sense of the importance of the study not just of Scholastic philosophy but more generally of the study of philosophy itself. I cannot fail to note with surprise and displeasure that this lack of interest in the study of philosophy is shared by not a few theologians" (*Fides et Ratio* 62).

One way to explore seriously the relationship of faith and reason is to look again, or perhaps for the first time, at the teaching of Aquinas. It is not an easy thing to master, but it is nevertheless of signal value for the intellectual life of the believer. With the help of contemporary guides to Thomas such as Ralph McInerny, Romanus Cessario, Russell Hittinger, John Haldane, and Jean-Pierre Torrell, all of us—theologians, aspiring theologians, and budding apologists alike—can make great strides in having a sure foundation and reason for the hope within us (1 Pet 3:15).

15. What is God?

Although concepts of God differ across the world, they all usually describe him as the supernatural creator of the universe. One useful but incomplete definition comes from the old *Baltimore Catechism*: "When we say that God is the Supreme Being we mean that he is above all creatures, the self-existing and infinitely perfect spirit. 'I am the first, and I am the last, and besides me there is no God (Is. 44:6).'"[28] *The Catechism of the Catholic Church* explains it this way:

> The revelation of the ineffable name "I AM WHO AM" contains then the truth that God alone IS. The Greek Septuagint translation of the Hebrew scriptures, and following it the Church's Tradition, understood the divine name in this sense: God is the fullness of

> being and of every perfection, without origin and without end. All creatures receive all that they are and have from him; but he alone is his very being, and he is of himself everything that he is (213).

God must exist because he is "the ground of existence"; existence is what he is, and every created thing exists only because God sustains it. As St. Paul says of God, "he himself gives to all men life and breath and everything. . . . In him we live and move and have our being" (Acts 17:25, 28). This makes God, in the words of Pope St. John Paul II, "the supreme being, the great 'Existent.'"[29]

16. What are some false views of God?

Before we explore the attributes and essence of the one true God, let's first examine three common false views of the nature of God.

Polytheism: Monotheists, such as Christians, Muslims, and Jews, believe that only one God exists. Polytheists, on the other hand, believe that many gods exist. The ancient followers of Greek and Roman mythology were examples of polytheists.[30]

Not all ancient Greeks and Romans believed in many gods, however. Philosophers such as Plato and Aristotle believed in a supreme being, or God, who created all of reality. In *Metaphysics*, Aristotle said that gods like Zeus were "myths" but the true God "is a living being, eternal, most good, so that life and duration continuous and eternal belong to God; for this is God."[31]

Unlike the gods of mythological pantheons, the one true God is not confined in any way, as he would be if the heavens were peopled with rival gods each with their own domain or jurisdiction. In fact, the orderly behavior of the universe according to fixed, natural laws is evidence for monotheism. If polytheism were true, we would expect the natural order to be disrupted by disagreements or infighting among the gods.[32]

Pantheism: The Pontifical Council for Interreligious Dialogue defined pantheism as the belief that "every element of the universe is divine, and the divinity is equally present in everything. There is no space in this view for God as a distinct being in the sense of classical theism."[33]

According to pantheists, God may be a personal being who comprises the universe or he may be an impersonal force that fills up the universe, but whatever God is, God is not a creator who exists apart from the universe.

Yet the universe began to exist from nothing in the finite past. Therefore, the universe's existence must be explained by a being who is eternal and exists independently of the universe (since it brought the universe into being)—what we know to be the traditional God of monotheism.

A modern variant of pantheism occurs when people reduce God to something in the universe, such as love. Now, it's true that 1 John 4:8 does say, "He who does not love does not know God; for God is love," but as C.S. Lewis said,

> Of course, what these people mean when they say that God is love is often something quite different: they really mean "Love is God" . . . What Christians mean by the statement "God is love" [is that] they believe that the living, dynamic activity of love has been going on in God forever and has created everything else.[34]

Deism: Deists believe that one God created the universe, but, unlike theists, they believe this God no longer interacts with the world he created. Some of the Founding Fathers, such as Thomas Jefferson, were deists. They rejected Christianity, but they did not reject what they called "nature's God." A derivative form of deism that commonly exists among the non-religious is what some call *moralistic therapeutic deism.*[35] According to this way of thinking, God

- exists and watches over the world,
- wants people to be nice; those nice people go to heaven; and
- is not needed in life unless there is a problem he can solve. This is because the purpose of life is to be happy, not to know and worship God.

The Christian God, though, is not a deistic "absentee landlord," or a shopkeeper who tries to respond to the whims of his human pets. Instead, he is the infinite act of being itself that sustains all of creation. God is just as active in creation now as he was when he brought it into existence in the finite past. According to the *Catechism*, "God does not abandon his creatures to themselves. He not only gives them being and existence, but also, and at every moment, upholds and sustains them in being, enables them to act and brings them to their final end" (301). In later answers we will see that God revealed himself through Jesus of Nazareth and so, unlike the God of deism, he certainly does care about the eternal fate of his creatures.

17. Is God's existence self-evident?

Do we really need any proof that God exists, through reason, revelation, or both? St. Thomas tells us that some people would answer no, we do not need proof, because God's existence is self-evident.[36]

People have argued that the existence of God is self-evident and undeniable because of one or more of the following three reasons:

1) Knowledge of God is implanted in us by nature.

2) Self-evident things are known as soon as their terms are known. For example, when the nature of a whole and a part are known, we instantly recognize that a whole is greater than its part. Similarly, as soon as the statement "God exists" is understood, his existence cannot be denied, because the word *God* means that thing than which nothing greater can be thought, but what exists in reality is greater than what exists only mentally. St. Anselm of Canterbury (c. 1133–1109) famously argued this point.

3) The existence of truth is self-evident and cannot be denied. If truth did not exist, then the statement "truth does not exist" would be *true*, so truth would still exist. And God is the truth (see John 14:6).

Yet we cannot mentally admit the opposite of what is self-evident—for example, that a part is greater than the whole—but people *do* deny that God exists. After all, Scripture tells us, "The fool said in his heart;There is no God" (Ps. 52:1). Therefore, Thomas explains, "that God exists is not self-evident."

For "a thing can be self-evident in either of two ways; on the one hand, self-evident in itself, though not to us; on the other, self-evident in itself, and to us." God's existence *would* be self-evident to us *if* God's essence were understood, but God's essence is imperfectly known to man, and our imperfect knowledge is achieved through reasoned argument or through revelation.

An awareness of God is indeed implanted in our natures, but in a confused way. All people seek happiness, but not all realize that our complete happiness (beatitude) lies only in God. As Boethius (c. 477-524) wrote, "There are some mental concepts self-evident only to the learned." We might think of the case of St. Augustine, who wrote that our hearts are restless until they rest in God. Augustine did not recognize this until he had learned and embraced the Catholic faith.

18. Can God's existence be proven by reason?

Although St. Thomas argues that God's existence is not self-evident to us[37], he goes on to show that God's existence can indeed be proved through reason alone (1:2:3). St. Paul tells us regarding God that "ever since the creation of the world his invisible nature, namely, his eternal power and deity, has been clearly perceived in the things that have been made" (Rom. 1:20). The Catholic Church agrees. The First Vatican Council would declare as dogma that certain knowledge of God can be attained "through the light of reason," and we read in the *Catechism* that "by natural reason man can know God with certainty, on the basis of his works" (50).

These proofs by the light of natural reason all employ *a posteriori* reasoning. That is, they start with the *undeniable evidence of our human senses* and then *rigorously reason backward* from these phenomena to their *ultimate cause*. In other words, they do not begin upon some abstract philosophical premise with which anyone may or may not agree.

By "ultimate cause," we do not mean a cause in the distant past, the first in a long series of successive causes, but one that is first in the order of actual causality. The point isn't so much that the universe was created at some precise moment in the past, as that the universe could not be actually sustained in existence without the causal power of God! Thomas's arguments do not require that we reason backward in time. Rather, all five of his arguments depend on a hidden principle—the *principle of final causality*, which says that anything that is brought from a state of *potentiality* to a state of *actuality* must be made actual by something else already in act.

All movement or change, efficient causality, perfection, order, and purpose require a cause for their existence—not merely sometime in the past, but *at this moment*. Sure, there's a chain of events that continues long after the initiator of those events has finished doing their initiating, but the system in which those events occur—the matter of the agents involved, the universe through which they move, the causal physical principles that govern their motion—remains *dependent* for its existence and its continuation on the presence and action of a *necessary being* from which all things derive. "We live, and move, and have our being" (Acts 17:28) right now through the grace, love, and power of an eternal God.

19. Does the Big Bang prove or disprove the existence of God?

In the early twentieth century, the Belgian priest and physicist Fr. Georges Lemaître concluded that Einstein's new theory of gravity, called general relativity, would cause a static eternal universe to collapse into nothingness. Since Einstein's theory was sound, this meant only one thing: the universe was not static but growing, and had a beginning in the finite past. Fr. Lemaître and Einstein even discussed the cosmic consequences of the theory while walking around the campus of Caltech. Although Einstein was skeptical at first, in 1933 he proclaimed that Fr. Lemaître's theory of an expanding universe was one of the most "beautiful theories he had ever heard."[38]

Fr. Lemaître called his theory "the primeval atom," but another physicist, Fred Hoyle, mocked it with the term "big bang." Hoyle wanted to discredit the theory as nothing more than religious propaganda, but the movement of stars away from each other and the cosmic radiation that permeated the whole galaxy provided almost indisputable evidence that the Big Bang did happen—evidence not for an *explosion in space*, but an *expansion of space* (as well as time, matter, and energy) from an infinitely dense point, called a singularity.[39] According to renowned Tufts University cosmologist Alexander Vilenkin, "All the evidence we have says that the universe had a beginning."[40]

Now, we should remember that all appeals to scientific evidence for the beginning of the universe can never be 100 percent certain. We should be open to where the evidence leads but we should also be aware of the history of cosmology, and how multiple, independent lines of evidence have been added to confirm the standard Big Bang model over the past century. The distinguished British astronomer Martin Rees wrote: "Cosmological ideas are no longer any more fragile and evanescent than our theories about the history of our earth. . . . The empirical support for a Big Bang ten to fifteen billion years ago is as compelling as the evidence that geologists offer on our earth's history."[41]

So if the universe began to exist, what can we conclude? One intuition most people have is summarized in the Latin phrase "*ex nihilo, nihil fit*," or "out of nothing, nothing comes."[42] It makes sense that "nothing" (not just black or empty space, but "no thing") is incapable of doing anything. As the song "Something Good" from the popular film *The Sound of Music* would have it, "Nothing comes from nothing. Nothing ever could."

Some atheists say that even if the universe began to exist at the Big Bang, it could have emerged from a state of nothingness similar to the way virtual particles have been observed in physics laboratories to come to be from nothing. Or the universe could have come from an infinite number of other universes stretching backward in time before the Big Bang. However, both of these explanations are problematic.

First, virtual particles do not pop into existence from pure nothingness. Instead, they come from a quantum vacuum, or a low-level energy field that can fluctuate. Philosopher and theoretical physicist David Albert writes,

> Vacuum states—no less than giraffes or refrigerators or solar systems—are particular arrangements of *elementary physical stuff*. . . . The fact that particles can pop in and out of existence, over time, as those [quantum] fields rearrange themselves, is not a whit more mysterious than the fact that fists can pop in and out of existence, over time, as my fingers rearrange themselves. And none of these poppings—if you look at them aright—amount to anything even remotely in the neighborhood of a creation from nothing.[43]

Even if an infinite regression of finite beings or causal relationships were possible, other physicists have shown that an infinite series of collapsing and expanding universes could not have caused the universe we observe today. Why? Because the amount of disorder we observe in our universe is far lower than it would be if the past were infinite.[44] A better explanation for the data we observe is that the universe, which includes all of space, time, matter, and energy, began to exist and that it came into existence from an "uncaused cause" that transcends space and time, or what we call God.

20. Does intelligent design prove the existence of God?

The *philosophical* argument for the existence of God by reason of intelligent design has a long tradition in the Catholic Church. It is the fifth of St. Thomas's five ways of proving the existence of God by inductive reasoning.

> Whatever lacks intelligence cannot move toward an end, unless it be directed by some being endowed with knowledge and

> intelligence; as the arrow is shot to its mark by the archer. Therefore some intelligent being exists by whom all natural things are directed to their end; and this being we call God.[45]

Proponents of what is popularly known as intelligent design (or ID) theory, however, claim that *science* can *detect* whether an intelligent agent designed certain features of the natural world. Rather than arguing for intelligent design in function of the *finality* that directs natural things to their end, the argument is that intelligent design alone can explain the *intricate structure* of these natural things, in their chemical or biological makeup.

For example, if you walked across the beach and saw the seashells arranged to spell "Sara, will you marry me?," you would probably assume that the shells didn't wind up that way on the beach by sheer chance. In the same way, ID advocates claim, some features in biology have these same markers of design (or intentional, specified patterns) that we can detect scientifically. Although they usually do not claim to know the identity of the intelligent designer, most ID advocates believe the designer is the Christian God. ID advocates differ among themselves over whether life evolved or was created directly by God several thousand years ago.

The Catholic physicist and ID advocate Michael Behe points to certain microscopic biological structures that are too complicated to be explained by natural theories of biological development. The most common examples cited by intelligent design advocates include

- "miniature machines in the cell" such as the bacterial flagellum,
- the immune system and blood clotting cascade, and
- DNA and the genetic code.

The Catholic Church has no specific teaching related to intelligent design theory. Although it embraces arguments of intelligent design from a philosophical level, theology is not equipped to pronounce on the value of scientific "proofs" of intelligent design. In 2004, the International Theological Commission, headed by Cardinal Joseph Ratzinger, issued a statement on the origins question that referred to intelligent design:

> A growing body of scientific critics of neo-Darwinism point to evidence of design (e.g., biological structures that exhibit specified complexity) that, in their view, cannot be explained in terms of a

> purely contingent process and that neo-Darwinians have ignored or misinterpreted. The nub of this currently lively disagreement involves scientific observation and generalization concerning whether the available data support inferences of design or chance, and cannot be settled by theology.[46]

As it falls outside the domain of faith, Catholics are free to give whatever value they choose to ID argumentation. Indeed, there is some controversy within the Catholic community about the merits of the intelligent design argument. Whereas some Catholics like Behe support intelligent design, others argue that intelligent design represents a mechanistic view of nature that is incompatible with a traditional Thomistic view of the world. They claim that Aquinas viewed nature being directed as a whole toward an intelligent end or goal. As a result, there would be no reason for God to intervene and specially create certain natural parts that make up the world.[47]

21. Do scientifically inexplicable things prove the existence of God?

A "God of the gaps" argument claims that a currently unknown feature of the natural world is proof that God exists because he is the cause of that feature. For example, ancient people who did not know what caused lighting could assume that a god caused it in order to punish mankind. These kinds of arguments for the existence of God ignore the fact that a suitable natural explanation for the phenomena we observe may eventually be discovered, and we will miss it if we rush to the conclusion "God did it!"

This happened when Isaac Newton said that the best explanation for the motion of the planets was that an intelligent agent or even angels were pushing them. We must also be wary of similar arguments today that claim certain features of the human cell, or certain organs, could not have arisen by natural means; therefore, a supernatural explanation is required. If a natural explanation is eventually found for what we can't explain, then our "evidence" for God will have disappeared as the gap in our understanding is closed by scientific discovery.

Science can't prove God exists simply by pointing to natural phenomena that human beings cannot currently explain. But it also can't disprove God exists, because science cannot make judgments about entities that exist beyond the natural world.

So how does science relate to God? Thomas Aquinas provides us with a model of the traditional relationship between science and the use of reason to prove God exists, or what is called natural theology. Aquinas used scientific facts such as the presence of change or the regularity of movement within natural bodies as premises in *philosophical* arguments for the existence of God.

The *Catechism* states that scientific discoveries should "invite us to even greater admiration for the greatness of the Creator" (283). We should use this knowledge about how the world *is*, or what we call *science*, to ground philosophical arguments for the fundamentals of our Faith, including the fundamental truth that God created the universe. We can use these arguments to demonstrate that the world has an origin outside of itself and a moral order within itself, facts that science cannot explain.

22. What are St. Thomas's five ways to prove the existence of God?

Thomas is perhaps best known for his five ways—proofs, using reason alone and not relying on divine revelation, for the existence of God. We'll examine them here in brief. (For more in-depth treatments from modern philosophers, you could start with Fr. Reginald Garrigou-Lagrange, Etienne Gilson, and Edward Feser.)

First is the *argument from motion or change*. Our senses tell us with certainty that material things are in motion. They change in various ways, such as in their location or in qualities such as size and temperature. They move from some state of potentiality (a capacity for change) to an actuality (an actual change). Matter in movement is the first and most obvious way in which we observe the primacy of what is in act over what is in potency. Inanimate matter does not move itself but is moved by another: a fire could not heat water unless the fire were already hot, and a stick moves something else only because it is put in motion by a hand. These outside sources of change cannot go on indefinitely, though, so there must be a first, unmoved mover, *already completely actualized* and put in motion by no other. This mover we call God.

Second is the *argument from the order of efficient causes* apparent in the world. A thing cannot cause itself, because then it would be prior to itself, which is impossible. The chain of causation cannot go into infinity because, without a first efficient cause, no intermediate causes would exist, and to take away the cause is to take away the effect, whereas effects clearly exist.

This argument, which St. Thomas lays out in succinct form, can be understood in two ways. A first, obvious sense in which his argument holds true is that anything that begins to exist has a cause for its existence. Most of the "coming into existence" that we observe in the material world, however, is simply the product of movement and change, which is already the subject of the first way. A second interpretation is possible if we consider the difference between inanimate realities (whether natural or artistic), which are moved by *another*, and animate realities, which possess an *interior efficient cause*. Just as inanimate matter is moved by the actuality of an exterior agent (natural forces or artistic processes), so the organic body is moved from within by the soul. But this principle of life, or agency, cannot cause itself. There must be a first efficient, uncaused cause, a Living One who is author of life. This we call God.

Third is the *argument from necessary being*. We find in nature things that exist but don't have to or that come to be but pass away. If everything in the universe is potentially nonexistent (i.e., is *contingent*, being dependent on something else for its act of being), then at one time or another there could have been no existing thing. But if that were true, there would be nothing now, because something that does not exist cannot give itself its own existence. There must therefore be some being that not merely *possibly*, but *necessarily* exists, having its existence not due to some other thing and causing all other things to exist. We call this necessary being God.

Fourth is the *argument from degrees of being*. Everything that exists has some measure of goodness by the fact that it exists. Still, we clearly see that some things in the world are better than others. They are better, nobler, more true or complete. But there is no standard to appreciate degrees of perfection unless there is an unchanging maximum, something with no imperfection at all in the given category of value. There must be some utmost being that exceeds and causes the various forms of goodness and various perfections in every other being. This ultimate being and source of all perfections we call God.

Fifth is the *argument from the governance of the world* (also known as the *argument from the final cause*). There are order and seemingly purposeful behavior even in inanimate natural bodies that follow the regular laws of nature. Although they lack awareness, they act in the same way, over and over again, achieving effective ends or goals. Unintelligent beings cannot reach specific goals unless directed by a being with intelligence, "as the arrow is shot to its mark by the archer. Therefore, some intelligent being exists by whom all natural things are directed to their end; and this being we call God."

In essence, Thomas's five ways prove not that God might exist, but that he *absolutely must exist*. Otherwise, the world brought to us by our own senses simply could not be.

23. Can the average person prove the existence of God?

There are many good reasons to think that God exists, reasons that the average person can understand without too much philosophical training. In their book *Handbook of Catholic Apologetics,* Peter Kreeft and Ronald Tacelli outline twenty arguments for the existence of God. Here we will look at three of the most compelling.

The Kalam Argument

The core of this argument, named after the Islamic philosophical tradition that refined it, can be phrased as follows:

1) Whatever begins to exist has a cause of its existence.
2) The universe began to exist.
3) Therefore, the universe has a cause of its existence: God.

The first premise seems obviously true by our experience. Things don't simply pop into existence, uncaused, out of nothing.[48] Indeed, if anything did appear simply to pop into existence, we would immediately begin asking why—what was the *cause* of this thing?

What about the second premise? Did the universe, all of time, space, matter and energy, begin to exist? Atheists have typically said that the universe exists without explanation and has been here forever. "The universe," claimed Bertrand Russell, "is just there. And that's all." Recent scientific discoveries, however, suggest otherwise. Today the standard view is that the universe—all space and time—sprang into existence around 13.7 billion years ago, in an event called the *Big Bang*.

These discoveries tend to put atheists in an awkward position, a position expressed well by former NASA scientist Robert Jastrow, who writes:

> For the scientist who has lived by his faith in the power of reason, the story ends like a bad dream. He has scaled the mountain of ignorance; he is about to conquer the highest peak; as he pulls himself over the final rock, he is greeted by a band of theologians who have been sitting there for centuries.[49]

Even if our universe emerged from an even larger "multiverse," which caused the Big Bang, scientists concur that even this larger multiverse must also have a finite past.[50] And so we reach our conclusion: since nothing can begin to exist without a cause, and since the universe began to exist, it follows that there is a cause of the universe.

What can we know about this cause? Since it created space, time, and matter, it must be greater than all those things. Furthermore, it must be personal, not a mere "force." For only a person with free will could create in time what had not been there before. As philosopher William Lane Craig put it,

> How else could a timeless cause give rise to a temporal effect like the universe? If the cause were an impersonal set of necessary and sufficient conditions, then the cause could never exist without the effect. If the cause were eternally present, then the effect would be eternally present as well. The only way for the cause to be timeless and the effect to begin in time is for the cause to be a personal agent who freely chooses to create an effect in time without any prior determining conditions. Thus, we are brought, not merely to a transcendent cause of the universe, but to its personal creator.[51]

The Kalam argument (which echoes the "second way" of St. Thomas) demonstrates the existence of an uncaused, spaceless, timeless, immaterial, all-powerful, personal creator of the universe. That sounds a lot like God.

The Contingency Argument

Our next argument (which parallels the "third way" of Thomas) goes like this:

1) Whatever exists that does not have to exist requires an explanation for its existence.

2) The physical universe does not have to exist.

3) Therefore, the universe requires an explanation in something that must exist.

4) God is the only being that must exist.

5) Therefore, God is the explanation for the existence of the universe.

The first premise of this argument reflects the human perception that there are reasons for the existence of the things we see around us. This is what drives science, as well as every other branch of study. It's the great question: "Why?" This question applies to anything that doesn't have to exist or that could be different from what it is (what philosophers sometimes refer to as *contingent* things).

For example, when astronomers discovered red-colored stars, they tried to explain their existence. To say that there isn't an explanation—not that we don't know it but that there actually *isn't* one—strikes at the foundation of rational thought. It's to reject the whole premise that underlies the quest for knowledge. The first premise of our argument thus seems secure.

So does the second premise. If we look around the physical universe, we see it filled with stars and galaxies. And we see that the things within it obey certain laws and those physical laws have certain constants, or unchanging values. For example, the constant *C* in E=MC2 refers to the speed of light, or 186,000 miles per second. This fact about light never changes, and so it is called a constant. There are many other constants, such as the gravitational constant: gravity is so strong and not stronger or weaker. We experience three dimensions of space and one of time, not more or less.

These things are constants in the physical world. But why are they such, and not otherwise?

Likewise, at one time the universe didn't contain stars and galaxies. Why do those objects exist now when they clearly don't have to? All of these matters are subjects of scientific inquiry, and they reveal that the physical universe as a whole is contingent. That is, the universe is one way but could be another, or it could simply not be at all. It therefore needs a reason for its own existence—an explanation.

But let's inquire a bit further and ask about what *could* explain the way the physical universe is. Whatever it is, it must be greater than the physical universe; it must be something beyond space and time, beyond matter and energy, but with the power to create each of these and to establish the laws that they obey. It would be something that explains its own existence and the existence of all else that exists, and that could not fail to exist.

Once again, that sounds a lot like God: what philosophers call a "necessary" being: God could not be different from what he is, which is what the third premise states.

This is something our intuition also tells us. There must be an ultimate explanation, one that doesn't depend on anything else, and thus one that explains everything else. There must be something fundamental, something that grounds all the contingent things we see around us. And thus there must be a God.

The Moral Argument

The third argument (a sort of modern composite of the "fourth way" and "fifth way" of Thomas) says,

1) If God doesn't exist, then objective moral values don't exist.

2) Objective moral values do exist.

3) Therefore, God exists.

The first premise is something that Christians and atheists may agree about. As we saw earlier, many Christians have argued that if God didn't exist, there could not be a rational basis for objective morality. Many atheists have said, yes, since there's no God, morality is a human construct. Good and evil aren't real—they're just words we use, concepts we've invented.

For example, the atheist philosopher Michael Ruse wrote that morality "is a biological adaptation no less than are hands and feet and teeth." It is "just an aid to survival and reproduction," and consequently, "any deeper meaning is illusory."[52]

But the second premise is that objective moral values and duties *do* exist. And if we're honest, mustn't we acknowledge this? When we hear stories of horrible crimes, for example, murders committed by a serial killer, we don't think, "A biological adaptation is causing me to apply feelings of disapproval toward these acts."

No, we think that these crimes are *evil,* because murder is *wrong*—not "wrong for me but perhaps right for you," but simply wrong in itself, *malicious.*

The intuition that such moral values are real is so deeply embedded in the human heart that even those who deny objective morality invariably can be found making moral judgments and expressing moral outrage. Ruse, who thinks morality is a "biological adaptation," wrote elsewhere, "The man who says that it is morally acceptable to rape little children is just as mistaken as the man who says, 2+2=5."[53]

So, the question is not whether objective morality exists, but what the basis for it might be. Here are four possibilities:

Nature. Moral laws could be part of the natural world, like the laws of physics. In that case they would be something that the natural sciences could detect. Yet they don't seem to be. You can't measure good and evil in a scientific experiment. Furthermore, we don't say that animals are acting immorally when they kill or steal from each other. Why doesn't our morality apply to them, too, just as the laws of physics do? The source of morality must therefore transcend the natural world and the realm of science.

Individual Choice. Perhaps we make our own morality, according to our choices. All of us, after all, have our own consciences and personal moral beliefs. This, however, wouldn't explain how things could be right or wrong even apart from (or in contradiction to) my choices. It also wouldn't result in a set of moral values that are binding on other people. What I think is right and wrong wouldn't apply to you.

Society. Perhaps moral values are established by what society decides and expresses through customs and laws. In other words, what is legal and acceptable or conventional is therefore moral. But this is really just a collective version of the individual choice idea, and so it too fails to establish a truly objective and binding set of moral values. And what if I disagree with society? What right do others have to tell me what I should and shouldn't do? On what grounds could any society deem immoral its own customs or the customs of another?

God. A final possibility is that objective morality might be grounded in God—flowing from his own nature and goodness, as well as his authority to prescribe certain kinds of behavior as adequate to the nature and ends of persons created in his image. It is in this sense that Catholic Tradition speaks of a "natural law" proscribing certain moral ends and boundaries in function of the ends and determinations inscribed in human nature by the Creator (not to be confused with "laws of nature," discussed above, observed in the physical world and discovered by science).

Only this final option seems to make sense; for only if morality originates in something *above* me would it have *authority* over me—the right to tell me what to do and what not to do. As Francis J. Beckwith and Greg

Koukl observe, "A command only makes sense when there are two minds involved, one giving the command and one receiving it."[54] If an objective moral law is indeed a command that we receive—whether in the form of natural law inscribed in us by the Creator or divine law transmitted to us by revelation—then there must be an objective, personal moral commander who transcends nature, the individual, and society.

Thus, it seems that apart from God there is no objective foundation for morality. This doesn't mean that *belief* in God is necessary to act morally; just that God—a perfectly good, transcendent lawgiver—is the only thing we can logically point to as a basis for saying that some things *are* just right or wrong, regardless of what any individual or society might prefer to believe.

24. Can we really know what God is like?

The human intellect does not have an immediate or comprehensive grasp of what God is, in his divine nature. Rather, we are better able to say what he is not, or "how" he is not, by comparing his way of existing to that of his creatures.

> God transcends all creatures. We must therefore continually purify our language of everything in it that is limited, image-bound or imperfect, if we are not to confuse our image of God—"the inexpressible, the incomprehensible, the invisible, the ungraspable"—with our human representations. Our human words always fall short of the mystery of God (CCC 42).

This theological method for approaching the mystery of God is called the *via negativa* (negative way) because it advances by eliminating characteristics that could not possibly describe a prime mover, a necessary being who is pure act. This is the method outlined by St. Thomas[55] for elaborating the principal attributes of God that we can attain through reason. Here is a summary of some of the attributes he considers in the following questions:

Simplicity. God is one, a perfect and infinite act of being. He is not composed of parts, such as body and spirit, nor does he enter into the composition of other things. St. Anselm of Canterbury declared, "There are no parts in you, Lord: neither are you many, but you are so much one and the same with yourself that in nothing are you dissimilar with yourself."[56]

Perfection. God lacks any kind of imperfection. There is no unfulfilled potential in God. God is pure act.

Infinity. When we say that God is infinite, we don't mean that God has an infinite number of thoughts or that he extends over an infinitely long cosmic distance. What we mean is that God lacks any limitation. Nothing precedes him, and nothing can be added to him. God alone is without beginning, end, or boundary of any kind. As the first-century text *The Shepherd of Hermas* puts it: "He contains all things while he himself is uncontained."[57]

Omnipresent: Because nothing limits God, God is present to all his creation. He is everywhere. This does not mean God is *identical* to everything (as in pantheism), nor does it mean he is *diffused* through the universe like an invisible gas. Instead, God is present in the universe by sustaining everything in being and governing everything by his providence.

Immutability. As there is no limit or divisibility to God's existence, there is also no potentiality for change. Anything that changes has a passive potential to become something different. God is pure act and perfectly complete. This view of God stands in contrast to that endorsed by the "process theologians," who say that God only has limited control over his creation and changes in response to it and so "gets better over time" as he governs the creation.[58] Such a perspective is at variance not only with reason but also with faith, as Scripture tells us that God is "the Father of lights with whom there is no variation or shadow due to change" (James 1:7) and that, if God's covenant toward us is stable it is because "I the Lord do not change" (Mal. 3:6).

Necessary: There is no limit to God's existence. For the same reason that God is immutable, he is also *necessary*—that is, he must exist and can never come into existence or go out of existence. God created all things, but nothing created God.

Eternal and immaterial: God is not limited by either space or time, by matter or movement. Tatian the Syrian deftly summarized God's eternality and immaterial nature back in the second century: "Our God has no introduction in time. He alone is without beginning, and is himself the beginning of all things. God is a spirit, not attending upon matter, but the maker of material spirits and of the appearances which are in matter. He is invisible, being himself the Father of both sensible and invisible things."[59]

Unity. On account of God's simplicity and infinity, he is utterly indivisible. If there were more than one God, then both of those beings would possess something of the Godhead that the other lacked. Each would limit each other in some way, thereby negating each being's claim to being infinite. We also see evidence of God's supreme oneness in the unity of the world. "For things that are diverse do not harmonize in the same order, unless they are reduced thereby to one".[60]

These are only some of the essential attributes of God's nature which can be known by human reason. Others include his goodness, love, omniscience, omnipotence, justice, mercy, and happiness. Although there is much of great value that can be discovered about God through the efforts of the natural intellect, our insights are never complete here on earth, nor will they be even if we are fortunate enough to see God face to face in the beatific vision. Even then, God's vastness exceeds beyond measure the comprehension of the gloried human intellect.

25. Can reason prove the existence of a personal God?

Although it is reasonable to believe in an immaterial, eternal, spiritual, and immensely powerful First Cause of the universe, there is still some difference between the First Cause of the universe and the personal God of the Bible. For example, the God of the Bible is said to be intelligent and good, but why should we think that the First Cause is intelligent or good?

St. Thomas Aquinas argues that the First Cause must be intelligent based on the universe's *order*.[61] In many ways it is easier today to argue for this premise than it was in the twelfth century, because contemporary science has made it even clearer that there is order in the universe. When chemists discover truths about how water molecules and sodium molecules interact, they are uncovering the order in the universe. When physicists discover that force equals mass times acceleration, they are uncovering the order in the universe. And where we find order in nonliving things, we know an *intelligence* exists behind the order.

Take, for example, any book. It would be absurd to think that the order of a book (pages in order, sentences in order, words in order) resulted from a random explosion at a factory containing paper, glue, and ink. The order of a book can only be explained by the intelligence of the author of the book. Likewise, the order of the universe (such as we find in chemistry and physics) is explained by the intelligence of the author of the universe. So it is reasonable to believe in an immaterial, eternal, spiritual, and immensely powerful First Cause of the universe who is intelligent. God's knowledge is perfect because God is the ultimate cause of whatever is in creation.

Even if it is true that the First Cause knows all things, though, do we have any reason to believe that the First Cause is *good*? It is reasonable to believe he is. Since you cannot give what you do not yourself have, God must have goodness. God has the good of existence. God has the good of intelligence. God has the good of immense power. God has the good of creativity, giving rise to the order of the universe. As the First Cause, God is the ultimate source of all other goodness, and cannot but be good himself.

26. Can God know things that aren't true?

Since God sustains all of existence, he knows all real and potentially real things. God knows not just everything that is true now, but also every real thing about the past (such as how many steps Alexander the Great took in his lifetime) and every real thing about the future (such as whether you will finish reading this answer).

However, some critics say God can't know everything because he personally doesn't know what it is like to be afraid or confused, for example. But omniscience only involves God's knowledge of real or possibly real things. Certainly, God knows how *we* feel when *we* are afraid or confused, but God cannot experience these emotions because such a condition is impossible for a being who, by definition, can't lack anything or lose anything that he has.

Since the statement "God is afraid" (and others like it) can't be true, it can't be known. God's omniscience involves his knowledge of only all real or potentially real things.

Other critics object that if God knows the future, then humans can't be free. In their view, if today God knows what I will do tomorrow (like choosing to wear a red shirt), then what I do tomorrow is fixed in advance because God's knowledge never changes. I seem destined to wear a certain shirt and do many other things tomorrow because God's foreknowledge cannot be thwarted and can never be incorrect.

Although this kind of puzzle seems troubling at first, we must remember that it does not disprove the existence of God. At best, it may only prove either that humans have no free will or that God doesn't know the future. Of course, Catholics believe that God both knows the future and allows our free choices to be part of his providential plan.

This is possible because God perceives the past, present, and future in one eternal moment. Whereas the future hasn't happened "yet" for us, God is aware of it "now," as if it were the present for him. God's knowledge of what I do in the future doesn't *determine* what I do at that time, any more than your knowledge of what I do now determines what I'm doing in the present moment. According to the *Catechism*, "to God, all moments of time are present in their immediacy" (600).

27. Is there anything that even God cannot do?

The classic argument against God's omnipotence is found in the age-old question: "Can God make a stone so heavy that even he could not lift it?" If there could be a stone he can't lift, then he's not all-powerful. If he couldn't make such a stone, then that's something God can't do, so he is not all-powerful.

Omnipotence relates to God's ability to actualize the *possible*, so God's omnipotence is not contradicted by his inability to actualize impossible states of affairs, notably anything that contradicts his own essential attributes.

For example, no artist, no matter how skilled, could draw a square circle or a four-sided triangle. We can speak of such things, but it doesn't mean they're possible; we're just combining words in a way that—if you stop to analyze them—makes no sense at all. We can't draw such objects or even imagine them. An all-powerful God could not make one. They're logical impossibilities.

The idea of an omnipotent being making a rock too heavy for him to lift is another such example. An omnipotent being has an infinite amount of lifting power, so anything too heavy for such a being to lift would have to have more than infinite weight. But "more than infinite" is one of those combinations of words that contain a logical impossibility. It's a nonsense phrase that can't correspond to anything in reality or in our imagination.

St. Augustine says that God "cannot do some things for the very reason that he is omnipotent."[62] What he means is that God's all-powerful nature would be contradicted if he engaged in acts that made him powerless in some way. To ask the question "Can God create a rock so heavy that he himself could not lift it?" is in effect to ask, "Is God powerful enough to fail?" This is as logically nonsensical as asking, "Can God purple toaster gremlin cupboard?" When asking questions of the form, "Can God X?", whatever stands in for *X* must be meaningful.

Just as an all-powerful God can't logically overcome his own power, an all-good God can't do things that violate his own wisdom and goodness. For example, he can't do evil acts or cause others to. Such acts would be contrary to his nature and therefore impossible. But in no way does God's inability to do the impossible make him self-contradictory and thus disprove his existence.

28. Does God have a body? Is God a "he"?

Even though the Catholic Church teaches that God is immaterial and transcends the universe, some religions, such as Mormonism, teach that God is a material being like you or me and has a physical body. Defenders of this view quote Genesis 1:26, which records God saying, "Let us make man in our image, after our likeness." If we are made in God's image, then shouldn't our bodies look like God's body?

Other critics defend the idea that God has a physical body by pointing to Scripture passages that describe God sitting on a throne (Psalm 47:8), having a right hand (Acts 7:55–56), and appearing to human beings in bodily form. One example of this would be Moses seeing God's "back" (Exod. 33:23) and speaking with God "face to face, as a man speaks to his friend" (Exod. 33:11). But we must be careful when we interpret verses that use non-literal language to communicate a spiritual truth about God. For example, Psalm 91:4 says God "will cover you with his pinions [feathers], and under his wings you will find refuge," but this passage teaches us about God's love for us, not his wingspan.

The biblical descriptions of God having a human body are not literal because reason shows us that God is the immaterial creator of the universe and Scripture teaches us that God is invisible (Col. 1:15, 1 Tim. 1:17). 1 Timothy 6:16 says that God "dwells in unapproachable light, whom no man has ever seen or can see." Yet Exodus tells us Moses spoke to God "face to face." This should be understood as an expression of the intimacy Moses had with God, rather than as a literal statement, in accordance with what God himself told Moses: "You cannot see my face; for man shall not see me and live" (Exod. 33:20). In addition, being "made in the image of God" means humans have rational abilities and resemble God in an immaterial way, such as by being loving or just (CCC 357). It does not mean God has a physical body like ours.

In fact, John 4:24 says, "God is spirit," and Jesus makes it clear in Luke 24:39 that "a spirit has not flesh and bones." The idea that God is a spirit and not a man was also the common understanding of God in the early Church. The second-century Church Father St. Irenaeus taught that God "is simple, not composed of parts, without structure, altogether like and equal to himself alone. He is all mind, all spirit."[63]

But if God doesn't have a body and isn't a man in his divine nature, then in what sense can God be called a "he"?

It has become fashionable in some circles to refer to God as "she" or to avoid gender pronouns entirely when referring to God. However, the *Catechism* explains:

> By calling God "Father," the language of faith indicates two main things: that God is the first origin of everything and transcendent authority; and that he is at the same time goodness and loving care for all his children. God's parental tenderness can also be expressed by the image of motherhood, which emphasizes God's immanence, the intimacy between Creator and creature . . . God transcends the human distinction between the sexes. He is neither man nor woman: he is God. He also transcends human fatherhood and motherhood, although he is their origin and standard: no one is father as God is Father (239).

The philosophers Peter Kreeft and Ronald Tacelli give us another reason to explain why God revealed himself as "he" instead of as "she" or "it." They say the Jewish religion was distinct in exclusively using male pronouns for the divine because this underscores how God is the distinct, transcendent creator of the universe. They write, "As a man comes into a woman from without to make her pregnant, so God creates the universe from without rather than birthing it from within."[64] Moreover, this is the language Jesus himself deemed appropriate to use when speaking of the God he had come to reveal as Father.

29. How can a good God exist if there is evil in the world?

The problem of evil is the greatest emotional obstacle to belief in God. It just doesn't *feel* like God should let people suffer.

The atheist philosopher J.L. Mackie maintained that belief in God was irrational, for if God were all-knowing (omniscient), he would know that there was evil in the world; if he were all-powerful (omnipotent), he could prevent it; and if he were all-good (omnibenevolent), then he would wish to prevent it. The fact that there is still evil in the world proves that God doesn't exist, or that if he did, he must be "impotent, ignorant, or wicked."

As keenly felt as the problem of evil may be, however, it doesn't represent a strong intellectual or logical obstacle to God's existence. Mackie was wrong: The existence of God and the existence of evil aren't mutually exclusive. Let's look at the three attributes of God that Mackie named.

Omnipotence: Omnipotence doesn't mean the ability to do what is self-contradictory or impossible. It's possible, therefore, for God to will the existence of beings that choose freely between good and evil, but willing this, he can't also force those creatures to choose freely to do good. If he *forced* their choice, it wouldn't be a *free* choice. Likewise, if God wills there to be a natural order, governed by internal principles of causality, he cannot at the same time be forever intervening to suspend those laws of nature.

Omniscience: If God has infinite knowledge, then he knows many things we don't. This means that he may, in fact, have good reasons for permitting things—such as evil and suffering—that seem inexplicable to us.

Human beings have a very limited vantage point, and so what appears to us to be a tragedy may have effects that bring about great good, and conversely, what appears to us as a good thing may, in the long run, prove harmful. Consider the analogy of a small child being taken to the doctor for his immunization shots. He knows the needle hurts, and he can't understand why his own parents are allowing the doctor to cause him pain—that the inoculations help prevent the much greater suffering of disease. He's unable to perceive the greater good.

In the same way, God may have good reasons for permitting, or even at times ordaining, what seems to us incomprehensible. And so he allows evil—and the suffering caused by evil—to exist because of his omniscience, not in spite of it.

Omnibenevolence: As we think about the goodness of God, we must be careful not to impose on him our inadequate understandings of what goodness is. In his book *The Problem of Pain*, the English author C.S. Lewis writes,

> By the goodness of God we mean nowadays almost exclusively his lovingness; and in this we may be right. And by love, in this context, most of us mean kindness. . . . What would really satisfy would be a God who said of anything we happened to like doing, "What does it matter so long as they are contented." We want, in fact, not so much a Father in heaven as a grandfather in heaven—a senile benevolence who, as they say, "liked to see young people enjoying themselves" and whose plan for the universe was simply

> that it might be truly said at the end of each day, "a good time was had by all."[65]

Most theists don't believe that God created us merely for happiness in this life, but also—and more importantly—for eternal happiness with him in the next. So, his omnibenevolence should be judged neither by our limited human standards of goodness nor by what happens in this world alone.

Putting these things together, we can recognize that an omnipotent, omniscient, and omnibenevolent God might have good reasons for tolerating abuses of human free will even though they lead to evil and suffering, either as their direct consequence or as their subsequent punishment. We may not know what all his reasons are, but we sense the value of freedom, including the value of being able to choose good freely rather than by compulsion. Likewise, we can see how in both his power and knowledge God can bring good out of evil, both moral and natural, in ways that we, in our limitations, aren't always able to comprehend. But in faith we can say along with St. Paul, "We know that in everything God works for good with those who love him" (Rom. 8:28).

In fact, rather than disproving God's existence, the reality of moral evil actually points to it, in an indirect way. If moral evil exists, then it follows that real morality exists. If there were no objective good, then we could say there are things we dislike, or what we call suffering, but there could be no such thing as evil, nothing objectively contrary to or lacking in goodness. Therefore, if objective morality exists, then it follows that God exists. Objective moral laws point to a perfect and unchanging moral lawgiver.

It's only within a moral framework, and ultimately within a Christian framework, that the sufferings of this life can have any meaning. It may be a mystery why an all-good God allows suffering and evil to take place, but at least there is meaning and purpose, and God can ultimately bring about justice and draw good out of the sufferings of this life, both now and in eternity. As St. Augustine famously concluded: "Since God is the highest good, he would not allow any evil to exist in his works unless his omnipotence and goodness were such as to bring good even out of evil."[66]

30. Does God use evil for good?

As we saw in the previous question, although the problem of evil is emotionally powerful, from a logical perspective it suffers from a glaring weakness. Specifically, it leaves out a key premise that is usually never argued for: "God can have no good reason to allow evil to exist." But St. Thomas Aquinas said that "God allows evils to happen in order to bring a greater good therefrom."[67] Several distinctions will help to understand this affirmation properly.

First, it's important to understand that evil is not created by God. Rather, evil is an absence of good. More precisely, it is a *privation* of good. As Thomas explains, "Not every defect of good is an evil, but the defect of the good which is naturally due. For the want of sight is not an evil in a stone, but it is an evil in an animal; since it is against the nature of a stone to see."[68]

Second, it is important to distinguish two types of evil—*moral* evil versus physical, or *natural*, evil. Moral evil occurs when an agent acts against freely against the good, such as a man poisoning his wife so he can marry another woman. Moral evil exists in the realm of voluntary action and dispositions for future action (vice). Natural evil, on the other hand, is the evil of not an *action*, but an *effect*. Natural evil is the privation that follows as the consequence of a natural cause such as a woman accidentally drinking poison and dying. Strictly speaking, natural evil is not "evil" in an absolute sense in the same way that moral evil is—it is regrettable for the one who endures it, but it is not *wrong*.

Moral evil and natural evil can be intertwined, as there can be repercussions in the natural realm of what began as moral evil in the human heart. Suffering the consequences of another's moral evil is not itself moral evil, but natural evil. As Thomas says, "Evil is caused in the action otherwise than in the effect".[69]

Third, when we say that God permits evil for the sake of a greater good, that does not mean that God "uses" evil for the sake of good, as we might reprehensibly use an evil means to a desired end (see Rom. 3:8). Rather, God tolerates privations that he does not create on account of a good that he *does* create: the good of our freedom, the good of the natural order of causes and effects existing in the world, or the good he is able to work in us gratuitously through the consequences of evil that we have wrongly chosen.[70]

God is always able to create goodness where goodness is lacking, in the same way that he can create being *ex nihilo* where being is lacking. Just as God does not "use" non-being to create being, so too he does not use evil to create good. Rather, God works the good freely, and often does so on occasions when a privation of goodness (evil) has made this abundantly necessary and possible.

So what reasons might God have for allowing evil to exist?

As we just noted, one reason might be on account of having willed creatures able to freely choose the good and avoid evil. If God always compelled us to choose the good then our actions would be morally insignificant. They would be no different from the preprogrammed actions of appliances or robots.

But what about natural evils like disease or disasters? Respect of human free will may not entirely explain the existence of such evils, although a good deal of the "groaning of creation" (Rom. 8:19-22) can indeed be explained by human negligence and abuse, and ultimately, by original sin. But there may be other reasons why God allows them to exist.

First, in a limited, physical world like ours, there will always be competing goods. What creates perfection in one natural good will create privation in another. For example, fire is a natural evil for a forest. And yet the effect of the fire will be to create a greater perfection of the soil, from which other trees will grow. According to the *Catechism*,

> God freely willed to create a world "in a state of journeying" toward its ultimate perfection. In God's plan this process of becoming involves the appearance of certain beings and the disappearance of others, the existence of the more perfect alongside the less perfect, both constructive and destructive forces of nature. With physical good there exists also *physical evil* as long as creation has not reached perfection (310).

Second, God willed the cause-effect relationships of the world (both natural and moral) to exist for our good. Imagine a world in which causes did not have effects, in which harmful actions did not have harmful consequences!

The condition of leprosy is a good example of what such a world would be like. Leprosy attacks only one type of cell in the body: the nerve endings. Ultimately, the reason leprosy destroys the body is that it *deprives its victim of the sense of pain*. Pain is normally considered an evil, but it is absolutely essential to the detection of harmful behaviors and the motivation to change them.[71] In the same way that leprosy destroys our capacity for physical pain, sin destroys our "spiritual nerve endings," making us insensible to the ways we are harming the image of God in ourselves and others.

A third reason why God might tolerate natural evils is that they serve to build our character. Confrontation with difficulty helps us to develop virtue, both natural and supernatural, in a way that would not be possible in a world immediately brought to perfection. St. Paul, who suffered a great deal during his ministry, considered "that the sufferings of this present time are not worth comparing with the glory that is to be revealed in us" (Rom. 8:18).

Ultimately, as limited human beings we are simply not in a good position to know the good that God can bring to bear in our lives and the lives of others through the evil and suffering we face in the present.

For whatever reason suffering and evil exist in the world, we know that they do not have the last word. In his own crucified son, God has taken upon himself suffering and the consequences of evil, so that "nothing in all creation will be able to separate us from the love of God in Christ Jesus our Lord" (Rom. 8:39).

31. Isn't it arrogant for you to think that your views are the correct ones and that everyone else is wrong?

We should first remember that *all people* think their views are correct. If they didn't, they wouldn't hold those views. Even the person who believes that it is arrogant for people to "think that their views are the correct ones and that everyone else is wrong" thinks *he* is correct in saying so, and those who disagree with him on it are wrong. There is nothing arrogant about having good reasons for a belief and thus really believing what you believe. Just as much as theists believe they are correct when they say God exists and those who disagree are mistaken, atheists believe they are correct when they say God doesn't exist and that the theists are wrong.

It must be recognized, too, that most theists don't believe "everyone else is wrong." Whatever their particular beliefs may be, most theists appreciate and share core essentials beliefs with other theists, even of different creeds: for example, that God exists, that he has revealed himself to humankind through chosen witnesses, and that our actions on earth have eternal consequences in his sight.

An atheist, on the other hand, must believe that the major claims of *all* religions are utterly false and that those who believe those claims are deluded. He must hold that *only* atheists are right about God and that the overwhelming majority of people who have ever lived have been completely wrong about what matters most to them.

Which sounds more humble to you?

32. Since atheism isn't a positive proposition, isn't the burden of proof on those who believe in God?

Theism, which is derived from the Greek word for God, *theos*, is the view that God exists. Atheism, in contrast, is the view that God does not exist. Like theism, atheism is a claim to knowledge—not merely a suspension of belief. In other words, an atheist is a person who *rejects* the existence of God, not a person who isn't sure if God exists or who is waiting to see more proof. We already have a perfectly good word in the English language for a person who withholds belief in God: *agnostic*.

Some atheists want to redefine atheism as something more like agnosticism, so they won't have to prove their position. This eagerness to redefine atheism all but admits the weakness of arguments against God's existence.

The person who is trying to convince someone else of his position must always shoulder the burden of proof. If I want to convince someone to abandon the belief that there is *not* good evidence for God, then I bear the burden of proof. But this applies to atheists as well. If they want to convince me to abandon my belief that there *is* good evidence for God, then they must offer proof. The rejection of God is as much a claim to knowledge as belief in God.

Atheists sometimes claim to be exempt from this obligation of bearing the burden of proof, as they claim that it's impossible to "prove a negative." On the contrary, people do it all the time. You can prove that there are no square circles, or that there are no lions in the room with you right now, or that there are no flaming snowflakes.

In fact, the claim "Negative propositions cannot be proved" is itself a negative proposition! So any argument in favor of it undermines the claim it's attempting to prove.

You don't have to scan everything in the universe to determine that there is no God to be found. If the idea of God is nonsensical, as atheists often claim, then you could demonstrate it logically the same way that you can demonstrate that there are no square circles. A mathematician doesn't have to search every inch of the universe to make sure there aren't any square circles lurking around. Geometry tells him there aren't.

On the other hand, if the idea of God *isn't* nonsensical, then the atheist must provide evidence to show why a believer should conclude that God doesn't exist. He must also refute the arguments that seek to prove God does exist. The traditional arguments for God's existence don't amount to "You can't prove there is not a God; therefore, there must be a God!" Rather, they offer positive reasons for believing in God as the universe's creator, designer, moral lawgiver, First Cause, and so forth.

33. If everything needs a cause, then God does, too, right?

Theists don't say that *everything* needs a cause—only things that began to exist. Or, to put it another way, that things that can fail to exist need a cause for their existence.

Things that come into being at a certain point in time must have a cause for their existence. But if something exists outside of time—such as God—then it never had a moment where it came into being and so doesn't need a cause.

Likewise, if something *doesn't have to exist,* then we need an explanation for why it does exist. But if something does have to exist—if it's a *necessary being* like God—then it doesn't need an explanation. Existence is simply part of what it is.

To our observation, the things around us in the universe appear to have had a beginning in time, and so they need a cause—a reason why they began to exist in the first place. All those bits of matter in the universe—the stars, blades of grass, the clock on your desk—don't seem to be necessary. They could, in theory, *not* exist. Therefore, we need an explanation for why they do exist.

God, according to the traditional theistic definition, can be the ultimate explanation for these things because he needs no further explanation. Indeed, the question "Who created God?" is nonsensical, because it amounts to asking, "Who created an uncreated being?"

34. How can we believe in God without scientific proof?

Science is a method for discovering truths about the natural world. But it has nothing to say about things *outside* the natural world—things that can't be observed or tested. Examining the material world, for example, can't disprove spiritual truths, such as the existence of an immaterial God. Even if science were to describe the physical universe exhaustively, it would still leave the question: Why does the universe, and the laws that govern it, exist?

Evolutionary biologist and atheist Stephen Jay Gould sums it up nicely: "To say it for all my colleagues and for the umpteenth million time

. . . science simply cannot (by its legitimate methods) adjudicate the issue of God's possible superintendence of nature. We neither affirm nor deny it; we simply can't comment on it as scientists."[72]

True science recognizes the limits of its sphere of knowledge. The view that science can or should provide the answer to *every* question is not true science, but a corruption of science called *scientism*. It claims that we shouldn't accept as true anything that we can't prove scientifically.

Yet clearly there are many things science can't prove:

1) It can't prove the laws of logic, or mathematical truths—it merely presupposes them.

2) It can't prove metaphysical truths, such as the primacy of being in act over being in potency or the existential goodness of your best friend. These are true judgments of the rational intellect, but they can't be proven scientifically.

3) It can't prove morality. Science can't show that we have a duty to help a starving child or that Nazi concentration camps were evil. Good and evil are not material entities that can be measured in a laboratory; therefore their existence and nature are beyond what science can prove.

There is also this fact: if scientism were true, then it should be scientifically provable.

Is it?

No, because the claim "You shouldn't believe anything unless it is proven by science" is a philosophical claim that you can't verify by any scientific experiment! Rather, it expresses a value judgment—what we *should* choose to believe—placing it in the realm of ethics and morals. We have already seen that science can't verify the existence of immaterial moral truths. This means that scientism is not only false, it is also self-refuting, because it can't meet its own test.

35. Don't people only believe in God or religion based on what their family and culture teach them?

It's certainly true that most people stick close to the belief system that they were trained in as children, and these systems vary from place to place and even from family to family. It's just a fact of history and human nature. But if this is meant to be an argument against God's existence, it is utterly fallacious.

Attempting to invalidate a belief based on how that belief originated is called the *genetic fallacy*. Obviously, people may come to hold all sorts of beliefs for inadequate reasons, and those beliefs could still be true. For example, a child may have learned from a cartoon that you could fit about a million earths into the sun. If we were to say to him or her, "That can't be true; you learned it from a cartoon," that would be committing the genetic fallacy.

Applied to God's existence, this faulty logic cuts both ways. If you were an atheist raised in an unbelieving family or in a secular culture, would being a product of your environment invalidate your atheism? Obviously, in neither case does how we were raised tell us whether our beliefs are *true*, which is the real question. In order to get at the answer to that question, you have to look at evidence.

36. How can God exist when religion is the number-one source of hatred and violence in the world?

Without conceding for a moment that "religion is the number one source" of these things, it needs to be understood that a belief's effects on society don't tell us whether that belief is true.

For example, the Soviet dictator Joseph Stalin ruled over an atheistic regime that killed tens of millions of people. That was an enormous crime against humanity, but we can't conclude from it that atheism is false and so there must be a God. Likewise we can't take crimes committed in God's name as proof that theism is false and so God doesn't exist.

37. How can I decide about God's existence if I'm not sure?

Sometimes, even after much reflection and study, people still feel that they can't decide between atheism and belief in God. The evidence seems so evenly weighted.

What then?

If it seems impossible to decide between these options based on the evidence, then perhaps you could consider the advantages of choosing one course over the other. That is, what could the results be of your choice? There are four possible scenarios:

1) You choose to live as if God exists, and you're correct: he does exist.
2) You choose to live as if God doesn't exist, and you're incorrect: he does exist.
3) You choose to live as if God exists, and you're incorrect: he doesn't exist.
4) You choose to live as if God doesn't exist, and you're correct: he doesn't exist.

This simple, structured reasoning is known as "Pascal's Wager" because it was advanced by Blaise Pascal, seventeenth-century mathematician, physicist, philosopher, and theologian.

In the first scenario, you stand to receive the infinite good of everlasting life, whereas in the second, you risk missing out on this infinite good, with eternally significant consequences.

In the third scenario, what awaits you after this life is not heaven but non-existence, but during life you would enjoy the consolation (and, studies suggest, more health and happiness) that comes from believing God exists. What would it matter that you were wrong? You wouldn't exist anymore.

In the fourth scenario, you'd be right about God's non-existence, but what difference would that make after you were dead? Meanwhile, you would be deprived of the sense of meaning and purpose in life that comes from a relationship with God and the community of believers.

Of these four options, believing in God offers either small or great rewards with little risk, whereas not believing poses potentially great risk with little reward. That being the case, when the evidence leaves you torn between belief and unbelief, the rational choice is to believe. Even basic self-interest, which is certainly part of human nature whether you believe God built it into us or not, clearly points toward believing in God.

Bear in mind that this is not an argument for God's existence but rather an argument for *believing* in God's existence. It's also not an argument for every possible situation. It's designed for those who feel torn between atheism and belief in the kind of God that Christianity proposes but who aren't at a point where they feel that they can settle the question by objective evidence. If you're in that situation, then this argument can help you.

If you think about it, there are many times in life when we must make decisions about what we will believe without having conclusive proof. If we waited, for example, to have conclusive proof that a prospective spouse will always be faithful and never betray us, we'd never get married. In fact, trying to get that kind of proof would likely crush the relationship before we could even get engaged! No, at some point we must make a leap of faith (and trust) and make the commitment, even without total proof.

Remember that no one is ever totally free of doubts. The question isn't whether you have them, but whether you'll let them challenge your commitment. As Lewis wrote, faith is not the absence of doubt, but "the art of holding on to things your reason has once accepted, in spite of your changing moods."[73]

If we were to change our beliefs whenever we have feelings of doubt, we wouldn't get very far in the pursuit of truth. When we recognize that doubts and fears can be random and temporary emotions, it helps us to set them aside and not be thrown into a tailspin. They will pass, and our fundamental commitment to our beliefs will remain. We can keep acting on the premise that God exists, that he loves us, and that we want to please him.

It's also important to remember that, if all that's true, we're not in this alone. We can entrust ourselves to God, to guide and illuminate us.

Here are four ways to grow in your faith, especially when having doubts:

> *Study:* Learn more about Christianity and what the great saints and Christian writers had to say about faith and doubt. You may be edified—and surprised—at what you find.
>
> *Read the Bible:* Begin with one of the Gospels in the New Testament, such as Luke or John, and gradually make your way through the New Testament, which is the part of the Bible most directly applicable to us today.
>
> The Bible is not simply words about God, but is the word *of* God, and the more you study it, the more you will learn about God and the way he interacts with us.
>
> *Pray:* Set aside a portion of time daily for personal prayer. You might spend this time conversing with God, telling him your fears and hopes in your own words and then spending some time in silence. You also might consider learning some structured prayers, such as the Lord's Prayer, which Jesus himself taught us to say. Or,

if you're skeptical, you might pray, "Lord, if you're real, would you reveal yourself to me in a way that I would understand?"

Get involved: God made us social creatures. We are meant to be with other people, to help them, and to receive help from them. That applies to our faith life as much as anything else. That is why Jesus founded a Church.

So get involved in your local church. Meet other Christians, and become part of the local Christian community. Take an inquirer's class. Go to Bible studies. Join a teen or young adult group. Go to church on Sundays. If you're Catholic, receive the sacraments, such as confession and the Holy Eucharist.

PART 2

DIVINE REVELATION

INTRODUCTION

All Christians generally agree that Christian doctrine must be determined in accordance with God's revelation. It makes sense that everything God has revealed is worthy of belief and, in many cases, necessary for salvation. Indeed, Jesus, quoting from Deuteronomy 8:3, emphasizes the importance of the *word of God*: "It is written, 'Man shall not live by bread alone, but by every word that proceeds from the mouth of God'" (Matt. 4:4).

Tragically, though, not all Christians agree on what God's word is, and thus do not agree on all matters of Christian doctrine.

Most non-Catholic Christians claim that the Bible alone is the word of God. This is a relatively novel idea in the history of Christianity, having come to the fore only since the time of the Protestant Reformation. For most of Christian history, Christians have believed that the deposit of faith was received long before a book of the New Testament was ever written (see Jude 3). That faith was first delivered to the early Church orally, not in writing.

Scholars nearly unanimously agree that the first books of the New Testament (1 and 2 Thessalonians) were not written until the middle of the first century, around A.D. 50-52. Yet, already, the revelation of Jesus Christ was being spread through the oral teaching of the apostles and their successors. The books of the New Testament were written over a period of several decades, and it was not always immediately apparent exactly how they should be understood (see 2 Pet. 3:16). So the early Christians came to interpret them correctly through authoritative oral teaching—what the Church calls *Sacred Tradition* (see 2 Pet. 1:20–21).

Most of Sacred Tradition contains the same material that is found in Sacred Scripture, only in different form. This makes the two useful for interpreting and confirming each other.

> This living transmission, accomplished in the Holy Spirit, is called tradition, since it is distinct from Sacred Scripture, though closely connected to it. Through tradition, the Church, in her doctrine, life and worship, perpetuates and transmits to every generation all that she herself is, all that she believes (CCC 78).

Without the living transmission and authoritative interpretation of divine revelation ensured by apostolic succession, believers would be left with

Scripture alone (*sola scriptura*), and their own fallible interpretations of it, to determine their doctrines and practices. This is indeed the situation of many Christians since the Reformation in the sixteenth century, since many early Reformers rejected Sacred Tradition—with the inevitable result of countless disagreements and widespread splintering into thousands of Christian denominations.

38. What is the "word of God"?

The term *word of God* refers to God's divine revelation to humanity, in which he reveals himself to us for the sake of our salvation. The Vatican II document *Dei Verbum* (DV) explains:

> Through divine revelation, God chose to show forth and communicate himself and the eternal decisions of his will regarding the salvation of men. That is to say, he chose to share with them those divine treasures which totally transcend the understanding of the human mind (6).

Christians generally agree that the *fullness* of God's revelation is the Son of God, Jesus Christ.[74] St. John begins his Gospel writing about the "Word" in this sense:

> In the beginning was the Word, and the Word was with God, and the Word was God. He was in the beginning with God; all things were made through him, and without him was not anything made that was made. In him was life, and the life was the light of men. The light shines in the darkness, and the darkness has not overcome it (John 1:1–5).

Quoting the *Catechism*, Pope Benedict XVI wrote in his post-synodal apostolic exhortation on the word of God, *Verbum Domini*,

> The Christian faith is not a "religion of the book": Christianity is the "religion of the word of God," not of "a written and mute word, but of the incarnate and living Word." Consequently the Scripture is to be proclaimed, heard, read, received and experienced as the word of God, in the stream of the apostolic Tradition from which it is inseparable (7).

The term *word of God* thus refers principally and primarily to the person of the incarnate and living Word of God, Jesus Christ. In a secondary sense, it refers to the spoken and written revelation of God upon which Christian teaching is based, and which is passed on from generation to generation.

For example, in the book of Acts, Luke writes about "preaching the word of God" (6:2) so that the word "increased" (6:7) as it "grew and multiplied" (12:24). The word of God is "proclaimed" (13:5), "spoken" (13:46), and people came to "hear" it (13:7, 44), being "taught" (18:11).

It is this secondary sense of the term that Christians most often have in mind when referring to the revelation of God, entrusted to the Church and taught throughout history. The word of God, spoken and written, contains the truths that Christians must believe and make active in their lives for the sake of their salvation and the salvation of others. St. Jude calls it "the faith which was once for all delivered to the saints" (Jude 3).

Jesus entrusted this *deposit of faith* to the apostles and their successors, guided by the Holy Spirit, to be safeguarded from corruption and taught in every age just as Jesus commissioned them to do before his ascension (see Matt. 28:19–20). *Dei Verbum* elaborates:

> In his gracious goodness, God has seen to it that what he had revealed for the salvation of all nations would abide perpetually in its full integrity and be handed on to all generations. Therefore Christ the Lord in whom the full revelation of the supreme God is brought to completion (see Cor. 1:20; 3:13; 4:6), commissioned the apostles to preach to all men that gospel which is the source of all saving truth and moral teaching, and to impart to them heavenly gifts. This gospel had been promised in former times through the prophets, and Christ himself had fulfilled it and promulgated it with his lips (7).

It is important to recognize that the apostles carried out their commission both through preaching *and* writing. The *Catechism Church* explains:

> In keeping with the Lord's command, the gospel was handed on in two ways:
>
> 1) *Orally* by the apostles who handed on, by the spoken word of their preaching, by the example they gave, by the institutions they established, what they themselves had received—whether

from the lips of Christ, from his way of life and his works, or whether they had learned it at the prompting of the Holy Spirit.

2) *In writing* by those apostles and other men associated with the apostles who, under the inspiration of the same Holy Spirit, committed the message of salvation to writing (CCC 76).

In the Catholic Church, we refer to the apostles' preaching, examples, and institutions as *Sacred Tradition* (or *apostolic Tradition*) and their writing (including the Old Testament that they received from the Jews) as *Sacred Scripture*. Many other Christians accept Scripture alone (the *written* word of God) as the only definitive source of divine truth. Catholics, however, believe that God did not limit his revelation to a book; instead he gave his saving truth to mankind in two complementary and equally authoritative forms.

> For Sacred Scripture is the word of God inasmuch as it is consigned to writing under the inspiration of the divine Spirit, while Sacred Tradition takes the word of God entrusted by Christ the Lord and the Holy Spirit to the apostles, and hands it on to their successors in its full purity, so that led by the light of the Spirit of Truth, they may in proclaiming it preserve this word of God faithfully, explain it, and make it more widely known. Consequently, it is not from Sacred Scripture alone that the Church draws her certainty about everything which has been revealed. Therefore both Sacred Tradition and Sacred Scripture are to be accepted and venerated with the same sense of loyalty and reverence (*Dei Verbum* 9).

Thus, the Catholic Church bases its teaching upon one source: the word of God, transmitted to his people in two ways.

39. What is Sacred Scripture?

Sacred Scripture is the written form of the word of God. It comprises the books of the Old and New Testament contained in the Christian Bible.

The Old Testament is important because it sets the foundation for the fullness of God's revelation in Jesus Christ. *Dei Verbum* explains:

> The plan of salvation foretold by the sacred authors, recounted and explained by them, is found as the true word of God in the books

> of the Old Testament: these books, therefore, written under divine inspiration, remain permanently valuable.
>
> The principal purpose to which the plan of the Old Covenant was directed was to prepare for the coming of Christ, the redeemer of all and of the messianic kingdom, to announce this coming by prophecy (Luke 24:44; John 5:39; 1 Pet. 1:10), and to indicate its meaning through various types (1 Cor. 10:12). Now the books of the Old Testament, in accordance with the state of mankind before the time of salvation established by Christ, reveal to all men the knowledge of God and of man and the ways in which God, just and merciful, deals with men. These books, though they also contain some things which are incomplete and temporary, nevertheless show us true divine pedagogy. These same books, then, give expression to a lively sense of God, contain a store of sublime teachings about God, sound wisdom about human life, and a wonderful treasury of prayers, and in them the mystery of our salvation is present in a hidden way. Christians should receive them with reverence (14–15).

So the Old Testament remains a valuable part of God's word as it prepares the way for Christ. Yet it cannot be fully understood apart from the New Testament, in which the preparation comes to fruition. In the New Testament we find the fulfillment of the revelation of the Old. *Dei Verbum* continues:

> The word of God, which is the power of God for the salvation of all who believe (see Rom. 1:16), is set forth and shows its power in a most excellent way in the writings of the New Testament. For when the fullness of time arrived (Gal. 4:4), the Word was made flesh and dwelt among us in his fullness of graces and truth (John 1:14). Christ established the kingdom of God on earth, manifested his Father and himself by deeds and words, and completed his work by his death, resurrection and glorious ascension and by the sending of the Holy Spirit. Having been lifted up from the earth, he draws all men to himself (John 12:32), he who alone has the words of eternal life (see John 6:68). This mystery had not been manifested to other generations as it was now revealed to his holy apostles and prophets in the Holy Spirit (Eph. 3:4–6), so that they

> might preach the gospel, stir up faith in Jesus, Christ and Lord, and gather together the Church. Now the writings of the New Testament stand as a perpetual and divine witness to these realities (17).

Thus, the Old Testament and the New Testament together bring us the revelation of salvation history. The Old Testament prepares us for the New. The New Testament brings to light and fulfills what was foretold in the Old. *Dei Verbum* once again:

> God, the inspirer and author of both Testaments, wisely arranged that the New Testament be hidden in the Old and the Old be made manifest in the New. For, though Christ established the New Covenant in his blood (Luke 22:20; 1 Cor. 11:25), still the books of the Old Testament with all their parts, caught up into the proclamation of the gospel, acquire and show forth their full meaning in the New Testament (Matt. 5:17; Luke 24:27; Rom. 16:25–26; 2 Cor. 14:16) and in turn shed light on it and explain it (16).

40. In what sense is the Bible the inspired word of God?

When Christians say the Bible is inspired, or that it is the word of God, that phrase can be misunderstood. Some people think that calling the Bible the "word of God" means God himself penned every word in it and used some kind of heavenly parcel delivery service to send it down to earth. But Jews and Christians have always known that the parts of the Bible that came directly from God, such as the Ten Commandments that God wrote on the tablets at Mount Sinai, are few and far between. Instead, it was men inspired by God who wrote the Bible's original manuscripts.

A more common mistake is to believe that these biblical authors acted merely as scribes; in other words, they were only the *mechanical* authors of Scripture. According to this view, none of the Bible's texts came from the human authors' minds, but from God's mind alone. The human authors either recorded the revelation God dictated to them, or God took control of their bodies and wrote his revelation through them. As Protestant author Jasper James Ray put it, "The very words of the Bible were given to the authors, and not just the ideas they convey. The writers were not left to choose the words."[75]

The idea that the human authors of Scripture recorded what God said just as a stenographer records courtroom testimony is common in certain kinds of biblical Fundamentalism, which, according to the Church's Pontifical Biblical Commission, "seeks to escape any closeness of the divine and the human . . . for this reason, it tends to treat the biblical text as if it had been dictated word for word by the Spirit. It fails to recognize that the word of God has been formulated in language and expression conditioned by various periods."[76]

This "dictation theory" of inspiration also doesn't make sense of passages such as 1 Corinthians 1:14–16, in which St. Paul wrote, "I am thankful that I baptized none of you except Crispus and Gaius; lest any one should say that you were baptized in my name. (I did baptize also the household of Stephanas. Beyond that, I do not know whether I baptized anyone else.)" Here it seems likely that Paul didn't write down whatever God told him, because God would have known whom Paul baptized. Instead, Paul appears to have used his own ideas and words to write to the Christians in Corinth.

That being said, God is still the author of Scripture even if its human authors used their own words and ideas when they wrote the Bible. According to *Dei Verbum*:

> The books of both the Old and New Testaments in their entirety, with all their parts, are sacred and canonical because written under the inspiration of the Holy Spirit, they have God as their author and have been handed on as such to the Church herself. In composing the sacred books, God chose men and while employed by him they made use of their powers and abilities, so that with him acting in them and through them, they, as true authors, consigned to writing everything and only those things which he wanted (11).

Another way to understand the inspiration of Scripture is to compare it to the Incarnation. Just as Christ is God's Word that became flesh and dwelt among us (John 1:14), Scripture is God's word made into written characters that dwells among us. *Dei Verbum* taught: "For the words of God, expressed in human language, have been made like human discourse, just as the word of the eternal Father, when he took to himself the flesh of human weakness, was in every way made like men" (13).

Pope St. John Paul II agreed, and said in an address to the Pontifical Biblical Commission, "After the heavenly glorification of the humanity of the

Word made flesh, it is again due to written words that his stay among us is attested to in an abiding way."[77]

Just as Christ's human nature did not contradict his divinity, the human words of Scripture do not contradict God's authorship of it, even though their finite nature limits what God can communicate through them. For instance, God allowed the human authors of Scripture to retain their own way of speaking about the natural world, even where that way of speaking does not correspond to our modern, scientific way of understanding it.

41. Why don't Catholics rely on the Bible alone?

Imagine if every American had the authority to decide what the U.S. Constitution means. Each person could claim that his actions fell under his own interpretation of the words in the Constitution. What would come of this approach? Anarchy. Fortunately, America's Founding Fathers created the Supreme Court to interpret the Constitution. Although the Supreme Court isn't divinely protected from error, as is the Church's Magisterium, its decisions ensure a uniform legal code that binds all citizens equally.

The Protestant Reformers believed that all the truth about Christianity comes from the Bible alone; or that the Bible is our sole, infallible rule of faith. They called this principle *sola scriptura* or "Scripture alone," but we might call it a "blueprint for anarchy."[78] Indeed, today we witness the proliferation of Protestant denominations that uphold contradictory positions on many important matters of faith. For just as personal interpretation of the Constitution would lead to chaos for the rule of law, relying solely on one's personal interpretation of the Bible as a guide to Christian doctrine leads to chaos for the rule of faith.

Interestingly, the Bible itself never asserts that all of divine revelation is found explicitly and only within its pages, despite assertions to the contrary.

One passage that Protestants usually cite in favor of *sola scriptura* is 2 Timothy 3:16–17. In this letter, St. Paul tells his disciple Timothy how he should behave and grow as a man of God and leader in the Church. He writes, "All Scripture is inspired by God and profitable for teaching, for reproof, for correction, and for training in righteousness, that the man of God may be complete, equipped for every good work." Thus, the argument goes, Scripture is sufficient to make the man of God "complete, equipped for every good work," and it is therefore sufficient to salvation.

Of course, Catholics agree that all Scripture is inspired by God and is useful for teaching and training. But just because Scripture is *profitable* for instruction in holiness and *necessary* for holiness to reach its completion, that does not mean it is the *exclusive* and *sufficient* means to attain this goal. Elsewhere Paul describes other things too equipping one for "every good work," without that making these things a Christian's sole source of saving doctrine. For example, Paul tells Timothy that if he cleanses himself from bad influences, he will be a vessel ready for "every good work" (2 Tim. 2:21), but that doesn't mean Timothy's prudence will cause him to know all the essential doctrines of the Faith.

Another passage often cited in favor of *sola scriptura* can be found in the Acts of the Apostles, where St. Luke briefly tells us about St. Paul's missionary work at Berea:

> The brethren immediately sent Paul and Silas away by night to Berea; and when they arrived they went into the Jewish synagogue. Now these Jews were more noble than those in Thessalonica, for they received the word with all eagerness, examining the Scriptures daily to see if these things were so. Many of them therefore believed, with not a few Greek women of high standing as well as men (Acts 17:10–12).

If the Bereans are commended for examining *Scripture* to test the word of Paul, does that not prove the sufficiency and supremacy of Scripture? In reality, what Luke commends them for is not their adherence to Scripture alone, but their eagerness in receiving "the word" that Paul delivered to them: the gospel message Jesus commissioned him to deliver (cf. Acts 9:15).

As a Jewish convert to Christianity himself, Paul knew the Old Testament well and he knew that it prophesied about Jesus. In the company of Jews he undoubtedly explained the Old Testament in light of Sacred Tradition in order to show them about the truth of Christianity. "I delivered to you as of first importance what I also received, that Christ died for our sins *in accordance with the Scriptures*; that he was buried, that he was raised on the third day *in accordance with the Scriptures*" (1 Cor. 15:3-4). The Bereans eagerly listened to Paul bringing the Old Testament to life through the teaching he received from Christ, and *this* is what Luke commends them for—their eagerness in receiving Sacred Tradition. They continued daily to revisit the Old Testament and see it come to life, discovering in the old familiar texts new depths of meaning they had never noticed or understood before. As a result, many Jews—including many of the Bereans—became Christians.

The Bereans, therefore, do not prove *sola scriptura*; nor did they even practice it themselves. If they did, they never would have "eagerly received" the Tradition that Paul preached.

42. How do we know which writings belong in the Bible?

The definitive list of books contained in the Bible is known as the *canon* of Scripture (from a Greek word meaning *rule*). The canon is not mentioned anywhere in the Bible itself. Rather, it was discerned and decided by the authority of the early Church and comes down to us through Sacred Tradition.

The earliest authoritative canon was given by Pope Damasus at a local synod held in Rome in the year 382. Up until that time, there had been disagreement over the canon, and there existed around ten different proposed lists that didn't correspond exactly to what the Bible now contains. To settle the matter, the early Church formally identified the canon in no fewer than five instances: the Synod of Rome (382), the Council of Hippo (393), the Council of Carthage (397), a letter from Pope Innocent I to Exsuperius, bishop of Toulouse (405), and the Second Council of Carthage (419). In every instance, the identified canon was identical to what the Catholic Bible contains today.

Because they dismiss the role of Sacred Tradition, Protestants claim that an authoritative Church is not needed to determine which ancient writings are inspired. Some defer to the Jewish rabbinic tradition, which, during the first centuries after Christ, limited the canon of Hebrew Scriptures to books older than the fourth century B.C. (or attributed to an author who had lived before that period) and originally written in Hebrew, among other criteria.

Others say it's simply obvious which books belong in the Bible and which do not.

But is it really so obvious?

After all, some books of the Bible don't seem very "biblical." Ecclesiastes contains what seems to be a cynical rejection of the afterlife, the third letter of John doesn't even mention the name of Jesus Christ, and the letter to Philemon doesn't teach any specific doctrine. The part of the book of Esther that Protestants do consider to be inspired Scripture never even mentions God! Yet, all these writings are found in the Bible, although other writings that were popular in the early Church, such as the *Didache* or the Letter of Clement (which was even read in early Church services) are not.[79]

Without an authoritative Church, how can the canonicity of this or that ancient writing be determined? Protestant theologian R.C. Sproul famously suggested that the best we can say is that the canon of Scripture is "a fallible list of infallible books."[80] It's fallible because, from Sproul's point of view, the Church that defined the canon had no real authority. But if a non-authoritative group of Christians in the third and fourth centuries could decide what the canon of Scripture was, then why couldn't another non-authoritative group of Christians do the same today?

For example, in 2013, Hal Taussig, a member of a group of skeptical scholars called the Jesus Seminar, published a collection called *A New New Testament*. Added to the traditional New Testament were second-century apocryphal gospels such as *The Gospel of Truth*, as well as texts from the Dead Sea Scrolls like *The Thunder: Perfect Mind*. Most Protestants would never accept such books as part of the Bible. But what authority do they have to say someone like Taussig is wrong?

Even some Protestants understand the difficulty that the question of canonicity poses for their theology. According to prominent Reformed theologian Douglas Wilson:

The problem with contemporary Protestants is that they have no doctrine of the Table of Contents. With the approach that is popular in conservative Evangelical circles, one simply comes to the Bible by means of an epistemological lurch. The Bible "just is," and any questions about how it got here are dismissed as a nuisance. But time passes, the questions remain unanswered, the silence becomes awkward, and conversions of thoughtful Evangelicals to Rome proceed apace.[81]

If the Catholic Church has divine authority from Christ, however, then Catholic Christians don't have to say that the Bible "just is." We can say that the Church has the power to recognize and pronounce the true canon of Scripture.

43. Why is the Catholic Bible bigger than the Protestant version?

The Protestant biblical canon has sixty-six books: twenty-seven in the New Testament and thirty-nine in the Old Testament. The Catholic Bible has the same number of books in the New Testament, but it has seven more books in the Old Testament (Tobit, Judith, Wisdom, Sirach, Baruch, and 1 and 2 Maccabees) as well as more chapters in the books of Esther and Daniel. Catholics refer to these books as *deuterocanonical*, whereas Protestants call them the *apocrypha*.

The Catholic Bible contains the deuterocanonical books because they were part of the biblical tradition that Jesus and the apostles were familiar with and made reference to. Called the *Septuagint*, the Greek translation of the Old Testament that contained these books was widely used in the early Church because Greek (like English today) was a universal language of commerce.

Some Protestants say we should not include the deuterocanonical books in the canon because Jesus and the apostles never quoted from them elsewhere in Scripture. But those aren't the only books that aren't quoted elsewhere. As Protestant scholar Bruce Metzger observes, "Nowhere in the New Testament is there a direct quotation from the canonical books of Joshua, Judges, Chronicles, Ezra, Nehemiah, Esther, Ecclesiastes, the Song of Solomon, Obadiah, Zephaniah, and Nahum; and the New Testament allusions to them are few in number."[82]

In fact, the New Testament authors never even *allude* to Esther, Ecclesiastes, or the Song of Solomon despite the fact that the content of these books was relevant to their own writings. They did, however, allude to the deuterocanonical books, such as in Mark 12:18–22, where the Sadducees question Jesus about a woman who was married to seven brothers who all died consecutively. That story is from the deuterocanonical book of Tobit, yet Jesus doesn't dismiss it as apocryphal.

Another example is Hebrews 11:35, where the author mentions how some women "received their dead by resurrection. Some were tortured, refusing to accept release, that they might rise again to a better life." This refers to persecutions found in 2 Maccabees 7, where a group of brothers suffer martyrdom instead of violating God's law. Their mother said, "Do not fear this butcher, but prove worthy of your brothers. Accept death, so that in God's mercy I may get you back again with your brothers" (2 Macc. 7:29).

Again, when the crowd and the Jewish leaders taunt Jesus because he declared himself to be the Son of God yet God didn't save him from being crucified (Matt. 27:39–43), it is a clear allusion to the deuterocanonical book of Wisdom, which says, "If the righteous man is God's son, he will help him, and will deliver him from the hand of his adversaries" (2:18). The crowd's gloating that God had failed to do this for Jesus makes sense only if they believed the book of Wisdom was inspired in what it said about the Son of God.

Some Protestants say that at the end of the first century A.D. a Jewish gathering called the Council of Jamnia definitively established the Hebrew canon, and Christians should abide by that decision. But, aside from evidence that there actually was no Council of Jamnia,[83] this argument would justify rejecting the canonical Gospels, too, because they were also allegedly rejected at this council! If certain books of Christian Scripture were suspect with Jewish authorities, it may well be precisely because these books had become popular with Christians, who in their eyes were just apostate Jews.[84]

So the real question is not "Why is the Catholic Bible bigger?" Rather, it's "Why is the Protestant version smaller?" By the time of the Reformation in the sixteenth century, Christians had been using the same seventy-three books in their translations of the Bible (forty-six in the Old Testament, twenty-seven in the New Testament) for more than 1,100 years. This practice changed with Martin Luther, who jettisoned them because they taught doctrines that conflicted with his novel theology. (The most famous example would be 2 Maccabees 12:46, which teaches the efficacy of praying for the dead in order to atone for their sins.[85]) Protestantism as a whole eventually following his lead, which led the Council of Trent (1545-1563) to infallibly affirm the full canon of Scripture.

Today, many Protestants do not realize that their versions of the Bible are lacking so much text that was originally included. However, anyone who studies the authentic history of the canon must admit that this is the case. As Anglican church historian J.N.D. Kelly acknowledge, for the great majority of the early Church Fathers "the deuterocanonical writings ranked as Scripture in the fullest sense."[86]

44. Isn't the Muratorian Fragment proof that the canon was settled long before the fourth century?

The Muratorian Fragment, the surviving portion of a second-century document discovered in 1740 by Lodovico Antonio Muratori, is the oldest extant listing of New Testament–era books revered by early Christians. It was written sometime between 155 and 200. Patristic scholars believe the unknown author originally wrote the list in Greek (since the Latin is very poor), but the oldest copy available is an eighth-century Latin manuscript.

Protestants sometimes cite the Muratorian Fragment in defense of an earlier dating of the canon, well before any synodal authority of the Catholic Church was engaged on the matter. But although the Muratorian Fragment is important for studying how the early Church developed the New Testament canon, it does not give exactly the same list of books that was later adopted as canonical at the Synod of Rome and councils of Hippo and Carthage. The Muratorian Fragment is just that: a portion of a larger list of books which were considered canonical or quasi-canonical by some Christians during the second century.

The Fragment itself provides us with a good, though incomplete, idea of this early list of books. Virtually the entire New Testament canon as we know it is represented: the Gospels of Luke and John (preceded by what seems to be an allusion to the Gospel of Mark), Acts, 1 and 2 Corinthians, Galatians, Romans, Ephesians, Philippians, Colossians, 1 and 2 Thessalonians, Philemon, Titus, 1 and 2 Timothy, Jude, two letters of John (since the Fragment simply says "the two ascribed to John," we don't know which two of his three letters are meant), and Revelation.

The unknown author includes non-canonical books in this lineup as well: the so-called Pauline epistles to the Laodiceans and to the Alexandrians (about which the Fragment's author expresses his conviction that they were not authored by Paul), the *Wisdom Written by the Friends of Solomon in His Honor*, the *Apocalypse of Peter*, and the *Shepherd* (written by Hermas). The Fragment's list is cut short with a final, enigmatic phrase that may indicate that the author had gone on to include still other non-inspired writings: "Those also who wrote the new book of psalms for Marcion, together with Basilides, the founder of the Asian Cataphrygians."

And so, although the Muratorian Fragment lists most of the New Testament books, it is missing a few (for example, Matthew and James), and it adds several works that are not inspired.

Although the Fragment came close, it did not represent the actual canon of inspired Scripture that would later be settled in accordance with Sacred Tradition by the authority of the Church. Indeed, there is no internal evidence in the document that it even sought to represent any kind of official canon that was regarded by the Church as binding.

In the first four centuries of the Church, many books, such as the seven letters of Ignatius, the Letter of Clement [the fourth pope] to the Corinthians, the Didache, and the Shepherd, were revered by many Christians as inspired but were later excluded from the canon of Scripture. It was not until the Synod of Rome and the subsequent councils of Hippo and Carthage that the Catholic Church defined which books made it into the New Testament and which didn't. Probably the council fathers studied the (complete) Muratorian Fragment as well as other documents, including, of course, the books in question themselves, but it was not until these much later councils that the Church officially settled the issue.

45. Are deuterocanonical books second-class Scripture?

The seven books in question—Tobit, Judith, 1 and 2 Maccabees, Wisdom, Sirach, and Baruch (and parts of Esther and Daniel)—are termed *deuterocanonical.* This term is not to be confused with the word *apocrypha*, which in modern usage denotes texts of dubious authenticity.[87]

What does *deuterocanonical* mean? The term, coined in 1566, technically means "second canon," but this is somewhat of a misnomer. The *Catholic Encyclopedia* explains:

> The terms *protocanonical* and *deuterocanonical*, of frequent usage among Catholic theologians and exegetes, require a word of caution.... It would be wrong to infer from them that the Church successively possessed two distinct biblical canons. Only in a partial and restricted way may we speak of a first and second canon. Protocanonical (*protos*, "first") is a conventional word denoting those sacred writings which have been always received by Christendom without dispute. The protocanonical books of the Old Testament correspond with those of the Bible of the Hebrews and the Old Testament as received by Protestants. The deuterocanonical (*deuteros*, "second") are those whose scriptural character was contested in some quarters, but which long ago gained a secure footing in the Bible of the Catholic Church, though those of the Old Testament are classed by Protestants as the "Apocrypha."[88]

Use of the terms *protocanonical* and *deuterocanonical* came about only in the sixteenth century, when the Protestant Reformers contested the canon of Scripture. The Church had never understood these terms to denote superior and inferior kinds of biblical books. The earliest Christians, the apostles, and even Jesus himself quoted from the Septuagint, a Greek translation of the Hebrew scriptures that contained these seven books, as is evidenced by the text of the New Testament as well as the writings of Church Fathers such as Clement of Rome, Irenaeus, Athenagoras, Clement of Alexandria, Origen, Methodius, Cyprian, Athanasius, and Augustine, who all cited the deuterocanonical books as Scripture.

In response to Protestantism's widespread rejection of so much of the Old Testament, the Catholic Church reaffirmed the ancient canon, infallibly defining it at the Council of Trent in 1546.[89]

46. How are the Old Testament and New Testament related?

The Old Testament provides the essential background needed to understand the New Testament. And the New Testament provides the ultimate fulfillment of those things that were lived or promised in the Old Testament, and thus the definitive light in which to understand them as part of God's provident design. Summarizing the relationship between the Testaments, the Second Vatican Council stated,

> God, the inspirer and author of both Testaments, wisely arranged that the New Testament be hidden in the Old and the Old be made manifest in the New. For, though Christ established the New Covenant in his blood (see Luke 22:20; 1 Cor. 11:25), still the books of the Old Testament with all their parts, caught up into the proclamation of the Gospel, acquire and show forth their full meaning in the New Testament (see Matt. 5:17; Luke 24:27; Rom. 16:25-26; 2 Cor. 14:16) and in turn shed light on it and explain it (*Dei Verbum* 16).

With this in mind, it is a tragedy that more Christians are not familiar with the books of the Old Testament. For the first Christians—including the authors of the New Testament—these books *were* the Scripture. They shaped their thought and life and informed their faith in a way that many modern Christians are almost completely unaware of. Not knowing well the Old Testament is a frequent cause of misunderstanding things in the New Testament.

An obvious way that the Old Testament relates to the New is that it provides the *historical background* of Israel as God's chosen people. It contains the record of God's dealings with Israel and introduces numerous concepts that are referred to in the New Testament. Without its books, for instance, one would have no understanding of the significance of Jesus as the "Son of David" or the "Lamb of God."

Another way that the Old Testament relates to the New is by providing *moral context*. The moral principles found in the Pentateuch—and elsewhere in the Old Testament—are expressions of God's will that hold true in the New Testament age, and that inform the basic Christian moral vision. These include its emphasis on the worship of the one, true God and of the moral duties we have to other human beings. The fundamental Christian ethic of love is rooted directly in the Old Testament, for in Matthew 22:37–39 Jesus tells us that the two great commandments are "You shall love the Lord your God with all your heart, and with all your soul, and with all your mind" (a quotation from Deut. 6:5) and "You shall love your neighbor as yourself" (a quotation from Lev. 19:18).

While building upon the moral foundation given in the Old Testament, Jesus goes even further in the New Testament, reinterpreting the demands of the Law in the light of the Father's perfect will (Matt. 5:17-48) and giving his own love as the measure for Christian morality: "A new commandment I give to you, that you love one another; even as I have loved you, that you also love one another" (John 13:34).

Finally, the Old Testament relates to the New by providing *prophetic context*. This happens in ways that are both obvious and subtle. For example, it is obvious that the Old Testament contains prophecies that relate directly to the Christian age. Thus the book of Jeremiah contains the promise that God will establish a "New Covenant" with his people, one that will be spiritually transformative, unlike the one made through Moses (Jer. 31:31–34); and on the night of his passion, Jesus declared this prophecy fulfilled, stating, "This cup which is poured out for you is the New Covenant in my blood" (Luke 22:20).

On a subtler level, prophecies like Isaiah 7:14 ("Behold, a young woman shall conceive and bear a son, and shall call his name Immanuel") had an initial fulfillment in the Old Testament era, but also a second and greater fulfillment in Jesus Christ. Many of the Psalms also contain hidden prophecies of the Messiah, such as Psalm 22:1 ("My God, my God, why hast thou forsaken me?"), which Jesus applied to himself on the cross (Matt. 27:46).

Subtler yet, Paul reveals how Sarah and Hagar represent two covenants: one bearing children for freedom in Christ, and the other bearing children still bound by the slavery of sin under the Law (Gal. 4:21–31).

These messianic prophecies—whether obvious or subtle—are why Jesus, when walking with the disciples on the road to Emmaus, was able "beginning with Moses and all the prophets" to interpret "to them in all the Scriptures the things concerning himself" (Luke 24:27).

Like Jesus, who exclaimed on the road to Emmaus, "O foolish men, and slow of heart to believe all that the prophets have spoken!" (Luke 24:26), Pope St. John Paul II decried the "ignorance of the deep ties linking the New Testament to the Old" in these terms:

To deprive Christ of his relationship with the Old Testament is therefore to detach him from his roots and to empty his mystery of all meaning. Indeed, to be meaningful, the Incarnation had to be rooted in centuries of preparation. Christ would otherwise have been like a meteor that falls by chance to the earth and is devoid of any connection with human history.[90]

47. Is the "God of the Old Testament" different from the "God of the New Testament"?

Old Testament professor David Lamb tells us in his book *God Behaving Badly* that he asks his students this question: "Why does the wrathful God of the New Testament seem so different from the loving God of the Old Testament?"[91]

Does Lamb's question seem backward? Don't you hear most people say that they like the God of the New Testament, who preaches love, but they hate the "fire and brimstone" God of the Old Testament? This attitude isn't new and can be traced all the way back to the second-century heretic Marcion of Sinope.

Marcion was at one time a faithful Christian who lavishly supported the Church at Rome with profits from his shipbuilding business.[92] But his donations were returned to him after he was excommunicated for advocating heresy. Marcion believed that there were actually two gods: the inferior god of the Old Testament, who directly created the material world, and the superior god of the New Testament, who created everything, including the god of the Old Testament.[93] Marcion also said the only books of the Bible that were inspired were those that advocated the worship of the superior god, which ended up including only St. Luke's Gospel and some of St. Paul's writings. The rest of the New Testament, as well as the entirety of the Old Testament, was declared to be uninspired rubbish.

Fortunately, Marcion's efforts to rewrite Scripture failed, and the councils of Hippo and Carthage reaffirmed the canonical status of all the books we recognize today as being part of the Bible. But Marcion's challenge still exists for many. Many people are under the impression that the Old Testament depicts God as angry and jealous, whereas the New Testament depicts him as loving and kind. They then ask how these two portraits can both describe the same God, with some arguing that they can't—that there is a fundamental contradiction in the way the two parts of the Bible depict him.

In reality, both Testaments describe God the same way. Though there are differences of emphasis, there is no difference in substance. Both the Old and the New Testaments reveal God's attributes of justice (associated with the pictures of him being angry or jealous) and mercy (associated with the pictures of him being loving and kind).

Thus in the Old Testament we do find depictions of the Lord as a jealous God, not wanting the Israelites to fall into idolatry: "Take heed to yourselves, lest you forget the covenant of the Lord your God, which he made with you, and make a graven image in the form of anything which the Lord your God has forbidden you. For the Lord your God is a devouring fire, a jealous God" (Deut. 4:23–24).

However, anyone who reads the Old Testament also encounters many references to God as loving and kind: "The Lord [is] a God merciful and gracious, slow to anger, and abounding in steadfast love and faithfulness" (Exod. 34:6; cf. Num. 14:18; Deut. 4:31; 2 Chron. 30:9; Neh. 9:17; Ps. 86:5).

In the New Testament we find many similar expressions indicating God's love: "God so loved the world that he gave his only Son, that whoever believes in him should not perish but have eternal life" (John 3:16). The New Testament even declares that "God is love" (1 John 4:8, 16).

However, anyone who reads the New Testament also encounters references to God's wrath: "It is a fearful thing to fall into the hands of the living God" (Heb. 10:31; cf. Matt. 25:41; Rom. 1:18; 2 Thess. 1:8–9; Rev. 20:11–15).

Both the Old and New Testaments thus depict God as stern *and* kind, as just *and* merciful. Therefore, there aren't two different Gods in the Bible, but one God who displays both attributes.

This is not to say that there are no differences in emphasis. There are, and they have to do with the different stages of God's plan, for "God has revealed himself to man by gradually communicating his own mystery in deeds and in words" (CCC 69).

The earlier portions of Scripture were written in a very violent period, and they reflect the character of the time. In the Old Testament, polytheism was a real threat to the Israelites, and there was constant oppression and exploitation of the poor and the weak. God thus used the image of himself as a powerful, heavenly king to warn the Israelites against polytheism and oppression—the sins that are most regularly singled out for the strongest condemnation in the Old Testament.

When Jesus came, a new phase in God's plan dawned—a phase in which God made himself vulnerable and offered himself on the cross, underscoring in the most dramatic way his love for mankind. The impact of this event naturally colored the way God is revealed in the New Testament and balances the emphases found in the Old.

Further, since the New Testament completes the Old, it is only with the arrival of God's son that we have his full and definitive revelation of himself. "In many and various ways God spoke of old to our fathers by the prophets," the letter to the Hebrews reminds its hearers, "but in these last days he has spoken to us by a Son" (Heb. 1:1). The New Testament thus provides the ultimate revelation of God's love and mercy.

> God has revealed himself fully by sending his own Son, in whom he has established his covenant forever. The Son is his Father's definitive Word; so there will be no further revelation after him (CCC 73).

48. Which translation of the Bible is the best?

The original manuscripts of the Bible were not written in English. Rather, the New Testament was written in ancient Greek and the Old Testament in ancient Hebrew, along with some Aramaic and Greek. The Old Testament was later translated into Greek, a translation known as the *Septuagint*. As time went on, the Church in the West translated these texts into Latin as well as popular languages such as German, French, and English. Today, the entire Bible has been translated into over 500 languages.

Even within one language there are usually many different translations, each with its own renderings of the passages found in the original languages. How can this be? The art of translation is not as simple as taking a word in one language and then using a dictionary to find the equivalent word in another language. Translators have different opinions about how words and phrases in a text should be reproduced into another language that has a different vocabulary, different rules of grammar, and different cultural attitudes than the language of the text being translated.

A translator's basic approach tends to fall into one of two kinds. One approach is called *formal equivalence*, and it strives to communicate, as literally as possible, translations of the original words the author used. The most formally equivalent translations of Scripture would be interlinear editions, which simply replace the original words in the biblical text with their modern counterparts. Using an interlinear translation, John 3:16 reads like this: "Thus indeed loved God the world that the Son the only-begotten he gave that everyone believing in him not should perish but might have life."

Interlinear translations sound stilted and can be confusing because they take words and word sequences that made sense in one language and blindly transfer them into another language without considering that language's grammar or idioms. Most other formally equivalent translations change the order and kinds of words that are used in order to help modern audiences understand the author's original meaning. The Revised Standard Version (RSV), which tends to be formally equivalent in its translation, renders John 3:16 in this way: "For God so loved the world that he gave his only son, that whoever believes in him should not perish but have eternal life."

The other approach to translation is *dynamic equivalence*, which strives to communicate the original *idea* the author intended to convey even if it does not use his original words.

Some dynamic-equivalence translations play very loose with the original-language text. *The Message* is an extreme example of this approach, especially since it is not technically a translation of the Bible, but more of a paraphrase that summarizes what the translator, in this case Eugene H. Peterson, thinks the Bible means or what he thinks Jesus would say to people today. For example, in the RSV Matthew 6:11 reads, "Give us this day our daily bread" but *The Message* renders it, "Keep us alive with three square meals." Likewise, *The Message* translates John 3:16 in this way: "This is how much God loved the world: he gave his son, his one and only son. And this is why: so that no one need be destroyed; by believing in him, anyone can have a whole and lasting life."

Dynamically equivalent and paraphrased translations may be easier for a modern person to understand, but there is a danger that the reader will encounter the interpretations of the translator more than the words of the sacred author. This can lead to faulty interpretations of the text. For example, in John 3:16, the Greek phrase *zoen aionion* literally means "life eternal" or "eternal life." *The Message*'s translation, "whole and lasting life," could cause readers instead to think faith in God's son assures them health and long life on earth.

Sometimes a translator's theology will even cause him to mistranslate a text in order to justify his beliefs. This is evident in the *New World Translation* of the Bible, which Jehovah's Witnesses use. In this Bible the first verse of John's Gospel does not say, as it does in the RSV, "In the beginning was the Word, and the Word was with God, and the Word was God" Instead it says, "In the beginning was the Word, and the Word was with God, and the Word was *a* god." Jehovah's Witnesses deny the co-substantial divinity of Christ and think he is just "a god" or a creation of the one almighty God Jehovah.

Although Catholics should be wary of non-Catholic translations of Scripture (especially since they usually lack the deuterocanonical books), there is no single translation of the Bible that all Christians must accept to the exclusion of others. An audience of people at Mass may appreciate a more dynamically equivalent translation of Scripture, such as the New American Bible (NAB), that refrains from using complex or outdated words that could obscure the author's meaning. A serious Scripture scholar, on the other hand, would prefer a formally equivalent translation, such as the RSV, that uses words that best convey what the sacred author was trying to say in his own language.

The best-known translations for Catholics include the RSV (Catholic Edition), the NAB that we hear at Mass, and the Douay-Rheims, which is an English translation of the Latin Bible translated by St. Jerome, called the Vulgate. What's the best translation for you? The one you will read!

49. How can we study the Bible?

Bible reading is the foundation of Bible study. We need to read and think reflectively about what we have read if we are to absorb the message of God's word. We are fortunate to live in an age in which not only are Bible translations common and inexpensive, but almost all of us have been blessed with an education that provided the gift of literacy.

Because the Bible is a complex and lengthy collection of books translated from languages and cultural contexts with which most people are not familiar, it may not be wise to read the books of the Bible in sequential order beginning with Genesis and ending with Revelation. Instead, you could try an order recommended in something like Jeff Cavins's *Bible Timeline*, or start with the Gospels and then read the New Testament letters. If you're pressed for time, you could try listening to something like the *Truth and Life Audio Bible.*

Regardless of what order we approach the books of the Bible, we need not be intimidated by the project of reading them all, little by little. Pope Benedict XVI recommended that we take time for this while on summer vacation:

> The Bible, as the name says, is a collection of books, a small "library" that came into being in the course of a millennium. Some of these "small books" of which it is composed are almost unknown to the majority, even people who are good Christians.
>
> Some are very short, such as the book of Tobit, a tale that contains a lofty sense of family and marriage; or the book of Esther, in which the Jewish queen saves her people from extermination with her faith and prayer; or the book of Ruth, a stranger who meets God and experiences his providence, which is even shorter. These little books can be read in an hour. More demanding and true masterpieces are the book of Job, which faces the great problem of innocent suffering; Ecclesiastes, which is striking because of the disconcerting modernity with which it calls into question the meaning of life and of the world; and the Song of Songs [Song of Solomon], a wonderful symbolic poem of human love. . . .
>
> To conclude, dear friends, today I would like to suggest that you keep the Holy Bible within reach, during the summer period or in your breaks, in order to enjoy it in a new way by reading some of its books straight through, those that are less known and also the most famous.[94]

Beyond simply reading, we can also take advantage of the many tools available today for deepening your understanding of what we find on the pages of the Bible. Many Bible editions today come with introductions and notes. Some even contain extensive study materials. Try, for example, Scott Hahn and Curtis Mitch's *Ignatius Catholic Study Bible* or the *Navarre Study Bible.*

Some study editions of the Bible are devoted to particular themes, such as devotion, life application, and apologetics. There are also "youth editions" designed to meet the needs and answer the questions of young people, as well as "365-day editions" designed to help you read through the entire Bible in a year.

We also are not confined to reading a single Bible, and it can be helpful to compare and contrast *different translations*, including non-Catholic ones, though we must be careful with the introductions and notes these contain.

In addition to reading a study Bible, you can go deeper by participating in the many *Bible studies* that have been authored in our day—whether they are devoted to particular books of the Bible or particular themes running throughout Scripture. We can do this privately, in parish groups, or online. Popular Catholic Bible studies include *Little Rock Scripture Study* and *Unlocking the Mystery of the Bible*. You can even take part in specialized studies that relate the Bible to the Catholic faith, such as Edward Sri's *A Biblical Walk Through the Mass*.

In addition to Bible studies, there are also extensive *commentaries* on all of the books of the Bible, from ones written by Fathers of the Church to ones written in our day. Commentaries help readers understand details about a passage's original language, its cultural context and literary context, its theological significance, and other elements that might be missed in a casual reading. A good one is the *Catholic Commentary on Holy Scripture*.

It is even possible—and easier than one might think—to begin studying the *original languages* in which the Bible is written: Hebrew, Aramaic, and Greek. Classes are taught on these around the country, and there are many textbooks and language-study programs that can be used on an individual basis—allowing people to encounter God's word in the languages in which it was composed, providing even greater insight.

There are also many additional resources that shed light on the Bible and world of the biblical authors, such as maps, atlases, and books on archaeology and culture.

Finally, if you want to better understand and defend God's word as it relates to the Church and Sacred Tradition, here are some *helpful books*, labeled as being either for beginners, intermediate study, or advanced study of a subject:

Beginners

- *20 Answers: Scripture and Tradition* by Jim Blackburn
- *Beginning Apologetics 7: How to Read the Bible* by Fr. Frank Chacon and Jim Burnham
- *The Bible Compass: A Catholic's Guide to Navigating the Scriptures* by Edward Sri
- *Exploring the Spirituality of the Gospels* by Fr. Patrick J. Hartin

Intermediate

- *The Case for the Deuterocanon: Evidence and Arguments* by Gary Michuta
- *Free from All Error* by Fr. William Most
- *Hard Sayings: A Catholic Approach to Answering Bible Difficulties* by Trent Horn
- *The Historical Reliability of the Gospels* by Craig Blomberg
- *The Historical Reliability of John's Gospel* by Craig Blomberg
- *Jesus and the Eyewitnesses: The Gospels as Eyewitness Testimony* by Richard Bauckham
- *The Meaning of Tradition* by Yves Congar
- *On the Reliability of the Old Testament* by K.A. Kitchen

Advanced

- *The Book of Acts in the Setting of Hellenistic History* by Colin Hemer
- *Spirituality in John's Gospel: Historical Developments and Critical Foundations* by Fr. Gabriel-Mary Fiore

Whichever path you choose in studying the Bible, a greater knowledge of it will benefit you by enriching your knowledge of God and his word, helping you understand the basis and background of the Christian faith (in the Old Testament) and the fulfillment of the hopes of Israel in Christ and the Church (in the New Testament).

50. How can I pray with Scripture?

Along with becoming familiar with Scripture through studying it, you could also try some of these ways to cultivate a devotion to God's word, by allowing it to animate your life of daily prayer:

- *Attend daily Mass.* Catholics who attend daily Mass will hear a large portion of the Bible read to them over the course of three years. They also have the benefit of meditating on Scripture in the context of the liturgy and the reception of the sacrament of the Eucharist.
- *Pray a scriptural rosary.* The rosary is "scriptural" by its very structure—its prayers come from Scripture and its mysteries take one on a meditative journey through the entire Gospel. But in addition to this, one can pray a "scriptural rosary" by including Scripture verses on each mystery for meditation.
- *Practice lectio divina.* Rooted in Benedictine spirituality, this prayerful approach to Scripture allows a person to immerse himself in it through a four-step process of reading, meditating, praying, and contemplating.

51. What exactly is Sacred Tradition?

The word *tradition* comes down to us from the Latin *tradere,* meaning to "transmit" or "deliver"—literally, to "hand on." It was a term used in Roman law to denote the legal transfer of property. The Greek word for this is *paradosis*, which has the connotation of something deliberately handed on over a long period of time.

This is precisely what Jesus commanded the apostles to do with all that he handed on to *them*: to "make disciples of all nations" (Matt. 28:19) and be his witnesses "in Jerusalem and in all Judea and Samaria and to the end of the earth" (Acts 1:8). Jesus intended his teaching to be carefully transmitted, continually handed down until his return. But prior to his ascension into heaven, so far as we know, Jesus never commanded the apostles to write anything down. Instead, their mission was to *preach* the gospel.

He even promised them the guidance of the Holy Spirit in order to accomplish this. At the Last Supper, Jesus promised the apostles that the Father "will give you another Counselor, to be with you for ever . . . the

Holy Spirit, whom the Father will send in my name, he will teach you all things, and bring to your remembrance all that I have said to you. . . . He will guide you into all the truth" (John 14:16, 26; 16:13).

Sacred Tradition is thus a living, breathing phenomenon that perpetuates the life of the Church down through the ages under the guidance of the Holy Spirit. It includes not only the doctrines handed down over the centuries—many of them consigned to writing in Sacred Scripture—but also all that encompasses the authentic life of the Church. Fr. Yves Congar calls Sacred Tradition "the communication of the entire heritage of the apostles, effected in a different way from that of their writings."[95]

> Now what was handed on by the apostles includes everything which contributes toward the holiness of life and increase in faith of the peoples of God; and so the Church, in her teaching, life and worship, perpetuates and hands on to all generations all that she herself is, all that she believes (*Dei Verbum* 8).

Sacred Tradition carries on the Great Commission of the apostles to this day, and will continue to do so throughout the life of the Church until the end of time for the sake of the salvation of souls.

> The Father's self-communication made through his Word in the Holy Spirit, remains present and active in the Church: God, who spoke in the past, continues to converse with the spouse of his beloved Son [the Church]. And the Holy Spirit, through whom the living voice of the gospel rings out in the Church—and through her in the world—leads believers to the full truth, and makes the word of Christ dwell in them in all its richness (CCC 79).

52. What is the relationship between Scripture and Tradition?

Sacred Scripture and Sacred Tradition both transmit to us the living word of God. They are related to one another in several significant ways.

First, *Tradition preceded Scripture.* This is true whether one considers the Hebrew Scriptures or the Christian Scripture. The stories contained in the Pentateuch, for example, were not written down until generations after they took place, carefully preserved in the oral tradition of the chosen people. Likewise, the first Christians didn't learn their faith from the New Testament, for the simple reason that it hadn't been written yet. Many Christians believed in Jesus and even died for his sake, without ever encountering the Christian Scripture.

During this time the word of God was transmitted orally, from Jesus to the apostles, and from them to other disciples, through what is called Sacred Tradition. Paul refers to this when he commends the Corinthians for "maintain[ing] the traditions even as I have delivered them to you" (1 Cor. 11:2) and instructs his disciple Timothy: "What you have heard from me before many witnesses entrust to faithful men who will be able to teach others also" (2 Tim. 2:2). Paul even thanked the Thessalonians for accepting his preaching, not as human words, but as the very words of God (1 Thess. 2:13).

As we know, eventually some of this apostolic Tradition was written down in the form of biographies of Christ (Gospels) or pastoral letters to the early churches. In this way, *Tradition gave birth to Scripture.*

> The Tradition here in question comes from the apostles and hands on what they received from Jesus' teaching and example and what they learned from the Holy Spirit. The first generation of Christians did not yet have a written New Testament, and the New Testament itself demonstrates the process of living Tradition (CCC 83).

The book of Acts is particularly interesting in this regard. In it, the life of the early Christian community is preserved as the "word of God" for future generations. Becoming Scripture, it did not cease to be Tradition, "perpetuating and handing on to all generations all that [the Church] herself is, all that she believes" (DV 8).

Not only did apostolic Tradition precede and consign to writing the New Testament Scripture, but it was this same living Tradition that discerned, among the many Christian texts of the first centuries, which carried the authority of divine revelation. There was some common consensus that certain books were inspired, but there was also dispute and error. Christians during that time did not have a complete and authoritative Bible, but they *did* have a living and authoritative Tradition from the apostles. The faithful had to rely on the authority Jesus gave to the leaders of the Church and their successors. It was that authority that eventually compiled the Bible, discerning which books to include and which not. Thus it is fair to say that apostolic *Tradition discerned and defined Scripture.* The Church's authority to affirm the canon doesn't mean, however, that the Church has a higher teaching authority than Scripture. On the contrary, the Second Vatican Council teaches that the *role of Tradition is to serve and guard the word of God*:

> This teaching office is not above the word of God, but serves it, teaching only what has been handed on, listening to it devoutly, guarding it scrupulously and explaining it faithfully in accord with a divine commission, and with the help of the Holy Spirit, it draws from this one deposit of faith everything which it presents for belief as divinely revealed (*Dei Verbum* 10).

One of the important ways in which Tradition faithfully preserves Scripture is by ensuring that it is interpreted correctly. Sincere, intelligent, faithful Christians of all kinds study the Bible, listen to Bible teaching, and pray for the grace of correct interpretation, yet come to different conclusions about what Scripture has to say about many important topics. They all genuinely believe their interpretations are *the* correct ones, and can't be convinced of any flaw in their understanding. Biblical doctrine is neither perfectly clear nor self-interpreting. Tradition helps draw out and correctly identify Scripture's true meaning. In other words, *Tradition guarantees the authentic interpretation of Scripture.*

If this was already necessary during the lifetime of the apostles, it became more and more so as Christianity spread in all directions and heresies began to proliferate.

St. Vincent of Lerins wrote in 434,

> With great zeal and closest attention, therefore, I frequently inquired of many men, eminent for their holiness and doctrine, how I might, in a concise and, so to speak, general and ordinary way, distinguish the truth of the Catholic faith from the falsehood of heretical depravity.
>
> I received almost always the same answer from all of them—that if I or anyone else wanted to expose the frauds and escape the snares of the heretics who rise up, and to remain intact and in sound faith, it would be necessary, with the help of the Lord, to fortify that faith in a twofold manner: first, of course, by the authority of divine law [Sacred Scripture] and then by the Tradition of the Catholic Church.

> Here, perhaps, someone may ask: "If the canon of the Scriptures be perfect and in itself more than suffices for everything, why is it necessary that the authority of ecclesiastical interpretation be joined to it?" Because, quite plainly, Sacred Scripture, by reason of its own depth, is not accepted by everyone as having one and the same meaning. . . .
>
> Thus, because of so many distortions of such various errors, it is highly necessary that the line of prophetic and apostolic interpretation be directed in accord with the norm of the ecclesiastical and Catholic meaning.[96]

Finally, Sacred Tradition remains always necessary in the Church because even the complete and correctly interpreted canon of Sacred Scripture can never fully suffice for passing on the Faith. St. John wrote:

> Now Jesus did many other signs in the presence of the disciples, which are not written in this book; but these are written that you may believe that Jesus is the Christ, the Son of God, and that believing you may have life in his name. . . . There are also many other things which Jesus did; were every one of them to be written, I suppose that the world itself could not contain the books that would be written (John 20:30–31; 21:25).

The Bible, by its own admission, is not the complete record of everything Jesus did, said, or taught. The early Christian leaders and writers clearly understood this and its implications, knowing that the deposit of faith is handed on not only in writing, but also in "mystery"—that is, sacrament and custom. In 375, St. Basil the Great wrote,

> Of the dogmas and messages preserved in the Church, some we possess from written teaching and others we receive from the tradition of the apostles, handed on to us in mystery. In respect to piety, both are of the same force. No one will contradict any of these, no one, at any rate, who is even moderately versed in matters ecclesiastical. Indeed, were we to try to reject unwritten customs as having no great authority, we would unwittingly injure the gospel in its vitals.[97]

Similarly, that same year Epiphanius of Salamis writes: "It is needful also to make use of tradition, for not everything can be gotten from Sacred Scripture. The holy apostles handed down some things in the Scriptures, other things in Tradition."[98]

Especially in the sacramental celebration of the Christian mystery, *Sacred Tradition celebrates and completes Scripture*, enabling it to become truly a "living word" in the lives of the faithful under the motion of the Holy Spirit. Citing the Second Vatican Council's dogmatic constitution on divine revelation, *Dei Verbum*, the *Catechism* summarizes:

> "Sacred Tradition and Sacred Scripture are bound closely together, and communicate one with the other. For both of them, flowing out from the same divine well-spring, come together in some fashion to form one thing, and move toward the same goal." Each of them makes present and fruitful in the Church the mystery of Christ, who promised to remain with his own "always, to the close of the age" (80).

53. Is Sacred Tradition mentioned in the Bible?

Many non-Catholic Christians mistakenly think that the Bible says that it alone—Sacred Scripture—is the sole rule of faith for Christians. However, nowhere in the Bible is this expressed or even implied. The Bible *does* express, however, that Sacred Tradition is crucially important for fully grasping the Christian faith.

Jesus' commandment to the apostles at the end of Matthew's Gospel logically assumes the necessity of Sacred Tradition:

> Go therefore and make disciples of all nations, baptizing them in the name of the Father and of the Son and of the Holy Spirit, and teaching them to obey all that I have commanded you. And remember, I am with you always, to the end of the age (Matt. 28:19–20).

Notice that Jesus did not tell the apostles to *write down* everything he had taught them. He simply commanded them to *teach* it. Much of this teaching later made its way into written form and became part of Sacred Scripture, but every bit of it was first—and still is—part of Sacred Tradition.

Consider St. Luke's introduction to his Gospel, in which he explains why he is writing:

> Inasmuch as many have undertaken to compile a narrative of the things which have been accomplished among us, just as they were delivered to us by those who from the beginning were eyewitnesses and ministers of the word, it seemed good to me also, having followed all things closely for some time past, to write an orderly account for you, most excellent Theophilus, that you may know the truth concerning the things of which you have been informed (Luke 1:1–4).

Luke, then, commits to writing what has *already been taught*. That teaching is Sacred Tradition just as surely as Luke's Gospel will later be recognized as Sacred Scripture.

In his writings, St. Paul provides even more explicit evidence of Sacred Tradition. For example, he tells the Corinthians, "I commend you because you remember me in everything and maintain the traditions even as I have delivered them to you" (1 Cor. 11:2). He also commands the Thessalonians, "So then, brethren, stand firm and hold to the traditions which you were taught by us, either by word of mouth or by letter" (2 Thess. 2:15). St. John Chrysostom (c. 347–407), writing shortly after the canon of Scripture was defined, commented on this verse:

> From this it is clear that [the apostles] did not hand down everything by letter, but there is much also that was not written. Like that which was written, the unwritten too is worthy of belief. So let us regard the Tradition of the Church also as worthy of belief. Is it a Tradition? Seek no further.[99]

Paul even goes so far as to caution the Thessalonians about people who do *not* hold to the Sacred Tradition he taught them: "Now we command you, brethren, in the name of our Lord Jesus Christ, that you keep away from any brother who is living in idleness and not in accord with the Tradition that you received from us" (2 Thess. 3:6).

Near the end of his ministry, Paul instructs Timothy to carry on the Sacred Tradition passed down to him: "Follow the pattern of the sound words which you have heard from me, in the faith and love which are in Christ Jesus; guard the truth that has been entrusted to you by the Holy

Spirit who dwells within us" (2 Tim. 1:13–14). To make sure that all this apostolic Tradition would be passed down after the deaths of the apostles, he tells Timothy, "You, then, my son, be strong in the grace that is in Christ Jesus, and what you have heard from me before many witnesses entrust to faithful men who will be able to teach others also" (2 Tim. 2:1–2). In this passage he refers to the first four generations of apostolic succession—his own generation, Timothy's generation, the generation Timothy will teach, and the generation they in turn will teach. Clearly, Paul had in mind that Sacred Tradition would continue to be an ordinary means of communicating the gospel.

Itself a fruit of Sacred Tradition, the Bible nowhere puts forth that the written word is to be the sole rule of the Christian faith. On the contrary, it is Sacred Tradition that is commanded time and again to be the ordinary, ongoing method of teaching the Christian faith.

54. Isn't the Bible all we really need to evangelize the world?

As Sacred Scripture itself attests, the preferred method of communicating the word of God is not in writing but by word of mouth. Much of the Old Testament was known and transmitted orally for centuries before it was written down. St. John emphasized the preference for spreading the gospel by Sacred Tradition when he wrote, "Though I have much to write to you, I would rather not use paper and ink, but I hope to come to see you and talk with you face to face, so that our joy may be complete" (2 John 12).

We see in Paul's epistles, too, how anxious he is about the welfare of the local churches he has established and how he wishes he could be there with them *in person* to guide and teach (Rom. 1:11; 15:24; 1 Cor. 16:7; 1 Thess. 2:17; 3:6, 10).

Clearly, Paul understood the value of human interaction when teaching the Christian faith! Sacred Tradition provides this in a way the Sacred Scripture alone does not.

All this is not to deny the value of the written word. Rather, it is to demonstrate the power of Sacred Tradition, which came long before a word of the New Testament was ever written. Jesus himself wrote none of the New Testament. He taught orally. He established a living Church founded on Peter and the apostles, and he told them to *preach*.

It might be helpful to imagine yourself living at the dawn of Christianity. There were nearly three decades between the Crucifixion and the writing of the first epistles of the New Testament, and nearly five more decades before the last New Testament book was written. Many Christians believed in Jesus and even died for his sake, without ever encountering the words of St. Paul—for the simple reason that Paul had not yet written them!

Not only did much of the New Testament not exist for the first generation of Christians, but for over two and a half centuries there was no authoritatively settled canon of Scripture. There was some common consensus that certain books were inspired, but there was also dispute and error. Christians during that time did not have a complete and authoritative Bible, but they *did* have a living and authoritative Tradition from the apostles. The faithful had to rely on the authority Jesus gave to the leaders of the Church and their successors. It was that authority that eventually compiled the Bible, discerning which books to include and which not.

The Bible is a testament to the oral tradition that was alive and already at work from the beginning of the Church. Sacred Scripture is itself a product of the Sacred Tradition of the Church. And it is through the continual handing on of Tradition that Scripture is authoritatively interpreted.

> Through the same tradition the Church's full canon of the sacred books is known, and the sacred writings themselves are more profoundly understood and unceasingly made active in her (*Dei Verbum* 8).

55. Is there any historical evidence that the apostles actually handed down Sacred Tradition through their successors?

Beyond the biblical accounts of Sacred Tradition being handed on, many bishops and other Christians who were contemporaries of the apostles, or who lived in the centuries after them, continued to write books and letters similar to those in the New Testament. Many of these writings of the "Church Fathers" have been preserved and come down to us through history, as testimony that Sacred Tradition was, indeed, handed on from the apostles to their successors, and so on, and so on, to present day.

> The apostles entrusted the "sacred deposit" of the Faith (the *depositum fidei*), contained in Sacred Scripture and Tradition, to the whole of the Church. By adhering to this heritage the entire holy people, united to its pastors, remains always faithful to the teaching

> of the apostles, to the brotherhood, to the breaking of bread and the prayers. So, in maintaining, practicing and professing the faith that has been handed on, there should be a remarkable harmony between the bishops and the faithful (CCC 84).

The Church Fathers, who were early links in the chain of succession, recognized the necessity of the traditions that had been handed down from the apostles, and guarded them scrupulously, as abundant testimony indicates. For example, St. Irenaeus wrote in opposition to heresies in A.D. 189:

> The Church, having received this preaching and this faith, although she is disseminated throughout the whole world, yet guarded it, as if she occupied but one house. She likewise believes these things just as if she had but one soul and one and the same heart; and harmoniously she proclaims them and teaches them and hands them down, as if she possessed but one mouth. For, while the languages of the world are diverse, nevertheless, the authority of the Tradition is one and the same.[100]

Later he added: "It is possible, then, for everyone in every church, who may wish to know the truth, to contemplate the Tradition of the apostles which has been made known throughout the whole world."[101]

In 225, Origen wrote: "The teaching of the Church has indeed been handed down through an order of succession from the apostles and remains in the churches even to the present time. That alone is to be believed as the truth which is in no way at variance with ecclesiastical and apostolic Tradition."[102]

Writing in the early fourth century, Church historian Eusebius attested:

> Papias [A.D. 120], who is now mentioned by us, affirms that he received the sayings of the apostles from those who accompanied them, and he, moreover, asserts that he heard in person Aristion and the presbyter John. Accordingly, he mentions them frequently by name, and in his writings gives their traditions [concerning Jesus] . . . . [There are] other passages of his in which he relates some miraculous deeds, stating that he acquired the knowledge of them from Tradition.[103]

> At that time [A.D. 150] there flourished in the Church Hegesippus, whom we know from what has gone before, and Dionysius, bishop

> of Corinth, and another bishop, Pinytus of Crete, and besides these, Philip, and Apollinarius, and Melito, and Musanus, and Modestus, and, finally, Irenaeus. From them has come down to us in writing, the sound and orthodox Faith received from Tradition."[104]

Around 400, St. Augustine wrote: "There are many things which are observed by the whole Church, and therefore are fairly held to have been enjoined by the apostles, which yet are not mentioned in their writings."[105] He went on to call apostolic Tradition "the fountain" that Christians should go back to for truth in matters of the Christian faith.[106]

In these examples and many others, we find clear historical evidence that the Christians of the first centuries of the Church did, indeed, hold fast to Sacred Tradition.

> The words of the holy fathers witness to the presence of this living tradition, whose wealth is poured into the practice and life of the believing and praying Church . . . and thus God, who spoke of old, uninterruptedly converses with the bride of his beloved Son; and the Holy Spirit, through whom the living voice of the gospel resounds in the Church, and through her, in the world, leads unto all truth those who believe and makes the word of Christ dwell abundantly in them (*Dei Verbum* 8).

56. Can Sacred Tradition be changed?

Because it is the word of God, Sacred Tradition is inerrant. *Human* tradition may contain mistakes, but Sacred Tradition does not. Therefore, though our understanding of it can grow and develop over time, Sacred Tradition cannot be changed any more than the Bible can be changed. They both come from God, whose truth is unchanging.

Clearly, it is crucial to be able to distinguish between Sacred Tradition, which is revealed by God and unchangeable, and human traditions, which can come and go over time. The *Catechism* notes:

> [Sacred] Tradition is to be distinguished from the various theological, disciplinary, liturgical or devotional traditions, born in the local churches over time. These are the particular forms, adapted to different places and times, in which the great Tradition is expressed. In the light of Tradition, these traditions can be

> retained, modified or even abandoned under the guidance of the Church's Magisterium (83).

The key to determining which traditions are sacred and which are merely human is the same as the key to telling which writings are sacred and which are merely human. The authoritative Magisterium—the official teaching authority—of the Church recognizes certain doctrinal and moral teachings taught since the beginning of Christian history as given by Jesus to the apostles and handed on by them to their successors down through the centuries. The Church recognizes these teachings, and those that have developed from them, as Sacred Tradition.

Other Catholic traditions, more aptly called *ecclesiastical* traditions (or disciplines or customs), are "man-made" in the sense that Christians developed them over the centuries as means to better live out their Christian faith. All Christian communities—not just Catholics—have human traditions in one form or another. But Sacred Tradition, as a direct expression of the authority Jesus gave to the apostles and their successors, is different. Whatever the Catholic Church teaches, it is bound to fidelity to Sacred Tradition and Sacred Scripture. It cannot sanction just anything it chooses, but only that which is in accord with what it has been given. Sacred Tradition comes from God and, as such, may not be altered by men. Other traditions originated with the Church's pastoral and disciplinary authority and, therefore, may change.

Admittedly, this can sometimes be confusing—even for Catholics. For example, consider the Church's teaching concerning the male-only priesthood. Some Catholics (mistakenly) believe that the Church can change this doctrine and that women can and should be ordained as priests. In other words, they believe this doctrine to be a changeable discipline.

On the contrary, the male-only priesthood is not only *implicit* in Sacred Scripture (in the Bible, Christ chooses only men as priests, and the apostles did likewise), but also *explicit* in Sacred Tradition. In fact, quite recently in Church history Pope St. John Paul II confirmed this doctrine in his 1994 apostolic letter *Ordinatio Sacerdotalis*, and the Church's Congregation for the Doctrine of the Faith subsequently attested to its certitude, and its place in Sacred Tradition: "This teaching requires definitive assent, since, founded on the written Word of God, and from the beginning constantly preserved and applied in the Tradition of the Church, it has been set forth infallibly by the ordinary and universal Magisterium."[107]

In contrast to the doctrine of the male-only priesthood is the discipline of celibacy in the priesthood. In the Roman rite of the Catholic Church, only men who are willing to commit to lifelong celibacy can be ordained to the priesthood. However, mandatory priestly celibacy is not revealed doctrine and does not carry the weight of authority of Sacred Scripture or Sacred Tradition. Most of the Eastern Catholic churches, in full communion with the Catholic Church, do ordain married men in keeping with their historical practice. Thus, the practice of priestly celibacy is more accurately described as an ecclesiastical tradition, and, as such, it could theoretically change—the Roman Church could choose to ordain married men. In fact, it already does so, in certain cases.[108]

57. Doesn't the proclamation of dogma add to public revelation?

Simply being infallible and binding does not make a document equal to Scripture, because Scripture is qualitatively something more: it is the inspired, inerrant word of God.

Even the most solemn and authoritative magisterial documents are purely human writings, not divine; they are *about* divine revelation, but are not themselves revealed. The notion that any inerrant document amounts to additional Scripture would betray a shockingly *low* view of Scripture, one which defines Scripture merely as that which is authoritative and without error.

Beyond this, the very charge of adding to the Bible presupposes that the writing of Scripture has ended—a doctrine that is contained in Sacred Tradition and affirmed by the authoritative teaching of the Church, but *nowhere* made explicit in Sacred Scripture itself. Ironically, this charge against the Church assumes a doctrine that is explicitly taught *only* in Church documents expounding Sacred Tradition!

The Catholic Church continues to teach this doctrine to the present day: "The Christian economy, therefore, since it is the new and definitive covenant, will never pass away; and no new public revelation is to be expected before the glorious manifestation of our Lord Jesus Christ" (CCC 66–67).

Even so, Sacred Tradition continues to develop, and the Church grows to understand it more fully. This sometimes is evidenced by magisterial documents. The *Catechism* continues: "Yet even if revelation is already complete, it has not been made completely explicit; it remains for Christian faith gradually to grasp its full significance over the course of the centuries" (66).

But it is important to understand that the Church does not equate this development to adding to the Bible. Not even private revelations made by God to Christians throughout history add to the word of God:

> Throughout the ages, there have been so-called "private" revelations, some of which have been recognized by the authority of the Church. They do not belong, however, to the deposit of faith. It is not their role to improve or complete Christ's definitive revelation, but to help live more fully by it in a certain period of history. Guided by the Magisterium of the Church, the *sensus fidelium* knows how to discern and welcome in these revelations whatever constitutes an authentic call of Christ or his saints to the Church (CCC 67).

Indeed, in that same passage the *Catechism* recognizes the dangers of claiming to be able to add new revelation to the deposit of faith, as some quasi-Christian groups do:

> Christian faith cannot accept "revelations" that claim to surpass or correct the revelation of which Christ is the fulfillment, as is the case in certain non-Christian religions and also in certain recent sects which base themselves on such "revelations."

Of final note, it should be mentioned that the warning in Revelation 22:18–19 does not actually refer to writing additional Scripture, but to tampering with "the words of this scroll," i.e., the book of Revelation itself:

> I warn everyone who hears the words of the prophecy of this book: if any one adds to them, God will add to him the plagues described in this book, and if any one takes away from the words of the book of this prophecy, God will take away his share in the tree of life and in the holy city, which are described in this book.

Similar warnings can be found in the Old Testament, long before the end of the age of revelation. For example, Deuteronomy 4:2 states: "You shall not add to the word which I command you, nor take from it; that you may keep the commandments of the Lord your God which I command you."

If this verse had been interpreted the same way many non-Catholics interpret Revelation 22:18–19 today, then nothing written after the book of Deuteronomy could be considered as Sacred Scripture!

58. What are the distinctions among a dogma, a doctrine, and a discipline?

Doctrine is the teaching the Church proposes for the faithful to believe. It can refer to an individual teaching (a doctrine) or to the totality of all the Church's teachings (Catholic doctrine).

Some of these teachings are *dogmas*, which the Church, either by its extraordinary or ordinary Magisterium, explicitly and infallibly defines as divinely revealed teachings that the faithful are obliged to believe.[109]

Although every dogma of the Faith is a doctrine, most doctrines are not dogmas, nor are they infallibly defined. For example, the truths contained in natural and moral law require no dogmatic definition, but they are nonetheless doctrine. Doctrine, unlike dogma, requires "religious submission of mind and will" rather than the "assent of faith."

The difference between the assent of faith and the religious submission of mind and will is not a license for Catholics to reject non-infallible teachings they simply do not like. It is instead a recognition that there is room for gradual development in Church teaching, which is why the Church does not always make its teaching definitive on a given matter. All the same, the faithful should still trust the shepherds Christ has left us even as they, under the guidance of the Holy Spirit, further clarify and present the Faith.

Nor should it be systematically assumed that because a doctrine is not defined dogmatically, it is less true or certain. Many things are held unswervingly to be true in the Church for which there has not yet been need to make a dogmatic proclamation. This could be the case because a matter implicitly believed from the beginning is now being called into question (this is how much of the Creed came to be developed) or has become particularly timely to place before the faithful as worthy of consideration. For example, it was not until relatively recently that the Church was obliged to define dogmatically a truth held from the beginning: that Catholic priesthood is reserved for males.[110]

So, for example, the *Catechism* says,

> The Church teaches that every spiritual soul is created immediately by God—it is not "produced" by the parents—and also that it is immortal: it does not perish when it separates from the body at death, and it will be reunited with the body at the final resurrection (366).

That human beings have immortal souls is a dogma of the Church that was infallibly defined at the Fifth Lateran Council in 1513. It has also been part of the continual, universal teaching of the Church, or the "ordinary Magisterium." That God creates those souls directly, however, is a doctrine rather than a dogma. The Church could declare this to be a dogma in the future, but for now it is a doctrine because it has not been infallibly defined as being divinely revealed.

The faithful cannot *openly* dissent against doctrine without falling into heresy, but unlike with dogmas, it is not a grave sin to personally fail to accept them. Still, it is a serious matter to withhold the submission of the mind and will, and the Church encourages theologians who, after careful study, remain unable to resolve the apparent difficulties, to cautiously express their concerns with the aim of helping the Magisterium better understand a disputed issue.[111]

> If, despite a loyal effort on the theologian's part, the difficulties persist, the theologian has the duty to make known to the magisterial authorities the problems raised by the teaching in itself, in the arguments proposed to justify it, or even in the manner in which it is presented. He should do this in an evangelical spirit and with a profound desire to resolve the difficulties. His objections could then contribute to real progress and provide a stimulus to the Magisterium to propose the teaching of the Church in greater depth and with a clearer presentation of the arguments (*Donum Veritatis 30)*.

Before we examine the Church's disciplines, we must distinguish doctrine from theological opinions. There are theological issues and questions to which the Church has not yet formulated a doctrinal response, but leaves open to theological examination.

One example of a matter left to theological opinion is the state of Mary's body upon her assumption into heaven. Although the fact that Mary's body was assumed into heaven is a dogma of the Church, the Church has not weighed in on the whether Mary was assumed before or after death. In his apostolic constitution that defined the dogma, Pope Pius XII said only that "the ever-virgin Mary, having completed the course of her earthly life, was assumed body and soul into heavenly glory" (*Munificentissimus Deus* 44). Notice how the pope spoke only of the end of Mary's earthly life and not of the manner in which it ended. Although most theologians, past and present, have speculated that Mary's body was assumed after death, a Catholic can believe she was assumed either before or after her death.

This leaves us with *disciplines*, which are the rules and laws the Church proposes by the authority given to it by Christ. Even though disciplines can be changed, the faithful are still obliged to obey them, just as citizens must obey speed limits that a municipal government can change when it deems it necessary.

An example of a discipline is the Communion fast. For most of Church history, the faithful fasted from midnight until they received the Eucharist that morning. Only after that would they have a meal that would "break the fast" (i.e., breakfast). However, in 1953, Pope Pius XII reduced the period of fasting to three hours before Communion to encourage greater reception of the sacrament.[112] In 1964, Pope Paul VI changed the period of fasting once again, this time to one hour before Communion. The current *Code of Canon Law* says, "A person who is to receive the Most Holy Eucharist is to abstain for at least one hour before Holy Communion from any food and drink, except for only water and medicine" (CIC 919).

To summarize, doctrine refers to all the teachings or beliefs the Church proposes for the faithful to believe. Dogmas are a subset of doctrines that are unchangeable and, because they are a part of divine revelation, require the assent of faith. Disciplines come from the Church and must be obeyed by the faithful even though the Magisterium can alter or abolish them.

59. Where can I find a list of all the teachings given to the apostles by divine revelation and contained in Sacred Tradition?

There is no such list, because some of the teachings have been passed down in implicit rather than explicit form, and it is impossible to list all of the implications of a set of doctrines.

Consider a similar question: Can any Christian list all the teachings divinely revealed in Sacred Scripture? Of course not! Our understanding of what is in Scripture (and Tradition) deepens and grows richer all the time; we have to contemplate it and apply it to new circumstances. In other words, teaching develops.

The opening verse of the book of Hebrews tells us, "In many and various ways God spoke of old to our fathers by the prophets." This was done fragmentarily, under various figures and symbols. Man was not given religious truth as though from a Sunday school teacher, nicely laid out and fully indexed. Doctrines had to be thought out, lived out in the liturgical life of the Church, even pieced together by the Fathers and ecumenical councils. In this way, the Church has gained an ever-deepening understanding of the deposit of faith that had been "once for all delivered" to it by Christ and the apostles (see Jude 3).

Non-Catholic Christians ordinarily admit that much. They recognize that there has been a real development in doctrine. There was an initial message, much clouded at the fall (Gen. 3), and then a progressively fuller explanation of God's teachings as Israel was prepared for the Messiah, until the apostles were instructed by the Messiah himself. Jesus told the apostles that in the Old Testament "many prophets and righteous men longed to see what you see, and did not see it, and to hear what you hear, and did not hear it" (Matt. 13:17).

Christians have always understood that at the close of the Apostolic Age—with the death of the last surviving apostle, John, around A.D. 100—public revelation ceased (CCC 66–67, 73). Christ fulfilled the Old Testament law (Matt. 5:17) and is the ultimate teacher of humanity: "You have one teacher, the Messiah" (Matt. 23:10). The apostles recognized that their task was to pass on, intact, the faith given to them by Christ: "And what you have heard from me before many witnesses entrust to faithful men who will be able to teach others also" (2 Tim. 2:2); "But as for you, continue in what you have learned and have firmly believed, knowing from whom you learned it" (2 Tim. 3:14).

However, this closure to public revelation doesn't mean there can't be progress in the understanding of what has been entrusted to the Church—an ever-fuller flowering of the deposit of revelation. Anyone interested in Christianity will ask of a given revealed truth, "What does this teaching imply? How does it relate to other teachings?"

A good example of why this is so can be found in the *Monothelite* controversy. The Monothelites were seventh-century heretics who claimed that Jesus had (and has) only one will, the divine. The orthodox position, defined at the Third Council of Constantinople (680–681), is that Jesus also has a human will that is distinct from—but never in conflict with—his divine will.

The Bible doesn't teach this in so many words. Neither did the writings of the earliest Church Fathers explicitly state that Christ has a human will distinct from but in harmony with his divine will. That doctrine was not handed on from the apostles in explicit form, but it was handed on in *implicit* form.

The apostles taught, as the Bible and the Church Fathers indicate, that Jesus was fully human and fully divine. This contains the implicit teaching of two wills, because if Christ is fully human, he must have a human will, and if he is fully divine, he must have a divine will. For Christ to lack one or the other would make him either not fully human or not fully divine.

Most non-Catholic Christians fully agree. They acknowledge that the doctrine of the two wills of Christ must be accepted as something coming to us from the apostles, even though it did not come in explicit form. It was a legitimate doctrinal development that emerged when a heresy struck and the Church sought a deeper, more explicit understanding of what it had already implicitly received.

Thus the Church does not try to make an exhaustive list of implicit doctrines, but allows new implications within the apostolic deposit to be realized over the course of time, as the Holy Spirit leads the Church into all truth (see John 16:13). If the Church did try to make such a list, it would be attempting to run ahead of the Holy Spirit by forcing the process of doctrinal development to a sudden and premature end. If the Church, for instance, had tried to make such a list before the outbreak of the Monothelite controversy, the list would not have included the proposition "Christ has a human will distinct from but entirely in harmony with his divine will."

60. Didn't Jesus condemn tradition?

Some Protestants object to the idea of Sacred Tradition because they believe Jesus condemned it. They refer to the time when Jesus told the Pharisees, "For the sake of your tradition, you have made void the word of God" (Matt. 15:6).

In this particular case, Jesus was condemning a man-made tradition that, when misapplied, was contrary to a divine commandment. Specifically, he criticized the religious authorities for abusing the tradition of *korban*, or sacrificial offering, to exempt themselves and others from the financial support due to parents—a tradition that nullified the Fourth Commandment, honor your father and mother.

Jesus' condemnation of a specific abuse of tradition in the former example seems to become a more general biblical rejection of "tradition" in this other passage often cited by *sola scriptura* advocates:

> Now when the Pharisees gathered together to [Jesus], with some of the scribes, who had come from Jerusalem, they saw that some of his disciples ate with hands defiled, that is, unwashed. (For the Pharisees, and all the Jews, do not eat unless they wash their hands, observing the tradition of the elders; and when they come from the market place, they do not eat unless they purify themselves; and there are many other traditions which they observe, the washing of cups and pots and vessels of bronze.) And the Pharisees and the scribes asked him, "Why do your disciples not live according to the tradition of the elders, but eat with hands defiled?" And he said to them, "Well did Isaiah prophesy of you hypocrites, as it is written, 'This people honors me with their lips, but their heart is far from me; in vain do they worship me, teaching as doctrines the precepts of men.' You leave the commandment of God, and hold fast the tradition of men" (Mark 7:1–8).

Here Jesus undeniably is condemning certain traditions, but it is important to recognize *which* traditions. In this case, they were "precepts of men" that were being put forth by the Pharisees and the scribes as doctrines. They were man-made rules imposed by the Pharisees that put an undue burden on the Jews. The Pharisees had no authority to represent such rules as doctrines. Jesus' rightful condemnation of the Pharisees' practice does not amount to a blanket rejection of Sacred Tradition.

Indeed, we know from other passages that Jesus did not reject the notion of an authoritative religious tradition when rightly exercised to expound the law of God. In Mathew 23:2–3 he told his disciples to obey the Pharisees because they sat on "Moses' seat," a term that referred to the Pharisees' teaching authority.

Another favorite verse of *sola scriptura* adherents is "See to it that no one makes a prey of you by philosophy and empty deceit, according to human tradition, according to the elemental spirits of the universe, and not according to Christ" (Col. 2:8).

Certainly the Catholic Church agrees with Paul that empty and deceitful human traditions are to be rejected. But Sacred Tradition is not such a tradition. It is the teaching of Jesus and the apostles, passed on over time and guided by the Holy Spirit. It is not deceitful but true; it is not human in origin but divine.

Having said all this, it is important to recognize that not *all* man-made traditions are bad. In addition to Sacred Tradition, Jesus also gave the apostles and their successors the authority to enact practices (which over time become traditions) that are not part of divine revelation but are nonetheless binding on the faithful. Jesus told Peter, "I will give you the keys of the kingdom of heaven, and whatever you bind on earth shall be bound in heaven, and whatever you loose on earth shall be loosed in heaven" (Matt. 16:19). Later on, Jesus gave similar authority to bind and loose to other apostles gathered together as a unit (see Matt. 18:18).

The *Catechism* explains that the power to bind and loose "connotes the authority to absolve sins, to pronounce doctrinal judgments, and to make disciplinary decisions in the Church. Jesus entrusted this authority to the Church through the ministry of the apostles and in particular through the ministry of Peter" (553).

Thus, it is necessary first to distinguish between Sacred Tradition and human tradition, always holding fast to the former. It is also necessary to distinguish between human traditions imposed with proper authority and those not, and to give due assent to the former. Although inferior to both Sacred Tradition and Sacred Scripture, human traditions may be lawfully enacted—and obeyed—in accordance with the Church's authority to bind and loose.

61. Can Scripture and Tradition contradict?

Any tradition that contradicts Scripture must be false, because God's revelation cannot contradict itself. But this doesn't make Sacred Tradition inferior to Scripture. For it is *likewise* true that any proposed Scripture or interpretation of Scripture that contradicts Sacred Tradition is false and must be rejected. Scripture must be tested against Tradition to see if it is apostolic.

This was, in fact, one of the ways in which the canon of the New Testament was selected. The Church Fathers who established the canon rejected any texts that contained doctrines contrary to the traditions the apostles had handed down to them.

Texts such as the gnostic gospels (for example, the *Gospel of Thomas*) and Marcion's modified version of Luke's Gospel and Paul's epistles were heretical writings proposed by different groups for inclusion in the New Testament. But the Church determined that they contradicted the Tradition handed down to them from the apostles, and so must have been forged or otherwise non-inspired writings.

The word of God cannot contradict itself, so if a tradition contradicts Scripture, then the tradition must be human. Conversely, if a document purporting to be Scripture (such as a forged or heretical gospel) contradicts Sacred Tradition, or if someone's interpretation of Scripture contradicts it, then we know that it, too, is of human origin.

62. Since Jesus commonly quoted Sacred Scripture in his disputes with the Pharisees and the Sadducees, doesn't this prove that he saw the Bible as the sole rule of faith?

Jesus did quote Scripture (the Old Testament) often, but this doesn't prove or even imply that he saw the Bible alone as authoritative. Jesus quoted from the Old Testament because it is the word of God and as such is authoritative for settling the theological questions it addresses. Furthermore, because both Jesus and his opponents accepted Scripture as an authority, he could appeal to it as common ground between them. Here he followed his usual practice of using what his opponents would, in theory at least, accept as binding. But consider his dispute with the Sadducees over the resurrection of the body:

> The same day Sadducees came to him, who say that there is no resurrection; and they asked him a question, saying, "Teacher, Moses said, 'If a man dies, having no children, his brother must marry the widow, and raise up children for his brother.' Now there were seven brothers among us; the first married, and died, and having no children left his wife to his brother. So too the second and third, down to the seventh. After them all, the woman died. In the resurrection, therefore, to which of the seven will she be wife? For they all had her." But Jesus answered them, "You are wrong, because you know neither the Scriptures nor the power of God. For in the resurrection they neither marry nor are given in marriage, but are like angels in heaven. And as for the resurrection of the dead, have you not read what was said to you by God, 'I am the God of Abraham, and the God of Isaac, and the God of Jacob'? He is not God of the dead, but of the living." And when the crowd heard it, they were astonished at his teaching (Matt. 22:23–33).

The Sadducees, who accepted as inspired only the Pentateuch (the first five books of the Old Testament), didn't believe in the resurrection of the body. In refuting them, Christ *quoted only from the Pentateuch* (Exod. 3:6), not because he didn't acknowledge other Old Testament books that explicitly mention the resurrection of the body (for example, Daniel), but because the Sadducees didn't accept these other books. An appeal to an authority they didn't accept would have been useless, so Jesus proved his point by referring to one the Sadducees would affirm.

This same type of approach is necessary no matter who a person is challenged by. Sticking to what is recognized as authoritative by both parties will often help to resolve a dispute. But such an approach should not be mistaken as an indication that the authority cited is the only one acknowledged by the person speaking. In fact, many of the disputes between Jesus and the Pharisees occurred precisely because Jesus spoke and acted in reference to his Father: "He who sent me is true, and I declare to the world what I have heard from him. . . . I do nothing on my own authority but speak thus as the Father taught me" (John 8:26, 28).

63. Does the Catholic Church discourage direct access to Scripture?

This is a common misconception. The truth is that Catholics meditate on Scripture every day at every Mass. The readings and the responsorial Psalm during the Liturgy of the Word are taken directly from the Bible. The prayers throughout are biblically based. In fact, every moment of the Mass is influenced by Sacred Scripture. But even outside the Mass, the Church teaches that Scripture should always be available to enrich the lives of Catholics as much as possible. *Dei Verbum* exhorts:

> Easy access to Sacred Scripture should be provided for all the Christian faithful. That is why the Church from the very beginning accepted as her own that very ancient Greek translation of the Old Testament which is called the Septuagint; and she has always given a place of honor to other Eastern translations and Latin ones especially the Latin translation known as the Vulgate (22).

From its earliest days, the Church has embraced Sacred Scripture and desired to give the faithful access to its richness. That's why St. Jerome, who said, "Ignorance of Scripture is ignorance of Christ," translated the Bible into Latin in the fourth century—it was the era's most popular language of the literate.

Dei Verbum goes on to promote the reading of Sacred Scripture in the daily lives of Catholics:

> The sacred synod also earnestly and especially urges all the Christian faithful, especially religious, to learn by frequent reading of the divine scriptures the "excellent knowledge of Jesus Christ" (Phil. 3:8).... Therefore, they should gladly put themselves in touch with the sacred text itself, whether it be through the liturgy, rich in the divine word, or through devotional reading, or through instructions suitable for the purpose and other aids which, in our time, with approval and active support of the shepherds of the Church, are commendably spread everywhere (25).

The Church wants the faithful to have ready access to Scripture and to make the study of it an ordinary part of Christian life. Dispelling any doubt about how important this is understood to be, the Church even grants indulgences (partial remission of the temporal punishment due for sin) for reading the Bible prayerfully and with reverence.

So what about stories of the Church trying to keep people from reading Scripture by chaining the Bible to churches or burning early printed copies of the Bible?

In the Middle Ages, copies of the Bible made by hand were sometimes chained up inside churches, but this was to *ensure* access to them, not to deny it. Such books were extremely rare and valuable—not something the average Christian (who was often illiterate, anyway) could buy and keep in his home like he can today—and the only way to give people access to them while at the same time preserving them from theft or damage was to lock them down securely. And what better place to do that than at church, where Christians gathered?

Johann Gutenberg, a German Catholic, is often credited with being the first printer of the Bible. The first book he printed was the Mazarin Bible, so called because a copy was discovered in Cardinal Jules Mazarin's library. It is more commonly known today as the Gutenberg Bible and it was printed more than sixty years before the advent of Protestantism. So the Church did not oppose the printing of the Bible, or, later, the translation of the Bible into vernacular languages.

Even so, very poor, even heretical, translations of the Bible have surfaced from time to time, and these can be a danger to anyone who is not aware of the problematic content they contain. In order to protect unwary faithful from studying them, the Church has condemned and even destroyed erroneous translations. Far from downplaying the importance of Scripture, the Church's vigilant concern for the integrity of God's written word demonstrates the great value it has historically placed on it.

Today, with widespread printing and even electronic editions of the Bible, the Church can't possibly monitor every translation that pops up. The Church does, however, offer guidelines for the benefit of the faithful: encouraging "suitable and correct translations" to ensure that Sacred Scripture "be accessible at all times," and charging bishops with the solemnly important task of instructing their flock in the "right use" of Scripture, "so that the children of the Church may safely and profitably become conversant with the Sacred Scriptures and be penetrated with their spirit" (*Dei Verbum* 25).

64. What does it mean for Scripture to be inerrant?

Because the Bible is *inspired* (God is its author), it follows that the Bible must be *inerrant,* or free from error. This means that God prevented the human authors of Scripture from asserting something false in the original biblical texts. Allegations of error in Scripture cannot be explained away as the inevitable by-product of the Bible's human authors. As St. Basil the Great said in the fourth century, "What is the distinctive mark of faith? Full and unhesitating certainty that the words inspired by God are true."[113]

Since before Basil's time, the Church has uniformly taught that Scripture is without error. Pope Leo XIII wrote in his 1893 encyclical *Providentissimus Deus*:

> Inspiration not only is essentially incompatible with error, but excludes and rejects it as absolutely and necessarily as it is impossible that God himself, the supreme Truth, can utter that which is not true. This is the ancient and unchanging faith of the Church, solemnly defined in the Councils of Florence and of Trent, and finally confirmed and more expressly formulated by the Council of the Vatican (20).

But what it means for the Bible to be inerrant is not as simple as that. Taken to an extreme, the claim that the Bible is without error would mean that the Bible could not possess any details that do not correspond to a modern, scientific worldview. The Pontifical Biblical Commission elaborates:

> With the progressive discoveries in the field of history, philology, and the natural sciences, and because of the application to biblical research of the historical-critical method, exegetes have had to recognize that not everything in the Bible is expressed in accordance with the demands of the contemporary sciences, because the biblical writers reflect the limits of their own personal knowledge, in addition to those of their time and culture. The Second Vatican Council had to confront this problem in the preparation of the dogmatic constitution *Dei Verbum*.[114]

There are a variety of genres in Scripture, and none of them asserts a scientific description of the natural world. That is why *Dei Verbum*, the Council's dogmatic constitution on divine revelation, does not teach that everything *written* in Scripture is without error. Instead, it teaches that

> since everything *asserted* [emphasis added] by the inspired authors or sacred writers must be held to be asserted by the Holy Spirit, it follows that the books of Scripture must be acknowledged as teaching solidly, faithfully and without error that truth which God wanted put into sacred writings for the sake of salvation (11).

The last phrase, "for the sake of salvation," is debated among some theologians. The traditional view is that this phrase refers to God's *purpose* in putting inerrant truth into the sacred writings: that it was done for our salvation. Another school of thought holds that it refers to *which truths* in Scripture God protected from error; that Scripture's inerrancy is restricted only to those parts of it that are "for the sake of [our] salvation." Other statements in the Bible not related to our salvation, especially those concerning scientific and historical facts, could be in error. Although some Catholic theologians and scholars endorse this latter view, it is not the historic view of inerrancy, and there are good reasons to be skeptical of it.[115]

Nearly twenty years before the Second Vatican Council (1962–1965), Pope Pius XII condemned the actions of those who "ventured to restrict the truth of Sacred Scripture solely to matters of faith and morals," and also said that Pope Leo XIII had "justly and rightly condemned these errors" in *Providentissimus Deus* (*Divino Afflante Spiritu* 1). *Dei Verbum* says that the human authors of Scripture were "true authors, consigned to writing everything and *only those things which he* [*God*] *wanted* [emphasis added]" (*Dei Verbum* 11).

This statement applies not just to truths given to us for the sake of our salvation, but to everything written in the Bible. Or rather, everything that is written in the Bible is for the sake of our salvation. To say that the Bible contains errors is to say that God wanted to inscribe errors into the biblical text, which would contradict his perfection and undermine our ability to trust the revelation he gave us. Of course, saying the Bible is free from error does not mean there are not apparent errors or difficult texts whose explanation is not clear.

Working through parts of Scripture that may seem to contain error takes time and careful study. Although the Church has taught that certain conclusions about the Bible (for example, that it is not divinely inspired) are opposed to the Faith, it has not explained the meaning of every passage in Scripture. That is an ongoing effort for all the faithful. As Pope Benedict XVI said,

> The correct interpretation of these [difficult] passages requires a degree of expertise, acquired through a training that interprets the texts in their historical-literary context and within the Christian perspective which has as its ultimate hermeneutical key "the gospel and the new commandment of Jesus Christ brought about in the paschal mystery." I encourage scholars and pastors to help all the faithful to approach these passages through an interpretation which enables their meaning to emerge in the light of the mystery of Christ (*Verbum Domini* 42).

65. Doesn't Vatican II say that Sacred Scripture is inerrant in only a very limited way?

No document from the Second Vatican Council limits Sacred Scripture's inerrancy. Confusion sometimes arises, though, in regard to this statement in *Dei Verbum*:

> Therefore, since everything asserted by the inspired authors or sacred writers must be held to be asserted by the Holy Spirit, it follows that the books of Scripture must be acknowledged as teaching solidly, faithfully, and without error that truth which God wanted put into the sacred writings for the sake of our salvation (11).

Proponents of "limited inerrancy" claim that the last clause of this paragraph is restrictive: that inerrancy extends *only* to those parts of Scripture pertaining to our salvation. However, in order to better grasp an authentic interpretation of this clause, *Dei Verbum*—as with *all* documents of the Magisterium of the Catholic Church—must be interpreted in continuity with what the same Magisterium has continually taught in the past.

In 1893, Pope Leo XIII issued the most comprehensive magisterial treatment of Scripture interpretation the Church had yet seen. *Providentissimus Deus* was a landmark encyclical that sought to correct the many errors about Scripture then circulating the world. In it, Pope Leo pointedly affirms the *unrestricted* inerrancy of Sacred Scripture:

> For all the books which the Church receives as sacred and canonical, are written wholly and entirely, with all their parts, at the dictation of the Holy Ghost; and so far is it from being possible that any error can co-exist with inspiration, that inspiration not only is essentially incompatible with error, but excludes and rejects it as absolutely and necessarily as it is impossible that God himself, the supreme Truth, can utter that which is not true. . . . It follows that those who maintain that an error is possible in any genuine passage of the sacred writings, either pervert the Catholic notion of inspiration, or make God the author of such error (20–21).

In 1920, Pope Benedict XV reaffirmed Pope Leo XIII's teaching in his own encyclical, *Spiritus Paraclitus*, and Pius XII did likewise in 1943 with *Divino Afflante Spiritu*.

Dei Verbum, then, must be interpreted within the context of, and in continuity with, these prior documents. In fact, the language of *Dei Verbum*, section 11 (cited above), is taken directly from them, and its footnotes even refer to them. The theological commission at Vatican II even made a point of stating that the Latin term *salutaris* ("for the sake of our salvation") does *not* mean that only the "salvific" truths of the Bible are inspired or that the Bible as a whole is not the word of God.

If the whole of Scripture is inspired—if what the biblical writer asserts the Holy Spirit asserts—and if the Holy Spirit can't err, then biblical inerrancy cannot be limited just to certain parts of the Bible.

In *Divino Afflante Spiritu*, Pope Pius XII uses the *incarnational analogy* to explain this: "For as the substantial Word of God became like to men in all things, except sin, so the words of God, expressed in human language, are made like to human speech in every respect, except error" (37). This analogy essentially compares the word of God in Scripture to the Word of God made flesh, Jesus. Just as the Word took on human flesh in Jesus, the Word took on human language in Sacred Scripture. And just as Jesus is fully human yet fully divine, Scripture is authored both by human authors and the divine author. Finally, just as Jesus is like men in all ways except sin, Scripture is like human language in all ways except error. This analogy may be equally applied to Sacred Tradition as well.

66. Is Church teaching infallible like the Bible?

It is important to distinguish between the terms *infallible* and *inerrant*. Non-Catholics often claim that the Bible is infallible, but that is a misuse of the term. *Infallible* means unable to make a mistake or to teach error, and the term is used in reference to people, not inanimate objects like books. And so the Bible is not infallible but *inerrant*. Everything the Bible asserts, correctly understood, is true and therefore without error.

Indeed, Sacred Scripture and Sacred Tradition, having God as their source, are both inerrant. Therefore, when the correct understanding of a doctrinal matter is at question, both Scripture and Tradition may be consulted in order to settle the matter. Both are the word of God and they never contradict each other.

How does this relate to the charism of infallibility? Normally, human beings are fallible—capable of making mistakes—but in order to preserve his teachings over time Jesus gave the charism (gift) of infallibility to certain people in the Church in certain circumstances. Such infallibility means that the pope and bishops are protected from error when they proclaim by a definitive act a doctrine pertaining to faith or morals (CCC 891). This does not mean, however, that they are otherwise inerrant, are inspired by the Holy Spirit to deliver new revelation, or are personally *impeccable* (incapable of sin).

Nor does it mean that the Church has an infallible ruling on every point of theological or human interrogation. However, when divergent interpretations arise touching fundamental truths of the faith, there arises the need to settle opposing views authoritatively. This is where infallibility is particularly valuable. Over the long history of the Church, heresies have been weeded out and doctrine has authoritatively developed under the assurance of the charism of infallibility.

Sacred Tradition fills out and interprets the revelation of Sacred Scripture in the light of the beliefs and practices that the early Church received from the apostles. Without such assurances as the *inerrancy of Sacred Tradition* and the *charism of infallibility*, non-Catholic Christians have no comparable to resolve disputes of doctrine.

67. What types of errors can be found in Scripture?

> The books of Scripture firmly, faithfully, and without error teach that truth which God, for the sake of our salvation, wished to see confided to the Sacred Scriptures (*Dei Verbum* 11).

So said the Second Vatican Council (1962–1965). And the Council was not teaching anything new. The conviction that the books of the Bible teach the truth, that they give us the word of God, has been part of the Christian faith since the very beginning.

Jesus himself declared that "Scripture cannot be broken" (John 10:35), and St. Paul affirmed that "all Scripture is inspired by God" (2 Tim. 3:16).

But not everything in Scripture is easy to understand (cf. Acts 8:30–31; 2 Pet. 3:15–16). Sometimes there are *difficulties*—places where, at least at first glance, it looks like Scripture might be saying something false.

These difficulties come in two kinds. First, there are *internal difficulties*, where one passage of Scripture looks like it might contradict another passage. Second, there are *external difficulties*, where something in Scripture appears to contradict something we know independently, such as a law of science, a fact of history, or a principle of morality.

Since all truth is God's truth, there must be solutions to these difficulties, but why do we encounter them in the first place? Partly it is because of the age in which Scripture was written. Language and culture change over time, creating challenges for us—the citizens of a much later age and culture—when we read ancient writings. Difficulties of this kind can often be cleared up by additional study.

But more fundamentally, it seems to be part of God's providential plan to allow us to wrestle with his word. By doing so, we learn his word even better. This is the way any learning experience works: if a teacher simply tells you the answer to every question as soon as it is posed, you won't learn the material nearly as well as if you studied it on your own, learned to apply key principles, and figured out the answers to problems for yourself.

Already in the year 405, St. Augustine sketched a general strategy for resolving difficult passages that seem to put in question the inerrancy of Scripture:

> Of [the canonical scriptures] alone do I most firmly believe that the authors were completely free from error. And if in these writings I am perplexed by anything which appears to me opposed to truth, I do not hesitate to suppose that either the manuscript is faulty, or the translator has not caught the meaning of what was said, or I myself have failed to understand it.[116]

Here Augustine names three ways of dealing with Bible difficulties, by appealing to mistakes made by one of three people:

The copyist: In his day, the printing press did not exist, and so every biblical manuscript was hand copied. Unfortunately, scribes were not divinely protected from making mistakes when they copied manuscripts, and so copyist errors are a real phenomenon.

The translator: Augustine spoke Latin, and he did not have a good grasp of the languages in which the Bible was written (Hebrew, Aramaic, and Greek). Consequently, like most of us today, he had to use translations. God also did not protect translators from making mistakes, and there have been translation errors in the history of the Bible.

The interpreter: Finally, Augustine humbly recognized that God did not protect him—as an interpreter of the Bible—from making mistakes. That's an important admission, and we need to have the humility to make it, too.

Although Scripture itself is without error, errors of transmission and interpretation can creep in. These types of errors are behind many of the difficulties that face scholars and believers who approach the text of Scripture and will be the topic of the following questions.

68. Are there copyist errors in the Bible?

If you've ever tried copying a long piece of text by hand, you know how easy it can be to make mistakes.

Since you can only hold a few words or phrases in mind at one time, you have to keep glancing back and forth between the original text and the copy you're making. It's thus easy to lose your place. As you copy the text, you can accidentally omit a word or phrase—or copy it twice.

You also might misspell a word, especially for sound-alike words (for example, *to* instead of *too* or *two*). You might unintentionally say the same thing in slightly different words ("he didn't" instead of "he did not").

You might hit a place where the original is illegible, forcing you to guess at what the writer meant to say. You might even come across an error made by a *previous* copyist and not be sure how to fix it.

All these problems are common in hand copying, and that was the only kind of copying available before the invention of the printing press in the 1400s.

As the Bible became the most popular book in world history, thousands of copies were produced, but in the age of hand copying this also meant that thousands of tiny copyist errors were created. Each time a copyist made a mistake, it introduced a variant reading into the manuscript he was creating.

Errors have even happened in the age of the printing press. A famous example is the "Adulterous Bible"—an edition of the King James Version that was printed in 1631. When the printers were typesetting the Ten Commandments, they accidentally left out the word "not" so that Exodus 20:14 ended up saying, "Thou shalt commit adultery"!

Sometimes skeptics portray the existence of manuscript variants as a huge problem—as if all the tiny copyist errors rob us of the ability to know what the Bible originally said—but this is not true.

Take the example of the Adulterous Bible. Its famous printer error was spotted because people knew what the Ten Commandments should say based on all the other translations of the Bible in circulation—ones that *didn't* have the typo. It was easy to compare the new copies to the old ones and see the problem.

The Bible's popularity—the fact there are thousands of early manuscripts—thus gives us a solution to the problem of copyist errors: if an individual manuscript contains slips of the pen, there are numerous other manuscripts with which we can compare it.

Over the last few centuries, a whole field of scholarship—known as *textual criticism*—has developed to identify the original readings of Bible passages. Scholars have surveyed and cataloged the variations copyists introduced in the early manuscripts, classified them, and developed techniques for identifying what the original readings would have been.

Not every question has been resolved, but textual criticism has made it easy to identify copyist errors. It has also shown that most of these are very minor and that none of them substantially affects Christian doctrine. Although the problem of copyist errors may have been significant in Augustine's day, it no longer affects most readers. The development of textual criticism and the invention of the printing press—which allows thousands of identical copies of a Bible to be produced at once—has largely cured it.

A modern reader thus can have great confidence that the Bible in his hands doesn't suffer from this kind of problem. Even when there is a significant variant in the early manuscripts—one that textual criticism hasn't resolved—modern editions of the Bible will contain a footnote telling the reader about the variant, allowing him to make up his own mind.

For Bible readers who want to go further in exploring variants, they are discussed in standard commentaries, and everyone is welcome to read the works of textual criticism that scholars have produced and thus assess the evidence for themselves. To do so, however, you'll need to know the languages in which the early manuscripts are written, which brings us to our next subject.

69. Are there translation errors in the Bible?

The Italians have a saying: *Traduttore, traditore.* It means "Translator, traitor," and it's a wry reflection on the fact that translation can be hard.

No language maps perfectly onto another one, with all the same meanings and nuances—especially when complex ideas are being translated. Every translator thus, at least in a minor way, "betrays" his source material by not bringing it across fully into the new language. He may be able to bring across the fundamental meaning, but not all the subtleties and connotations.

Here's a famous example: in Greek, the final clause of the Lord's Prayer asks God to deliver us from *tou ponêrou.* In English, you could translate that one of two ways—either "evil" or "the evil one" (i.e., the devil). English doesn't have a way to capture that ambiguity in a single word or phrase, so the translator must make a choice. In doing so, he has to sacrifice the ambiguity that's in the Greek and say something more definite in English.

Translators face this kind of choice even when they are doing their jobs well, but sometimes translators lack skill or are motivated by ideological biases. An example of the latter is the Jehovah's Witnesses' *New World Translation*, which deliberately twists what is in the original languages to fit the group's theology. But although translator mistakes and biases are always possible, modern, mainstream Bible translations keep them to a minimum.

This is possible because the way biblical languages work is now well understood, and scholars in every Christian community recognize that their counterparts are doing good, competent work in Bible translation. If a Bible translation appeared that had major problems, these would be quickly spotted by scholars of *every* persuasion, and the translation would be severely critiqued (as the *New World Translation* has been).

Despite the high quality of modern Bible translations, though, the process of translation can still lead to difficulties that puzzle readers.

Consider how the Revised Standard Version translates passages in Acts that describe St. Paul's conversion and what happened when Jesus spoke to him. In one passage, we read, "The men who were traveling with him stood speechless, hearing (*akouontes*) the voice (*phônês*) but seeing no one" (Acts 9:7). In another passage, Paul says, "Now those who were with me saw the light but did not hear (*êkousan*) the voice (*phônên*) of the one who was speaking to me" (Acts 22:9). Both verses have forms of the Greek verb *akouô* for "hear" and the noun *phônê* for "voice." One seems to say that the men with Paul heard the voice and the other that they didn't.

The solution to this seeming contradiction has to do with the meaning of the Greek words. *Akouô* doesn't just mean "hear." If you check a standard Greek dictionary, you'll see it also means "understand." And *phônê* doesn't just mean "voice"; it also means "sound."

Since St. Luke—the author of Acts—is unlikely to contradict himself in recounting a story he undoubtedly heard from Paul multiple times, the logical thing to do is read the passages in harmony with each other, letting the relevant Greek words have their true range of meanings.

That's what the *New International Version* does in translating these passages: the men traveling with Paul "heard the sound" (Acts 9:7, NIV), but "they did not understand the voice of him who was speaking to me" (Acts 22:9, NIV).

The takeaway for Bible readers is that, when we encounter a Bible difficulty, we should consider whether the problem may be generated by the way the text is being translated. Could there be another translation that would clear up the difficulty? One way to investigate this possibility is to look at other translations and see what they say. Someone puzzled by the way the *Revised Standard Version* translates Acts could consult the *New International Version* and see the solution.

We are blessed today by having a large number of high quality, professional Bible translations, and even if you don't have knowledge of the biblical languages, you can consult other translations and see if they render the text in a way that doesn't produce the difficulty. Some websites (e.g., BibleHub.com) even specialize in showing you the same passage in multiple translations at once.

If you need to dig deeper, you can always consult detailed Bible commentaries or even start studying the biblical languages for yourself.

70. Are there historical errors in the Bible?

Our knowledge of the ancient world is limited. Most events were never recorded in writing, and the records of many that were written down have been lost. Further, reports can conflict, with ancient authors disagreeing about exactly what happened on a particular occasion. This poses a challenge for historians in every field, and that includes scholars of biblical history.

Keeping a number of principles in mind can help resolve these difficulties. First, there is the incompleteness of our sources. Sometimes skeptics have accused the biblical authors of being in error because they mention something not recorded in extrabiblical sources. However, just because something isn't independently attested to does not mean that it didn't happen. The accounts in the Old Testament themselves provide historical evidence for the events they describe, and this evidence cannot simply be dismissed.

Second, just because we may not currently have extrabiblical confirmation for an event does not mean we will not one day get it. As archaeology has developed, it has provided confirmation for biblical claims that were previously disputed. For example, skeptics at one time questioned whether the Israelites were around as early as the 1200s B.C. However, in 1896, the British archaeologist Sir Flinders Petrie discovered an Egyptian record, known as the Merneptah Stele, which documents the existence of the Israelites around 1210 B.C.

Third, in cases where the biblical and extrabiblical sources conflict, one cannot simply assume that the biblical sources are wrong. For example,

Egyptian scribes studiously avoided portraying their pharaohs as losing battles. Consequently, we would expect Egyptian records either to omit or misrepresent the defeat that Pharaoh Neco II suffered at the hand of the Babylonian king Nebuchadnezzar in 601 B.C., whereas Jeremiah's reference to it would be accurate (Jer. 46:2).

Fourth, we need to be sensitive to the way that the ancients wrote history. The techniques used in different time periods vary, and we cannot expect ancient historians—biblical or otherwise—to write in a modern fashion. For example, ancient histories involved a greater degree of approximation than modern ones do. There were no tape recorders, and so paraphrases and reconstructed conversations were expected in historical records. They were meant to convey the gist of what happened, but the details often were understood to be approximations.

Fifth, we need to be sensitive to the genres that the ancient authors employed. This is particularly the case when we are dealing with accounts of events that would have occurred long before they were written down. In these cases, the authors necessarily had less specific information about the events, and so they needed to adopt a genre capable of recording them in narrative form.

Thus in 1950, Pope Pius XII wrote,

> The first eleven chapters of Genesis, although properly speaking not conforming to the historical method used by the best Greek and Latin writers or by competent authors of our time, do nevertheless pertain to history in a true sense, which however must be further studied and determined by exegetes; the same chapters ... in simple and metaphorical language adapted to the mentality of a people but little cultured, both state the principal truths which are fundamental for our salvation, and also give a popular description of the origin of the human race and the chosen people (*Humani Generis* 38).

Sixth, we need to be careful about whether a text is even attempting to offer a literal account or whether it is employing some degree of symbolism. We have already seen that Genesis 1 is not meant to offer chronological information about how God created the world and instead uses a symbolic, topical way of organizing the work of the Creator, and we've looked at the proposal made by some Church Fathers and modern authors that aspects of the conquest narrative are not meant to be taken literally.

In some cases, entire books that might at first glance appear to be historical could turn out on closer reading to be something else. Pope St. John Paul II stated, "The Books of Tobit, Judith, and Esther, although dealing with the history of the chosen people, have the character of allegorical and moral narrative rather than history properly so called."[117]

There are thus a variety of principles that need to be kept in mind when considering proposed historical difficulties involving the Old Testament.

71. What about the thousands of contradictions in the Bible?

Have you ever heard someone tell you that there are hundreds, if not thousands, of alleged contradictions within the Bible's pages? Maybe they sent you to a website such as www.1001biblecontradictions.com? This kind of argument is nothing new; already the early Church Fathers were diligent in resolving alleged contradictions put forward by their pagan opponents. So how should believers respond to these allegations?

First, there are some simple rules to remember when reading the Bible that can help you resolve many alleged contradictions:

- *Read it in context.* Sometimes biblical passages only sound contradictory because they are isolated from their original context. Find the context and you'll usually find the explanation of the passage.
- *Consult a reliable commentary.* Commentaries provide details or facts not found in Scripture that can help explain alleged contradictions.
- *Differing descriptions do not equal contradictions.* The authors of Scripture may have differed in their descriptions of an event's details, but not in the essential truths they were asserting about those events. Some of them may have also written in different styles (topical vs. chronological), which can explain alleged discrepancies between them.
- *Incomplete is not inaccurate.* Just because the sacred author did not record something another author recorded does not mean his text is in error.
- *Only the original texts are inspired, not their copies.* Errors that came about through the copying process do not fall under the doctrine of inerrancy and can usually be located and corrected with ease.

- *The burden of proof is on the critic, not the believer.* If a critic alleges that Scripture is in error, he has the burden of proving that is the case. If the believer even shows a *possible* way of resolving the text, then the critic's objection that there is an intractable contradiction is refuted.

Second, you can consult one of the large encyclopedias of Bible difficulties published by Christians who have addressed these issues in detail. Unfortunately, the majority of the authors of such works are non-Catholics, so some of their explanations may conflict with Catholic teaching.[118]

Finally, we should give God's word the benefit of the doubt. Even if we can't resolve a difficulty at the present moment, it doesn't mean that the Bible is in error or that it is uninspired. It just means *we* don't know how to resolve the difficulty in question. This attitude is seen in early Church Fathers such as Justin Martyr, who told critics in the second century, "[Since] I am entirely convinced that no Scripture contradicts another, I shall admit rather that I do not understand what is recorded, and shall strive to persuade those who imagine that the scriptures are contradictory, to be rather of the same opinion as myself."[119]

Maybe someone else has already resolved a particular difficulty but we aren't aware of it, or perhaps an explanation will arise when additional evidence is discovered in the future. The bottom line is that the truth of what God has revealed to us does not depend on our ability to defend that revelation in discussions or debates with non-believers. The *Catechism* teaches,

> Faith is certain. It is more certain than all human knowledge because it is founded on the very word of God who cannot lie. To be sure, revealed truths can seem obscure to human reason and experience, but "the certainty that the divine light gives is greater than that which the light of natural reason gives" (157).

Karl Keating offers a good attitude to have in the face of alleged contradictions:

> If you think [the Bible] is supposed to be a listing of theological propositions, you won't make heads or tails of it. If you think it is written in literary forms you're most familiar with, you'll go astray in interpreting it. Your only safe bet is to read it with the mind of the Church, which affirms the Bible's inerrancy. If you do that, you'll see that it contains no fundamental contradictions

because, being God's inspired word, it's wholly true and can't be anything else.[120]

72. Do James and Paul contradict each other?

As in the famous story of blind men trying to describe an elephant based on individual parts they have touched, individual human beings are only capable of grasping part of the infinite mystery of God. The authors of the Bible thus have their own theological approaches and themes that they emphasize.

Sometimes the differences in how they express themselves, including the way they use terms, can generate Bible difficulties. Perhaps the most famous involves statements made by St. James and St. Paul on the topic of justification.

James famously says, "You see that a man is justified by works and not by faith alone" (James 2:24), whereas Paul says, "We hold that a man is justified by faith apart from works of law" (Rom. 3:28), and, "A man is not justified by works of the law but through faith in Jesus Christ" (Gal. 2:16).

Paul's teaching was widely misunderstood (Rom. 3:8; cf. 2 Pet. 3:15–16), and it is possible that James had encountered distorted reports of what Paul was teaching and decided to clarify matters. However, a careful reading shows he is not contradicting Paul. In actuality, the two are using key terms—faith, works, and justification—in different senses.

First, regarding the Greek term for faith/belief, James uses it to refer to intellectual assent to the truths about God. Thus he says, "You believe that God is one; you do well. Even the demons believe—and shudder" (James 2:19). But Paul refers to what theologians call "formed faith" or "faith formed by charity." Thus he says what counts is "faith working through love" (Gal. 5:6).

Second, regarding works, James uses this term to refer to positive actions flowing from belief in God—good works—such as giving food and clothing to the needy (James 2:15–16) or the actions performed by Abraham and Rahab in God's service (James 2:23, 25).

In Paul's key passages, however, he refers not to "works" but to "works of the law"—works done because they're required by the Law of Moses. He thus sees works of the law as characteristic of Jews but not Gentiles (Rom. 3:28–30; Gal. 2:11–16), and the main work he is concerned with is the Jewish initiation ritual of circumcision (Rom. 2:25–29, 3:30; Gal. 5:6, 6:13–15).

Third, James and Paul are discussing different kinds of justification. In addition to the justification that occurs when we first come to God and are forgiven, there is an ongoing growth in righteousness throughout the Christian life.

Thus James refers to Abraham as being justified when he offered Isaac on the altar (James 2:21). This occurred in Genesis 22, long after Abraham was initially justified. Indeed, he had been explicitly pronounced righteous/justified as early as Genesis 15:6.

However, Paul is principally concerned with initial justification—the kind that occurs when we first come to God. Thus he speaks of justification in the context of Christian conversion (1 Cor. 6:9–11, Gal. 2:16), and he stresses that this grace is not obtained by circumcision or other legal/ceremonial observances of the Law of Moses, but by the gift of the Holy Spirit through faith in Christ (cf. Gal. 5:4, 6:15).

James thus holds that intellectual faith alone does not save and that our ongoing growth in righteousness *after* conversion is furthered by doing good works. Paul says as much himself by affirming that, in so far as the Christian hope of righteousness is concerned, "neither circumcision nor uncircumcision is of any avail, but faith working through love" (Gal. 5:5-6). We thus find the two authors expressing complementary—not contradictory—views.

73. How should Catholics interpret Scripture?

The *Catechism of the Catholic Church* tells us that there are two different senses of Scripture: the *literal* sense conveyed by the words of Scripture and the *spiritual* sense conveyed by the realities and events within those words (115–118). If we don't understand both senses we risk misunderstanding the sacred author's meaning.

Take Matthew's assertion that the infant Jesus' departure from Egypt fulfilled Hosea's prophecy, in which God says, "out of Egypt have I called my Son" (Matt. 2:15; Hos. 11:1) This prophecy is literally about Israel, and Matthew knows this, but it was also spiritually fulfilled in Jesus. Matthew shows us that God, in his providence, used the Exodus as a "type" or "precursor" to model his future call, which brought his only-begotten Son out of Egypt and into Nazareth as an infant. In other words, the literal sense of Scripture recognizes how humans use *language* to communicate what they mean, whereas the symbolic sense recognizes how God, in his all-powerful and all-knowing providence, can use *events* in history to communicate what he means.

The Church also makes a crucial distinction between what is *written* in Scripture and what is *asserted* in Scripture. According to *Dei Verbum*, "everything asserted by the inspired authors or sacred writers must be held to be asserted by the Holy Spirit" (*Dei Verbum* 11). If I say, "It's raining cats and dogs outside" or "I have a million things to do today," the average listener will know that I am asserting a message that differs from what my words literally mean.

Of course, although it may be easy for modern English speakers to understand a fellow English speaker's assertions, understanding statements originally made in other languages and translated into one's own language becomes more difficult.

That's why it is helpful to examine the *genre* of the biblical text in question—the literary category to which it belongs. As the Pontifical Biblical Commission notes, "In the Bible, we find different literary genres in use in that cultural area: poetry, prophecy, narrative, eschatological sayings, parables, hymns, confessions of faith, etc., each of which has its own way of presenting the truth."[121]

Another principle of interpreting Scripture is the *analogy of faith*, or the idea that Scripture ought to be read against the whole of divine revelation (CCC 114). According to *Dei Verbum*: "Serious attention must be given to the content and unity of the whole of Scripture if the meaning of the sacred texts is to be correctly worked out. The living Tradition of the whole Church must be taken into account along with the harmony which exists between elements of the faith (12)." Indeed, 2 Peter 1:20 says that "no prophecy of Scripture is a matter of one's own interpretation," and the author later warns his readers that some passages in the Bible are "hard to understand, which the ignorant and unstable twist to their own destruction" (2 Pet. 3:16).

Fortunately, Christ did not leave us as orphans (John 14:18). Instead, he gave us his Church guided by the Holy Spirit to be an infallible teacher on the nature and meaning of Sacred Scripture. Scripture is correctly interpreted when it is done so in continuity with *Sacred Tradition*. That is why St. Paul called the Church "the pillar and foundation of truth" (1 Tim. 3:15) and the Second Vatican Council said, "The task of authentically interpreting the word of God, whether written or handed on, has been entrusted exclusively to the living teaching office of the Church, whose authority is exercised in the name of Jesus Christ" (*Dei Verbum* 11).

74. What is the most important question a Bible interpreter needs to ask?

Although Bible difficulties can arise from the process of copying or translating, most of the time the problem is generated when the text is being *interpreted*. In other words, when the interpreter has trouble understanding the text correctly. Fortunately, there is a central question that can help an interpreter focus his thoughts when trying to resolve a Bible difficulty: What, precisely, is the author of Scripture trying to *assert*?

To understand the importance of this question, we need to look at what the Second Vatican Council says about the way Scripture was written:

> In composing the sacred books, God chose men and while employed by him they made use of their powers and abilities, so that with him acting in them and through them, they, as true authors, consigned to writing everything and only those things which he wanted.

Therefore, since everything asserted by the inspired authors or sacred writers must be held to be asserted by the Holy Spirit, it follows that the books of Scripture must be acknowledged as teaching solidly, faithfully, and without error that truth which God wanted put into sacred writings for the sake of salvation (*Dei Verbum* 11).

We can rephrase the logic of this passage like this:

- Under divine inspiration, the biblical authors wrote everything God wanted and no more.
- Therefore, everything the biblical authors assert is asserted by the Holy Spirit.
- Everything the Holy Spirit asserts is true.
- Therefore, everything the biblical authors assert is true.

This is why it is important, when resolving a Bible difficulty, to determine what the biblical author is asserting. But that task is not always easy. Sometimes we think that the biblical author is asserting something that he isn't. This is a particular danger since the biblical texts were written centuries ago and in a different culture. In 1943, Pope Pius XII commented:

> What is the literal sense of a passage is not always as obvious in the speeches and writings of the ancient authors of the East, as it is in the works of our own time. For what they wished to express is not to be determined by the rules of grammar and philology alone, nor solely by the context; the interpreter must, as it were, go back wholly in spirit to those remote centuries of the East and with the aid of history, archaeology, ethnology, and other sciences, to accurately determine what modes of writing, so to speak, the authors of that ancient period would be likely to use, and in fact did use.
>
> For the ancient peoples of the East, in order to express their ideas, did not always employ those forms or kinds of speech which we use today; but rather those used by the men of their times and countries. What those exactly were the commentator cannot determine as it were in advance, but only after a careful examination of the ancient literature of the East (*Divino Afflante Spiritu* 35–36).

The difference in time and culture between the biblical age and ours can make it difficult for modern interpreters to determine what the authors of the Bible were asserting, and when they get this wrong, Bible difficulties can result. To resolve these difficulties, therefore, we have to figure out what the authors were asserting and what they were not.

For example, early Christians often assumed that the Second Coming of Jesus would occur within their own lifetimes. St. Paul seems to assume this when he writes, "We who are alive, who are left, shall be caught up together with them in the clouds to meet the Lord in the air" (1 Thess. 4:17). Yet Jesus did not return in Paul's life.

This would be a problem if Paul had indeed asserted that Jesus *would*. In that case, Scripture would be wrong. But that isn't what's happening in this passage. Paul may be tentatively *assuming* that Jesus would return quickly, but he isn't *asserting* it. The point he is asserting is that those who are alive at the Second Coming (whoever they may be) will be caught up to be with Jesus. Elsewhere Paul expresses doubt that he would remain alive (Phil. 2:17), and by the end of his career he was certain he would die (2 Tim. 4:6–8).

Being sensitive to the difference between a definite assertion and a tentative assumption allows us to resolve this potential difficulty, and similar techniques will allow us to resolve others.

75. What is the role of theology in interpreting Scripture?

The nature and extent of sacred doctrine are explored at the very beginning of the *Summa Theologiae* of St. Thomas Aquinas, because upon this understanding hinges the whole possibility of theologians to contribute something of value in the transmission of divine revelation.

Thomas first asks[122] "Whether besides philosophy, any further doctrine is required?" Although human reason and philosophy can most definitely lead us to some important truths, nonetheless,

> it was necessary for man's salvation that there should be a teaching revealed by God beyond the philosophical disciplines, which are investigated by human reason. First, indeed, because man is directed to God, as to an end that surpasses the grasp of his reason: *The eye hath not seen, O God, besides thee, what things thou hast prepared for them that love thee* (Isa. 64:4). But the end must first be known by men who are to direct their thoughts and actions to the end.

The exalted nature of man's end is not the only reason for a science dedicated to the study of God's self-revelation. Faith surpasses reason, but it also calls upon reason to clarify and defend the truths of faith, which might otherwise be misunderstood. Theology is precisely the science that is built up when the human intelligence places itself at the service of revealed truth. On this subject, Pope John Paul II summarizes:

> Without philosophy's contribution, it would in fact be impossible to discuss theological issues such as, for example, the use of language to speak about God, the personal relations within the Trinity, God's creative activity in the world, the relationship between God and man, or Christ's identity as true God and true man. This is no less true of the different themes of moral theology, which employ concepts such as the moral law, conscience, freedom, personal responsibility and guilt, which are in part defined by philosophical ethics.
>
> It is necessary therefore that the "mind" of the believer acquire a natural, consistent and true knowledge of created realities—the world and man himself—which are also the object of divine

> Revelation. Still more, reason must be able to articulate this knowledge in concept and argument (*Fides et Ratio* 66).

Thus, although "theology's source and starting point must always be the word of God revealed in history" (73), it employs the noblest insights of human reason to help us understand and live out the supernatural truths that God has revealed to us.

Two particular domains in which the theologian makes use of human reason in interpreting the word of God are in deciphering metaphors and the diverse senses of Scripture. St. Thomas dedicates an article to each of these themes, arguing that Scripture rightly uses metaphors, because comparisons with material things help us to comprehend spiritual truths[123], and providing some useful insights on how to interpret Scripture in both its literal and spiritual senses[124].

76. What is literal versus spiritual interpretation?

One of the most essential keys to properly interpreting any Bible passage is to distinguish between what are known as the literal and the spiritual senses of a text (cf. CCC 115). There is a considerable amount of confusion about these, so it is important to understand what the terms mean in their proper sense.

Put simply, the *literal sense* is whatever the author of Scripture intended to communicate, based on the words he uses. Scholars determine the literal sense of a text by looking at what an author wrote—the words themselves—and engaging in a process known as *exegesis* (Greek: "interpretation").

Because the biblical authors intended to communicate *something* in every text they wrote, each passage of the Bible has a literal sense, which is always the primary sense of the text. The *Catechism* states: "The literal sense is the meaning conveyed by the words of Scripture and discovered by exegesis, following the rules of sound interpretation: all other senses of Sacred Scripture are based on the literal" (116).

The human authors of Scripture were writing not simply on their own. Since "all Scripture is inspired by God" (2 Tim. 3:16; cf. 2 Pet. 1:20–21), God is the ultimate author of Scripture, and he knows more than the human author does. Consequently, there can be additional meanings in Scripture that are intended by God even if they were not something that occurred to the human author. This is what is known as the *spiritual sense* of the text.

The *Catechism* explains that the spiritual sense exists because, "thanks to the unity of God's plan, not only the text of Scripture but also the realities and events about which it speaks can be signs" (117).

To make this clear, let us consider an example. The book of Genesis records the circumstances surrounding the birth of Abraham's sons Ishmael and Isaac. Ishmael's mother was the maidservant Hagar, and Isaac's mother was Abraham's wife, Sarah (see Gen. 16–18, 21). The author of Genesis recounts this as information concerning the origin of the Jewish people, who are descended from Isaac, and other peoples, who are descended from Ishmael. That is what is happening in the literal sense of the text.

However, God also intended there to be a spiritual understanding of the text, and this is explored by St. Paul in Galatians 4:21–31, where he uses Isaac—the son of the free woman—as a symbol of Christians who are children of the promise, born of the Spirit. He uses Ishmael—the son of the slave woman—as a symbol of those who remain subject to the Law of Moses and seek their justification from it.

Based on what Genesis says, one could never show that this allegory was intended by the human author. But the fact that Paul writes about it under divine inspiration shows that it was intended by God. It is thus part of the spiritual sense of the text.

There is an important mistake we need to avoid when attempting to determine the literal sense of a text: thinking that the literal sense of a text can not involve symbols. This would be to misunderstand the relationship between the literal and the spiritual senses of a text. Literal does not mean "non-symbolic," and spiritual does not mean "symbolic."

For example, when Jesus tells the parable of the prodigal son (Luke 15:11–32), he uses a symbolic narrative to teach us a lesson about God's mercy. That lesson is the literal sense of the text. It would be a mistake to read the text *literalistically*—by failing to recognize that Jesus is using symbols—and start asking questions like "What was the prodigal son's name? What was his birthday?"

Only after the literal sense has been correctly identified are we ready to proceed to additional meanings, which are found in the "spiritual" sense of the text. This is traditionally divided into:

1) The *allegorical* sense. We can acquire a more profound understanding of former events by recognizing their ultimate fulfillment in Christ;

thus the crossing of the Red Sea is a sign or type of Christ's victory over death and also of Christian baptism.

2) The *moral* sense. The events reported in Scripture ought to lead us to act justly. "For whatever was written in former days was written for our instruction" (Rom. 15:4).

3) The *anagogical* sense (Greek: *anagōgē*, "leading"). We can view realities and events in terms of their eternal significance, leading us toward our true homeland: thus the Church on earth is a sign of the heavenly Jerusalem (CCC 117).

We see the New Testament authors identifying each of these senses in various texts, and applying them for their readers. Paul gives an *allegorical* reading to the story of Sarah and Hagar, mentioned above, in light of the freedom we have as sons of God in Christ. Similarly, he sees the rock which miraculously gave the Israelites water (Num. 20) as an allegory of Christ (1 Cor. 10:4).

Paul draws out the *moral* sense of various Old Testament texts where the Israelites indulged in immorality (Exod. 32:1–6; Num. 14:2, 21:6, 25:1–9) and concludes, "Now these things happened to them as a warning, but they were written down for our instruction, upon whom the end of the ages has come" (1 Cor. 10:11).

Finally, the author of Hebrews explores the *anagogical* sense of Old Testament texts in which the Israelites who disobeyed God failed to enter his rest in the promised land (e.g., Ps. 95:11)—and how the Sabbath rest itself points forward to the eternal rest that awaits those who believe the gospel, concluding, "Let us therefore strive to enter that rest, that no one fall by the same sort of disobedience" (Heb. 4:11).

Ultimately, the same principles of interpretation that the New Testament authors employed are open to us today, allowing us to mine the riches of the Old Testament for a wealth of insights. However, we must do so carefully, recognizing both the importance of the literal sense and the differences between the Old Testament era and the new era ushered in by Christ and his death for us on the cross.

77. Why is genre important?

The word *genre* refers to a type of composition. Genres occur in every kind of media: classical and hip-hop are genres of music; sitcoms and news programs are genres of television; westerns and science fiction are genres of movies; and so on.

Each work in a genre is composed according to certain conventions or rules, which define the genre. Classical music uses orchestral instruments, whereas hip-hop uses synthesizers and record sampling. Sitcoms use laugh tracks, but news programs don't. Westerns have cowboys and horses, and science fiction has aliens and space ships. Sometimes you even find works that fuse two genres, such as sci-fi westerns, which feature both cowboys and aliens.

In written literature, there are many genres, and that also applies to the literature in the Bible. Originally, the Bible was not a single book but a collection of books written in different genres. Some of them contain biographies (the Gospels), some histories (1–2 Samuel, Acts), some hymns (the Psalms), some prophesies and visions (Isaiah, Revelation), some wise sayings (Proverbs, Sirach), some laws (Leviticus, Deuteronomy), and some are letters (Romans, 1–2 Corinthians).

Individual books of the Bible also can fuse different genres. Thus the Gospels contain not only biographical information about what Jesus did and what happened to him in his life, they also contain his teaching, which is expressed in a variety of genres, including ethical discourse (Matt. 5–7), parables (Matt. 13), and prophecy (Matt. 24–25).

When interpreting the Bible, it is important to identify the genre that a biblical author is using and to understand the rules by which that genre works. If you don't know those things, Bible difficulties are sure to result.

For example, prophecies and parables make heavy use of symbolism in their narratives, but historical narratives generally don't. It would be a mistake to read Revelation 13 and conclude that John means that a literal seven-headed beast rise out of the sea and begin persecuting Christians. It also would be a mistake to read Jesus' parable of the sower (Matt. 13:3–9) and conclude that he was telling a story about a specific farmer who lived in his own day.

The rules that different genres obey are like rules of grammar: they help the author communicate his meaning to the audience, and if you don't understand the rules, you won't be able to figure out what the author is asserting and what he isn't. As Pius XII indicated, in order to know the rules of a genre, we need to make "a careful examination of the ancient literature of the East" (*Divino Afflante Spiritu*).

When reading the Bible, we must be sensitive to small cues in the text that can help us identify the genre we are reading and the rules that it obeys, because it can sometimes be difficult for a modern reader to figure this out.

For example, some modern readers look at the book of Judith and assume it is a work of history. This immediately generates a difficulty, as the first verse describes Nebuchadnezzar as the king of the Assyrians. "But," some say, "everybody knows that Nebuchadnezzar was the king of the Babylonians, not the Assyrians!" And yes, that's the point: everybody *did* know this. The first verse deliberately combines the two great enemies of Israel (the Babylonians and the Assyrians).

As you keep reading, you discover the book is about a conflict between one of Nebuchadnezzar's generals and Judith, a heroine whose name means "Lady Jew" and who thus personifies the Jewish people.

The effect is as if a modern person read a story that pitted Miss America against a general sent by Adolf Hitler, leader of the USSR, thus combining America's two great opponents of the twentieth century—the Nazis and the Soviets. The content of the book—right from the first verse—thus signals to the reader that he isn't reading a historical work but a kind of extended parable. Identifying the genre of Judith thus clears up the historical difficulties that would otherwise result.

Another example of how understanding genre is important is found in the book of Proverbs. Sometimes people confuse proverbs with laws, and if you do that, problems will result. For example, Proverbs 26:4 says, "Answer not a fool according to his folly, lest you be like him yourself." But the next verse says, "Answer a fool according to his folly, lest he be wise in his own eyes."

If these were laws that always had to be obeyed, there would be a problem, because they conflict. But they are not laws. They are proverbs, or wise sayings. By juxtaposing the two sayings, the author of Proverbs is telling us that *sometimes* it is wise not to answer a fool in kind, but *sometimes* it is. Rather than always doing one or the other, we need to use our prudential judgment to determine which is the wise course of action in a particular case.

78. What role does approximation play?

We live in a detail-oriented age. People today like exact records and precise measurements.

There is even a whole field—known as *metrology*—devoted to the scientific study of measurement. It allows us to say things like, "The speed of light in a vacuum is 186,282 miles per second," and, "The average atomic weight of an iron atom is 55.845."

Although this degree of precision is useful in some circumstances, we don't use anything like it in everyday life. Most of the time, we have no need for it, and it would actually get in the way if we had to specify everything down to the last decimal place.

Consequently, when we describe things we normally use *approximations*. We say, "It rained a lot yesterday," not, "There was 4.781 inches of precipitation yesterday." It would be absurd to expect people to use scientific levels of precision when an approximation would allow them to make their basic point.

Ancient people also used approximations. Indeed, they had to, because metrology and scientific measurement hadn't been invented yet. For many things, approximations were all they had—but they were all they needed to communicate their message.

Understanding this plays a role in resolving Bible difficulties, because to grasp what a biblical author is asserting, you need to know what degree of approximation he was using.

For example, some have seen a difficulty in the measurements the Bible gives for the metal basin or "sea" used for ceremonial washings in Solomon's temple. Scripture says it was ten cubits across, and "a line of thirty cubits measured its circumference" (1 Kings 7:23; 2 Chron. 4:2). That would imply that the value of π (*pi*) is 3, which is too small. π is an irrational number slightly greater than 3.14159, and the sea should have had a circumference of more than thirty-one cubits.

This example involves expecting a modern, scientific degree of approximation when it's not appropriate. The difficulty vanishes when you realize the biblical author wasn't asserting that the sea had a diameter of *exactly* ten cubits and a circumference of *exactly* thirty cubits. He was just approximating, the same way a modern person likely would in ordinary speech.

Approximation doesn't occur just when numbers are involved. It also occurs when words are involved, and difficulties arise if you don't recognize this. Many have seen Bible difficulties in the fact that the Gospels sometimes phrase things Jesus said in different ways or report him giving long speeches that would not have been memorized at the time.

But suppose that, today, you are telling a coworker about something your boss said. Unless you tape-recorded your boss or took shorthand dictation, you probably won't use his exact words. Instead, you'll give an approximation of what he said. You'll express the same meaning, but you'll use somewhat different words to convey it: a *paraphrase.*

In the ancient world, they didn't have tape recorders, and knowledge of shorthand was rare. This meant that, whenever one person quoted another, it was almost always a paraphrase. The only exceptions—also rare—were when one person made a deliberate effort to memorize something someone said in a word-for-word fashion.

In the case of a great teacher, someone might make the effort to memorize his sayings. Some of Jesus' sayings are short and vivid and structured in a way that would aid memorization, such as "the last will be first, and the first last" (Matt. 20:16). But paraphrases were the norm, and even sayings like that one could be paraphrased (see Matt. 19:30, Mark 10:31, Luke 13:30). If a stranger came up to Jesus and asked to be healed, nobody would expect the disciples to memorize *exactly* what the person said or what Jesus replied. When the event was recounted later, the audience would have expected the disciples (including the biblical author) to approximate what was said.

One thing we often do when paraphrasing is to flesh out the implications of what a person said and cover them in more detail. The ancients did that, too, and this is the likely explanation for the long speeches in John's Gospel. As an eyewitness (John 21:24), John knew Jesus and understood his thought intimately, allowing him to flesh out its meaning even when reporting one-time speeches that he would not have memorized on the spot.

79. How did the biblical authors select which facts to record?

Modern printing technology has made it possible to print lengthy books very cheaply. Today you can buy a 2,000-page Bible for twenty dollars or less.

This is not the way it was in the ancient world. Back then, when you had to pay scribes to write out every copy of a book by hand, books were fantastically expensive, and only the rich could afford them. Furthermore, books didn't have square spines the way modern books do. Instead, they were written on scrolls that you had to roll and unroll as you read them.

Both these facts meant books were smaller. Virtually nobody could afford a 2,000-page book, and absolutely nobody would want to roll through a 2,000-page scroll! Considerations of affordability and usability therefore led authors to keep their works concise. That's why you can read an individual Gospel, an ancient biography of Jesus, in just two or three hours.

But Jesus lived for more than thirty years, and his ministry lasted for more than three. If an ancient author wanted to write Jesus' biography, he would have to be very selective in what material he decided to include. That's why John closes his Gospel by saying, "But there are also many other things which Jesus did; were every one of them to be written, I suppose that the world itself could not contain the books that would be written" (John 21:25).

Other factors aside from length also influenced which episodes or details were included in any given biblical text. Different Evangelists had access to different details and, among those, would have chosen which to include and which to omit according to their audience and intended focus. The same would have been true for the authors of the epistles, addressed to particular communities in particular circumstances.

For example, sometimes one Gospel will tell of an incident and mention it involving a single individual, whereas another Gospel will mention it involving two. Thus Mark 5:2 tells of Jesus exorcising a single demoniac, but Matthew 8:28 mentions two demoniacs. Similarly, in Matthew 28:2 there is mention of one angel announcing Jesus' resurrection at his tomb, whereas in Luke 24:4 there are two.

Some have seen these as contradictions, but they are not. The authors are simply making different choices in which details to record. In reality, there were two demoniacs who were exorcised, and there were two angels at the tomb. One author mentions this, whereas another omits the detail and shortens the report to its essentials.

We see choices being made in which details to include in theological discussions also. For example, in the Sermon on the Mount, Jesus says, "Let your light so shine before men, that they may see your good works and give glory to your Father who is in heaven" (Matt. 5:16). But a little later, he says, "Beware of practicing your piety before men in order to be seen by them; for then you will have no reward from your Father who is in heaven" (Matt. 6:1).

By placing both of these sayings in the same context, Matthew is not contradicting himself. He expects us to read them both and to understand them in harmony with each other. Each expresses part of the truth but not the whole truth: we *should* let others see our good works when it would help them glorify God, but we *should not* do so out of a desire to glorify ourselves.

Making decisions about which facts to include on which occasions is something we do all the time. We almost never give technical, exhaustive statements of what we know about a subject. Instead, we mention certain facts on certain occasions, as determined by what we need to communicate at the moment. We then expect others to understand such partial statements in harmony with each other.

The biblical authors did the same things. They chose which facts to include based on what they were trying to communicate. Sometimes they mentioned more details to communicate a fuller message. Sometimes they mentioned fewer in order to save space or communicate more simply. By recognizing this and reading their statements in harmony with each other, we can resolve many Bible difficulties.

80. How did the biblical authors sequence their material?

Unless you have a freakishly detailed memory or keep detailed diaries, you likely can remember many significant events of the past without being able to recall the exact dates or the sequence in which these events happened. Our memories are good enough to preserve the essence of these experiences, but the knowledge of precisely when they happened fades quickly.

Ancient authors—both biblical and secular—had memories that worked the same way. Unless someone made a written, chronological record of an event, they would remember *what* happened, but not precisely *when* it happened. This meant that they would have to make choices about the sequence in which they presented their material.

For example, in *The Lives of the Twelve Caesars* by the Roman historian Suetonius, the biographies have a kind of loose chronological structure: they begin with an account of the caesar's family history and early life; they cover his rise to power; and they end with an account of the caesar's death and legacy.

But in the middle, things can be organized in a non-chronological way. Suetonius frequently groups the *positive* things a caesar did in office in one section, and he recounts the *negative* things the same caesar did in another section.

We find something similar in the Gospels: they also have a loose chronological structure, beginning (in Matthew and Luke's case) with his birth, covering his baptism by John and the beginning of his ministry, recounting the growth of his popularity (as illustrated by events like the feeding of the 5,000), and concluding with his death and resurrection. That's the natural structure of his life and ministry, and all the Gospels reflect it.

But apart from these key events, the Gospels vary the order in which they relate what Jesus said and did. Some people have noticed that and accused the Gospels of contradicting each other.

The solution to this difficulty is recognizing that the biblical authors—like other ancient authors—were not trying to give a strictly chronological account. Sometimes they used chronology, which is why they all record Jesus' baptism before his death. Sometimes they even give us very specific chronological information (such as in Luke 3:1–3).

But other times they arranged material by different criteria, such as by topic. Matthew's Gospel provides very clear examples of this. In Mark and Luke, we find sayings of Jesus scattered in many places, but Matthew gathers the same sayings up and groups them together by topic. He has Jesus' major ethical teachings in the Sermon on the Mount (Matt. 5–7), he has Jesus' major parables in a single discourse (Matt. 13), and he has Jesus' prophecies in the Olivet Discourse (Matt. 24–25).

By adopting a topical arrangement for Jesus' sayings, Matthew is doing essentially the same thing that Suetonius did. Ancient readers knew that authors wrote in this manner, sometimes arranging material chronologically and sometimes topically, and we need to understand this, too.

If we don't, we may falsely conclude that the biblical authors are *asserting* that the events they record happened in a particular sequence, when in fact they aren't. They are asserting *that* something was said or done, but often they aren't asserting anything about precisely *when* it happened. An awareness of the way biblical authors sequenced their material thus clears up many potential Bible difficulties.

In addition, it is important to realize that the teachings and parables of Jesus would have been repeated on numerous occasions in different places and circumstances. Even from a purely chronological perspective, there is no inherent contradiction in recording these teachings in different contexts, with different nuances, and in different sequences.

81. How are different modes of speech important?

We use figures of speech all the time, without even realizing it. They are part of how we naturally think. But if we stop to analyze what we say, they leap out at us.

The ancients, including the biblical authors, did the same thing. But because their culture was different from ours, we may not recognize the figures of speech they used.

Sometimes our Bible translations render the stranger expressions in idiomatic English. For example, in the RSV, Exodus 34:6 says that God is "slow to anger." What it literally says in Hebrew is that God is "long of nose." Being long of nose was a Hebrew figure of speech for being patient.

Other times, modern Bible editions leave it up to the reader to identify and interpret non-literal modes of speech. Sometimes recognizing them is easy. We all know that prophetic books like Revelation contain a large number of symbols and that Jesus' parables aren't meant to be accounts of historical incidents. We may still have to work to figure out what they mean, but we recognize that they aren't intended to be taken literally.

In some cases, however, it isn't so easy to spot non-literal speech in the Bible, and that can lead to Bible difficulties. For example, Mormons sometimes appeal to passages that refer to God's "outstretched arm" or his all-seeing eyes (Deut. 4:34; Prov. 15:3) as evidence for their view that God is an "exalted man." But elsewhere the Bible forthrightly states that God is "not a man" (Num. 23:19; 1 Sam. 15:29).

They key to resolving this difficulty is recognizing that the former passages are not meant literally. They involve a figure of speech known as *anthropomorphic language*—that is, language that depicts something (or someone, in this case God) *as if it* were human. The literal truth is that God is not a man, but the biblical authors use human symbols like arms and eyes to convey a sense of his power and knowledge.

Difficulties can also arise when a person fails to recognize a mode of figurative speech known as *phenomenological language*, which describes phenomena according to their appearances. For example, some passages in Scripture speak of the dead as being asleep (Ps. 13:3; Dan. 12:2; Matt. 9:24), but others indicate that the dead are conscious in the afterlife (Luke 16:19–31; 2 Cor. 5:8; Rev. 6:9–11, 7:13–15).

The solution is that the former passages describe the condition of the dead based on appearances—they *appear* to be asleep (they don't stand up, don't move around, and typically have their eyes closed). But in reality their souls are conscious and with God.

Another famous example of phenomenological language in the Bible is references to the sun rising and setting (Ps. 113:3, Eccles. 1:5, Isa. 45:6)—figures of speech that we still use today.

Finally, Bible difficulties can be generated when we fail to appreciate a concept known as the *universe of discourse* (also known as the domain of discourse). This refers to the range of things that are under discussion. For example, in Romans 3:23, St. Paul says that "all have sinned." This would create a problem if Paul was speaking absolutely. In that case, both Jesus and Mary would be counted as sinners.

But Paul is not discussing them. He has a restricted universe of discourse, as can be shown by the fact that later in the same letter he refers to unborn children who have not sinned (Rom. 9:11). Paul is discussing ordinary individuals, not people who aren't old enough to make moral choices, like infants, or who have a special place in God's plan, like Jesus and Mary (cf. Heb. 4:15).

82. Why is identifying the author's attitude important?

Bible difficulties often come up when people do not correctly discern the biblical author's attitude toward what he is describing. If we fail to do this, we may conclude that the Bible is endorsing something when it is not.

Consider an obvious example: Scripture sometimes quotes the devil (e.g., Job 1:9–10; Matt. 4:3, 6, 9). Obviously, the biblical authors do not endorse things said or done by Satan. Indeed, they acknowledge that he "has nothing to do with the truth, because there is no truth in him. When he lies, he speaks according to his own nature, for he is a liar and the father of lies" (John 8:44).

Likewise, there can be other biblical spokesmen whose point of view falls short of the truth of God. Consider the example of Job's three friends. Although they come to console with him and exhort him by every means possible to turn from sin so as to experience the Lord's salvation, they fundamentally err in interpreting his suffering as a divine chastisement for personal sin. Ultimately, it is they who are reprimanded by God for "not speaking of me what is right, as my servant Job has" (Job 42:7).

This presents us with an important caution against taking biblical passages out of context. Just because the Bible reports something, that doesn't mean it approves of it. In fact, the biblical author may be doing just the opposite.

Consider some of the crimes committed by Israel's leaders. In the literature of some ancient peoples, rulers are consistently portrayed in a positive light. In Egypt, for example, pharaohs were always depicted as winning battles, never as losing them. By contrast, the Old Testament historical books are remarkably frank about the defeats and flaws of the Hebrew kings. In fact, among ancient authors the men who wrote the Bible were uniquely straightforward about the sins of their kings, and even offer a critique of the institution of kingship itself, pointing out the abuses to which monarchy can lead (see 1 Sam. 8:10–18).

This applies even for kings with otherwise good reputations, such as David. Thus Scripture doesn't shy from reporting David's seduction of Bathsheba, the wife of another man. This could have been portrayed positively, as an act illustrating the king's machismo and his skillful outmaneuvering of a lesser man. But the biblical author presents it as sinful. He further reports that when Bathsheba becomes pregnant, David tries to avoid responsibility. He first tries to convince her husband that he is actually the father and, when this fails, he arranges for him to be killed in battle. God then sends a prophet to denounce David for his actions and proclaim judgment upon him (2 Sam. 11–12).

Sometimes the biblical authors convey their disapproval of a given violent or sinful act without recording an explicit divine judgment on the person in question. This kind of reportage is similar to modern accounts in which a news reporter or historian relates events in a straightforward way and allows the character of what happened to speak for itself, without offering editorial comment. Modern authors may expect their audience to recognize that something was bad without stopping to say, "And this was wrong," and biblical authors do the same thing.

The biblical authors were, however, men of their own day, and their attitudes reflect this fact. In some cases, they held attitudes that would later be supplemented and corrected by further revelation. In these cases, they may view incidents more positively or leniently than we would today, which brings us to our next point.

83. What role does progressive revelation play?

The Bible was written over a period of around a thousand years. The first books of the Old Testament were written around the time of King David, or perhaps a few centuries earlier, and the last books of the Bible—those of the New Testament—were written in the first century A.D.

This means that God did not give his revelation all at once. As the *Catechism of the Catholic Church* says, "God has revealed himself to man by gradually communicating his own mystery in deeds and in words" (68). Theologians refer to this gradual process as *progressive revelation*.

One consequence of progressive revelation is that people living in earlier ages did not have all of the information that those living in later ages did. This is why some passages in the Old Testament do not clearly envision the resurrection of the dead. The Israelites, like people of every culture, believed in an afterlife, but the specific form of the afterlife, involving resurrection, was only revealed gradually (CCC 992).

The progressive nature of revelation has other implications. In 2010, Pope Benedict XVI explained,

> God's plan is manifested progressively, and it is accomplished slowly, in successive stages and despite human resistance. God chose a people and patiently worked to guide and educate them. Revelation is suited to the cultural and moral level of distant times and thus describes facts and customs, such as cheating and trickery, and acts of violence and massacre, without explicitly denouncing the immorality of such things. This can be explained by the historical context, yet it can cause the modern reader to be taken aback, especially if he or she fails to take account of the many "dark" deeds carried out down the centuries, and also in our own day. In the Old Testament, the preaching of the prophets vigorously challenged every kind of injustice and violence, whether collective or individual, and thus became God's way of training his people in preparation for the gospel (*Verbum Domini* 42).

One aspect of God's progressive revelation is that he was initially willing to tolerate certain things because of human weakness, and then gradually showed his people a better way, ultimately revealing the fullness of his will in the example of Jesus Christ.

Thus Jesus indicated that God initially tolerated divorce because the Israelites were stubbornly attached to the institution: "For your hardness of heart [Moses] wrote you this commandment" (Mark 10:5). Jesus then gave the full revelation of God's will: "What therefore God has joined together, let not man put asunder" (Mark 10:9).

Parents may tolerate behavior from a small child that they would not allow once the child has matured, and in the same way, God allowed the early Israelites to do things that—by the time of Jesus—he revealed were not his will. This is a recurring theme in Jesus' teaching, as when he says, "You have heard that it was said, 'An eye for an eye and a tooth for a tooth.' But I say to you, do not resist one who is evil. But if any one strikes you on the right cheek, turn to him the other also" (Matt. 5:38–39).

This principle of God tolerating things temporarily as he leads people toward moral and spiritual maturity applies even in our own lives (cf. 2 Cor. 10:5b–6), and it explains many Bible difficulties involving the harsher laws in the Old Testament.

These laws were based on the harsh culture that prevailed when God first began working with the Israelites, and over time he gradually corrected them, ultimately revealing the ethic of love even for one's enemies (Matt. 5:44), as demonstrated when Jesus willingly went to the cross and prayed that those who executed him would be forgiven (Luke 23:34).

84. How was Scripture interpreted in the early Church?

Even in the early Church, interpretation of Scripture was an issue that demanded serious attention.

For example, St. Peter wrote, "There are some things in [St. Paul's letters] hard to understand, which the ignorant and unstable twist to their own destruction, as they do the other scriptures" (2 Pet. 3:16). Here we see that even during the apostolic era there was concern about misguided interpretations of the scriptures. Peter goes on to warn Christians, "You therefore, beloved, knowing this beforehand, beware lest you be carried away with the error of lawless men and lose your own stability" (v. 17).

The early Christians were hearing many interpretations of Scripture, and they couldn't *all* be correct. Sacred Tradition provided the way to discern the correct understanding. Early Christians knew they could trust Peter's teaching because he was one of Jesus' apostles, those whom Jesus first appointed with authority to teach. They recognized that the apostles were sent by Christ endowed with special authority to teach in his name.[125]

Peter also taught, "First of all you must understand this, that no prophecy of Scripture is a matter of one's own interpretation, because no prophecy ever came by the impulse of man, but men moved by the Holy Spirit spoke from God" (2 Pet. 1:20–21). In other words, just as Scripture was written under the inspiration of the Holy Spirit, so too, the only guarantee of its authentic interpretation is the Holy Spirit's guidance, promised in a special way to the apostles and their successors (John 14:26; 15:12-13). It is their apostolic teaching that is called Sacred Tradition.

Peter went on to warn about those who taught without authority: "There will be false teachers among you, who will secretly bring in destructive heresies, even denying the Master who bought them, bringing upon themselves swift destruction" (2 Pet. 2:1). The author of the Letter to the Hebrews issues a similar warning:

> Remember your leaders, those who spoke to you the word of God; consider the outcome of their life, and imitate their faith. Jesus Christ is the same yesterday and today and forever. Do not be led away by diverse and strange teachings. . . . Obey your leaders and submit to them; for they are keeping watch over your souls, as men who will have to give account. Let them do this joyfully, and not sadly, for that would be of no advantage to you (Heb. 13:7–9, 17).

We see an interesting example of how the early Church interpreted Scripture, to avoid the intrusion of any such diverse and strange teachings, in the Council of Jerusalem (Acts 15). Paradoxically, the subject in question on this occasion was the ceremonial and legal restrictions of the Mosaic Law, which certain members of the Jewish Christian community were teaching must also be observed by Gentile Christians. The experience of the apostles, on the contrary, was that the Holy Spirit "made no distinction between us and them, but cleansed their hearts by faith" (15:9). The testimony of Peter and James, Barnabas and Paul, ultimately led the assembly to discern the intent of Scripture and which parts of the Law should be extended to Gentiles and which not: "For it seemed good to the Holy Spirit and to us to lay upon you no greater burden than these necessary things" (15:28).

Thus, whether it concerned the prophecies and observances of the Old Testament or the epistles of the apostles themselves, Sacred Scripture did not stand alone in the early Church. It was never intended to. The assurance of correctly passing on the Faith comes through Sacred Tradition handed on by those with teaching authority.

> The task of giving an authentic interpretation of the word of God, whether in its written form or in the form of tradition, has been entrusted to the living teaching office of the Church alone. Its authority in this matter is exercised in the name of Jesus Christ. This means that the task of interpretation has been entrusted to the bishops in communion with the successor of Peter, the bishop of Rome (CCC 85).

85. How can the Bible be inspired when the book of Genesis contradicts science?

According to "young-earth" creationists, the book of Genesis says that God created the world in six twenty-four hour days. According to the theory of evolution, life evolved over billions of years through a slow and gradual process.[126] Doesn't it follow then that Genesis contradicts modern biology? You may be surprised to learn that already long before Darwin's theory of evolution was published in 1859, critics of the Church attacked the creation account in Genesis. In the fourth century, for example, a group of heretics called the Manichees challenged the authority of Scripture by asking how day and night could have existed before the creation of the sun on the fourth day.[127] Indeed, any reader, ancient or modern, should be puzzled by the fact that Genesis 1:3 describes how God created "light" on the first day, but created the sun, the thing that makes the light, on the fourth day. How do we explain this odd sequence of events?

Imagine that you're trying to recount what happened on a recent family vacation. How would you tell the story? You could present it in *chronological* order and talk about the long drive to the beach, the mix-up checking into the hotel, the visit to Grandma, then lounging on the beach, getting lost downtown, and stopping at a cheesy tourist trap on the way home.

Or, you could present it in *topical* order. You could first tell someone about your favorite parts of the trip—going to the beach, seeing Grandma, stopping at the tourist trap. Then, you might follow this with a description of your least favorite parts of the trip—the boring drive, the mix-up at the hotel, and getting lost in an unfamiliar place. Both approaches would be valid ways of retelling the story, even though one of them, the topical method, seems inaccurate if the listener assumed you were telling the story in chronological order.

The early Church Fathers and ecclesial writers understood this distinction and responded to critics accordingly. St. Augustine told the Manichees that the fourth day of creation symbolically demonstrates how God gave the sun and moon authority to rule over the kingdoms created during the first three days. Augustine went on to say that he believed God created the world instantly: "The sacred writer was able to separate in the time of his narrative what God did not separate in time in his creative act."[128] He even proposed the idea that God could have planted within the universe "dormant seeds" that would grow and take different forms over time—not unlike the change that occurs in living species through the process of evolution.[129]

The Catholic Church teaches that the first eleven chapters of Genesis contain fundamental truths of creation: that is, God created everything and made humans in his image so that they could know and adore him as the one, true God. But those chapters, in the words of Pope Pius XII, in "simple and metaphorical language adapted to the mentality of a people but little cultured, both state the principal truths which are fundamental for our salvation, and also give a popular description of the origin of the human race and the chosen people" (*Humani Generis* 38).

Think about how a parent might explain to his child that babies "come from seeds daddies give to mommies that grow inside the mommy's tummy." That's a true explanation but it shouldn't be taken literally since it was accommodated for a child's level of understanding. Likewise, the stories in Genesis are true but consist of non-literal language that comes down to the level of understanding found in the audience that first heard these stories. Pope St. John Paul II even referred to the creation stories in Genesis as "myths," but he was also adamant that they were not mere fictions:

> The language in question is a mythical one. In this case, the term "myth" does not designate a fabulous content, but merely an archaic way of expressing a deeper content. Without any difficulty we discover that content, under the layer of the ancient narrative. It is really marvelous as regards the qualities and the condensation of the truths contained in it.[130]

The *Catechism* says, "The account of the fall in Genesis 3 uses figurative language but affirms a primeval event, a deed that took place at the beginning of the history of man" (390). So, for example, the language of Genesis about talking snakes and eating forbidden fruit may be a figurative way of describing our first parents' sin.

The Catholic Church has infallibly taught that God created the world from nothing by his own free choice and that he made man's immortal soul in his image.[131] The Church has not, however, taught about the precise method God used to create the world or how old it is. Since a Catholic is free to form his own opinion on those questions, the critic can't say that our faith asserts a scientifically inaccurate description of the world.

86. Why does God callously strike people down in the Bible?

It is true that the Bible recounts many times when death is inflicted by the hand of the Lord upon those who sin against him or his chosen people. Consider only a few examples: the plagues of Egypt (Exod. 7-12), the destruction of the Egyptian army by the waters of the Red Sea (Exod. 14), the earthquake that swallowed the men of Korah's rebellion (Num. 16), the fire from heaven that swallowed king Ahaziah's cohorts (2 Kings 1), or the angel of the Lord who slew the Assyrian army encamped around Jerusalem (2 Kings 19).

One would hardly argue that these are occasions of God *callously* striking people down. But what about when death strikes those who have done nothing to deserve such severe punishment? What about the children of Job, for example, or the children who teased the prophet Elisha? A closer reading of these texts is instructive.

Although the reader knows the death of Job's children to be the devil's handiwork, Job receives the distressing news with an attitude of abandonment to the Lord: "Naked I came from my mother's womb, and naked shall I return; the Lord gave, and the Lord has taken away; blessed be the name of the Lord" (Job 1:21). Notice that when Job speaks of the Lord "taking away" the lives of his children, he is speaking of the gift they were *to him*. He is not saying that the Lord killed his children, but rather, that the Lord's gift to him of their presence has come to an end. None of us did anything to earn the gift of our lives or the lives of those we love, and so we have no basis for saying God wrongs us by taking to himself the gifts he entrusted to us for a time.

What about the children who teased the prophet Elisha? 2 Kings 2:23–25 describes an event that disturbs many people:

> [Elisha] went up from there [Jericho] to Bethel; and while he was going up on the way, some small boys came out of the city and jeered at him, saying, "Go up, you baldhead! Go up, you baldhead!" And he turned around, and when he saw them, he cursed them in the name of the Lord. And two she-bears came out of the woods and tore forty-two of the boys. From there he went on to Mount Carmel, and thence he returned to Samaria.

Notice that Scripture does not explicitly affirm a causal relationship linking the bear attack to the prophet's curse. It may be the case that the catastrophe was interpreted in that light by those who witnessed it and transmitted as such for the religious education of the youth. Regardless, the intent of the passage clearly to seems be that disregard for God's prophets has dire consequences.

Note, however, that the oncoming youths weren't a couple of small children harmlessly teasing Elisha; they were more likely a large, threatening group of young men. The Hebrew words often translated as "small boys" are *hunearim qetannim*. *Hunearim* is derived from the Hebrew *na'ar*, which means "boy," "lad," or "youth." In Scripture this word is predominantly used of young men who are over the age of twelve, such as Isaac (Gen. 22:12) and Joseph (Gen. 37:2), as one would expect of a group of young persons left to themselves outside the city limits.

Now, imagine if over forty teenage boys started making fun of you as you walked by yourself across a desolate area. You might become nervous, knowing that such a large group could cause you serious harm. In some third-world countries, gangs of children as young as eleven commonly rob and even kill people in broad daylight.[132]

The boy's taunt to "go up" was almost certainly a reference to Elijah's assumption into heaven. It represented a desire for Elisha and his God to "get out of here" and disappear in a similar way. The boy's taunts about his baldness may have been directed not at his mere appearance but toward his decision to serve the God of Israel (some prophets shaved their heads). It also could have been an epithet on par with calling someone an "idiot" regardless of his actual intelligence. Either way, the boys demonstrated profound lack of respect both for God and the prophets he sent. Rachelle Gilmour, in her study of the Elisha narratives, wrote: "It is no longer just an insult to Elisha, it is an insult to the Lord, and the bears appear only after a curse in his name."

Modern people balk at the violence and loss of life in biblical stories like this one, but what is usually absent from their criticisms is a concern about the sins these individuals and groups were guilty of committing. If we recognize that avoiding sin and seeking God with our heart, mind, and strength is what our focus in life should be, then we can understand why gruesome stories that treat sin with a heavy hand are included in Scripture. They serve as warnings not to follow the path that leads to death but to follow the path that leads to eternal life.

At the same time, even if death is ultimately a penalty for original sin and is, at times, inflicted as a penalty for personal sin, that does not mean that those who suffer it should be unilaterally judged as the objects of divine chastisement:

> Do you think that these Galileans were worse sinners than all the other Galileans, because they suffered thus? I tell you, No; but unless you repent you will all likewise perish. Or those eighteen upon whom the tower in Silo′am fell and killed them, do you think that they were worse offenders than all the others who dwelt in Jerusalem? I tell you, No; but unless you repent you will all likewise perish (Luke 13:2-5).

Clearly, Jesus is not suggesting that righteousness is an alternative to earthly death, since both the sinner and the just man die. He is warning, however, in a very concrete way, that imminent destruction awaits Jerusalem unless its inhabitants radically turn away from sin. This disaster will come upon them at the hands of their enemies, unless they take refuge in the Lord.

87. How could God command the Israelites to kill innocent women and children?

For many people this is the most difficult problem they encounter in Scripture—passages that record God ordering the massacre of innocent human beings. One example would be 1 Samuel 15:3, where God tells King Saul to "go and strike Amalek [a tribe that constantly fought with Israel], and utterly destroy all that they have; do not spare them, but kill both man and woman, infant and suckling, ox and sheep, camel and donkey."

What could explain such a harsh command?

In the book of Genesis, God told Abraham that he would "be buried in a good old age. And they [Abraham's descendants] shall come back here [to the land of Canaan] in the fourth generation; for the iniquity of the Amorites is not yet complete" (Gen. 15:15–16). The Amorites were one among many groups of mountain-dwelling Canaanites, but the iniquity God referred to was also present in the other Canaanites who inhabited the land. This includes worship of deities that committed murder, incest, and even bestiality. Fr. Raymond Brown wrote:

> Canaanite worship was socially destructive. Its religious acts were pornographic and sick, seriously damaging to children, creating early impressions of deities with no interest in moral behavior. It tried to dignify, by the use of religious labels, depraved acts of bestiality and corruption. It had a low estimate of human life. It suggested that anything was permissible, promiscuity, murder, or anything else, in order to guarantee a good crop at harvest. It ignored the highest values both in the family and in the wider community—love, loyalty, purity, peace and security—and encouraged the view that all these things were inferior to material prosperity, physical satisfaction, and human pleasure. A society where those things matter most is self-destructive.[133]

God was committed to shepherding a chosen people from which would come the Messiah, who would atone for the sins of all people, including the Canaanites. But this chosen people had to be protected from idolatry and other sins that would cause them to turn away from the one, true God. God had to forcibly create a space where his chosen people could prosper and eventually bring their knowledge of him to the entire world.

Remember also that God has the right to set limits to any human being's life, regardless of age or moral character. None of us has a limitless lease on earthly life, and the giver of life does no injustice to establish for any one of his creatures an early entrance to eternal life. St. Thomas Aquinas put it this way:

> All men alike, both guilty and innocent, die the death of nature: which death of nature is inflicted by the power of God on account of original sin, according to 1 Samuel 2:6: "The Lord killeth and maketh alive." Consequently, by the command of God, death can be inflicted on any man, guilty or innocent, without any injustice whatever.[134]

It could also be the case that the language used in some of these texts is exaggerated, non-literal "warfare rhetoric." Phrases such as "all were struck down with the edge of the sword," repeated over and over again in these passages, are typical of the hyperbole used in ancient battle accounts. For example, the Egyptian Merneptah Stele says that Israel was "laid waste and his seed is not," even though the nation of Israel continued to exist for several centuries after the stele was erected. Other ancient Syrian and Egyptian texts describe how opposing armies were "completely destroyed," even instantaneously, but those same texts also refer to the continued existence of the supposedly decimated forces.[135]

There is support for such an interpretation in the Bible, for example, where the book of Judges records the Israelites' destroying only the Canaanite idols (Judg. 6:25–27)—not the people as a whole, as the book of Joshua seems to describe. Judges 1:28 even says, "When Israel grew strong, they put the Canaanites to forced labor, but did not utterly drive them out." This stands in contrast to Joshua's hyperbolic description of the Canaanites being "utterly destroyed" (Josh. 6:21, 11:21).

Granted, there would still have been civilian casualties when Israel fought the Canaanites, just as there are in modern wars, but Richard Hess has argued that Jericho and many other conquered cities described in the book of Joshua were primarily military forts and so there would have been few civilian casualties. Most non-combatants would have resided in the countryside surrounding the fort and fled when the battle began.[136]

In sum, the Church has not definitively taught how we should interpret these kinds of Scripture passages. They might be literal accounts of the past that challenge our moral intuitions, or they might be non-literal accounts that demand an understanding of ancient genres and literary forms. Or they may be a blend of the literal and the non-literal. The fact that these texts are challenging does not mean that they are untenable; as we've seen, there are several plausible ways to explain them without sacrificing God's goodness or the inerrancy of his sacred word.

88. Why doesn't the Bible condemn slavery?

Slavery was a universal institution in the ancient world that, like poverty and war, had no place in God's ultimate plan for humanity. God's desire was that there would be no poverty (Deut. 15:4), and that his people would transform their weapons of war into agricultural tools and never fight again (Isa. 2:4). In order to overcome the effects of sin and hardened hearts, God progressively revealed himself to his people and meanwhile tolerated certain evils that their hard hearts embraced. But these evils were not meant to last forever, which is why God's word contained regulations designed to mitigate and eventually eliminate them.

For example, the Old Testament does not instruct the Israelites to treat slaves in the same way one would treat an animal or a chair. If a master seriously injured a slave by knocking out a tooth or an eye, he had to set the slave free (Exod. 21:26–27). Slaves could not work on the Sabbath (Exod. 20:10), and were allowed to participate in religious festivals, a freedom that was unheard of elsewhere in the ancient world (Exod. 12:44). Slaves could marry free persons (1 Chron. 2:34–35), own property, and even own other slaves (2 Sam. 19:17). If an ox killed a slave, then the ox would be stoned, which was the same punishment that was administered for the killing of a free person (Exod. 21:28–36). Fugitive slaves from other nations could not be returned to their masters and were allowed to live without oppression in the land of Israel (Deut. 23:15–16).

In many respects, Israel's slave laws were superior to those in the surrounding cultures. The Code of Hammurabi, for example, prescribed the death penalty for sheltering fugitive slaves and only required a modest fine for the crime of injuring someone else's slave.[137] The code did not prescribe a punishment for mistreating one's own slave. According to Old Testament scholar C.J. Wright: "No other ancient Near Eastern law has been found that holds a master to account for the treatment of his own slaves (as distinct from injury done to the slave of another master), and the otherwise universal law regarding runaway slaves was that they must be sent back, with severe penalties for those who failed to comply."[138]

This incremental approach to eliminating slavery could be compared to the current incremental approach many pro-life advocates take toward eliminating abortion in the United States. In the same way, the authors of the Old Testament passed laws that helped remove some of the worst abuses that were present in ancient Mesopotamian slavery and set the stage for God's people to eventually reject the institution of slavery in its entirety.

St. Paul encourages slaves to acquire their freedom if they can. But in the end, he would have both slave and free remain peaceful, whatever their state of life might be, for true freedom is the freedom we have in Christ.

> Every one should remain in the state in which he was called. Were you a slave when called? Never mind. But if you can gain your freedom, avail yourself of the opportunity. For he who was called in the Lord as a slave is a freedman of the Lord. Likewise he who was free when called is a slave of Christ (1 Cor. 7:20–23).

Developing this theme at length in Romans 6, Paul draws a contrast between two types of slavery and two types of freedom:

> Do you not know that if you yield yourselves to any one as obedient slaves, you are slaves of the one whom you obey, either of sin, which leads to death, or of obedience, which leads to righteousness? But thanks be to God, that you who were once slaves of sin have become obedient from the heart to the standard of teaching to which you were committed, and, having been set free from sin, have become slaves of righteousness (Rom. 6:16-18).

Regardless of socioeconomic background, all Christians share the same fundamental condition of having been "set free from sin and hav[ing] become slaves of God" (Rom. 6:22) through heartfelt obedience to the gospel. That's why elsewhere Paul says, "There is neither Jew nor Greek, there is neither slave nor free, there is neither male nor female; for you are all one in Christ Jesus" (Gal. 3:28). This was a revolutionary idea, given that Roman intellectuals, although lamenting some aspects of slavery, generally held slaves to be of lesser worth than free men.[139] Slaves in the early Church, however, were not stigmatized, and some, like Pius I (140–155) and Callixtus I (218–223), even held the office of pope.

In conclusion, it's important to remember that just because the Bible *regulates* a practice, even an evil one, that doesn't mean God *recommends* that practice. Instead, God progressively revealed his revelation to hard-hearted people who had to be incrementally led away from the evils of this world. Slavery was a universal feature of ancient economies just as credit is a universal feature of today's economies. God's people could not end slavery outright but they did promote the humane treatment of slaves as well as the intrinsic dignity of all people, which led to slavery being abolished by later Christians.

89. What is the Bible's attitude toward women?

There is no doubt that attitudes toward women were very different in ancient times compared to today. This has led some to propose Bible difficulties on the subject, sometimes charging that the Bible is misogynistic and that it fundamentally devalues women.

Space does not allow us a detailed survey of passages involving women, but several general points need to be made. First, because of the age in which the Bible was written, it is natural that its authors would write in terms of their own culture and the roles that women played in the society of their day.

Second, as we noted earlier, we must be careful to identify the author's attitude toward the subject under discussion. For example, Deuteronomy 21:10–14—which deals with taking as wives women captured in battle—is actually meant to restrain the lust of their captors and to provide protections for the women, who, the text says, have been "humiliated" (v. 14).

Third, Bible passages—including those regarding women—must be read in terms of the stage of progressive revelation that had been reached. This particularly affects Old Testament passages, which were written before God's definitive revelation of his will in Jesus Christ.

God initially took the Israelites for himself as a people when they were at a very low stage of cultural and spiritual development. They were even worshiping idols at the time God led them out of slavery in Egypt (Lev. 17:7; Deut. 32:17), and it took a centuries-long process for God to educate them spiritually and wean them away from pagan practices.

Jesus indicated that while this process was underway, God tolerated certain practices on account of Israel's hard-heartedness, and the way women were treated in the Old Testament certainly falls under that heading.

Fourth, God eventually brought about the definitive revelation of his will in Christ (cf. Heb. 1:1–2; Jude 3). Despite the low social status of women in the first century, Jesus freely associated with and showed compassion for women (e.g., Mark 5:25–34; Luke 7:11–17; 13:10–17), and he counted women among his key disciples (Luke 8:2–3).

Indeed, the New Testament depicts women as among his most faithful disciples, witnessing his crucifixion and burial and coming to anoint his body after death, whereas the male disciples had fled (Matt. 26:31) and were in hiding (John 20:19). This is why the women were privileged to be the first witnesses of the Resurrection (Matt. 28:9–10; Mark 16:9; John 20:14–17).

Jesus showed high regard for his mother. It was by her intercession that he performed his first public sign (John 2:1–11); he made provision for her care after his death (John 19:26–27); the New Testament describes her as the most blessed of women (Luke 1:42); and in the Catholic view she is the most blessed among all God's creatures, male or female, human or angelic (CCC 967, 1172).

Fifth, there *are* differences between men and women. This is obvious, though some moderns have sought to minimize these to the point of denying them and any implications they may have for the roles men and women most naturally fulfill in society. This is an area in which modern attitudes should not simply be uncritically accepted. Whatever natural differences in gender roles may exist, though, do not imply an inequality of the sexes.

Finally, the Bible recognizes the fundamental equality of men and women, and it does so from the very beginning. Thus the *Catechism* notes,

> God created man and woman together and willed each for the other. The word of God gives us to understand this through various features of the sacred text. "It is not good that the man should be alone. I will make him a helper fit for him" (Gen. 2:18). None of the animals can be man's partner. The woman God "fashions" from the man's rib and brings to him elicits on the man's part a cry of wonder, an exclamation of love and communion: "This at last is bone of my bones and flesh of my flesh" (Gen. 2:23). Man discovers woman as another "I," sharing the same humanity (371).

God thus created men and women "to be a communion of persons, in which each can be 'helpmate' to the other, for they are equal as persons ('bone of my bones') and complementary as masculine and feminine" (CCC 372).

The text of Genesis thus indicates that women, like men, are made in the image of God: "God created mankind in his image; in the image of God he created them; male and female he created them" (Gen. 1:27, NABRE; cf. CCC 369). The fundamental equality of men and women in God's eyes is expressed even more clearly in the New Testament, which proclaims, "There is neither Jew nor Greek, there is neither slave nor free, there is neither male nor female; for you are all one in Christ Jesus" (Gal. 3:28).

90. Are some of the teachings of Jesus unreasonable?

Because Jesus lived in a foreign culture thousands of years ago, it can be easy to misunderstand many things he said.

Take, for example, where Jesus says, "To you has been given the secret of the kingdom of God, but for those outside everything is in parables; that they may indeed see but not perceive, and may indeed hear but not understand; lest they should turn again, and be forgiven" (Mark 4:11-12). Does this mean Jesus deliberately confuses people so they will be damned?

To understand this passage we must recognize that Jesus is quoting part of Isaiah's call to be a prophet in Isaiah 6:9. In that context, God is essentially saying to Isaiah, "Go ahead and preach my judgment, but don't expect anyone to listen to you." Part of God's providence involves proclaiming judgment against sin and carrying out punishment for those who defy his judgment (even if he knew in advance they would defy his warning anyway—which happens often with human parents). The parable of the sower illustrates that God's message will sometimes be received by hard-hearted people who will not "turn and be forgiven," but the message is preached nonetheless to all, for the benefit of the open hearted, who are like "good soil"—who *will* turn and be forgiven.

Another example that troubles many is Jesus' assertion that "if any one comes to me and does not hate his own father and mother and wife and children and brothers and sisters, yes, and even his own life, he cannot be my disciple" (Luke 4:26). Does Jesus really want us to hate our families and even ourselves?

First, we should remember that as a good Jew, Jesus obeyed all of the Ten Commandments, including the fourth: "Honor your father and mother." He even criticized the Pharisees for shirking this responsibility (see Mark 7:9-13). However, Jesus knew that our love for God must come first, and that nothing on earth, even the people closest to us, can be more important than that love. Furthermore, in the idiomatic usage of the Hebrew language, to "hate" someone does not necessarily mean to unconditionally despise him. It can also simply mean "to love less than others."[140]

On this occasion, Jesus means that even family must always be secondary to the love of God. Matthew 10:37-38 recounts the same saying, but rephrases it slightly so that the meaning is easier to discern: "Whoever loves father or mother more than me is not worthy of me, and whoever loves son or daughter more than me is not worthy of me; and whoever does not take up his cross and follow after me is not worthy of me." This also explains Jesus' seemingly harsh words in Matthew 10:34: "I have not come to bring peace, but the sword." What Jesus means is that his gospel is not going to unite people under comfortable truths, but divide them by uncomfortable truths. He knows that the Church will be persecuted for its beliefs (the sword) and, therefore, that Christians must be ready for hatred and rejection.

Moreover, if we loved someone else more than God, putting them in the place of God, then our love for them would not be based in reality but in an illusion and a lie. Our relationship with them would be grossly distorted, making us unable to love them for who they really are. And at the same time, we would fail to properly love God, for we would be setting up an idol to replace him. So the words of Jesus are misunderstood if we fail to recognize the deliberate exaggeration that Jesus is using. He wants us to love all people, including our family. But he does not want us to love anyone, even our family, as if they were God.

Another troublesome passage recounts Jesus saying, "If your hand or your foot causes you to stumble, cut it off and throw it away. It is better for you to enter life maimed or crippled than to have two hands or two feet and be thrown into eternal fire" (Matt. 18:8).

Although this teaching of Jesus seems unreasonable if understood in a simplistic, literalistic way, it is this interpretation that is unreasonable, not what Jesus meant. In this passage, Jesus is using hyperbolic language: a deliberate exaggeration to make a point. We still do this today. A man might say to his buddy, "My wife is going to kill me for getting home so late." The husband does not actually mean that his wife is a killer and that he will be in the morgue the next day. Rather, he's using colorful and memorable language to make the point that his wife will be extremely angry with him.

By using such strong language, Christ is emphasizing the vital importance of turning away from sin and embracing a life of love for God and neighbor. Sin is like cancer. It damages us, impeding our functioning, and if not treated it can kill us. If we get cancer, it is utterly foolish not to try to eliminate the disease. We may have to get radiation treatments. We may have to get chemotherapy. We may have to get surgery to remove the tumors. But all these treatments, even painful and difficult ones, are worthwhile if they get rid of what is causing our suffering and what threatens to kill us.

So too, with sin. If not treated, it can kill our relationship with God, our relationships with others, and even our relationship with ourselves. Sin can lead us to hate God, hate other people, and hate ourselves. When this hatred is complete and lasts forever, that is the condition known as hell. Because Jesus loves us, he wants us to be cured; he wants us to have love in our lives. Just as the good physician hates the cancer, so Jesus the physician hates the cancer of sin and warns us in vivid and memorable language to get rid of sin.

Finally, there is the enigmatic incident where Jesus curses a fig tree for its unfruitfulness (Matt. 21:18-22; Mark 11:12-25). What sane person would curse a tree for not bearing fruit, especially when it wasn't even the season for fruit? Here Jesus is using the example of the fig tree to make a larger point about Jerusalem. Just as the fig tree has disappointed his hopes for fruit, on account of it not being the season for figs, so too Jerusalem has perennially frustrated the expectations of the Lord, claiming that the time of repentance had not yet come, and will soon be destroyed.

At the same time, Jesus uses this occasion, shortly before his Passion, to show his astonished disciples the absolute authority of his word, promising the same efficacity to their prayer of faith (Matt. 21:21-22; Mark 11:22-25; John 14:12-14.)

There are many other examples of Jesus' saying things that, to our modern ears, may seem absurd or even impossible. But it's important to remember that theologians and biblical scholars have examined these sayings and have provided explanations that help us more clearly understand what Jesus said. In order that we may profit from Scripture more fully, God gave us not only the Bible but also a reliable *interpreter* of the Bible. In the words of the *Catechism*, "Sacred Scripture must be read and interpreted in the light of the same Spirit by whom it was written" (111), the Spirit that animates and protects "the living Tradition of the whole Church" (113). Otherwise, we may be lead to make false and unreasonable interpretations of Christ's teachings.

91. How can I believe in Jesus if he was wrong about the end of time?

This is often called the "problem of the delayed Parousia," or the delay of Jesus' promised Second Coming. Yet this problem is only problematic if Jesus was definitely teaching that the *end of the physical world* would take place within the lifetime of his followers (say, within eighty or ninety years at the most). It's also possible that when Jesus said he was coming in his kingdom or that there would be apocalyptic signs of destruction, he was not talking about the end of *the* world, but rather the end of *a* world.

For the scenes of destruction Jesus predicted in Matthew 24 *would* come to pass only forty years later: in the Roman siege of Jerusalem that resulted in the destruction of the Jewish temple. His prediction of coming again, then, may have referred to his coming in judgment against the city of Jerusalem. Fr. William Most writes:

> The *coming* is best understood within the common scriptural concept of *visitation,* God intervening to help, to save, to punish. The intervention of Jesus, his coming, probably refers to the wars of A.D. 66-70 and the fall of Jerusalem, which put an end to the Jewish persecutions before the disciples ran out of places in which to preach. In the city's destruction, Jesus "visited Jerusalem," as we gather from chapter 24 of Matthew. Further, in view of the fact that Scripture often utilizes multiple fulfillments of prophecies (and Matthew 24 is a specially good instance), this saying may also have another fulfillment at the end-time.[141]

For a deeper explanation of this theory, and the various clues we find in the biblical passages that support it, a helpful resource is David Currie's book *What Did Jesus Really Say About the End of the World?*

Another interpretation of Mark 9:1 claims that when Jesus said that "there are some standing here who will not taste death before they see the Son of Man coming in his kingdom" he was referring to his disciples who would see him "come in glory" during his Transfiguration, which would begin six days later and is described in the very next verses of Mark's Gospel. Pope Benedict XVI writes in his book *Jesus of Nazareth*, "If we learn to understand the content of the Transfiguration story in these terms—as the irruption and inauguration of the messianic age—then we are also able to grasp the obscure statement that Mark's Gospel inserts between Peter's confession and the teaching on discipleship, on one hand, and the account of the Transfiguration, on the other."[142]

We should treat this "hard saying" the same way we would treat other unclear teachings or sayings of Jesus. If Jesus is the Son of God as he claimed to be, then there must be an explanation for why Jesus uttered these words besides, "He was just wrong." It turns out that in order to answer the question, "What did Jesus mean?" we have to answer the even more fundamental question Jesus posed to his disciples: "Who do you say that I am?"

92. If we forgive as Jesus calls us to do, won't this harm us psychologically?

Jesus clearly and emphatically taught his followers to forgive others. "If you forgive others their transgressions, your heavenly Father will forgive you. But if you do not forgive others, neither will your Father forgive your transgressions" (Matt. 6:14–15). The centrality of forgiveness is emphasized in every Gospel, in every liturgy, and in every "Our Father" in which we pray, "Forgive us our trespasses as we forgive those who trespass against us." Even as Jesus was dying on the cross, he gave an example of forgiveness, praying, "Father, forgive them, they know not what they do" (Luke 23:34). The ancient rabbis taught that we ought to forgive three times, and then we no longer need to forgive. Peter suggested to Jesus that maybe we would forgive seven times, more than doubling what the rabbis taught. Jesus said in reply that we should forgive seventy times seven (Matt. 18:22). By this he did not mean 490 times, and then stop on the 491st time. Rather, Jesus—using the biblical language of seven as the symbol of perfect fullness—meant we should forgive limitlessly.

Now, this teaching of Jesus can be easily misunderstood if we misunderstand what forgiveness is. Forgiveness is not *forgetting*. If someone does something incredibly horrible to you, like killing your mother, you will never forget it. But you can still forgive it. Forgiveness is also not *pretending* that nothing wrong was done. Murder, adultery, theft, and assaulting an innocent person are always wrong, but we can forgive someone who has done these things against us or those we love. Indeed, forgiveness presupposes that something wrong was done, rather than denying something wrong was done. If nothing wrong was done, there really is no need for forgiveness. Forgiveness is also not *reconciliation*. If someone who has wronged us remains dangerous, we may not be able to reconcile with him and restore the relationship to what it once was. So what is forgiveness? Following Everett Worthington's book *Forgiving and Reconciling*, we can distinguish two types.

Decisional forgiveness is forgoing personal vengeance and treating the wrongdoer with basic respect. *Emotional forgiveness* is forgoing personal vengeance, treating the wrongdoer with basic respect, and also feeling inner peace about the person. Decisional forgiveness is a choice. Emotional forgiveness goes beyond choice and includes our emotional state. When we have unforgiveness, we are like a man carrying around a bunch of burning hot coals who is looking for an opportunity to throw these coals back into the wrongdoer's face. The entire time the man carries the burning coals, he is getting burned and suffering pain. To forgive is to free ourselves from this burden.

So if we forgive others as Jesus calls us to do, will this harm us psychologically? The answer is emphatically no. It is *unforgiveness* that harms us, damaging our health by putting us in a chronic "fight or flight" mode of living. Many studies have discovered that "forgiving people are less likely to be hateful, depressed, hostile, anxious, angry, and neurotic. They are more likely to be happier, healthier, more agreeable, and more serene."[143]

Forgiveness is essential for human happiness because love is absolutely essential for human happiness. Without long-term loving relationships of family and friends, people lead lives of loneliness and isolation. Such lives are not only unhappy but typically very short. Given the human condition, friends and family invariably will do things that cause us pain and make us angry. If we do not have the ability to forgive others, we reject them and write them out of our lives. Since almost everyone will make a misstep, cause us some harm, and disappoint us in some way, if we do not forgive others, we will find ourselves with no long-term relationships with friends and family. Forgiveness is essential for our happiness because it allows us to preserve these most vital relationships.

Now, it is important to emphasize that to forgive others does not mean to be a doormat for them. The victim of a crime does not have an obligation to allow the criminal to get away with what he has done. This is not forgiveness. On the contrary, it can be a loving action to call the police, for example, because legal punishment can be medicinal for the wrongdoer, and justice done pleases God.

Forgiving and filing charges are not contradictory actions. In any case, the evidence is abundant that the teaching of Jesus about forgiveness is extremely beneficial when put into practice.

PART 3

THE BOOKS OF THE BIBLE

INTRODUCTION

The Bible (named from the Greek word for *book*) is a collection of books and letters, written over a period of centuries, that describe God's revelation to man and man's response to that revelation. The Bible, also called Sacred Scripture, is divided into two main parts: the Old Testament and the New Testament.

The first book of the Bible, Genesis, teaches that God created the world and made human beings in his image. It describes how our first parents rebelled against God and how God revealed himself to human beings in order to save them and their descendants from sin. This revelation took the form of *covenants*, such as those God made with Noah and Abraham, the latter of whom became the father of God's chosen people, Israel. God decreed that this group of people, named after Abraham's grandson Jacob, whom God later renamed Israel, would bless the entire world.

The next books of the Bible describe how Israel was enslaved in Egypt until God formed a covenant with Moses. Moses led Israel to freedom out of Egypt and into the desert, where they wandered for forty years before settling in a land God had promised to them in Canaan (located in modern-day Israel). The first five books of the Bible, which Jewish people call the Torah and scholars call the Pentateuch, end with the death of Moses and the installation of his successor, Joshua. The books of Joshua and Judges continue Israel's story and describe how Israel contended with the hostile tribes that inhabited the land of Canaan.

Along with books that tell the story of God's people, the Old Testament (or Hebrew Bible) contains literature that teaches God's people wisdom and right living (such as the book of Proverbs). It also contains collections of prayers and hymns, such as those found in the book of Psalms. Other books in the Old Testament include stories that were written to teach people to have faith in God, such as the story of Job, who kept his faith in spite of tremendous suffering.

The remaining historical books of the Old Testament, for example, Samuel and Kings, describe how Israel became a nation, and then a kingdom, and then a divided kingdom. The most famous of Israel's kings was David, whom most people remember as the shepherd boy who defeated the Philistine giant Goliath with a sling and a stone. David's son Solomon succeeded him but, despite his great wisdom, he failed to keep God's people from falling into idolatry and wickedness. This led to the nation being divided into northern and southern kingdoms.

After this division, God sent a series of prophets to exhort his people to repentance, but these prophetic reforms were either ignored or did not last. Other nations conquered both kingdoms and took God's people into captivity. The final historical books of the Old Testament reveal how God's people were freed from captivity and returned to their promised land. Unfortunately, even after their return God's people suffered under the rule of foreign powers such as the Greeks (and later the Romans). Through all this, they patiently awaited the Messiah: a savior promised in Scripture who would restore God's kingdom.

The New Testament is the story of that Messiah, Jesus Christ. The four Gospels (Matthew, Mark, Luke, and John) tell us that Jesus existed as the Son of God before the creation of the world and that he became man in order to save humanity from its sins. The Gospels describe how Jesus gathered twelve disciples, taught, healed, performed miracles, and died on a cross to atone for the world's sins. The Gospels end with an account of Christ's resurrection from the dead and his commissioning of the disciples to become apostles (a Greek word that means *messenger*) who would share this good news throughout the world.

The Acts of the Apostles is the book that picks up where the Gospels leave off (its author also wrote the Gospel of Luke) and describes how Christ's Church flourished in spite of the persecution it faced from Jewish and Roman leaders. The remainder of the New Testament includes a collection of letters the apostles sent to various communities in order to teach and encourage them to keep the Faith. The majority of these letters were written by St. Paul, a Jewish leader who persecuted the Church until he encountered the risen Christ and became a Christian.

The last book of the Bible is Revelation, which contains visions of God's heavenly kingdom given to the apostle John. It also contains prophecies about the end of the world and descriptions of how God will conquer evil and gather his people, both the living and the dead, unto himself in order to share glorious, eternal life with them.

BIBLICAL TIMELINE

Scholars debate the exact chronology of the following events. For helpful resources, see Jack Finegan, *Handbook of Biblical Chronology* (2nd ed.) and Andrew E. Steinmann, *From Abraham to Paul: A Biblical Chronology* (St. Louis, MO: Concordia Publishing, 2011).

c. 2000 B.C.	Life of Abraham (early dating)
c. 1800 B.C.	Life of Abraham (late dating)
c. 1400 B.C.	Exodus from Egypt (early dating)
c. 1200 B.C.	Exodus from Egypt (late dating)
1048 B.C.	Reign of King Saul begins
1009 B.C.	Reign of King David begins
971 B.C.	Reign of King Solomon begins
932 B.C.	Kingdoms of Israel and Judah separate
723 B.C.	Israel falls to Assyrians
586 B.C.	Jerusalem falls to Babylonians (temple destroyed; Exile begins)
515 B.C.	Dedication of rebuilt temple after return from Exile
331 B.C.	Palestine conquered by Alexander the Great
169 B.C.	Antiochus IV desecrates temple; Maccabees rebel
36 B.C.	Herod the Great becomes king of Jerusalem
3/2 B.C.	Birth of Jesus Christ
1 B.C.	Death of Herod the Great
A.D. 10	Jesus found in the temple
A.D. 14	Augustus dies; Tiberius becomes emperor

A.D. 26	Pontius Pilate becomes governor of Judea
A.D. 29	Baptism of Jesus
A.D. 33	Crucifixion of Jesus
A.D. 36	Pontius Pilate recalled to Rome; martyrdom of Stephen; conversion of Paul
A.D. 37	Tiberius dies; Caligula becomes emperor
A.D. 41	Caligula assassinated; Claudius becomes emperor
A.D. 43	James, son of Zebedee, martyred at Jerusalem
A.D. 43-49	Paul's First Missionary Journey
c. A.D. 48	The letter of James written
A.D. 49	Council of Jerusalem
A.D. 49-51	Paul's Second Missionary Journey
c. A.D. 50	1 Thessalonians, 2 Thessalonians, Galatians written
A.D. 51-55	Paul's Third Missionary Journey
c. A.D. 53	1 Corinthians written
A.D. 54	Claudius poisoned; Nero becomes emperor
c. A.D. 54-55	2 Corinthians, Romans written
A.D. 55	Paul arrested in Jerusalem
c. A.D. 55	Gospel of Mark written (early dating)
A.D. 57	Paul sent to Rome for trial before Nero
A.D. 58	Paul arrives in Rome
A.D. 59	Gospel of Luke written (early dating)
c. A.D. 59-60	Ephesians, Philippians, Colossians, Philemon written

A.D. 60	Book of Acts written
A.D. 62	James the Just martyred at Jerusalem
c. A.D. 62-63	1 Peter written
c. A.D. 63	Gospel of Matthew written (early dating)
c. A.D. 64-65	2 Peter and Jude written
c. A.D. 65	Gospel of John written (early dating); also 1 Timothy, Titus, and 1–3 John
A.D. 65-66	Peter martyred at Rome
A.D. 66	Great Jewish Revolt begins
c. A.D. 66	2 Timothy written
A.D. 67	Paul martyred at Rome
A.D. 68	Nero forced to commit suicide; Galba becomes emperor
c. A.D. 68	Hebrews written, Revelation written (early dating)
A.D. 69	The chaotic "Year of Four Emperors": Galba, Otho, Vitellius, and Vespasian each serve in turn as emperor
A.D. 70	*1 Clement* written; Roman forces raze Jerusalem and destroy the temple
A.D. 79	Titus becomes emperor
A.D. 81	Domitian becomes emperor
c. A.D. 95	Revelation written (late dating)

93. What is the Old Testament?

Simply put, the Old Testament is the collection of inspired books that God gave the Jewish people prior to the time of Christ.

The precise books that it contains are debated by Jews and Christians, but for Catholics it contains forty-six books. The first of these—Genesis—opens by describing the creation of the world, and the last to be written—probably Wisdom—was penned in the first century B.C. or even the early first century A.D. All told, its books were written over a period of about a thousand years.

The Old Testament takes its name from the covenant God made with the Jewish people. *Testament* is another word for covenant, and during the course of history, God made covenants with and through a number of individuals, including Abraham, Moses, and David.

To Abraham, God gave the promise that he would become the father of a multitude, and this promise was fulfilled in a special way through the people of Israel. Through Moses, God gave Israel his law for their nation. And to David, God gave the promise of an eternal kingdom, which was ultimately fulfilled in Jesus Christ.

A special moment came around 600 B.C., when the prophet Jeremiah revealed that God would create a new covenant:

> Behold, the days are coming, says the Lord, when I will make a new covenant with the house of Israel and the house of Judah, not like the covenant which I made with their fathers when I took them by the hand to bring them out of the land of Egypt, my covenant which they broke, though I was their husband, says the Lord. But this is the covenant which I will make with the house of Israel after those days, says the Lord: I will put my law within them, and I will write it upon their hearts; and I will be their God, and they shall be my people (Jer. 31:31–33).

On the eve of his passion, Jesus announced the fulfillment of this prophecy, stating:

> This cup which is poured out for you is the new covenant in my blood (Luke 22:20).

Because Jesus inaugurated in his Pascal mystery the New Covenant that Jeremiah had prophesied, and the books written about Jesus by the apostles and their associates came to be known as the books of the New Covenant or the *New Testament*. By contrast, the books that covered God's former dealings with the Israelites came to be known as the books of the Old Covenant or the *Old Testament*.

Although it is very common in our culture, the term *Old Testament* is not commonly used in Jewish circles, since it presupposes the Christian understanding of the New Covenant. Instead, these books are called the *Jewish Scriptures*, the *Hebrew Scriptures*, or the *Tanak*—an acronym based on the threefold classification of these books as the Law (*Torah*), the Prophets (*Neviim*), and the Writings (*Kethuvim*).

This way of classifying the books of the Old Testament is commonly used in Jewish circles today, but it is not the only way of grouping them. In the New Testament era, it was common to use a twofold division, distinguishing between "the law and the prophets" (Matt. 5:17, 7:12, 22:40; Luke 16:16; John 1:45; Acts 13:15; Rom. 3:21)—that is, between the Pentateuch and everything else.

Today it is common to divide the books of the Old Testament into several groups, including the Pentateuch, the historical books, the wisdom literature, and the prophets. We will discuss each of these categories.

Another way of dividing them is between the protocanonical ("first canon") and deuterocanonical ("second canon") books. The former refers to the books that are considered canonical in Jewish and Protestant circles and the latter to the additional books considered canonical by Catholics and Eastern Christians.

The original language of the Israelites was Hebrew, and most of the Old Testament was written in this language. However, after they were conquered by the Babylonians around 587 B.C., many Jews began to speak Aramaic, and so small portions of the Old Testament are written in that language. Finally, following the conquests of Alexander the Great around 330 B.C., many Jews began to speak Greek, and a few of the deuterocanonical books of the Old Testament were written in that language, just as the New Testament is. In addition, a major translation of the entire Old Testament, known as the *Septuagint*, was produced for the benefit of Greek-speaking Jews. (This translation is traditionally dated to the reign of Ptolemy II Philadelphus of Egypt, 285-246 B.C.).

94. What is the Pentateuch?

The Pentateuch consists of the first five books of the Bible. Its name comes from the Greek word *pentateuchos*, which means a five-book work. It is also known by several other names: The *Torah* (Hebrew for "instruction"), the Five Books of Moses, the Law of Moses, or simply, the Law.

The Pentateuch is the most fundamental part of the Old Testament—as important for Jews as the four Gospels are to Christians. It focuses on the origin of the people of Israel, how they came to possess the promised land, and God's instructions for governing their national and religious life.

1) *Genesis* is the first book of the Pentateuch. Its name is a Greek word that means "creation" or "origin." It's an appropriate title because Genesis describes the creation of the world and the origins of God's people, Israel.

The first eleven chapters of Genesis are often referred to as the *primeval history*. A lot happens in these early chapters. Genesis 1 gives us a powerful account of the creation of the world in six days; Genesis 2 provides an account focusing specifically on the creation of man; Genesis 3 explains how man fell into sin and thus became subject to death; Genesis 4 records the first experience of death (the murder of Abel); and Genesis 5 explains how mankind began to spread over the earth.

Because man continued in his wicked ways, God decided to cleanse the world. Genesis 6–9 recounts the flood he sent to accomplish this goal. The righteous man Noah and his family are preserved in the ark, and the story ends with God promising never to send another great flood. Genesis 10 and 11 then tell how mankind spread once more, bringing us to the close of the primeval history.

We then meet Abraham, the first of the Old Testament patriarchaps. His story runs from Genesis 12 to 25. Although Abraham is childless, God promises to give him many descendants, who will become a great nation. He also swears to give Abraham the promised land and make of him a blessing to all peoples.

These promises begin to be fulfilled through Abraham's son Isaac. The story of his miraculous birth is found in Genesis 17, and the events of his life are recorded in chapters 21 to 35.

The third of the great patriarchs is Isaac's son Jacob, to whom God gives the new name *Israel*. Peoples in the Ancient Near East were often named after one of their key ancestors, and so Jacob's descendants become known as the *nation of Israel*. The first generation of these descendants—Jacob's twelve sons—become the founding fathers of the twelve tribes of Israel. Jacob's story is the main focus of Genesis from chapter 25 to 36.

The final part of Genesis—from chapter 37 to 50—deals with Jacob's son Joseph. Because his brothers are jealous of him, Joseph is sold into slavery, but he rises to become a key official in Egypt. God uses these events to preserve both Jacob's family and many other people through a devastating famine. The book closes with the whole family reunited in Egypt, but with the assurance that God will eventually bring the family back to the promised land.

By our reckoning, the events of Genesis 12–50 would fall in the second millennium B.C., and the book as a whole covers the period from the creation of the world through the time of the patriarchs of Israel.

2) *Exodus* is the second book of the Pentateuch. Its name is a Greek word that means "departure" or "going out." It tells the story of how the nation of Israel left Egypt and began its journey to the promised land.

The account begins several centuries after the time of Joseph. Although the latter had been a key court official, eventually a new ruler arose who had no respect for the Hebrews and subjected them to slave labor. Because of the growing number of Israelites, Pharaoh devised a plan to weaken them as a people, ordering that newborn boys be put to death.

However, God providentially preserved the life of baby Moses and arranged for him to be brought up in Pharaoh's own household. As an adult, Moses defended one of his fellow Israelites, taking the life of an Egyptian in the process, which led him to flee to the neighboring land of Midian. There, God appeared to Moses in a burning bush and commissioned him to return to Egypt and deliver his people from slavery (Exod. 3).

Moses returns and, in keeping with the instructions that God has given him, demands that Pharaoh release the Israelites so they can worship God in the desert. But Pharaoh refuses to do so. Consequently, God sends a series of ten plagues on the Egyptians, culminating in the death of every firstborn son. The Israelites, however, are protected from the plagues, including the last one. To avoid being visited by the angel of death, they smear lamb's blood on their doorposts and celebrate the first Passover meal (Exod. 12). Afterward, Pharaoh finally lets the people go.

He soon has a change of heart, and he and his army pursue the Israelites into the desert. But God miraculously parts the waters of the Red Sea (Heb., *yam suph*: literally, "Sea of Reeds") and allows the Israelites to escape. He then drowns Pharaoh and his army when they try to pursue their former slaves through the waters (Exod. 14).

The Israelites then journey in the wilderness in Sinai to the mountain of God. There they encounter a powerful, storm-like manifestation of God's presence, and he gives them the Ten Commandments (Exod. 20), as well as other instructions, and Moses ratifies their covenant with God (Exod.

24). They also receive the plans for the tabernacle—a tent that functioned as a portable temple—and instructions for the ceremonies to be performed in it (Exod. 25–31).

When the people see that Moses is spending a long time on the mountain, his own brother Aaron misguidedly builds a golden calf for the Israelites to worship, and God becomes angry with his people. Upon seeing what they have done, Moses is so aghast that he smashes the tablets on which God had written the Ten Commandments, signifying how Israel had broken God's law (Exod. 32).

However, God renews his covenant with Israel, and has Moses create a new copy of the Ten Commandments. He also gives the people many more instructions through Moses, and the book closes with the construction of the tabernacle, and with Israel still on its journey to the promised land (Exod. 40).

3) *Leviticus* is the third book of the Pentateuch. Its name is based on a Greek word that alludes to the tribe of Levi, to which the line of Jewish priests belonged. The book consists almost entirely of instructions about holiness. It records the regulations to be used for making sacrifices (Lev. 1–7), laws regarding clean and unclean things (Lev. 11–16), and practical instructions for holiness (Lev. 17–27). It contains very little narrative material, the most significant example being the ordination of Aaron and his sons as priests, and the early events of their priesthood (Lev. 8–10).

4) *Numbers* is the fourth book of the Pentateuch. Its name is based on the fact that, at the beginning of the book and near its end, two censuses ("numberings" or countings) of the Israelites are taken. Although Numbers contains additional instructions regulating the life of Israel, it is primarily an account of the Israelites' journey to the promised land.

A key turning point in this journey occurs when Moses sends spies into the promised land to see what the conditions are like. When ten of the twelve spies report that the inhabitants of the land are too strong for the Israelites to defeat, a great crisis in national morale occurs, the people lose faith in God's promise, and he swears that this faithless generation will not enter the promised land. Instead, they wander in the desert for forty years and their children inherit the land (Num. 13–14).

At one point, even Moses becomes so frustrated with the Israelites that he oversteps God's instructions. On this account, he too die before they entered the promised land (Num. 20).

God guides his people through many trials during the forty years of wandering, and at their conclusion, a second census is taken (Num. 26) and other preparations are made for the Israelites' arrival in the promised land (Num. 27–36).

5) *Deuteronomy* is the fifth book of the Pentateuch. Its name is based on a Greek word that means "second law." It takes the form of a farewell discourse by Moses, because he is preparing to die and the people are preparing to enter the promised land. He reviews the history of God's dealings with his people (Deut. 1–4), instructs the new generation in God's law (Deut. 5–28), and renews the Lord's covenant with them (Deut. 29–30). The book then closes with a description of the events leading up to and including Moses' death (Deut. 31–34).

95. Is Genesis based on pagan narratives?

In the nineteenth century, archaeologists began to translate the literature of a number of ancient peoples, including the Egyptians, Babylonians, and Sumerians. As they did so, they discovered a variety of accounts that have similarities to the early chapters of Genesis. They contain creation narratives, flood stories, and so forth.

Strikingly, some of these accounts were written earlier than Genesis was. Most scholars hold that the material in Genesis was written sometime between the tenth and eighth centuries B.C., though some scholars say it was a few centuries earlier. Given the similarities between the texts, the question of the extent to which the author of Genesis borrowed from them was certain to arise.

From a Catholic perspective, the idea that the text of Genesis was in some way influenced by these accounts does not create a Bible difficulty. As Pope Pius XII explained,

If, however, the ancient sacred writers have taken anything from popular narrations (and this may be conceded), it must never be forgotten that they did so with the help of divine inspiration, through which they were rendered immune from any error in selecting and evaluating those documents (*Humani Generis* 38).

The idea that Genesis would be influenced by such texts should not be surprising. The Israelites were surrounded by powerful civilizations, and they were in contact with the oral traditions and literature of those peoples. It would be natural for Israelites to want to know how to respond to the claims made by their neighbors. We thus find the author of Genesis offering a critique of pagan views, and this critique manifests itself in a number of ways.

For example, although Genesis 1 describes God creating the sun and the moon (vv. 14–18), it never uses the Hebrew words for these bodies. Instead, it describes them simply as "lights" and explains that their function is "to give light upon the earth" and to provide ways of reckoning "for signs and for seasons and for days and years."

The reason the author does this is to correct the pagan view that the sun and the moon were deities. That's why he never uses their names: the Hebrew words for *sun* and *moon* were the names of the Canaanite solar and lunar deities, and the author wants to avoid the idea that God was the creator of a pantheon that included the sun and moon gods. Thus he describes them simply as lights and describes their functions. The message is: *they're not gods; don't worship them!*

Pagan narratives typically focused on the creation of a pantheon of gods, often by sexual reproduction, and they sometimes presented the creation of the world as due to a violent conflict among the gods. For example, in the Babylonian *Enuma Elish*, the god Marduk tears apart the corpse of the primordial mother goddess Tiamat to make the heavens and the earth. Then Marduk kills Tiamat's husband Kingu and fashions mankind from his blood as a slave race to free the gods from their labor.

A related work known as the *Atrahasis Epic* agrees that men were created so that the gods wouldn't have to work, but it says that men made so much noise that it disturbed the gods' sleep, and it was decided to wipe them out with a great flood.

By contrast, Genesis reveals that the world was created by a single God, and that it was not done in a sexual manner. God merely spoke, and reality obeyed. Creation did not involve a conflict between gods, and it resulted in a good and beautiful world that God entrusted to man.

Furthermore, God did not create man to get out of doing work. Instead, he put man in paradise and gave him the dignified task of stewarding his creation. We only experience suffering and drudgery because we sinned and rebelled against the role God had given us (Gen. 3:16–19). Similarly, disasters like the Flood are brought about by human sin (Gen. 6:5–8).

Genesis thus presents a theological vision according to which the world is created and ruled by a single, supreme God, who is good, generous, and just—not a pantheon of squabbling, selfish godlings.

Rather than saying Genesis is "based on" or "borrows from" pagan accounts, it would be more accurate to say that Genesis *responds to* and *corrects* pagan ideas so that we have a true theological understanding of God and his creation.

96. Does Genesis contradict modern science?

The first chapter of Genesis contains a creation narrative in which God is depicted as creating the world in a period of seven days. This is markedly different from the proposals made by scientists, who point to evidence that the universe and life developed gradually, over a period of billions of years.

Some have proposed that this difficulty can be resolved by the fact the Hebrew word for *day* (*yom*) can refer either to a twenty-four-hour period or to a longer period of time. The latter use is present even in English. We sometimes use *day* to refer to historical periods—for example, "Conditions were different in Napoleon's day." Some thus have proposed that the days of Genesis 1 could refer to periods of time that were billions of years long.

There are two problems with this view. First, even if it were true, it would not harmonize with the findings of science; for Genesis 1 depicts the birds being created before the land animals (vv. 20–25), yet paleontology indicates it was the other way around. Second, the text depicts the days as twenty-four-hour periods, for each is divided into "evening" and "morning" (vv. 5, 8, 13, 19, 23, 31), so either they are literal twenty-four-hour days or they are non-literal symbols.

A better solution to the difficulty is found when we pay careful attention to the text of Genesis itself. A close reading reveals that, despite what one might initially think, the text is not attempting to give us chronological information about the origin of the world. Instead, as the *Catechism* points out, it presents "the work of the Creator symbolically as a succession of six days of divine 'work'" (337).

The symbolism is revealed by the way the passage is structured. Initially, we are told that "In the beginning God created the heavens and the earth" (v. 1) and "The earth was without form and void" (v. 2)—in other words, it was unstructured and empty.

Over the first three days, God solves the formlessness problem by giving structure to the world: on day one he separates day from night; on day two he separates sky from sea; and on day three he separates the waters of the sea so that dry land appears (vv. 3–13).

Having solved the formlessness problem, God then solves the emptiness problem, and over the next three days he goes back over the same realms—in the same order—and populates them: on day four he populates the day and the night with the sun, moon, and stars; on day five he populates the sky and sea with the birds and the fish; and on day six he populates the land with the animals and man (vv. 14–31).

Once the earth is no longer formless and empty, God rests on the seventh day (2:1–3).

For our purposes, it's important to note that the sun is not created until the fourth day. The ancients knew just as well as we that the presence or absence of the sun is what causes the day/night cycle. The creation of the sun on the fourth day is thus a signal to the audience that the text is not meant to be taken literally but symbolically: it fits the work of the Creator into the framework of a Hebrew week, telling us *what* God did, but without intending to give us literal, chronological information about *when* God did it. Instead, it arranges the material *topically*, as God progressively solves the problems of formlessness and emptiness.

The difficulty is thus solved by careful attention to the genre of the text, to the sequencing of the material in a topical rather than chronological fashion, and to the text's use of non-literal language.

Consequently, St. John Paul II noted,

> Above all, this text has a religious and theological importance. It doesn't contain significant elements from the point of view of the natural sciences. Research on the origin and development of the individual species in nature does not find in this description any definitive norm or positive contributions of substantial interest. Indeed, the theory of natural evolution, understood in a sense that does not exclude divine causality, is not in principle opposed to the truth about the creation of the visible world, as presented in the book of Genesis.[144]

97. The Old Testament is full of archaic laws. Do we have to follow them?

The laws of God recorded in the Pentateuch can be classified in more than one way. In the Jewish Talmud (a collection of commentaries on them), there are said to be 613 laws, which are divided into 248 positive commandments ("do this") and 365 negative commandments ("don't do this").

Christian scholars have often proposed a threefold division of the laws (St. Thomas Aquinas, *Summa Theologiae* I–II:99:2–3). According to this system, the laws in the Pentateuch can be divided into three general categories: moral precepts, ceremonial precepts, and judicial (or civil) precepts.

The *moral precepts* are expressions of basic ethical principles. Examples include "You shall not kill" (Exod. 20:13) and "You shall not commit adultery" (Exod. 20:14).

The *ceremonial precepts* deal with the worship of God, the Israelites' religious activities, and the rituals they were to employ. Examples include the requirement of circumcision, the celebration of Passover and other feasts, dietary and other laws distinguishing between ritually clean and unclean things, and the way different types of sacrifices were to be offered.

The *judicial precepts* regulated aspects of Israel's civil life as a nation. Examples include establishing cities of refuge where people who accidentally killed a person could flee to find asylum (Num. 35:9–15), how much people should be fined for particular offenses (Exod. 22:1–15), the number of witnesses needed to convict someone of a crime (Deut. 19:15), and the penalties to be applied to false witnesses (Deut. 19:16–19).

The ceremonial and judicial precepts were given specifically to the people of Israel to prepare them for the coming of Christ and were not binding on other nations. Thus Gentiles do not have to be circumcised or establish cities of refuge (*Summa Theologiae* I–II:98:5). The moral laws, however, dealt with principles of right and wrong that are equally applicable to all, Jew and Gentile, both before and after the coming of Christ. According to Scripture professor Mark Giszczak, "Aquinas teaches that the ritual and judicial laws have been abrogated, but that the moral law still holds. So we *can* eat bacon, but we can't eat our neighbor."[145]

Here's an analogy to help us understand this distinction. When I was a child, my mom gave me two rules: hold her hand when I cross the street, and don't drink from the bottles under the sink. Today, I have to follow only the latter rule. The former rule is no longer needed to protect me; in fact, following it could do me more harm than good. But it's just as unhealthy for me to break the latter rule now as it was then.

The ritual/judicial laws were like mom's hand-holding rule. They helped the Israelites understand the purity God's law requires, just as hand-holding helped me understand the vigilance that crossing the street required. These laws also protected the Israelites from pagan influences, just as the hand-holding rule protected me from careless motorists. But by the time of the New

Covenant, these laws were no longer needed. In fact, the burden of following some of them (such as the requirement to be circumcised) hindered the goal of bringing non-Jews into communion with God.

But because the moral precepts are part of natural law, they apply to all peoples in all times. Of special note are the Ten Commandments. These express key moral principles that the *Catechism of the Council of Trent*, in its section on the third commandment, calls "precepts of the natural and perpetual law, under all circumstances unalterable," explaining that "notwithstanding the abrogation of the Law of Moses, all the commandments contained in the two tables are observed by the Christian people . . . because they agree with the law of nature, by the dictates of which men are impelled to their observance."

Even the ceremonial requirement to keep the Sabbath (Saturday) holy—which, "if considered as to the time of its observance, is not fixed and unalterable, but susceptible of change, and belongs not to the moral but ceremonial law"—reflects the underlying moral requirement is to devote adequate time to rest and worship. This obligation is fulfilled in the Christian age on Sunday, "the Lord's day" (Rev. 1:10; see 1 Cor. 16:2).

Which Old Testament precepts were obligatory for Christians is a question that dates all the way back to the time of the apostles, and even to the life of Christ. For example, Jesus "declared all foods clean" (Mark 7:19), which the *Catechism* explains in this way: "Jesus perfects the dietary law, so important in Jewish daily life, by revealing its pedagogical meaning through a divine interpretation . . . 'What comes out of a man is what defiles a man. For from within, out of the heart of man, come evil thoughts'" (582).

This pedagogical nature of the Mosaic Law was also underlined by St. Paul: the Law was useful in teaching the Jews how to be holy, but it was incapable of saving them from sin (Gal. 3:10). That's because no one could perfectly follow the Law and the Law didn't fix the root of why we sin—our fallen nature. The Law was holy, good, and just (Rom. 7:12), but it made nothing perfect (Heb. 7:19).[146] It contained what the Second Vatican Council calls "imperfect and provisional" things like animal sacrifices or ritual cleansing that would not be a part of God's final, universal plan to redeem all of humanity (*Dei Verbum* 15).

Simply put, we are not saved by obeying the Law of Moses, but by obeying the Law of Christ (Gal. 6:2). We rely on his grace (Eph. 2:8–10) to purify us from sin (1 John 1:7) and make us God's adopted children (Rom. 8:15). It is only through grace that we are able to follow Jesus' command to be perfect "as your heavenly Father is perfect" (Matt. 5:48). As a result, Christ's Church, endowed with his authority (Matt. 16:18, Luke 10:16), removed the necessity of following the provisional laws of the Old Testament (Acts 15:6–21).[147]

98. What is the point of Jewish purity laws?

Ritual and ceremony are human universals. Every culture has rituals—both secular and religious—that its members observe, from ways of greeting one another to ways of saying goodbye, and everything in between. People all over the world celebrate special days, have rites commemorating birth and death, and have ways of honoring God—or at least the gods they worship. Consequently, it was only natural for God to incorporate rituals and ceremonies into the instructions he gave his people Israel.

One function the Jewish purity laws (ceremonial precepts) performed was to make Israel holy. This was one of the key goals of the Pentateuch: "For you are a people holy to the Lord your God; the Lord your God has chosen you to be a people for his own possession, out of all the peoples that are on the face of the earth" (Deut. 7:6).

The Hebrew word for "holy"—*qadōsh*—does not just mean morally pure. It also means set apart from common things as something sacred. By giving the Israelites ceremonial precepts, God marked them off as separate from all the other peoples of the earth, as his own special possession—a nation specially consecrated to him.

Although, in the absolute sense, nothing God has made is unclean and no food defiles a man (Mark 7:14–23), by giving the Israelites dietary laws, God made them culturally separate from the peoples that surrounded them. Israelites could not eat things that their Gentile neighbors could, which helped create a cultural wall around them. This not only reinforced their identity as a distinct people dedicated to God, but it also helped protect them from temptations to worship the gods of the Gentiles, since they could not accept invitations to eat with pagans.

Similarly, there was a requirement that only Israelites could eat the Passover meal. If a foreigner wanted to eat it, all the males of his household had to be circumcised and become like native Israelites (Exod. 12:48). This also helped protect against mingling religious observances with pagans and their practices.

The same principle of keeping the Israelites distinct is found in many other ceremonial requirements of the Law. Unlike the Gentiles, the Israelites could not cut the edges off their beards (Lev. 19:27), have tattoos (Lev. 19:28), or wear clothes made by mixing wool and linen fibers (Deut. 22:11). In this way, the Israelites would even be visually distinct from their neighbors.

Many things that the Israelites encountered in everyday life could make them ceremonially unclean, requiring them to take a ritual bath to become clean again (Lev. 11:25; 15:5, 16, 18, 21; 22:6, and elsewhere). These practices not only reinforced Israelite cultural identity, but they also taught a deeper lesson that one must separate oneself from what is morally unclean. The ceremonial purity requirements of the Mosaic Law thus pointed to the realm of moral purity as well.

Finally, these aspects of the Law of Moses also pointed forward to Christ and the "law of Christ" that he would reveal (1 Cor. 9:21; Gal. 6:2). Thus the ceremonial baths pointed forward to Christian baptism, and the Passover meal pointed forward to Christ—the ultimate "Lamb of God" (John 1:29)—so that St. Paul could say, "Christ, our paschal lamb, has been sacrificed. Let us, therefore, celebrate the festival, not with the old leaven, the leaven of malice and evil, but with the unleavened bread of sincerity and truth" (1 Cor. 5:7–8).

99. Why do some Old Testament laws seem harsh?

The Old Testament contains various laws that do not accord with modern sensibilities. There are a number of things to keep in mind when considering these passages.

First, just because modern sensibilities do not like something does not mean that it must be false. The idea that our ideas today are automatically superior to those of the ancient world reflects a form of *chronological snobbery*; it needs to be asked whether perhaps the *modern* ideas are the problematic ones. Compared to people in the ancient world, we lead very soft and comfortable lives, and it is reasonable to ask whether some of our views may have consequently become unrealistic or even degenerate.

Second, we should recognize that many of the laws in question are found in the Pentateuch (the books of Genesis through Deuteronomy) and that they thus reflect an earlier stage of progressive revelation. Jesus indicated that Moses gave the Israelites some laws only because of the hardness of their hearts (Mark 10:5). God was willing to tolerate certain practices among the

Israelites for a time, though he ultimately revealed the fullness of his will through Christ. The difficulty caused by a particular law thus may be due to the fact it represents something God was tolerating since the Israelites had not yet reached a more advanced stage of cultural and spiritual development.

Third, a careful reading of the legal texts shows that, rather than implying an endorsement, the Law was actually trying to limit the damage caused in a situation. For example, some have been shocked by the regulations saying what Israelite men should do when they have captured women in battle and wish to marry them (Deut. 21:10–14), but the purpose of this law actually is to restrain what the men would otherwise do and to provide protections for the captive women.

Thus the men are not allowed to marry the women immediately. There is a waiting period in which the woman makes herself unattractive and mourns for her parents, giving the man a chance to reconsider (vv. 12–13). The text warns the man who still insists on marrying such a woman that he has "humiliated her" (v. 14), and if he decides to divorce her then she has the right to go wherever she wants, including back to her own people. He is not allowed to sell her or treat her as a slave. The text thus seeks to restrain the way the Israelites treated captive women.

Fourth, we should seek to understand the principles on which the laws were based. For example, many moderns criticize harsh-sounding Old Testament statements that speak of taking "an eye for an eye and a tooth for a tooth," but, properly understood, the passages expressed a principle of justice and sought to promote the common good.

Three passages mention the "eye for an eye" principle: Exodus 21:22–25, Leviticus 24:17–21, and Deuteronomy 19:16–21. The first deals with the case of men who are fighting and accidentally injure a pregnant woman, causing miscarriage. The second deals with a man who attacks and maims another. The third deals with a witness who lies in court to harm an innocent person. In each passage a similar formula occurs: "you shall give life for life, eye for eye, tooth for tooth, hand for hand, foot for foot, burn for burn, wound for wound, stripe for stripe" (Exod. 21:23–25).

Note that these passages are intended to be used by a court when a crime has been committed. They aren't instructions telling people to take personal revenge. The point of having a court system is to *prevent* people from doing that by seeing that justice is done when an innocent party is harmed.

If people take their own revenge, they may often do so excessively. A person who has been wounded or seen a loved one wounded may *kill* the perpetrator, for example. Courts exist to keep this from happening. To do their job properly, courts need to be seen as administering justice fairly. If they are too lenient, people may take matters into their own hands. Thus the "eye for an eye" passages. They direct courts to let the punishment fit the crime, which is a fundamental principle of justice. This principle promoted the common good and order of society by discouraging people from taking their own revenge.

In a world without an extensive prison system, this may have literally meant "an eye for an eye," though not always. Numbers 35:31 specifies that no ransom can be accepted in a case of murder, suggesting that in lesser cases the guilty party could pay compensation. A person thus might avoid "an eye for an eye" if he provided appropriate compensation to the injured party.

Justice can also be tempered by mercy in other ways. Thus Jesus counseled individuals to "turn the other cheek" rather than pressing for "an eye for an eye" justice (Matt. 5:38–39).

100. What are the historical books?

The historical books of the Old Testament are those that record the history of Israel after the time of Moses' death. Here we will cover the historical books that are found in the Hebrew Bible. Those that belong to the deuterocanonical books will be covered later.

1) *Joshua* is the first of the historical books. It begins immediately after Moses and describes the conquest of the Holy Land under the leadership of his successor, Joshua the son of Nun. The book concludes with Joshua telling the Israelites that they need to decide which gods they will serve, and the people reaffirm their loyalty to the Lord, the God who brought them up from the land of Egypt and fulfilled his promises by giving them the land (Josh. 24:14–28).

From a Christian perspective, the figure of Joshua has a special significance. The name *Yehōshua* is the Hebrew equivalent of *Jesus*, and Jesus is in a special way the successor of Moses, who leads God's people into the spiritual promised land.

2) *Judges* deals with the time in Israel's history before they had a king. In this period, God raised up warrior chieftains known as *judges* to defend his people against foreign aggression. These judges came from different tribes, in keeping with Israel's nature as a tribal confederacy rather than a nation with a centralized government. The story of Judges describes how, when

Israel sinned, God allowed them to be defeated at the hands of their enemies. He would then send them saviors in the form of judges who would restore peace to the land. The judges themselves are described honestly, with a frank recognition of their flaws. Famous—and flawed—judges include Jephthah, who made a foolish vow (Judg. 11:30–40), and Samson, who foolishly married a pagan woman (Judg. 14:1–10), slept with a harlot (Judg. 16:1–3), and became infatuated with Delilah, leading to his downfall (Judg. 16:4–31).

3) *Ruth* is a more positive book. It is only four chapters long, but it reveals the touching story of a pagan woman who turns to the God of Israel and ends up becoming the grandmother of King David (Ruth 4:13–17) and thus an ancestor of Jesus (Matt. 1:5).

The longest of the historical books are Samuel, Kings, and Chronicles. Originally, each of these was written as a single book, but in our versions of the Bible today, they have each been split in two, producing 1 and 2 Samuel, 1 and 2 Kings, and 1 and 2 Chronicles.

4) *1 Samuel* tells the story of the last of Israel's judges, Samuel. When Israel demanded a king, the Lord instructed Samuel to anoint Saul. But Saul disobeyed God and fell from his favor. This led to the rise of David, whose early adventures are related in this book.

5) *2 Samuel* picks up the story just after Saul's death, when David becomes king in his stead. David is a key figure in Israel's history, and this book records the main events of his reign, including God's establishing a covenant with him and promising that his descendants would have an everlasting reign (2 Sam. 7), a promise ultimately fulfilled in Jesus, the "Son of David" (Matt. 22:42). We are also told of David's flaws, notably, his affair with Bathsheba and how he engineered the death of her husband (2 Sam. 11), and his census of Israel's fighting men, considered a lack of trust in God (2 Sam. 24). In both cases, when he is reproved for his sin, Davids shows exemplary contrition.

6) *1 Kings* begins by relating the final days of King David, and how Solomon became his successor. The book then recounts the events of Solomon's reign and how, because of his sins, the kingdom was broken in two during the reign of his son Rehoboam. The ten northern tribes defected from the Davidic dynasty to become the kingdom of Israel, leaving two tribes—Judah and Benjamin—as the southern kingdom of Judah. Each then had its own line of kings, and the book takes us up through the reigns of Jehoshaphat of Judah and Ahaziah of Israel (c. 853 B.C.). A major figure toward the end of the book is the prophet Elijah.

7) *2 Kings* continues the story of Elijah and introduces his successor, the prophet Elisha. It also covers the period leading up to the conquest of both the northern and southern kingdoms. Because Israel went after other gods, the Lord allowed them to be conquered by the Assyrian empire in 723 B.C., during the reign of the northern king Hoshea, and its people were taken into exile (2 Kings 17). Later, because of its own unfaithfulness to God, the kingdom of Judah was conquered by the Babylonians in 587 B.C., during the reign of King Zedekiah (2 Kings 25). The Jerusalem temple was destroyed, and the population was deported, leading to the Babylonian Exile.

1 and 2 Chronicles cover much of the same ground as 1 Samuel through 2 Kings, but they tell it from a different perspective, just as the four Gospels recount the events of Jesus' ministry from different perspectives.

8) *1 Chronicles* begins with an extensive genealogy that stretches back to Adam (1 Chron. 1–9) and describes the end of the reign of King Saul. It then records the events of the reign of King David, ending with the coronation of his son Solomon.

9) *2 Chronicles* describes Solomon's reign and the subsequent kings of Judah, leading up to the conquest of Jerusalem and the Babylonian Exile. One difference between 2 Chronicles and the books of Kings is that it focuses primarily on Judah and does not offer as detailed a history of the northern kingdom of Israel. The book also ends on a more hopeful note, describing the end of the Exile during the reign of Cyrus the Persian (2 Chron. 36:22–23).

Two books that explore this period in more detail are Ezra and Nehemiah. Originally, these formed a single book, Ezra, but they are separated in modern Bible editions.

10) *Ezra* begins with the decree of Cyrus allowing exiles to return to Jerusalem and rebuild the temple. After the temple is rededicated, the book focuses on the activity of Ezra, a priest and scribe, and his ministry helping the people of Judah restore their national and religious life, including sending away pagan wives the men had taken.

11) *Nehemiah* contains the first-person narrative of another returning exile, who was a cupbearer for the Persian king Artaxerxes I. Nehemiah is allowed to travel to Jerusalem and help the Judahites rebuild and restore their national life. His ministry overlaps that of Ezra, and the book concludes around the year 428 B.C.

12) *Esther,* the final book of the Hebrew Bible, is often grouped with the historical books. It is set during the middle of the reign of the Persian king

Xerxes I (486-465 B.C.) and tells the story of how its heroine and her guardian Mordecai thwart a genocidal plan against the Jewish people. Although it is grouped with the historical books, modern scholars debate its precise relationship with history. According to Pope St. John Paul II, this book—as well as Tobit and Judith—"although dealing with the history of the chosen people, have the character of allegorical and moral narrative rather than history properly so called."[148]

101. Is the Old Testament historically reliable?

The Old Testament relates to history in more than one way, so the modern reader has to be careful when posing questions of historical reliability. Many books of the wisdom literature (e.g., Psalms, Proverbs, Ecclesiastes, Song of Solomon, Wisdom, Sirach) do not use historical narrative at all, though they may occasionally refer to events in history (as with Sirach's celebration of famous Jewish leaders). This means that what we can learn about history from them is limited, because telling us about history is not their primary purpose.

The prophets relate to history in a more direct way. The prophets lived in specific times, and their oracles refer backward to historical events (e.g., the sins of the people) and forward to future ones (e.g., coming divine judgment and the consolation and restoration that will follow it). However, they do so in a symbolic fashion that also limits what we can learn about history from them. Nevertheless, individual passages in the prophets (e.g., Jeremiah's descriptions of events that he experienced) can be very informative and fill in events not mentioned in the historical books.

Some books use narrative that at first glance looks like straightforward history, but clues in the text reveal that the reader was not meant to understand it in this way. Thus, Pope St. John Paul II stated: "The books of Tobit, Judith, and Esther, although dealing with the history of the chosen people, have the character of allegorical and moral narrative rather than history properly so called."[149] These books thus function like extended parables, like the parables of Jesus but longer and with more detail. The wisdom book of Job, which is hard to locate in any particular period and is primarily written in the form of poetry, likely belongs in this class as well.

The books that relate to history in the most direct way are, of course, the historical books; these are our richest source of historical information, because their primary purpose is to give us such information. However, even then we have to be careful, because the ancient writers used methods of historiography that were common in their day, not those common in ours. This is particularly true of the first eleven chapters of Genesis, which describe the remote origins of the human race and events taking place centuries (or longer) before the author wrote. These chapters pertain to history in a true sense, but they are written according to a set of literary conventions that conveys truth using more symbolism than later passages.

The Magisterium has indicated this for Genesis 1, stating, "Scripture presents the work of the Creator symbolically as a succession of six days of divine 'work,' concluded by the 'rest' of the seventh day" (CCC 337). It has said the same for Genesis 3, stating, "The account of the fall in Genesis 3 uses figurative language, but affirms a primeval event, a deed that took place at the beginning of the history of man" (390).

The Magisterium has not yet similarly commented on other events in Genesis 1–11 (e.g., the Flood, the Tower of Babel), but it likely would take the same approach. Thus, in 1950, Pius XII stated:

> The first eleven chapters of Genesis, although properly speaking not conforming to the historical method used by the best Greek and Latin writers or by competent authors of our time, do nevertheless pertain to history in a true sense, which however must be further studied and determined by exegetes; the same chapters ... in simple and metaphorical language adapted to the mentality of a people but little cultured, both state the principal truths which are fundamental for our salvation, and also give a popular description of the origin of the human race and the chosen people (*Humani Generis* 38).

One reason for the greater use of symbolism in these chapters is the remoteness of the events in time. This period is before Israel's recorded history began, and truth concerning this period cannot be conveyed the same way it can for the period after detailed historical records began to be kept. A different set of literary conventions were thus used for describing the period before the arrival of Abraham in Genesis 12.

From Abraham onward, the account becomes less symbolic until, finally, a more conventional way of recording history begins with the advent of the kings and the keeping of court records. Consequently, the later historical books provide historical information presented in the way most like modern works of history. Some Old Testament passages even represent first-person, eyewitness testimony, which historians today highly prize.

102. Why are there so many violent and sinful acts in the Old Testament?

Because it is honest about the ancient world. People then lived in very violent times, and the historical record of the period naturally reflects that. Warfare was so common that in many places, every year when the weather allowed, new conflicts would break out. The Old Testament even refers to spring as "the time when kings go forth to battle" (2 Sam. 11:1, 1 Chron. 20:1).

The records of our time also report violence. A typical newspaper does so every day. A newspaper's job is to report significant things that happened. That doesn't mean it approves. Newspapers report rapes, murders, and crimes the papers do not approve of. They also report people saying and doing things that the paper's reporters and editors completely disagree with.

Similarly, just because Scripture records something doesn't mean it endorses it. It does mean the biblical author thought the event was significant for his audience to know, but it doesn't mean that he—or God—approved.

Consequently, one cannot simply note that Scripture *reports* someone saying or doing something abominable and conclude that it *teaches* something abominable. When evaluating such passages, one must ask whether the proposed evil is condemned.

Sometimes, there will be an explicit condemnation (thus the biblical author condemns Solomon's idolatry: 1 Kings 11:9–10). Other times, the condemnation will be implicit, but clues in the text reveal the horrific nature of an act (for example, the yearly observance of mourning for what happened to Jephthah's daughter on account of his rash vow—Judg. 11:39–40). Or disapproval can be inferred because the action is condemned elsewhere in Scripture (e.g., even if David's initial act of adultery wasn't explicitly condemned in 2 Sam. 12, we know his act was wrong because it violates the Ten Commandments—Exod. 20:14; Deut. 5:18).

Finally, our native moral sense can be a clue to the biblical author's disapproval (e.g., even though David didn't personally kill Uriah the Hittite, he engineered the man's death, and even without the explicit condemnation in 2 Samuel 12, the audience would sense he violated the biblical prohibition on killing). In general, when our moral sense tells us that something Scripture reports is problematic, it is intended to be perceived as such.

103. What is wisdom literature?

The wisdom literature is a collection of books that are neither straightforward historical narratives nor straightforward prophetic texts. They are frequently of a poetic character and deal with a variety of themes, often philosophical, making them sources of scriptural wisdom. Here we will look at the five books of wisdom literature found in the Hebrew Bible. Additional books of wisdom are found among the deuterocanonical books and will be discussed later.

1) *Job* is a poetic book that contains a meditation on human suffering—part of the philosophical problem of evil. In it, God allows Job—a righteous man—to suffer a series of calamities. Job is visited by three friends who propose different solutions for why these things have happened to him, until finally, God intervenes to settle the matter: it is a mystery why innocent people sometimes suffer, but it is allowed as part of God's plan. In the end, God rewards Job for his humility and restores his fortunes.

2) The *Psalms* are a collection of hymns, many of which are associated with King David. They contain many expressions of praise, thanksgiving, and petition directed to God; and reflect many circumstances in life, from exaltation and triumph to sorrow and penitence. The Psalms were used as hymns in the Jerusalem temple and in the broader life of Israel.

3) *Proverbs* is primarily a collection of short, wise sayings (i.e., proverbs). After the first nine chapters, which present longer discourses on the importance of wisdom, the proverbs themselves begin, often taking the form of two-part statements—e.g., "A wise son makes a glad father, but a foolish son is a sorrow to his mother" (Prov. 10:1). The book as a whole is associated with King Solomon (Prov. 1:1), though sections of the book are also attributed to other authors (Prov. 25:1; 30:1; 31:1). One of the key themes of the book is the reverence due to God: "The fear of the Lord is the beginning of knowledge; fools despise wisdom and instruction" (Prov. 1:7).

4) *Ecclesiastes* is very similar in name to one of the deuterocanonical books—Ecclesiasticus (i.e., Sirach)—and so today it is often referred to by its Hebrew title, *Qōheleth*, a term translated "the Preacher" in most English versions. The author is described as "the son of David, king in Jerusalem" (Eccles. 1:1) and is often identified as Solomon. The book itself is a meditation on the apparent futility of life: "Vanity of vanities, says the Preacher, vanity of vanities! All is vanity. What does man gain by all the toil at which he toils under the sun?" (Eccles. 1:2–3). Despite this seemingly negative

outlook, the author recognizes that "there is nothing better for [men] than to be happy and enjoy themselves as long as they live; also that it is God's gift to man that everyone should eat and drink and take pleasure in all his toil" (Eccles. 3:12–13).

5) *Song of Solomon* also goes by more than one name. It is also called the *Song of Songs* (i.e., the greatest song) and *Canticles*. It is associated with King Solomon (Song 1:1), and it is devoted to the theme of love between a man and a woman. It is often compared to modern love poetry, though as its title indicates, it was meant to be a musical composition, and it is known to have been sung aloud by people in the ancient world.

104. How should we interpret the wisdom literature?

Because the books of wisdom literature belong to five different genres, they each present their own interpretive challenges and opportunities.

For example, the various human figures who speak in Job (e.g., the title character and his three friends) struggle to understand the problem of innocent suffering, and as they do so they propose ideas that are flawed in different ways. This means that one cannot simply take any of them as entirely reliable, though the speeches contain recognizable elements of truth. This reflects the fact that, in this life, we can only partially understand the mystery of suffering (see *Catechism of the Catholic Church* 324).

The Psalms are poetic compositions, which means they contain many non-literal figures of speech—a fact modern interpreters must take into account. Because of the powerful voice they show in expressing praise and petition to God, they have been extraordinarily influential in the life and liturgy of the Church. Together with Deuteronomy and Isaiah, the Psalms are one of the Old Testament books that the New Testament quotes most often.

One of the reasons for this is that the New Testament writers recognized that the Psalms operate on more than one level and frequently contain messianic prophecies that point forward to Jesus. Thus, Jesus himself quoted from Psalm 22, which begins "My God, my God, why hast thou forsaken me?", and applied it to himself while he was suffering on the cross (Matt. 27:46). (It should be noted that in Psalm 22 the author expected himself to be ultimately vindicated by God—see Psalm 22:22–31—and we may infer that Jesus did not regard himself as truly abandoned by God, and he expected to be vindicated by his resurrection from the dead.)

The fact that Proverbs is a collection of wise sayings has important implications for the way we interpret it. A wise saying is not the same thing as a law, and whereas a law is meant to be obeyed in all (or almost all) circumstances, a wise saying is meant to form one's prudential judgment, and hence, to be applied on a case-by-case basis.

Proverbs vividly illustrates this point by giving contrasting pieces of advice, such as when one verse says, "Answer not a fool according to his folly, lest you be like him yourself" (Prov. 26:4) and the next verse states, "Answer a fool according to his folly, lest he be wise in his own eyes" (Prov. 26:5). By directly juxtaposing these two statements, Proverbs indicates that we must use judgment to wisely discern which course of action is appropriate in a particular circumstance.

Ecclesiastes, as an extended meditation on the meaning of life, poses special challenges for the interpreter. Its overall negative, at times despairing tone is remarkable, but despite this it places human experience in an overall framework that recognizes God's role. Despite the challenges we face, the book concludes by saying, "The end of the matter; all has been heard. Fear God, and keep his commandments; for this is the whole duty of man. For God will bring every deed into judgment, with every secret thing, whether good or evil" (Eccles. 12:13–14).

Finally, the interpretation of the Song of Solomon is very interesting. On the literal level, this book is a celebration of human love. However, Scripture operates on more than one level, and since early times it has also been understood in an allegorical way. Thus early Jewish interpreters saw it as a reflection of God's love for Israel, and Christian interpreters have naturally seen it as reflecting Christ's love for his Church. All three of these interpretations are compatible.

105. Who are the Major and Minor Prophets?

The prophetic books of the Hebrew Bible are divided into two groups: the Major Prophets and the Minor Prophets.

The Major Prophets consist of Isaiah, Jeremiah, Lamentations, Ezekiel, and Daniel. The deuterocanonical book of Baruch is sometimes grouped with them. They are called "major" because they include the longest prophetic books.

1) *Isaiah* lived in the 700s B.C. The book that bears his name is the longest prophetic book of the Old Testament. It is sixty-six chapters long,

and scholars are generally agreed that chapters 1–39 collect oracles given by the original eighth-century prophet.

2) *Jeremiah* lived in the late 600s and early 500s B.C . His ministry began during the reigns of the final kings of Judah and continued into the Babylonian Exile. Jeremiah was assisted in ministry by a man named Baruch, who was his scribe and friend. Because of his sorrowful message and the strong emotion he shows, Jeremiah is often called "the weeping prophet."

3) *Lamentations* is a short book. It consists of five chapters, each of which is a lament or sorrowful poetic composition. They mourn the destruction of Jerusalem by the Babylonians, and though the book does not identify its author, it is historically attributed to Jeremiah and so grouped with the Major Prophets.

4) *Ezekiel* exercised his prophetic ministry from 593 to at least 571 B.C. It appears that Ezekiel was taken into captivity after Nebuchadnezzar's second assault on Jerusalem, in 597 B.C. (see 2 Kings 24:10–16). This was before the destruction of the temple, which occurred in a later assault (2 Kings 25:8–9). In the interim, the prophet was relocated to a colony of Jewish exiles on the Chebar canal in Mesopotamia, where he received his prophetic call (Ezek. 1–3).

5) *Daniel* was a young Judean nobleman taken into captivity following Nebuchadnezzar's first siege of Jerusalem in 605 B.C. (Dan. 1:1–7). He was active as a prophet until the reign of Darius I, who came to power in 521 B.C.

The Minor Prophets are a group of twelve short books by or about prophets who were active between roughly the 800s and the 400s B.C. In the ancient world, they were presented in a single scroll known simply as *The Twelve.* They can be briefly described as follows:

Hosea and *Amos* both ministered in the 700s B.C. and were sent by God to prophecy against the northern kingdom of Israel, prior to the Assyrian captivity in 723 B.C.. *Micah*, in the meantime, prophesied both in Samaria and Jerusalem.

The prophetic missions of *Jonah* and *Nahum* were directed against the Assyrian city of Nineveh, Jonah in the 700s and Nahum likely in the 600s, prior to the city's fall to the Babylonians in 612 B.C.

The prophets *Habakkuk* and *Zephaniah* ministered in the 600s. Their prophecies deal with God's judgment of Judah and the surrounding nations.

Haggai, *Zechariah*, and *Malachi* were prophets in Judea after the return from exile in Babylon. *Haggai* can be dated, very precisely, to the year 520 B.C., when God sent a message to the Jewish governor, Zerubbabel, by the mouth of the prophet. *Zechariah* began his ministry at the same time as Haggai, followed by *Malachi* around 500 B.C. or somewhat later, after the Jerusalem temple had been rebuilt and sacrifices had been restored.

Finally, the dating of the prophets *Joel* and *Obadiah* is unclear and little is known about their personal background.

106. What are the deuterocanonical books?

The deuterocanonical books are parts of the Old Testament that are considered canonical by Catholics and many Eastern Christians, including the Orthodox, but not by Protestants or modern Jews. Most were written in Hebrew or Aramaic, but they survive primarily in the Septuagint, the main Greek translation of the Old Testament. They consist of seven books, plus parts of two others.

1) *Tobit* tells the story of God's mercy in the life of a righteous man and his family. The title character was deported to the city of Nineveh after the northern kingdom of Israel was conquered by the Assyrians. To aid them, God sends the angel Raphael, who travels in disguise in human form (see Gen. 19:1–3; Heb. 13:2) and brings them relief from the misfortunes they have suffered. Although set during a particular period of Israel's history, modern scholars have concluded based on clues in the text that the book has "the character of allegorical and moral narrative rather than history properly so called."[150]

2) *Judith* describes how God used a righteous woman to deliver her people from the plots of their enemies. Judith's name means "Lady Jew," and she represents a female personification of the Jewish people. In the book she is pitted against a general sent by the Babylonian king Nebuchadnezzar, who is nevertheless described as the king of the Assyrians (Jth. 1:1). We thus have the personification of God's people depicted in a conflict with their two greatest enemies—the Babylonians and the Assyrians. Because of this, scholars have concluded that Judith—like Tobit and Esther—has an allegorical rather than strictly historical character.

3) *1 Maccabees* is a straightforward historical book. It deals with the period after the Babylonian Exile and the conquests of Alexander the Great. When the latter died, his empire was divided, and one of the resulting kingdoms became a new persecutor of God's people. This persecution came to a head under the Seleucid ruler Antiochus IV, who tried to stamp out Judaism, defiled the Jewish temple with pagan sacrifices, and put himself forward

as a living god. This was too much for pious Jews to bear, and a rebellion began, leading to the establishment of an independent Jewish state under the leadership of a priestly family known as the Maccabees (also known as the Hasmoneans).

4) *2 Maccabees* is another historical book and recounts many of the same events as 1 Maccabees, though from a different perspective, the same way the books of Chronicles offer a supplemental perspective on the events recorded in the books of Samuel and Kings.

5) *Wisdom*, also called the *Wisdom of Solomon*, is—as its title suggests—a work of wisdom literature. It is written in the voice of King Solomon, who serves as a symbol of great wisdom. Early Christian authors recognized this as a literary device, and it was most likely written by a learned man in the Jewish colony at Alexandria, Egypt, who wished to help Jewish people have a Hebrew perspective on the issues that confronted them, including Greek ideas they were encountering. It is probably the last of the Old Testament books to be written, being composed in the first century B.C. or the early first century A.D.

6) *Sirach* is known by several names. It is sometimes called *Ecclesiasticus* or the *Wisdom of Jesus ben-Sira*. It is a work of wisdom literature that was written in Hebrew by a man named Jesus the son of Sirach (Sir. 50:27) and translated by his grandson into Greek. Much of it resembles the book of Proverbs, and it contains a celebration of famed Jewish leaders down to Sirach's own time (c. 180 B.C.).

7) *Baruch* is a prophetic work attributed to Jeremiah's secretary of the same name and set during the Babylonian Exile (Bar. 1:1–4). It contains penitential prayers, wisdom material, and themes of lamentation and consolation. The sixth and final chapter of the book—sometimes called the *Letter of Jeremiah*—takes the form of a letter written by the prophet to the exiles in Babylon.

8) *Esther*, in its deuterocanonical edition, includes additional sections that bring out more clearly the role of God in delivering his people from calamity. (The Hebrew edition, strikingly, does not contain any explicit references to God.)

9) *Daniel*, in its deuterocanonical edition, includes several additional sections. One ("The Song of the Three Young Men") is a hymn sung by Daniel's companions when they were placed in the fiery furnace. The other two ("Susannah" and "Bel and the Dragon") display Daniel's wisdom and show how God delivered him from danger.

107. How did the Old Testament canon develop?

The books of the Old Testament were written during a period stretching around a thousand years, and they were not the only books to be written in that time. The Old Testament even refers to additional works that are now lost (e.g., Num. 21:14; Josh. 10:13; 1 Chron. 29:29; 2 Chron. 9:29, 12:15, 33:19). So how did the canon of the Old Testament develop?

It is widely agreed that the first group of books to achieve canonical status were those of the Pentateuch. These came to be recognized as the most important books of the Old Testament and were universally accepted as Scripture among the Jewish people. Some groups—such as the Sadducees and the Samaritans—appear to have had a canon that included *only* these books.

Over time, additional books came to be recognized as Scripture by major Jewish groups, though the canon did not have precise boundaries. One prominent group that arose in the centuries just before the time of Christ was the Pharisees. They recognized more books of Scripture than their counterparts, the Sadducees, though it took time for the canon that grew from their tradition to be solidified.

By the first century, the Pharisees appear to have recognized basically the same books that are found in the modern Jewish bible (i.e., all of the protocanonical books). However, their successors—the rabbis—continued to dispute about several books for a few centuries after Christ. Some opposed the inclusion in Scripture of books like Esther, Proverbs, Ecclesiastes, Song of Solomon, and Ezekiel. These are sometimes referred to as the Old Testament *antilegomena* (Greek: "ones spoken against"). In addition, some rabbis favored including the deuterocanonical book of Sirach as Scripture.

Another group of first-century Jews was the sect that composed the Dead Sea Scrolls. Scholars generally believe them to have been a group known as the *Essenes*. It is clear from the scrolls they left behind that they broadly accepted the protocanonical books, with the possible exception of Esther. However, they also accepted certain additional works as Scripture, including 1 Enoch, Jubilees, and a work known as the *Temple Scroll*.

The Sadducees, the Pharisees, and the Essenes were all based in the Holy Land, which shows how even there Jews had a diversity of opinion about which books should be recognized as Scripture. But they were not the only Jewish groups of the time. In addition, there were many Greek-speaking Jews, both in the Holy Land and in the broader Roman world.

To meet the needs of these Greek speakers (referred to in the New Testament as "Hellenists"; see Acts 6:1), translations of the Hebrew and Aramaic scriptures were made. A translation of the Pentateuch was made, and it became known as the Septuagint (Latin, *septuaginta*: "the seventy") on account of a tradition that it was made by seventy translators. Over time, translations of the rest of the books of the Hebrew Bible and the deuterocanonical books were included. A few of the latter (e.g., Wisdom) were even originally composed in Greek.

These books were influential in the Holy Land, including among the authors of the New Testament, who were primarily Jews born or raised in Palestine (e.g., Matthew, Mark, John, Paul, Peter, James, Jude). The only author who definitely didn't belong to this category was Luke.

In composing the New Testament, its authors overwhelmingly used the Septuagint when they quoted the Old Testament. Around 80 percent of the Old Testament quotations found in the New Testament are based on the Septuagint, and the New Testament authors also make allusions to the deuterocanonical books. (For example, Hebrews 11:35 refers to 2 Maccabees 7.)

As a result, the Septuagint canonical tradition was naturally adopted by the Christian community, including both Jewish and Gentile Christians. At the time, like the Pharisee canonical tradition, the Septuagint tradition had fuzzy boundaries, with some books floating on the edge of it. These included additional works like 1 and 2 Esdras, 3 and 4 Maccabees, and the Prayer of Manasseh, which were not ultimately included in the Catholic canon.

Over the first few centuries of the Christian age, the Holy Spirit led the Church to recognize more clearly the books of the Old Testament canon, as well as those of the New Testament. This was done in a particular way through a series of local councils in North Africa in the late 300s and early 400s. Later, the ecumenical Council of Florence (1438–1445) authoritatively taught which books should be included in the Bible, and the Council of Trent (1545–1563) reaffirmed its teaching infallibly.

The reason that Trent needed to rule infallibly was that the Protestant Reformers, beginning with Martin Luther, had objected to certain Catholic teachings that were supported in the deuterocanonical books. They thus sought to deny these books scriptural status, appealing to the fact that contemporary European Jews (the only ones who they were aware of) did not include these books in their canon. The Protestant Old Testament canon thus uses only the protocanonical books.

However, contemporary European Jews were religiously descended—via the early rabbis—from the Pharisees, who represented only one strand of early Jewish opinion. Christians had received the broader Septuagint tradition that the New Testament authors used, and so Trent infallibly reaffirmed the Church's belief in the books of Scripture that the Church had historically recognized.

108. How do we know that the text of the Old Testament is accurate?

Given the age of the Old Testament books, people sometimes ask how we know we have accurate texts. After all, before the invention of the printing press in the 1400s, books had to be hand copied by scribes, who invariably make at least small mistakes. After so many centuries of hand copying, could serious errors have been introduced into the text?

Could some of them even have been introduced deliberately, in the service of some theological agenda, perhaps by people who purposely suppressed certain texts?

Several factors worked to prevent this. The first is the fact that the books of the Old Testament are considered sacred. This meant that scribes took great pains not to make mistakes when copying them, and to quickly fix mistakes if they did.

In particular, a group of Jewish scribes known as the *Masoretes* were active in Palestine and Babylonia between around A.D. 600 and 950. They developed elaborate procedures for the accurate copying of the Hebrew scriptures. The version they produced—known as the *Masoretic Text*—served as the basis of later versions of the Old Testament.

The fundamental accuracy of the Masoretic Text was confirmed in the 1940s with the discovery of the Dead Sea Scrolls. These were hidden in caves surrounding the Dead Sea in Palestine during the First Jewish Revolt (A.D. 66-73), and they contained copies of Old Testament scriptures, some of which have been carbon-dated to centuries before Christ. Suddenly scholars had access to copies of biblical books from the Old Testament period itself, and they confirmed that the text had not been fundamentally altered.

Though it is a Greek translation, the Septuagint also played a role in preserving knowledge of what the biblical text originally said. So did translations into other languages, such as the Old Latin versions that preceded St. Jerome's Vulgate translation, as well as the Vulgate itself. We thus have many ancient manuscripts of the Old Testament books in Hebrew, Greek, Latin, and other languages. Each of these allows scholars a way to cross-check what the originals said.

In addition to Old Testament manuscripts, we have many quotations of the Old Testament from ancient authors, such as the Jewish rabbis, who wrote extensive commentaries on the texts. Similarly, the first-century Jewish historian Josephus uses a great deal of material from the Old Testament in his monumental history *Jewish Antiquities*. Even the Church Fathers quote frequently from the Old Testament in their writings.

Of course, scribes did make mistakes, but they were minor, and today scholars have a wealth of material they can use to establish what the original text of the Old Testament was. A special science—known as textual criticism—has even developed to allow scholars to do this. And, although there are passages whose exact wording is debated, scholars are not in doubt that the texts we have are fundamentally accurate. There are too many independent and converging lines of evidence supporting it.

This also reveals how impossible it would have been for anyone to deliberately introduce false readings or suppress texts in the service of a theological agenda. Even if someone wanted to, copies of the Old Testament books were in too many hands.

If a Jewish group wanted to alter a passage they objected to, they would never be able to go through the entire Jewish world and get their coreligionists to take it out or alter it, and they certainly wouldn't be able to get Christians to take it out of their Bible. The same would be true of a Christian group wanting to do this: too many other Christians would refuse to do so, and non-Christian Jews would never remove or alter an Old Testament passage on Christian say-so.

Further—precisely because the Dead Sea Scrolls were hidden for almost 2,000 years—*nobody* would have had the ability to tamper with them.

Thus there is no basis for challenging the fundamental reliability of the Old Testament text.

109. What is Bible prophecy?

Today we think of *prophecy* as a near synonym for "prediction." If someone makes a prophecy, he is issuing a prediction about the future.

The biblical prophets did often make predictions, but that was only part of what they did.

The Greek word *prophet* (*prophētēs*) comes from roots that indicate a person who speaks in front of a group of people (*pro-* "in front of" + *phētēs* "speaker"). If we were to give it a fresh translation into English, *spokesman* would be a good equivalent.

That's what the prophets were: God's spokesmen. As a result, they were tasked with giving people whatever message God wanted delivered, whether or not that message had to do with the future.

Sometimes people even wanted prophets to reveal information about things that had happened in the *past*. Thus, when Jesus' opponents were mocking him, they first blindfolded and then slapped him, saying, "Prophesy! Who is it that struck you?" (Luke 22:64).

God wasn't interested in satisfying facetious demands like that one, but he was interested in warning his people against sin—and that's what the biblical prophets did much of the time. Warning Israel against its sins—idolatry, bloodshed, oppression of the poor—was one of the principal tasks of the biblical prophets. Of course, warning people about sin involves warning them about what will happen if they *don't* repent, and so the prophets also discussed future events.

In the Old Testament, the focus was not on what the consequences of sin would be in the next life, but on what they would be in this one. The prophets regularly warned people about consequences like famines, diseases, and military invasions. These were consequences God would allow if people persisted in their sins.

God also promised rewards if people acted in accord with his law. If they turned from idols, bloodshed, and oppression, he would give them prosperity, health, peace, and security. He also revealed that, even when they were being chastised for their sin, he still loved them and that—once they did repent—he would show mercy and bring times of blessing again.

On other occasions, when a particular danger threatened—such as a military invasion by a powerful enemy—he would assure them he would protect them and that the invasion would not succeed.

In all these ways, God acted as a father toward Israel, warning his children of the consequences of bad behavior, promising rewards for good behavior, reassuring them of his love even amid discipline, and assuaging their fears.

Through all of this, the prophets acted as God's spokesmen, delivering these messages to the children of Israel.

The prophets had a privileged place in God's plan, not to be confused with other figures who also claimed to reveal hidden knowledge. The Old

Testament warns against "any one who practices divination, a soothsayer, or an augur, or a sorcerer, or a charmer, or a medium, or a wizard, or a necromancer" (Deut. 18:10–11). These individuals claimed to give people information from supernatural sources, but they weren't getting it from God. Such false prophets, the Lord said, "are prophesying lies in my name; I did not send them, nor did I command them or speak to them. They are prophesying to you a lying vision, worthless divination, and the deceit of their own minds." That the Israelites might be able to recognize who were his authorized spokesmen, he gave them tests they could use to tell true prophets from false ones (Deut. 13:1–5; 18:20–22).

And ultimately, he told them to expect the coming of another great prophet, one like Moses, who spoke to the Lord face to face:

> I will raise up for them a prophet like you from among their brethren; and I will put my words in his mouth, and he shall speak to them all that I command him. And whoever will not give heed to my words which he shall speak in my name, I myself will require it of him (Exod. 18:18-19).

Because the focus of prophecy, especially in the Old Testament, tended to be on the consequences of good and bad behavior in this life, prophecies often had a shorter time frame for fulfillment than we today might expect. Because prophecy often has to do with the future, we can mistakenly assume that a given prophecy has to do with *our* future. But usually the prophets warned their audience of consequences that would happen soon—either in their own generation or within a few generations of when the prophecy was given. This is a theme we will see repeatedly.

110. Who were the biblical prophets?

There were a large number of prophets in biblical times, only a few of whom we have any written record.

For example, we are told that when the wicked queen Jezebel was killing the prophets of the Lord, a man named Obadiah (not the prophet of the same name) "took a hundred prophets and hid them by fifties in a cave" (1 Kings 18:4).

Imagine that! There were at least a hundred prophets living at this one time! Yet we know nothing about them as individuals.

Moses is the most famous Old Testament prophet, though we often don't think of him that way because of his special role as Israel's lawgiver.

The prophets most familiar to us today include Isaiah, Jeremiah, Ezekiel, and Daniel. Together, they are known as the *Major Prophets*—and they have something in common: they all wrote lengthy books that are part of the Bible.

There were also twelve Minor Prophets, whose books are shorter; they include figures like Hosea, Joel, and Jonah. In the ancient world, they were often simply called "the Twelve," and their books were written in a single scroll, which was also called "the Twelve."

Sometimes these prophets are referred to as "literary prophets" because they recorded their prophecies in writing. However, the literary prophets whose books are in the Bible today are not the only literary prophets there were. We know that there were others who also wrote books. For example, various passages in the Old Testament refer to books written by prophets such as Nathan, Gad, Abijah, Shemaiah, and Iddo (1 Chron. 29:29; 2 Chron. 9:29; 12:15).

In addition, there were many prophets who did not write down their prophecies (so far as we know). In fact, one of the most famous prophets of the Old Testament, Elijah, was a non-literary prophet. He is the subject of a lengthy treatment in the books of Kings (see 1 Kings 17 through 2 Kings 2), and he is remembered for being taken directly up into heaven (2 Kings 2:1–12).

Another famous non-literary prophet is Samuel, whose story is extensively recorded in the first book that bears his name (see 1 Sam. 1–25).

Given the number of prophets known to have been alive at any one time, it is probable that most were non-literary.

Although some men devoted their lives to prophetic ministry, the Bible also regards other figures as prophets. For example, Genesis describes Abraham as a prophet (Gen. 20:7), even though he did not act regularly in this capacity. Similarly, King Saul is known to have prophesied (1 Sam. 10:10–13).

If a broad standard is used, so that anyone to whom God gave special revelation counts as a prophet, then many biblical figures among the patriarchs, judges, and kings count as prophets, including Jacob, Joseph, Joshua, Gideon, Solomon, and others.

By one definition, all the authors of the Bible count as prophets. Since "all Scripture is inspired by God" (2 Tim. 3:16), it all counts as God's message to man, and so the messengers—the biblical authors—can be seen as prophets.

Thus, if one looks in a modern Jewish bible, one will find certain historical books—Joshua, Judges, 1–2 Samuel, 1–2 Kings, and 1–2 Chronicles—listed as "the former prophets," in contrast to "the later prophets": Isaiah, Jeremiah, Ezekiel, and the Twelve. (Daniel belongs to the "writings" in the Jewish Bible, not to the prophets.)

Prophets also appeared in the period between the Old and New Testaments. Just before the ministry of Jesus began, John the Baptist began to prophesy, and Jesus confirmed that John was a prophet "and more than a prophet" (Matt. 11:9).

Jesus himself was a prophet (Matt. 13:57; 21:11; Luke 24:19; John 4:44), the great prophet foretold by Moses (Exod. 18:15-18), sent into the world to speak all things he had heard from the Father (John 15:15; 12:49-50; 17:6-8).

Several disciples of the early Christian church were prophets as well. In the book of Acts, for example, we meet prophets such as Agabus, Judas Barsabbas, and Paul's companion Silas (Acts 11:28; 15:32; 21:10). For a time, it was common for there to be multiple prophets in a single Christian congregation, as Paul indicates was the case at Corinth (1 Cor. 14:29–33).

The most famous New Testament prophet is John, who saw the vision recorded in the book of Revelation (1:1, 4, 9; 22:8).

Finally, we should note that although most of the biblical prophets were men, the gift of prophecy was also given to women. Thus Moses' sister Miriam was a prophetess (Ex. 15:20). Other prophetesses include Deborah (Judg. 4:4), Huldah (2 Kings 14), and Anna (Luke 2:36). Paul also speaks of women prophesying in church (1 Cor. 11:5).

111. How does biblical prophecy work?

The starting point to understanding how biblical prophecy works is to understand the role of prophets *in biblical times*. God did not send prophets to Israel simply to satisfy people's curiosity about the future. They had a practical purpose. Their principal role was to encourage people to remain faithful to God and his laws.

At times, this meant giving predictions. A prophet might foretell a coming disaster—like a war, a famine, or a plague—if people did not repent of their sins. He might foretell a blessing if they repented. Or he might assure them that victory would be theirs if they only stayed true to God. However, predictions were not the principal thing that prophets were sent to communicate. Their primary message was the need to remain faithful to the Lord.

Consequently, when prophets did make predictions, they were normally directed to their own day and age—so that the people then living could act on them and heed the message to be faithful. There are examples of prophets speaking to people in a distant age (e.g., Dan. 12:4), but this is not the norm. Usually, their predictions concerned either their own generation or one closely following it.

An instructive example is found in Isaiah 7. In this chapter, the kings of Syria and Ephraim have combined forces to conquer Jerusalem and install a new king as their puppet. The current king in Jerusalem—Ahaz—is rightly concerned about this, and God sends the prophet Isaiah to Ahaz to assure him that the forces arrayed against him will not succeed. The king only needs to remain faithful and trust in God.

To provide proof, Isaiah tells Ahaz to name a sign for God to give him: "Let it be deep as Sheol or high as heaven" (Isa. 7:11). But, overcome by false piety, Ahaz refuses to name a sign, and so the prophet tells him:

> The Lord himself will give you a sign. Behold, a young woman shall conceive and bear a son, and shall call his name Immanuel. He shall eat curds and honey when he knows how to refuse the evil and choose the good. For before the child knows how to refuse the evil and choose the good, the land before whose two kings you are in dread will be deserted (Isa. 7:14–16).

For this to serve as a sign to Ahaz, who reigned in the 700s B.C., the child would need to be born very soon—before the conflict with the other two kings was over. Otherwise, it could not serve as a sign to Ahaz that the Lord would keep him on the throne. Scholars have consequently speculated on who this child of prophecy was. One of the leading suggestions is that it was Ahaz's own son, Hezekiah, who would be king after him. However that may be, the prophecy had a fulfillment in the time of King Ahaz.

Yet it was not limited to that time, because it would go on to have a greater fulfillment centuries later. The Hebrew name *Immanuel* means "God with us," and eventually God would come to be with his people not only in a spiritual sense but also by taking on human form. Thus, the birth of Jesus—God incarnate—also fulfills the Immanuel prophecy (Matt. 1:23).

This shows that, although prophecies are normally directed to the near future of when they were originally given, they also can have additional fulfillments in later ages.

112. How does prophetic symbolism work?

Bible prophecy often uses symbolism, but sometimes it does not.

Shortly before the Crucifixion, Jesus told his disciples: "Behold, we are going up to Jerusalem; and the Son of Man will be delivered to the chief priests and the scribes, and they will condemn him to death, and deliver him to the Gentiles; and they will mock him, and spit upon him, and scourge him, and kill him; and after three days he will rise" (Mark 10:33–34).

This prophecy is presented in a straightforward, non-symbolic manner. Jesus states that a series of specific events will happen. He identifies the parties involved (the chief priests, scribes, and Gentiles). He identifies the place (Jerusalem). And he indicates times involved (once they arrive in Jerusalem, with the Resurrection occurring "three days" after his death).

Much of the time, however, Bible prophecy is not presented in such straightforward a manner. Usually, it is cloaked in symbolism. The Old Testament prophets regularly used symbolism, and the book of Revelation is famous for it. Why God usually uses symbolism in prophecy is an interesting question. Symbolism can make prophecy more compelling, inviting us to think more deeply about it and thus better internalize its message than if God just gave us a list of things that will happen in the future. Also, symbols can have more than one meaning, allowing God to use a single passage to communicate multiple things—giving us a richer, more informative message.

Sometimes we are directly told what a symbol means. John tells us that the fine linen the bride of Christ is clothed with represents "the righteous deeds of the saints" (Rev. 19:8). Most of the time, though, we are not directly told the meaning of a symbol. In these cases, we have to do our best to figure it out based on clues in the text and our knowledge of how other, similar symbols are used in Scripture.

We need to pay careful attention to the fact that biblical symbols can have multiple meanings. For example, when John sees the beast with seven heads, he is told, "The seven heads are seven hills. . . . They are also seven kings" (Rev. 17:9–10).

Sometimes the Bible uses symbolism in ways that are surprising to us today, as when we encounter "cosmic cataclysm" language, where the prophets talk about the sun darkening, the moon not giving its light, the stars falling, etc. (Isa. 13:10; 24:18–23; 34:4; Ezek. 32:7; Joel 2:10, 31; Amos 8:9; Hag. 2:22; Mark 13:24–25).

Some understand this imagery as indicating familiar phenomena: solar eclipses (sun darkening), lunar eclipses (moon not giving light), meteor showers (stars falling). However, there is another understanding that takes this language as symbolizing God's judgment on a people. For example, Isaiah 13 contains an oracle against Babylon that says, "The stars of the heavens and their constellations will not give their light; the sun will be dark at its rising and the moon will not shed its light.... [God] will make the heavens tremble, and the earth will be shaken out of its place" (vv. 10, 13). But God makes it clear *how* this judgment on the Babylonians will be accomplished: "I am stirring up the Medes against them" (v. 17). This shows us that, in this case, the cosmic cataclysm language is symbolic. God is using these images to describe the conquest of the Babylonian empire by the ancient Medes. It thus refers to an event in our past—as admitted even by commentators who usually are quick to see prophecies as applying to our future, such as dispensationalists.

The cosmic cataclysm imagery is a poetic expression of what living through judgment would be like. For those experiencing it, it would be *as if* the sun and moon darkened and the stars fell from the sky. Further, some interpreters have seen the celestial bodies as symbols of the rulers of the people, who would quake and lose their positions in the turmoil.

This symbolic view is not a new interpretation. The prophets' language has been understood this way for a long time. For example, it was taken this way by the twelfth-century Jewish scholar Moses Maimonides (*Guide for the Perplexed* 2:29), and it is widely understood this way by scholars of all persuasions today.

113. How does prophetic fulfillment work?

When a true prophet says something about the future, at some point it must be fulfilled. This raises the question of how the concept of fulfillment works.

In cases of non-symbolic prophecy, it is often easy to identify the fulfillment, as when Jesus said he would rise from the dead.

The concept of fulfillment is not always so straightforward, however. One reason is that even in the *literal sense* of the text, biblical *symbols can have more than one meaning* and thus be fulfilled in more than one way. In

Revelation, the beast's seven heads are fulfilled *both* by there being seven mountains (17:9) *and* in the persons of seven kings (17:10). In addition, there are the *spiritual senses* of the text, which can point to *additional fulfillments*.

In the book of Hosea, God declares, "When Israel was a child, I loved him, and out of Egypt, I called my son" (11:1). In its original context, the meaning of this text is clear: it refers back to the Exodus event, centuries earlier, when God used Moses to deliver the Israelites from slavery in Egypt. That's the *literal sense* of the text.

But there is also a *spiritual sense* of which the prophet Hosea was likely not conscious. This is brought out by Matthew, who recognized a fulfillment of this prophetic text when the Holy Family returned from their flight to Egypt. Thus, Matthew writes: "This was to fulfill what the Lord had spoken by the prophet, 'Out of Egypt have I called my son'" (Matt. 2:15).

The literal sense of Hosea 11:1 thus refers to one event, which is part of Old Testament history, and there is also a spiritual sense that applies to Christ in the New Testament.

This is not the only time this happens. For example, in the time of King Ahaz (732–716 B.C.), Syria had forged a military alliance with the northern kingdom of Israel that threatened to conquer Ahaz in Jerusalem (Isa. 7:1–2). God sent Isaiah to assure Ahaz that the alliance would not succeed (vv. 3–9) and told him to name a sign for God to give him as proof (vv. 10–11).

Ahaz refused to name a sign (v. 12), so God declared: "Therefore the Lord himself will give you a sign. Behold, a young woman shall conceive and bear a son, and shall call his name Immanuel. . . . For before the child knows how to refuse the evil and choose the good, the land before whose two kings you are in dread will be deserted" (vv. 14–16).

For this sign to be meaningful to Ahaz, it would have to be fulfilled in his own day—indeed, very quickly. It therefore points, on the primary, literal level, to a child conceived at that time (perhaps Ahaz's son, the future King Hezekiah).

The Evangelist Matthew recognized that the prophecy *also* pointed to Christ, who was "Immanuel," or, in Hebrew, "God with us" (Matt. 1:23).

This shows us several things:

1) A prophecy can have more than one fulfillment.

2) It may have a fulfillment shortly after it was given and another fulfillment centuries later.

3) If we know about a New Testament fulfillment, we should not assume that this was its only one. There may have been another, earlier fulfillment in the Old Testament.

4) In fact, the Old Testament fulfillment may have been meant in the literal sense of the text, whereas the New Testament fulfillment is to be found in the spiritual sense of the text.

At times, the biblical authors' understanding of fulfillment can be very broad. Thus, Isaiah 6:9–10 speaks of the Israelites of his day as being spiritually hard of hearing and uncomprehending of Isaiah's message. The Israelites of Jesus' day were similarly unresponsive, and in Matthew 13:14–15, the Evangelist says this "fulfilled the prophecy of Isaiah."

It appears that the New Testament authors could potentially see any later events that echoed an earlier prophetic text as in some sense fulfilling it. This points us toward a broad understanding of the concept of fulfillment.

Finally, we should note that God sometimes fulfilled prophecies in ways that would have been surprising to the ancient audience. When this happens, the fulfillment can be much greater than what was expected. The fact that the Messiah would be a divine and suffering savior who would die to save the world—not a merely human military leader who would expel the hated Romans—is one example.

114. What procedure should we use when interpreting a prophetic text?

By its nature, prophecy can be difficult to interpret. It uses many symbols, and these can be taken in more than one way.

The key to understanding biblical prophecy is to determine its literal sense—that is, what it meant in its original context, what the prophet was trying to communicate to his audience for their benefit. Normally Old Testament prophecies have their primary fulfillment within the generation to which they were given or within a few generations. However, they can have additional fulfillments later in time. Thus many Old Testament prophecies have further fulfillments at the time of Christ.

Knowing all this, there are a series of principles to keep in mind when reading the prophets:

1) The first thing to do is set aside expectations you have about the text. In particular, do not look to a text to validate a particular view you already hold. Ask what the text is saying, not what you want it to say.

2) To the best of your ability, identify who wrote a prophetic text, who the original audience was, and when the text was composed. Sometimes this is difficult or can be done only within broad limits, but situating a text in its historical circumstances is important.

3) Seek to establish the literal sense of the text by focusing on the words the author wrote and interpreting them in the historical context in which they were composed (this will mean temporarily setting aside what we may know about this text from other sources, such as how it was used in the New Testament). Specifically, ask how these words would have been understood by the original audience.

4) Ask what overall message the prophet was trying to communicate to his audience. Bear in mind that this was not to satisfy our curiosity about the future, but rather, to warn the Israelites about misbehavior, promise rewards for good behavior, assure them of God's love, and help them live through historical circumstances they would face. Which kind of message is being given in the text you are examining?

5) Ask what elements in the text are symbolic (or may be symbolic) and what these symbols likely mean for the literal sense of the text, based on what the author says and how similar symbols are used elsewhere.

6) Look for clues in the text that give an idea of when the prophet and his audience would have expected the prophecy to be fulfilled. Bear in mind that this would normally be within the prophet's own generation or within a few generations.

7) Ask what events occurring in that time frame could have fulfilled the prophecy. Sometimes it may not be possible to identify a specific event due to the fact that many details of ancient history have been forgotten, but this does not mean there was not an event that fulfilled it. Look the passage up in commentaries to see what scholars have proposed as fulfillments.

8) Ask if there could have been other fulfillments, in view of the fact that a symbol can sometimes point to more than one thing.

9) Having sought to establish the original, literal sense of the text, explore what spiritual senses may exist. At this point, it is appropriate to bring back the knowledge of how the text was later used in the New Testament, and whether there may be further fulfillments of the text (e.g., additional Christological interpretations).

This procedure is, by necessity, a simplified one. However, it will serve as a sound starting point for interpreting prophetic texts. Violating these principles is a recipe for misinterpreting, truncating, and distorting a text's meaning.

115. What are the biggest mistakes people make when interpreting prophecy?

Since people know that prophecy contains predictions, they often assume that prophetic passages in the Bible must refer to things in *their* future. Rather, because of prophecy's practical orientation, we should *first* look for a fulfillment near the prophet's own time and only *then* ask whether it may have more distant fulfillments.

Assuming that prophecies automatically refer to events in *our* future is one of the most common mistakes people make, but it is far from the only one. Another is adopting what may be called an "egocentric" interpretation: when people think Bible prophecy is *about them*.

At the extreme, this involves the interpreter thinking that he, personally, is a figure mentioned in biblical prophecy. Throughout the centuries various people—including recent ones like Charles Manson or David Koresh—have claimed that they were figures whose coming was prophesied in the Bible.

The vast majority of people do not claim such things, but a less extreme form of this tendency is very common. Even if they do not think that Scripture speaks of them *specifically*, some people assume that biblical prophecy concerns them in a more general way—that it speaks of things in their location or time period.

Advocates of the second-century heresy known as *Montanism* claimed that the new Jerusalem would descent from heaven on the small town of Pepuza in modern Turkey, where they happened to have their headquarters. And throughout the centuries, many have thought that they were living immediately before the end and that the Second Coming would happen within just a few years. Some even set dates for when it would occur, only to see these dates pass.[151]

Another common mistake is failing to recognize the amount of symbolism biblical authors use. For example, sometimes the Bible uses "cosmic cataclysm" language—speaking of the sun darkening, the moon not giving its light, the stars falling, etc. (Isa. 13:10; 24:18–23; 34:4; Ezek. 32:7; Joel 2:10, 31; Amos 8:9; Hag. 2:22; Mark 13:24–25). Some understand this imagery literally, as referring to solar eclipses (the sun darkening), lunar eclipses (the moon not giving light), or meteor showers (stars falling).

However, this language usually is a symbol of God's judgment on a people. Isaiah 13 contains an oracle against Babylon that says, "The stars of the heavens and their constellations will not give their light; the sun will be dark at its rising and the moon will not shed its light. . . . [God] will make the heavens tremble, and the earth will be shaken out of its place" (vv. 10, 13). God makes it clear how this judgment on the Babylonians will be accomplished: "I am stirring up the Medes against them" (v. 17).

This shows that God is using the cataclysm imagery to describe the conquest of the Babylonian empire by the ancient Medes. It is a poetic expression of what living through the judgment will be like. For the Babylonians, it will be *as if* the sun and moon darkened and the stars fell from the sky. Further, some interpreters have seen the celestial bodies as symbols of the rulers of the people, who would quake and lose their positions in the turmoil.[152]

To avoid making these mistakes, it's helpful to keep several principles: (1) don't assume that biblical prophecy automatically refers to the future; (2) don't assume it's about your time or place; and (3) don't assume it is literal rather than symbolic. A given prophecy might turn out to be each of these things, but that can't simply be assumed. It needs to be proven.

116. How did prophecy develop through the Old Testament?

God has spoken in "many and various ways" (Heb. 1:1) to mankind, even from the beginning (CCC 54). The early section of Genesis (chaps. 1–11) shows God revealing himself to primordial figures such as Adam and Noah, and later chapters record his dealings with the patriarchs of Israel, including Abraham, Jacob, and Joseph.

A turning point came with Moses. He functioned as both prophet and lawgiver for Israel, and God declared that in the future, he would send the nation another prophet on the model of Moses (Deut. 18:15).

After the conquest of the promised land, Israel was led by a series of judges—warrior chieftains who helped protect the nation from its enemies. They sometimes received divine revelation, and one of them—Deborah—is described as a prophetess (Judg. 4:4). There were also other prophets in this period who were not judges (6:8).

Samuel is often considered the last of the judges and the first of the main series of prophets. In his time, Israel transitioned to a monarchy, and Samuel anointed the first two kings, Saul and David (1 Sam. 10, 16). The monarchy was instituted in the eleventh century B.C., and this seems to have inaugurated a prophetic golden age, in which prophets began to appear with great frequency.

We are told that when Samuel was a boy, revelations from God were rare (1 Sam. 3:1), but, as we have noted, in the time of Queen Jezebel (ninth century B.C.), there were more than a hundred prophets at one time (1 Kings 18:4).

During this age, as recorded in the historical books (1 Samuel through Nehemiah), we find the prophets giving many messages to the kings of Israel and Judah—alternatingly counseling, reassuring, warning, and rebuking them. The messages God gave in this age centered on how his people and their leaders could navigate the turbulent times in which they lived.

The major age of prophecy continued through the Assyrian and Babylonian Exiles and into the post-exilic age. All told, it appears to have lasted for about six hundred years—until the fifth century B.C., when Malachi, the last of the Minor Prophets, wrote.

Even during this highly prophetic age, there were periods in which prophetic activity subsided—as attested in various texts, such as Psalm 74:9 ("there is no longer any prophet") and Lamentations 2:9 (Zion's "prophets obtain no vision from the Lord").

The fact that these passages are part of Scripture reveals that even if overt prophetic activity could temporarily subside, this did not stop divine inspiration from happening. After all, these scriptures were written *during* prophetic lulls.

Even after the fifth century B.C., we see God giving periodic revelations to individuals, even though they did not function as formal prophets (2 Macc. 3:24–28; 5:2–4; 15:12–16). And there remained an expectation that there would be prophets in the future (1 Macc. 4:46; 14:41).

After this extended lull, a new flowering of prophecy began in the late first century B.C., with the events leading up to the birth of Jesus and the dawning of the Christian age.

Finally, we should note that because Scripture itself is a form of prophecy. Because of divine inspiration, scriptural texts have spiritual senses that the human authors may not have been aware of. These can contain information about later times.

In particular, since many of the Psalms are ascribed to David, it was natural for Christians to see many passages in this book in reference to the Son of David. Thus, we speak of the "messianic Psalms," because their spiritual and prophetic dimensions deal with Jesus.

117. Who is the prophet Isaiah?

Isaiah son of Amoz lived in the 700s B.C. He was married to a woman he refers to as "the prophetess" (Isa. 8:3)—either because she was a prophetess herself or because she was married to him—and they had at least two sons (7:3; 8:3–4).

His ministry spanned the reigns of several kings of Judah (Uzziah, Jotham, Ahaz, and Hezekiah). A tradition found in both Jewish and early Christian circles holds that he was martyred by Hezekiah's son, the wicked king Manasseh, by being sawn in two. (Heb. 11:37 may refer to this tradition.)

The book that bears his name is the longest prophetic book of the Old Testament, and it is placed at the front of the Major Prophets. It is sixty-six chapters long, and scholars are generally agreed that chapters one through thirty-nine collect oracles given by the original eighth-century prophet. Based on various factors, most modern scholars propose that chapters forty through sixty-six were written by one or more later prophets.

The Church has no teaching on this proposal one way or another, but recent popes—including St. John Paul II and Benedict XVI—have favored it. Thus, John Paul II stated: "In the book that bears the prophet Isaiah's name, scholars have identified various voices all of which are placed under the patronage of this great prophet who lived in the eighth century B.C."[153]

From the Church's perspective, the key thing is that the entire book of Isaiah was written under divine inspiration. Who wrote individual parts of it is regarded as a matter of history rather than a matter of faith.

Isaiah is a significant book, and it is quoted more than any other prophetic book in the New Testament, which has literally hundreds of citations and allusions to it.

Many of Isaiah's prophecies deal with the coming conquest of Judah by Babylon and the resulting exile. However, the book also contains messages relating to the post-captivity era and a new golden age.

One reason Isaiah is quoted so frequently in the New Testament is that it contains a series of important messianic prophecies (see 7:11–17; 9:1–7; 11:1–10; 40:3–5).

Of special note are a series of texts describing a figure referred to as the Lord's servant. These "servant songs" (42:1–9; 49:1–12; 50:4–11; 52:13–53:12; and possibly 61:1–3) have a messianic dimension. The most famous is in chapter 53, which the New Testament applies to the sufferings of Christ. Also noteworthy is that these texts indicate that the servant will serve as the embodiment of a new covenant (see 42:6; 49:8).

We must be careful, however, when reading the messianic prophecies in Isaiah, that we do not assume they refer *only* to Christ.

For example, the prophecy of Isaiah 7:14 ("Behold, a young woman shall conceive and bear a son, and shall call his name Immanuel") was a sign given to assure King Ahaz that enemy kings would not conquer him. For this prophecy to be effective as a sign, it needed to be fulfilled during Ahaz's reign (732–716 B.C.). The Christological fulfillment of the text is thus a later one found within the text's spiritual sense.

Similarly, the second servant song identifies the servant as "Israel, in whom I am glorified" (49:3), and scholars have long debated whether the text suggests that the servant is an individual or a corporate entity. None of this excludes the Christological fulfillment of these passages, but it does mean that their fulfillment by Christ may not be the only one.

In addition to passages dealing with the Messiah specifically, Isaiah contains passages forecasting a new golden age, in which the Gentiles come to worship God (49:6; 56:6–8; 60:3; 66:18–20). God even says, "And some of them I also will take for priests and for Levites" (66:21).

Finally, Isaiah describes a future era in which God will make "new heavens and a new earth" (65:17; 66:22).

118. Who is the prophet Jeremiah?

Jeremiah son of Hilkiah lived in the late 600s and early 500s B.C. He was the son of a priest and a native of the town of Anathoth (Jer. 1:1). God forbade him to marry or have children in Israel, in view of the calamities that were coming on the land (16:1–4). He was called to be a prophet as a young man (1:6), and his ministry spanned the reigns of several kings (Josiah, Jehoahaz, Jehoiachin, Jehoiakim, and Zedekiah). It continued into the Babylonian Exile.

After the Babylonians conquered Jerusalem, Jeremiah chose to remain there. Eventually, he was forced to relocate to Egypt, where he continued his prophetic ministry. The exact circumstances of his death are not known, and traditions about it conflict with one another.

Jeremiah was assisted in his ministry by a man named Baruch son of Neriah, who was his scribe and friend.

Because of his sorrowful message and the strong emotion he shows, Jeremiah is often called "the weeping prophet."

The book of Jeremiah is the second longest of the Major Prophets, comprising fifty-two chapters. The first edition of it was a scroll Jeremiah dictated to Baruch, which contained the prophecies he had been given to that time. However, when Baruch read the scroll publicly, King Jehoiakim burned it, forcing Jeremiah and Baruch to write a new version, which they supplemented with later prophecies (chap. 36).

The book is challenging in that it is not written in chronological order, but it contains many biographical accounts of incidents in Jeremiah's life, giving us more knowledge of this prophet and his struggles than we have of others.

Jeremiah is often grouped with two other books—Lamentations and Baruch—which, historically, have been attributed to the prophet and his scribe, respectively. The first is a series of laments about the destruction of Jerusalem, and the second continues themes developed in Jeremiah. It also contains a letter ascribed to the prophet.

A major theme in Jeremiah is the need for the people to repent to avoid God's judgment. When they refuse to do so, doom becomes certain and Jeremiah urges the people to accept the Babylonian conquest as God's judgment on their sins. They refuse to comply, and Jeremiah is persecuted.

The book contains a variety of oracles, both against the southern kingdom of Judah and against other nations. It also indicates that after Babylon has served as the instrument of God's judgment, it also will be punished for its sins.

One of the most memorable actions occurs when God has Jeremiah visit a potter's house, and he sees a vessel the potter is working on become ruined, leading the potter to refashion it into a new vessel. God then says, "O house of Israel, can I not do with you as this potter has done? . . . If at any time I declare concerning a nation or a kingdom, that I will pluck up and break down and destroy it, and if that nation, concerning which I have spoken, turns from its evil, I will repent of the evil that I intended to do to it" (18:6–8).

Prophecy thus can contain a contingent element: If people repent in time, doom can be avoided.

Jeremiah is known for prophesying a period of "seventy years" in connection with the Exile (25:11–12; 29:10). It is unclear whether the prophecy means that Babylon's dominance would last seventy years, that Judah's captivity would last seventy years, or both (in view of prophecies having more than one fulfillment). Scholars have proposed a number of possible fulfillments of this prophecy, including the seventy years between the destruction of the Jerusalem temple in 586 B.C. and the dedication of the rebuilt temple in 515 B.C.

The book also contains messianic prophecy, with the forecast of the rise of a new ruler from David's stock, a man whom Jeremiah refers to as "the Branch" (23:5–6; 33:14–16).

Finally, the book contains the promise that God will establish a "new covenant" with his people, one that will be spiritually transformative, unlike the one made through Moses (31:31–34).

119. Who is the prophet Ezekiel?

Ezekiel son of Buzi acted as a prophet from 593 to 571 B.C., if not later. Like Jeremiah, he was the son of a priest, and he refers to himself as a priest (Ezek. 1:3). He was married, and when his wife died unexpectedly, he was forbidden to mourn her, as a prophetic sign to the people of their own tragedies (24:19–24).

It appears that Ezekiel was taken into captivity after Nebuchadnezzar's second assault on Jerusalem, in 597 B.C. (see 2 Kings 24:10–16), before the destruction of the temple, which occurred in a later assault (2 Kings 25:8–9). The prophet was relocated to a colony of Jewish exiles on the Chebar canal in Mesopotamia, where he received his prophetic call (Ezek. 1–3). We do not have reliable information regarding his death.

The book of Ezekiel is the third longest of the Major Prophets, comprising forty-eight chapters.

During his ministry, Ezekiel is directed to carry out a number of unusual prophetic actions to signify the strained situation between God and his people (e.g., 4:1-17; 5:1-17).

Ezekiel also gives various oracles against the nations that oppress Israel, and he experiences a number of famous visions, including visions of the glory of God (1:4–28), the valley of dry bones (37:1–28), and a restored temple and nation of Israel (40:1–48:35).

In the prophecy about the dry bones, Ezekiel is commanded to speak to them so that flesh may come upon them and they may live again. Christians have sometimes read this as a straightforward prophecy of the resurrection of the dead. That is certainly so in the spiritual sense, but in the literal sense, it refers to the restoration of Israel to its land after the dry, withering state of exile (37:11–14).

The vision of the restored temple and nation includes details that do not match up easily with any period in history—either past or future (given what we know from other prophecies)—leaving scholars to puzzle over the extent to which they are meant to relate to history or to an idealized state.

Ezekiel also contains messianic prophecy, such as when he predicts that the restored nation will be ruled by a Davidic king in an age when a new covenant will be made (37:24–28).

Finally, it is noteworthy that Ezekiel is regularly addressed (more than ninety times) as "Son of Man" in his visions. It would later become one of Christ's preferred designations for himself.

120. Who is the prophet Daniel?

Daniel was a young Judean nobleman. He was taken into captivity following Nebuchadnezzar's first siege of Jerusalem in 605 B.C. (Dan. 1:1–7). He was active as a prophet until the reign of Darius I, who came to power in 521 B.C.

We know nothing of Daniel's family life. There is no mention of a wife or children, and since he was placed under the care of Nebuchadnezzar's "chief of the eunuchs" (1:7), Daniel and his companions may have been made eunuchs—as later Jewish tradition held.

The book of Daniel is the shortest of the Major Prophets. It has two editions—a twelve-chapter edition considered canonical by Jews and Protestants and a fourteen-chapter edition considered canonical by Catholics and Orthodox.

The text of the book is unusual in that it is written in more than one language. The shorter edition contains passages in both Hebrew and Aramaic, and the longer edition also contains passages in Greek (though these are likely translations of Hebrew or Aramaic originals).

The book of Daniel does not claim to be written by the prophet. The narrative sections are written in the third person. However, several prophetic sections are written in the first person and thus are ascribed to Daniel.

The book contains a mixture of narrative sections and prophetic ones. The latter are found in chapters 2 and 7–12. Because of the brevity of the prophetic material, it can be summarized as a series of five visions:

In chapter 2, Nebuchadnezzar has a dream of a great idol made out of different kinds of metals. Daniel interprets this as representing a series of kingdoms, beginning with the Babylonian empire. The idol is destroyed when its feet, the final empire, are smashed by a stone that becomes a great mountain, representing the kingdom God establishes.

In chapter 7, Daniel has a dream of four strange beasts that combine parts of different animals. The last is a monster with many horns. One horn blasphemes against God and makes war against his saints until the beginning of God's kingdom, when "one like a Son of Man" arrives and is presented to God. Daniel is made to understand that these beasts also represent a series of kingdoms that precede God's.

In chapter 8, Daniel sees a vision of a ram and a he-goat, and we again have a drama involving a horn that persecutes God's people. This time, we are told that the ram symbolizes the Medo-Persian empire and the he-goat symbolizes the Greek empire.

In chapter 9, Daniel reflects on Jeremiah's prophecy of seventy years, and the angel Gabriel reveals to him a prophecy of seventy weeks of years (i.e., 490 years) concerning Israel's future. It includes the arrival of an anointed prince and the destruction of the rebuilt temple.

In chapters 10–12, Daniel is given a revelation unlike the previous ones in that it is not cloaked in symbolism, but is told in a straightforward manner. It concerns the fall of the Persian empire and the rise of the Greek, under a great king whose empire is then divided into four parts. Daniel is told about the politics that ensue among these four successor kingdoms, including a king who profanes the Jerusalem temple and erects "the abomination that makes desolate" or "desolating sacrilege" (11:31; 12:11; see 9:27).

The revelations in Daniel involve a succession of kingdoms or empires that had power in the period after the fall of Jerusalem in 587 B.C. As the book progresses, attention is drawn to the conquests of Alexander the Great, the four kingdoms his empire gave rise to, and the Greek-speaking ruler Antiochus IV (i.e., "Antiochus Epiphanes," who ruled 175–164 B.C.), who persecuted the Jewish people.

These events parallel those recorded in the books of the Maccabees, which report that the men of Antiochus IV set up the abomination of desolation in the temple at Jerusalem (1 Macc. 1:54). This was not the prophecy's only fulfillment, however, as Jesus indicated that it would have a later one as well (Matt. 24:15).

And although the prophecies of Daniel have fulfillments in the time of the Maccabees, they also have fulfillments in Jesus'. Notably, Jesus refers to himself throughout his ministry as "the Son of Man," identifying himself unmistakably as the "one like a Son of Man" who received from the "Ancient of Days" a universal authority: "And to him was given dominion and glory and kingdom, that all peoples, nations, and languages should serve him; his dominion is an everlasting dominion, which shall not pass away, and his kingdom one that shall not be destroyed" (Dan. 7:13-14; see Rev. 1:13; 14:14).[154]

At some point, the prophecies of Daniel begin to have fulfillments in the far future, as they contain an unmistakable prophecy of the resurrection of the dead (Dan. 12:2–3). Because of its fulfillments in Jesus' day and at the end of the world, Daniel became one of the most influential books in New Testament prophecy.

121. Who were the Minor Prophets?

The Minor Prophets are a group of twelve short books by or about prophets who were active between roughly the 800s and the 400s B.C. In the ancient world, they were presented in a single scroll known simply as "The Twelve."

Because of the symbolic number twelve, they were likely collected from a larger body of prophetic works, during or somewhat after the time of Malachi, the last of the Minor Prophets.

They can be briefly described as follows:

1) *Hosea* ministered in the 700s B.C. He was from the northern kingdom of Israel.

His ministry was based on a powerful prophetic action in that God directed him, "Go, take to yourself a wife of harlotry and have children of harlotry, for the land commits great harlotry by forsaking the Lord" (Hos. 1:2).

The marital drama that ensues forms an allegory for God's relationship with his unfaithful, idolatrous people. The sins of Israel will eventually lead the northern kingdom into captivity by the Assyrians, but in his love, God will eventually take them back.

2) *Joel*'s dating is unclear, and little is known about the prophet's personal background.

The book deals with devastation left by a horde of locusts. It also focuses on "the day of the Lord" and how it will bring both judgment and mercy.

In the New Testament, on the day of Pentecost, Peter applies Joel 2:28–32 to the dawning Christian age (Acts 2:17–21).

3) *Amos* ministered in the 700s B.C. He came from a humble background, being an agricultural worker—"a herdsman, and a dresser of sycamore trees" (Amos 7:14). Although he was from Judah, he ministered in the northern kingdom of Israel.

Amos preached against both foreign nations and God's people, faulting the latter for failure to observe the Mosaic Law (2:4). He also condemns the haughty behavior of the rich with respect to the poor (8:4–6). Despite the judgment that will come upon the people, Amos prophesies an eventual restoration and period of prosperity (9:9–15).

4) *Obadiah*'s dating is unclear. It is the shortest book of the Old Testament, consisting of only a single chapter, and we are not given much information about the prophet.

The book consists of an oracle of judgment against the nation of Edom, which was descended from Jacob's brother Esau.

5) *Jonah* ministered in the 700s B.C. He is sometimes called "the reluctant prophet" because he initially fled his prophetic mission, leading him to be swallowed by a "great fish" (Jon. 1:17).

When he finally accepted his call, he went to the Assyrian city of Nineveh and prophesied its destruction. The Ninevites repented, and God called off the doom he had planned for the city—illustrating the contingent element in prophecy mentioned in Jeremiah 18:6–8.

Jonah objected to this, but God stressed his love for all people—including the Gentiles who lived in Nineveh.

6) *Micah* ministered in the 700s B.C. He was from rural Judah and prophesied about Samaria and Jerusalem (Mic. 1:1).

The book contains a beautiful prophecy of the messianic age in which the Gentiles come to worship God (4:1–5). The same passage is found in Isaiah (Isa. 2:1–4), and it includes the famous prophecy of swords being beaten into plowshares.

Micah also contains the famous prophecy of the coming Davidic king who will be born in Bethlehem (Mic. 5:2).

7) *Nahum* likely ministered in the 600s B.C. His prophecy is directed against the Assyrian city of Nineveh. Like Jonah, he prophesied its doom, but unlike in the time of Jonah, the Ninevites did not repent, and the city fell to the Babylonians in 612 B.C.

8) *Habakkuk* likely ministered in the 600s B.C. He asks why God does not punish the wicked in Judea (Hab. 1:2–4), and God indicates he will use the Babylonians (Chaldeans) to punish them (1:5–11). The prophet then asks how God can use such a wicked nation to do this (1:12–17), and God replies that he will also punish the Babylonians for their sins (2:1–20).

The book is famous for the statement that "the righteous shall live by his faith" (2:4; see Rom. 1:17; Gal. 3:11; Heb. 10:38).

9) *Zephaniah* ministered in the 600s B.C. He is apparently a descendant of King Hezekiah (Zeph. 1:1). He describes God's judgment as a virtual reversal of creation (vv. 2–3), brought on by the idolatry being committed in Judea (vv. 4–6).

God will judge not only Judah, but also the surrounding nations, as far south as Ethiopia and as far north as Assyria (2:12–15). But beyond this there will be a time of joy and blessing in which God rules as king of Israel (3:15).

10) *Haggai* can be dated, precisely, to the year 520 B.C., when God sent a message to the Jewish governor Zerubbabel by the mouth of the prophet.

The Babylonian Exile was over, but people were saying the time had not yet come to finish rebuilding the temple in Jerusalem, citing their poverty. God said it was not right for them to live in their houses while his lay in ruins and that if they would rebuild the temple, he would pour out prosperity upon them.

11) *Zechariah* ministered at the same time as Haggai—520 B.C.—and afterward.

The book of Zechariah is the longest of the Minor Prophets and contains many unusual visions. It falls into two parts (chapters one through eight and nine through fourteen). In the first part, the prophet encourages the rebuilding of the Jerusalem temple, like Haggai, and in the second part, he delves deeper into the future, including the messianic age.

The book is influential in the New Testament. It includes a text (Zech. 9:9) that foreshadows Jesus' triumphal entry into Jerusalem (see Matt. 21:5) and one that foretells the sorrow people will have when they look upon the messianic figure whom they have pierced (Zech. 12:10; see John 19:37 and Rev. 1:7).

12) *Malachi* (Hebrew, "my [i.e., God's] messenger") may be either a personal name or the symbolic designation of an otherwise anonymous prophet.

Malachi ministered around 500 B.C. or somewhat later, after the Jerusalem temple had been rebuilt and sacrifices had been restored. The prophet criticizes the people for offering blind and lame animals on God's altar (Mal. 1:6–8).

The book contains a key prophecy that "Elijah" will be sent before the coming of the day of the Lord (4:5–6)—a prophecy Jesus indicated was fulfilled in the ministry of John the Baptist (Matt. 17:10–13; see Luke 1:17).

122. What are the principal prophetic themes in the Old Testament?

Old Testament prophecy contains countless individual themes, but some of the most important include:

1) *Blessing and punishment.* Perhaps the most fundamental theme in prophetic texts is that God will give his people blessings for doing right and punishments for doing wrong.

A particularly noteworthy text on this theme is found in Deuteronomy 28, where, just as the Israelites are about to go into the promised land, Moses prophesies the blessings and punishments they will receive, depending on what they do.

This theme is developed in numerous passages in the prophets, and most of what they have to say can be seen as applications of this one general theme.

2) *God's visitations/comings.* The prophets commonly envision God "visiting" or "coming" to a people to accomplish his purpose among them.

God's coming might be an occasion of judgment (Gen. 18:21; Ps. 50:3–6; 96:13), benediction (Ex. 3:8; Deut. 33:2–3; Ruth 1:6; 1 Sam. 2:21; Ps. 65:9;

Jer. 27:2), vindication of the righteous, or punishment of evildoers (Gen. 11:5–8; 1 Sam. 4:6–7; Ps. 18:6–19; 97:5–8; Isa. 19:1; 23:17; 31:4–5; 64:1–3; 66:15–17; Mic. 1:3–7).

3) *The Davidic Monarchy.* God promised King David that he would establish an enduring house for him and that his descendants would continue to rule after him.

The key text for this prophecy is 2 Samuel 7:11–16, but it is discussed in multiple other passages (e.g., 2 Sam. 23:5; 1 Chron. 17:11–14; 2 Chron. 6:16; Ps. 89:3–4; 132:10–18; Isa. 9:6–7; 11:1–5; Jer. 23:5; 30:9).

4) *Exile.* Having brought the Israelites out of slavery in Egypt, God warned them through Moses that if they behaved wickedly, he would send them into foreign captivity again (Deut. 28:62–68).

Eventually, the northern kingdom of Israel would be taken into exile by the Assyrian empire in the eighth century B.C., and the southern kingdom of Judah would be taken into exile by the Babylonians in the sixth century B.C.

These exiles are a major theme in the prophets (see Isa. 5:13; 39:5–7; Jer. 13:19; 20:4–6; 52:27–30; Ezek. 12:1–16; Dan. 1:1–4; Amos 5:27; 9:4; Mic. 1:6; Zech. 14:2).

5) *Return.* God promised that his people would repent of their sins while in exile and would eventually be restored to the land—both the inhabitants of the northern kingdom of Israel and the southern kingdom of Judah.

Return from exile is also a major theme in the prophets (Isa. 11:11–12; 43:5–6; Jer. 16:15; 23:3; 24:5–7; 25:11–12; 19:10; Lam. 4:22; Ezek. 20:34; 34:12–14; 36:8; Hos. 1:10–11; Zeph. 3:20).

6) *The New Covenant.* God made a covenant with Israel through Moses, but this covenant did not bring about a spiritual transformation of the people, and they broke it, leading to exile. Consequently, God promised that after the Exile, he would make a new covenant with his people, which would be spiritually transformative.

The key text for the prophecy of the New Covenant is Jeremiah 31:31–34. Aspects of it are discussed in many other passages (e.g., Isa. 55:1–5; 59:21; 61:8–9; Jer. 32:37–41; 50:4–5; Bar. 2:35; Ezek. 11:17–20; 16:60; 36:22–27).

7) *The Messiah.* The term *messiah* means "anointed one." Because God anointed many individuals for different purposes, the subject of messiahship is complex, with many potential messiahs. Notably, Jewish kings were

anointed, and thus the successors of David were considered messiahs. Even the Persian king Cyrus the Great had a place in God's plan and is thus described as one of his messiahs (Isa. 45:1).

Which prophecies deal with *the* Messiah are debated, especially as the term *messiah* often is not used even when the concept is being discussed. Over time, literally hundreds of texts have been proposed as dealing with the Messiah, either in their literal or in their spiritual sense. Some of the most notable will be discussed as we go along.

Once the Davidic dynasty ceased to rule at the Babylonian exile, prophecies concerning the messianic rule of a son of David become more striking. By predicting a ruler who would spring from David's family and reign in righteousness and peace (Isa. 11:1–9), the prophets were influential in preparing the coming of the Lord.

123. How does the New Testament fulfill the Old Testament prophecy?

The New Testament picks up the major themes explored in the Old Testament prophets, sometimes fulfilling them in an even greater way than could have been understood by the original audience (Matt. 13:17; Eph. 3:4–6; Col. 1:26).

1) *Blessing and punishment*: These remain themes in the New Testament, but the focus has shifted. Whereas the Old Testament focused on blessings and punishments people would receive in this life, the New Testament takes a broader perspective and focuses on the eternal rewards and punishments one will receive in the next (Rom. 2:6–7; Gal. 6:6–10).

2) *Exile and return*: By the time the New Testament authors wrote, the Babylonian Exile is over, many of the Jews have returned to the land, and the temple has been rebuilt. We are now in an age where the restoration predicted by the Old Testament prophets—or much of the restoration—has taken place.

A question that remains outstanding, however, during the New Testament era, is the re-gathering of the ten tribes from the northern kingdom of Israel, which was also predicted. Although these tribes are often described today as being "lost," it is not clear that they were considered lost in the first century A.D. There were descendants of these tribes still to be found in Palestine and Samaria (Luke 2:36), and New Testament figures still spoke of there being twelve tribes (Acts 26:7; James 1:1). Their re-gathering may have been accomplished through small migrations that have not been fully documented (even if many stayed in the lands of exile, just as many Jews did in the Diaspora). It also may have been accomplished spiritually through the conversion to Christianity of Jews and Samaritans descended from these tribes, some perhaps who were now considered "Gentiles" after they began to lose their distinctive identity as Israelites and thus became "lost."

3) *Davidic monarchy and the Messiah*: Although there had been a partial restoration of Davidic rule through the governor Zerubbabel in the 500s B.C., the definitive and eternal fulfillment of this promise occurred through Jesus Christ.

Before Jesus was born, it was revealed that "the Lord God will give to him the throne of his father David, and he will reign over the house of Jacob for ever; and of his kingdom there will be no end" (Luke 1:32–33).

Jesus also fulfilled numerous messianic prophecies—based either on the literal or the spiritual senses of Old Testament texts—so that when he met disciples on the road to Emmaus, "beginning with Moses and all the prophets, he interpreted to them in all the scriptures the things concerning himself" (Luke 24:27).

4) *The New Covenant*: Prophets not only predicted that God would establish a new covenant but also indicated that the "the servant of the Lord" would personally embody this covenant (Isa. 42:6; 49:8).

This was fulfilled in a dramatic way when Jesus established the Eucharist, declaring, "This cup which is poured out for you is the new covenant in my blood" (Luke 22:20; 1 Cor. 11:25). The New Covenant is further explored elsewhere in the New Testament, particularly in Hebrews (see chapters eight through ten).

5) *God's visitations/comings*: When Christians consider this topic, they naturally think of Christ's Second Coming, which will occur at the end of time (Acts 1:11; 1 Cor. 15:21–26).

Critics sometime charge Jesus with having falsely predicted his Second Coming as taking place during the first century, saying, for example, "This generation will not pass away before all these things take place" (Mark 13:30). However, the prophets understood God as "visiting" or "coming" to his people when judging them, defending them, blessing the righteous, or punishing evildoers. This is important background when we encounter similar discussions in the New Testament, which depicts God/Jesus/the kingdom as coming in multiple ways (see Luke 1:68; 9:27–36; 17:21; 19:41–44).

124. How was Jesus a prophet?

Moses prophesied: "The Lord your God will raise up for you a prophet like me from among you, from your brethren—him you shall heed" (Deut. 18:15).

God gave Israel a whole series of prophets, but it was recognized that this passage promised the coming of a single prophet *par excellence*—"the prophet"—who would be like Moses in a way no other would be.

Thus, when John the Baptist appeared, people asked if he was "the prophet" (John 1:21). John answered, "No," and pointed to the one who came after him: Jesus Christ.

Jesus was the prophet who equaled and surpassed Moses. In his own day, the people recognized his prophetic status. After his triumphal entry into Jerusalem, they acclaimed him as "the prophet Jesus from Nazareth of Galilee" (Matt. 21:11).

Christ acted as a prophet in many ways. Many of his parables had a prophetic function, explaining the future growth and development of God's kingdom (Matt. 13; Mark 4). He also told parables about the fates people would have at the end of time (e.g., Matt. 20:1–16; 22:1–14; 25:1–46).

Jesus also made predictions in non-symbolic form, particularly when he predicted his own passion, crucifixion, and rising from the dead (e.g., Mark 8:31; 9:9, 31; 10:32–34). Interestingly, his disciples did not always recognize that he was speaking non-symbolically and thus discussed among themselves "what rising from the dead might mean" (9:10; see 9:32).

Critics have sometimes said Jesus incorrectly predicted that his Second Coming would occur in the first century A.D. This misreads the texts in question. When Jesus says, "There are some standing here who will not taste death before they see that the kingdom of God has come with power" (Mark 9:1; see Matt. 16:28; Luke 9:27), Jesus was not referring to the end of the world. Instead, he was referring to the Transfiguration.

In each of the synoptic Gospels, the Transfiguration *immediately* follows Jesus' announcement (Matt. 17:1–9; Mark 9:2–10; Luke 9:28–36). Jesus takes three of the disciples—Peter, James, and John—up a mountain. His clothing becomes dazzlingly bright; Moses and Elijah appear beside him; everyone is enveloped in a cloud; and God the Father speaks from heaven, identifying Jesus as his Son and his chosen, and declaring, "Hear him!"

This manifestation is the coming of the kingdom "with power" Jesus referred to, and the text of each Gospel suggests that this is the way the Evangelists understood it.

Not only does the Transfiguration happen right after the announcement, but each Gospel says it was about a week later (Matt. 17:1; Mark 9:1; Luke 9:28). (The slight difference in the number of days may reflect reckoning parts of days as wholes and counting days as beginning at sunset, midnight, or dawn.)

Thus Peter, James, and John were the ones who did not taste death before they saw the kingdom coming with power.

Similarly, when Jesus said, "This generation will not pass away before all these things take place" (Mark 13:30; see Matt. 24:34; Luke 21:32), "these things" does not refer to the end of the world, but to the events leading up to the destruction of the rebuilt Jerusalem temple in A.D. 70.

The "this generation" statement occurs in Jesus' longest prophetic statement, which is a speech known as the Olivet Discourse, because he gave it on the Mount of Olives. The speech occurs after Jesus makes a prediction about the temple: "Do you see these great buildings? There will not be left here one stone upon another, that will not be thrown down" (Mark 13:2). Afterward, "as he sat on the Mount of Olives opposite the temple, Peter and James and John and Andrew asked him privately, 'Tell us, when will this be, and what will be the sign when these things are all to be accomplished?'" (13:3–4).

The disciples asked not about the end of the world, but about the destruction of the temple. Jesus answered that his generation would not pass away before the temple was destroyed, and he was correct.

The Gospels record the speech occurring just before the Crucifixion, in A.D. 33. The temple was destroyed in A.D. 70 by forces under the command of the Roman general Titus. There would have been many people of Jesus' generation who were still alive when the temple was destroyed.

Note that Luke introduces Jesus' speech on the Mount of Olives the same way as Mark does, with the disciples asking when his prediction about the temple would be fulfilled (Luke 21:7–9).

In Matthew, they ask about the temple, but they also ask, "And what will be the sign of your coming and of the close of the age?" (24:3). These added questions may refer to the end of the world.

Matthew has several parables at the end of his account that are not in Mark and Luke, and these seem to deal with the end of the world (25:1–46). This suggests that the additional material deals with the additional questions, and the statement about "this generation" still refers to the destruction of the temple.

Jesus thus was correct in his predictions regarding the Transfiguration and the destruction of the temple—as well as those regarding his suffering, death, and resurrection.

125. What prophecies are found in the New Testament letters?

Much of the New Testament consists of letters written by various early Christian figures, notably St. Paul. These letters contain prophecies.

The non-Pauline letters do not contain a great deal of prophetic material. However, they do stress certain common themes, such as the Second Coming of Christ on the Last Day (Heb. 10:37; James 5:7–8; 1 Pet. 1:7, 13; 2:12; 1 John 2:28), when the living and the dead will be judged (1 Pet. 4:5; 2 Pet. 2:9; Jude 1:6, 15) and the righteous saved and rewarded (Heb. 9:28; 1 Pet. 1:5; 5:4). They also note that in the end times, there will be scoffers who doubt the accomplishment of these things (2 Pet. 3:3–4; Jude 1:18), but that God will fulfill them in his own time (2 Pet. 3:8–9).

In addition to these general themes, some specific prophecies include that the current world will perish by fire (2 Pet. 3:7–12), that we await new heavens and a new earth (v. 13), and that we will be transformed to become like Jesus when he appears (1 John 3:2).

A theme of special note is that of the Antichrist. This term is found only in 1 and 2 John, where it refers both to a category of people (individual antichrists) and, apparently, to a single Antichrist. What characterizes Antichrist (in both senses) is the denial that Jesus is the Christ (1 John 2:22). John also notes that the spirit of Antichrist was already in the world in his day (4:3; see 2:18; 2 John 7).

Like the other New Testament letters, Paul's are not primarily devoted to prophecy. However, they do contain prophetic elements, and the large number of letters Paul wrote leads to a significant number of prophetic passages.

Paul regularly stresses general themes like the Second Coming of Christ, the Final Judgment, and the salvation and rewarding of the righteous. He does so often enough that we do not have space to review these themes here. Instead, we will look at some of the more notable, specific prophecies he makes.

For example, Paul predicts that there will be a major conversion of the Jewish people to Christ (Rom. 11:11–12, 25), which apparently will occur shortly before the end of the world (11:15).

Paul reveals that, in the next age, the saints (i.e., faithful Christians) will judge the world, including angels (1 Cor. 6:2–3).

He also provides an extended discussion of the resurrection of the dead (1 Cor. 15:12–58). This event will occur at the end of the world (11:23–26), and it will involve a transformation that will change our current mortal bodies into glorious immortal ones (15:35–44), which will be like Jesus' resurrected body (15:49)—a theme he also stresses elsewhere (Phil. 3:20–21). For those who are alive at the time of the Second Coming, this transformation will occur "in the twinkling of an eye," without their dying first (1 Cor. 15:51–52).

Paul revisits some of these themes in 1 Thessalonians, where he discusses the fact that, at the Second Coming, "those who have fallen asleep" (i.e., died) will rise from the dead (4:14–17). The apostle writes, "Then we who are alive, who are left, shall be caught up together with them in the clouds to meet the Lord in the air; and so we shall always be with the Lord" (4:17).

This passage has given rise to much problematic speculation. Among dispensationalists, the event Paul here describes has come to be known as the "Rapture." The problem is that dispensationalists assume that the Second Coming will occur some years before an earthly millennial reign of Christ, which itself precedes the final resurrection of the dead and Last Judgment.

Instead, in the prophetic statements of Paul, the Second Coming and the gathering of believers to be with Christ will occur at the end of the world, with the Last Judgment quickly ensuing.

Thus, Paul emphasizes that "*when* the Lord Jesus is revealed from heaven" (2 Thess. 1:7, emphasis added) the wicked "shall suffer the punishment of eternal destruction and exclusion from the presence of the Lord . . . when he comes on that day to be glorified in his saints" (1:9–10)—an overall event that Paul describes as "the coming of our Lord Jesus Christ and our assembling to meet him" (2:1).

Paul also gives a number of details about signs that will precede this event, saying, "That day will not come, unless the rebellion comes first, and the man of lawlessness is revealed, the son of perdition, who opposes and exalts himself against every so-called god or object of worship, so that he takes his seat in the temple of God, proclaiming himself to be God" (2:3–4).

He also indicates that something is currently holding back these events (2:6–7) but that eventually, "the lawless one will be revealed, and the Lord Jesus will slay him with the breath of his mouth and destroy him by his appearing and his coming" (2:8).

He further states that the coming of the lawless one will be accompanied by false signs and wonders that will deceive many (2:9–12). This apparently plays a role in the "rebellion" (Greek: *apostasia*, "apostasy") that will accompany the man of lawlessness (see 2 Tim. 3:1–9).

This final villain of world history has often been referred to as the Antichrist, and he has often been linked with the beast of Revelation, though there are reasons to be cautious about this identification.

126. What is apocalyptic prophecy?

The book of Revelation has given its name—or at least its Greek name—to a whole type of literature. As we noted, the Greek word for revelation is *apokalupsis*, and older Bible editions sometimes call the book the Apocalypse of St. John.

For several centuries before and after the time of Christ, works like Revelation were very popular, and scholars refer to these books as "apocalyptic literature." Although in contemporary English the word *apocalypse* is associated with the end of the world, this theme isn't required for a book to be an apocalypse.

A characteristic of apocalyptic literature—one of the main things that distinguishes it from ordinary prophecy—is that it uses a lot of symbolism, especially when representing history and what God plans to do in it. This symbolism is often interpreted for the visionary by a heavenly figure, such as an angel, and sometimes the visionary is given a tour of the invisible world and gets to see places like heaven and hell.

Daniel 7–12, where the rise and fall of various empires is depicted as a series of strange animals, is considered an early example of apocalyptic literature. And Jesus' discussion of the destruction of the Jerusalem temple in the Olivet Discourse (Matt. 24, Mark 13, Luke 21) is often called the "little apocalypse" because of its similarity to Revelation.

The book of Revelation is a definitive example of apocalyptic literature. In it, John sees God's purposes in history depicted using symbolism, some of which is interpreted for him by heavenly figures, although most remains enigmatic, leaving readers to search out meaning through reference to other biblical prophecies or events in history.

Another characteristic of apocalyptic literature found in Revelation is that John gets to see parts of the invisible world, including God's heavenly throne room and temple (4:1–5;14, 11:19, 14:15–17, 15:5–8), the abyss or "bottomless pit" of the demons (9:1–2, 11; 11:7, 17:8, 20:1–3), and the lake of fire where the condemned are sent (19:20; 20:10, 14–15).

127. Have the prophecies in the book of Revelation already been fulfilled?

The book of Revelation is one of the most enigmatic of all biblical prophecies, and one which especially intrigues interpreters, as it remains an open question as to when the prophecies it contains will be (or have been) fulfilled.

Interpreters generally agree that the beginning of the book of Revelation (at least Rev. 1–3) deals principally with events in the first century A.D. They also agree that the end of the book (20:7 through 22:21) deals principally with events at the end of the world and that are thus in our future.

The major question is how the remaining bulk of the book is to be related to history. On this question, there are four major schools of thought:

Preterism holds that the bulk of the book deals with events toward the beginning of Christian history—either the first century or the first few centuries.

Historicism holds that the bulk of the book forms an outline of Church history so that as you proceed through the book, you move through the different centuries, until at last you arrive at the end of time.

Idealism holds that the bulk of the book describes the conflict between good and evil that plays out in Church history, but it does not relate this conflict in the form of a simple timeline (as does historicism). Instead, it presents elements that occur over and over again during Church history in a cyclical pattern.

Futurism holds that the bulk of the book deals with material that lies in our future.

Which of these views is to be preferred?

The natural starting point is preterism. As previously discussed, the biblical prophets focus primarily on events to occur in their own generation or within a few generations—not thousands of years later.

Also, some of the major symbols of Revelation fit a first-century context very well.

Finally, both the beginning and the end of the book say the events it describes are "what must soon take place" (1:1; 22:6).

Combined, these facts create a strong initial case for the view that most of Revelation deals with the beginning of Christian history. Can a case be made for any of the other views that would overturn this?

The prospects for historicism are not good. This view is held by very few scholars today, as it is impossible to match up the events of Revelation with Church history in any objective way. Where in Revelation should one see the rise of Islam? Or the Protestant Reformation? Or the Napoleonic Wars? Or World Wars I and II? How is one to know which events are represented and under which symbols? There is no objective way to establish these things.

The prospects for idealism might seem better, because prophecies can have more than one fulfillment, and the struggle between good and evil does go on throughout the Christian age. Therefore, it is possible to see things from Revelation being fulfilled at different points in Church history.

However, prophecies tend to have a single primary fulfillment—described in the literal sense of the text—with other fulfillments belonging to the spiritual sense. We would expect the same to be true of Revelation.

Only if one could establish that Revelation is *not* principally about the beginning of the Christian age—that it is not principally about *any* part of the Christian age—would idealism be established. It is not clear how one would argue this, particularly since idealism acknowledges that the events in Revelation *do* apply to the beginning of Church history.

Futurism is popular today in many Evangelical Protestant circles, especially among dispensational premillennialists. However, it faces a significant problem: if the beginning of the book applies to the first century, when does it suddenly start talking about events two thousand or more years later? There is no point in the text that indicates that a long period of time has elapsed—no clear jump between the past and the future.

Also, futurism would require us to take the book's emphasis that it describes what will happen "soon" in a very counterintuitive sense. Although such a sense is not *impossible* (see 2 Pet. 3:8), the starting point of our interpretation should be taking words in their natural sense, and that would point us toward preterism.

A futurist could pose a counter-argument and note that if most of Revelation deals with the beginning of Church history, but the end deals with events in our future, where is the indication that a long period of time elapses before the end of the book? In other words, where is the jump from past to future that we would expect?

The answer is in Revelation 20:1–6, where a long period of time—described as "a thousand years"—is discussed.

If the number is taken as a stock figure representing just a long period of time, then we see exactly what we would expect on a preterist interpretation: most of the book (1:1–19:21) deals with events early in Church history, then there is a long period of time (20:1–6) in which we are now living, and finally (20:7–22; 21), we come to events still in our future.

On this view, Revelation would principally be about the convulsions that happened at the beginning of Church history—the persecutions and martyrdoms of Christians that happened at that time (1:9, 6:9, 7:14, 17:6), and God's judgment on the persecutors (pagan Rome and/or Jerusalem). Eventually, however, Christianity will prevail, leading to a new, spiritual age in which the gospel will be preached and that will last for many centuries before the Second Coming and the end of the world.

We should point out that although preterism is the natural starting point for interpreting Revelation, this does not altogether exclude other views. Since prophecies can have multiple fulfillments, Revelation may primarily apply to the early Christian age but also have secondary fulfillments throughout Church history—including at the end of the world.

This would be similar to the way Daniel's "abomination of desolation"/"desolating sacrilege" (Dan. 9:27; 11:31; 12:11) could be fulfilled both in the time of the Maccabees (1 Macc. 1:54) and again in the generation that followed Jesus (Matt. 24:15).

The Catholic Church does not have a detailed set of teachings regarding precisely what will happen in our future and exactly how or when the end times prophesized in Scripture will be take place. It largely leaves the interpretation of biblical texts to individual scholars. There is thus no official teaching regarding how the book of Revelation is to be interpreted. Although many Catholic scholars advocate some form of preterism, the Church allows the book to be understood in historicist, idealist, or futurist senses—or as some combination of these.

128. What is the New Testament?

The New Testament is the collection of inspired books that are regarded as sacred and canonical by Christians.

Testament is another word for covenant—a type of solemn and binding agreement. Over the centuries, God has made a number of covenants, either with mankind as a whole, with a particular people, or with a particular individual.

Among the most famous is the one made through Israel's founding lawgiver, Moses. This covenant, which is described in the first five books of the Bible (Genesis, Exodus, Leviticus, Numbers, and Deuteronomy), became the basis of the Jewish faith and Israel's national life. The sacred books that were written as a result of this covenant are known as the books of the Old Testament.

However, the Old Testament prophet Jeremiah declared that one day God would institute a "new covenant" (Jer. 31:31), and Jesus announced the coming of this covenant on the night of his Passion. When he instituted the Eucharist, he declared, "This cup which is poured out for you is the New Covenant in my blood" (Luke 22:20). The New Covenant—which makes salvation possible for all mankind—was then put into effect when he shed his blood on the cross.

Consequently, the twenty-seven books of the New Testament are the ones that deal with Jesus and the covenant God made through him.

They were written in the first century, in the decades following the ministry of Jesus (c. A.D. 29–33), and they fall into four general categories:

- Four of the books are known as Gospels and are biographies of Jesus Christ and chronicles of his ministry.
- One—the book of Acts—is a history that continues the story of the early Church from the time of Jesus to about the year A.D. 60.
- Twenty-one books take the form of letters (also called *epistles*) that were written to groups and individuals.
- Finally, one—the book of Revelation—is a work of prophecy.

129. Who wrote the New Testament?

Some of the documents of the New Testament explicitly name their authors. This happens in most of the letters.

The reason is that, at the time, it was customary for letters to begin with an address that took the form "X to Y," where X was the sender and Y was the recipient. Thus the address of the letter of James reads, "James, a servant of God and of the Lord Jesus Christ, to the twelve tribes in the Dispersion" (James 1:1).

Almost all of the New Testament letters list their authors. Sometimes more than one author is indicated, as in 1 Thessalonians, which begins, "Paul, Silvanus, and Timothy, to the church of the Thessalonians" (1 Thess. 1:1). It is unusual for ancient letter writers to list coauthors, but Paul valued the contributions of his coworkers, like Silvanus and Timothy, and often lists them as coauthors.

At times the author of a letter was so well known to his readers that he didn't name himself explicitly. This is the case with 2 and 3 John, where the sender simply identifies himself as "the Elder" (2 John 1; 3 John 1). The same is true of Hebrews and 1 John, where the author assumes that the readers know who he is and so does not identify himself.

Based on the attributions given in the letters themselves, the principal authors were Paul, James, Peter, "the Elder," and Jude, along with Paul's coauthors, including Silvanus, Timothy, and Sosthenes.

The only other book of the New Testament that explicitly names its author is Revelation, which has the same kind of address as a letter (Rev. 1:4) and identifies the sender as "John."

The Gospels and Acts do not name their authors. The likely reason for this is that they are works of history, and they were being modeled on the Old Testament historical books, which also did not name their authors.

This does not mean that the original readers weren't expected to know who the authors were. Luke and Acts are addressed to an individual called Theophilus (Luke 1:3), who was likely the patron that underwrote the costs of producing these two books. Thus when the author says things like, "In the first book, O Theophilus, I have dealt with all that Jesus began to do and teach" (Acts 1:1), Theophilus knew who was writing.

Similarly, the Gospel of John reveals that it was written by an eyewitness we refer to today as "the beloved disciple" because the text describes him as "the disciple whom Jesus loved" (John 21:20; see John 21:24). The author also takes pains to debunk a rumor that he would not die before the Second Coming (John 21:21–23). He expects the original audience to know about this rumor and thus to know who he is.

Beyond the statements found in the New Testament documents themselves, we have evidence in the writings of the early Church Fathers, who add more information about who wrote them. Thus they state that the first three Gospels were written by the apostle Matthew, by Mark the companion of Peter, and by Luke the companion of Paul, who also wrote Acts.

In recent times, some skeptical scholars have doubted the accuracy of these attributions, as they have the attributions of some of the New Testament letters. However, the case for the traditional authors is strong.

The value of external testimony of this nature is not to be underestimated. Many ancient books did not name their authors. For purposes of comparison, Plato's most famous dialogue—*The Republic*—never mentions the name of its author. We know that it was written by Plato because of external testimony to this fact, and his authorship of the work is not doubted by scholars.

The authorship attributions of the Gospels are all very early and date to the first century. As the scholar Martin Hengel pointed out, as soon as the second Gospel was written, there was a need for them to be named so that they could be distinguished from one another, and the method that was chosen was to name them after their authors.[155]

The external testimony regarding the authors of the New Testament is very strong. There are only a few cases where the early Church Fathers had any doubt about who wrote particular books.

For example, there was some question about who wrote the books attributed to John—whether some of them were written by John the apostle or by another eyewitness of Jesus named John the Elder. Thus St. Jerome mentions that many held 2 and 3 John were written by John the Elder,[156] and Eusebius argues that it was the Elder rather than the apostle who wrote Revelation.[157] Some recent authors have also held that John the Elder had a role in writing the Gospel of John.[158]

Regardless of these questions, it is certain that the New Testament books were written by first-century figures who were either apostles (e.g., Matthew, Paul, Peter) or companions of the apostles (e.g., Mark, Luke, Timothy, John the Elder). They all count as among the group that Luke refers to as "eyewitnesses and ministers of the word" (Luke 1:2).

Ultimately, what is important is not the exact authorship of particular books. What counts is the fact that these books—like those of the Old Testament—are the inspired word of God (2 Tim. 3:16) and that they were received into the canon of Scripture by the Church under the guidance of the Holy Spirit (John 16:13). They are therefore authoritative for Christian faith.

130. What are the Gospels?

The four canonical Gospels are biographies of Jesus Christ. As Luke states, they record "all that Jesus began to do and teach" (Acts 1:1).

Naturally, they were written according to the literary conventions that were employed in the first century. Because they stand in the same overall tradition as the books of the Old Testament, they have some elements in common with its historical books. However, they closely approximate the Greek style of biography, which is known as a *bios* ("life").

They are called *Gospels* rather than *Lives* because of the message that Jesus came to proclaim—"the gospel." The Greek word for gospel (*euangelion*) originally meant "good news," and in the first century it was often used to characterize royal decrees, such as the decrees of Augustus Caesar.

When Jesus came preaching "the gospel of the kingdom" of God (Matt. 4:23), this was the true good news that mankind had been awaiting—that the God of all creation had sent his Son to usher in his kingdom and make salvation possible. The gospel was so central to the teaching of Jesus that his entire ministry reflected it, and so the biographies that were written about him came to be called Gospels.

Like other ancient biographies of public figures, the Gospels do not focus much on his childhood and youth. Instead, they focus on his public ministry, which began shortly after John the Baptist launched his own ministry "in the fifteenth year of Tiberius Caesar" (Luke 3:1) or A.D. 29.

They then describe the activities that characterized his ministry, including preaching and performing miracles, and they conclude by focusing on the events leading up to his death and resurrection. Many ancient biographies focus on the death of the person they are written about, particularly if the death is thought to be instructive or important. It thus was natural for the Gospel authors to focus on Jesus' death and resurrection, for it was by these events that he made salvation possible.

Why are there four Gospels rather than one? Part of the answer has to do with the way ancient books worked. At the time, they had to be hand copied, and they were fantastically expensive. A single copy of a Gospel would cost the ancient equivalent of thousands of dollars to produce (which is why Luke would need a patron like Theophilus).

Because of the cost, books had to be short—typically just one scroll in length. Consequently, no single Gospel could record all of the things Jesus said and did. Thus John states, "there are also many other things which Jesus did; were every one of them to be written, I suppose that the world itself could not contain the books that would be written" (John 21:25).

To preserve knowledge of different things Jesus did and taught, the four Evangelists each wrote a Gospel. Since each of these is a biography of the same figure, they contain some overlap (e.g., accounts of Jesus' death and resurrection). This is similar to how the historical books of the Old Testament frequently parallel each other (e.g., the events of 1 Samuel and 2 Kings are paralleled in 1–2 Chronicles) to provide a supplemental perspective on the same happenings.

Since the earliest centuries, scholars have noted that three of the Gospels—Matthew, Mark, and Luke—recount Jesus' life in very similar ways. They are therefore called *synoptic* Gospels, because they give a common view of his ministry (Greek: *sun*, "together"; *opsis*, "seeing").

The synoptic Gospels contain many passages that are almost word-for-word identical, and not just in the sayings of Jesus (which one might expect to be memorized). The narrative portions also are sometimes worded very similarly, which has led scholars from ancient times to speculate on how the three are related to each other.

An early proposal known as the *Augustinian Hypothesis*, because it was proposed by St. Augustine, is that Matthew wrote first, Mark abbreviated Matthew, and then Luke wrote third.

Today the most popular proposal is known as the *Two-Document Hypothesis*. It holds that Mark wrote first and that Matthew and Luke independently expanded upon Mark using a second, hypothetical source called Q (from *Quelle,* the German word for "source"). According to this view, Mark and Q were the two documents on which Matthew and Luke were principally based.

In recent years, additional proposals have begun to gain popularity. These include:

- the *Griesbach Hypothesis*, which holds that Matthew wrote first, Luke used Matthew, and then Mark fused material from both;
- the *Farrer Hypothesis*, which holds that Mark wrote first, Matthew expanded on Mark, and then Luke used both; and
- the *Wilke Hypothesis*, which holds that Mark wrote first, Luke expanded on Mark, and then Matthew used both.

The Church does not have a teaching of which of these solutions to the synoptic problem—or another one—is true. It leaves this matter for scholars to discuss.

131. What is the book of Acts?

Unlike the Gospels, Acts is not a biography but a history, written by the Evangelist Luke for the benefit of a certain Theophilus (Acts 1:1). It covers the period between the resurrection of Jesus (A.D. 33) and a two-year period of house arrest that Paul experienced in Rome (c. A.D. 58-60).

Acts is often dated to A.D. 75–90, but—as with the Gospels—there is reason to think it was written earlier. It is noteworthy that the narrative in Acts cuts off suddenly, with Paul still under house arrest. This strongly suggests that the book was written at the end of this two-year period.

In Acts, Luke has been building up to Paul's trial before Nero for many chapters (since at least 20:22–23), and the reader naturally expects him to relate what happened. Either outcome would suit his literary purpose: if Paul was condemned then Luke could use this as an inspiring example of suffering for the Faith, and if he was released then Luke could show this as a glorious vindication.

Later historical sources suggest that Paul was—indeed—vindicated at his first Roman trial (before Nero became hostile to Christians), but the fact that Luke does not tell the reader this and abruptly ends his narrative before its natural climax suggests that the trial had not yet happened.

Therefore, Acts was likely written two years into Paul's detention in Rome, around A.D. 60. Because the end of the Gospel of Luke shows signs of being written to set up the beginning of Acts, it was probably also written during the detention, around A.D. 59.

Luke's principal sources for Acts are easy to determine. The first twelve chapters of the book focus almost exclusively on Peter, and Luke likely got the information for this part of the book from him during Paul's house arrest in Rome. The rest of the book focuses on Paul, who was a source for much of that material. In addition, chapter 8 focuses on Philip the Evangelist, and he is the likely source of much of this information, as Luke later met him (Acts 21:8). Finally, Luke himself was an eyewitness source for the book, as illustrated by what are known as the *we passages* (Acts 16:10–17; 20:5–15; 21:1–18; 27:1–28). In these, Luke uses the first-person plural, saying things like, "we sought to go on to Macedonia" (16:10), indicating that he was present for these events.

The outline of the book of Acts is given when Jesus tells the disciples, "You shall be my witnesses in Jerusalem and in all Judea and Samaria and to the end of the earth" (Acts 1:8), and it then chronicles the expansion of the Gospel, beginning in Jerusalem on the day of Pentecost (Acts 2), spreading to Samaria (Acts 8), and then through the rest of the Mediterranean world, reaching as far as Rome (Acts 13–28).

A special focus of Acts is how the gospel spread to people from formerly excluded groups, including Samaritans (Acts 8:5–25), eunuchs (Acts 8:26–39), and Gentiles (Acts 10:1–11:18). Particularly noteworthy is the Jerusalem Council (Acts 15), which decreed that Gentiles did not need to be circumcised to be Christians.

Acts is an extraordinarily valuable source of information about early Church history, and our knowledge of this period would be incredibly impoverished if we did not have it. Among the many facts it relates is the origin of the name of our faith, stating that it was "in Antioch the disciples were for the first time called *Christians*" (Acts 11:26).

132. Who is St. Paul?

The apostle Paul is a major author of the New Testament documents, having composed most of the letters that it contains.

He was born in the city of Tarsus, in modern-day Turkey, but he was raised in Jerusalem, where he received a religious education in the tradition of the Pharisees from the scholar Gamaliel the Elder (Acts 22:3).

His father was a member of the tribe of Benjamin (Phil. 3:5) and a Roman citizen (Acts 22:28). This explains why Paul is known by two names. His Jewish name was Saul, a name that may have been popular among Benjaminites because of Israel's King Saul, who had come from that tribe. However, his Roman name was Paulus. It is likely that Paul's father or grandfather became a Roman citizen in Tarsus in the first century B.C.

We know little of the rest of Paul's family, though we do know that he had a sister and a nephew living in Jerusalem (Acts 23:16).

By profession, Paul was a tentmaker (Acts 18:3), and he used this trade to support his apostolic work so that he did not need to be a financial burden to the churches he founded (1 Cor. 9:1, 4, 6; Thess. 2:9; 2 Thess. 3:8).

Paul was not an eyewitness of Jesus' ministry, and initially he was quite hostile to the early Christian movement. As a young man, he was present at and consented to the martyrdom of St. Stephen around A.D. 36 (Acts 7:58; 8:1). He then took a leading role in persecuting the church in Jerusalem "and entering house after house, he dragged off men and women and committed them to prison" (Acts 8:2).

He then secured letters from the high priest to the synagogues of Damascus, Syria, allowing him to arrest Christians there and bring them to Jerusalem (Acts 9:1–2). However, on the road to Damascus, Jesus appeared to him (Acts 9:3–6), blinding him for three days (Acts 9:8–9, 17–19).

After his conversion, Jesus sent Paul to the Jewish people and the Gentiles to preach the message of salvation to them (Acts 26:17–18). Because he had been commissioned directly by Christ (Gal. 1:1; 1 Cor. 9:1), Paul is counted an "apostle" even though being an eyewitness of Jesus' ministry like the Twelve.

Initially, Paul preached the message of Jesus in Damascus and Jerusalem (Acts 9:19–22, 26–28) before Barnabas brought him to Antioch, Syria, which became his home base for evangelization (Acts 11:25).

As the companion of Barnabas, Paul embarked on what is known as the *First Missionary Journey* (Acts 13–14)—a major evangelistic mission to the island of Cyprus and the mainland of modern Turkey that took place around A.D. 43–49. He was then present at the Council of Jerusalem (Acts 15).

After dissolving his partnership with Barnabas over a dispute about Mark, Paul embarked on the *Second Missionary Journey* (Acts 15:40–18:22), in which he traveled through modern Turkey, Macedonia, and Greece around A.D. 49–51.

After a brief return to Antioch, he then conducted the *Third Missionary Journey* (Acts 18:23–21:17) around A.D. 51–55. He returned from this trip bearing a gift for the poor of the church in Jerusalem (Acts 24:17). He did so having been warned ahead of time that he faced persecution and arrest there (Acts 21:10–14), and he was indeed arrested (Acts 21:27–36).

He then spent two years in detention by the Roman governor Felix, before the new governor—Porcius Festus—arrived around A.D. 57 (Acts 24:27). Paul then used his Roman citizenship to have his case transferred to Rome so that it could be personally judged by Nero (Acts 25:7–12).

Paul was thus sent to Rome, where he spent two years under house arrest, awaiting trial (Acts 28:30). It is at this point, around A.D. 60, that the narrative of Acts ends, without revealing the outcome of the trial. However, we have evidence from later sources indicating that Paul was released and was able to fulfill his desire to go as far as Spain to preach the gospel (Rom. 15:24, 28; see 1 Clement 5:7a).

The great fire of Rome in A.D. 64 caused Nero's attitude toward Christians to turn hostile, and he used them as public scapegoats for the fire.[159] Consequently, when Paul was arrested again, he was put to death at Rome under Nero's officials.[160] This occurred around A.D. 67.

Although Paul did make Jewish converts, his preaching bore special fruit among the Gentiles (Gal. 2:8; Eph. 3:8), and today he is known as the "apostle to the Gentiles."

133. What are the Pauline epistles?

During the course of his ministry Paul wrote numerous letters. Some of these are lost (see 1 Cor. 5:9; 2 Cor. 2:3–9; 7:8–12; Col. 4:16), but letters that he wrote to seven churches have been preserved in the New Testament.

1) *Romans* was written in late A.D. 54 or early 55, while Paul was staying at Corinth at the end of the Third Missionary Journey, as he was preparing to return with a gift for the church in Jerusalem. At this point, Paul had never visited Rome, but he hoped to travel there on his way to Spain (Rom. 15:24, 26).

Despite his lack of personal connection with the Roman Christians, he wrote to combat the idea that one must be circumcised and become a Jew in order to be saved—an idea that was still present in many circles, despite it having been rejected by the Jerusalem Council (Acts 15).

He devotes a great deal of his letter to the subject of how both Jews and Gentiles are justified through their faith in Christ and not by works of the Mosaic Law (Rom. 3:28–30). He also provides an extended discussion of divine Providence and the role of Israel and the Gentiles in God's plan (chaps. 9—11).

2) *First Corinthians* was written while Paul was in Ephesus during the Third Missionary Journey, around A.D. 53. He wrote it after receiving a report from Corinth that the church there was being plagued by factions, based on which religious leaders they admired. The first part of the letter is thus devoted to combating factionalism.

Paul also responded to several questions that the Corinthians had sent him in a letter, dealing with topics such as marriage and sexual relations, eating food that had been offered to idols, spiritual gifts such as speaking in tongues, and the collection he was taking up for the poor in Jerusalem. He also combated the idea, which some Corinthians were entertaining, that the dead would not be raised at the end of time.

3) *Second Corinthians* was written while Paul was in Macedonia, toward the end of the Third Missionary Journey, placing it in late A.D. 54 or early 55. He wrote it in response to problems that had developed between him and some at Corinth. Not everyone there was devoted to Paul (1 Cor. 1:12), and after he sent the previous letter, matters with his opponents reached a crisis point.

He therefore wrote them a letter "out of much affliction and anguish of heart and with many tears" (2 Cor. 2:4) that he "might test you and know whether you are obedient in everything" (2 Cor. 2:9). He was therefore relieved when his coworker Titus arrived with news that the Corinthians had reaffirmed their love for him (2 Cor. 7:6–7).

Despite this, word apparently reached Paul while he was preparing 2 Corinthians that some still scorned him, and he undertook a heated and extended defense of his apostolic ministry (2 Cor. 10:1–13:11).

4) *Galatians* was written shortly after the Jerusalem Council, which it discusses (Gal. 2:1–10). It likely was composed around A.D. 50, though a date around 53 also is possible.

Paul wrote because the idea that one must be circumcised as a Jew to be saved had begun to take root in churches he had founded in the province of Galatia (Acts 16:6). Paul insists that this idea is contrary to the true gospel, telling the Galatians that "even if we, or an angel from heaven, should preach to you a gospel contrary to that which we preached to you, let him be accursed" (Gal. 1:8).

5) *Ephesians* is something of a puzzle. Although some manuscripts list the letter as being addressed "to the saints who are at Ephesus" (Eph. 1:1), others lack the words "at Ephesus." The contents of the letter do not reflect the intimate familiarity Paul had with the Ephesian Christians, whose church he founded and among whom he had spent three years (Acts 18:19–21; 20:31). Consequently, many have proposed that this letter was originally a circular letter intended to be read in many churches, not all of which Paul had visited. One copy may have been sent to Ephesus, but it was written without presupposing that the readers knew him.

It is clear that Paul was in prison at the time he wrote (Eph. 3:1). It is thus known as one of his *prison letters*, and various factors point to it being composed during Paul's first Roman imprisonment, around A.D. 59 or 60. As a circular letter, Ephesians reflects on spiritual themes such as the Father's eternal plan of salvation in his Son (Eph. 1:3-14), the salvation of Jews and Gentiles through faith in Christ (Eph. 2:4–22), and the concord to which Christians are called within the believing community and within families.

6) *Philippians* is another prison letter (Phil. 1:17), and it also was likely written during Paul's first Roman imprisonment (see Phil. 1:13). Paul had founded the church at Philippi (Acts 16:12–40), and they had helped him financially in his ministry to other churches (Phil. 4:15–16). He is grateful for additional support they have sent him during his imprisonment (Phil. 4:18).

The letter is famous for preserving a first-century hymn to Christ (Phil. 2:6–11). As in other letters, Paul warns against the idea that one needs to be circumcised to be saved, using himself as an example of hope in Christ (Phil. 3:2–14).

7) *Colossians* was written at the same time as Ephesians, and was delivered by the same courier, a man named Tychicus (Eph. 6:21-22; Col. 4:7-8). It was sent to the church at Colossae, which Paul had not visited (Col. 2:1), and it shares many of the same themes as Ephesians. One of them is a warning against the idea they need to embrace Jewish practices such as circumcision, eating a kosher diet, or observing Jewish feast days (Col. 2:11–23).

8) *First Thessalonians* may be the first of Paul's surviving letters. It was written around A.D. 50, just a few months after he had founded the church of Thessalonica (Acts 17:1–10). He had been forced to flee this city after only three weeks because of anti-Christian violence, and he was naturally concerned about whether his new converts would remain faithful. He therefore sent Timothy to visit the church and was overjoyed when his protégé returned with the news that the Thessalonians remained faithful (1 Thess. 3:6–10).

In addition to his standard exhortations to living a moral life in Christ, including an exhortation not to be idle (1 Thess. 5:13), Paul also gives the Thessalonians supplemental instruction on the fate of the dead and the end of the world (1 Thess. 4:13–5:11).

9) *Second Thessalonians* was written shortly after its predecessor, likely later in A.D. 50. The principal reason was to encourage the new converts in their faith and to correct confusion about the end of the world. Apparently, some thought Paul had indicated that the return of Christ was so close that it had already begun or already happened. He thus tells them that the end will not come before certain signs are fulfilled (2 Thess. 2:1–15).

134. What are the pastoral epistles?

In addition to the letters Paul wrote to local churches, the New Testament also reserves four letters addressed to individuals. Three of these are known as the *pastoral epistles* because they are written to Paul's protégés Timothy and Titus, and he gives them instructions on how to conduct their ministry as pastors.

The final letter is written to an individual named Philemon, who may well have been a pastor because a church met in his house (Philem. chap. 1–2). However, Paul gives him no instructions concerning pastoral ministry. It is thus not classed as a pastoral epistle.

1) *First Timothy* appears to have been written around A.D. 65, after Paul's first Roman imprisonment had ended. Paul had urged Timothy to remain in Ephesus and instruct certain people not to teach false doctrines (1 Tim. 1:3–8). He also gives him instructions concerning appointing bishops and deacons (1 Tim. 3:1–13) and the proper behavior of various groups in the Church, including consecrated widows (1 Tim. 5:3–16).

2) *Second Timothy* likely was written in A.D. 66, the year before Paul's martyrdom. He had already been arrested (2 Tim. 1:8) and taken to Rome a second time (2 Tim. 1:17), and he senses that the date of his death is approaching, writing, "I am already on the point of being sacrificed; the time of my departure has come. I have fought the good fight, I have finished the race, I have kept the Faith. Henceforth there is laid up for me the crown of righteousness, which the Lord, the righteous judge, will award to me on that Day" (2 Tim. 4:6–8).

Paul is almost alone in his imprisonment, with only Luke available to him (2 Tim. 4:10–12). He urges Timothy to come before the travel season closes in winter (2 Tim. 4:21) and to bring certain personal possessions so that he may make use of them in the time he has left (2 Tim. 4:13).

3) *Titus* appears to have been written about the same time as 1 Timothy, around A.D. 65. The letter reveals that Paul has left his coworker Titus on the island of Crete, telling him to "amend what was defective, and to appoint elders in every town" (Titus 1:5). He thus reviews the qualifications for the office of elder, which at this time overlapped with the office of bishop (Titus 1:6–9).

Paul tells Titus to offer instruction on Christian living to members of the churches of Crete (Titus 2:1–15), including the proper attitude toward secular rulers and other non-Christians (Titus 3:1–2).

4) *Philemon* is unique among Paul's letters in several respects. It is much shorter than any of the others, which actually makes it a normal size for an ancient letter. It also deals with a very private matter. This letter sent at the same time as Colossians (Col. 4:7–9 with Philem. 10) to a man named Philemon who hosted a church in his house in Colossae. It is thus a private letter accompanying the public letter to the Colossians.

Paul writes that he was found during his imprisonment by Onesimus, a runaway slave of Philemon's, whom Paul has now converted to the Faith. The letter is meant to encourage the master and slave to reconcile as brothers in Christ. Many scholars have understood Paul to be appealing for Philemon to emancipate Onesimus. One way or another, the book testifies to God's compassion for those experiencing slavery.

135. What is the epistle to the Hebrews?

In canonical order, Hebrews is placed after the pastoral epistles and before the Catholic epistles. It does not begin as a letter, as it does not open with a reference to a sender, recipients, or a greeting. Instead, it immediately begins discussing its subject matter.

However, it does have letter-like characteristics. It has a postscript of the sort we would expect in a letter, and the author asks the readers to heed the "word of exhortation" that "I have written to you" (Heb. 13:22). He relates news concerning Timothy, says he hopes to visit the recipients, and conveys greetings (Heb. 13:23–25). Hebrews thus may be considered a letter, though some have proposed alternatives, such as it being a homily or theological treatise that was then used as a letter after the postscript was supplied.

Through much of Church history, Paul was regarded as the author of Hebrews, though there was doubt about this early on. For example, Jerome notes that Pope St. Zephyrinus (A.D. 119–217) denied that it was by Paul.[161] TTertullian held that it was written by Barnabas,[162] and Origen preserved reports that it was written by Luke or Pope St. Clement I, though he concludes, "But who wrote the epistle, in truth, God knows."[163]

The author was Jewish and writing to a predominately Jewish audience, writing that "God spoke of old to our fathers by the prophets" (Heb. 1:1). He has a position of teaching authority (note the way he addresses the audience in Hebrews 5:11–14), and he was a second-generation Christian, not an eyewitness of Jesus, for he spoke of how salvation "was declared at first by the Lord, and it was attested to us by those who heard him" (Heb. 2:3).

Modern scholars generally think it unlikely Paul would have written in this way, as he stresses that he received the gospel by revelation, as a result of his encounter with Jesus (Gal. 1:11–12).

The letter was written either to or from Italy, as it contains greetings from Italian Christians (Heb. 13:24), and it speaks as if the Jewish priests in Jerusalem are still offering sacrifice in the temple (Heb. 8:4), which would put the composition before A.D. 70. It may have been written after the Jewish War began in A.D. 66 because it refers to the Old Covenant as being "ready to vanish away" (Heb. 8:13), in fulfillment of Jesus' prophecy of the temple's destruction (Mark 13:1–2). It likely was written around A.D. 68.

The chief subject of Hebrews is Jesus Christ, and the letter opens with an extensive discussion of how—as God's Son—Jesus is superior to all angels (Heb. 1:4–14), to Moses (Heb. 3:1–6), and to the Jewish high priests (Heb. 4:14–5:10). There are also multiple exhortations to the readers to persevere and not to fall away (Heb. 2:1; 3:6–4:13; etc.), which in context would mean abandoning the Christian faith and resuming the practice of non-Christian Judaism. This is also a sign that the book was written before A.D. 70, because if the temple had been destroyed, it would have been mentioned as clinching proof of the author's entire line of argument.

136. What are the catholic epistles?

The final seven letters in the New Testament are called *catholic* (Greek: *katholikê*, "general, universal") because none of them is addressed to an individual church. They were already grouped together in this way by the early fourth century, when Eusebius writes of them by this name.

1) The letter of *James* is attributed to "James, a servant of God and of the Lord Jesus Christ" (James 1:1). Tradition knows him as James the Just, the first bishop of Jerusalem. St. Jerome identified him as being the same James known as "the brother of the Lord" (Gal. 1:19) and as James the Less, son of Alphaeus, one of the Twelve.[164] The letter is addressed to "the twelve tribes in the Dispersion" (James 1:1), indicating a wide audience of Jewish Christians in the many nations to which they had been scattered (see Acts 26:7).

James the Just was martyred in A.D. 62[165] indicating that the letter was written before this year. The content of the letter suggests that it was written quite early, though likely after early reports of Paul's First Missionary Journey to the Gentiles had begun to be received at Jerusalem (c. A.D. 48), as indicated by its discussion of justification by faith in relationship to works

(James 2:14–26). This points to a composition around A.D. 48, though a later date is not impossible.

The letter focuses primarily on ethical teaching, and it echoes many points discussed in the Gospels, particularly in Matthew's Sermon on the Mount (Matt. 5–7).

2) *First Peter* is addressed to "the exiles of the Dispersion in Pontus, Galatia, Cappadocia, Asia, and Bithynia" (1 Pet. 1:1)—all parts of modern Turkey. The reference to "the exiles of the Dispersion" could be taken as a reference to Jewish Christians, but there are indications that Peter actually has Gentiles in mind (1 Pet. 1:18; 2:10; 3:6; 4:3–4). It was likely written not long before 2 Peter, perhaps around A.D. 62–63.

The letter was written from Rome ("Babylon"; 1 Pet. 5:13), and its purpose was to exhort Christians to live lives of faith and obedience, particularly in light of the hostility they faced from others.

3) *Second Peter* does not identify where its audience lived, but it refers to itself as "the second letter I have written you," indicating the same audience as 1 Peter. It is also therefore later than 1 Peter, and since Peter says that he knows his death will be soon (2 Pet. 1:12–15), it was likely written around A.D. 64–65, shortly before his martyrdom in A.D. 65 or 66.

The purpose of the letter was to exhort Christians to remain faithful, to lead moral lives, to await the coming of the Lord, and to avoid false teachers, including those who were perverting the writings of St. Paul (2 Pet. 3:15–17).

4) *First John* is similar to Hebrews in that it lacks standard features of a letter (sender, recipients, greeting), making it read more like a homily. The lack of letter-like features may mean it was meant for several congregations rather than a specific one.

It shows notable similarities to the Gospel of John. Not only is the style similar, but it shares many of the same themes (being born of God, the new commandment of love, light and darkness, etc.), and the opening of the letter (1 John 1:1–7) is strongly reminiscent of the opening of the Gospel (John 1:1–9). External tradition consequently attributes it to the same author as the Gospel (i.e., John).

The letter does not contain many concrete clues about when it was written, and scholars generally date it to the same period as the other literature attributed to John, either the A.D. 90s or in the A.D. 60s.

The purpose of the letter is pastoral, and John exhorts his readers to live as Christians should and to avoid certain false teachers who have withdrawn from the community (1 John 2:18–23).

5) *Second John* is only a single chapter long, making it one of the few New Testament epistles that was of normal length for an ancient letter (the others are Philemon, 3 John, and Jude). It is written by "the Elder," whom external tradition identifies as John, though there is a question whether it is John, son of Zebedee, or John the Elder.

He is writing to "the elect lady and her children." In keeping with the early practice of personifying churches as women (see 1 Pet. 5:13), scholars have understood this to be a reference to a local church and its members.

Like 1 John, 2 John does not contain concrete indications of when it was written, and scholars generally date it to the same period as the other works they attributed to John.

The Elder encourages the readers to love one another and to be on guard against "men who will not acknowledge the coming of Jesus Christ in the flesh; such a one is the deceiver and the Antichrist" (v. 7).

6) *Third John* is the shortest book of the New Testament, being just 218 words in Greek. It is from the Elder to a man named Gaius. The Elder commends him for his service to fellow Christians, including traveling missionaries (vv. 5–8). He also warns Gaius against a community leader named Diotrephes, who was critical of the Elder and refused to welcome others from the Elder's circle (vv. 9–10).

This letter may be a companion to 2 John, since the Elder says he has "written something to the church" (v. 9). If so, it would be dated to the same period.

7) The letter of *Jude* is only a single chapter long. Its sender is "Jude, a servant of Jesus Christ and brother of James." The use of the name James, without qualification, points to the most famous James at the time—that is, James the Just. This makes the author likely one of the "brethren of the Lord" (see Mark 6:3), and has traditionally associated him with Jude "of James," one of the Twelve.

Jude and 2 Peter have a great deal of overlap (see especially Jude 1:6–13 with 2 Peter 2:4–17). The parallels are so close that one must be borrowing from the other, or there must be a common source behind the two. Without a sure way of resolving this matter, we date Jude to approximately the same time as 2 Peter—that is, around A.D. 64–65—though it could have been earlier or later.

The letter was written for a very specific purpose: to warn against false teachers and their immoral lifestyle, and Jude uses many colorful illustrations in his critique of them.

Depending on whether or not the authorship of the letters of James, John, and Jude can be traced to the apostles bearing those names (along with those written by Peter), the four "Catholic" epistles may have originally been grouped together under that title on account of representing the apostolic exhortations of the Twelve.

137. What is the book of Revelation?

The book of Revelation is a book of prophecy. Its purpose is "to show to [Christ's] servants what must soon take place; and he made it known by sending his angel to his servant John" (Rev. 1:1). It is intended to encourage them to hold fast to their Christian faith in the face of persecution and the traumatic events that were soon to come.

Most have understood the John in question to be John, son of Zebedee, though some in the early Church, and some recent scholars, have understood it to be John the Elder.

Revelation is addressed to "the seven churches that are in Asia" (Rev. 1:4)—that is, Ephesus, Smyrna, Pergamum, Thyatira, Sardis, Philadelphia, and Laodicea (Rev. 1:11). There were actually more churches in the Roman province of Asia Minor at the time (e.g., the church of the Colossians), and these seven are likely selected because John was personally familiar with them and the number seven is a biblical symbol for completeness.

The book was written while John was in exile on the island of Patmos (Rev. 1:9), and although many have dated the book to the A.D. 90s, there is evidence it was written earlier. It speaks as if the Jerusalem temple is still operating (Rev. 11:1–2), and the most precise clue as to its dating may be its interpretation of the seven heads of the beast John sees: "The seven heads are seven mountains on which the woman is seated; they are also seven kings, five of whom have fallen, one is, the other has not yet come, and when he comes he must remain only a little while" (Rev. 17:9–10).

The seven mountains have been identified since ancient times as the seven hills of Rome, and the seven kings involve a reference to the Roman emperors. Note that—like the Roman emperors—the beast blasphemes God, persecutes the saints, rules the world, and receives worship from all but Christians (Rev. 13:6–8).

If the seven heads are the line of first-century Roman emperors, then the five who "have fallen" would be Augustus, Tiberius, Caligula, Claudius, and Nero. The one who "is" would be Nero's successor, Galba, and the other who "has not yet come" would be Otho, who did—indeed—reign "only a little while" (three months). This would place the composition of Revelation during the reign of Galba (A.D. June 9, 68–January 15, 69).

Revelation draws heavily from Old Testament imagery, and it is not possible to correctly interpret the book without a thorough understanding of the symbols on which it draws. This has contributed to the widely divergent interpretations of the book.

138. How did the New Testament canon develop?

The books of the Old Testament were written during a period of around a thousand years. By contrast, the books of the New Testament were written in less than a century. This did not mean that they were all instantly recognized as canonical. It took some time for the Holy Spirit to guide the Church into a definitive recognition of what belonged in the canon.

The process of canonization began as the authors of the New Testament began composing their books and handing them on to the Christian community as reliable and authoritative guides to the Faith.

For many years, it was the fashion among scholars to envision each author producing only a single copy of each work and sharing it with only a single community, for whom he had tailored it specifically. This applied not only to letters to churches but also to works like the Gospels, which were assumed to be written for single churches.

The idea was that, over time, the churches in different communities began making additional copies of the New Testament documents, sharing them with each other; and gradually the whole body of New Testament documents was gathered together, somewhat like a snowball increasing in size.

Such "snowball" theories have come under increasing criticism in recent years, with some scholars arguing that the New Testament documents were aimed at much broader audiences. In particular, it is argued that the Gospels were not written for individual churches but were meant to be shared broadly among Christians.[166] Even Luke, which is addressed to Theophilus, was unlikely to be meant solely for him to read. Instead, Theophilus was likely the patron who paid for multiple copies of Luke to be distributed in the churches. The same is true of Acts.

What about Paul's letters? In the case of other published collections of letters from the ancient world (Cicero's being a famous one), recent studies dismiss the idea of haphazard assembly as people gradually collected single copies that had been sent out.

Instead, the first edition of an author's letters was usually produced by the author himself from copies he had retained in his archive. He determined which letters would be published and the principle by which they would be organized (e.g., by date, topic, or length). After his death, his literary executors might produce expanded editions, which followed the same organizing principle the author had established.[167]

There are clues indicating that this happened in the case of Paul's letters as well. They are organized by length, beginning with the largest—Romans—and then growing smaller as we proceed toward 2 Thessalonians. However, there is a hiccup in this pattern: Ephesians is somewhat longer than Galatians, and it may represent the beginning of an expanded edition compiled at a later date. The first edition of Paul's letters then would have been Romans (A.D. 54), 1–2 Corinthians (A.D. 53-54), and Galatians (A.D. 50).

The first edition of Paul's letters was likely prepared by the apostle himself—just like other famous writers of the period. An expanded collection including Ephesians through 2 Thessalonians and his letters to individuals (1–2 Timothy, Titus, and Philemon) would have been issued at some later date, perhaps after his death.

A guiding principle in the collection of the New Testament letters may have been the number seven, which represented completeness. Like the book of Revelation, Paul's letter collection is addressed to churches in seven locations (Rome, Corinth, Galatia, Ephesus, Philippi, Colossae, and Thessalonica), and if Hebrews is grouped with the Pauline letters, there are fourteen in total. Similarly, there are seven Catholic epistles. The desire to produce collections based on the number seven could explain why the short letters (Philemon, 2–3 John, Jude) were included.

Although we have evidence that the core of the New Testament came together quickly, not every question was settled at once, and it had fuzzy boundaries for some time. Thus, some early writers expressed doubt about the canonicity of some works, such as Hebrews, 2 Peter, 2–3 John, Jude, and Revelation.

On the other hand, some early writers considered books to be scriptural that were not ultimately included in the New Testament. Clement of Rome was an associate of the apostles, and some in the early Church considered *1 Clement* to be canonical. Others regarded the work of first-century prophecy known as *The Shepherd of Hermas* to be Scripture. Another early work that some considered canonical was the letter of pseudo-Barnabas.

The second century saw a proliferation of allegedly scriptural works, such as the *Gospel of Thomas*, the mutilated edition of the New Testament produced by the heretic Marcion, and the apocryphal gospels written to support the emerging Gnostic movement. However, these were quickly dismissed as they had not been handed down from the time of the apostles, and they disagreed with apostolic teaching (see St. Irenaeus of Lyons's *Against Heresies*).

The New Testament continued to have a solid core but fuzzy boundaries into the early 300s. Eusebius of Caesarea summarized the state of opinion in his day.[168] He divided the books into several categories:

Undisputed books:

- The Gospels of Matthew, Mark, Luke, and John
- Acts of the Apostles
- The letters of Paul
- 1 John
- 1 Peter

Disputed books:

- Letter to the Hebrews
- James
- 2 Peter
- 2–3 John
- Jude
- Revelation of John
- Shepherd of Hermas
- Gospel of the Hebrews

Rejected books:

- Revelation of Peter
- Pseudo-Barnabas
- The Didache
- Gospels of Peter, Thomas, and Matthias
- Acts of Paul, Andrew, and John

The situation was soon clarified, and a series of local councils in North Africa in the late 300s and early 400s endorsed the New Testament as we have it today. Later, the ecumenical Council of Florence (1438–1445) authoritatively taught on which books should be included in the Bible, and the Council of Trent (1545–1563) reaffirmed its teaching infallibly.

The reason Trent needed to rule infallibly was that the Protestant Reformers, beginning with Martin Luther, had objected to certain Catholic teachings that were supported in the deuterocanonical books of the Old Testament and in certain New Testament books. In particular, Luther rejected or questioned the canonicity of Hebrews, James, Jude, and Revelation.

Fortunately, later Protestants have recognized the canonicity of these works, and today there is virtual agreement among Christians on the content of the New Testament canon.

139. How do we know that the text of the New Testament is accurate?

Some people question the validity of the New Testament because they are very old, and because we don't have any of the original manuscripts but only copies of them. This is true, but irrelevant, because there are practically no original copies of *any* ancient manuscript of any kind. For example, the hundreds of copies of Plato, Aristotle, and Thucydides (considered the ancient world's most reliable historian) that we possess were written over a thousand years after their originals, yet hardly anyone doubts that the texts we now possess correspond to what those authors originally wrote. In fact, we only have one manuscript copy of the first six chapters of Tacitus's *Annals*, our main primary source about Roman history, and it was written nearly seven hundred years after the original copy.

But perhaps serious errors were introduced into the text of the New Testament by early scribes? Could some even have been introduced deliberately?

Several factors make this hypothesis impossible. The first is the fact that the books of the New Testament were (and are) considered sacred. The task of copying them was thus considered an act glorifying God. Scribes took great pains not to make mistakes when copying the texts entrusted to them and to quickly fix mistakes if they did, knowing that the texts they produced so laboriously would be revered and protected for centuries. In the sixth century, the monk Cassiodorus, who was a contemporary of St. Benedict, said, "What happy application, what praiseworthy industry, to preach unto men by means of the hand, to untie the tongue by means of the fingers, to bring quiet salvation to mortals, and to fight the devil's insidious wiles with pen and ink!"[169]

No scribe would undertake such a task with a levity of spirit. In fact, because Christianity was illegal within the Roman Empire until the edict of Constantine in A.D. 313, Christians who copied the New Testament were risking painful deaths just so others could have a copy of Scripture.

Another major factor protecting the integrity of the manuscripts was the enormous number of copies that were made. There currently exist over 5,500 complete or partial copies of New Testament manuscripts written in Greek, as well as 15,000 manuscripts written in other languages, including Latin, Coptic, and Syriac. Fifty of the Greek manuscripts can be dated to within 250 years of the original copies. The first complete copy of the New Testament, called *Codex Sinaiticus* (because it was discovered in a monastery at the foot of Mount Sinai), can be dated to within 300 years of the original documents.

Modern scholars have recovered these ancient manuscripts from places like monastery libraries and archaeological sites—especially in Egypt where the dry, desert conditions help preserve buried writing materials. Many of them date to very early times—the A.D. 200s and 300s—and some even earlier. For example, we have part of the Gospel of John—in a manuscript known as the *Rylands Papyrus* or *P52*—dating to around A.D. 140, just a few decades after this Gospel was written.

At the time these copies were made, the original New Testament books—known as the *autographs*—were still in circulation. Recent studies of the Dead Sea Scrolls and ancient library practices have revealed that individual copies of books remained in use for up to 500 years, though 150 years was more common.[170]

This means that original New Testament manuscripts would have remained in use in the second and third centuries and able to influence copies made in this period, such as the Rylands Papyrus. In fact, the early Church Father St. Peter of Alexandria (died c. A.D. 311) mentions that in his day, the original copy of the Gospel of John "written by the hand of the Evangelist" was still "preserved in the most holy church of Ephesus, and is there adored by the faithful" (Fragment 5:1:7).

This is an abundance of evidence compared to what we have for other works of ancient literature. For example, consider Julius Caesar's popular autobiographical work *The Gallic Wars*, which was written about 50 B.C. We have only around 260 manuscripts of it, ten of which are in good condition, and the earliest of which dates 900 years after the original was written. Or Homer's *Iliad*, which was written in the eighth century B.C. Although a few fragments of the *Iliad* can be dated to within 500 years of Homer, the oldest complete copy of the *Iliad* (a manuscript scholars refer to as Venetus A) was written in the tenth century A.D., that is, 1,800 years later! Biblical scholar F.F. Bruce put it bluntly: "There is no body of ancient literature in the world which enjoys such a wealth of good textual attestation as the New Testament."[171]

Along with faithful scribes, we also have the testimony of faithful Church Fathers, who glorified God by teaching and commenting on the Bible. Even though the Bible manuscripts they consulted no longer exist, they have survived through quotations in the Fathers' commentaries on Scripture. Even Bart Ehrman, a critic who often claims that the Bible has been hopelessly corrupted, admitted that this is a resource for textual critics: "so extensive are these citations that if all other sources for our knowledge of the text of the New Testament were destroyed, they would be sufficient alone for the reconstruction of practically the entire New Testament."[172]

Of course, scribes did make mistakes, but they were minor, and today scholars have a wealth of material they can use to establish what the original text of the New Testament was. A special science—known as *textual criticism*—has even developed to allow scholars to do this. And, although there are passages whose exact wording is debated, scholars are not in doubt that the texts we have are fundamentally accurate. There are too many independent and converging lines of evidence supporting it.

This also reveals how impossible it would have been for anyone to deliberately introduce false readings or suppress passages in the service of a theological agenda. Even if someone wanted to, copies of the New Testament books were in too many hands.

If a heretical group wanted to alter a passage they objected to, they would never be able to go through the entire Christian world and get their coreligionists to take it out or alter it. Too many would refuse to do so, and it would have caused a huge theological dispute that we would have a record of. St. Augustine once told St. Jerome that the people of Tripoli rioted in the streets because Jerome's new translation of the book of Jonah was so unfamiliar to them.[173] Imagine what these people would do if a completely new story about Christ were presented to them!

In addition, no one would have been able to change all the manuscripts that modern scholars have discovered but that at the time lay forgotten in monastery libraries or in archaeological sites. The evidence we possess provides no basis for challenging the fundamental reliability of the New Testament text.

140. What is a Gospel?

In the simplest terms, a *Gospel* is an ancient Christian book about Jesus. When people refer to "the Gospels," they're typically referring to the four canonical ones. However, there also are non-canonical gospels that are not included in the New Testament.

The Greek term for *gospel* (*euangelion*) means "good news," and it could be used in a variety of senses. Naturally, it could refer to hearing about any good thing that had happened. However, it often was used to refer to announcements by or about the Roman emperor.

The emperor often was regarded as the son of a god, and his person represented the peace and security of the empire. Whatever he announced purported to be good news for the people, and was declared as such (whether it really was or not).

It thus was natural for Christians to announce the coming of the true Son of God and his kingdom as good news, and so St. Mark begins his book with these words: "The beginning of the gospel of Jesus Christ, the Son of God." It is probably from this verse that the book of Mark came to be known as a "Gospel," and from there the term spread to other canonical and non-canonical works.

Because the canonical ones are known as Gospels (Greek: *Euangelia*), their authors are known as the four Evangelists—with a capital *E*, to distinguish them from ordinary evangelists, who share the message of Jesus generally.

When it comes to the *kind* of books the canonical Gospels are, they are essentially biographies. That is, they tell us about the life and teachings of Jesus of Nazareth.

Biographies were common in the ancient world. The Greek term for a biography is *bios* ("life"), and many ancient authors wrote *bioi*—or lives—of important men, including emperors, kings, statesmen, generals, and philosophers. Some of the most famous include Plutarch's *Parallel Lives* and Suetonius's *Lives of the Twelve Caesars*.

There are differences between modern biographies and ancient lives. Today, authors may write biographies about people just because they've had interesting lives. Ancient biographies, however, had an instructional purpose. Readers were meant to learn *lessons* from the lives of the people they read about.

Thus, in his *Parallel Lives*, Plutarch wrote about two noble figures—a Greek in parallel with a Roman—so that his readers could learn what made the men great and what they might want to imitate. Similarly, in *Lives of the Twelve Caesars*, Suetonius discusses both the good things and the bad things the first twelve Roman emperors did—partly so that people would know what good rulers should *and should not* do.

The four Gospels share this instructional quality, and we are meant to take away important lessons for our lives. John states, "Now Jesus did many other signs in the presence of the disciples, which are not written in this book; but these are written that you may believe that Jesus is the Christ, the Son of God, and that believing you may have life in his name" (20:30–31).

Similarly, in Matthew, Jesus says, "Everyone then who hears these words of mine and does them will be like a wise man who built his house upon the rock" (7:24).

Sometimes people wonder whether the Gospels were meant for Christian audiences or whether they were evangelistic documents meant to convince people to become Christian. The answer is the former, and the reason is the cost involved in producing copies of the Gospels.

Today, individual Gospels and even entire New Testaments can be mass-produced cheaply and given away for free, making them usable as evangelistic tools. But before the printing press, every word had to be handwritten by a scribe, and every sheet of papyrus or parchment had to be painstakingly manufactured by hand.

As a result, a single copy of one of the Gospels was fantastically expensive, with Matthew costing the equivalent of around $2,200, Mark around $1,400, Luke around $2,400, and John around $1,900.[174] Only rich people and congregations that pooled resources could afford them, making it clear that they could not be handed out as evangelistic tracts, so they were meant for people who were already committed Christians.

141. What is the Gospel of Matthew?

The Gospels have been arranged in different orders, but today Matthew is placed first in the New Testament, and so it is commonly referred to as the "first Gospel."

Historically, many people have also regarded it as the first Gospel to be written, but today, most scholars hold that it was the second or third.

The traditional author is St. Matthew the tax-collector (Matt. 9:9), who became one of the twelve apostles (10:3).

Scholars have noted that the Gospel of Matthew is the most Jewish in orientation and devotes particular attention to Jewish concerns. Some Christians—like St. Paul—were accused of overturning the Law of Moses (Rom. 3:31), and so Matthew made sure to record Jesus saying, "Do not think that I have come to abolish the law and the prophets; I have come not to abolish them but to fulfill them" (Matt. 5:17).

However, Matthew also ensures that the reader knows that Gentiles have a place in the Church, too, and so he points out that Jesus had multiple Gentile ancestors (Rahab, Ruth, and the "wife of Uriah" the Hittite; 1:5–6).

He then concludes his Gospel with Jesus' command: "Go therefore and make disciples of all nations"—that is, the Gentiles—"baptizing them in the name of the Father and of the Son and of the Holy Spirit, teaching them to observe all that I have commanded you" (28:19–20).

It thus appears that Matthew's Gospel was written for an audience of Jewish Christians, and one of its goals was to help them understand the place of Gentiles in the Church.

Matthew is one of two Gospels (the other being Luke) that has an *Infancy Narrative* or information about Jesus' early life. The Evangelist begins by presenting a genealogy of Jesus tracing his line back to Abraham via David's son Solomon (1:1–17). He then turns to the birth and early life of Jesus, focusing on his foster father, Joseph (1:18–2:23).

After this, Matthew records Jesus' earthly ministry, which mostly took place in Galilee (chaps. 3–20), before turning to the last week of Jesus' life and the Passion and Resurrection Narratives (chaps. 21–28).

Inserted into this material about Jesus' life are five major speeches that contain the majority of Jesus' teachings in the Gospel. Matthew is an organizer, and one of the things he does is collect sayings of Jesus that are scattered in different places in other Gospels and arrange them by topic into major speeches. The five speeches are:

- The Sermon on the Mount (chaps. 5–7)
- The Evangelistic Discourse (chap. 10)
- The Kingdom Parables (chap. 13)
- The Church Discipline Discourse (chap. 18)
- The Olivet Discourse (chaps. 23–25)

These speeches are arranged in a kind of literary pyramid known to scholars as a *chiasm*. The first speech gives Jesus' ethical teachings, corresponding to the Law of Moses, and the last contains his prophetic teachings, corresponding to the Old Testament prophetic books. These two speeches thus correspond to the Law and the Prophets—the principal parts of the Hebrew scriptures (see 22:40).

Between them are two shorter speeches dealing with the Church. Chapter 10 deals with the Church's relationship with outsiders and the need to bear witness to and evangelize them, whereas chapter 18 deals with problems inside the Church and how Christians relate to one another.

At the center of the discourses are Jesus' parables about the central mystery of his teaching—the kingdom of God.

It is easy to see how Matthew composed these speeches by collecting sayings from different places. The core of the Sermon on the Mount is found in Luke 6:20–49, but Matthew added sayings found elsewhere in Luke, such as Jesus' parables about salt and light (Matt. 5:13–16; Luke 14:34–35, 8:16, 11:33).

Similarly, the core of Matthew's Olivet Discourse is found in Luke 21:5–36, but Matthew adds sayings here, too (see Matt. 24:23–28; Luke 17:23–24, 37).

Another of Matthew's interests is showing how Jesus fulfilled Old Testament prophecies. All of the Evangelists do this, but Matthew often points it out explicitly, using a formula like "All this took place to fulfill what the Lord had spoken by the prophet: 'Behold, a virgin shall conceive and bear a son, and his name shall be called Emmanuel'" (1:22–23; see Isa. 7:14). Matthew has ten such fulfillment notices in his Gospel (1:22; 2:15, 17, 23; 4:14; 8:17; 12:17; 13:35; 21:4; 27:9).

Matthew also points out in a subtler way how Jesus fulfilled prophecy—for example, the prophecy of Moses that the "Lord your God will raise up for you a prophet like me from among you" (Deut. 18:15). Matthew subtly portrays Jesus as that prophet, recording how Jesus escaped death as a small child (Matt. 2:13–14/Exod. 1:15–2:10), how he passed through water (Matt. 3:13–17/Exod. 14:21–22), how he spent time in the desert (Matt. 4:1–11/Exod. 15:22–Deut. 34:12), and how he announced God's law from a mountain (Matt. 5–7/Exod. 19:16–20:21). Matthew thus shows both explicitly and implicitly how Jesus fulfilled prophecy.

142. What is the Gospel of Mark?

The Gospel of Mark is placed after Matthew, and so it is often referred to as the "second Gospel."

It is attributed to John Mark, a young man whom we meet in Acts (12:12) and who became the traveling companion of St. Peter (1 Pet. 5:13).

Early Christian sources indicate that Mark wrote his Gospel at Rome, that it was based on the preaching of St. Peter, and that it was written for a Gentile audience—a fact confirmed by the way Mark explains Jewish customs for the reader (7:3–4).

Historically, many people thought Mark was written after Matthew, but today, most scholars believe that it actually was the first Gospel written. Mark may have been the first person to try to tell the story of Jesus in written form, making him the pioneer who laid the foundation the other Evangelists would build on.

This could explain why Mark's Gospel is rough around the edges—*literally*. It both begins and ends in abrupt ways.

Ancient biographies didn't always begin with a discussion of their subject's family and birth, but they usually did. Mark, however, has no Infancy Narrative telling where Jesus came from. He simply says, "The beginning of the Gospel of Jesus Christ, the Son of God" (1:1)—as if he's expecting us to know already who Jesus is. He then says, "John the Baptist appeared in the wilderness" (1:4), expecting us to know who John the Baptist is.

This is possible because Mark was written for people who were already Christians and would know about Jesus and John the Baptist. But the way Mark ends is even more startling.

According to some of our most important manuscripts, Mark ends very suddenly after the women have found the empty tomb and encountered an angel. Mark states, "And they went out and fled from the tomb; for trembling and astonishment had come upon them; and they said nothing to anyone, for they were afraid" (16:8). Surprisingly, these manuscripts do not go on to mention any of Jesus' post-Resurrection appearances to the disciples.

The twelve verses that follow (16:9–20)—although regarded as canonical—are different in style and largely repeat things found in other Gospels and the Acts. Most scholars regard them as a later—but still early—composition to give the Gospel a sense of completeness by relating what happened next.

Many have wondered how to explain Mark's apparent, abrupt original ending. One suggestion is that the original ending was lost, but if so, this would have had to happen *very* early, or copies would have been made that preserved it.

Another suggestion is that Mark was interrupted before he could finish writing, but that seems unlikely. Why didn't he go on to complete it, and why don't we have other manuscripts—written in Mark's style—that preserve his ending?

Some have suggested that Mark is doing something super clever by ending his Gospel at this point, as if he's saying to the reader, "The women didn't tell people about Jesus. What about *you*? Are *you* going to tell them about him?" But this *avant-garde* move seems too clever by half.

A recent suggestion is that Mark's Gospel was never *meant* to be a finished, polished work. Instead, it belongs to a class of ancient writings known as *hupomnemata* (Greek: "memoirs"). These were collections of research notes intended to be the *basis* of later, polished works. They were meant to be supplemented and reworked—sometimes by another author.[175]

If so, it looks as though that's exactly what Matthew and Luke did—took Mark, supplemented it, and polished it so that it was in good literary form. For example, Mark repeatedly uses the Greek word *euthus* ("immediately") to convey a sense of dynamic urgency: *immediately*, Jesus did this, and then *immediately* he did that. Repetition of *euthus* is one of the things Matthew and Luke eliminate in polishing Mark's prose.

Also, like the other synoptic Gospels, Mark spends most of his time discussing Jesus' ministry in Galilee (chaps. 1–10), followed by an account of his last week, passion, and death (chaps. 11–16), but he gives few of Jesus' teachings. This is odd, since Mark regards Jesus as a great teacher (4:38, 5:35, 9:17, etc.), and one of the things Matthew and Luke do is supplement Mark's action-oriented narrative by including more of Jesus' teachings.

Despite its roughness, Mark became one of the most influential books in history, and it provided a good foundation for the other Evangelists to build upon.

143. What is the Gospel of Luke?

Luke is commonly referred to as the third Gospel, because of its placement after Matthew and Mark. It is generally thought that it was the second or third Gospel to be written.

It is attributed to St. Luke—a physician and traveling companion of Paul (see Acts 16:11; Col. 4:14). It is generally held that Luke—alone among the New Testament authors—was a Gentile, and like Mark, his Gospel was written principally for Gentile Christians. Luke also is the author of the Acts of the Apostles, which covers the history of the Church from the Resurrection to about A.D. 60.

Luke begins with a preface in which he explains the purposes for which he wrote:

> Inasmuch as many have undertaken to compile a narrative of the things which have been accomplished among us, just as they were delivered to us by those who from the beginning were eyewitnesses and ministers of the word, it seemed good to me also, having followed all things closely for some time past, to write an orderly account for you, most excellent Theophilus, that you may know the truth concerning the things of which you have been informed (1:1-4).

Luke acknowledges that others had previously written about Jesus, and he indicates that his own sources included "eyewitnesses and ministers of the word"—that is, people who personally saw Jesus and his ministry, as well as others who were considered qualified ministers of Christ.

Luke wished to write an "orderly account" for a man called Theophilus, who was likely the patron that financed the production of the Gospel. What Luke means by "orderly account" is uncertain. He may be referring to an account in *chronological* order or in good *literary* order.

His Gospel beings with an Infancy Narrative covering Jesus' early life (chaps. 1–2). It discusses the birth of Jesus' older kinsman John the Baptist, relates events from Mary's perspective rather than Joseph's, and includes an incident when Jesus was twelve—the Finding in the Temple (2:41–52). Luke twice mentions that Mary "kept all these things, pondering them in her heart" (2:19, 51), indicating that Mary was the source of this material.

Luke includes chronological information, telling us that John the Baptist began his ministry in the "fifteenth year of the reign of Tiberius Caesar" (3:1)—that is, A.D. 28—and that Jesus "was about thirty years of age" when he began his ministry (3:23). Luke also gives a genealogy of Jesus, but—unlike Matthew's—it traces Jesus' descent through David's son Nathan rather than Solomon, and it goes all the way back to Adam, the original son of God (3:23–38).

As a physician, Luke is especially interested in Jesus' role as a healer, and he is more positive toward doctors than Mark. Discussing a woman with a persistent hemorrhage, Mark states that she "had suffered much under many physicians, and had spent all that she had, and was no better but rather grew worse" (5:26). Luke softens this to say that she "had spent all her living upon physicians and could not be healed by anyone" (8:43).

His Gospel is the longest of the four and contains memorable passages not found in the others. These include the parables of the good Samaritan (10:25–37), the prodigal son (15:11–32), and Lazarus and the rich man (16:19–31).

Luke's Gospel was written principally for Gentile Christians. This is illustrated by its dedication to "Theophilus" (a Greek name) and by how Luke clarifies Jewish matters for his audience. For example, Matthew and Mark link the coming destruction of Jerusalem to the "desolating sacrilege spoken of by the prophet Daniel" (Matt. 24:15; see Mark 13:14). But non-Jewish readers would not be familiar with Daniel's prophecy, and Luke omits this and instead says, "When you see Jerusalem surrounded by armies, then know that its desolation has come near" (21:20).

144. What is the Gospel of John?

St. John's Gospel is commonly called the "fourth Gospel" because of its placement in the New Testament, but it also is thought to be the last written.

It is attributed to a man named John who was an eyewitness of Jesus' ministry (21:20–24), and he has classically been regarded as St. John, son of Zebedee, one of the Twelve (Matt. 10:1–2).

John's Gospel begins with the famous declaration, "In the beginning was the Word, and the Word was with God, and the Word was God." This is an allusion to the first verse of Genesis ("In the beginning God created the heavens and the earth"), and it indicates the divinity of Jesus ("the Word"; see 1:14).

John also closes his Gospel with an affirmation of Christ's divinity, when the apostle Thomas falls at the feet of the resurrected Jesus and confesses him to be "my Lord and my God" (20:28).

John is different in many ways from the other Gospels. It omits much that they include and includes much that they omit. Except for the last week of Jesus' life, the other Gospels focus almost entirely on his ministry in Galilee, but John focuses more on his ministry in Judea and Jerusalem. The other Gospels mention Jesus taking only one trip to Jerusalem—at the end of his life—but John mentions multiple trips. And the others mention only one Passover—when Jesus was crucified—but John mentions three Passovers (2:13; 6:4; 11:55).

It's because of how John ties Jesus' activities to feasts that we are able to tell that his ministry lasted three years. If we had only the others to go by, we might have concluded that it lasted only a year.

Another difference is the way John presents Jesus' teaching. Matthew, Mark, and Luke record Jesus teaching in pithy, memorable statements (e.g., "the last will be first, and the first last"; Matt. 20:16) or parables like the parable of the Sower (Matt. 13:3–9). When they do present Jesus giving longer blocks of teaching, these tend to be collections of shorter sayings—like Matthew's Sermon on the Mount (chaps. 5–7), which compiles Jesus' sayings on moral subjects.

By contrast, John presents longer discourses, often as part of ongoing conversations with his critics or disciples. The longest of these is the Farewell Discourse, which stretches over four of John's twenty-one chapters (chaps. 13–16). John is also the only Evangelist to record at length the prayer of Jesus, which he does at the conclusion of the Farewell Discourse (chap. 17).

Not only the style, but also the content of Jesus' teaching is different in the Gospel of John. The other Gospels record Jesus teaching on a variety of subjects, including specific moral questions like anger (Matt. 5:21–26), adultery (5:27–30), and divorce (5:31–32).

However, John mentions only Jesus' general command to love one another (13:34–35, 15:9–12) and focuses on Jesus' teachings about his identity as God's Son. In the Old Testament, God uses "I am" as one of his names (Exod. 3:14), and Jesus also applies "I am" to himself to indicate he is Yahweh, as in his famous statement, "before Abraham was, I am" (8:58; see 8:24, 28; 13:19; 18:5–9). John also contains seven "I am" sayings that deal with aspects of Jesus' identity (e.g., "I am the Bread of Life," 6:35; see 8:12; 10:9; 11–14; 11:25; 14:6; 15:1–5).

Additionally, John records more of Jesus' teachings regarding the third Person of the Trinity—the Holy Spirit. In John, Jesus stresses the role of the Holy Spirit in salvation (3:3–8), promises to give the Spirit (7:37–39), emphasizes the role of the Spirit in the life of the disciples as the "Paraclete" (14:16–17, 26; 15:26; 16:7–11, 13–15), and bestows the Holy Spirit on the disciples so they can forgive or retain sins (20:21–23).

In light of this strong emphasis on such exalted subject matter—the persons of the Trinity—Clement of Alexandria said John had written a particularly "spiritual Gospel."[176]

145. Are the Gospels anonymous?

It is sometimes claimed that the four Gospels are anonymous, with the implications that we don't know who wrote them, that they likely weren't written by their traditional authors, and that they may not be very accurate.

Critics claim that the names of the authors of the Gospels were added after they had already been in circulation in the Church. Instead of Matthew, Mark, Luke, and John, they say, the real authors were anonymous Christians who relied on hearsay and legend rather than eyewitness testimony. But is there evidence for this claim?

It is true, the names of the Evangelists don't appear in the *text* of the Gospels—only in ascriptions at the front of the documents. If you wanted, you could say that the *text* of the Gospels is formally anonymous due to authors' names not appearing in it, but the books are *not* anonymous. They have author attributions right up front, being identified as the Gospels "according to" Matthew, Mark, Luke, and John.

This is normal for books—both ancient and modern. In his dialogues, Plato never identifies himself by name as the author. He never inserts himself into the flow of the narrative and says, "I—Plato—wrote this." Neither do most other ancient authors.

Modern ones also tend not to. For example, skeptical scholar Bart Ehrman's book *Misquoting Jesus* never names Ehrman as the author in the text of the book. *Misquoting Jesus* thus is anonymous *in the same sense* that the Gospels are! But we wouldn't seriously say that the book is anonymous or that we don't know who wrote it. The author's name is right up front! It's on the cover!

It could be claimed that *Misquoting Jesus* is a modern book, and its author's name was printed on the first edition, but that wasn't true of the Gospels. They circulated anonymously, and the names were put on them only in the late second century.

Even if the earliest copies of the Gospels did not bear the names of their authors, that would not disprove the traditional authorship of those texts. The works of the ancient Roman historian Tacitus often do not bear his name, but very few historians have ever questioned that Tacitus wrote them. We know Tacitus is the author of these works because other ancient writers, such as St. Jerome, identify him as the author.

St. Augustine dealt with the charge that the Gospels were anonymous in the fourth century in his reply to a heretic named Faustus:

> How do we know the authorship of the works of Plato, Aristotle, Cicero, Varro, and other similar writers, but by the unbroken chain of evidence? So also with the numerous commentaries on the ecclesiastical books, which have no canonical authority, and yet show a desire of usefulness and a spirit of inquiry. . . . How can we be sure of the authorship of any book, if we doubt the apostolic origin of those books which are attributed to the apostles by the Church which the apostles themselves founded?[177]

Furthermore, there is no compelling evidence that the first manuscripts of the Gospels *did* lack attribution to their traditional authors. There are no manuscripts that simply lack titles, as lay critics might imagine), and academic critics say the variants in the titles of those early manuscripts prove the authors' names were added at a much later date.[178] However, the usual variant is just the absence of the word *Gospel*, which leaves a title that begins with "According to . . ." followed by the author's name—a name that is never absent from these manuscripts. Biblical scholar Brant Pitre says, "According to the basic rules of textual criticism, then, if anything is original in the titles, it is the names of the authors. They are at least as original as any other part of the Gospels for which we have unanimous manuscript evidence."[179] But let's suppose for a moment—that the Gospels didn't originally have author attributions. Would that mean people didn't know who wrote them?

Consider the Gospel of Luke: he dedicates it to his patron Theophilus (1:3; see Acts 1:1). Obviously, Theophilus knew who the author was—especially if he was paying for it to be produced!

Similarly, in the Gospel of John, we find this passage:

> Peter turned and saw following them the disciple whom Jesus loved.... When Peter saw him, he said to Jesus, "Lord, what about this man?" Jesus said to him, "If it is my will that he remain until I come, what is that to you? Follow me!" The saying spread abroad among the brethren that this disciple was not to die; yet Jesus did not say to him that he was not to die, but, "If it is my will that he remain until I come, what is that to you?" This is the disciple who is bearing witness to these things, and who has written these things (21:20–24).

This reveals the beloved disciple as the one writing the Gospel, and it reveals that his identity was known. There was a rumor that Jesus said he would never die!—a rumor he went out of his way to debunk, explaining that Jesus said only, "*If* it is my will that he remain until I come." Obviously, the identity of the author was known and intended to be crystal-clear to the audience. We would scarcely call a modern book anonymous if an author telegraphed his identity *that clearly* to the audience.

Matthew and Mark don't contain passages like this, but their identities also would have been known to the original audiences. It's not as if they would have written their Gospels completely in secret and then pitched them into a church in the dead of night to keep their identities from being known. Had they done something so ridiculous, their books would have fallen under suspicion and never been copied and passed on.

Reason indicates that the identities of all four Evangelists were known in the early Church, which would have thanked and honored them for producing such precious records of the Savior.

This brings us back to whether the Gospels circulated without the authors' names on them. This is not impossible, though if so, the period could not have been long.

As soon as a church had more than one Gospel in its possession, it needed a way to distinguish them. For example, in the liturgy, the lector needed to tell the congregation what he was reading from.

If the Gospels had been long in circulation without written titles, churches would have called them different things. In one community, the Gospel of Matthew may have been called by that name, but in another, it would be called *The Life of Christ* or *The Gospel for the Jews*—or if people didn't know who wrote it, they may have attributed it to an important figure like Jesus' famous "brother" and called it *The Gospel According to James the Just.*

But we never see this. The four Gospels are always referred to by the same set of names. This means that if they *ever* circulated without names, the churches had to agree very early on what to call them, and so the current names were in use in the first century.[180]

146. Do we really know who wrote the Gospels?

The identities of the men who wrote the Gospels is not a matter of faith. What the Church teaches is that these are divinely inspired records of the life of Christ, but we do not have to know who wrote them for this to be the case.

We do not know the identities of the authors of many books of the Old Testament, but that didn't stop Jesus and the apostles from recognizing them as inspired. Nor did it stop the Holy Spirit from guiding the Church to recognize this.

Yet we do have evidence regarding the authorship of the Gospels. The early Church's unanimous attribution of the Gospels to Matthew, Mark, Luke, and John provides us with evidence that these were the men who wrote them. The fact that these attributions were made in the first century—when the authors' identities would have been known—only strengthens the case for their authorship.

Further, in the case of Matthew's Gospel, we can speculate that Matthew was only a mid-level apostle, as his name appears only in the middle of the lists of the Twelve (Matt. 10:3; Mark 3:18; Luke 6:15; Acts 1:13). If he was not in Jesus' inner circle, his name would be an unlikely choice to give the Gospel extra authority.

The apostle Matthew was a tax-collector (Matt. 10:3), and—as they were collaborators with the Romans—tax-collectors were despised in the Jewish community (5:46, 9:11, 11:19, 18:17, etc.). Yet Matthew's Gospel is clearly written for a Jewish audience. In view of how Jews regarded tax-collectors, it would be very unlikely for Matthew's name to become associated with the most Jewish Gospel if he had not actually written it.

In the case of Mark, we have first-century testimony that it was written by John Mark, the companion of Peter. This testimony comes from a first-century figure—who was also an eyewitness of Jesus' ministry—named John the Elder. He informs us:

> Mark, having become the interpreter of Peter, wrote down accurately, though not indeed in order, whatsoever he remembered of the things said or done by Christ. For he had not heard the Lord, nor had he followed him, but later on, as I said, followed Peter, who used to give teaching as necessity demanded but not making, as it were, an arrangement of the Lord's oracles, so that Mark did nothing wrong in thus writing down single points as he remembered them. For to one thing he gave attention, to leave out nothing of what he had heard and to make no false statements in them.[181]

Writing around A.D. 200, Clement of Alexandria tells us that

> when Peter had publicly preached the word at Rome, and by the Spirit had proclaimed the Gospel, that those present, who were many, exhorted Mark, as one who had followed him for a long time and remembered what had been spoken, to make a record of what was said; and that he did this, and distributed the Gospel among those that asked him.[182]

The fact that Mark wasn't even an apostle also is evidence that he authored this Gospel. When ancient documents *were* falsely attributed to someone, that person was important. It was an attempt to get the document taken seriously by giving it a prestigious author.

Mark was a comparative nobody. He wasn't an apostle or an eyewitness of Jesus. He was only an apostolic companion, and not always a good one! Acts records that at one point, he abandoned the mission field, causing the apostles Paul and Barnabas to quarrel and dissolve their partnership (15:36–41). Mark later proved himself to Paul (see Col. 4:10; 2 Tim. 4:11; Philem. 24), but he had a blemished record and was not the kind of authoritative figure to whom you'd want to falsely attribute a Gospel.

Luke has an unblemished record as a companion of Paul, but he too was a comparative nobody, being neither an apostle nor an eyewitness of Jesus, so he wasn't the kind of person a Gospel would end up falsely attributed to, either.

John alone among the Evangelists is commonly held to be among the inner circle of Jesus' apostles—together with Peter and James (see Matt. 17:1; Mark 5:37)—and thus the kind of individual people might falsely attribute a Gospel to.

However, John's was the last Gospel written, and since the names of the Evangelists go back to the first century, that means that "according to John" was attached to it when the author's identity was still known. After all, there was the rumor he wouldn't die! It is thus highly likely that it was written by an eyewitness of Jesus' ministry named John.

This was the near-universal understanding in the early Church, though it is not always clear which John the earliest Church Fathers had in mind, as he is sometimes described as an apostle of Jesus and sometimes only as a disciple. A consensus view emerged that the Gospel was authored by John the apostle, and this has been the dominant view in Church history.

But again, which John was the author is not as clear as is often assumed.[183] The internal evidence for it being John, son of Zebedee, is based on the author's description of himself as the disciple whom Jesus loved (John 19:26, 20:2, 21:7, 20) and who leaned against his breast at the Last Supper (13:23). From this it is inferred that the disciple must have been one of the inner circle of the Twelve. But it could not have been Peter (see 13:23–25), or James, the first of the Twelve to die (Acts 12:1–2). That would leave John, son of Zebedee.

This chain of reasoning depends on the inference that the beloved disciple must be one of the Twelve, but that is not guaranteed. It is likely Jesus had friendships with people who weren't among his traveling companions, so we need to consider whether there is evidence that could point toward one of them. Some scholars have proposed that the fourth Gospel was written by a man from Jerusalem named John, perhaps an eyewitness of Jesus' ministry known as John the Elder (quoted above).[184]

According to this view, the Gospel was later accidentally attributed to John, son of Zebedee because it was known to have been written by a friend and eyewitness named John, and the son of Zebedee was the most famous man meeting that description after memories of John the Elder began to fade.

In sum, we have good evidence—which dates from the first century—that the Gospels were written by identifiable persons known to the early Church community, though there remains a question about which John.

147. How did the Evangelists get their information?

To accurately report on what Jesus said and did, the Evangelists needed good information about him, and the question of how they got it is important.

Today, many scholars hold that the Gospels were not written until A.D. 70–100, though there is reason to challenge this. How was the information preserved between Jesus' ministry and the writing of the Gospels?

One proposal is that it was preserved by oral tradition passed down from one Christian to another in an elaborate, unreliable game of "telephone," with many links between the original witnesses and the Evangelists. Each time a story about Jesus was retold, it would have been altered slightly, such that, after many retellings, the Gospel accounts would have become unreliable, though they contain accurate elements.

This view was popular in the first part of the twentieth century in a movement known as *form criticism*, which classified passages according to their literary form (e.g., saying, parable, miracle story) and sought to understand how the material had changed before it was written down.

In the second half of the twentieth century, form criticism began to be criticized, and it is now widely rejected, though its legacy is still with us.

Any view that proposes a long period of oral tradition depends on the idea that the Evangelists were not actually the people to whom the Gospels were attributed, but later, unknown individuals. This view is highly problematic, and there is good evidence that the authors really were Matthew, Mark, Luke, and John. In that case, where did they get their information?

Matthew was an eyewitness of Jesus' ministry, so his own experiences would have been one of his sources. This doesn't mean he didn't use others. Approximately 90 percent of Mark is found in Matthew, so Matthew likely used and supplemented Mark. Some have questioned whether an eyewitness like Matthew would use Mark, but there were no copyrights in the first century, and if Matthew had a written account that he liked, he could easily use it rather than reinvent the wheel. This would particularly be true if the source were based on the preaching of Peter—the head apostle—and even more so more if the Gospel of Mark was meant to be *hupomnemata*—notes intended for the production of later, polished works.

We have explicit testimony regarding Mark's primary source: the preaching of Peter. Peter was an eyewitness, and so there was only one link—Peter—in the chain of tradition between the events and the Evangelist.

Luke contains approximately 50 percent of Mark, so the second Gospel was apparently one of his principal sources, meaning this material was also just one link away from the events. Luke also tells us he had received information from "those who from the beginning were eyewitnesses and ministers of the word" (Luke 1:2).

We can even determine some of the eyewitnesses whom Luke may have interviewed. In his Infancy Narrative, Luke twice mentions that Mary "kept all these things, pondering them in her heart" (2:19; see 2:51). That identifies Mary as the source of this material, meaning either that Luke interviewed her or that he spoke with someone who did. Either way, there weren't many links in the chain of tradition.

Luke and Acts were likely written during Paul's two-year house arrest in Rome (A.D. 58–60), and Luke would have interviewed the two apostles in Rome at the time: Peter and Paul. This explains why Peter dominates the first part of Acts (chaps. 1–12) before the narrative starts following Paul (chaps. 13–28).

If Luke interviewed Peter for Acts, he also would have asked him about his experiences with Jesus, and so Peter was likely one of the sources Luke used in composing his Gospel.

Paul wasn't an eyewitness of Jesus' ministry, but he had his own post-Resurrection experiences with Jesus, and he was one of the "ministers of the word" Luke refers to. Not just anybody could become a minister in the first century. There was an approval process the apostles oversaw (Acts 13:2–3, 14:34; Titus 1:5). This shows that the early Church was concerned with quality control regarding information about Jesus. It was not a chaotic, free-for-all game of "telephone."

Regardless of which John wrote the Gospel, he was an eyewitness, and so his Gospel is direct, eyewitness testimony.

We thus see that the Gospels either were composed by eyewitnesses or are based on eyewitness testimony, with only one or two links in the chain of transmission.[185]

148. What are the synoptic Gospels?

Three of the Gospels—Matthew, Mark, and Luke—have a special name. They are called the *synoptic Gospels*.

Synoptic comes from Greek roots meaning "seeing" (*opsis*) and "together" (*sun*). The three are called synoptic because they present the story of Jesus in similar ways. They share a common perspective ("see together") on how to relate Jesus' life.

All four Gospels deal with Jesus' ministry, teaching, crucifixion, and resurrection. But Matthew, Mark, and Luke have many additional similarities. The material they share is known as the "triple tradition" because it appears in all three, and it contains fifty-four passages (sayings, parables, and stories) found in *each* of the synoptics.

These include Jesus' forty days in the wilderness, the call of the fishermen disciples, the healing of Simon (Peter)'s mother-in-law, the raising of Jairus's daughter, the Transfiguration, the rich young ruler, paying taxes to Caesar, the institution of the Eucharist, and many more.

The synoptic Gospels often relate their content in almost identical words in Greek. This even shines through in English translation.

> And Jesus said to them, "Whose likeness and inscription is this?" They said, "Caesar's." Then he said to them, "Render therefore to Caesar the things that are Caesar's, and to God the things that are God's" (Matt. 22:20–21).

> And he said to them, "Whose likeness and inscription is this?" They said to him, "Caesar's." Jesus said to them, "Render to Caesar the things that are Caesar's, and to God the things that are God's" (Mark 12:16b–17).

> "Whose likeness and inscription has it?" They said, "Caesar's." He said to them, "Then render to Caesar the things that are Caesar's, and to God the things that are God's" (Luke 20:24–25).

There are only slight variations in wording, and the same is true in Greek. This happens in many passages throughout the synoptics.

Because of this—and the fact that John contains *some* material in common with the synoptics—it's possible to arrange the Gospels in four parallel columns so you can see which material is in each Gospel and how the four Evangelists treat it. This kind of work is known as a *synopsis* of the four Gospels, and it is often used by Bible students and scholars.

At the same time, there *are* differences among the synoptics. Each has sayings and stories that are unique (Mark having the fewest), and each Evangelist has his own style or way of relating material.

For example, Matthew prefers to use the phrase *kingdom of heaven*, whereas Mark and Luke prefer *kingdom of God*. Similarly, Matthew and Mark prefer the term *disciples*, whereas Luke commonly uses *apostles*. And Mark uses the term *gospel* much more than Matthew or Luke.

149. Why is John so different?

There are only sixteen passages (all narratives) in John that are present in all three of the synoptics. One mentions the role of John the Baptist at the beginning of Jesus' ministry, one is the feeding of the five thousand (the only miracle besides the Resurrection in all four Gospels), and the rest are events in the last week of Jesus' life.

And even these are told differently—in John's unique style, which records longer conversations and is more explicit about Jesus' divinity and the role of the Holy Spirit.

How can we explain these differences? There are two basic options:

1) John hadn't read the synoptics and so didn't interact with them. He was simply pursuing his own interests as he wrote, and these didn't overlap much with the synoptics.

2) John *had* read some or all of the synoptics and was deliberately doing something *different* from what they were doing.

The second option has been the most common in Church history, but through a good part of the twentieth century, the first became popular among scholars. In recent years, the first option has lost ground, and today, scholars are more open to the historic view.

What evidence is there concerning the two views? The evidence for the first would be based on how *different* John is from the synoptics—almost as if he's not aware of them. But the differences in John also are consistent with the view that he *did* know them and was deliberately doing something different.

A close reading of John suggests that the historic view is the true one, but what was it that John was trying to do differently? We can determine this by looking at some curious omissions in the fourth Gospel.

The synoptics all have an account of Jesus' baptism, and although John does discuss John the Baptist, he never actually *says* that John baptized Jesus. Instead, he says John saw the Holy Spirit descending on Jesus in the form of a dove—something we know from the synoptics—but he doesn't say it happened *during* the baptism (see John 1:32–33). This is a curious omission we might not understand if we didn't have the synoptics.

Another is found in John 3, where the Evangelist is discussing a location where John the Baptist was performing his ministry, and out of nowhere, he says, "For John had not yet been put in prison" (3:24). To someone who had only the Gospel of John, this would make no sense, for he nowhere else mentions John being put in prison.

We know from the synoptics that Herod Antipas imprisoned and eventually executed John the Baptist. The fourth Gospel doesn't mention any of that. Yet the Evangelist seems to expect us to know about it, for he mentions that John's imprisonment hadn't *yet* happened as a way of explaining how John was baptizing when and where he was.

Another curious omission is the institution of the Eucharist. This is found in each of the synoptics, and John *has* an account of the Last Supper, but he doesn't mention the institution of the Eucharist. It's not as if John is uninterested in this topic. Just after the feeding of the five thousand, John has a lengthy discussion of the Eucharist (6:26–58). Yet when he relates the Last Supper, he curiously omits the institution of the sacrament for which he previously supplied a major discussion.

Why would he omit these things? John is clearly interested in the baptism of Jesus, the arrest of John the Baptist, and the Eucharist. Otherwise, he wouldn't mention them at all. But if he's interested in them, why would he fail to include descriptions of the key events? The synoptics all have them!

And that's the point: the synoptics *do* describe these events. They were already on record in the Christian community, and so John doesn't *need* to record them. As the last of the Evangelists, John can assume that his readers were familiar with the synoptics, and that frees him up to record material not found in them.

Book production was fantastically expensive in the first century, and there was price pressure on John to keep his work affordable for the Christian community. Since he had a great deal of non-synoptic material to record, he chose to omit things he knew that the synoptics contained so that he would have space for his own material.

That explains what he's trying to do differently from the synoptics: he's trying to *supplement* them.[186] Even then, he knows he can't include everything, for in the end, he says, "There are also many other things which Jesus did; were every one of them to be written, I suppose that the world itself could not contain the books that would be written" (21:25).

150. What is the synoptic problem?

The fact that Matthew, Mark, and Luke have so much in common has led scholars to investigate the relationship among the three. The issue of how they are related is known as the *synoptic problem*, and there have been many attempts to solve it.[187]

It would be hypothetically possible for each of the synoptic Evangelists to write his own Gospel from scratch—based only on oral tradition. However, if that happened, we wouldn't expect to see the amount of convergence we do among them. We wouldn't expect to see lengthy passages of almost word-for-word agreement in the triple tradition. This agreement applies not only to the sayings of Jesus (which might have been memorized), but also to the narrative that surrounds them.

Scholars since ancient times have concluded that there is a *literary relationship* among the three—meaning that one Evangelist wrote first and then the other two used his work when composing their own.

A key question in solving the synoptic problem is answering the question "Which Evangelist wrote first?"

We should note that the Church does not have a teaching on this question or on the synoptic problem in general. It leaves these matters to scholars to explore.

One strand of early tradition in the Church Fathers, which eventually became dominant and remained so for a long time, is that Matthew was the first Evangelist to write. It was often held that he wrote his Gospel in Hebrew or Aramaic, and it was then translated into Greek.

According to a hypothesis entertained by St. Augustine, Mark then wrote an abbreviated version of Matthew, and Luke wrote third, using both Matthew and Mark. This is known as the *Augustinian Hypothesis* because the saint proposed it at the beginning of his *Harmony of the Gospels*, though by the end of the work it isn't clear that he definitely believed it.

The idea that Matthew wrote first is known as *Matthean priority*. This view was common until the late 1700s, when it was proposed that Mark wrote first (*Marcan priority*), and this view gained ground. Today, the large majority of scholars—of all persuasions—hold that Mark was the first Gospel written.

One reason is that Mark's style is less polished than what we find in Matthew and Luke. Another reason is that Mark tends to use more words to relate an incident than the others. It looks as though part of Matthew's and Luke's polishing process was *shortening* Mark's version so they'd have additional space to relate their own stories about Jesus.

Further, Mark omits really important material from Matthew (e.g., the Infancy Narrative and most of Jesus' teachings, including the Lord's Prayer). If Mark were based on Matthew, it's hard to explain why he would omit such things in favor of *yet another* healing story, similar to so many others. It looks more likely that Mark wrote first and then Matthew chose selectively among Mark's narratives, while leaving room for more important material.

The synoptic problem also deals with the relationship between Matthew and Luke. These Gospels contain about 235 verses in common, most of which deal with sayings of Jesus. To explain this, some scholars have proposed that the two Evangelists relied on a now lost source, which has been dubbed Q, from the German word *Quelle* ("source").

This led to what is known as the *Two-Source* hypothesis, according to which Mark and Q were the two sources combined by Matthew and Luke.

This leaves some of the material in the latter two Gospels unexplained. Both have passages unique to them (the Infancy Narratives being key examples). Such unique passages are referred to as the "special material" of each Gospel, and some scholars have proposed additional written sources for it. The source for the special material in Matthew has been dubbed *M*, and the source for Luke's special material has been dubbed *L*.

This led to a *Four-Document* hypothesis, with the four sources behind the synoptic Gospels being Mark, Q, M, and L. Currently, the Four-Document hypothesis and variants on it are popular among scholars.

151. What alternatives are there to the Four-Document hypothesis?

Despite its popularity, the Four-Document view is far from universally agreed upon by scholars, and in recent decades, it has been increasingly challenged.

Q is only a hypothetical source. We have no copies of it, and there are other ways of explaining why Matthew and Luke have 235 verses in common, so Q may never have existed.

Even less certain is the existence of documents like M and L. Not only are they purely hypothetical, but it isn't clear that Matthew or Luke would have used *documents* for this material.

Luke may have interviewed Mary *orally* for the material in his Infancy Narrative. Or, if he did have a written source for this, why should it be the *same* document from which he got the parable of the prodigal son (15:11–32)? It is more likely that Luke was combining material from multiple sources, both oral and written (see 1:1–2).

We thus should look at alternatives to the Four-Document hypothesis. One—known as the Griesbach hypothesis—holds that Matthew wrote first, Luke used Matthew, and then Mark edited Matthew and Luke together and produced a shorter, condensed account. This view is consistent with the fact that Mark contains almost nothing that isn't found in either Matthew or Luke.

However, this view does not explain why Mark's language is less polished than Matthew's and Luke's, why Mark uses more words to relate incidents, or why Mark omits so much high-value information contained in Matthew and Luke such as the Virgin Birth, the Lord's Prayer, etc.

Further, the Griesbach hypothesis directly contradicts the earliest information we have about Mark's Gospel, which holds that it was based on Peter's preaching—*not* Matthew and Luke. This information comes from John the Elder, who was a first-century eyewitness of Jesus' ministry, who was within the circle of those who wrote the New Testament, and who may have been one of its authors. Such testimony is not to be lightly set aside.

Another alternative is known as the Farrer hypothesis. According to this view, Mark wrote first, Matthew expanded Mark, and then Luke used both Mark and Matthew. This view does away with the need for a Q document, for the 235 verses that Matthew and Luke have in common could have been taken *directly from Matthew*, without needing an additional source.

A challenge for this view is how to explain the organization of this material in Luke. In Matthew, Jesus' sayings have been arranged into orderly speeches by topic—Matthew's five major discourses. However, if Luke took this material from Matthew, then he had to pull apart these speeches and scatter sayings here and there in his Gospel.

Some scholars have looked very unfavorably on this idea. Reginald Fuller said that if Luke did this, it would be "a case of unscrambling the egg with a vengeance!"[188] B.H. Streeter put the matter even more brusquely, saying that "a theory which would make an author capable of such a proceeding would only be tenable if, on other grounds, we had reason to believe he was a crank."[189]

An alternative that avoids this difficulty is known as the Wilke hypothesis. According to it, Mark wrote first, Luke expanded Mark, and then Matthew used Mark and Luke. This also does away with the need for Q. On this view, Matthew took the 235 verses directly from Luke, where they were scattered in different places. Being the organizer that he was, Matthew then took them and other sayings of Jesus and arranged them in orderly speeches by topic.

Although today almost all scholars agree that Mark was written first, and the Four-Document hypothesis remains popular, the alternatives are gaining ground.

152. Did Matthew write a Hebrew gospel?

According to various sources, Matthew originally wrote a Gospel in Hebrew (or Aramaic) that was later translated into Greek and became part of the New Testament.

Whether this would be considered a lost gospel—or merely an alternate-language version of a gospel that we have—would depend on the definition you use. But even if it were just an original-language version, its discovery would be tremendously exciting to scholars, as having an original-language text would shed light on multiple passages.

Possibly the earliest reference we have to the idea is found in the late first- and early second-century author Papias. After discussing the origin of Mark, he states,

> So then Matthew compiled the oracles in the Hebrew dialect, and everyone interpreted them as he was able.[190]

It isn't clear from context whether this statement comes from John the Elder or from Papias, and this makes it less certain what weight it should be given.

Another difficulty is that the passage is notoriously difficult to translate. The key terms can be understood in multiple ways:

- "Compiled" (*sunetaxeto*) could also mean "composed" or "arranged."
- "Oracles" (*logia*) could also mean "sayings."
- "Hebrew" (*hebraidi*) could mean the *actual* Hebrew language *or* Aramaic, which was the common language among Hebrews at the time.
- "Dialect" (*dialektô*) could also mean "language," "idiom," or "style."
- "Interpreted" (*hêrmêneusen*) could also mean "translated," "transmitted," "communicated," or "explained."[191]

As a result, Papias's statement can be understood different ways, a few of which include:

1) Matthew wrote his Gospel in Hebrew or Aramaic, and everyone translated it into Greek as best he could.
2) Matthew compiled the Old Testament oracles about Jesus in a Hebrew style, and everyone sought to understand them as best he could.
3) Matthew arranged the sayings *of* Jesus in a Hebrew style, and everyone sought to understand them as best he could.
4) Matthew wrote the sayings *about* Jesus in a Hebrew style, and everyone sought to understand them as best he could.

The first option would mean that Matthew originally wrote his Gospel in a Semitic language, and then multiple people translated it into Greek.

The second option would mean that Matthew composed some kind of collection of Old Testament prophecies about Jesus. These could have been in a separate document, possibly one that was later incorporated into Matthew. Or he could have written them directly into his Gospel as he composed it (i.e., the fulfillment passages that characterize Matthew; see 260).

The third would mean that Matthew collected Jesus' sayings (as in the Sermon on the Mount and the other major discourses in Matthew). Again, this could have been in a separate document that was later incorporated into Matthew, or he could have collected them *as* he was composing the Gospel.

Finally, the fourth would mean that Matthew collected the sayings *about* Jesus (i.e., stories of his words and deeds) and put them together in a Hebrew style, which Gentile readers then sought to understood as best they could.

Many in the early Church took Papias to mean the first possibility. However, if Matthew wrote any such document, we do not have it.

Furthermore, if "everybody translated [it] as he was able," you might expect us to have multiple Greek versions of Matthew, but we don't. We have only one, and it doesn't read like a translation. Its Greek is too good for that, and—like other books of the New Testament—Matthew normally quotes the Septuagint, the Greek Old Testament, rather than directly translating the Hebrew. This suggests that it was composed in Greek.

Particularly noteworthy is 1:23, where Matthew quotes Isaiah's prophecy from the Septuagint: "Behold, a *parthenos* shall conceive and bear a son" (Isa.7:14) *Parthenos* is a Greek word that specifically means "virgin." However, the Hebrew term Isaiah used—*`almah*—is more general and just means a young woman old enough to marry, not a virgin specifically. This suggests that Matthew deliberately used the Greek, because the Greek version brings out more clearly the miraculous nature of Jesus' birth.

Also against this interpretation is the fact that Matthew uses 90 percent of Mark, and Mark was written in Greek.

All except the first option are consistent with the idea of Matthew writing his Gospel in Greek, though in a Hebrew style that Gentile readers understood as best they could. Matthew certainly was written for a Jewish audience, and Gentile readers would have faced challenges in understanding some of the Jewish references it contains.

In favor of the second is the fact that the term *oracles* would most commonly mean Old Testament prophecies. Against this is that Matthew's fulfillment passages are a lesser element in his Gospel. They're not prominent enough that one would expect Papias to comment on them.

In favor of the third is the fact that Matthew obviously collected the sayings of Jesus into his five discourses, which are one of the most prominent features of his Gospel. Also, in context, Papias is contrasting what Matthew did with what John the Elder says Mark did. Mark wrote accurately but did not make "an arrangement of the Lord's oracles," whereas Matthew *did* "arrange the sayings in a Hebrew style" that wouldn't always be clear to Gentile readers.

Given the difficulties with the first and second options, it is probable that one of the other two is what Papias meant (either that or he was simply mistaken). It remains *possible* that Matthew wrote something in Hebrew or Aramaic—a kind of *proto-Matthew*—and this *may* have been incorporated into the canonical Gospel. However, this—like Q—is hypothetical, and Matthew as we have it appears to have been both based on Mark and written in Greek.

153. When were the Gospels written?

Throughout Church history, Christians held that the Gospels were written in the first century by the individuals whose names they bear. However, both their authorship and dates came to be challenged.

Under the influence of skeptical nineteenth-century German scholars, it was popular for a time to hold that they were written very late, with John being written as late as A.D. 170! However, archaeological discoveries (including a fragment of the Gospel of John dated to around A.D. 125) pushed the proposed dates back into the first century.

Today, many scholars accept dates that are roughly as follows: [192]

- Mark: 60-75, most likely between 68 and 73
- Matthew: 80-90, give or take a decade
- Luke: 85, give or take five to ten years
- John: 80-110

These dates are not impossible, but a careful study of the evidence suggests that the Gospels were actually written earlier.

The particular dates that the Gospels should be assigned will depend on which view of the synoptic problem you accept. Here we will proceed on the Wilke hypothesis.

A key to dating the Gospels is the book of Acts, which spends its last seven chapters building toward Paul's trial before Nero Caesar. Yet it suddenly cuts off without telling us what happened at the trial it has been building to. The narrative suddenly stops around A.D. 60, with Paul under a two-year house arrest in Rome (28:30–31).

Luke spent a quarter of Acts dealing with Paul's trial, and it is inexplicable why he would stop at this point if he knew the outcome of Paul's trial. The obvious solution is that he didn't know the outcome of the trial because it hadn't happened yet. In Acts, Luke wrote as far as the events of his own day and then stopped. This would put the composition of Acts in the second year of Paul's imprisonment.

That gives us a probable date for Luke's Gospel, whose conclusion shows signs that it was written with the beginning of Acts in mind, suggesting that Acts was written immediately after the Gospel of Luke was finished. We may thus estimate that Luke was written in the first year of Paul's house arrest (A.D. 59) and Acts was written in the second (A.D. 60).

Since Luke uses Mark, the latter must have written earlier. But if Mark is based on Peter's preaching, it must have been penned after Mark became a companion of Peter. Mark was a companion of Barnabas and Paul between A.D. 43 and 49 (Acts 15:36–39; see 13:1–13), so his time as Peter's companion must have begun in the A.D. 50s, making that the decade the second Gospel was written. We may thus estimate that Mark was written around A.D. 55.

On the Wilke hypothesis, Matthew was written after Luke, but it should not have been long afterward, for Matthew speaks as if the Jerusalem temple is still functioning (5:23–24; 12:5; 23:20–21), and it was destroyed in A.D. 70. He also speaks of the cataclysm of the Jewish War as still future (24:15–16, 20). Matthew thus would have been written after Luke in A.D. 59 but before the war, which began in A.D. 66, allowing us to estimate a date of 63 for Matthew.

It appears John was writing to supplement the synoptics. He also speaks of architecture in Jerusalem (destroyed in A.D. 70) as still standing (5:2). And when he discusses the martyrdom of Peter, he uses the future tense, indicating that Peter was not yet dead. Despite what you read in English translations, what he says in Greek is that Jesus predicted "by what death he [Peter] *shall* glorify God" (21:19, Young's Literal Translation). Since Peter was martyred in A.D. 66 or 67, we will estimate that John wrote in A.D. 65.

We thus propose the following approximate dates for the Gospels:

- Mark: 55
- Luke: 59
- Matthew: 63
- John: 65[193]

154. Are there lost gospels?

There are books about Jesus and his life that we no longer have. We know the names of several from the Church Fathers.

One was the *Gospel According to the Hebrews*, and in the early 300s, Eusebius tells us it was disputed, with some considering it canonical, whereas others did not. He remarked that it was a work "in which the Hebrews who have accepted Christ especially delight."[194]

It was significant enough that St. Jerome translated it into Greek and Latin, and he relates that it included a passage about the otherwise obscure post-Resurrection appearance of Jesus to his "brother" James the Just (1 Cor. 15:7):

> The Lord, however, after he had given his grave clothes to the servant of the priest, appeared to James, for James had sworn that he would not eat bread from that hour in which he drank the cup of the Lord until he should see him rising again from among those that sleep. . . . "Bring a table and bread," said the Lord." . . . He brought bread and blessed and broke it and gave to James the Just and said to him, "My brother, eat your bread, for the Son of Man is risen from among those that sleep."[195]

In other cases, we don't know the name of a lost gospel, but we still have fragments of it. In 1905 a parchment fragment of an unknown gospel was found at Oxyrhynchus, Egypt. Today it is known as *Papyrus Oxyrhynchus 840*, and it includes a story about Jesus having a dispute with a Pharisee high priest about ritual purity in the temple courts. During the course of the conversation, Jesus says:

> Woe to you blind who do not see. You have washed in these waters that have been poured out, in which dogs and swine have wallowed night and day. And when you washed you scoured the outer skin, which even prostitutes and flute girls anoint, wash, scour, and beautify for human lust. But inside they are full of scorpions and every evil.[196]

We have fragments from other works we can tell were gospels, but unless fuller copies of them are found, they will remain lost.

It is important not to treat every claim of a lost gospel as automatically true. Some have proposed that Q should be considered a lost gospel, but we do not know that Q even existed, as it's a purely hypothetical source.

There have been reports of lost gospels that turned out to be false. One came to public attention in 1973, when historian Morton Smith claimed to have discovered a letter from Clement of Alexandria in which the Church Father discussed a "secret" version of Mark that included additional passages. The letter Smith claimed to have found was unavailable for study, but some in the scholarly community were open to the idea that there was a *Secret Gospel of Mark*. More recently, a strong case has emerged that the letter was a hoax perpetrated by Smith himself.[197]

In 2012, American scholar Karen King announced the discovery of a fragment in which Jesus referred to "my wife." The fragment then was said to be from a lost gospel, and it was immediately dubbed the *Gospel of Jesus' Wife*. However, in 2016, *The Atlantic* published an investigative piece that revealed that King had been taken in by a forger, and King herself acknowledged that this was what the new evidence suggested.[198]

Although there are lost gospels, we need to be careful and should not get overly excited. There have been forgeries and hoaxes, and even if genuine lost gospels were rediscovered, they would not be on the same level as the canonical ones. Matthew, Mark, Luke, and John came to be recognized as canonical *because* they were the earliest, most reliable writings about Jesus and were handed on to the Church by the apostles as authoritative. Anything else does not have the same reliability or authority.

155. What about non-canonical gospels?

In addition to the lost gospels we know existed, we have several non-canonical gospels that survive in whole or in part, with many being discovered only recently. These surviving, non-canonical gospels include:

- the *Infancy Gospel of James* (*Protoevangelium of James*), which relates the birth and life of the Virgin Mary, including Jesus' birth and the flight to Egypt
- the *Infancy Gospel of Thomas*, which covers Jesus' life from ages five to twelve

- the *Gospel of Thomas*, a collection of 114 sayings attributed to Jesus, some of which are based on ones found in the canonical Gospels
- the *Gospel of Judas*, which concerns a dialogue set during the Last Supper
- the *Gospel of Nicodemus*, which concerns Jesus' trial before Pilate and his descent into hell
- the *Gospel of Peter*, which concerns Jesus' crucifixion and resurrection
- the *Gospel of Mary*, which concerns a dialogue set after the Resurrection between Jesus and "Mary" (probably Mary Magdalene)

A notable thing about these gospels is that none follows the pattern of the canonical Gospels—that is, telling a complete story of Jesus' ministry, death, and resurrection.

They thus *presuppose* the canonical Gospels. Once again, the fantastic price of books and the need to keep them short meant that their authors did not have the space to do yet another narrative retelling of Jesus' career. Instead, they focus only on individual aspects of his story. This has important implications. The fact that these authors *presuppose* and *rely on* the canonical Gospels testifies to the canonical Gospels' importance in the early Christian community.

Another important implication of the authors' reliance on the canonical Gospels is that they are *later* works. They date to the second and third centuries—or even later—and so scholars do not regard them as reliable sources of information about Jesus. Some of the earliest and most orthodox ones (e.g., the *Infancy Gospel of James*) may contain *some* accurate traditions regarding Jesus and his family, but they simply are not as reliable as the first-century, canonical ones.

Further, many of these works contain ideas belonging to the Gnostic heresy that emerged in the second century. That is why many non-canonical gospels take the form of dialogues between Jesus and various disciples after his resurrection (the *Gospel of Mary* being an example). In these dialogues, Jesus is shown imparting "secret" Gnostic teachings to select disciples—allowing later Gnostics to explain why their views were not supported by the Catholic Church and were not openly taught by the apostles.

Scholars freely admit that the Gnostic gospels don't tell us anything reliable about Jesus. Instead, their historical value is in telling us about *later heretical groups of Christians* and what they believed.

156. How can I grow closer to Jesus by reading the Gospels?

Matthew, Mark, Luke, and John are by far our best sources of information about Jesus, and one of the best ways to grow closer to Jesus is by reading them. We should do everything possible to learn about our Lord and Savior, and this definitely includes studying what God's inspired word has to say about him.

The Gospels are available in many translations, editions, and formats. The Douay-Rheims (the Catholic equivalent of the King James Version) uses elevated, Elizabethan English for those who prefer that, and there are numerous modern versions with different reading levels, from the more challenging to the very simple. Some translate the Greek in a formal, word-for-word manner, whereas others render it in a more dynamic, thought-for-thought way.

When it comes to editions of these translations, some come with only a few footnotes, whereas others are accompanied with extensive study notes, introductions, maps, timelines, and other study aids.

The Gospels are published in formats including everything from leather-bound, hardbound, and paperback to individual pocket editions containing just the four Gospels to electronic versions that can be found in special Bible study apps or as e-books or web pages. There are even audiobook editions.

If you've never read the Gospels, they can take getting used to, for they are written differently from how books are written today. There is a learning curve when reading the Gospels, so persevere! You will come to understand and appreciate what the authors are doing.

To get the most out of the Gospels, it is important not just to read them, but to read them multiple *ways*. For example, you initially might read them individually, a bit at a time—maybe a chapter or two a day—starting with Matthew and ending with John.

However, later, you should try reading the Gospels in single sittings so that you get the whole flow of a Gospel at once. Set aside two or three hours, read a Gospel, then reflect on its meaning and appreciate what that Evangelist was doing. After you've had time to digest it, set aside a few more hours to read another Gospel and do the same.

In addition to reading the Gospels individually, you can also read them together. For this, having a synopsis that arranges their text in parallel columns is helpful. This will let you see the choices the Evangelists made about what to include, what to omit, what themes to bring out, and what details to emphasize.

At times, you will want to read the Gospels slowly, taking each word in a passage one at a time, thinking about all the possible meanings it might have, and then using clues in the context to help figure out the most probable meanings.

Bear in mind that the Gospels were never meant to be read *alone*. They were meant to be accompanied by apostolic preaching, which could fill in and clarify things. The Gospels do contain "hard sayings" (see John 6:60), and you will encounter things you need to consult other resources to understand.

One of the best things you can do is read the *Catechism of the Catholic Church* (all of it!) so that you have a good grounding in the Faith as a whole. When it comes to specific aids to study the Gospels, there are study guides, commentaries, and books on Bible difficulties that can clarify many points.

Reading the Gospels must not be just an intellectual exercise, for they were meant to enrich us spiritually. There should be a spiritual focus to your study.

Many people pray before and after they study Scripture, asking the Holy Spirit to enlighten their understanding as they read, and afterward thanking God for sharing his word with us.

Another good technique is imagining yourself as present at the events you are reading about. How would you have reacted? What would you have thought and felt? If Jesus is giving an ethical teaching, how can you apply it in your life? If he's giving a warning, to what extent does it apply to you? If he's giving encouragement, how can you appropriate it? And what do his actions reveal about his love both for people in general and for you in particular?

Many engage in a practice known as *lectio divina* (Latin, "divine reading"), which involves a four-stage process of reading, meditation, prayer, and contemplation. This also can be a valuable spiritual approach to the Gospels.

Never before in history have the Gospels been available in so many formats and made accessible to so many people. Never before have there been so many aids to help us get the most out of them. But we need to actually read them if we want to know and grow closer to Jesus.

157. Is there any evidence that Jesus really existed?

To judge by some very recent controversies, you might think that scholars are bitterly divided over this question. But in reality, that Jesus really existed is a mundane and rarely contested fact of history. As Bart Ehrman, an agnostic scholar who is widely regarded as an expert on New Testament documents, writes, "The view that Jesus existed is held by virtually every expert on the planet."[199]

When skeptics ask, "Is there evidence for Jesus?" they usually mean "Is there *non-biblical* evidence for Jesus?" Their question betrays the hidden assumption that the Bible does not count as "historical evidence." But why should we rule out the Bible as evidence that Jesus existed?

Some critics will say that the Bible is biased text that contains stories of miracles, which means it's unreliable as history. But such criteria would make it virtually impossible to do *any* ancient history, since ancient historians were also biased, and many of them (such as Tacitus or Herodotus) also recorded miracle stories. Yet modern historians don't discard ancient accounts of history, but investigate them and critically examine their historical content. And even if skeptics were determined to dismiss the historical reliability of the Gospels, we could use the principles of historical inquiry to come to the conclusion that Jesus existed by examining another biblical source: the letters of St. Paul.

Sometime in the early A.D. 30s, Paul underwent a conversion: from persecutor of the fledgling Church to an apostle who went on to write several letters defending and clarifying Christian theology. His authorship of major New Testament epistles such as Romans, Corinthians, and Galatians is well established even among skeptical scholars. In those letters Paul makes it clear that the Jesus he believed in was a man who was descended from David (Rom. 1:1-3), was born of a woman (Gal. 4:4), had a Last Supper with his disciples (1 Cor. 11:26), was crucified and rose from the dead (1 Cor. 15:3-7).

Paul was able to corroborate this information because he met the disciples of Jesus; he recorded that meeting in Galatians 1:18-19. In fact, the Greek word that Paul uses to describe this discussion with the apostles about Jesus is *historesai*, from which we get the word "history." In that passage, Paul describes a personal meeting he had in Jerusalem with Peter and James, the latter of whom he described as "the brother of the Lord." If Jesus had been a mere legend, then surely one of his alleged relatives, not to mention his chief apostle, would have known it.

Some of those who deny that Jesus existed claim that "brother of the Lord" does not mean that James was Jesus' flesh-and-blood relative, (The Greek word can mean brother, cousin, or another close relative.) but rather a spiritual "brother"—just as today Christians will call each other "brother" and "sister." But if that is what Paul meant, then why isn't Peter also described that way? Moreover, why is James called *the* brother of the Lord as opposed to *a* brother? Other critics claim that James was really the leader of a pre-existing Jewish monastic group called "the brothers of the Lord."[200] But we have no corroborating evidence that such a group existed in Jerusalem at that time.

Instead, a fair reading of Paul's letters shows that he believed Jesus was a real person and since he met the apostles who actually knew Jesus during his ministry, we have a great piece of evidence for the existence of Jesus.

158. Do we know anything about Jesus from outside the Gospels?

The Gospels are our *best* source of information about Jesus but not our *only* source. If we didn't have Matthew, Mark, Luke, and John, we would still know a good bit about him.

Our second-best source is the other books of the New Testament, which also date to the A.D. 50s and 60s. None of these is a book *about* Jesus' life (otherwise, they'd *be* Gospels). For example, Paul's letters are about addressing pastoral situations in various churches. But they contain significant information about Jesus, and we learn dozens of things about him.[201]

From them we know that Jesus was regarded as the Jewish Messiah and was crucified (1 Cor. 1:22–23), that he was descended from David and also the Son of God (Rom. 1:3), that he had a group of followers known as "the Twelve" and "apostles" (1 Cor. 5:5, 7), that Jesus' own countrymen sought to have him killed (1 Thess. 2:15), that Pontius Pilate tried him (1 Tim. 6:15), that he rose "on the third day" (1 Cor. 15:3–4), and that he ascended to heaven (Eph. 4:8–10), where he is now (Rom. 10:6).

We also learn about Jesus' family, including his "brethren" and his notable kinsman James (1 Cor. 9:5; Gal. 1:19), and that Jesus had a particularly notable follower named Cephas—that is, Peter (1 Cor. 5:5; Gal. 1:18–19, 2:9).

We learn that he instituted the Eucharist on the night he was betrayed (1 Cor. 10:23–25) and that he gave teachings on subjects like divorce (1 Cor. 7:10–11).

Even though Paul doesn't attribute certain teachings directly to Jesus, we find him stating that love is the fulfillment of the Mosaic Law (Rom. 13:8), that we should bless those who persecute us (Rom. 13:14), and that we should not pass judgment on others (Rom. 14:4). Given Paul's attitude toward Jesus, we might then infer that Jesus also taught these things.

We also know about Jesus from the writings of the Jewish historian Josephus, who mentions him twice, though one of the passages has been partially corrupted.[202]

We even know of sayings attributed to Jesus that are not in the Gospels. These sayings are referred to as *agrapha* since they are not written in the Gospels (Greek: *a-*, "not" + *graphê*, "writing").

The clearest and most certain is in Acts, where Paul remembers "the words of the Lord Jesus, how he said, 'It is more blessed to give than to receive'" (20:35).

Other *agrapha* are not as certain, but scholars have identified a number of other sayings attributed to Jesus in early Christian sources that may be authentic.[203]

Papias—a late first- and early second-century author—records a saying from "John, the disciple of the Lord" (John the Elder?) in which Jesus taught about the glories of the coming of God's kingdom and said,

> The days will come, in which vines shall grow, each having ten thousand branches, and in each branch ten thousand twigs, and in each true twig ten thousand shoots, and in each one of the shoots ten thousand clusters, and on every one of the clusters ten thousand grapes, and every grape when pressed will give five and twenty measures of wine. And when any one of the saints shall lay hold of a cluster, another shall cry out, "I am a better cluster, take me; bless the Lord through me."[204]

Papias also records that when Judas objected, questioning how this would be possible, Jesus enigmatically replied, "Those who live until those times will see."[205]

Similarly, the first-century document known as the *Letter of Barnabas* records Jesus as saying, "Those who desire to see me and to take hold of my kingdom must take hold of me through affliction and suffering" (7:11). And, writing around A.D. 150, St. Justin Martyr records Jesus as saying, "In whatever state I lay hold of you, in this state I will also judge you."[206]

These sayings are not found in the inspired documents of the New Testament, so they are not certain. However, they are found in very early, orthodox Christian sources, and they should be given consideration as things Jesus *may* have said.

159. Is there evidence outside of the Bible that Jesus existed?

The first-century Jewish historian Josephus mentions Jesus twice in his monumental history of the Jewish people called Antiquities of the Jews. The shorter reference is in book 20, where Josephus describes the stoning of lawbreakers in A.D. 62. One of the criminals is described as "the brother of Jesus, who was called Christ, whose name was James." What makes this passage authentic is that it lacks Christian terms like "the Lord," it fits into the context of this section of the *Antiquities*, and it's found in every manuscript copy of the Antiquities. According to New Testament scholar Robert Van Voorst, "The overwhelming majority of scholars hold that the words 'brother of Jesus, who was called Christ,' are authentic, as is the entire passage in which it is found."[207]

The longer passage in book 18 is called the *Testimonium Flavianum*. Scholars are divided on this passage because although it does mention Jesus, it contains phrases that were almost certainly added by later Christian copyists. These include phrases that would never have been used by a Jew like Josephus, such as, "He was the Christ" or "He appeared alive again on the third day."

Those who deny that Jesus existed, called *mythicists*, maintain that the entire passage is a forgery because it is out of context and interrupts Josephus's previous narrative. But this view neglects the fact that writers in the ancient world did not use footnotes, and would often wander into unrelated topics in their writings. According to New Testament scholar James D.G. Dunn, the passage has clearly been subject to Christian additions, but there are also words Christians would never use of Jesus. These include calling Jesus "a wise man" or referring to themselves as a "tribe"—which is strong evidence Josephus originally wrote something very close to the following:

> At this time there appeared Jesus, a wise man. For he was a doer of startling deeds, a teacher of people who received the truth with pleasure. And he gained a following both among many Jews and among many of Greek origin. And when Pilate, because of an accusation made by the leading men among us, condemned him to the cross, those who had loved him previously did not cease to do so. And up until this very day the tribe of Christians (named after him) has not died out.[208]

The Roman historian Tacitus also records in his *Annals* that after the great fire in Rome, Emperor Nero fastened the blame on a despised group of people called Christians. Tacitus identifies this group thus: "Christus, the founder of the name, was put to death by Pontius Pilate, procurator of Judea in the reign of Tiberius." This corroborates the Gospel data about the basic circumstances of Jesus' life and death.

Mythicists usually claim that the first Christians believed Jesus was just a cosmic savior figure who communicated to believers through visions. Later Christians then added the apocryphal details of Jesus' life (such as his execution under Pontius Pilate) in order to ground him in first-century Palestine. However, if the mythicist theory is true, then at some point in Christian history there would had to have been a break or outright conflict between new converts who believed in a real Jesus and the older establishment view that Jesus never actually existed.

The curious thing about this theory is that the early Christian leaders, known as Church Fathers, loved to stamp out heresy. They wrote massive treatises criticizing heretics, and yet in all of their writings, the heresy that Jesus never existed is never mentioned.[209] In fact, no one in the entire history of Christianity (not even early pagan critics like Celsus or Lucian) seriously argued for a mythic Jesus until the eighteenth century. Heresies of every kind plagued the Church for centuries, yet mythicism is simply unheard of. Christians always believed in a historical Jesus because such a person really did exist.

160. If Jesus really existed, why didn't more historians write about him?

In their book *The Jesus Mysteries*, Timothy Freke and Peter Gandy raise this point, consulting a list of twenty-four ancient authors who lived within 100 years of Jesus.[210] This style of argument actually goes back to a list of forty-two authors devised by the skeptic John Remsburg in 1909. The list contains some impressive names:

> Philo-Judaeus, Seneca, Pliny the Elder, Suetonius, Juvena, Martial, Persius, Plutarch, Justus of Tiberius, Apollonius, Quintilian, Lucanus, Epictetus, Silius Italicus, Statius, Ptolemy, Hermogones, Valerius Maximus, Arrian, Petronius, Dion, Pruseus, Paterculus, Appian, Theon of Smyrna, Phlegon, Pompon Mela, Quintius

> Curtius, Lucian, Pausanias, Valerius Flaccus, Florus Lucius, Favorinus, Phaedrus, Damis, Aulus Gellius, Columella, Dio Chrysostom, Lysias, Appion of Alexandria . . .

Although this list can seem daunting, when each author is examined individually we find that Remsburg's "argument from silence" is faulty, because sometimes silence is justified. For example, many of the authors on these lists didn't even write about history at all. Pausanias and Pompon Mela wrote Greek and Roman geographies. Ptolemy, Columella, and Pliny the Elder were scientists who recorded information about the natural world. Theon of Smyrna, Favorinus, and Gellius wrote reflections on philosophy, and Theon's only surviving work is entitled *On Mathematics Useful for the Understanding of Plato.* Other writers, such as Hermogenes, Quintilian, Apollonius Dyscolus, and Dio Chrysostom focused on practical subjects like speech-making. And Columella limited his writing to the subject of trees that existed within the Roman Empire!

The ones who *were* historians often did not even write about the time period in which Jesus lived. Statius, Flaccus, and Appolonius the Sophist only wrote about ancient Greek subjects. Other writers, such as Arrian, were devoted to writing about the world conqueror and larger-than-life legend Alexander the Great—who lived four hundred years before Christ.

What about authors whose subject might have reasonably included mention of Jesus? Atheist David Fitzgerald notes, for example, that the first-century writer Justus does not mention Jesus in his *History of the Jewish Kings*.[211] And yet, although Jesus might at first seem like a related topic for this writer, a faithful Jew like Justus would not have written about a disgraced and executed criminal. Expecting Justus to mention Jesus in a history of Jewish kings would be like expecting a faithful Catholic author to mention some obscure cult leader in his history of the popes.

More generally, that many ancient authors did not mention Jesus simply underscores how little Jesus meant to the ancient world. As scholar John Meier put it, from the perspective of ancient people, Jesus was a "marginal Jew" who was executed in a backwater Roman province. As a result, most ancient historians would not have written about a man who would only later be known as the object of worship in a persecuted cult movement.

Finally, it's interesting to note, by way of comparison, that the only written sources we have for the existence of Pontius Pilate are Josephus, Tacitus, and the Jewish historian Philo. If we only have these few sources to account for the administrator of an entire Roman province, then why should we expect there to be a wealth of literature about an obscure itinerant preacher like Jesus?

161. How reliable are the Gospels?

From the perspective of faith, the four Gospels—like all books of the Bible—are divinely inspired, and this has implications for their truth and reliability. According to the Second Vatican Council:

> To compose the sacred books, God chose certain men who, all the while he employed them in this task, made full use of their own faculties and powers so that, though he acted in them and by them, it was as true authors that they consigned to writing whatever he wanted written, and no more.
>
> Since therefore all that the inspired authors or sacred writers affirm should be regarded as affirmed by the Holy Spirit, we must acknowledge that the books of Scripture firmly, faithfully, and without error teach that truth which God, for the sake of our salvation, wished to see confided to the sacred scriptures (*Dei Verbum* 11).

Since, under divine inspiration, the Evangelists wrote "whatever [God] wanted written, and no more," whatever the Gospels affirm is "affirmed by the Holy Spirit" and so teaches the truth "without error." The Gospels are thus completely reliable.

This doesn't mean that what the Evangelist is affirming is always obvious, but it does mean that if we have properly understood what the Evangelist is saying, God guarantees that it's true.

Even with the assurances that faith gives, it is also a valuable exercise to demonstrate the reliability of the Gospels from the perspective of reason.

In a wave of skeptical scholarship that began a little more than two hundred years ago, everything was questioned and challenged. Skeptics came to hold that the Gospels were written by anonymous individuals, long after the events they portray, and that the stories and sayings of Jesus were the product of long periods of oral transmission in an unreliable game of "telephone."

There are reasons to reject each of these claims. The Gospels were in fact written quite early, by men whose names are on them, and are based on eyewitness or near-eyewitness testimony. But even if one were to admit a lapse of forty or fifty years since the events (if one follows the later dating proposed by some scholars), would that make impossible to accurately remember the events being described?

Consider that the events surrounding Jesus' life and ministry would have left an indelible mark on the apostles' memories. Their ability to remember the events of Jesus' life would be comparable to a veteran in the year 2016 remembering what he did during the Vietnam War.

We also have to remember that our "memory muscles" atrophy as a result of using electronic recording devices (such as when we fail to remember telephone numbers and rely on the directory in our phones). This was not the case in Jesus' time, and the Jewish Talmud even records how some rabbis could memorize the entire Old Testament.[212]

In addition, Jesus was a traveling preacher who delivered the same sermons throughout his travels, many of which contain poetic structure or memorable puns. The apostles would have heard his teachings dozens if not hundreds of times and then repeated them in their own preaching, thus making the deeds and teachings of Christ easy to remember. In any case, in a world before tape recorders, audiences did not expect verbatim transcripts, particularly of speeches that were given only on one occasion, such as the long discourses in John's Gospel. Instead, they expected a competent author to accurately express the *thought* of the figure in question. We can trust that the beloved disciple did so faithfully, all the more so because Jesus had explicitly promised his apostles the help of the Spirit of truth to "bring to your remembrance all that I have said to you" (John 14:27).

There are also a good many details in the Gospels that point toward their authenticity.[213] For example, in John, when Jesus is about to miraculously feed the five thousand, he asks Philip where it would be possible to buy bread (John 6:5–6). Luke, meanwhile, records that the feeding of the five thousand occurred in a desolate place near the town of Bethsaida (Luke 9:10–13). That would explain why Jesus would ask Philip where bread could be bought. We know from John that Philip was from Bethsaida—the town from which Peter and Andrew also originally hailed (John 1:44; 12:21). Why then did Jesus ask Philip, and not Peter or Andrew?

The matter is clarified in Mark, who indicates that Peter and Andrew were now living in the village of Capernaum (Mark 1:21–29). They no longer lived in Bethsaida and would not have up-to-date knowledge of where bread could be bought. Jesus thus asked Philip.

It is striking that each fact is mentioned in only one of the Gospels:

- Only John mentions that Jesus asked Philip where to buy bread and that Philip was from Bethsaida.
- Only Luke mentions that the feeding of the five thousand took place near Bethsaida.
- Only Mark mentions that Peter and Andrew were now living in Capernaum.

Yet when careful attention is paid to the details of each Gospel, a coherent picture emerges of why Jesus specifically asked Philip where bread could be bought. This is not the kind of situation that would arise if the Evangelists were making up details at random. The Gospels are all too short for chance to explain the matter. Neither does the situation reflect a collusion of authors, for the relevant details are mentioned only in passing and nothing is ever made of them.

This indicates that the Evangelists are accurately recording historical details, whose integrity is shown when their accounts are compared.

Other details point to authenticity because they contain confusing and often embarrassing elements that a fabricator would have removed. These include the apostles' cowardly and stupid behavior (and Jesus' rebuking them for it), Jesus' hard sayings, and the overall high ethical demands of the Gospel. Historians call this the *criterion of embarrassment*, and it makes these portions of the New Testament very reliable.

Furthermore, if the Gospels had been invented by the early Church, then we would expect to find Jesus being used as a ventriloquist dummy on behalf of the factions within the early Christian community, which was divided over issues such as the eating of meat sacrificed to idols. Since we never read in the Gospels of Jesus speaking on many issues that later affected the early Church, we can have increased confidence in their early dating, and in taking the Gospel accounts not as purely theological treatises but as *bioi*, or ancient biography.[214]

In addition, because Luke is also the author of Acts, which ranges all over the Greco-Roman world, it is possible to prove that Luke was extraordinarily accurate as a historian. British scholar William Ramsay did a study of Acts—expecting it to be unreliable—only to conclude that "Acts may justly be quoted as a trustworthy historical authority" and "Luke is a historian of the first rank. . . . In short, this author should be placed along with the very greatest of historians."[215]

In sum, as the Greco-Roman Historian A.N. Sherwin-White writes, "It is astonishing that while Greco-Roman historians have been growing in confidence, the twentieth century study of the Gospel narratives, starting from no less promising material, has taken so gloomy a turn in the development of form criticism." When it comes to the standards of ancient history, the Gospels are among our best and most reliable sources for the life of Christ.[216]

162. Aren't the stories about Jesus simply copied from pagan mythology?

Similarities among religions shouldn't surprise us. Most religions, after all, try to answer the same fundamental questions in life: "Where did we come from?" "Is there an afterlife?" "How should we live?" Most religions have rituals, sacred stories, and moral codes. It would be surprising if there *weren't* some similarities among them. In fact, you might say that the similarities are a sign that God does exist—you might expect different religions in different eras and cultures to reach many similar conclusions about what he's like and how to relate to him.

But when we examine the alleged dying and rising gods that are supposed to be the inspiration for Christianity, we find that the supposed parallels between them and Jesus have no basis in fact. Let's examine two of the most popular alleged pagan inspirations for Christianity—Mithra and Horus.[217]

Mithra was the deity of a Roman mystery religion who, some mythicists say, was allegedly born of a virgin on December 25, had twelve disciples, enjoyed a last supper with his disciples, was crucified, and then rose from the dead. That does sound a lot like Jesus, but is it true?

Well, history does mention a god named Mithra (also called Mitra) in a treaty discovered in Iran that is dated to 1400 B.C., but this Persian god (who was invoked to uphold contracts) was not the same Roman warrior Mithra alleged to be the model for Jesus. And although it was once thought that belief in *the latter* Mithra pre-dated Christianity, modern mithraic scholars have almost universally rejected the idea.[218] It seems that the Roman cult of Mithra came *after* Christianity, so there's no way that a mythic Jesus could have been based on it.

Furthermore, the connections between the Roman Mithra and Jesus are spurious at best. Although there is evidence that the Romans had a festival on

December 25 in honor of their sun god, there is no real evidence to connect this feast with the birth of Mithra.[219] Mithra was *not* said to have been born of a virgin, but emerged fully grown from a rock. Yes, there is a painting of him standing next to twelve figures, but there is no evidence they are disciples (they were probably just references to the Zodiac). Finally, there is simply no ancient record of Mithra being crucified or rising from the dead.[220] Such claims are fanciful embellishments or outright lies.

What about Horus? He was the Egyptian sky god who was said to have been born of a virgin, baptized by Anup (who was later beheaded, like John the Baptist), had twelve disciples, was crucified, and rose from the dead.

Much of the Jesus/Horus connection has been fueled by the bad scholarship of the nineteenth-century amateur Egyptologist Gerald Massey. It was he who asserted that Horus was baptized by Anup, that Anup was later beheaded, and that Horus had twelve disciples. There's only one problem: nowhere in Egyptian literature is there evidence for such claims. Unsurprisingly, Massey's work is largely ignored by modern Egypt scholars, but the internet and popular media keep his claims alive.

The parallels between Jesus and Horus for which there is some evidence tend to be ambiguous or subject to misinterpretation. For example, Horus was said to be conceived when his mother Isis engaged in sexual relations with the dead body of his father Osiris. This hardly seems comparable to the virgin birth of Jesus. Likewise, the claim that Horus was crucified is based solely on images of Horus standing with his arms spread wide. This could mean almost anything, of course—though probably not crucifixion, since there's no evidence that the ancient Egyptians used that method to execute people.

Similarly, Horus's "resurrection" consists of his grieving mother bringing him back to life after he was stung by a scorpion so that he could go on to attain his father Osiris's throne. Indeed, many of the so-called resurrections in ancient mythology are just reanimations of the deceased, far different from Jesus' glorious rise to immortal life. This includes Horus's own father Osiris, whose dead body was dismembered and scattered around Egypt before being re-assembled, allowing Osiris to become ruler of the underworld.

T.N.D. Mettigner writes in his scholarly monograph *Riddle of the Resurrection: Dying and Rising Gods in the Ancient Near East*, "There is, as far as I am aware, no *prima facie* evidence that the death and resurrection of Jesus is a mythological construct, drawing on myths and rites of the dying and rising gods of the surrounding world. While studied with profit against the background of Jewish resurrection belief, the faith in the death and resurrection of Jesus retains its unique character in the history of religions."[221]

163. Are there contradictions in the Gospels?

Sometimes skeptics assert that there are contradictions in the Gospels. It is important to know how to address these claims.

In the first place, the alleged contradictions are never about major matters. Skeptics are not able to point to passages saying that Jesus was a Greek rather than a Jew, that Joseph was his biological father, or that he was stoned rather than crucified. Invariably, the alleged contradictions are minor. Thus, even if there were discrepancies among the Gospels, they would be on lesser matters, and their substance would still be correct.

However, it turns out that the alleged, minor discrepancies are not contradictions. They might appear so to skeptics reading the Gospels as if they were written according to modern conventions. But when we examine the way ancient literature was written, we find they are not.

The Second Vatican Council points out the need to study the way ancient authors wrote:

> Seeing that, in Sacred Scripture, God speaks through men in human fashion, it follows that the interpreter of sacred scriptures, if he is to ascertain what God has wished to communicate to us, should carefully search out the meaning which the sacred writers really had in mind, that meaning which God had thought well to manifest through the medium of their words (*Dei Verbum* 12).

Here we will look at three ancient writing practices that can trip up modern readers: selection, paraphrase, and sequencing.

Selection deals with what material an author chooses to include. Because books were fantastically expensive and the Evangelists wanted to keep their works small enough to fit on a single scroll, they had to choose which details to include and which to omit. John even alludes to the fact that he knew much more than he was able to write (21:25).

The Evangelists made choices about what details to mention and omit, and sometimes skeptics portray these as contradictions. For example, Mark 10:46–52 records how Jesus healed blind Bartimaeus at Jericho, although Matthew 9:27–31 indicates that he healed two blind men on that occasion.

This is not a contradiction. Mark simply focuses on Bartimaeus, whereas Matthew mentions the other blind man. This has been compared to how witnesses to a car crash may report different details without contradicting each other.

Paraphrase is using different words to convey the same meaning. We do this constantly in everyday speech. We communicate the gist of what someone said to us without using his exact words. But in written works, we don't expect to see paraphrases put between quotation marks. This is partly because we live in a world of recording devices, and it's much easier to check what someone said and give his words exactly.

But they didn't have recorders in the ancient world. They also didn't have quotation marks (those are added by Bible translators), and so ancient audiences didn't expect authors to always give exact wording. They expected authors to accurately give the gist of what someone would have said on an occasion, but not the precise wording.

For example, Matthew gives the opening of the Lord's Prayer like this: "Our Father who is in heaven, hallowed be your name. Your kingdom come. Your will be done on earth as it is in heaven" (6:9–10), whereas Luke gives it in a shorter form: "Father, hallowed be your name. Your kingdom come" (11:2).

Ancient audiences would regard this not as a contradiction, but as the kind of paraphrase they would normally expect. Both authors preserve the same meaning; it's just that the wording of the prayer is slightly different.

Sequencing deals with the order in which an author presents his material. This can be done different ways. Sometimes an author may present material in a strict chronological sequence, but other times, he may arrange it by topic.

This can trip up modern readers because we live in an age in which records are kept about precisely when things occurred. In the ancient world, this usually wasn't the case. People would remember *what* happened, but not the *exact date*. As a result, ancient audiences didn't expect an author to keep things in strictly chronological order unless he said that is what he was doing.

Thus, when Matthew collects different sayings of Jesus and arranges them into speeches by topic, such as in the Sermon on the Mount (Matt. 5–7), the original audience would not have understood him as claiming that Jesus literally delivered all these sayings, in this order, on a single occasion.

For them, the important thing would have been *that* Jesus said them, not *when* he said them.

An awareness that the Evangelists—like other ancient authors—may use topical rather than chronological sequencing thus resolves alleged discrepancies regarding chronology in the Gospels.

Ultimately, there are no contradictions in the Gospels, but showing this requires us to understand what the Evangelists were and weren't affirming, which requires a knowledge of how ancient literature worked.

164. Do the infancy narratives contain contradictions or historical errors?

Sometimes skeptics have claimed that the infancy narratives found in Matthew 1–2 and Luke 1–2 contradict each other. For example, it is pointed out that Luke has Mary living in Nazareth before going to Bethlehem, whereas in Matthew they don't go to Nazareth until later. It has also been claimed that they contain historical errors, such as Matthew's mention of Herod's slaughter of boys in Bethlehem (Matt. 2:16) or Luke's mention of the enrollment that took place when Jesus was born (Luke 2:1–5).

All these difficulties are resolvable. First, the infancy narratives don't contradict each other. They fit together very well. Here's an interwoven narrative:

Initially, Gabriel appears to Zechariah to announce the birth of John the Baptist (Luke 1:5–25). A few months later, Gabriel appears to Mary in Nazareth to announce the birth of Jesus (Luke 1:26–38), and Mary goes to visit Elizabeth before returning to Nazareth (Luke 1:39–56). Then John the Baptist is born (Luke 1:57–80).

Around this time, Joseph is informed that Mary is pregnant. He plans to divorce her, but an angel tells him to continue the marriage (Matt. 1:18–23). The two begin cohabiting (Matt. 1:24). This would be in Nazareth, per Luke's account.

Because of the enrollment announced by Caesar Augustus, the Holy Family travels to Bethlehem (Luke 2:1–5), where Jesus is born (Matt. 1:25a; Luke 2:7). That night, the shepherds visit them (Luke 2:8–20). Around the same time, the Magi observe the star in their homeland (see Matt. 2:2, 9).

Eight days after birth, Jesus is circumcised and named (Matt. 1:25b; Luke 2:21), and after forty days he is presented at the temple (Luke 2:22–38).

At this point, the Holy Family either returns to Nazareth or remains in Bethlehem (which of the two they did is not clear). If they returned to Nazareth, they continued to visit Jerusalem and their relatives in Bethlehem multiple times every year for the three annual pilgrimage feasts (Exod. 23:14–17; see Luke 2:41).

Between one and two years after the birth (see Matt. 2:16), the Magi arrive and are directed to Bethlehem, where they find the Holy Family (Matt. 2:1–11). They are warned in a dream to return to their country by a different route (Matt. 2:12). Also warned in a dream, the Holy Family flees to Egypt (Matt. 2:13–15) to avoid the Slaughter of the Innocents (Matt. 2:16–18).

When Herod the Great dies, the Holy Family returns to Israel (Matt. 2:19–21), but Joseph learns Herod Archelaus is ruling in Judea and so takes the family to Nazareth (Matt. 2:22–23).[222]

Herod's slaughter of Bethlehem's baby boys is sometimes claimed to be a myth, as we don't have extrabiblical records of it happening. However, the Gospel of Matthew is *itself* a record, and it cannot simply be set aside.

Further, we would not expect surviving extrabiblical records to mention the event. Bethlehem was small (Mic. 5:2), and in Jesus' day its population was between 300 and 1,000. The number of males under two was likely no more than twenty-five to thirty; perhaps no more than six or seven.[223] In comparison to the other atrocities of Herod, it may not even have been particularly surprising or memorable to those not directly impacted.

We don't have any of Herod's court records, and what knowledge we have of his acts is spotty, being principally derived from the Jewish historian Josephus, who was born decades after Herod died.

Despite this, the story fits what was known about Herod. During the latter part of his reign he became paranoid and obsessed with keeping power. He saw plots everywhere and consequently executed his favorite wife and three of his sons. Caesar Augustus allegedly quipped, "It is better to be Herod's pig than son"[224]—the joke being that, as a Jew, Herod wouldn't eat pork, and his pig would be safe. Herod is also known to have ordered mass executions. As his own death approached, he had a large number of prominent men confined in a stadium and ordered that they be killed so every family would grieve upon his death.[225]

The Slaughter of the Innocents is precisely what we would expect of Herod upon learning a baby was born who had a rival claim to the Jewish throne.

Concerning Luke's "enrollment," claims are made that it wouldn't have been empire-wide, that Joseph wouldn't have gone to Bethlehem, and that Mary wouldn't have accompanied him. However, there are solutions to each challenge.

Augustus was emperor from 27 B.C. to A.D. 14, and he began the practice of empire-wide census taking: "Every five years, the Romans enumerated citizens and their property to determine their liabilities. *This practice was extended to include the entire Roman Empire in 5 B.C.*"[226] Because of the size of the empire, census taking was done in stages, taking place in different countries in different years. The decree of 5 B.C. thus likely wasn't implemented in Palestine for a few years. If the census was being done for tax purposes—as was normal—it would explain why Joseph returned to Bethlehem: he was from there and still had property there.

However, the enrollment may not have been a census. It may be an event that took place in 3–2 B.C. when the people of the empire swore allegiance to Augustus. In this case, Joseph may have returned to Bethlehem because Israel was organized tribally, and the Romans may have used the tribal structure to ensure that the locals took the oath. Since Bethlehem was the ancestral home of Joseph's clan, that is where he went.

Mary went with Joseph because she was his wife and could be better cared for by him and other relatives in Bethlehem than if left at home. Contrary to popular depictions in art, we need not suppose that she made the journey to Bethlehem in the last stages of pregnancy. Luke merely says that "while they were there, the time came for her to be delivered" (Luke 2:6).

Finally, Luke and his readers were familiar with the way such enrollments worked. They had taken part in such events themselves. Even critical scholar Raymond Brown notes, "It is dangerous to assume that [Luke] described a process of registration that would have been patently opposed to everything that he and his readers knew."[227]

165. Does the Passion narrative contain contradictions or historical errors?

Various claims have been made regarding the narrative that chronicles the events that led up to Jesus' crucifixion. For example, it has been asserted that the Gospels contradict each other regarding the day and time of the Crucifixion and that events like the release of Barabbas would not have occurred.

Regarding the day on which Christ was crucified, all four Gospels indicate it was a Friday, which was then known as the *Day of Preparation*—that is, the day on which people cooked food and made other preparations since they would not be allowed to work on Saturday—the Sabbath—which began at sundown (Matt. 27:62, Mark 15:42, Luke 23:54, John 19:31, 42).

The point that is disputed is the relationship of this Friday to the feast of Passover. The synoptic Gospels (Matthew, Mark, and Luke) indicate that Jesus celebrated the Last Supper as a Passover meal (Matt. 26:19, Mark 14:16, Luke 22:13, 15). Since he was crucified on the afternoon of the following day, this would place the Crucifixion on the same day by Jewish reckoning—that is, on the day of Passover.

However, some claim that John places the crucifixion of Jesus, the Lamb of God, at the same time the lambs were being slaughtered at the temple in preparation for the Passover feast. As the Jewish authorities did not want to enter Pilate's headquarters "so that they might not be defiled, but might eat the Passover" (John 18:28), this would suggest Jesus was crucified the day *before* the Passover meal was eaten.

There are multiple solutions to this difficulty. One of them consists of two points: first, John *never says* Jesus was crucified when the lambs were being slaughtered. This myth is so commonly repeated that people think it's in the Bible when it is not. It is simply a theological explanation of why John may have thought it appropriate to place the Crucifixion in parallel with the eve of the Passover, if this is what he did.

Second, the reason that the Jewish authorities didn't want to defile themselves was because Passover continued for a week after the lamb was eaten (Exod. 12:15, 18–20), and they wanted to *continue* to eat sanctified food during the festival.

John thus does not contradict the synoptics' indication that Jesus was crucified on the first day of Passover, following the eating of the Passover lamb the previous evening.

Regarding the time of day, Mark says Jesus was crucified at "the third hour" (Mark 15:25), and all three synoptics record the darkness from "the sixth hour" to "the ninth hour" while he was on the cross (Matt. 27:45; Mark 15:33; Luke 23:44), but John indicates that Jesus wasn't yet crucified at "the sixth hour" (John 19:14).

The solution is straightforward: in first-century Judea, the custom was to count twelve hours from sunrise, as illustrated in Jesus' parable in Matthew

20:1–16, where a man hires workers at the third, sixth, ninth, and eleventh hours of daytime.

John, however, was using the Roman practice of counting hours beginning at midnight. Thus in John 1:39 two disciples are said to spend "that day" with Jesus, even though they met him "about the tenth hour." This would make more sense if John were counting from midnight (making the tenth hour 10 a.m.) than if he was counting from dawn (making the tenth hour 4 p.m·).

The timing of the Crucifixion thus is clear if we take account of the two systems of reckoning hours. In John, Pilate brings Jesus out to the crowd at "about the sixth hour" after midnight (around 6 a.m.). According to Mark he is then crucified at "the third hour" after dawn (around 9 a.m.). And according to all three synoptics, darkness covered the land from the sixth to the ninth hours after dawn (from around noon to 3 p.m.).

As to the release of Barabbas, we do not have an extrabiblical record that says, "Pilate customarily released a prisoner at Passover," but that's hardly surprising. Releasing a prisoner at the Jewish capital on a Jewish feast would be a purely local custom, and we don't have detailed records of the Roman administration in Judea.

However, leaders often pardon popular political prisoners to curry favor with their subjects. We have records of ancient rulers in Judea doing just that. Both Herod Archelaus (4 B.C.–A.D. 6) and the Roman governor Albinus (A.D. 62–64) did so.[228] And the Jewish *Mishnah* (a collection of oral traditions) contains provisions for slaughtering the Passover lamb for prisoners released at Passover.[229]

Even if we didn't know all that, the Gospels are historical records in their own right, they must be taken seriously, and *all four* mention the custom (Matt. 27:15, Mark 15:6, Luke 23:18, John 18:39).

166. How do we know that Jesus truly died and was buried?

The main groups who deny that Jesus was crucified are a) mythicists who deny that Jesus even existed and b) Muslims who believe in the Quran's teaching that Jesus was not crucified but that a "look-alike" was put on the cross in his place.[230] However, religious and non-religious scholars who do not have a preconceived attitude about Jesus' death agree that Jesus of Nazareth was crucified in first-century Judea. For example, the famous skeptical critic John Dominic Crossan denies that Jesus rose from the dead, but even he admits, "That he was crucified is as sure as anything historical can ever be."[231] It is the uniform testimony of the New Testament, as well as ancient historians such as Josephus and Tacitus, that Jesus was crucified under Pontius Pilate.

But can we be certain that Jesus actually died on the cross and didn't simply pass out and wake up later in the tomb? Medically speaking, it seems pretty certain. In 1986, the American Medical Association published a paper that analyzed the Gospel accounts, as well as ancient records of crucifixion. It came to the conclusion that Jesus' survival of both the intense flogging that flayed his skin as well as the asphyxiation brought on by crucifixion would have been almost impossible.[232]

Even if Jesus did somehow survive the Crucifixion, it is very unlikely that the apostles would have believed that he triumphantly rose from the dead. Even the famous nineteenth-century skeptic and "de-mythologizer" David Strauss rejected this theory, writing, "It is impossible that a being who had stolen half dead out of the sepulchre, who crept about weak and ill and wanting medical treatment . . . could have given the disciples the impression that he was a conqueror over death and the grave, the Prince of life: an impression that lay at the bottom of their future ministry."[233]

Nearly every historian, both secular and Christian, agrees that Jesus died from crucifixion. Where they disagree is on what happened to Jesus' body after he was crucified. The Gospels say that Jesus was buried in a tomb owned by Joseph of Arimathea, a member of the Sanhedrin council that condemned Jesus.[234] There is no ancient account of Jesus' being thrown in a ditch, or given to his family, or eaten by vultures on the cross, to contradict the Gospel's descriptions.

But did the burial really happen? Wouldn't a condemned criminal have simply been thrown into a pit (as Crossan argues), or even just left on the cross?

In ancient Judea, as in our cultures today, most people who died were buried in some kind of tomb or plot. According to Deuteronomy 21:22-23, the Jewish people were forbidden by their law to leave a criminal hanging on a tree and had to bury him immediately. We can also conjecture that the Roman occupiers of Judea, constantly worried about Jewish uprisings, would have removed Jesus from the cross rather than leave him up as an inducement to riots during the Passover.

Assuming it evident that Jesus was taken down from the cross, what evidence is there that he was buried in a tomb? First, Jesus' burial is described in all four Gospels and corroborated in Paul's first letter to the Corinthians. The Greek word for "buried" used in these accounts is *hetaphe*, which is derived from the root *thapto*: "to bury." The word is also used in Matthew 14:12 to describe John the Baptist's disciples formally burying him after his execution. But would a condemned criminal have received such a burial? Why wasn't Jesus simply thrown into the communal plot in the criminal's graveyard?

First of all, the only skeleton we know of from a first-century crucifixion victim, that of Yehohanan of Giv'at Ha-Mivtar, was found in a tomb.[235] This shows that it was not unheard of for Jewish criminals to be allowed a proper burial. Plus, if the Gospel writers had invented the burial story, it is unlikely that they would have concocted a tale of him receiving funeral rites at the hands of Joseph of Arimathea, who was a member of the council that condemned Jesus to death. If Jesus had merely been thrown into a common grave, there is no reason to believe that fact would have been changed or omitted from the Gospels. The Christian movement did not attempt to hide the fact that Jesus was shamefully executed, so why bother hiding a shameful burial?

Finally, it is worth remembering that if burial was an act of reverence on the part of Jesus' disciples, it was also an act of prudence on the part of the Pharisees and Roman authorities, who could thereby guard a sealed tomb against any hoaxsters (Matt. 27:62-69). So evidence and logic suggest that Jesus was indeed buried in a tomb as the Gospels say he was.

167. How do we know that Jesus' tomb was really empty on Easter Sunday?

We should first remember that bodies *do* go missing from graves from time to time. Jesus' tomb being found empty is not an extraordinary event that requires mountains of evidence to corroborate it. Indeed, the empty tomb is recorded in all four Gospels, which provide multiple independent sources for the event's authenticity. Critics may object that St. Paul does not describe the empty tomb, saying only that Jesus was buried and then raised. But it would have made no sense for Paul to say Jesus was raised if he thought his body remained in the tomb.

Another piece of evidence for the empty tomb is the fact that the disciples preached the empty tomb in the city of Jerusalem.[236] If the tomb were not empty, enemies of the early Church could have easily exhumed the body and quashed the first Easter proclamation. Critics may argue that the apostles did not begin preaching until fifty days after the Crucifixion, on Pentecost, and by that time the body would have been so badly decomposed that it would have been unidentifiable. However, even after that amount of time (especially in the arid climate of Jerusalem) an exhumer would be able to identify a corpse with crucifixion wounds. It would then have been up to the apostles to prove this corpse was not Jesus.

Even the earliest enemies of the Church affirmed that Jesus' tomb was empty. The Gospel of Matthew records that the guards at the tomb were told to say, "His disciples came by night and stole him while we were asleep" (Matt. 28:13-15) and that this explanation was still being circulated when Matthew wrote his Gospel. In Justin Martyr's dialogue with the Rabbi Trypho in the second century, he refers to claims by critics, like Trypho, who argue that the disciples stole Jesus' body from the tomb.

One of the most powerful pieces of evidence that the empty-tomb tradition is historical is that the Gospels record *women* discovering the tomb. In first-century Palestine the testimony of women was considered completely unreliable, and it was an embarrassment to rely upon it. The Jewish Talmud says, "The words of the Torah should be burned rather than entrusted to women" and that the testimony of women in court held the same weight as that of a criminal.[237]The Jewish historian Josephus also wrote in favor of forbidding the testimony of women on account of the "levity and boldness of their sex."[238] The Jewish historian Josephus also wrote in favor of forbidding the testimony of women on account of the "levity and boldness of their sex."[223] Because of how embarrassing this detail was, the Gospel writers would have included it only because that is simply what happened.

Finally, the empty tomb is a very simple story that lacks signs of legendary embellishment. Unlike the apocryphal Gospels written centuries later, which include lavish miracles and feature entire Jewish and Roman assemblies at the tomb, Mark's Gospel (likely our earliest source) is very simple and only includes the women meeting a young man seated beside Jesus' grave clothes. The most plausible explanation for this simple account, the embarrassing use of women's testimony, the preaching in Jerusalem that went unchallenged, as well as the arguments from early opponents that the disciples stole the body is that Jesus' tomb was indeed empty on the Sunday following his crucifixion.[239]

What of the alternative explanation that the disciples stole Jesus' body? It's not impossible but this theory—called the fraud theory—seems extremely unlikely. First, because there's no evidence of any crack in the conspiracy—no record of a single Christian admitting after the fact that it was all a hoax. Moreover, fraud is normally committed for personal gain; however, the only thing the disciples had to gain from their fraud was a martyr's death. The fearless zeal, in the face of much persecution, with which the apostles preached (and suffered for) the gospel after Jesus' resurrection seems incompatible with the fraud theory.

168. How can we deal with the differences in the Resurrection narratives?

Critics have pointed to differences in the Gospel accounts of what happened after Jesus' resurrection and charged them with contradicting each other. However, this is not the case.

St. Paul indicates that Jesus made multiple post-resurrection appearances (1 Cor. 15:5–8), and Luke indicates that Jesus appeared repeatedly over a period of forty days (Acts 1:3). Consequently, the Evangelists needed to make choices about what appearances to include in their Gospels.

The solutions to the proposed difficulties become apparent when we recognize the different choices the authors made in selecting and sequencing their material. Here is an interwoven narrative:

All four Gospels agree that women went to Jesus' tomb after the Sabbath, around dawn on the first day of the week (Matt. 28:1; Mark 16:1–2; Luke 24:1; John 20:1). The stone was rolled away, the body was gone, and they had an angelic encounter (Matt. 28:2–7; Mark 16:4–7; Luke 24:2–7, 10; John 20:1, 11–13).

The Evangelists vary in which details they mention. All four indicate that Mary Magdalene was among the women, whereas Matthew, Mark, and Luke also mention her companions.

Matthew mentions there were guards at the tomb (Matt. 27:62–66; 28:4, 11–15). He also records that an angel rolled back the stone. Matthew thus makes explicit something that is implicit in the other three accounts. The way he records the angel's action could be read as a flashback (to what happened before the women arrived). Regardless, the Evangelists were not bound to record events in chronological order.

Matthew and Mark mention one angel, whereas Luke and John mention two, and they record different parts of the angels' message. Matthew and

Mark mention that Jesus will appear to the disciples in Galilee, whereas Luke and John omit this.

What the women experience at the tomb provokes different initial reactions. Mary Magdalene runs to Peter and John, the beloved disciple (John 20:2), whereas some of her companions leave the tomb without initially saying anything to anyone (Mark 16:8).

After Peter and John visit the tomb and return home (John 20:3–10; see Luke 24:12), Jesus appears to Mary Magdalene, who is still at the tomb (John 20:14–17; Mark 16:9), and then to the other women who have already left it (Matt. 28:9-10). Once again, Mary Magdalene runs directly to the apostles to tell of having seen the Lord (John 20:18; Mark 16:9), a report that her companions then confirm (Matt. 28:8; Luke 24:9-11).

Luke further mentions appearances Jesus made the same day in the Jerusalem vicinity (Luke 24:13–44), whereas Matthew chose one in Galilee (Matt. 28:16–20). Mark also indicates Jesus' appearance in Galilee (Mark 14:28; 16:7), but his original ending (which may be paralleled in Matthew) appears to have been lost. John records post-resurrection appearances in both Galilee and Jerusalem (John 20:19–29; 21:1–23).

Luke tells us that, after visiting Galilee, the disciples were back in the Jerusalem area before the Ascension (Luke 24:50–53, Acts 1:9–12), and on this occasion Jesus tells them to remain in the city until the descent of the Holy Spirit on Pentecost, when they will begin their major evangelistic work (Luke 24:49, Acts 1:4; 2:1–47). Luke focuses on the appearances in and around Jerusalem, because he is planning to chronicle, in Acts, how the Christian faith began spreading in stages, through the apostles' witness "in Jerusalem and in all Judea and Samaria and to the end of the earth" (Acts 1:8).

Matthew and Mark, not planning on writing sequels to their Gospels, focus instead on an appearance in Galilee, bringing closure on a literary level by taking us back to where Jesus' ministry began. And John, writing to supplement the synoptic Gospels, records additional appearances in both places.[240]

169. Can we trust the stories about Jesus appearing to people after he died?

It's true, an empty tomb does not by itself prove a resurrection has taken place. This is evidenced by Mary Magdalene, who thought that the empty tomb meant that someone had simply taken Jesus' body (John 20:2).

However, the empty tomb coupled with the fact that the apostles saw Jesus alive after his death (which is what convinced Mary Magdalene) provides powerful evidence for his resurrection.

So how do we know that the stories of the apostles' seeing a resurrected Jesus are indeed authentic and not mere legends? The best evidence for the historical reliability of the post-Resurrection appearances is 1 Corinthians 15:3-7. This passage in Paul's letter proceeds as follows:

> For I handed on to you as of first importance what I also received:
>
> that Christ died for our sins in accordance with the scriptures;
>
> that he was buried;
>
> that he was raised on the third day in accordance with the scriptures;
>
> that he appeared to Cephas, then to the Twelve.
>
> After that, he appeared to more than five hundred brothers at once, most of whom are still living, though some have fallen asleep.
>
> After that he appeared to James, then to all the apostles.

Paul ends this creed in verse eight, saying that after those other appearances Jesus appeared also to him. A linguistic analysis of this passage shows that verses 3-7 were not something that Paul composed when he wrote his letter to the Corinthians in A.D. 55. Instead, this is a creed, or statement of faith, which summarizes the earliest beliefs of the Church about the Resurrection. Paul uses traditional rabbinic language of "receiving" and "handing on" to describe material that is not original to him. Each line of the passage also begins with, "And that," which is typical in creeds so that they can be easily memorized. The creed also uses the Aramaic name for Peter, *Cephas*, which signifies that it comes from an early tradition.

In Galatians 1:19, Paul says that he visited the apostles three years after his conversion and they confirmed what he had been teaching. This may have been the time they passed this creed on to him. The fact that the creed can be dated to within a few years of Jesus' death shows that the appearances could not be mere legends, since eyewitnesses were still alive with fresh memories to correct the facts. However, Paul received this testimony directly from the apostles, so there was no need for correction.

But how do we know that these appearances weren't just made up by the apostles and then passed on to other people? Just as with the empty tomb, we can have confidence in the sincerity of their testimony because the apostles were willing to die for it.

Of course, people throughout history have died for many things they thought were true. For example, Muslim suicide bombers die for the Islamic faith because they believe Allah will reward them in heaven, but such sincerity does not prove Islam is correct. The key difference here is that whereas Muslim suicide bombers are not in a position to know if Islam is false (they never interacted with the Muslim prophet Muhammad), the apostles were in a position to know whether Christianity was false and they were perpetuating concocted lies. There was no chance that they were all deceived. This gives us confidence that the apostles sincerely believed Jesus rose from the dead and allows us to conclude that the best motivator for such a belief was an actual resurrection.

170. How do we know the apostles weren't suffering from a group hallucination?

Even Gerd Ludemann, a scholar who denies the Resurrection, affirms that the apostles had *some* sort of experience of the risen Christ. He writes, "It may be taken as historically certain that Peter and the disciples had experiences after Jesus' death in which Jesus appeared to them as the risen Christ."[241] The question we must ask is "What explains these appearances?"

The most common alternative explanation for the appearances to the disciples is a grief-induced hallucination. Skeptics claim that many people, when grieving the death of a loved one, often report seeing and even touching a living apparition of the deceased person. This type of hallucination, they say, could have explained what happened to the apostles.

This explanation seems far-fetched, though, because hallucinations are always experienced by individuals, not groups. As psychologist Gary Collins writes, "By their very nature only one person can see a given hallucination at a time. They certainly aren't something which can be seen by a group of people. . . . Since an hallucination exists only in the subjective, personal sense, it is obvious that others cannot witness it."[242]

A further problem with the hallucination theory is that a physical resurrection from the dead was probably beyond even the apostles' imagination. Historian N.T. Wright, in his book *The Resurrection of the Son of God*, scoured the ancient literature and found no examples in the pagan world or in Jewish thought of the belief in a person dying, experiencing the afterlife, and then returning to a glorified, immortal, bodily existence. If the apostles had somehow all hallucinated, projecting something that would have been plausible and familiar to them, most likely they would have imagined the return of a glorified spirit. However, the apostles emphatically did not preach this.[243]

Even if the disciples could find some motivation to believe in Jesus even without seeing him resurrected, no such motivation existed for Jesus' enemies. Saul of Tarsus (later known as Paul the apostle) was a Pharisee who persecuted the ancient Church. However, after an encounter with the risen Christ, Saul completely reversed his beliefs and joined the Jewish heresy he had been persecuting.

Perhaps the simplest and most commonsensical argument against the hallucination theory is that at any time it would have been possible for the apostles themselves to test it: by visiting the tomb and seeing if there was a body in it.

171. How does the book of Revelation work?

Revelation is one of the books of the New Testament. Many assume that it was the last book of the Bible to be written, but this is something we do not know. Other books may have been written later.

One reason people think Revelation was written last is the fact that it's printed in the back of the Bible, making it last in *canonical* order. This is because Revelation contains prophecies that describe the end of the world, so it's logical to place it last in sequence.

The Old Testament contains many prophetic books, but Revelation is the only one in the New Testament. The four Gospels and the New Testament letters contain individual prophecies, but only Revelation is entirely devoted to the subject of prophecy.

Revelation also is different from the prophetic books of the Old Testament. Works like Isaiah, Jeremiah, and Ezekiel contain revelations that the prophets received at various points in their careers, and the books collect these prophecies and weave them together with historical incidents from their lives.

By contrast, Revelation presents its prophetic material as a single, grand vision. We even know what day of the week the author began receiving it—a Sunday—because he tells us it began when "I was in the Spirit on the

Lord's Day" (Rev. 1:10). It's possible that he saw the vision all on a single day or that he saw it in parts and just doesn't mention the gaps between individual visions. One way or the other, he apparently received it all in a short space of time rather than over a lengthy prophetic career.

The book is different in another way. Whereas the Old Testament prophetic books are written to a general audience, Revelation is written to a specific one. In fact, its literary form is that of a letter. It uses the standard opening for first-century letters, which involved a sender-to-receivers formula. Thus, after an opening title and exhortation, we read, "John to the seven churches that are in Asia" (1:4).

Revelation is, in essence, a letter communicating the prophetic material the author received. And, by ancient standards, it was gigantic. The average length of letters from that time and place was eighty-seven words;[244] Revelation is 9,852 words long in Greek, making it more than a hundred times the size of a normal letter. It's longer than any other letter of the New Testament, and it's almost as long as the Gospel of Mark. John's readers must have been astonished when they got it!

When inspiring Scripture, God used the knowledge and background of the biblical authors, and it is clear that John had a detailed, intimate knowledge of the Old Testament prophetic books. Revelation contains more than a hundred references to them.

Now that Jesus had come, the author realized that the whole prophetic enterprise of the Hebrew Bible was coming together and being crowned by his own work. As scholar Richard Bauckham states, John "understood his prophecy to be the climax of the tradition of Old Testament prophecy, because in the revelation made to him by Jesus Christ was disclosed the secret of the divine purpose for the final coming of the kingdom of God."[245]

172. Who wrote Revelation and why?

Four times, the book of Revelation identifies its author as "John" (1:1, 4, 9; 22:8). This was an extremely popular name at the time. In fact, *John* was fifth most common among names for Jewish men in Palestine in this period.[246]

The fact that John does not further identify himself (e.g., as John Mark, John son of Zebedee, or John of Jerusalem) shows that he must have been well known to his audience. He only says that he is "your brother and partner in the tribulation and the kingdom and the patient endurance that are in Jesus" (1:9a, ESV).

The only biographical detail he adds is that, when he saw the vision, he "was on the island called Patmos on account of the word of God and the testimony of Jesus" (1:9b).

Patmos is a Greek island in the Aegean Sea, only thirteen square miles in size. John says he was on the island because of "the testimony of Jesus," which could mean that he was there on an evangelizing mission, but the context of persecution and tribulation has convinced scholars that John was on Patmos as a punishment for his Christian preaching.

This has led some to claim that Patmos was a penal colony, but evidence does not support that. It is more likely that John had been banished or exiled to Patmos from a major city. Banishment was a common way of dealing with troublesome upper-class individuals as an alternative to execution or forced labor. A person in exile would be allowed to live in a remote location—away from where he had been causing trouble. This seems to have been why John was on Patmos.

Is John of Patmos identical to any of the other known Johns of the early Christian world? Historically, the most popular view is that it was John, son of Zebedee, one of the twelve apostles. This view can be traced to as early as A.D. 155, when it was endorsed in the writings of St. Justin Martyr.[247]

However, there was a dispute about this among the early Church Fathers. Some say that they do not know who wrote Revelation and doubt its apostolic authorship. Others suggest that it was written by a figure known as John the Elder or John the Presbyter.[248] According to early sources, John the Elder was not one of the Twelve but he was an eyewitness of the ministry of Christ, and in later years he—like John son of Zebedee—lived in Ephesus, resulting in two famous Johns having their tombs there.

This may be supported by the fact that John the apostle was an uneducated, Galilean fisherman from the lower class (Acts 4:13) and not the kind of person who would receive the mild punishment of exile. It has been argued that John the Elder was a member of the Jerusalem aristocracy,[249] and the option of exile was often applied to members of the upper class in place of the death penalty, which would have been used on members of the lower class who had committed the same crime.

Whoever wrote the book, the reason why it was written is made clear in its opening verse, which describes it as "The revelation of Jesus Christ, which God gave him to show to his servants what must soon take place" (1:1). The Greek term for revelation—*apokalupsis*—is the origin of our word *apocalypse*. In the first century, this meant "a revealing," so the book reveals information given by Jesus Christ about his bride, the Church. In fact, the term *apokalupsis literally means* "unveiling," and at the time John was writing, was commonly to describe a particular moment of their week-long wedding festivities: "the lifting of the veil of a virgin bride, which took place immediately before the marriage was consummated."[250]

This information concerns "what must soon take place" from John's first-century perspective. He was writing to warn his readers of a series of events in the Roman world that would involve the persecution of Christians and God's judgment on the pagan world order that oppressed them, and to strengthen them in hope through the vision of the victorious Church as "bride of the Lamb."

173. When was Revelation written?

The book of Revelation was written during the Apostolic Age, but precisely when is debated. Today, there are two principal schools of thought. The first dates Revelation to the reign of the emperor Domitian (A.D. 81–96), and specifically toward the end of his reign (c. 95), whereas the second school places it earlier, following the persecutions of the emperor Nero (A.D. 54–68) but before the destruction of the Jerusalem temple in A.D. 70. From the late second century A.D. until the nineteenth century, and again today, the most common view is the former. During the nineteenth century, the earlier date was the most favored.[251]

The view that places Revelation in the nineties is based on statements in some of the early Church Fathers that John was banished to Patmos during the reign of Domitian. This view is thought to have been held by Irenaeus of Lyons around A.D. 180.[252]

However, there is ambiguity in what Irenaeus said. In Greek, he can be understood to say either that "it" (the revelation of John) was seen during the reign of Domitian or that "he" (John himself) was seen during this time. If the latter is the case, Irenaeus is commenting not on when the book was written but on how long John lived.

> Other early Christian sources seem to have placed the banishment of John several decades earlier. For example,
>
> According to the confused tradition in Epiphanius (*Pan.* 51.12.1–2), John left Patmos when he was over ninety years old during the reign of Claudius Caesar (A.D. 41–54). Some confusion results

> from the fact that Claudius was one of the names of Nero, who is referred to both as Nero Claudius and as Nero Claudius Caesar.[253]

It seems unlikely that John would have been over ninety years old during the reign of Claudius Caesar, especially if one maintains the traditional authorship of Revelation by the Evangelist John, held to be the youngest of the apostles[254] and the last to die (see John 21:23). Interpreting the assertion of Epiphanes in reference to the reign of Nero Claudius instead would also make John older than tradition would have him, although less egregiously. Such a date became popular in the nineteenth century due to the apparent connections between Nero and Revelation.

A clue supporting an earlier date is the fact that Revelation describes the Jerusalem temple as still operating, for John says, "I was given a reed like a measuring rod and was told, 'Go and measure the temple of God and the altar, with its worshipers. But exclude the outer court; do not measure it, because it has been given to the Gentiles. They will trample on the holy city for forty-two months'" (11:1–2, NIV).

This depicts "the temple of God" in Jerusalem ("the holy city") "and those worshiping it it"—using the present tense. But the temple was destroyed by the Romans in A.D. 70 when Jerusalem was conquered and "given to the Gentiles," who trampled it. Because the passage describes the temple before its destruction, this suggests a date for the book prior to 70.

The most precise clue to its dating may be the interpretation it gives of the seven heads of the beast that John sees: "The seven heads are seven mountains. . . . They are also seven kings, five of whom have fallen, one is, the other has not yet come, and when he comes he must remain only a little while" (17:9–10).

The seven mountains have been identified since ancient times as the seven hills of Rome, and so the seven kings involve a reference to Roman emperors, who, like the beast, blaspheme God, persecute the saints, rule the world, and receive worship from all but Christians (13:6–8).

If the seven heads are the line of first-century emperors, the five who "have fallen" would be Augustus, Tiberius, Caligula, Claudius, and Nero. The one who "is" would be Nero's successor, Galba, and the other who "has not yet come" would be Otho, who did—indeed—reign "only a little while" (three months). This would place the composition of Revelation during the reign of Galba (June 9, A.D. 68–January 15, A.D. 69).[255]

174. How is Revelation structured?

It is clear to everyone who studies Revelation carefully that the book is intricately structured, with both large and small patterns that keep recurring. The problem is how to fit these patterns into an overall outline.

The most obvious structures in the book are based on the number seven. Early in the book, there are messages given to seven churches (2:1–3:22). Later, seven seals are removed from a scroll (6:1–8:1). Then seven angels blow trumpets (8:7–11:19). And finally, angels pour out seven bowls containing plagues (16:2–21). The parts dealing with the messages, seals, trumpets, and bowls are major sections around which the book is written.

But there is a great deal of material inserted in and around these blocks, making it harder to discern the overall structure. Some of these sections also seem to be built around the number seven, but in a less obvious way.

For example, Revelation 12:1–14:20 describes what may be understood as seven signs that John sees. The first two—a woman in heaven and a dragon—are explicitly called signs (12:1, 3), and the remaining five are introduced by the formula "and I saw" (Greek: *kai eidon*). Similarly, Revelation 19:11–21:8 describes what may be called seven sights, each of which is introduced by the formula "and I saw."

If this is taken as a guide, an outline of the book can be proposed as follows:[256]

1. *Introduction* (1:1–8)—This section contains the superscription of the book (1:1-3) and its opening in the form of a letter (1:4–8).

2. *Seven Messages* (1:9–3:22)—This section contains an introductory vision of Jesus (1:9–20), after which Jesus dictates individual messages to the seven churches to whom the letter is being sent (2:1–3:22).

3. *Seven Seals* (4:1–8:1)—John is caught up to heaven, where he has an introductory vision of the worship in heaven (4:1–11) and sees a scroll that only Jesus can open (5:1–14). Jesus then proceeds to remove each of the seven seals that close the scroll. A dramatic event occurs as each seal is removed, until the final seal, which is followed by silence in heaven (6:1–8:1). This section also contains an interlude in which John sees Jesus with 144,000 Israelites (7:1–8) and a great multitude from every nation (7:9-17).

4. *Seven Trumpets* (8:2–11:19)—John sees seven angels who blow trumpets, and a dramatic event occurs as each trumpet is blown. This section also contains an interlude in which John is given a scroll to eat (10:1–11) and is told to measure the temple in Jerusalem (11:1–14), after which the holy city

will be trampled underfoot by the Gentiles during the prophetic career of the Lord's two witnesses (11:1–14).

5. *Seven Signs* (12:1–14:20)—John sees a series of seven signs, including a woman in heaven (12:1–2), a dragon with whom she is in conflict (12:3–17), a beast from the sea (13:1–10), a beast from the land (13:11–18), the Lamb and the 144,000 (14:1–5), a group of three angels flying in heaven (14:6–13), and two harvests of the earth (14:14–20).

6. *Seven Bowls* (15:1–16:21)—John sees an introductory vision of seven angels that have seven last plagues (15:1-8), after which the angels pour out these plagues using ceremonial bowls (16:1–21).

7. *The Whore of Babylon* (17:1–19:10)—An angel takes John to witness the downfall of a figure known as the whore of Babylon, who is associated with the beast from the land. When at last the judgment against her is complete, the wedding feast of the Lamb is announced as imminent, because his bride is now ready (19:5–10).

8. *Seven Sights* (19:11–21:8)—John sees a series of seven sights: Jesus and his heavenly army (19:11–16), an angel standing on the sun (19:17–18), the beast and his earthly army (19:19–21), an angel who comes down from heaven and binds the devil for a thousand years (20:1–3), the thrones of martyrs who reign during the thousand years (20:4–10), the throne of God and the Final Judgment (20:11–15), and the appearance of the new heaven and the new earth (21:1–8).

9. *The Bride of the Lamb* (21:9–22:11)—An angel takes John to witness the glory of the bride of the Lamb—the heavenly city, the new Jerusalem, which descends from heaven to the new earth. Its temple and glory are the Lamb, its twelve foundations are the twelve disciples, and its twelve gates the twelve tribes of Israel.

10. *Conclusion* (22:12–21)—John concludes the letter by emphasizing the nearness of the events it describes and attesting, in the name of Jesus, to its authenticity.

There are various themes running through these segments. Some of them (the seals, trumpets, and bowl segments) focus on divine judgments; others (the sign and sight segments) focus on the conflict between the forces of good and evil; others contrast the glory of this world and that of heaven using the images of two women (the whore of Babylon and the bride of the Lamb).

Once we have a grasp of the structure of the book, it is easier to make sense of the sections and the individual symbols they contain. This provides a basic overview, though there are more subtle structures in the book than can be described here.[257]

175. Where does John get his symbols, and how can we understand them?

One of the greatest mistakes people make when interpreting Revelation is failing to understand where it draws its images from. Readers practicing "newspaper exegesis" seek to interpret things in the book in terms of things that they are familiar with rather than what John and his audience would have thought about.

For example, 9:1–11 describes the opening of the supernatural location known as the abyss or "bottomless pit" where demons are housed. Smoke emerges from the abyss, and out of the smoke come "locusts on the earth, and they were given power like the power of scorpions of the earth." John describes these terrifying creatures:

> In appearance the locusts were like horses arrayed for battle; on their heads were what looked like crowns of gold; their faces were like human faces, their hair like women's hair, and their teeth like lions' teeth; they had scales like iron breastplates, and the noise of their wings was like the noise of many chariots with horses rushing into battle. They have tails like scorpions, and stings.

Despite what this passage would have meant to John and his audience, some recent interpreters have seen the locusts as representing the Cobra helicopters that were used in the Vietnam War of the 1960s, with nerve gas being sprayed from their tails.[258]

Apart from the fact that mechanical Cobra helicopters do not look like the biological description John gives of the locusts, this is not how the original audience would have understood them. The locusts are monstrous creatures confined in a supernatural location (the abyss) with demons, and they are led by "the angel of the bottomless pit," whose name means Destroyer in Greek. Confronted with these facts, we should interpret them as demonic creatures, not helicopters.

This kind of error stems from a lack of familiarity with biblical imagery. Most of the symbols appearing in John's visions have parallels in the Old Testament. Others make reference to known people, places, or literature of the period. On other occasions, Revelation helps us understand its own symbolism when Jesus, an angel, or John himself tells us the meaning of a symbol. For instance:

- Seven stars represent the angels of seven churches (1:20).
- Seven lampstands represent seven churches (1:20).
- Seven torches of fire before God's throne represent the seven spirits of God (4:5).
- Seven eyes of the Lamb represent the seven spirits of God sent throughout the earth (5:6).
- Golden bowls full of incense represent the prayers of the saints (5:8).
- People wearing white robes represent those coming out of the tribulation (7:13–14).
- Two witnesses represent two olive trees and two lampstands before the Lord (11:3–4).
- Seven heads of the beast represent seven hills and seven kings (17:9–10).
- Fine linen represents the righteous deeds of the saints (19:8).

These interpretations are helpful in figuring out the symbolism of Revelation, and they teach more than one lesson that may not be obvious.

For example, the two witnesses of chapter 11 are interpreted as "the two olive trees and the two lampstands which stand before the Lord of the earth" (v. 4). As a result, we have a symbol (the witnesses) interpreted by *reference to other symbols* (the olive trees and lampstands)! This shows us that we need to be sensitive to the complex relationship that can exist between symbols. It is not always the case in Revelation that a symbol stands for a single, easily identifiable thing.

Another lesson is found when we are told in chapter 17 that the seven heads of the beast "are seven hills on which the woman is seated; they are also seven kings" (vv. 9–10). Here we have a *single* symbol (the heads) that stands for *more than one thing* (the hills and the kings). This reveals that an individual symbol in Revelation can stand for multiple items, not just one.

Using the passages where Revelation interprets itself, it is possible to get clues about how other passages should be understood. Since we know that in stars represent angels (1:20), we should consider the possibility that the *same symbolism* is being used elsewhere in the book.

For example, when a third of the stars are swept from heaven and cast down to the earth (12:4), and individual stars fall (8:10; 9:1). We could interpret these passages naturalistically and suppose that they represent meteor showers or asteroid strikes, but the symbolic key given by the text suggests that we should consider whether they involve fallen angels instead. This does not mean that stars *always* represent angels in Revelation, but it is a possibility that needs to be considered in these passages.

The interpretations Revelation provides of some of its symbols are helpful, but they explain only a small portion of the symbolism in the book. If we want to understand other passages, we need to look elsewhere.

For example, when the two witnesses described in 11:3–4 are said to be "the two olive trees," this is a reference to Zechariah 4:3–12, which was a familiar passage to those brought up on the Hebrew scriptures.

This brings us to a key principle of interpretation: whenever Revelation does not interpret an image for us, our *first* move should be checking to see if it was *used in the Old Testament* or *other apocalyptic literature* of John's period.

This can be done by checking any of the many scholarly commentaries on Revelation. Popular commentaries are unreliable for this purpose and may not mention prior uses of John's imagery, but scholarly commentaries will provide a good survey of what John is likely alluding to.[259]

An awareness of Old Testament background can help us avoid mistakes even when Revelation does interpret its own symbolism. Though stars *can* be used to represent angels (1:20), this is not always the case. In 12:1, John sees a woman clothed in the sun, standing on the moon, and wearing a crown of twelve stars. This imagery is also used in Genesis 37 and represents the family of Israel. Thus, in Revelation 12 the stars are not meant to be angels but identify the woman in some way with Israel.

We also need to be sensitive to the ways that Revelation can change and adapt imagery taken from the Old Testament. Take, for instance, this passage:

> Round the throne, on each side of the throne, are four living creatures, full of eyes in front and behind: the first living creature like a lion, the second living creature like an ox, the third living creature with the face of a man, and the fourth living creature like a flying eagle. And the four living creatures, each of them with six wings, are full of eyes all round and within, and day and night they

never cease to sing, "Holy, holy, holy, is the Lord God Almighty." (Rev. 4:6-8)

This imagery is paralleled in visions given to two Old Testament prophets: the cherubim that Ezekiel sees around God's throne (Ezek. 1:5–14) and the seraphim Isaiah sees surrounding it (Isa. 6:2–3). The living creatures seen by John contain elements from the descriptions of both the cherubim and the seraphim, but they are not identical to either of them. They thus represent a fusion of two Old Testament images and should not be identified simply as one or the other.

Something similar happens in 13:1–2, where John sees "a beast rising out of the sea, with ten horns and seven heads, with ten diadems upon its horns and a blasphemous name upon its heads. And the beast that I saw was like a leopard, its feet were like a bear's, and its mouth was like a lion's mouth."

This imagery is drawn from Daniel 7, where the prophet sees a series of four strange beasts that represent empires that oppressed God's people. The beast that John sees combines characteristics of all four of Daniel's, suggesting that it is another persecuting empire like the others, but without being strictly identified with any of the four that Daniel saw.

Finally, in addition to looking at the Old Testament, we need to be sensitive to *other cultural or historical sources* John may be drawing on.

For example, the two witnesses of chapter 11 are also said to be "two lampstands which stand before the Lord of the earth" (v. 4). Although there *is* a single lampstand mentioned in Zechariah 4, there aren't *two* of them, indicating that John is drawing on something more than this. As ancient illustrations of synagogues show two menorahs (lampstands) in front of the shrine containing the synagogue's copy of the Torah, John may be drawing on the common arrangement of synagogues in his day.

176. How do historicists interpret Revelation?

Revelation says it describes what will "soon" occur (1:1, 22:6), but it also describes events taking place centuries after John's time (20:7) and at the end of the world (21:1). So, how do the contents of the book relate to history?

It's clear that the beginning of the book (chaps. 1–3) deals with events in John's own day and the end of the book (chaps. 21–22) deals with the distant future, but what about the middle of the book (chaps. 4–20)? How does it relate to history? Over time, several views have developed, and we will look at four: historicism, idealism, futurism, and preterism.

Historicism holds that the middle of Revelation describes events that are roughly evenly spread out between the first century and the end of the world, so they essentially form a roadmap or timeline of what will happen between John's day and the end of the world.

It is easy to see how a view like this could develop. Many early Christians assumed that Jesus would be returning within their own lifetimes (see 1 Thess. 4:15), though eventually they learned that this would not be the case (see 2 Tim. 4:6–8). The disclosure in Revelation that a millennium would occur before the end of the world (20:1–6) also made that clear.

For many living in the first and second century, it would be natural to assume that they were living in the middle of the book of Revelation and that "soon" the later events of the book would arrive. However, as Church history progressed, Christians in the third, fourth, and subsequent centuries would need to extend the timeline that the middle of the book was supposed to cover. Eventually, the timeline was stretched to cover the entirety of the Middle Ages, the Renaissance, and the Reformation.

Some Catholic authors in the Middle Ages adopted the historicist view, but it became extremely popular later among Protestants and it was the dominant view among the Reformers, who identified the beast/Antichrist figure of the book with the papacy and used this to demonize the Catholic Church:

> For example, the breaking of the seven seals (chaps. 6–7) is often said to be the barbarian invasions that sacked the western Roman Empire. The scorpion/locusts that come out of the bottomless pit (chap. 9) are the Arab hordes attacking the eastern Roman Empire, followed by the Turks, represented as the horses with serpents for tails and flame-throwers for mouths. "The beast" (chap. 13) represents the Roman papacy.[260]

Historicism continued to be popular in Protestant circles until the nineteenth century, but it rapidly fell out of popularity, as its shortcomings were becoming more obvious. Although still held among Seventh-day Adventists, it has otherwise completely fallen out of favor among Protestants, and it is not taken seriously by New Testament scholars of any persuasion today.

The reason is that, as time advanced, the arbitrariness of historicist interpretations became ever clearer. Interpreters tended to assume that they were living near the end of Revelation, so as the number of centuries the book needed to cover increased, the interpretations of particular passages kept having to change.

For example, a historicist living before the time of Muhammad (c. 570–632) would not see him in the book at all. But after the devastating invasions of Christendom by Muslim forces, a place for the rise of Islam needed to be found in Revelation, and the later in history that a commentator was writing, the earlier in the book the mention of Muhammad would need to be.

Similarly, interpreters living before the Reformation or Hitler or Communism would not see these in the book, but afterward could want to find them there, forcing a reinterpretation of passages. As the amount of time Revelation needed to cover stretched, more and more historicist commentaries that disagreed with each other came to be written, leading to a realization that identifications of particular symbols within the book with particular historical events was essentially arbitrary and not grounded in good exegesis.

Another factor leading to the realization of historicism's arbitrariness is that commentators sought to interpret the book almost exclusively in terms of European Christendom, with European popes, kings, wars, and invasions dominating the interpretations of the book's symbols. But after the age of exploration, Christianity was a global phenomenon, and it was not clear why Revelation should be exclusively focused on Europe and ignore developments in the rest of the Christian world.

By the nineteenth century, the Protestant denominations were sufficiently established and felt secure enough that they no longer needed to demonize Catholicism to the same degree, and as passions cooled, Protestant scholars realized that the papacy does not fit the biblical data regarding the Antichrist. They thus no longer needed to interpret Revelation in a historicist way to justify their rejection of the Catholic Church, and the view rapidly fell out of favor—except among Seventh-day Adventists, who maintain a connection between the Antichrist and the papacy.

In addition to the arbitrariness that historicism involves, scholars today also fault it because this view would make the book totally unintelligible to its original audience. If Revelation were a roadmap of Church history, with specific judgments corresponding to events in distant centuries, there is no way John's original readers could have understood what they were referring to. Yet he emphasizes that the contents of the vision are to happen "soon" and expects the reader to be able to figure out symbols in the middle of the book, as when he says, "let the one who has understanding calculate the number of the beast, for it is the number of a man" (13:18, ESV).

177. How do idealists interpret Revelation?

The *idealist* view of Revelation—which goes by a variety of names, including the *spiritual* or *symbolic* view—is similar to the historicist view in that it sees the middle of the book as relating to all of Church history. However, it does not see it as providing a roadmap or timeline of this period. Instead, it relates to history in a more general way.

Idealism began to be popular in the nineteenth century as the historicist view was falling out of favor. It is easy to see how a view like this would arise. If it proved impossible to match passages in Revelation to specific events in the course of Church history—as in historicism—then it would be natural to ask if they might apply to history in a less specific fashion.

Thus, Revelation came to be understood by idealists as describing the great conflict between God and Satan that plays out in every part of Church history. Although God will ultimately be victorious, believers in every age will need to face the challenges that the book describes, including persecutions and other disasters.

For example, Revelation 6:3–8 describes a series of horsemen who unambiguously represent war, famine, and death. Idealists would take this as a sign that Christians in every age must be prepared to face these challenges, without seeing the passage as referring to an occasion where a *specific* war led to famine and death. On this view, the passage represents a principle that can occur over and over again in history rather than referring to one particular occasion.

Because idealism holds that Revelation deals with themes that recur throughout history as it builds to its ultimate climax, some have referred to this as the "philosophy of history" interpretation, as Revelation would be seeking to provide a Christian perspective on the meaning of Church history.

Some idealists also have seen Revelation as employing a technique called *progressive parallelism*, telling and retelling the same basic story of the Church's struggles. For example, the well-known Protestant author William Hendriksen argued in his book *More Than Conquerors* that Revelation contains seven segments, each of which tell the same story but with different symbols and emphases.

Idealism has become very popular in modern commentaries on Revelation, especially in the scholarly community. Perhaps one reason for this is that it frees the commentator from the need to identify passages in Revelation with specific historical events and allows him to write a commentary that can be read by advocates of the other schools (historicism, futurism, preterism), without having to decide the contentious questions that separate them.

The chief problem with idealism is that John does seem to be predicting things that are rather specific when he emphasizes that Revelation was written "to show to his servants the things that must soon take place" (1:1; see 22:6, ESV).

As a result, many idealists combine their approach with one of the others. Given the first-century context in which John is writing, idealism is most commonly combined with preterism, though it also is sometimes combined with futurism.

178. How do futurists interpret Revelation?

Rather than seeing Revelation as applying to the whole of Church history—as historicists and idealists do—*futurists* hold that the bulk of the book (chaps. 4–20) apply to events that are still in our future.

When the Protestant Reformers began using historicism to attack the Catholic Church, two Spanish Jesuits proposed alternative readings. One of them, Francisco Ribera (1537–1591), said that John "only foresaw events of the near future and of the final things at the end of the world, but had none of the intervening history in view. The Antichrist was defined as a future individual who would arise in the end times. Babylon was seen as Rome—not under the popes—but in a future corrupted state. This was the beginning of many of the ideas that are now a part of the *futurist* approach to Revelation."[261]

Initially, futurism was not popular among Protestants, who saw it as a Catholic attempt to avoid their criticisms. However, this began to change in the nineteenth century, and futurism became more popular.

In particular, it was adopted by the Anglo-Irish clergyman John Nelson Darby (1800–1882). Darby became a leader in a sect known as the Plymouth Brethren, and he incorporated futurism as a pillar in a theological system he developed, known as *dispensationalism*. According to this view, world history is divided into a number of periods or "dispensations" in which God deals with mankind in different ways.

One of these dispensations is a future thousand-year reign of Christ on earth known as the *millennium* (see Rev. 20:1–6). Dispensationalism introduced the idea that this period would be preceded by a "rapture" in which all true believers would be caught up to be with Jesus in heaven while the Antichrist reigned on earth in a period called the *tribulation*. After the tribulation, Christ would return, slay the Antichrist, and inaugurate a thousand-year earthly kingdom. Only after this would the end of the world come.

Dispensationalism was promoted in America by the theologian C.I. Scofield (1843–1921), who incorporated it into the notes of his popular study Bible, *The Scofield Reference Bible*. By the mid-twentieth century, dispensationalism had become extremely popular in American Evangelicalism, and it was further popularized by books such as Hal Lindsey's *The Late Great Planet Earth* in the 1970s and Tim LaHaye's *Left Behind* series in the 1990s.

These proved so popular that the dispensationalist understanding of Revelation, with its belief in a rapture and an earthly reign of Christ, entered pop culture, and many today assume that it is the standard or even the only way to understand Revelation. Even some futurists, however, do not accept a dispensationalist interpretation of the book—not to mention the many scholars and believers who reject futurism altogether.

Futurists often claim that Revelation should be taken in a highly literal sense, and by confining its events to our future, their view is uniquely able to do this. "For example, there has never been a time in the past when a third of the sea turned to blood, killing a third of the fish and sinking a third of the ships (Rev. 8). If this is to have a literal fulfillment, it must still be in the future. Other approaches must take the passage nonliterally."[262]

Despite their emphasis on a literal interpretation, futurists acknowledge that Revelation contains a large number of symbols. For example, there will not be a literal red dragon that sweeps a third of the stars out of the sky with its tail (12:3–4). Consequently, it is not a question whether Revelation *should* be read literally but *what mix* of literal and symbolic readings best explains the book.

Since people are naturally curious about the future, a chief attraction of futurism is that it would allow Revelation to give us a detailed map of events that are still to come. However, just because we might like a theory does not mean that it is true.

One of the main problems of futurism is that, if it were true, it would make the large majority of the book irrelevant to its original audience, as it would be describing events that occurred thousands of years after John's time. This would not sit easily with John's repeated assurances to his audience that the events of the book will happen "soon" (1:1; 22:6). Neither would they be able to understand the prophecy, as John expects them to when he tells the original audience to calculate the number of the beast (13:18).

In fact, the bulk of the book would be irrelevant to Christians living in *every* generation—except the last. Only the final Christians would be able to correctly interpret the events of the book and draw practical lessons from them.

Another problem for the futurist reading is that the beginning of the book does not contain a large jump in time. The material in chapters 1–3 explicitly deals with the first century, but futurists hold that at the beginning of chapter 4 there is a sudden leap of 2,000 or more years into the future.

They attempt to find this leap in 4:1, which says: "After this I looked, and behold, a door standing open in heaven! And the first voice, which I had heard speaking to me like a trumpet, said, 'Come up here, and I will show you what must take place after this.'"

Since the Rapture is not mentioned in the book, dispensationalists also frequently see the command to John to "come up here" as indicating the point at which the Church is raptured. However, this is not a literal reading of the text. The text does not say anything about Jesus descending from heaven to rapture his Church away so that they will be protected from the reign of the Antichrist. Instead, it refers to John being caught up to heaven to see the vision that the book contains.

More fundamentally, a leap of 2,000 or more years is not indicated. The text simply says John will be shown what will take place "after" what he has already seen, but "after" would not be understood by the original audience to mean thousands of years after—not when they have been told that the events will happen "soon" and when John has been told, "Do not seal up the words of the prophecy of this book, for the time is near" (22:10).

In part because of these difficulties, futurism is most common in popular-level expositions of Revelation, though there are a few scholarly commentaries with this perspective.

179. How do preterists interpret Revelation?

The Latin word *praeter* means "before," and *preterists* hold that the bulk of the book of Revelation was fulfilled before our time and applies to the early part of Church history. On this view, chapters 1–19 deal with events in or near John's own time, then there is a long period described symbolically as a thousand years (20:1–6), after which comes the end of the world (20:7–22:1).

This solves the problem of how to get from the past to the future in the book. The great majority of the text *does* deal with events that would happen "soon" from John's perspective, then there is the long period of time indicated—the period in which we are now living—and finally there are the events still in our future.

There had been preterists earlier in Church history, but the view received new attention after the Protestant Reformers began using historicism to demonize the Catholic Church. Whereas one Spanish Jesuit—Francisco Ribera—proposed a futurist reading, another, named Luiz de Alcazar (1554–1613), proposed a preterist reading, "in which chapters four through eleven were interpreted as depicting the church's struggle against Judaism, culminating in the fall of Jerusalem in A.D. 70; chapters twelve through nineteen as the church's struggle with paganism, ending in the fall of Rome in 476; and chapters twenty through twenty-two as the triumph of the church in papal Rome."[263]

Because it undermined Reformation-era rhetoric, preterism was not popular with Protestants. However, after the passions of the period had cooled, it began to attract Protestant adherents. Variations on preterism are common in scholarly commentaries on Revelation—often combined with the idealist view—and in recent years there have been an increasing number of popular-level works advocating preterism.

When it comes to Revelation, there are several versions of preterism. The main differences concern whether the book deals with God's judgment on Jerusalem, Rome, or both. One view holds that the book covers the same events that Jesus did in his Olivet Discourse, in which he prophesied the destruction of the Jerusalem temple in A.D. 70 (see Mark 13, esp. vv. 1–5). This view identifies the whore of Babylon (Rev. 17–18) as the apostate city of Jerusalem, which executed the Messiah.

Another view holds that the whore of Babylon is pagan Rome, which persecuted Christians. On this view, Revelation may deal with God's judgment on Roman paganism and its defeat by the advance of the gospel.

Some, such as Luiz de Alcazar, have thought that the book deals with the judgment on both Jerusalem and Rome. He did this by dividing the book into two sections, one for each city, but others have proposed that the whore of Babylon represents *both* Jerusalem and Rome—or any great city that sets itself in opposition to God.

Even adopting a broadly preterist viewpoint does not mean we must completely exclude other views. Prophecy can have more than one fulfillment. For example, in the 700s B.C., God gave King Ahaz a sign that he would not be defeated by his enemies: "Behold, a young woman shall conceive and bear a son, and shall call his name Immanuel" (Isa. 7:14). This child had to be born in Ahaz's day to serve as a sign for him, but the prophecy had another, greater fulfillment when Jesus was born (Matt. 1:23).

Consequently, even though the bulk of Revelation may have had its literal fulfillment early in Church history, this does not prevent it from also having fulfillments in other ages, including just before the end of the world.

Thus, we might reasonably argue, in the words of Scripture scholar Robert H. Mounce,

> In John's vision the beast is the Roman Empire [preterism]. It is that concentration of secular power which claims a religious sanction for its cruelty and injustice. Yet the beast is more than the Roman Empire. In a larger sense it is the spirit of godless totalitarianism that has energized every authoritarian system devised by man throughout history [idealism]. At the end of time, the beast will appear in its most malicious form. It will be the ultimate expression of deified secular authority [futurism].[264]

180. What are the seven churches?

The book of Revelation is addressed to "the seven churches that are in Asia" (1:4). Today, we think of Asia as a vast continent that includes nations like India and China. In John's day, however, the term referred to a single Roman province that is in the western part of what is now Turkey.

In 1:11, we learn the identities of these seven churches, as John is told, "Write what you see in a book and send it to the seven churches, to Ephesus and to Smyrna and to Pergamum and to Thyatira and to Sardis and to Philadelphia and to Laodicea."

We know that there were more than seven churches in Asia at this time. One of them—the church of the Colossians—is famous because St. Paul wrote one of his letters to it. Another—Hierapolis—is less well known but also was present at the time (Col. 4:13).

So, why does John speak of "the seven" churches of Asia if there were more than that? The number seven is extremely important in Revelation. It occurs 275 times in Revelation's 404 verses. The number clearly has symbolic value, but its precise meaning is debated.

One proposal is that seven can stand for completion—like the seven days in a week—and so John may have selected seven churches to represent the conditions of churches everywhere in his day. Others challenge this and argue that the number seven may simply convey the divine authority of his message.

Can we determine why these particular seven churches were selected? It may be because John had visited them and the Christians there knew who he was, allowing him to simply introduce himself as "John," without saying anything more about his identity (1:1, 4, 9; 22:8).

Another factor is that they are all connected by a single path along the Roman road network, and they would be visited in the same order given in 1:11. The letter courier John used would have sailed from Patmos to Ephesus, the closest port city, then worked his way north to Pergamum and then turned southeast and worked his way down to Laodicea, delivering the letter at each of the seven churches in sequence.

Chapters two and three contain a series of messages that are given to these churches. Sometimes, they are called the "letters" to the seven churches, but they do not fit the format of a first-century letter. Revelation itself is written as a letter, and these are short, more personalized messages within it.

Each message is addressed to "the angel of the church" in a given town. Since the Greek term *angelos* can simply mean messenger, some have suggested that these "angels" may be human figures, such as the bishop of each church. However, most commentators understand *angel* in its familiar sense and see the messages as addressed to the guardian angel of each church.

Each message is addressed to the angel from Jesus, and they draw imagery from John's initial vision of Christ (1:12–20). They also are described as "what the Spirit says to the churches" (2:7, 11, 17, etc.), indicating that they are jointly sent by the Son and the Spirit.

The body of each message typically contains a word of commendation for the local church—things that its members are doing right—as well as a word of condemnation—things they are doing wrong.

For example, the church of Ephesus is given this compliment: "I know your works, your toil and your patient endurance, and how you cannot bear evil men but have tested those who call themselves apostles but are not, and found them to be false; I know you are enduring patiently and bearing up for my name's sake, and you have not grown weary" (2:2–3).

But then, the Ephesians are told, "I have this against you, that you have abandoned the love you had at first. Remember then from what you have fallen, repent and do the works you did at first. If not, I will come to you and remove your lampstand [i.e., church] from its place, unless you repent. Yet this you have, you hate the works of the Nicolaitans, which I also hate" (2:4–6).

There are exceptions to this pattern of compliment and condemnation. Two of the churches—Smyrna and Philadelphia—receive only praise, whereas one church—Laodicea—receives only criticism.

Each message concludes with an exhortation to hear what the Spirit is saying and with a promise to "him who conquers"—that is, he who succeeds in living the Christian life despite its difficulties. The promises vary from one church to another but represent aspects of eternal life, as we see in the promise given in the message to the Ephesians: "To him who conquers I will grant to eat of the tree of life, which is in the paradise of God" (2:7).

Scholars have noted that the messages reflect the conditions in the seven cities in the first century, and archaeology has shed light on the meaning of some of the things said in them.[265] We also learn about individual members of some of these congregations. For example, in Pergamum there was a Christian named Antipas who had been martyred, and in Thyatira there was a woman John refers to as "Jezebel" (after the wicked Israelite queen; see 1 Kings 21, 2 Kings 9), who claimed to be a prophetess but taught Christians to do immoral things.

The messages in chapters two and three unambiguously deal with conditions in the first century, but futurists believe that there is a sudden jump to the distant future at the beginning of chapter four. To ease this transition, some futurists have proposed that the seven churches represent seven ages in church history, with Ephesus representing the Apostolic Age and Laodicea representing the current and final period.

This view has found favor among some dispensationalists, and it papers over an otherwise inexplicable lurch from the first century to the end of the world, but it has absolutely no foundation in the text. Thus the view is not taken seriously in the scholarly community, and it does not easily fit with the Protestant principle of *sola scriptura* (that the Bible is our only rule of faith) as there is nothing in the text that would tell the reader these seven churches represent seven ages of history. Consequently, most Protestant authors reject it as nothing more than convenient supposition.

181. What are the seals, trumpets, and bowls?

In addition to the messages to the churches, several other sections of the book are clearly organized around sequences of seven elements. We later read about the seven seals (6:1–8:1), the seven trumpets (8:7–11:19), and the seven bowls (16:2–21).

In the overarching narrative of Revelation, after John writes the messages to the seven churches, he is caught up to heaven to see a vision of "what must take place after this" (4:1). There, he witnesses the worship that continually takes place in God's heavenly temple.

He observes that God is holding a scroll in his right hand, and the scroll is "written within and on the back, sealed with seven seals" (5:1). Most scrolls in the ancient world had writing only on one side and were secured with only one seal. This one is different: it has a lot to say and is very secure.

Scholars have debated the meaning of the scroll. It clearly represents God's authoritative word (being in his right hand), and perhaps the most natural understanding of it in context is that it is a decree describing the events that John is assigned to prophesy.

The only person able to open the scroll is Jesus, who begins removing the scroll's seven seals one at a time. As each seal is removed, a dramatic event takes place.

Once the scroll has been fully opened, John writes, "I saw the seven angels who stand before God, and seven trumpets were given to them" (8:2). These angels then blow the trumpets in sequence, and again dramatic events take place.

Since trumpets were used to announce important events, a natural way to understand the blowing of the trumpets is that they announce the events described in the unsealed scroll.

Finally, after the last of the trumpets has been blown, John sees "seven angels with seven plagues, which are the last, for with them the wrath of God is ended" (15:1). These plagues are given to them in the form of "seven golden bowls full of the wrath of God" (15:7), which they then pour out to release the judgments.

Today we think of bowls as simple kitchen vessels, but the Greek word used here—*phialê*—refers to a ceremonial bowl used to carry sacred offerings, such as libations of wine. The use of bowls in this section thus represents a liturgical action taking place in God's heavenly temple.

Judgment is the overarching theme connecting the seals, trumpets, and bowls. God's decree of judgment is first unsealed, then the judgment is announced by the trumpets, and finally it is brought to completion by the pouring out of the ceremonial bowls.

But who is being judged?

On a preterist understanding of the book, it could be apostate Jerusalem, pagan Rome, or both of them. In an idealist understanding of the book, the judgment would refer to something more general, such as corrupt systems that set themselves up in opposition to God.

When it comes to the individual events associated with each of the seals, trumpets, and bowls, some are easier to interpret than others.

For example, when Christ opens the first four seals (6:1–8), John sees a series of four riders on horseback, which have become known as the four horsemen of the Apocalypse (i.e., of Revelation). The horses are of different colors—white, red, black, and "pale" (literally, "green")—and because Christ is later depicted riding a white horse (19:11–16), many have interpreted the first horseman as Jesus.

However, in context the first horseman is described as a conqueror who "went out conquering and to conquer." The next three horsemen unambiguously represent war, famine, and death, and they thus form a natural progression: conquerors start wars, wars lead to famines, with wars and famines leading to death. This sequence may reflect the "wars and rumors of wars" Jesus warned of (Mark 13:7), including the Jewish War of the A.D. 60s or the Roman civil wars taking place in 69, the "Year of Four Emperors."

Other judgments are more difficult to match with historical events, such as when the third bowl is poured out and the rivers become blood (16:4). This may have a more symbolic meaning, perhaps echoing the deliverance of the Israelites after God turned the Nile to blood, or it may reflect actual historical conditions, such as waterways bloodied by those who fell in combat.

182. What is the Great Tribulation?

In life, people experience trouble—or "tribulation" to use an old-fashioned word—and this applies to Christians as much as anyone else. St. Paul said that it is "through many tribulations we must enter the kingdom of God" (Acts 14:22).

Sometimes God prophetically warns his people about times of trouble, and various passages of Scripture speak of tribulation. Because prophecy usually applies to the near future of when it is given, most of these belong to history. However, some passages speak of future times of trouble.

Daniel 12:1–2 speaks of a tribulation that will occur just before the resurrection of the dead: "There shall be a time of trouble, such as never has been since there was a nation till that time. . . . And many of those who sleep in the dust of the earth shall awake."

Because this time of trouble is unprecedented, it is often called "*the* great tribulation," and people have naturally sought to learn more about it.

One way they've done this is by looking for other passages that speak of tribulation, and especially severe tribulations, on the assumption that they refer to the same event. And if a Bible passage speaks of "great tribulation," it's guaranteed someone will propose this.

But we need to be careful, because the Bible can speak of tribulations—even great ones—without intending to speak about the final trial that precedes the resurrection of the dead. Before assuming that a passage that mentions a tribulation is talking about the last one, we first need to read it and determine its meaning in its own context.

For example, in the Olivet Discourse, Jesus says, "Then there will be great tribulation, such as has not been from the beginning of the world until now, no, and never will be" (Matt. 24:21). However, this part of the discourse is speaking about the destruction of the Jerusalem temple in A.D. 70, and it refers to a local tribulation, not a global one, as Jesus warns, "Let those who are in Judea flee to the mountains" (Matt. 24:16; see 24:17–20).

There was reason to flee! The Jewish historian Josephus reports that, of the approximately three million people who had gathered in Jerusalem for Passover, more than a third were killed, so that "the victims thus outnumbered those of any previous visitation [of wrath], human or divine."[266] Except for a few, select structures, the city itself was almost totally destroyed, and the Romans razed it to the point that it "was so completely leveled to the ground as to leave future visitors to the spot no ground for believing that it had ever been inhabited."[267]

Still, these events may foreshadow the tribulation that will precede the Final Judgment. Revelation records that, after the millennium, "Satan will be released from his prison and will come out to deceive the nations which are at the four corners of the earth" (Rev. 20:7–8), resulting in a persecution.

According to the *Catechism*, "The Church will enter the glory of the kingdom only through this final Passover, when she will follow her Lord in his death and Resurrection" (677). This suggests that the Church will be persecuted almost to the point of extinction (see Luke 18:8), but Jesus will return to save it at the last moment.

183. Who is the woman clothed with the sun?

After the seven trumpets have been blown, we read, "And a great sign appeared in heaven, a woman clothed with the sun, with the moon under her feet, and on her head a crown of twelve stars; she was with child and she cried out in her pangs of birth, in anguish for delivery. She brought forth a male child, one who is to rule all the nations with a rod of iron, but her child was caught up to God and to his throne" (12:1–2, 5).

What does this woman represent? Note that the woman gives birth to a male child who is to rule the nations with a rod of iron. This is a reference to the messianic prophecy in Psalm 2:8–9, and Jesus fulfilled this prophecy. The fact that the child is caught up to the throne of God is a reference to Jesus' ascension into heaven, so we have another confirmation that the child is Jesus. That would indicate that the woman is his mother, the Virgin Mary.

However, the symbolism connected with the woman is drawn from Genesis, where the patriarch Joseph has a dream involving the sun, the moon, and the stars (37:9–10). In the dream, the sun and moon represent Joseph's father and mother and the stars represent his brothers, the patriarchs of the tribes of Israel. This has led many to say that the woman in Revelation 12 is Israel.

You could go further and note that the Church is the *spiritual* Israel, leading some to suggest that the woman is the Church. This can be supported by the verse saying that the woman has other children who are "those who keep the commandments of God and bear testimony to Jesus" (12:17)—in other words, her other children are Christians, suggesting that she is the Church.

So, is the woman Mary, Israel, or the Church? It is important to recall that in Revelation a symbol can point to more than one thing. As a result, we do not have to choose between these meanings. The text contains indications that point to all three, and so the woman can represent all of them.

This view was supported by Pope Benedict XVI, who wrote,

> When the book of Revelation speaks of the great sign of a woman appearing in heaven, she is understood to represent *all Israel*, indeed, the *whole Church*.... On the basis of the "corporate personality" model—in keeping with biblical thought—the early

> Church had no difficulty recognizing in the Woman, on the one hand, *Mary herself* and, on the other hand, transcending time, the Church, bride and mother, in which the mystery of Mary spreads out into history.[268]

On another occasion, he said, "This woman represents Mary, the mother of the Redeemer, but at the same time she also represents the whole Church, the people of God of all times, the Church which in all ages, with great suffering, brings forth Christ ever anew."[269]

We thus don't have to force a choice between the possible meanings of what the woman represents. In keeping with the richness of the way Revelation uses symbolism, to use Pope Benedict's phrases, she can be Mary *and* "all Israel" *and* "the whole Church" in different ways.

This understanding also may allow interpreters to understand more easily some of the things Revelation says about the woman. For example, 12:2 describes her crying out in the pangs of childbirth, but Mary is traditionally thought to have had a painless delivery. These pangs might then refer to the national pain that Israel was experiencing at the time of Christ's birth, such as the difficulties inflicted by the Roman occupation they were under in this period, or to the birth pangs of the Church, who labors to bring forth children to God in the midst of persecution and the consequences of sin.

184. Who is the beast and what is his mark?

At the time of the Reformation, it became common for Protestant interpreters to identify the papacy with the Antichrist and "the beast" of Revelation. There are several problems with this view.

First, the Antichrist is not mentioned in Revelation. The term appears only in John's letters (1 John 2:18, 22; 4:3; 2 John 7). It is speculative to identify the Antichrist with the beast.

Second, John says that "men who will not acknowledge the coming of Jesus Christ in the flesh; such a one is the deceiver and the Antichrist" (2 John 7). But popes do not deny that Jesus Christ has come in the flesh. Their very job is based on the fact that Jesus *did* become incarnate and die for man's sins. Identifying the papacy and the Antichrist violates the biblical data.

Third, the book of Revelation contains more than one beast, but the most famous is one John sees rising from the sea in chapter 13. It incorporates animal symbols that had previously been used in the book of Daniel to represent a line of pagan kingdoms that oppressed God's people (Dan. 7).

This beast has seven heads, and we are told, "The seven heads are seven mountains on which the woman is seated; they are also seven kings, five of whom have fallen, one is, the other has not yet come, and when he comes, he must remain only a little while" (Rev. 17:9–10).

The seven mountains have been identified since ancient times as the seven hills of Rome. Interpreters thus have commonly understood this beast as the pagan Roman Empire that persecuted Christians in John's day and in the early centuries.

As seven kings, the beast's heads are seen as connected to the line of first-century Roman emperors. Like these emperors, the beast blasphemes God, persecutes the saints, rules the world, and receives worship from all but Christians (Rev. 13:6–8). It also has the number 666 (Rev. 13:18), which is what "Nero Caesar" (NRWN QSR) adds up to in Hebrew and Aramaic according to the numerical values the letters have in these languages (N+R+W+N+Q+S+R = 50+200+6+50+100+60+200 = 666).

This would suggest that the literal fulfillment of the beast is to be found in the first-century line of Roman emperors. However, this would not prevent there from being another fulfillment of this prophecy before the end of the world. It could be similar to the way Daniel's "abomination of desolation"/"desolating sacrilege" (Dan. 9:27, 11:31, 12:11) could be fulfilled both in the time of the Maccabees (1 Macc. 1:54) and again in the generation that followed Jesus (Matt. 24:15).

Thus the world's final villain—described by Paul as "the man of lawlessness" and commonly called "the Antichrist"—is likely to echo the beast of Revelation and Roman emperors like Nero.

Many have wondered about the "mark of the beast" that its followers receive on their right hands or foreheads, allowing them to buy and sell (Rev. 13:16–18). Some have suggested that this might involve modern technologies like implanted RFID chips, but this is not what the passage would have meant in its original context.

In the first century, disobedient slaves were sometimes tattooed or branded to show who owned them, but the beast's servants seem willing rather than disobedient. On the other hand, the devotees of some pagan gods also were marked for the one they worshiped, so that may be in view.

Yet there is reason to think that Revelation does not intend this to be a literal, visible mark. In the Old Testament, God spoke of his laws being a mark on the Israelites' hands and foreheads (Exod. 13:9, 16). In Ezekiel, the righteous are invisibly marked on their foreheads by an angel (Ezek. 9:4), as are a group of 144,000 Israelites in Revelation (7:3–8, 14:1). Indeed, Christians in general are said to be sealed by God (2 Cor. 1:22, Eph. 1:13, 4:30).

Understood in light of these parallels, the mark of the beast would not be a physical brand or tattoo—much less an undreamt-of future technology—but a symbol of a pagan's willingness to employ his head and his hand in the service of the Roman cult of emperor worship and thus reap the economic rewards of participating in imperial public life—from which Christians were often excluded.

If this mark has a parallel in the future, its form can only be a matter of speculation. From an idealist perspective, it speaks of the complicity with evil that, in every generation, seduces the children of this world by promises of political, social, and economic advantage.

185. Who is the false prophet?

In chapters twelve and thirteen of Revelation, we meet three sinister figures that are sometimes referred to as an unholy trinity. The first is a red dragon with seven heads and ten horns (12:3), the second is the beast that emerges from the sea, which also has seven heads and ten horns (13:1), and the last is a beast "which rose out of the earth; it had two horns like a lamb, and it spoke like a dragon" (13:11).

The dragon is elsewhere identified as Satan (20:2), and we've seen that the beast from the sea is identified in a special way with the line of first-century Roman emperors. But who is the beast from the land?

Later in the book, the devil and the beast from the sea are associated with a third figure known as "the false prophet" (16:13, 19:20, 20:10), and most interpreters have understood the beast from the land and the false prophet to be identical. This is partly because the second beast acts like a priest and prophet of the former beast in the chapter where they are introduced.

We are told that the beast from the land "makes the earth and its inhabitants worship the first beast" and "works great signs." By means of these signs, "it deceives those who dwell on earth, bidding them make an image for the beast," and it is able to animate the image "so that the image of the beast should even speak, and to cause those who would not worship the image of the beast to be slain." Finally, it compels people to take the mark of the beast so that no one can buy or sell without the mark (13:12–17).

When it comes to the identification of the false prophet, some have pointed to its two lamb-like horns, and that it comes from "the land," to identify it as Jewish in origin. The lamb was a sacrificial animal for Jews, Jesus is depicted in Revelation as a lamb (5:6), and Israel dwelled in the promised land. On this proposal, it might represent Jewish leaders who rejected and killed the Messiah and then formed an alliance with Rome to persecute Christians.

However, the false prophet is portrayed as a strong supporter of the cult of emperor worship, and Jewish leaders were very much opposed to that. This suggests that we should consider other possible meanings for the symbol.

The fact that it looks like a lamb but speaks like a dragon may simply mean that the false prophet outwardly seems harmless but nevertheless carries a satanic message, and the land it comes from may be the land where John and his readers are—Asia—rather than the Holy Land. In that case, it could represent something native to Asia rather than brought there by means of the sea, like the first beast (the Roman Empire), which arrived by sea.

Consequently, most interpreters have understood the false prophet to represent the cult of emperor worship in Asia. With the exception of Caligula, Nero, and Domitian, first-century Roman emperors were not worshiped in Rome during their lifetimes. It was considered improper for them to demand divine honors in their own capital. However, there was no problem with people in other parts of the empire worshiping the emperor, and many people in the provinces sought to prove their loyalty by treating him as a god and building temples to him. There were several such temples in Asia.

As a result, the false prophet fits well with the native Asian cult of emperor worship and the local officials who promoted it.

The image that the false prophet sets up would naturally be understood as an idol of the emperor. Promoters of various cults in the Greco-Roman world would sometimes equip statues of divinities with hidden speaking tubes that allowed oracles to be given through them by their priests.[270] They also used an early form of animatronics or robotics to cause the idols to move.[271] Such trickery may have been employed by advocates of emperor worship to produce "pretended signs and wonders" (see 2 Thess. 2:9).

When it comes to the false prophet imposing the mark of the beast so that people may buy and sell, many interpreters have understood this as referring to the need to participate in emperor worship as a condition of conducting business. Trade guilds had religious rites that could involve the imperial cult;

boycotts could be targeted against merchants who were perceived as disloyal; businesses might refuse to sell to unpatriotic customers; and even the coins people used to buy and sell often carried depictions of the emperor as a god. Refusing to participate in emperor worship could have serious economic consequences even when martyrdom did not result.

186. What is the battle of Armageddon?

In popular speech, *Armageddon* has become a term for the final military battle of world history. It also has an extended meaning and can refer to any devastating conflict, whether or not it would be the final one. Thus, during the Cold War, people feared that World War III would bring about a "nuclear Armageddon."

The basis for this idea is found in a passage in Revelation that describes the trio of evil beings—the dragon (i.e., the devil), the beast, and the false prophet—who disgorge "three foul spirits like frogs" that "go abroad to the kings of the whole world, to assemble them for battle on the great day of God the Almighty." These kings then assemble "at the place which is called in Hebrew Armageddon" (Rev. 16:13–16).

We are told that "they will make war on the Lamb [i.e., Jesus], and the Lamb will conquer them" (17:14). This conflict is described in Revelation 19:11–21, and the outcome is that the beast and the false prophet are captured and thrown alive into hell, while the devil is bound for a thousand years, so that he cannot deceive the nations during the millennium (Rev. 20:1–6).

However, the devil is afterward released, and he deceives the nations and again gathers them for battle. His army is then destroyed by fire, and he is thrown into hell alongside the beast and the false prophet.

Thus, contrary to popular usage, Revelation does not depict Armageddon as the final battle of history but as one *preceding* the reign of Christ.

Scholars debate the precise meaning of the name *Armageddon*. The Greek word John uses is *harmagedôn*, but he tells us it is of Hebrew or Aramaic origin. The term *har* means "mountain," and Megiddo was an ancient city in Israel, so most scholars have understood Armageddon to mean "the mount of Megiddo."

Megiddo sits in the middle of a valley, but, as an ancient settlement that long predates the founding of Israel, it has been rebuilt numerous times, resulting in it sitting atop an artificial hill made up of the residue of all its earlier versions. This artificial hill may be the "mount" that John is referring to. Alternately, some scholars suggest, it may be a true mountain that is *near* Megiddo, such as Mount Carmel.

Whatever the case, Megiddo has a long history as the site of battles. It was a strategically important location, and numerous battles have been fought there, both before and after the founding of Israel. Revelation thus invokes its history as a site of warfare.

The question is how literally the conflict involving it should be understood. Many premillennialists—especially dispensationalists—see this as a literal military conflict that will occur in Israel, with forces led by the Antichrist, just before the beginning of the earthly reign of Christ in the millennium.

However, in a Catholic perspective, there will not be an earthly reign of Christ before the end of the world. Instead, the millennium is best understood as the reign of Christ that is occurring now in heaven and, through his Church, on earth (CCC 680).

The battle of Armageddon thus might be understood as related to the Jewish War of the A.D. 60s, when the forces of pagan Rome ("the beast") attacked Jerusalem and destroyed its temple.

Alternately, it may be understood not as a literal military conflict but as a spiritual conflict between the forces of paganism and the gospel, which led to the devil being bound so that he could not stop the proclamation of Christ to the nations. Revelation would be depicting this spiritual conflict in military terms and drawing on the history of Megiddo as a site of warfare as part of that imagery.

However Armageddon is to be understood, Revelation does predict a future conflict at the end of the Christian age, and it may involve military as well as spiritual elements, including the involvement of the Antichrist.

187. Who is the whore of Babylon?

We first hear of the "whore of Babylon" shortly after the two beasts are introduced, but we are given very little detail. John simply hears an angel crying, "Fallen, fallen is Babylon the great, she who made all nations drink the wine of her impure passion" (14:8).

The next clear mention occurs after the seventh bowl is poured out and John writes, "And God remembered great Babylon, to make her drain the cup of the fury of his wrath" (16:19).

These enigmatic references are then clarified in chapters seventeen through nineteen, which are devoted principally to elaborating on Babylon and its fall. At the beginning of this section, an angel takes John to the wilderness to show him God's judgment on "the great harlot."

> I saw a woman sitting on a scarlet beast which was full of blasphemous names, and it had seven heads and ten horns. The woman was clothed in purple and scarlet, and adorned with gold and jewels and pearls, holding in her hand a golden cup full of abominations and the impurities of her fornication; and on her forehead was written a name of mystery: "Babylon the great, mother of harlots and of earth's abominations." And I saw the woman, drunk with the blood of the saints and the blood of the martyrs of Jesus (17:3–6).

Babylon was a city in ancient Mesopotamia (modern Iraq), but scholars recognize the use of "Babylon" in Revelation as a symbolic designation of another city (11:8; see 1 Pet. 5:13, where Peter, who is known to have been in Rome, refers to being in "Babylon"):

- The whore is depicted persecuting Christians (17:6, 14).
- She is seated on the beast with seven heads, which is likely Rome (17:3).
- The beast also has ten horns, which hate the whore, attack her, and burn her with fire (17:16).
- The whore is said to be "the great city which has dominion over the kings of the earth" (17:18).

Most scholars see these as pointing to the ancient pagan city of Rome, which persecuted Christians, was built on seven hills, had a line of emperors plausibly identified with the beast, and was the capital of the major empire of the day.

Some scholars have seen the clues as pointing instead to another city—Jerusalem—which also persecuted Christians in the first century, whose authorities were allied with and supported by the Roman Empire (and thus "seated" on the beast), and which was attacked and burned by an alliance of Roman and other troops in A.D. 70, as Jesus predicted (Mark 13).

Further, Revelation 11:8 speaks of "the great city" as being where the "Lord was crucified." Given the contrast between the old Jerusalem and the new Jerusalem elsewhere in Scripture (see Gal. 4:21–31)—and the fact that the Old Testament speaks of Jerusalem as a whore (Isa. 1:21; Ezek. 16:1, 15–35)—some conclude that if the bride is the new Jerusalem, then the whore must be the current, apostate Jerusalem.

In Revelation 17:16, the beast and its allies attack the whore and burn it with fire. If the whore is Jerusalem, this would refer to the sack of Jerusalem that occurred in A.D. 70.

On the other hand, if the whore is Rome, it could refer to the great fire of Rome in A.D. 64 (which Nero allegedly set) or to the calamitous Year of Four Emperors in A.D. 69, in which the city was convulsed by civil war and destruction, including fire.

Both identifications are possible, and some have even suggested that the whore may represent *both* Rome and Jerusalem.

The devastation of the whore is described in detail in Revelation 18:1–19:3. Afterward, Jesus appears and destroys the beast and its allies (Rev. 19:11–21), signifying the destruction of the pagan Roman system and the beginning of the new, Christian age, in which the devil is bound "that he should deceive the nations no more, till the thousand years were ended" (Rev. 20:3).

188. What is the millennium?

The term *millennium* comes from Latin roots that mean "thousand" (*mille*) and "year" (*annus*). In the context of biblical prophecy, the millennium refers to the thousand-year period mentioned in Revelation 20:1–6. Although some interpreters take the number 1,000 literally, others see it as a symbolic figure that simply indicates a long period of time (see Psa. 50:10, as when God says that "the cattle on a thousand hills" are his—meaning that the animals on *all* the hills are his).

During the millennium, the devil is bound so "that he should deceive the nations no more, till the thousand years were ended," during which time a group of Christian martyrs who had refused to worship the beast "came to life and reigned with Christ a thousand years."[272]

A key question is how this event is to be understood, and historically there have been three major options. In Protestant circles, these have been dubbed *premillennialism*, *postmillennialism*, and *amillennialism*.

According to *premillennialists*, Christ's Second Coming will occur *before* (pre-) this thousand-year period, and Jesus will physically reign on earth (likely from Jerusalem) during it. This view was common among some early Christian writers, and in the twentieth century it became popular among Evangelical Protestants. In Catholic circles, this view has often been called *millenarianism*.

According to *postmillennialism*, the Second Coming will occur *after* (post-) the millennium, and during that period Christ reigns from heaven, along with his saints, in a way that produces a golden age on earth. This view was popular in the nineteenth and early twentieth centuries among English-speaking Protestants. It became less popular after the horrors of the twentieth century's two world wars and growing secularization led many to conclude that we were not moving toward such a golden age in which the Church progressively triumphs.

According to *amillennialism*, we are now living in the millennium, which spans the Christian age and will be followed by the Second Coming. Christ is currently reigning in heaven, and the saints live and reign with him there. On earth, the devil is bound so that he cannot deceive the nations by stopping the spread of the gospel, though this does not result in a paradisiacal golden age where all earthly problems vanish. This view has been the position of most scholars throughout history, including the original Protestant Reformers.

Although Catholics tend not to use the word *amillennial*, this term best corresponds to the Church's understanding of the millennium. The Magisterium has specifically rejected premillennialism (or millenarianism). According to the *Catechism*, "The Antichrist's deception already begins to take shape in the world every time the claim is made to realize within history that messianic hope which can only be realized beyond history through the eschatological judgment. The Church has rejected even modified forms of this falsification of the kingdom to come under the name of millenarianism" (676).

The Magisterium also has warned against expecting a golden age of the kind predicted by postmillennialism before the Second Coming: "The kingdom will be fulfilled, then, not by a historic triumph of the Church through a progressive ascendancy, but only by God's victory over the final unleashing of evil, which will cause his bride to come down from heaven" (CCC 677).

The millennial reign of Christ spoken of in Revelation 20 is thus taking place right now, for as he said, "All authority in heaven and on earth has been given to me" (Matt. 28:18), and as St. Paul declared, "He must reign until he has put all his enemies under his feet. The last enemy to be destroyed is death" (1 Cor. 15:25–26).

189. How does the book of Revelation end?

The final part of Revelation contains a number of elements: the final defeat of the devil, the Final Judgment, the apparition of new heavens and a new earth, the description of the bride of the Lamb, and an epilogue.

The first of these events, the *final defeat of the devil*, takes place immediately after the millennium: "When the thousand years are ended, Satan will be released from his prison and will come out to deceive the nations which are at the four corners of the earth" (20:7–8). He will then gather them for battle and surround "the camp of the saints and the beloved city" (20:9), which is naturally interpreted either as a reference to Jerusalem or to the Church. However, fire comes down from heaven to defeat them, and the devil is thrown into the lake of fire where the beast and the false prophet had been confined after the battle of Armageddon.

Following this, the *Final Judgment* takes place, and "the dead, great and small" are judged. Everyone who has ever lived is brought back to life, for "Death and Hades gave up the dead in them" (Hades being the place that houses the dead). This is a permanent resurrection, because "Death and Hades were thrown into the lake of fire," since there will no longer be a need for them. At the same time, the dead are assigned their fates, being judged "by what they had done," and "if any one's name was not found written in the book of life, he was thrown into the lake of fire" (20:11–15).

John then writes, "I saw a *new heaven and a new earth*; for the first heaven and the first earth had passed away" (21:1). This prophecy of a new heaven and earth goes back to the book of Isaiah (Isa. 65:17; 66:22) and is repeated elsewhere in the New Testament (e.g., 2 Pet. 3:13). The *Catechism* speaks of this change as a renewal rather than a complete annihilation and replacement of the current cosmos.

A feature of the renovated cosmos is "the holy city, new Jerusalem," which comes down out of heaven, "prepared as a *bride* adorned for her husband" (21:2). This expectation of a new or heavenly Jerusalem is also found elsewhere in the New Testament (Gal. 4:25–26, Heb. 11:10, 16; 12:22).

Its descent to earth marks a radical change in the order of things, for now "the dwelling of God is with men. He will dwell with them, and they shall be his people" (21:3). Ever since the fall, there has been a separation between

God and man, but now that is overcome, with the result that God "will wipe away every tear from their eyes, and death shall be no more, neither shall there be mourning nor crying nor pain any more, for the former things have passed away" (21:4).

We then encounter a section of the book devoted to the new Jerusalem (21:9–22:11). This section parallels the section on the whore of Babylon (17:1–19:10), and they both begin and end the same way. Both start when one of the angels of the seven bowls takes John to a distant location to view the city in question, and both conclude with John being so overcome that he attempts to worship the angel and is told not to. This makes it clear that the two cities/women are mirror images of each other. One is unholy, the other holy; one is a prostitute, the other a bride.

The section dealing with new Jerusalem is the source of popular images of heaven, including "pearly gates" (i.e., gates cut out of giant pearls) and streets paved with gold (21:21). It also describes mankind once again having access to the tree of life from Genesis, since he is now immortal (22:2; see Gen. 3:22).

The images used in this section convey a sense of the glory and joy of our final destiny, but they need to be understood as symbols. The next age transcends what we can imagine, and we should recognize the symbolic nature of the images used to describe it. They are hints meant to convey a much greater reality.

For example, new Jerusalem is described as being 12,000 stadia long, wide, and tall (21:16). The number 12,000 combines the symbolic numbers 12 and 1,000, but we are not meant to take the distance literally. This distance is equivalent to 1,500 miles, but the city's wall is only 144 cubits high (21:17). This is another symbolic number (144 = 12 x 12), and if taken literally it would represent a wall 216 feet high. But how could a city 1,500 miles tall be protected by a wall only 216 feet tall? This underscores the symbolic nature of these numbers—and of the images of this section in general.

According to the *Catechism,* "This mystery of blessed communion with God and all who are in Christ is beyond all understanding and description. Scripture speaks of it in images: life, light, peace, wedding feast, wine of the kingdom, the Father's house, the heavenly Jerusalem, paradise: 'no eye has seen, nor ear heard, nor the heart of man conceived, what God has prepared for those who love him' (1 Cor. 2:9)" (1027).

The final part of Revelation is a closing epilogue that stresses the nearness of the events in the book. In the final chapter, there are five assurances on this point. Three times, Jesus says, "I am coming soon" (22:7, 12, 20), once John is told that the events of the book "must soon take place" (22:6), and he also is told, "Do not seal up the words of the prophecy of this book, for the time is near" (22:10). This is in direct contrast to Daniel, who was told to seal up one of his visions, as it pertained to a distant, future time (Dan. 8:26).

The Spirit and the bride then implore Jesus to come, and the one who hears the book read aloud in church is urged to implore Jesus to come (22:17). Finally, John himself urges Jesus to come (22:20). These would seem primarily to be references to Jesus coming in judgment on those who oppress his people—whether Jewish, Roman, or otherwise—although they also express the Church's expectation of his Second Coming at the end of time.

Although Revelation ends with a discussion of events that were in the far future from John's perspective—and that are still in the future from our perspective—the heavy emphasis on the nearness of the book as a whole strongly argues for an early fulfillment of the material in the book preceding the millennium.

That is what John led his readers to expect, it's the natural interpretation of the book, and it should be our interpretation as well—regardless of the application this material may also have to our future by way of additional fulfillments.

PART 4

THE CHRISTIAN MYSTERY

INTRODUCTION

Our Christian faith is the *good news* that God has delivered to humanity. He first prepared us for his gospel by a progressive revelation of himself and his eternal truths. He took a people to himself: teaching them, guiding them, disciplining them, setting them apart from the world. He made a covenant with them, binding himself to them and giving them a law by which they could bind themselves to him.

Many times, God's people strayed from their covenant and broke his law. But God was always faithful to them.

Finally, at the time and in the place for which God had been preparing his people for thousands of years—the time and place he had preordained since the beginning of the world—he completed his self-revelation and capped off the arc of his grand plan by sending his divine Son into the world: the God who became man to save mankind.

In this section we will examine the core truths and key players of this central salvific mystery: the natures of God and man, and of the God-man; the ministers of God's power in the order of creation and grace; and the destiny that awaits the universe and each of us in it.

190. Is the God of philosophers the same as the God of the Bible?

As we've already seen, when the Bible describes God having a body or being a "he," it is using metaphors to explain eternal truths about God to finite human beings—us. But its use of such metaphors doesn't mean that the biblical God is different from the infinite, necessary, simple, and flawless being posited by philosophers.

Some atheists object that the God of the Bible seems emotionally dysfunctional because the Bible says he is "wrathful" toward sinners and "jealous" when they worship other gods. But we need not take these descriptions to mean that the biblical God has emotions in the sense that we do—immediate, affective responses to stimuli. Nothing can change or surprise the all-knowing God. He doesn't exhibit the emotions we do when we react to new situations. So when the Bible describes God having emotions like anger, regret, or pleasure, it is using metaphors to describe how human beings relate to God—not the other way around. Catholic philosopher Patrick Lee writes that God can be said to be pleased or angry with us "in the relational sense"; that is, "we are related to God as one who pleases is related to the one who is pleased. . . . We are related to God as one who elicits anger is related to the one who is angry."[273]

In other words, saying that God is angry at our sin, or pleased with our obedience, doesn't describe God reacting to something we have done. Instead, it is a non-literal way of describing the consequences our own actions have regarding our relationship with God. Positive actions draw us closer to God whereas negative actions push us away from him. Saying that God is jealous of other gods means that God does not will that we worship false gods, who are morally and metaphysically inferior to the one true God.

Other passages in Scripture that ascribe emotions to God must also be understood in this non-literal, relational sense. For example, the last verse of the book of Jonah says, "When God saw what they did, how they turned from their evil way, God repented of the evil which he had said he would do to them; and he did not do it" (Jon. 3:10). But how can an immutable God change his mind? Wouldn't an omniscient being know about his future change of mind before it occurred? The phrase "God repented" tells us that God would no longer execute his judgment upon the people of Nineveh. When the Bible says that God changed or repented from evil, it is a metaphorical way of saying that human beings have changed, or that human beings have repented, not that God has changed in any way. God knew the people of Nineveh would eventually repent, but he sent Jonah to them because *the people of Nineveh* did not know they were capable of such repentance.

When we encounter biblical descriptions of God that seem "too human," we must remember a principle of revelation called *divine condescension*. This is the act by which God stoops down to our level so that we finite humans can better understand him. For example, God must assume some kind of visual or auditory form to relate to humans, even though he is not composed of matter. He must speak to humans in sentences, even though his knowledge exists as a perfect, timeless whole and not in the form of discursive reasoning.

St. John Chrysostom says that even the angels who surrounded God's throne in Isaiah 6:1–2 did not see God's true glory:

> Yet they did not see the pure light itself nor the pure essence itself. What they saw was a condescension accommodated to their nature. What is this condescension? God condescends whenever

> he is not seen as he is, but in the way one incapable of beholding him is able to look upon him. In this way God reveals himself by accommodating what he reveals to the weakness of vision of those who behold him.[274]

191. Is it a contradiction to say that one God is Father, Son, and Holy Spirit?

At first glance, it appears as if it is a contradiction to hold both that there is only one God and that God is Father, Son, and Holy Spirit. But this is only an apparent, not a real contradiction.

First, we must define what is meant by a contradiction. In his book *Socratic Logic*, Peter Kreeft points out, "In logic, 'contradiction' does not mean the subjective, psychological relation between two human beings who disagree with each other, but the objective, logical relation between two propositions that cannot both be true at the same time and also cannot both be false at the same time."[275] So if I say, "My favorite baseball team is the Mariners," and you say, "My favorite baseball team is the Red Sox," we do not have a logical contradiction. By contrast, the following two propositions are in logical contradiction to each other:

> A) "Babe Ruth hit more home runs than any other major league ball player."
>
> B) "Babe Ruth did not hit more home runs than any other major league ball player."

Proposition A and proposition B cannot both be true at the same time and in the same respect. If we accept A, we must reject B. If we accept B, we must reject A.

Are the propositions "There is only one God" and "God is Father, Son, and Holy Spirit" logically contradictory to each other? If we are monotheists believing in just one God, must we reject trinitarian belief in God the Father, Son, and Holy Spirit? If we believe in the Trinity, must we reject monotheism?

In fact, belief in one God and belief in the Trinity are not contradictory. There is only one God. But the one God is three divine persons: Father, Son, and Holy Spirit. It would be a logical contradiction to say, "There is only one God" and "There is more than one God; indeed there are three Gods." It would also be a logical contradiction to say "There is only one Person in God" and "There are three persons in God." But the Church teaches neither of these contradictions. "We do not confess three Gods, but one God in three persons, the 'consubstantial Trinity'" (CCC 253). There is no logical contradiction in claiming that there is only one God and that this one God is three divine persons: Father, Son, and Holy Spirit.

The Trinity of persons in one God is not a logical contradiction, and it is also not a logical conclusion, either. We know about the Trinity only because we accept what Jesus teaches about himself, about his Father, and about the Holy Spirit. Interpersonal communion did not begin with creation. Rather, from all eternity, the Father was knowing, loving, and delighting in the Son. The Son was knowing, loving, and delighting in the Father. Both Father and Son were knowing, loving, and delighting in the Holy Spirit and vice versa. The foundation of both creation and redemption is a loving communion of persons knowing, loving, and delighting in one another. So when we act to promote the communion of persons made in God's image here on earth—when we know, love, and delight in one another and in God—we are in harmony with the ultimate foundation of the entire universe and hasten in its supernatural fulfillment in Christ.

192. What is the Trinity?

Put simply, the Christian doctrine of the Trinity states that God is one being who exists as three divine persons—the Father, Son, and Holy Spirit. As we saw in the previous question, "We do not confess three Gods, but one God in three persons, the 'consubstantial Trinity'" (CCC 253).

The mystery of the Trinity does not contradict God's simplicity because each person fully dwells in each other person and they are distinguished *relationally*, not spatially or temporally. The different persons are not different "parts" of God.[276]

In order to understand this doctrine, we must first understand three key words: being, nature, and person. *Being* refers to a unified act of existence, that is, "that something is." *A being* is thus a unified entity. *Nature* refers to "what something is" or to what specific kind a being belongs. Finally, *person* refers to "who someone is" and can be said only of individuals possessing intellect and will. We are persons of a specific nature, just as we are beings of a specific nature: we are *human* beings and *human* persons.

So how does this relate to God? Christians do not believe that God is *one person* with infinite attributes. That belief, held for example by Jews and Muslims, is called *unitarianism*. Christians instead believe that God is *one being* who exists as *three persons*, each of whom fully possess the divine *nature*. Christians are not unitarians, but trinitarians. They believe that, because there is only one God, and the Father is God, the Son is God, and the Holy Spirit is God, it follows that this one God must exist as three coequal and co-eternal persons.

The Trinity can't be grasped if we think of "beings" and "persons" as the same thing. But if we recognize that there are beings that are zero persons (such as rocks and trees) and there are beings that are one person (humans and angels), then we see that it is not impossible for there to exist a being that is three persons.

It's also important to avoid confusing analogies that misrepresent the Trinity. For example, saying the Trinity is like one clover with three petals may be helpful for explaining the Trinity to children but actually translates into the heresy of tritheism, or the belief that the Father, Son, and Holy Spirit are individual beings who share a part of the divine nature, not three persons united in one indivisible co-extensive Godhead.

Another faulty analogy is saying that the Trinity is like one man being a father, husband, and son at the same time. This is not Trinitarianism but the heresy of modalism, which says that the Trinity is made up of three aspects or *modes* of God, each of which has a different role in relation to creatures. However, modalism doesn't make sense of passages in Scripture in which the Son is clearly relating to the Father as to another person, for example, praying to the Father (Matt. 11:25-26; John 11:41-42; 17), returning to the Father (John 14:12, 14:28, 16:10), and together with the Father sending the Holy Spirit (John 14:16–17, 14:26, 15:26, 16:13–15; Acts 2:32–33).[277]

In addition to its disregard of Scripture, modalism undermines the essence of Christian hope. Rather than inviting humanity to share in the beatitude of the eternal Son of the Father—"the glory which I had with thee before the world began" (John 17:5)—modalism makes God's fatherhood and sonship *relative to us*. In this view, God is only Father insofar as he is Creator and Son insofar as he became man to save us. Modalism erases the eternal interpersonal relationship—"thou in me and I in thee"—which constitutes the "glory" that Jesus wants to share with us (John 17:21-23).

Although it is a complex mystery ultimately beyond our human reason, the doctrine of the Trinity is not just some theological fine point and it is not, as some critics assert, a pagan idea that crept into the Church after many centuries. It flowed organically from the early Church Fathers and their understanding of Scripture. In fact, the doctrine demonstrates one of God's most amazing attributes: that he is *love* (1 John 4:8). As love itself, God is a relationship of divine persons: a Trinity of Father, Son, and Holy Spirit who eternally give and receive love. God is not a solitary being who has existed alone from ages past.

193. What distinguishes the three persons of the Trinity?

If the Father, the Son, and the Holy Spirit are one indivisible and consubstantial God, what distinguishes one person from another?

Drawing on both faith and reason, St. Thomas Aquinas outlines three fundamental issues in response to this question: first, the origin or *procession* of the persons; second, their *relations*; and third, the *persons* themselves.

Concerning the *divine processions*, we have the witness of Scripture, as Jesus tells us, "From God I proceeded'" (John 8:42). Likewise, he tells us that the Holy Spirit "proceeds from the Father" (15:26).

The Son and the Holy Spirit proceed from the Father not by means of an external, outward act like that of creation. Their procession is an *inward* act within God, analogous to procession in the human mind and heart.

For example, when we understand a thing in our intellect, a concept comes forth from our intellectual power and proceeds from our knowledge of that object. As God's divine intelligence is perfect and substantial, "the divine Word is of necessity perfectly one with the source whence he proceeds."[278] The Word proceeds from the Father's perfect and total knowing, somewhat like the way our concepts and words proceed from our imperfect, partial manner of knowing.

This analogy is founded on Scripture. As we read in John 1:1: "In the beginning was the Word, and the Word was with God, and the Word was God." And because the Word is substantial and of the same nature as the Father, he is also Son—"the only Son, who is in the bosom of the Father" (John 1:18)—such that this procession is properly called *generation*.

Our intellects are one way we were formed in the image and likeness of God, but they're not the only way. The other way lies in our possession of will. "The operation of the will within ourselves," Thomas writes, "involves also another procession, that of love, whereby the object loved is in the lover; as, by the conception of the word, the object spoken of or understood is in the intelligent agent. Hence, besides the procession of the Word in God, there exists in him another procession called the procession of love."[279] This procession is called *spiration*, which derives from our words for "breathing" and for "spirit."[280]

This procession of *love* flows from the procession of the Word, since nothing can be loved unless it is known by the intellect. This is why, every time we recite the Nicene Creed at Mass, we declare that we believe in the Holy Spirit, "who proceeds from the Father and the Son."

These two processions underlie the *relations* of the Holy Trinity—that is, the ways in which the persons can be referred to or contrasted in some way to each other.

The Father is relative to the Son, whom he generates: this is the relation called *paternity*. The Son is begotten by the Father, and this relation is called *filiation*. Meanwhile, the relation of the Father and Son to the Spirit, and of the Spirit to the Father and Son, are called by the general names of *spiration* and *procession*, respectively.[281]

It is these substantial relations which differentiate the *persons* of the Trinity among themselves, says Aquinas, citing the sixth-century Christian philosopher Boethius: "Relation alone multiplies the Trinity of the divine persons."[282]

The persons of the Trinity—whom we know from Scripture as Father, Son, and Spirit—are rightly called "person" because they are indeed, following the classical definition of Boethius, "an individual substance of a rational nature."[283] Although the word *person* is not found applied to God in Scripture, what that word means is found many times, because God is regularly described, as Thomas puts it, as "the supreme, self-subsisting and the most perfectly intelligent being."[284]

> Person signifies what is most perfect in all nature—that is, a subsistent individual with a rational nature. Hence, since everything that is perfect must be attributed to God, forasmuch as his essence contains every perfection, this name *person* is fittingly applied to God—not, however, as it is applied to creatures, but in a more excellent way.[285]

If *person* is aptly applied to God in his essence, it is also applicable to the *three* subsisting relations that exist in God.

Fatherhood in God *is* God the Father, the "principle of the whole deity" as St. Augustine says (see ST I:33:1), unbegotten and proceeding from no other principle.[286] Likewise, the filiation in God *is* God the Son, the Word of God, consubstantial with the Father. He is also called the *image* of God. (Man is *made in* the image of God, whereas the Son alone *is* the actual image of God.) Finally, the Holy Spirit—whose proper name of "holy" and "spirit" reflects attributes shared in common with the Father and Son—can fittingly be named *Love*, because "the Holy Ghost is said to be the bond of the Father and the Son, inasmuch as he is Love" (ST I:37:1).

194. Does the Bible say that Jesus and the Holy Spirit are divine?

Yes, Scripture explicitly testifies to the divinity of Jesus and of the Holy Spirit, and they were recorded with this end in mind.

The divinity of Christ is evident in passages of Scripture in which Jesus spoke with unparalleled authority and made claims that elevated him to the status of God himself. Here are just a few examples:

- In Matthew 11:27, Jesus claims to have an exclusive and absolute relationship with God the Father when he says, "All things have been delivered to me by my Father; and no one knows the Son except the Father, and no one knows the Father except the Son and any one to whom the Son chooses to reveal him."
- In Luke 22:29, Jesus claims to have the authority to confer kingdoms, just like the Father does.
- In John 5:17-18, we are told that the Jews sought to kill Jesus "because he not only broke the Sabbath but also called God his Father, making himself equal with God." This same charge of "making himself Son of God" is brought against Jesus before the Sanhedrin (Luke 22:69-71) and before Pilate (John 19:7). It was for this unprecedented claim that he was put to death.
- In John 8:58, Jesus uses the unpronounceable divine name for himself when he says, "before Abraham was, I AM," implying that he existed—eternally—before Abraham lived thousands of years before. This act drove the Jews, who were only just now claiming to be his disciples, to take up stones to put him to death, as they understood it to be blasphemy.

- In John 20:28, Thomas addresses Jesus as "My Lord and my God." Jesus does not correct Thomas for uttering what would have been blasphemy if it were not true.

Some critics object that these references to Jesus' claims of divinity all come from later sources (especially the Gospel of John) and are the product of legendary development. However, even in the earliest Gospel, there is evidence of Jesus' divine stature. For example, in Mark 2:5, after healing the paralytic, Jesus claims to be able to forgive the man's sins, something that only God has the authority to do. In Mark 6:7, Jesus gathers twelve disciples, which is symbolic of the twelve tribes of Israel. Rather than representing one of the tribes himself, such as the tribe of Levi, which had a claim to the priesthood, Jesus stands apart from the Twelve and gathers them together in the same way that God called the twelve tribes of Israel.

Along with the evidence from the Gospels, the letters in the New Testament confirm that the first Christians worshiped Jesus as God and did not think of him as just a wise human being. They say that Jesus Christ is the "image of the invisible God" (Col. 1:15), in whom the "fullness of deity dwells bodily" (Col. 2:8–9). Jesus has the "form of God" and a name to which every knee shall bend (Phil. 2:6, 10). Finally, Jesus is "our great God and Savior" (Titus 2:13).

The Gospel of John and the letter to the Hebrews even go so far as to identify the incarnate Son of God as the Creator, through whom the world was made in the beginning and by whose power it continues in being:

> In the beginning was the Word, and the Word was with God, and the Word was God. He was *in the beginning with God; all things were made through him, and without him was not anything made that was made* (John 1:1-3).

> In many and various ways God spoke of old to our fathers by the prophets; but in these last days he has spoken to us by a Son, whom he appointed the heir of all things, *through whom also he created the world.* He reflects the glory of God and bears the very stamp of his nature, *upholding the universe by his word of power* (Heb. 1:1-3).

The Christians who came after the apostles also recognized the divinity of Christ. For example, St. Ignatius of Antioch, in the year A.D. 110, referred to "the Church beloved and enlightened after the love of Jesus Christ, *our God*."[287]

The divinity of the Holy Spirit is also explicitly testified in the New Testament, as well as alluded to in Old Testament passages speaking of the "Spirit of God."

Scripture says that the Holy Spirit will guide us "into all the truth" (John 16:13), and that the Spirit alone comprehends the thoughts of God (1 Cor. 2:11). Who else but God can know all truth or comprehend God's thoughts?

Jesus tells us that the Spirit of truth and the Son both "proceed from" God the Father (John 8:42, 15:26). This is something no mere prophet could ever claim, as it means not only being "sent" by God but coming forth from the interior of God. Likewise, Jesus instructs the apostles to "go therefore and make disciples of all nations, baptizing them in the name of the Father and of the Son and of the Holy Spirit" (Matt. 28:19), giving to the Spirit the same divine name as the Father and Son.

St. Peter also testifies to the divinity of the Holy Spirit when he asks Ananias, "Ananias, why has Satan filled your heart to lie to the Holy Spirit and to keep back part of the proceeds of the land? . . . How is it that you have contrived this deed in your heart? You have not lied to men but to God" (Acts 5:3–4). Not only is the Holy Spirit a person who cannot be lied to, but lying to the Holy Spirit is the same as lying to God, because the Holy Spirit is the third person of the Holy Trinity.

Using language that would have been easily understood by both Jews and Gentiles alike, the New Testament letters attest to the divinity of the Spirit by speaking of Christians as the *temple* of the living God (2 Cor. 6:16). If the Spirit dwells in us as in a temple, that means he is God.

> Do you not know that you are God's temple and that God's Spirit dwells in you? (1 Cor. 3:16).
>
> Do you not know that your body is a temple of the Holy Spirit within you? (1 Cor. 6:19).
>
> By this we know that we abide in him and he in us, because he has given us of his own Spirit (1 John 4:13).

Rereading the prophecies and the practices of Israel in the light of Christ, even the Old Testament scriptures bear witness, albeit enigmatically, to the divinity of the Son and the Spirit. For example, Jesus and the Spirit are the divine emissaries spoken of in the book of the prophet Isaiah:

> Hearken to me, O Jacob,
> and Israel, whom I called!
> I am He, I am the first,
> and I am the last.
> My hand laid the foundation of the earth,
> and my right hand spread out the heavens;
> when I call to them,
> they stand forth together.
>
> Draw near to me, hear this:
> from the beginning I have not spoken in secret,
> from the time it came to be I have been there.
> *And now the Lord God has sent me and his Spirit.* (Isa. 48:12-13, 16)

The one who is "sent" to earth along with the Spirit is no mere mortal. He is the first and the last, the Creator of heaven and earth. It is he who, along with the Lord God who sent him and the Creator Spirit, established all the ends of the earth:

> Who has gone up to heaven and come down?
> Whose hands have gathered up the wind?
> Who has wrapped up the waters in a cloak?
> Who has established all the ends of the earth?
> *What is his name, and what is the name of his son?*
> Surely you know! (Prov. 30:4)
>
> O Lord, how manifold are thy works!
> In wisdom hast thou made them all;
> the earth is full of thy creatures.
> *When thou sendest forth thy Spirit, they are created;*
> and thou renewest the face of the ground (Ps. 104: 24, 30).

195. What are angels?

Angels are purely spiritual beings created by God. Strictly speaking, the word *angel* (from the Greek for "messenger") refers to their office, not their nature. In other words, the good spirits who interact with human beings are called *angels*, whereas those who operate strictly in heaven are more precisely called *spirits*. However, it is traditional and acceptable to call all of them angels.

Whereas God continues to create new human beings, he created all the angels at the beginning of the world. Just as we don't know how many human beings God will create, we also don't know how many angels he created. According to the prophet Daniel, "Thousands upon thousands were ministering to him, and myriads upon myriads stood before him" (7:10).

Angels are not eternal in the way that God is, that is, existing before and outside of time. Rather, they are eternal in the same way human souls are: once created, they exist forever. Because they do not have bodies, they do not experience the separation of body and soul which we call death. Like human beings, angels are created in the image of God, which means they have intellect and free will; they are capable of thought and can choose courses of action. However, being purely spiritual, the exercise of their intellect and will differs in many ways from that of human beings.

Because the angelic intellect is intuitive, not discursive (rational), angels do not reason step by step to a conclusion as human beings do; instead, they have concepts in mind all at once. For example, when choosing a course of action, angels do not spend time considering different possibilities; they can see all the possibilities at once and immediately make their decision.

Because their knowledge is not limited by physical senses, angels also have the ability to know anything that is happening throughout the material world. Should they have the need, angels can intellectually apprehend the temperature at the North Pole, the flow of lava under the earth's crust, or the rate of speed of a distant galaxy hurtling through space. Of course, angels would have no reason to focus their intellect on all such things as they occur, but instead apply their intellect to those things that pertain to God's will for them.

Furthermore, angels do not have emotions as human beings do, so their choices are not influenced by passions such as fear and anger. What they chose, they chose based on their intelligence and will. Nor do they have to deliberate about what God wants them to do, as humans do. When the Lord has a mission for them to accomplish, he enlightens them directly. "They speak to him by consulting him about what ought to be done whenever they have to perform any new work, concerning which they desire enlightenment."[288]

196. Where are the angels and what do they do?

Because angels are purely spiritual beings, they cannot be said to be in a particular place in the same way as a material object, as being contained by it or commensurate with it. Nor can they be said to be everywhere, as God is, by acting upon all that is. Rather, the place where an angel can be said to be at any moment is where it is exerting its power.[289]

Angels cannot be in two places at once; in other words, they cannot exert their power in two different places at the same time. But the place where they exert their power need not be a small point; for example, it is just as easy for an angel to be present with a person to give an inspiring thought, as to protect a city, or to change the course of a planet.[290]

Time is also different for angels from how it is for material beings. Angels don't use physical agency in moving from place to place or in accomplishing the tasks assigned to them, so they do not experience time passing in the same way. The succession of events has meaning for them; in other words, an event succeeds some events and precedes others. But lengths of time do not mean anything to angels: angels do not tire, do not grow bored, and do not wonder how long until God wills them to do something else.

Scripture tells us they constantly behold the face of our heavenly Father; as the *Catechism* states, "The role of the angels is to glorify God without ceasing" (350). The prophet Isaiah had a vision of angels crying to one another, "Holy, holy, holy is the Lord of hosts; the whole earth is full of his glory" (6:3). At the birth of Christ, after an angel announced the good news to the shepherds, there was a multitude of the heavenly host with the angel, praising God and saying, "Glory to God in the highest, and on earth peace among men with whom he is pleased!" (Luke 2:14). Similarly, St. John had a vision of numerous angels in their worship of the Lamb, that is, God the Son.

And even though they may be in different places, according to St. Thomas, "the angels do not go abroad in such a manner as to lose the delights of inward contemplation."[291] In other words, since their adoration of God is an act of their intellect and will, angels are in continual worship no matter what other action they may be carrying out. The angels carry heaven with them.

197. Can angels change their mind?

The angels were all created good, for nothing that God creates is evil. But some rebelled against him, and "rejected God and his reign" (The Catechism of the Catholic Church 392). This rebellion was irrevocable: the fallen angels, led by one called Lucifer, are completely evil and never will repent of their sin. Similarly, the angels who chose obedience to God made a permanent choice: none of them would ever decide later to rebel against him.

The permanence of the angels' choice is a result of their being pure spirits. We human beings often change our minds about things after gaining further knowledge and seeing the results of our decisions. There are times we make decisions based on heightened emotions and sensual desires, and later—when those influences have calmed—we may repent of a particular choice and make a better one.

The angels are different: from the moment God created them, they had all the knowledge they needed to choose good or evil. Unlike us, they do not have senses and emotions that could affect their decisions. Whether an hour or a million years later, nothing in the angels' thinking or experience is different, so the idea of changing their mind does not even make sense to them. Those who rebelled preferred unhappiness to obedience, and nothing they would learn later—not even an eternity of complete misery—would induce them to regret their choice.

198. How do angels interact with one another?

As described by the prophet Isaiah (6:2–3), St. Luke (2:13–14), and St. John (Rev. 4:8), angels' primary interaction consists in their united worship of God. But the Bible also describes instances in which a number of angels act together.

For example, two angels appeared to Lot to warn him of the impending destruction of Sodom and Gomorrah (Gen. 19). In the book of the prophet Daniel (chap. 10), there is an enigmatic interplay between an angel assigned to Israel (possibly Gabriel, who is named in chap. 9) and the angel of Persia.

The clearest example of both angelic cooperation and resistance on a massive scale is described in the book of Revelation: "Now war arose in heaven, Michael and his angels fighting against the dragon; and the dragon and his angels fought, but they were defeated" (12:7–8). The same book recurrently describes numerous angels taking part in pronouncements and preparations at the end of the world. Jesus, moreover, said that angels will accompany him on Judgment Day (Matt. 16).

Angels do not converse with each other in a human way, since they do not have vocal cords or eardrums with which to talk and hear. But angels do make mental concepts known to one another, and this can be called speech. Superior angels speak to inferior ones to enlighten them about things of God. Inferior angels may speak to superior angels to make known their own interior thoughts, such as, "I wish to learn this from you," or, "God wills that I do that."

This illustrates an important point: one angel cannot read the mind of another, for only God knows the thoughts of angels and human beings. A fascinating corollary is that not all angels know when one speaks, but only those being spoken to. Since their speech is purely mental—one mind communicating with another—it is not as if angels converse with audible voices that others can hear. Another consequence of angelic speech being mental is that distance does not affect it. Angels who are acting upon material realities light years apart from one another communicate just as easily as if they were side by side.

199. Are some angels superior to others?

It is believed that angels differ from one another more than human beings differ from one another. In the animal world, each species may have many individuals, whether lobsters, llamas, or human beings. This is because animals have physical bodies, so the nature of each species is the same in every member of that species: every lobster has the same lobster nature, every llama has the same llama nature, and every human has the same human nature.

But angels do not have bodies, so they have no common nature. In other words, one angel does not differ from another angel as one lobster differs from another lobster, but as a lobster differs from a llama. Or as St. Thomas said more elegantly, as one star differs from another in glory, all the more do angels differ from one another.[292]

Keeping in mind that the powers of angels are their intellect and will, if some angels are superior to others, their superiority must be through their greater intellect and more powerful will. Since all angels have an equal ability to know the material universe, any differences in intellect must consist in the fact that some were given to understand more deeply the mind of God. Thus, Thomas considered that superior angels sometimes enlighten inferiors on things related to God. But this would not result in equality between them, since the superior would understand the knowledge more deeply.

Aquinas also wrote that when acting on behalf of a superior angel, an inferior angel has the power of their superior. He gives the example of an inferior angel using the power of a superior to drive off a demon that would otherwise be too powerful. This implies that the angels are superior and inferior not only in their intellect, but also in the strength of their will. The same truth may also be seen in cases of fallen angels possessing a human being: some demons seem more difficult to drive out than others.

200. Where do we get names for angels and angel choirs?

Angels do not use names among themselves in the sense of informing one another of who they are, since they know one another through mental concepts. However, in the Bible there are four angels who have names associated with their identity or function.

The leader of the fallen angels is addressed by several names: *Satan*, the name by which Jesus refers to him several times, means "enemy" or "adversary"; *Beelzebul*, another term Jesus used, comes from a derogatory name for a god of the Canaanites and means "lord of the flies"; and *Lucifer*, a metaphorical reference to the king of Babylon (Isa. 14:12), means "light-bearer "or "morning star," reminding us that the devil is a fallen angel.

In regard to the good angels, the name *Michael* means "who is like unto God": this was Michael's response to the devil's declaration, "I will be like God." Michael appears in the books of Daniel, Jude, and Revelation. *Gabriel* means "God is my strength"; he is also in the book of Daniel, and (of course) in Luke's Gospel. *Raphael* may be translated "God heals"; he is a key personage in the book of Tobit. We also see in Scripture that angels do not always reveal their names. On one occasion Menoah, father of Samson, asked an angel its name; the angel replied, "Why do you ask my name, seeing it is wonderful?" (Judg. 13:18).

Concerning the fallen angels, the Rite of Exorcism instructs the exorcist to ask the name of the possessing evil spirits. Exorcists say these demons resist giving their names, because doing so gives the exorcist more authority over them. But the possessing demons are forced to reveal their names when the exorcist repeatedly invokes the more powerful name of Jesus.

The names of nine different groups or "choirs" are found in Scripture and in the Mass, but there is nothing in Scripture or in Church doctrine that specifies what these different names imply about the actual differences between the choirs. St. Thomas Aquinas, St. Gregory the Great, and Dionysius the Areopagite organized the nine choirs into three groups, or hierarchies, according to the depth of their knowledge and understanding of God. The first hierarchy consists of seraphim, cherubim, and thrones; the second of dominions, virtues, and powers; the third of principalities, archangels, and angels.

Seraphim means "fiery ones," referring to their burning love of God; they are mentioned in the Bible just once, in the book of Isaiah. *Cherubim* means "winged messenger"; they are mentioned several times in the Old Testament, as when God instructed Moses to build the Ark of the Covenant with winged cherubim made of gold on the lid.

Other choirs of angels are mentioned in St. Paul's letter to the Ephesians, in which he describes Jesus as "far above all rule and authority and power and dominion, and above every name that is named, not only in this age but in the age to come" (1:21). This list is similar to that found in Paul's letter to the Colossians, in his beautiful explanation of Jesus as the second person of the Triune God: "He is the image of the invisible God, the first-born of all creation; for in him all things were created, in heaven and on earth, visible and invisible, whether thrones or dominions or principalities or authorities—all things were created through him and for him" (1:15–16).

The word *archangel* is found twice in the Bible, both times in the New Testament. Paul says that the end of the world will be signaled by the call of an (unnamed) archangel (1 Thess. 4:16), and St. Jude (v. 9) refers to Michael as an archangel. The last choir, simply called *angels*, are mentioned dozens of times throughout the Bible, including numerous references by Jesus.

201. How do angels interact with us and with the material world?

There are several places in the Bible where angels are described as having wings. Although they can manipulate air and solid matter to take any physical appearance they desire, they remain pure spirit, and so do not actually have wings by nature. The symbolism of wings represents their ability to move from one place to another almost instantaneously.

Angels can also communicate through visions, in which there is no actual physical appearance, as in St. Joseph's dream and the vision of St. John described in the book of Revelation. Angels also have the ability to give us ideas and inspirations, just as other human beings do; the difference is that angels do so in a nonverbal way.

Well-known angelic messages in the Bible include those to Isaiah (6:7), Manoah and his wife (Judg. 13), Zechariah (Luke 1:1–25), and of course Mary (Luke 1:26–38), Joseph (Matt. 1:18–21), and the shepherds (Luke 2:8–14). People should not be too quick, however, to believe that an angel is speaking to them, even though one should not deny it as a possibility.

Angels cannot see the future as God can. But they may sometimes appear to us to do so in two ways. First, God may reveal future events to them as he did to the prophets, which the angels may in turn proclaim to human beings (e.g., the destruction of Sodom and Gomorrah in Genesis 18–19, or the births of John the Baptist and of Jesus in Luke 1).

Second, because they are capable of focusing their attention on external events occurring in the world, angels can predict many events that human beings cannot. For example, someone's guardian angel may know of a dangerous situation that the person cannot see, and may give him an inspiration to avoid the danger. The angel does not see the future, but does have a wider view of events that may affect the person.

Neither angels nor human beings can read hearts and minds as God can. But just as humans can sometimes guess what others are thinking or feeling by nonverbal signs such as body language or facial expression, so angels can do the same. Because they can see more subtle signs and know people more thoroughly through long observation, angels are much better at inferring their thoughts and emotions.

Angels also have great power in regard to the material universe. When moving an object in the physical world, angels do not use physical exertion, for they do not have physical bodies. Rather, they move things by a simple act of the intellect and will, and therefore it takes no more strength for an angel to move a planet than to move a peanut.

Angels can also manipulate physical matter in more subtle ways. As Moses looked on, an angel made a bush appear to be burning without being consumed. An angel cooled the inside of the fiery furnace where three Israelites (Shadrach, Meshach, and Abednego) had been thrown for refusing to worship a gold statue; they emerged unscathed. St. Peter's guardian angel tapped his shoulder, made light appear in his prison cell, made the chains fall off his wrists, and led him through locked doors and iron gates. These examples illustrate not only angels' power over the material world, but also their role in protecting human beings.

But it would be a mistake to think of angels only as servants of human beings. God has appointed them to serve us, but he also assigns them to carry out his judgment.

After Adam and Eve sinned, God expelled them from the garden of Eden; in a mysterious reference, Genesis says that at the east of the garden of Eden God "placed the cherubim, and a flaming sword which turned every way, to guard the way to the tree of life" (3:24). When the Assyrians were about to invade Jerusalem, God answered the prayer of the Israelite King Hezekiah and sent one angel who killed 185,000 enemy soldiers. In his parable of the weeds and the wheat, Jesus described the role of the angels at the end of the world: "The Son of Man will send his angels, and they will gather out of his kingdom all causes of sin and all evildoers, and throw them into the furnace of fire; there men will weep and gnash their teeth" (Matt. 13:41–42).

On a brighter note, it is helpful for Catholics at Mass to keep in mind that angels are present, assisting the priest. In the extraordinary form of the Mass, while he incenses the bread and wine, the priest prays, "Through the intercession of blessed Michael the archangel standing at the right hand of the altar of incense, and of all his elect, may the Lord vouchsafe to bless this incense and to receive it in the odor of sweetness." The Roman Canon, also known as Eucharistic Prayer I, includes this request: "In humble prayer we ask you, Almighty God, command that these gifts be borne by the hands of your holy angel to your altar on high." In the Byzantine Liturgy, the Cherubic Hymn reminds the faithful that angels surround the body of Christ:

> We who mystically represent the cherubim, and who sing to the life-giving Trinity the thrice-holy hymn, let us now lay aside all earthly cares that we may receive the King of all, escorted invisibly by the angelic orders. Alleluia.

202. What is the role of guardian angels?

"Beside each believer stands an angel as protector and shepherd leading him to life." This is how St. Basil, quoted in the *Catechism* (336), described the role of the guardian angels. Obviously, God does not need the assistance of the angels; he is capable of taking care of people without them. But in his wisdom God has seen fit to assign angels to watch over human beings. Perhaps because Lucifer, the leader of the fallen angels, led human beings to their downfall, it is appropriate that other angels take part in leading people to salvation. Another reason for this provident design of God is that human beings, in their weakness, can take comfort in knowing that they each have an angel specifically designated by him to watch over them.

There are differing opinions regarding when a person's guardian angel is assigned to him. St. Anselm thought the assignment took place at the time of *ensoulment*, when one's body and soul are created, more commonly referred to as *conception*. St. Jerome speculated that only Christians had guardian angels, receiving them when they were baptized. St. Thomas Aquinas, on the other hand, thought people received their guardian angel at birth; perhaps the mother's angel, he reasoned, watched over the unborn child until he left the womb and his own guardian was given to him. Along with St. Jerome, he argued that all men, not only Christians, were assigned to the guardianship of an angel, as all need assistance in their journey through life.[293]

There are many scriptural references to people being protected by angels. In the book of the prophet Daniel, the three Israelites who refuse to worship a golden idol are cast into a fiery furnace. They survive without even the smell of smoke touching their clothes, thanks to the protection of an angel. In the book of Tobit, Tobit is cured of blindness by the archangel Raphael, who also protects Tobit's son Tobias from the demon Asmodeus. In the Acts of the Apostles, St. Peter is freed from his chains and from prison by an angel. When Jesus, in the Gospel of Luke, endured the agony in the garden of Gethsemane, "there appeared to him an angel from heaven, strengthening him" (22:43). As God the Son, he did not need an angel, but Jesus was also human; this event shows that angels give people strength in times of suffering.

In addition to guarding individuals, angels protect nations, cities, and even parishes. An angel helped lead the Israelites out of slavery in Egypt, and the book of the prophet Daniel names the archangel Michael as the guardian of the nation of Israel. During the time of the prophet Isaiah, an angel protected the city of Jerusalem from an imminent invasion by the Assyrians: "the angel of the Lord went forth, and slew a hundred and eighty-five thousand in the camp of the Assyrians; and when men arose early in the morning, behold, these were all dead bodies" (Isa. 37:36).

The book of Revelation mentions angels of churches in particular cities, but since these are sometimes reprimanded for their faults, the word *angel* in this context seems to refer to the bishop of the city. Nevertheless, there is a pious belief that every parish has its own guardian angel; for example, the archives of St. Columba Church in Ottawa, Illinois, reveal that the painting of an angel above the altar depicts the guardian angel of the parish.

In a Vatican document approved by Pope St. John Paul II ("Directory on Popular Piety and the Liturgy," 2001), the practice of assigning names to angels was discouraged as a deviation from authentic spiritual piety.

Because angels were created at the beginning of the world, it is incongruous to think that after many eons of time, a human being can suddenly give a name to an angel.

Furthermore, assigning a name implies that the one giving it has authority over the one receiving it, as when parents name their children. Human beings are assisted and protected by angels, but that does not mean humans have authority over them.

Instead, just as people generally refer to their parents as Mom and Dad, the traditional practice is to refer to one's angel simply as "Guardian Angel."

203. Did God create the world?

The Fourth Lateran Council tells us that God is the "creator of all things invisible and visible, spiritual and corporeal; who by his almighty power at the beginning of time created from nothing."[294] The *Catechism* also affirms that "God needs no pre-existent thing or any help in order to create, nor is creation any sort of necessary emanation from the divine substance. God creates freely 'out of nothing'" (CCC 296).

This doctrine is called *creatio ex nihilo*, or "creation from nothing," and can be known from reason as well as from the clear affirmation of Scripture.

First, the universe cannot be explained by an infinite regression to causes in the material order, as both matter and the laws of nature require explanation for their existence. God could not have rearranged eternally pre-existing matter in order to make the universe. He must instead have brought the universe into being from nothing through an act of his will.

But why believe that the "Unmoved Mover" at the origin of the material world is God? Why couldn't things come into existence from nothing through some kind of impersonal immaterial force?

This is the question known as the argument from contingency. An eternal, impersonal force having a necessary effect would automatically generate its effect for all eternity. But since the universe is not eternal, it follows that its cause is determined not by impersonal necessity but by the free agency of a personal being. Since the universe did not *have* to exist and there is good evidence that it *began* to exist, it requires an explanation for why it *does* exist. This reason is the free creative act of God.

The Bible and the Church Fathers also testify to this doctrine. The psalmist tells the stars to "praise the name of the Lord! For he commanded and they were created" (Ps. 148:5). The heroic mother in 2 Maccabees told her sons, "Look at the heaven and the earth and see everything that is in them, and recognize that God did not make them out of things that existed" (2 Macc. 7:28). Hebrews 11:3 says that "the world was created by the word of God, so that what is seen was made out of things which do not appear" (or, in other translations, "was not made out of visible things"). The first-century author of *The Shepherd of Hermas* declares that God "created all things and set them in order and brought out of nonexistence into existence everything that is."[295]

Other critics object that if God is perfect then why did he create the universe? Wouldn't God only have created the universe because he lacked something, and if he lacked something, then wouldn't that mean he was not perfect? However, there's no need to presume that God would only have created the universe to fill some void in his life, or out of loneliness or boredom. Since God is the perfection of goodness and self-giving love, the creation of the universe must be understood as the freely chosen result of his superabundant love and self-gift. God created the universe not for his good, but for ours (CCC 293).

St. Theophilus of Antioch wrote in the second century, "God made all things out of nothing; for nothing was co-eternal with God: but he being his own place, and wanting nothing, and existing before the ages, willed to make man by whom he might be known; *for him* [man], therefore, he prepared the world."[296]

204. Hasn't science shown that something can indeed come from nothing?

Physics describes how objects move and behave in the world, but traditional physics has a limit when it comes to describing really small objects, such as electrons or quarks. For that we need quantum physics (also called quantum mechanics), which explains the nature and motion of atoms as well as the particles that make up atoms. Because these particles are so small, they can act in strange ways. For example, scientists have observed so-called "virtual particles" emerging, apparently without a cause, from an empty vacuum. If these particles can come into existence without a cause in the quantum realm, then couldn't the universe have come into being from nothing?

The problem with this argument is that a quantum vacuum is not "nothing." It is a very low state of energy that boils and froths almost like the foam on the surface of the ocean. To say our universe emerged from such a vacuum is not the same as saying it came from nothing. The quantum vacuum has properties and needs an explanation of where it came from. It will not suffice to say that the vacuum has simply existed forever, because this would not explain why our universe is of a finite age and isn't as old as the vacuum from which it came.

Philosopher and theoretical physicist David Albert of Columbia University wrote in the *New York Times* that physicists are not solving any mysteries when they try to use the spontaneous emergence of virtual particles from vacuums to explain the origin of the universe. Albert writes, "None of this amounts to anything even remotely in the neighborhood of a creation from nothing."[297]

It is impossible to provide a scientific explanation of how the universe emerged from pure nothing, because scientific explanations involve the use of natural laws and processes. Natural laws and processes do not exist in a void but in natural realities. Any law or scientific process one uses to explain why the universe came from nothing would be a part of the universe you're trying to explain! Instead, the explanation for the universe's origin from nothing would have to be a supernatural explanation, that is, an explanation that transcends matter, energy, space, and time—in other words, what we call God.

205. When was the world created? How long did it take?

Some Christians who call themselves *young-earth creationists* claim the Bible teaches that the universe is 6,000 to 10,000 years old, based on the ages of people listed in the genealogies in the Old Testament. The most famous attempt to date the creation event in this way comes from the seventeenth-century Anglican archbishop James Ussher, who said the world was created in the year 4004 B.C. on the night before Sunday, October 23.

But the Bible never states that the earth or the universe is of a certain age. The Bible was never intended to be a cosmological textbook. This doesn't mean that the Bible errs when it describes the creation of the world, just that it describes it in a particular way for a particular purpose. According to the

Catechism of the Catholic Church, the creation passages in Genesis "express in their solemn language the truths of creation—its origin and its end in God, its order and goodness, the vocation of man, and finally the drama of sin and the hope of salvation" (289).

In contrast to Ussher's exactness, the First Vatican Council requires only that Catholics believe "the world and all things which are contained in it, both spiritual and material, as regards their whole substance, have been produced by God from nothing."[298]

In fact, Christian writers from the early centuries, 1,500 years or more before Darwin, realized the need to interpret the six biblical "days" of creation as something other than literal twenty-four-hour periods.

For example, in the A.D. 200s, Origen of Alexandria noted that day and night are made on the first day but the sun is not created until the fourth. The ancients knew as well as we do that the presence or absence of the sun is what makes it day or night, and so he took this as an indication that the text was using a literary device and not presenting a literal chronology. "I don't suppose," he wrote, "that anyone doubts that these things figuratively indicate certain mysteries, the history having taken place in appearance, and not literally."[299]

Although Genesis can be read as a literal explication of God's creating the world in six twenty-four-hour days (a view held by many of the Church Fathers), there has long been an alternative interpretation that has come to be called the *framework interpretation*. This is the view that the six days of creation do not consist of a literal, chronological description of events, but rather, a topical way of describing how God created the world. In the first three days God creates the realms where creation will reside (the sky, the waters, the land, and vegetation); then God fills those realms in the next three days (with the lights in the sky, the birds and fish, and the land animals).

The fact that a non-literal interpretation of Genesis was proposed nearly 1,500 years before Darwin shows that such an interpretation is not a desperate attempt to explain away Genesis in light of the findings of evolutionary biology. Rather, the Catholic Church teaches that the first chapters of Genesis contain truths about what really happened in the world, but those chapters also use "simple and metaphorical language adapted to the mentality of a people but little cultured, both state the principal truths which are fundamental for our salvation, and also give a popular description of the origin of the human race and the chosen people" (*Humani Generis* 38).

The recognition that the creation accounts must be understood with some nuance is not new. Only modern skeptics try to force this novel and literal interpretation on the Bible. The Church has affirmed only that Scripture infallibly teaches that God created the world from nothing by his own will and made man's immortal soul in his image. The Church has not issued an infallible interpretative judgment on the precise method God used to create the world or how long that process took. As a result, a Catholic is free to believe in either a literal view of Genesis or another interpretation that allows for a long period of time in which life evolves from a common ancestor.

206. Doesn't evolution contradict belief that life was created by God?

The theory of evolution proposes an explanation for how life on earth arose and developed. It holds that there was a long period in which natural processes gave rise to life and that life changes over time from one generation to the next. As life changes and adapts to survive in changing environments, new creatures begin to emerge. According to the theory of evolution, this process has given rise to all the different life forms on earth, including man.

Whether true or false, this in no way conflicts with the idea of creation by God. As the omnipotent creator, God is free to create quickly or slowly, directly or through intermediate processes. He can create the universe in an instantaneous big bang and then put it through a long, slow period of development, giving rise to stars and planets and eventually life forms. Since he directs and sustains those processes, he can even intervene in them: such as when he creates a soul for each human being or when he performs a miracle.

Consider an analogy: Suppose that after a thorough scientific investigation of the famous painting *Mona Lisa*, a scientist concluded that it was the result of collisions of paint and canvas gradually leading from indecipherable shapes and patches of color to a beautiful and intriguing picture of a woman.

The scientist's analysis of the painting would be correct. That is, in fact, what the *Mona Lisa* is and how it developed. But this analysis by no means disproves or makes unnecessary Leonardo DaVinci as the painter. And which seems more reasonable: that the collisions of paint and canvas occurred randomly until a masterpiece emerged, or that they were directed by some intelligence?

Recognizing that there is no contradiction between faith and reason on this point, the Catholic Church is open to the idea of an old universe and to the idea that God used evolution as part of his plan for creating life. According to the *Catechism*,

> the question about the origins of the world and of man has been the object of many scientific studies which have splendidly enriched our knowledge of the age and dimensions of the cosmos, the development of life forms and the appearance of man. These discoveries invite us to even greater admiration for the greatness of the Creator, prompting us to give him thanks for all his works and for the understanding and wisdom he gives to scholars and researchers (283).

Or, as Joseph Cardinal Ratzinger (Pope Benedict XVI) beautifully put it, the biblical account of man's creation doesn't

> explain how human persons come to be but rather what they are. It explains their inmost origin and casts light on the project that they are. And, vice versa, the theory of evolution seeks to understand and describe biological developments. But in so doing it can't explain where the "project" of human persons comes from, nor their inner origin, nor their particular nature. To that extent we are faced here with two complementary—rather than mutually exclusive—realities.[300]

Twenty years later, in a 2007 address, Pope Benedict XVI encouraged believers to look to the deeper truths that the theory of evolution in no way contradicts, but also in no way explains:

> There are so many scientific proofs in favor of evolution, which appears to be a reality we can see and which enriches our knowledge of life and being as such. But . . . the doctrine of evolution does not answer every query, especially the great philosophical question: Where does everything come from? And how did everything start which ultimately led to man? I believe this is of the utmost importance.[301]

For example, evolution is one way of explaining how life developed. But "How is it that we live in a universe where the evolution of life is even possible?" In the past fifty years, scientists have discovered that there is a wide variety of constants and conditions that make up the laws of nature. Even a slight variation in many of these finely tuned laws would have spelled disaster for life as we know it. For example, gravity is 10^{36} times weaker than competing forces within atoms, a critical fact for all living things.[302] As a 2009 article in *New Scientist* magazine put it:

> The feebleness of gravity is something we should be grateful for. If it were a tiny bit stronger, none of us would be here to scoff at its puny nature . . . Only the middle ground, where the expansion and the gravitational strength balance to within one part in 10^{15} [a quadrillion] at one second after the Big Bang, allows life to form.[303]

Another example is the cosmological constant, which represents the strength of gravity in an empty vacuum of space and controls how fast the universe expands. Once thought to be zero, this constant is actually fine-tuned to the 120th power—a decimal point with 119 zeros and a one. What is the explanation for this incredibly small, yet nonzero value? Alexander Vilenkin wrote: "A tiny deviation from the required power results in a cosmological disaster, such as the fireball collapsing under its own weight or the universe being nearly empty. . . . This is the most notorious and perplexing case of fine-tuning in physics."[304]

String theorist Leonard Susskind, like Vilenkin a non-religious scientist, writes in his article, "Disturbing Implications of the Cosmological Constant," that unless this constant was fine-tuned, "statistically miraculous events" would be needed for our universe to be life-permitting. He suggests that, in light of this, it is possible that an unknown agent set the early conditions of the universe we observe today.[305]

Reflection on Darwin's newly published theory of evolution, Cardinal Henry Newman mused that it "need not be atheistical, be it true or not; it may simply be suggesting a larger idea of Divine Prescience and Skill."

In this light, according to Pope Pius XII's encyclical *Humani Generis*, a Catholic is free to believe that life (including the bodies of modern human beings) was formed via the evolutionary process. Catholics are simply not free to believe that our *souls* were part of the evolutionary process, since the soul is immortal and immaterial, meaning it cannot evolve but must be created directly by God within each human person.

207. What is the soul?

All physical objects are composed of matter, but there is an observable difference between living and nonliving matter. Living matter is able to grow and adapt over time, sense the material world (in the case of animals), and even think rationally about it (in the case of humans).

This is amazing given that in humans, for example, 99 percent of our bodies are composed of only six nonliving elements: hydrogen, carbon, oxygen, nitrogen, calcium, and phosphorus.[306]

Since living and nonliving things are composed of roughly the same elements, the difference between them cannot be purely physical. Instead, the difference between living and nonliving matter is found in the presence of the soul, which St. Thomas Aquinas called "the first principle of life."[307]

Realities without a principle of life are called *inanimate* objects. Those that do have a principle of life are called *animate* beings (*anima* being Latin for "soul").

Some people mistakenly think that only human beings have souls, but in fact, all living things have souls. However, unlike humans, the souls of other living things are just as material and just as mortal as the parts they animate. When a plant or animal ceases to exist, the soul that animated this being ceases to exist as well.[308] But human souls are different because they are *immaterial*, and so they continue to exist after death and cannot be destroyed.

We alone among of all creatures on earth possess an *immaterial, immortal spirit* (a soul) as an integral part of our nature. It is through the unique powers of the human *soul* that we are made in God's image and likeness.

The rutabaga in your garden, and all plant life on earth, can nourish itself, grow, and reproduce. These are called the *vegetative powers of the soul.*

Animals can do those things, too, and can also *see, hear, smell, taste,* and *touch* things. In addition to vegetative powers, they have *sensitive powers of the soul.* They are likewise blessed with *motor capacity*—so they can not only sense the things they desire, but carry themselves to where they can get those things—and rudimentary forms of four *interior* senses:

- *Common sense* is the capacity to perceive that the disparate information coming in from multiple senses represents one thing, like the sight and the taste of their next meal.

- *Imagination* is the power to form images of things that no longer impinge on their senses.
- *Memory* is the power to hold onto these images in the absence of their objects.
- *Cogitative sense* is the power to detect whether the objects of their senses are good or bad for them. A lamb not only perceives the wolf but instinctively grasps its dangerousness.

Humans alone can rise above the vegetative and sensitive powers of the soul, through the powers of *intellect* and *will*.

The Latin word *intellectus* derives from *intus* (inside) and *legere* (to read). The intellect looks below the surfaces of experience to abstract (draw forth) the essences of objects that stimulate our senses. It sorts the jumble of sensory data to conceptualize a thing's essential, universal nature. This capacity to form abstract universals is the first indication that the human soul possesses a capacity that transcends the organic body (though it uses material organs, like the brain, as its instruments). Thomas points out that "if the intellectual soul were composed of matter and form, the form of things would be received into it as individuals, and so it would only know the individuals; just as it happens with the sensitive powers which receive forms from a corporeal organ; since matter is the principle by which forms are individualized. It follows, therefore, that the intellectual soul—and every intellectual substance which has knowledge of forms absolutely—is exempt from composition of matter and form."[309]

Because the human, intellectual soul is *immaterial*, it cannot be the result of biological generation; instead, the Church teaches that "every spiritual soul is created immediately by God—it is not 'produced' by the parents" (CCC 366). Likewise, as the soul has no parts that can decompose, barring an act of annihilation from God himself, the human soul is thus *immortal*: "it does not perish when it separates from the body at death" but "will be reunited with the body at the final resurrection."

Not only do human intellectual powers point to the existence of an immaterial soul, but they also give human persons a power unlike any other species on earth: the power of the intellectual appetite, or *will*. Animals' appetites and actions are guided by instincts or training, whereas we can freely decide what goals we will pursue, guided by our intellectual powers of *reasoning* and *judgment*, which enable us to discern the difference between right and wrong and determine what must be done or left undone in deference to higher goods.

208. How are human beings made in God's image?

It is through the intellect and will that we are made in God's image. Each *individual human* person carries this image within himself by nature and is called to welcome its fulfillment by grace.

- Like God, our soul is *immaterial*, and, although created in time, it is *immortal*, called by grace to share in God's eternity.
- Like God, we are persons, possessed of *intellect* and *free will*. We are able to know the truth and to freely love and choose the good. It is through the proper use of these spiritual powers that we are called to work out our salvation and attain the happiness that is God's own delight.
- Like God, we are called to exercise our capacities for *creativity* and *dominion*, safeguarding and perfecting the material world that is entrusted to us. Our creativity and dominion, however, remain always subordinate to God's creation and law, and it is when they are exercised responsibly in accord with his provident design that we are truly "lords" of creation.

In addition to the many ways that each one of us individually is made in the image of our Creator on account of our spiritual souls, we are also "in the image of God" as a *community of persons*. By existing "face to face" with other human persons, we reflect the image of God, who is a triune communion of persons. This is particularly evident in the fruitful communion of married love, where human persons, by their substantial union and openness to the Lord's creative work, pro-create other human persons also in God's image. In this way, even the body expresses the "image of God," designed in such a way as to express the fruitful unity in diversity that is God's own mystery.[310]

209. Couldn't moral behavior and intelligence have come from evolution?

Hasn't science demonstrated that moral and intelligent behavior can be explained by evolution? What need is there then to believe in a spiritual soul created by God?

Primatologist Jane Goodall claims that chimpanzees exhibit a sense of fairness and that when two or more begin to quarrel over food, for instance, other chimps intervene and divide what they are fighting over.[311] But this "sharing" is merely a way to stop a potentially violent situation from escalating. But morality is about doing what's *right*, not about doing what is most efficient or beneficial. We know very well that chimps are operating on instinct and don't deserve praise or blame, because they don't choose their behavior.

In his book *The Atheist's Guide to Reality*, philosopher Alex Rosenberg admits that it would be radically unlikely for humans to randomly evolve behaviors that also happened to correspond with objective moral rules. As a result, Rosenberg concludes that morality is simply a human convention and has no objective existence of its own.[312]

The alternative conclusion—that some things really are wrong regardless of whether they offer evolutionary advantage for our species (such as parents' drowning disabled infants)—points to the existence of an objective grounding for morality that is not a product of evolutionary processes.

If *we* were the product of random evolutionary processes, without anyone directing them, then we'd have good reason to doubt our mental faculties when it comes to knowing the truth about morality and everything else as well. Why? Because biologists tell us that evolutionary development is not aimed at producing true beliefs, but at helping creatures survive. Mental processes evolved in this way would be aimed not at objective truth, but at survival.

Charles Darwin seems to have understood this when he wrote, "With me the horrid doubt always arises whether the convictions of man's mind, which has been developed from the mind of the lower animals, are of any value or at all trustworthy. Would anyone trust in the convictions of a monkey's mind, if there are any convictions in such a mind?"[313]

An atheist could reply to this objection by saying that true beliefs are the ones that are most likely to help us survive, and therefore evolution will give rise to creatures whose minds are ordered toward acquiring true beliefs. This would be the case, however, only of judgments directly related to survival in this world and not to those professing to discern the existence of God, the origins of human nature, or the moral goodness of any given action. If an atheist's mind has no higher claim to truth than what evolution has given him for survival, why should anyone take seriously its propositions about the rest?

210. Hasn't science proven there is no such thing as the soul?

Some modern critics say that the soul does not exist, because science has shown that thought and personality can be affected by injuries to the brain. For example, due to a terrible work-related accident, a nineteenth-century railroad worker named Phineas Gage had a railroad spike lodged in his brain. Gage miraculously survived, but his friends and family noticed that his personality changed abruptly after the incident and he seemed like a "different person." Critics argue that if a person is a soul, then how could his personality change just because his body is damaged? They conclude that a person is not a soul but is simply his brain and that when the brain perishes, so does the person.

In reality, because our souls and bodies are so intimately joined, what happens to one will affect the other. The personality change of Phineas Gage or anyone else can be explained without discarding belief in an immaterial soul. The soul continues to animate the body and provide the foundation for rational thought. However, if the body—in this case, the brain—is damaged, the soul may not be able to manifest itself properly or even at all.

Consider a car whose axle is warped so that the car always veers to the left. You might think the person driving the car is a bad driver, but he may simply be unable to compensate for the damage to the vehicle he is driving—just as the soul cannot compensate for the damage to the body it is united to and display a proper rational function.

Also, when scientists show that certain portions of the brain become active or emit electrical impulses during particular actions, they have not proven that these actions or thoughts are *caused* by the material interactions in the brain. All they have proven is that there is a *correlation* between certain actions or thoughts and electrical signals in the brain. This correlation can just as easily indicate that the activity of the soul has repercussions in the organic body that it animates.

The question of whether or not an immaterial soul exists is a not scientific question; it is instead a philosophical or a theological one. In fact, there are powerful philosophical arguments in favor of the existence of the soul, because human beings are capable of *judgment and choice*. If we were merely our brains and were subject to how the molecules in our brains randomly collide with one another, then we would have no reason to trust any of the randomly generated beliefs our brains generate, nor any choice to adhere to them or not.

211. How is it possible for God to become a man?

Christians believe that God is a trinity of persons, Father, Son, and Holy Spirit, who each fully possess the divine nature. Upon his Incarnation, God the Son became man within the body of his mother, Mary. He did all of this while remaining one divine person and retaining his fully divine nature, even as he took on a fully human nature through the Incarnation. This mystery is called the *hypostatic union*, and it means that Jesus was not half God and half man (like a Greek demigod) but was 100 percent God and 100 percent man. How is this possible? According to the *Catechism*:

> Christ's human nature belongs, as his own, to the divine person of the Son of God, who assumed it. Everything that Christ is and does in this nature derives from "one of the Trinity." The Son of God therefore communicates to his humanity his own personal mode of existence in the Trinity. In his soul as in his body, Christ thus expresses humanly the divine ways of the Trinity (470).

Saying that "Jesus is God" means that Jesus is a divine person. Although human nature and divine nature in Jesus remain distinct—"without confusion, without change, without division, without separation," in the words of Council of Chalcedon (A.D. 451)—whatever is true of Jesus is also true of God in Christ.

For example, since Jesus died on the cross it is also true that "God died on the cross," because Jesus is God. Similarly, Scripture tells us that "Jesus increased in wisdom and in stature, and in favor with God and man" (Luke 2:52), even though, as God, he was already perfect in wisdom and goodness.

In these examples, and others like them, the key is to remember that Christ had a truly human body and a truly human soul, possessing human knowledge and a human will, even while possessing a divine will and divine knowledge as a part of his divine nature.

212. Why would God become man?

God became incarnate as man as the most fitting way to restore our corrupted human nature after the sinful fall of Adam and Eve. The fittingness of this divine choice is seen in many ways, as St. Thomas outlines in the first question of the third part of the *Summa*.

Among these are the building up of our *faith*, since we could hear God himself speak; *hope*, since Christ's presence shows us God's love for us; *charity*, since we could desire to love God in return for his presence among us; and *well-doing*, since God himself served as our example—indeed, "the full participation of the divinity, which is the bliss of man and end of human life; and this is bestowed on us by Christ's humanity; for Augustine says in a sermon (8, *De Temp*): God was made man, that man might be made God."[314]

Not only did Christ open to us a new destiny as sons of God, sharing in his fullness of grace, but he walked with us, tracing out the way in our own humanity.

> The way, it has been said, is Christ himself, so he says, "I am the way." This is indeed true, for, as stated in Romans (Rom. 5:2), it is through him that we have access to the Father. . . . Because this way is not separated from its destination but united to it, he adds, "and the truth, and the life." So Christ is at once the way and the destination. He is the way by reason of his human nature, and the destination because of his divinity. Therefore, as human, he says, "I am the way"; as God, he adds, "and the truth, and the life."[315]

And as Thomas wrote elsewhere, one of our great joys in heaven will be to look upon Christ's glorified body in the flesh!

213. What are some of the common errors about the Incarnation?

One of the core truths of Christianity is that God the Son is begotten, not made, one in being with the Father, was incarnate of the Virgin Mary, suffered, died, and rose from the dead. Unfortunately, many heresies developed over the centuries that deny some of these basic truths about Christ. Here are the best known:

Adoptionism: This is the view that Jesus Christ was a mere human being whom God adopted and upon whom he bestowed a special divine status (generally thought to occur at Jesus' baptism). Pope Victor I condemned Adoptionism as heretical at the end of the second century.

Docetism: This second-century heresy claimed that Jesus was fully God but that his humanity was an illusion. Gnostics, or heretics who believed the body was evil and that matter in general was to be avoided, held this view because they could not tolerate the notion of an embodied savior. But Docetism is refuted by scriptural passages that describe Christ's suffering and death as well as his burial and resurrection. It was condemned at the ecumenical council of Nicaea in 325, which is why the Nicene Creed says that we believe Jesus "suffered death and was buried."

Arianism: This fourth-century heresy claimed that Jesus was *like* God the Father but was not of the same substance as the Father (meaning that Jesus wasn't God, but merely God's greatest creation). Arians defended this view by citing passages such as Colossians 1:15, which says of Christ, "He is the image of the invisible God, *the first-born* of all creation." But these passages only show that Jesus has a special authority and relationship with the Father, not that he is a created being.

The title "firstborn of creation" doesn't mean that Jesus was created first and then the rest of creation was made after him. It means that Jesus inherits all of creation and has dominion over it, just as in many cultures in human history a first-born human son has rights over his father's property. The very next verse in Colossians explicitly says that Jesus created "all things." Jesus can't be a part of God's creation if he is the true God who created all things.

Like Docetism, Arianism was condemned at the ecumenical council of Nicaea and again at the Council of Constantinople in 381. This is why the Nicene Creed says that Jesus is "God from God, Light from Light, true God from true God, begotten, not made, consubstantial [of the same substance] with the Father; through him all things were made."

Nestorianism: This heresy holds that Christ is not one person but two, God the Son and Jesus Christ. It came from a bishop named Nestorius, who believed that Mary was not the Mother of God, but only the mother of the human Christ (he called Mary the "Christ-bearer," or *Christotokos*, and not the "God-bearer," or *Theotokos*).

According to Nestorians, since Mary gave Jesus his human nature but God the Father gave Jesus his divine nature, Mary can only be thought of as the mother of Christ, not the Mother of God. Now, it's true that Mary is not the source of Christ's divinity, but mothers give birth to *persons*, not natures. If Jesus is God, and Mary is his mother, then it follows that Mary, in the words of St. Irenaeus in the second century, "bore God," and is the *Theotokos*, the Mother of God.[316]

Nestorianism was officially condemned at the ecumenical councils of Ephesus in 431 and Chalcedon in 451, which reaffirmed that Christ is one divine person with a fully human nature and a fully divine nature.

Monophysitism: In contrast to Nestorianism, this heresy correctly taught that Christ is one person, but it erred in teaching that Christ only has one (*mono*) human-divine nature (*physis*). This contradicts the traditional teaching of the hypostatic union that Jesus is one person with two natures, one fully human, which "grew in wisdom and understanding," and the other fully divine, which provided an adequate atonement for sin. The Council of Chalcedon condemned Monophysitism in 451.

Monothelitism: This is the view that Jesus had only one will. But since Christ has two natures, it follows that he has two wills, one human and the other divine. This is evidenced in the agony in the garden, where Jesus said, "If it be possible, let this cup pass from me; yet, not as I will, but as thou wilt" (Matt. 26:39). This heresy was formally condemned at the Third Council of Constantinople in 681.

214. Is it reasonable to believe that Jesus is God?

Some people think of Jesus as a remarkable man but basically in the same category as Buddha, Moses, Confucius, and Gandhi: a good man, a holy man, but just a man.

This view, however, is hard to reconcile with what Jesus says and does. Jesus claims to be Lord over the Sabbath (Luke 6:1–5). Jesus forgives sins committed against God (Mark 2:5–12). Jesus says he is the one who gives eternal life (John 3:16). Jesus says no one can convict him of sin (John 8:46). Jesus says, "I am the way, the truth, and the life. No one comes to the Father except through me" (John 14:6). The fact that Jesus changed the name of Simon to Peter is also significant in this respect (Matt. 16:13–19). As Peter Kreeft and Ronald Tacelli point out, "For a Jew, changing names was something only God could do, for your name was not just a human, arbitrary label but your real identity, which was given to you by God alone. In the Old Testament, only God changed names, and destinies—Abram became Abraham, Sarai became Sarah, Jacob became Israel."[317]

And when his life was threatened and his enemies surrounded him, Jesus said, "Amen, amen, I say to you, before Abraham came to be, I AM." In attributing to himself the sacred name of God, "I AM," Jesus was making himself equal to God. His enemies understood this as blasphemy: "So they picked up stones to throw at him; but Jesus hid and went out of the temple area" (John 8:57–59). Given the claims that Jesus makes about himself, is it reasonable to believe that Jesus was simply a holy man and wise teacher?

In his classic book *Mere Christianity*, C.S. Lewis says this is the one thing we *can't* say about Jesus. "A man who was merely a man," Lewis writes, "and said the sort of things Jesus said would not be a great moral teacher. He would either be a lunatic—on the level with the man who says he is a poached egg—or else he would be the devil of hell. You must make your choice." Lewis outlines three possibilities. Jesus is either a liar, a lunatic, or the Lord. He could not have been simply a good person, a saintly sage.

Was Jesus a liar?

One possibility is that Jesus knew he was not God but said he was; in other words, he deliberately lied. But it is hard to believe that a man hailed throughout the centuries as a paragon of goodness could have spent his life intentionally misleading and deceiving his disciples in this way. If Jesus knew he was not God but claimed to be God nevertheless, he wasn't a good person—he was the worst religious charlatan of all time. If Jesus lied to his disciples about being God, then he misled to their violent deaths those who trusted him most. He also led billions of people into the sin of idolatry. No, if he deliberately deceived others about his identity, Jesus was not a holy man, but a deeply narcissistic and malicious person.

This is not how most people perceive the Jesus of the Gospels. His life was so radically unlike other religious hucksters who claim to be God (or a prophet of God). Con artists claim to be God in order to amass wealth and a harem of young women to be their brides. But the character of Jesus is radically unlike that of a con man. He amassed no wealth and did not have even one wife, let alone a harem. Jesus did not seek power—"My kingdom is not of this world," he said (John 18:36)—but rather laid down his life as a suffering servant. Jesus did not *act* like a lying con artist.

Was Jesus a lunatic?

If Jesus was not a liar, was he perhaps just mistaken about his identity? Maybe he wasn't a liar because although he was not God he really *thought* he was God. In other words, Jesus was massively mistaken, but not a deliberate deceiver.

If Jesus was not divine but honestly and mistakenly thought he was, then Jesus was not a wise person. He was, therefore, very unlike Confucius, or Moses, or a sage. Kreeft and Tacelli note, "There are lunatics in asylums who sincerely believe they are God. The 'divinity complex' is a recognized form of pathology. Its character traits are well known: egoism, narcissism, inflexibility, dullness, predictability and an inability to understand and love others as they really are and creatively relate to others."[318] But Jesus is radically unlike a lunatic babbling in an insane asylum. His moral teachings stressed the importance of loving your neighbor, forgiving your enemies, and caring for those in need.

Moreover, the way Jesus responds to the traps set for him indicates not a raving madman totally disconnected from reality but someone with practical wisdom. Consider, for example, when his enemies bring to him a woman caught in adultery. They set a brilliant trap: "Teacher, this woman was caught in the very act of committing adultery. Now in the law, Moses commanded us to stone such women. So what do you say?" If Jesus says she should not be stoned, then he is acting against the laws of the community and against the authority of Moses. His enemies could then accuse him of heresy and rebellion. If Jesus says that she *should* be stoned, then he is acting against his own teaching to show mercy to others. His enemies can then accuse him of self-contradiction. Whatever he says, his enemies think they have him trapped.

Jesus replies, "Let the one among you who is without sin be the first to throw a stone at her." In saying this, Jesus avoids acting against the Law of Moses, avoids contradicting himself, and convicts those who want to stone her of their own sin. In the wisdom of his teaching and in the prudence of his actions, Jesus shows he is no madman.

Now, if Jesus was not a liar (because that would make him evil), and Jesus was also not a lunatic (because everything he says and does in the Gospel suggests otherwise), this only leaves the option that Jesus was who he claimed to be: one with the Father; the Way, the Truth and the Life; and the Son of God.

215. Is there evidence that Jesus originally claimed to be the Son of God?

If Jesus were merely a teacher, then he would have been an extremely arrogant if not mentally ill one.

Compare Buddha's humble teachings to the bold claims of Jesus Christ. Buddha said, "Therefore, be ye lamps unto yourselves, be a refuge to yourselves. Hold fast to Truth as a lamp; hold fast to the truth as a refuge."[319] Where Buddha encouraged his followers to find the truth and be lights for themselves, Jesus said "*I* am the light of the world. Whoever follows me will not walk in darkness, but will have the light of life" (John 8:12). He also said, "I am the way, and the truth, and the life. No one comes to the Father except through me" (John 14:6).

There is abundant evidence in the New Testament that Jesus saw himself as being more than a wise sage or even a prophet. Jesus spoke with an unparalleled authority and made claims that elevated him to the status of God himself. Here are just a few examples:

- In Matthew 11:27, Jesus claims to have an exclusive and absolute relationship with God the Father when he says, "All things have been delivered to me by my Father; and no one knows the Son except the Father, and no one knows the Father except the Son and any one to whom the Son chooses to reveal him."

- In Luke 22:29, Jesus claims to have the authority to confer kingdoms just like the Father.

- In John 8:58, Jesus uses the unpronounceable divine name for himself when he says that "before Abraham was I AM," implying that he existed—eternally—before Abraham lived thousands of years before. This act sent the high priests into a frenzy and motivated them to kill Jesus for blasphemy.

- In John 20:28, Thomas addresses Jesus as "my Lord and my God." Jesus does not correct Thomas for uttering what would have been blasphemy if it were not true.

Critics may claim that these references to Jesus' divinity all come from later sources (especially the Gospel of John) and are the product of legendary development. They counter that the earliest recorded sayings of Jesus reveal a merely human teacher and not someone who considered himself divine. But although it is true that earlier Gospels, such as Mark's, emphasize the humanity of Jesus more than John's Gospel (which was written last), that doesn't mean they denied Jesus' divine nature.

In Mark 2:5, after healing the paralytic, Jesus claims to be able to forgive the man's sins, something that only God has the authority to do. In Mark 6:7, Jesus gathers twelve disciples, which is symbolic of the twelve tribes of Israel. Rather than representing one of the tribes himself, such as the tribe of Levi which had a claim to the priesthood, Jesus stands apart from the twelve apostles, and gathers them together in the same way that God called the twelve tribes of Israel.

Later in the same Gospel, Jesus tells the story of the vineyard whose wicked tenants kill the servants sent by the owner (Mark 12:1-12). In the parable, the owner finally sends his son, whom the wicked tenants also kill. This parable is similar to other illustrations from the prophets, who identified the vineyard with Israel and the servants with the prophets Israel previously rejected.[320] But, remarkably, Jesus identifies himself not with a servant of the owner of the vineyard, but with the son of the owner of the vineyard. Just as the son of the vineyard owner was killed because of his relationship to the father, so too would Jesus be killed because of his claim to having a special and unique relationship with the heavenly Father.

216. Didn't Jesus call himself the "Son of Man" and even deny his divinity?

On a few occasions in the Gospels, Jesus seems explicitly to deny equality with the Father, so that the hearts of his listeners will focus on the Father alone. How then did Christians come to see Jesus as divine?

For example, Jesus tells a young scholar of the law who praises him that "no one is good but God alone" (Mark 10:18). Later, on the eve of his Passion, he tells the Twelve that "The Father is greater than I" (John 14:28). Was Jesus denying he was divine in these situations?

In the first instance, Jesus is testing the young man who asked what he needed to do to get to heaven. The man begins by flattering Jesus, hoping to get a satisfying answer. Jesus sees through this and says, "Why do you call me good [as if a man can give you special access to heaven]? No one is good but God alone." Is the young man addressing him as a good rabbi or as the Son of God?

The statement of Jesus in the Gospel of John must be taken in the context of his other affirmations concerning unity with the Father and understood in the light of his incarnation. According to his human nature, it is entirely true that the "Father is greater." And according to his divine nature, for a time Jesus allowed the manifestation of his divine glory to be diminished. Paul refers to this in Philippians 2:7 when he writes that even though Jesus "was in the form of God," he "emptied himself" and took "the form of a servant." So the same Jesus who shares the Father's divine nature and claims to be one with him (John 10:30) can also say, "The Father is greater than I."

Finally, when Jesus refers to himself as the "Son of Man," he is not denying his divinity. On the contrary, by applying to himself this messianic title from the book of the prophet Daniel, Jesus is claiming divinity, something his listeners understood very well (Luke 22:69-71).

> I saw One like a Son of Man coming, on the clouds of heaven; When he reached the Ancient One and was presented before him, He received dominion, glory, and kingship; nations and peoples of every language serve him. His dominion is an everlasting dominion that shall not be taken away, his kingship shall not be destroyed (Dan. 7:13-14).

217. Did the Church suppress gospels that depict Jesus as an ordinary man?

The theory that some grand conspiracy has kept the real Jesus from us grew in popularity after the 2005 novel *The Da Vinci Code*, which put forward several shocking claims about Jesus. Though wrapped in the guise of a fictional detective story, the book also claimed that "all descriptions of artwork, architecture, documents, and secret rituals in this novel are accurate." As a result, many readers were taken in by the novel's historian, Teabing, who casually tells us, "Jesus was viewed by his followers as a mortal prophet . . . a great and powerful man, but a man nonetheless. A mortal."[321] Jesus was also married, he says, because it would have been completely unheard of for a Jewish man to live a celibate life.

The idea that Jesus was divine, this fictional historian says, did not become a part of Christianity until the council of Nicaea in 325. This change in doctrine was supposedly made at the request of Emperor Constantine, who was eager to have a new religion under which to unite the Roman Empire. Under Constantine's direction, the Church subsequently destroyed and tried to hide those Gospels that recorded Jesus' mortal life—Gospels that were recently rediscovered.

The problem with such claims, which, even though they come from a fictional novel, have captivated the minds of many readers, is that they're completely without evidence. In fact, they're often contradicted by historical facts that have been known for centuries.

The best evidence we have of early Christian devotion to Jesus as God, and not a mere mortal teacher, comes from ancient writers who were hostile to the Christian faith. Lucian of Samosata was a second-century playwright who thought Christians were gullible and ignorant fools. In his work *The Passing of Peregrinnus* he says that Christians still worship a man who was crucified in Palestine. Pliny the Younger, the second-century governor of the Roman province of Bythinia, interrogated Christians who refused to sacrifice to the gods, and observed in a letter to the emperor Trajan that Christians "were in the habit of meeting on a certain fixed day before it was light, when they sang in alternate verse a hymn to Christ as to a god, and bound themselves to a solemn oath." These two hostile sources provide solid evidence that early Christians worshiped Jesus as God centuries before Constantine allegedly invented the practice.

Along with the evidence from the Gospels that we've already looked at, Paul's letters also confirm that Christians worshiped Jesus. Paul says that Jesus Christ is the "image of the invisible God" (Col. 1:15), in whom the fullness of deity dwells bodily (2:8-9), has the "form of God" and a name to which every knee shall bend (Phil. 2:5-11), and that he is our "great God and Savior" (Titus 2:13).

Any counter-claim that Paul's letters and the canonical Gospels are later, unreliable sources about Jesus is simply untrue. They were in fact the *only* sources about Jesus from the first century. The allegedly suppressed Gospels, such as the Gospel of Phillip or the Gospel of Judas, that deviate from the traditional view Christians have about him were written 100 to 300 years after Jesus' death. What's more, these later "apocryphal" Gospels did not even deny that Jesus was divine. They were more likely to deny Jesus was truly *human*, claiming instead that he was God who had simply assumed a human appearance.

The argument that Jesus must have been married because celibacy for Jewish men was unheard of is hardly airtight. The testimony of consecrated virginity dates to apostolic times, lauded by Church Fathers as the state of life chosen by the Lord and his mother, as well as other notable figures such as John the Baptist, St. Paul, and earlier prophets. And it would hardly make sense for Jesus to advocate "celibacy for the sake of the kingdom" if he himself was not living it. Paul, who was celibate, freely advised others to be celibate as well (1 Cor. 7:32-38).

When we truly understand the nature of the apocryphal Gospels we can see how foolish it is to base our knowledge of the real Jesus upon them. Not only were they written centuries after the events they describe, their descriptions of Jesus contradict the earlier and more reliable canonical Gospels found in modern Bible editions.

Rather than being reliable, historical accounts of the life of Jesus, these later Gospels were simply concocted to justify the heresies of Gnostic Christianity—sects that taught that followers needed special knowledge (Greek: *gnosis*) in order to be saved. New Testament scholar Craig Blomberg says in his book *The Historical Reliability of the Gospels* that these accounts are not historical but are instead "little more than an artificial framework for imparting Gnostic doctrine."[322]

218. What does it mean to believe in Jesus?

If it's important to have a correct picture of who Jesus *was* during his earthly ministry, it's even more important to know who Jesus *is* at this very moment. Jesus is not a deceased prophet, preacher, zealot, or guru. He is the living and resurrected Son of God who came to earth to redeem mankind from all of its sins. He is the incarnation of God's love for humanity and the hope for salvation open to all people at all times in all places. And he wants you, personally, to know him.

How can people come to know Jesus and find in him salvation from their sins?

"Repent and believe in the gospel," Jesus says when he first begins his apostolic ministry (Mark 1:15). First, one must *repent*. In Greek, the word for repent is *metanoia*, which literally means, "to be of another mind." One who repents changes the direction of life and signals that he no longer wants to sin.

A person who repents must do so *believing* that Jesus Christ is God's Son who has come to redeem us from sin and give us grace to become children of God who will dwell with him forever. This grace doesn't just hide our sins or make us appear righteous: It actually transforms us so that we become holy, so that we "partake in the divine nature" (1 Pet. 4:8).

The ability to believe in Jesus and the desire to change one's life is already a grace, a free gift of God. Desiring to receive God's grace in greater fullness, according to Jesus' instruction, involves being baptized, which washes away the stain of sin and allows us to be a part of God's family.

After being baptized, a Christian is able to participate in the sacraments of the Church (Matt. 16:18), which effectively nourish divine life within us and make us "new creations" in Christ. For example, in the sacrament of the Eucharist, Catholics are able to receive the body and blood of Christ, under the form of bread and wine, so that they can have the ultimate gift of God dwelling inside of them in a tangible way.

219. Who is Mary of Nazareth?

Though she became the most famous woman in the history of the world, Mary was born a simple Jewish girl from a poor family in the house of David,[323] some 2,000 years ago. God chose her to be the mother of Jesus Christ, God incarnate; this simple teenage girl then became *the Mother of God*.[324] She was, as a matter of history, called to the unique task of bringing the Messiah into the world.

Mary is a sign to us all of how God loves to choose "what is weak in the world to shame the strong" (1 Cor. 1:27).

Mary's life and identity are really all about her divine son, Jesus Christ. Her greatness, her holiness, in fact, anything of eternal value in her at all comes entirely through her relationship with him. In Mary's words, "All generations will call me blessed; for he who is mighty has done great things for me, and holy is his name" (Luke 1:48–49).

According to the context of Luke 1 (especially verses 26–38), "great things" refers to Mary having just conceived Jesus in her womb. Mary's "blessed" state, then, exists because of the divine Christ child within her and the faith she has in him: "Blessed is she who believed that there would be a fulfillment of what was spoken to her from the Lord" (Luke 1:45).

When Mary encountered her cousin Elizabeth soon after conceiving Jesus, Elizabeth exclaimed in awe: "Why is this granted me, that the mother of my Lord should come to me?'" (Luke 1:42–43)

The reference to Mary as "Mother of the Lord" is an obvious indication of the lordship of Jesus Christ. But if we understand its Old Testament antecedent, this God-inspired declaration becomes even more illuminating. Elizabeth was referring, almost verbatim, to a text from 2 Samuel 6:9, wherein David exclaims, concerning the Old Testament Ark of the Covenant, "How can the ark of the Lord come to me?"

The Ark of the Covenant, we know, was especially holy and called *the ark of Almighty God*. It contained within it three *types* or prefigurations of Jesus Christ: the high priest Aaron's miraculous staff, a sample of the miraculous bread from heaven—the *manna*—and the Ten Commandments, or "Ten Words" (Heb. 10:4).

Because Mary carried within her our true High Priest (Heb. 3:1), the true "manna from heaven" (John 6:31–32), and the Word made flesh (John 1:14), she is the true ark of the New Covenant. The *Catechism of the Catholic Church* elaborates on this passage:

> Called in the Gospels "the mother of Jesus," Mary is acclaimed by Elizabeth, at the prompting of the Spirit and even before the birth of her son, as "the mother of my Lord." In fact, the One whom she conceived as man by the Holy Spirit, who truly became her Son according to the flesh, was none other than the Father's eternal Son, the second person of the Holy Trinity. Hence the Church confesses that Mary is truly "Mother of God" (495).

Mary is correctly called Mother of God because Jesus Christ, her son, is God. To deny this essential truth of the Faith, as the Council of Ephesus (431) declared, is to cut oneself off from full communion with Christ and his Church. The Council decreed,

> If anyone does not confess that God is truly Emmanuel, and that on this account the Holy Virgin is the Mother of God (for according to the flesh she gave birth to the Word of God become flesh by birth), let him be anathema.

In its dogmatic definition, the Council made reference to the prophecy of Isaiah 7:14, which prophesied over seven hundred years before the birth of Christ that the Messiah was to be born of a woman and was to be "God with us." Thus, we have evidence from both the Old and New Testaments testifying to Mary as Mother of God.

220. What do Catholics believe about Mary?

Non-Catholics can be taken aback by the fact that there are several Catholic "dogmas" about Mary. Specifically, there are four truths about Mary that all the faithful are bound to accept as divinely revealed and infallibly true: her divine motherhood, her perpetual virginity, her immaculate conception, and her assumption body and soul into heaven.

It could seem as though these dogmas are adding to revelation or somehow overshadowing the importance of truth about Christ. Why exactly does the Church bother with Marian dogma?

The answer to that is simple. Theologically speaking, it's vitally important to understand the truth about Mary *because of what it means about Christ.*

For example, if someone denies Mary is the Mother of God, the question becomes "Who, then, is Jesus Christ?" Jesus necessarily becomes either a mere man, or two different persons (one divine, one human), or else not a person at all but some sort of amorphous and unknowable *thing*.

Correct doctrine about Mary eliminates the confusion, and points us to correct doctrine about Jesus.

Marian doctrine also points to truths about who we are as human beings, and what the Lord wants to accomplish *in each one of us*. The Immaculate Conception, for example, displays the full grandeur of the redemptive grace of Christ, bestowed on us by the Father:

> Blessed be the God and Father of our Lord Jesus Christ, who has blessed us in Christ with every spiritual blessing in the heavenly places, even as he chose us in him before the foundation of the world, that we should be *holy and blameless before him*. He destined us in love to be his sons through Jesus Christ, according to the purpose of his will, to the praise of his glorious grace which he freely bestowed on us in the Beloved (Eph. 1:3-6).

As the merits of Christ were applied in advance to preserve Mary from the blemish of original sin, so too the merits of Christ will be applied to all the redeemed that they might be *immaculate* (literally, without blemish):

> Christ loved the Church and gave himself up for her, that he might sanctify her, having cleansed her by the washing of water with the word, that he might present the Church to himself in splendor,

without spot or wrinkle or any such thing, that she might be *holy and without blemish* (Eph. 5:25-27).

The same can be said of the other privileges of Mary. Although grace is given to her in a unique way and to an exceptional degree, in essence her grace is also our grace. As she is Mother of God, so too, those who hear the word of God and keep it are declared by Christ to be his mother (Matt. 12:48-50). As Mary is assumed into heaven body and soul, so too one day we will all be taken into glory, body and soul (Col. 3:1-4; 1 Thess. 4:16-17). As she is ever-virgin, so must we be in our faith (2 Cor. 11:1-4; Rev. 14:4-5).

If the Church sets before us the glories of Mary, it is so that we might have "the eyes of our hearts enlightened, that [we] might know what is the hope to which he has called [us], what are the riches of his glorious inheritance in the saints, and what is the immeasurable greatness of his power in us who believe" (Eph. 1:18-19).

221. How can God have a mother?

First of all, when we say *God*, we may be referring to all three persons of the Blessed Trinity, but not necessarily so. The three persons in the Trinity are distinct within the eternal relations, so we can speak of them individually. Thus, when we say that Mary is the Mother of God, we mean more precisely that Mary is the mother of the *Second Person* of the Trinity.

But we must also remember that the three persons share the same divine nature; they are each fully God. There are not three Gods, nor are there "parts" with God. God is absolutely one in essence or nature. Thus, if Mary is the mother of the Second Person of the Trinity, she is rightly said to be "Mother of God."

But even if Mary is the mother of only the second person of the Blessed Trinity, that person is just as eternal as the other two divine persons. In order to give birth to the eternal God, wouldn't Mary would have to *be* eternal like God?

Just as above we distinguished the three persons in the one God, here we need to distinguish between the two natures in Christ. The Catholic Church does not say Mary is the source of the divine nature (which is eternal) of the second person of the Blessed Trinity. That would be both heretical and absurd. But it does not then follow that she cannot be his mother.

We can use the example of normal human reproduction to help clarify this point. When a woman bears a child, she is not the source of the child's immortal soul. God, the source of all life, directly creates each individual soul.[325] However, we do not conclude from this that the mother is merely the mother of the *body* of the child. Instead, she is the mother of a whole *person* who is a body-soul composite.

Analogously, though Mary did not provide Jesus with either his divine nature or his immortal human soul, she was more than the mother of a body or a "nature." Mary, like any other mother, gave birth to a *person*; and that person is God.

And this leads to the real crux of the issue. Ultimately, rejecting Mary as Mother of God results in one of three serious Christological errors:

1) The denial of the divinity of Christ
2) The creation of two persons to represent Jesus Christ, one human and one divine
3) Some form of unintelligible Christology leaving Jesus Christ as something less than a fully divine person

Understanding Mary to be Mother of God guards and defends the truth that Jesus Christ is the second person of the Blessed Trinity incarnate. That person must be understood to be God—or else you've got the wrong person.

222. How could a mother be a virgin?

Only the power of God can explain *how* a mother can be a virgin. And this is indeed the answer that Scripture gives: "The Holy Spirit will come upon you, and the power of the Most High will overshadow you; therefore the child to be born will be called holy, the Son of God."

The fact that Mary was both mother and virgin is also attested to in Scripture. For example, in Luke 1:34, when Mary was told by the angel Gabriel that she was chosen to be the mother of the Messiah, she asked the question, literally translated from the Greek, "How shall this be, since I know not man?" This question makes no sense unless Mary had intended to honor a vow of virginity.

It is important to keep in mind that Mary and Joseph were already "espoused" (1:27). They were married! Normally, in ancient Israel, after the espousal the husband would go off and prepare a home for his new bride, then receive her into his home, where the union would be consummated. Thus we read that Joseph intended to "divorce her quietly" (Matt. 1:19) when he discovered she was pregnant. He had not yet taken her to his home, but was already in a ratified marriage covenant that required divorce to be dissolved.

This background is significant because a newly married woman would not, when told she would conceive and bear a child, ask the question, "How shall this be?" She would know! Unless, of course, she had already had a vow of virginity. Mary believed the message but wanted to know how it was going to be accomplished. This indicates she was not planning on the normal course of events for her future with her husband, Joseph.

Likewise, Matthew tells us that "all this took place to fulfill what the Lord had spoken by the prophet: 'Behold, a virgin shall conceive and bear a son'" (Matt. 1:23; Isa. 7:14). Although he was writing for a Hebrew-speaking audience, he did not use Isaiah's term *`almah*—which means simply a young woman old enough to marry. Instead, he chose the Greek Septuagint translation: "Behold, a *parthenos* shall conceive and bear a son"—a word that specifically means "virgin." For a young woman, or even a virgin, to one day conceive is not a miracle, in the normal course of events. But to say that "the virgin *is* with child"—following the alternate translation of Isaiah's prophecy (RSV-CE)—makes clear that her motherhood did not alter her virginity. The Greek version brings out more clearly the miraculous nature of Jesus' birth.

The virgin birth of Christ was believed and defended since the time of the apostles, as we perceive in such early witnesses as the second-century Rule of Faith, which survives to this day as the basis of the Apostles' Creed. Accordingly, we believe what the Church has always believed:

> In one God, the Father Almighty, who made the heaven and the earth and the seas and all the things that are in them; and in one Christ Jesus, the Son of God, who was made flesh for our salvation; and in the Holy Spirit, who made known through the prophets the plan of salvation, and the coming, and *the birth from a virgin*, and the passion, and the resurrection from the dead, and the bodily ascension into heaven of the beloved Christ Jesus, our Lord, and his future appearing from heaven in the glory of the Father to sum up all things and to raise anew all flesh of the whole human race.[326]

An even earlier text, by St. Justin Martyr (c.A.D. 100-165), tells us,

> He became man by the Virgin, in order that the disobedience which proceeded from the serpent might receive its destruction in the same manner in which it derived its origin. For Eve, who was a virgin and undefiled, having conceived the word of the serpent, brought forth disobedience and death. But the Virgin Mary received faith and joy, when the angel Gabriel announced the good tidings to her that the Spirit of the Lord would come upon her, and the power of the Highest would overshadow her: wherefore also the Holy Thing begotten of her is the Son of God; and she replied, "Be it unto me according to your word" (Luke 1:38).[327]

223. If Jesus had brothers wouldn't that mean that Mary had other children?

Protestant apologist Eric Svendsen plainly states: "The New Testament mentions several times that Jesus had biological brothers and sisters."[328] Matthew 13:55–56 says:

> Is not this the carpenter's son? Is not his mother called Mary? And are not his brethren James and Joseph and Simon and Judas? And are not all his sisters with us?

On the surface, these texts seem troubling for the Catholic position. If Jesus had brothers, how could Mary have remained a virgin?

We must first remember that the Gospels weren't originally written in English but Greek, and that the common language of Christ and his contemporaries was Aramaic. In both Aramaic and the Greek of the New Testament, the word used for *brother* was also commonly used to mean cousins, uncles, nephews, and other relatives. This probably stemmed, at least in part, from the fact that neither Aramaic nor Hebrew had a specific word for *cousin*. It became common to use *brother* or *sister* when speaking of cousins, which led to using the term for other family relations as well.[329] The *Catechism* cites Abraham and Lot as classic examples of this, in Genesis 13:8 and 14:16. Though they were uncle and nephew by relation, they called one another *brother* (500).

It is not a surprise, then, that in both the Septuagint (the Greek translation of the Hebrew scriptures) and in the New Testament, even though there was a word for "cousin" in Greek (*anepsios*, as found in Colossians 4:10), we find the same phenomenon. In the Septuagint, we have multiple examples. Leviticus 10:4 uses a form of *adelphos* ("brother") to refer to the cousins of Moses and Aaron. In 1 Chronicles 23:22, the cousins of the daughters of Eleazar are called *adelphoi*. And in Tobit 7:2–4 we have forms of both *anepsios* and *adelphos* used as synonyms within two verses of each other: "Then Raguel said to his wife Edna, 'How much the young man resembles my *cousin* Tobit!' . . . So he said to them, 'Do you know our *brother* Tobit?'"

The New Testament also clearly uses *adelphos* to refer generally to *relatives*, just as the Septuagint does. For example, John 19:25 refers to Jesus' "mother's sister (*adelphe*), Mary the wife of Clopas," being present at the foot of the cross along with Mary and Mary Magdalene. It is highly unlikely that there would be two *uterine* sisters with the same name of *Mary*. This is surely an example of some other kind of relation being called *sister*.[330]

Further, Matthew tells us explicitly who is mother of these *brothers of the Lord*, "James and Joseph and Simon and Judas" (Matt. 13:55), when he speaks of the women present at the cross, one of whom was "Mary, the mother of James and Joseph" (27:56). It would be utterly incongruous for Matthew to speak of Jesus' own mother Mary in this way at the moment of the crucifixion, rather than calling her the mother of Jesus, or mother of the Lord.

Finally, Galatians 1:17–19 is another biblical prooftext often used to argue that Jesus had at least one uterine brother:[331]

> Nor did I go up to Jerusalem to those who were apostles before me, but I went away into Arabia; and again I returned to Damascus. Then after three years I went up to Jerusalem to visit Cephas, and remained with him fifteen days. But I saw none of the other apostles except James the Lord's brother.

But notice that James, whom Paul calls a *brother of the Lord*, is an *apostle*.

Now, there were some called apostles, such as Barnabas, who were not of the Twelve.[332] But here Paul is writing about those who "were apostles before him," only a few years after the resurrection of Christ.[333] As "the apostles" were still in Jerusalem at that time,[334] it is unlikely that Paul is referring here to later "apostles" in an extended sense. In fact, there is no record in Scripture of the title "apostle" in an extended sense—beyond the twelve—called such before Paul. Paul is thus referring to James, the *Lord's brother*, as being one of the twelve apostles.[335]

From there it's a matter of simple deduction. There were only two apostles named James among the Twelve. The first was the son of Zebedee. But he could not be the one Paul speaks about in Galatians 1, because he was martyred very early according (Acts 12:1-2). That leaves the other apostle James. And according to Luke 6:15–16, his father's name was Alphaeus—not Joseph. That means that the apostle James whom Paul calls *the Lord's brother* could not have been Jesus' uterine brother.[336]

With Origen (c. 230), then, we can say that "Mary, as those declare who with sound mind extol her, had no other son but Jesus."[337]

224. What other arguments do Protestants make against the perpetual virginity of Mary?

We read in Matthew 1:18: "Before they came together [Mary] was found to be with child of the Holy Spirit." Some would argue that "before they came together" makes sense only "if Mary *did not* make a vow of lifelong virginity. Matthew is making a point of letting his readers know that the child was conceived before any sexual union took place."[338]

Svendsen might have a point if the word *before* necessarily implied that circumstances changed *after.* But just as in English, the Greek word for *before* (*prin*) does not necessitate any event *after* the time of emphasis. It can be used to emphasize either a present or past event or state of being rather than a future event.

For example, consider this statement: "Tom dropped out of high school before he graduated." This statement uses the word *before* to emphasize what Tom did at a particular time in his life. In no way does it imply that he *later* graduated from a different school, got his GED, or anything else.

Svendsen is half-right: Matthew's purpose is to emphasize the virginal conception of Jesus. But there is no evidence that the text is concerned with whether or not Joseph and Mary had sexual union at a later time. There would need to be more information to demonstrate whether or not that took place.

A similar and equally common argument involves the word *until*, as it appears in Matthew 1:24–25:

> When Joseph woke from sleep, he did as the angel of the Lord commanded him; he took his wife, but knew her not until she had borne a son; and he called his name Jesus.

The late Christian apologist Dave Hunt made a lot of hay from these verses, claiming that they meant "Mary was a virgin until the time that Jesus was born. Subsequently, she had a number of other children by Joseph, her husband."[339]

Does Matthew's use of the word *until* mean that Joseph eventually did come to know Mary conjugally? No. As with the word *before*, this implication is unfounded. The word *until* can be used to mean "leading up to the time of" without implying a change afterward. For example, I may say to a friend, "Until we meet again, God bless you!" Does that mean that after we meet again, I want God to *stop* blessing him?

The fourth-century Father of the Church and great Scripture scholar St. Jerome responded to this very question:

> And the Savior in the Gospel tells the apostles, "Lo, I am with you always, even unto the end of the world." Will the Lord then after the end of the world has come forsake his disciples, and at the very time when seated on twelve thrones they are to judge the twelve tribes of Israel will they be bereft of the company of their Lord?
>
> I could give countless instances of this usage . . . a cloud of proofs; I shall, however, add only a few, and leave the reader to discover others for himself.[340]

Here are some of the plain biblical examples confirming St. Jerome's words:

> 2 Samuel 6:23: "And Michal the daughter of Saul had no child to the day of her death." Does this mean she had children after she died?
>
> 1 Timothy 4:13: "Till I come, attend to the public reading of Scripture, to preaching, to teaching." Does this mean Timothy should stop teaching after St. Paul arrives?
>
> 1 Corinthians 15:25: "For he [Christ] must reign until he has put all his enemies under his feet." Does this mean Christ's reign will end after that happens?
>
> Matthew 28:20: "And lo, I am with you always, to the end of the age." In this verse as in 2 Samuel 6:23 above, the Greek word translated "to" is the same—*heos*—as the word translated "until"

> in Matthew 1:25. As Jerome asked, does this verse mean Christ will not be with us after the end of the age?
>
> 1 Timothy 6:14: "I charge you to keep the commandments unstained and free from reproach until the appearing of our Lord Jesus Christ." Does this mean they can break the commandments after Jesus comes?

225. What is the Immaculate Conception?

The Immaculate Conception refers to Mary's preservation from original sin from the very moment of her conception. The formal definition of this dogma was given to the Church by Pope St. Pius IX in 1854:

> We declare, pronounce, and define that the doctrine which holds that the most Blessed Virgin Mary, in the first instance of her conception, by a singular privilege granted by Almighty God, in view of the merits of Jesus Christ, the Savior of the human race, was preserved free from all stain of original sin, is a doctrine revealed by God and therefore to be believed firmly and constantly by all the faithful (*Ineffabilis Deus*).

This teaching is very much rooted in Scripture, particularly in the event of the Annunciation, as contained in the Gospel of Luke:

> And [the angel Gabriel] came to [Mary] and said, "Hail, full of grace, the Lord is with you!" But she was greatly troubled at the saying, and considered in her mind what sort of greeting this might be. And the angel said to her, "Do not be afraid, Mary, for you have found favor with God" (Luke 1:28-30).

According to many biblical scholars, what on the surface looks like a simple greeting is much more than that. Greeting Mary with the salutation *kaire kecharitomene*, the angel communicated to Mary a new name or title.[341] Generally speaking, when one greeted another with *kaire* (hail), a name or title would often be found in the immediate context.[342] The fact that the angel replaces Mary's name in the greeting with "full of grace" is significant.

In Hebrew culture, names and name changes tell us something *permanent* about someone.[343] When you add to this the fact that St. Luke uses the perfect passive participle—*kekaritomene* literally means "she who has been graced" in a completed sense—we have a profound indication of Mary's uniquely holy state.[344] This verbal adjective, "graced," is not just describing a simple past action. Greek has the *aorist* tense for that. The perfect tense is used to indicate that an action has been completed in the past, resulting in a present state of being. That's Mary's name!

So what does it tell us about Mary? Well, the average Christian is *not* full of grace in a permanent sense (see Phil. 3:8–12). But according to the angel, Mary *is*. You and I sin, because of a lack of cooperation with grace in our lives. This greeting of the angel is one clue into the unique character and calling of the Mother of God. Although Mary continued to grow in grace and holiness throughout her life, she was at every moment full of grace, with a unique fullness troubled neither by sin nor by the inclination to sin.

It is important for us to recall that New Covenant fulfillments are always *more* glorious than—*perfections of*, if you will—their Old Testament types, which are "but a shadow of the good things to come" in the New Covenant (see Heb. 10:1). The fall of Adam and Eve is an excellent example of this. In Genesis 3:15 we find, immediately after the fall of our original parents, God telling Satan about the advent of "the woman" (Mary) and her "seed" (Jesus), who would *reverse the curse*, as it is said, that Adam and Eve had brought upon humanity through their disobedience:

> I will put enmity between you and *the woman*, and between your seed and her seed; he shall bruise your head, and you shall bruise his heel.

In the beginning, Adam and Eve are named simply "the man" and "the woman." When we then look at the New Covenant, Jesus is explicitly referred to as "the man" (John 19:5) and the "New Adam" (1 Cor. 15:45). And Jesus himself indicates Mary to be the prophetic "woman," or "New Eve," of Genesis 3:15, when he refers to his mother as "woman" in John 2:5 and 19:26. As the first Eve brought death to all of her children by heeding the words of the ancient serpent, the "New Eve" brings life and salvation to all of her children through her obedience.

The same "serpent" who deceived the first woman is unable to overcome this *New Woman, who takes refuge in God* (Rev. 12:1-16). The New Eve overcomes the serpent, and as a result, "the serpent was angry with the woman, and went off to make war on the rest of her offspring, on those who keep the commandments of God, and bear testimony to Jesus" (Rev. 12:17).

Since she is revealed to be the *New Eve*, it would be unthinkable for Mary to be conceived with original sin. If she were, she would be inferior to Eve of old, who was created in a perfect state, free from all sin.

226. How can Mary be without sin?

Scripture tells us that all have sinned. How then can Mary be without sin?

> All have sinned and fall short of the glory of God (Rom. 3:21).
>
> If we say we have no sin, we deceive ourselves, and the truth is not in us (1 John 1:8).
>
> None is righteous, no not one (Rom. 3:10).

A superficial understanding of these texts would lead us to say that Mary couldn't have been sinless as Catholics believe she was. She must have been a sinner like every other human being, and so she needed redemption.

How should Catholics respond to this?

First of all, we need to know that all three of those prooftexts are dealing with personal sin, not original sin. Original sin is not something we do; it is something we've inherited. Or rather, it is a part of our inheritance that was lost as a result of the sin of Adam.

So when it comes to these verses, we are not dealing with the question of whether anyone is exempt from original sin but rather, from personal sin. Although there are only two members of the human race free from original sin—Jesus and Mary—there are plenty of persons who have no personal sin!

Has a baby in the womb, or a child of two, ever committed a personal sin?

Or how about the severely mentally challenged who do not have the use of their intellects and wills; have they committed personal sins?

No. In order to commit a sin, a person must have knowledge of the sinful act and full use of his will in performing that objectively sinful act.

Clearly, then, the statements of St. Paul and St. John are not meant to exclude any and all exceptions, but to include all humanity within the number of those who stand in need of the grace of Christ's redemption. And this Mary did in a preeminent way from the moment of her conception. As the papal bull *Ineffabilis Deus* (Pius IX, 1854) declares, it was "by a singular grace and privilege granted by Almighty God, *in view of the merits of Jesus*

Christ, the Savior of the human race, [that she] was preserved free from all stain of original sin.

227. What does it mean to say that Mary is mediatrix?

The word *mediatrix* is the feminine form of *meditator*, one who serves as a go-between. Speaking of Mary as mediatrix refers to her role in helping to bring us to God and God to us.

This is a point upon which Protestant Christians are particularly sensitive, in light of what St. Paul says in his first letter to Timothy:

> For there is one God, and there is *one mediator* between God and men, the man Christ Jesus, who gave himself as a ransom for all, the testimony to which was borne at the proper time (1 Tim. 2:5–6).

In teaching this doctrine, is Paul precluding any collaboration between the disciples and Christ in his saving work? On the contrary. In the immediately preceding verses of the same letter, Paul explains that we are to work with Jesus in advancing the salvation of the whole world.

> I urge that supplications, prayers, intercessions, and thanksgivings be made for all men, for kings and all who are in high positions, that we may lead a quiet and peaceable life, godly and respectful in every way. This is good, and it is acceptable in the sight of God our Savior, who desires all men to be saved and to come to the knowledge of the truth (1 Tim. 2:1-4).

Intercession is a synonym for mediation. Christian intercessory prayer is good and acceptable in God's sight, so that all might be saved and come to the knowledge of truth. This is the role that Hebrews 7:24–25 ascribes to Jesus, our mediator at the right hand of the Father:

> He holds his priesthood permanently, because he continues for ever. Consequently he is able for all time to save those who draw near to God through him, since he always lives to make intercession for them.

And yet, even though Christ is our one mediator/intercessor, Paul commands *all Christians* to be intercessors/mediators. Another way of understanding this is to consider that a priest is also, by definition, "a mediator between God and men." And yet, according to 1 Peter 2:5–9, *all Christians are priests*:

> And like living stones be yourselves built into a spiritual house, to be a holy priesthood. . . . You are a chosen race, a royal priesthood, a holy nation, God's own people.

Some Protestants might thus concede that disciples *on earth* can intercede for each other, including offering up their suffering (2 Cor. 1:6), but those who have died cannot, and so their assistance should not be sought. However, the faithful departed are alive in the Lord (Matt. 22:32), as Jesus affirms through his encounter with Moses and Elijah at the Transfiguration (Luke 9:30-31).

The idea of members of the Church acting as mediators is ultimately rooted in the radical union between Christ and the Church, a union described by St. Paul in terms of the body (1 Cor. 12) and by Jesus in terms of a vine and its branches (John 15).

Just as the head of the body works in and through the members, so too, Christ is "the head over all things for the Church, which is his body, the fullness of him who fills all in all" (Eph. 1:22–23). Likewise, just as the life of the vine bears fruit in and on the branches, so, too, Christ says, "He who abides in me, and I in him, he it is that bears much fruit" (John 15:5).

Remember, we are not talking about *necessity* here. Christ could save us all by himself—if he wanted to. But he *chooses* not to do everything himself, strictly speaking. He delights in using the members of his body to communicate his life and love to the world.

Is Christ, then, our one, true mediator? Absolutely! And it is this same Christ who has chosen to use his body to mediate God's grace to the world *in and through him*.

This is how we should understand the role of Mary as mediatrix. The difference with her is not a matter of *essence*, but of *degree*. Mary's role is unique because in cooperating with God to bring Christ into the world, she alone among human beings brings the source of all grace to the entire world. Individual Christians are called to mediate grace to various other members of Christ, and to those they encounter who are outside of Christ as well, in accordance with their individual gifts. Mary alone was called to bring the source of *all* grace to the *entire* world. She brought "grace and truth" (John 1:17) to the world in her son, Jesus Christ.

Nor did her role as mediatrix end with the birth of Christ. Mary's powerful role as mediatrix of grace is manifested in the first of his signs, at the wedding feast at Cana.

> On the third day there was a marriage at Cana in Galilee, and the mother of Jesus was there. . . . When the wine failed, the mother of Jesus said to him, "They have no wine." And Jesus said to her, "O woman, what have you to do with me? My hour has not yet come." His mother said to the servants, "Do whatever he tells you." (John 2:1-5).

Jesus here uses the strongest of language to demonstrate Mary's essential role in God's plan of salvation. He simply will not enter into his ministry, perform his first miracle, and bring his disciples to faith, *until Mary intervenes*. "My hour is not yet come," he says. And yet he responds to Mary's intercession and performs his inaugural miracle through her intercession.[345]

Mary and the other saints are not would-be competitors with Christ, but God-ordained collaborators with Jesus. Their prayerful collaboration—like ours on earth—is rooted in and made possible by Jesus. In other words, the fact that our Lord is mediator does not make our prayer for one another unnecessary; it makes it effective.

228. What does it mean to call Mary co-redemptrix? Isn't Jesus alone the Redeemer of the world?

Co-redemptrix means Mary cooperates with Christ in the salvation of souls. But this does not deny that Jesus alone is the one who redeems and saves the world.

There is no essential difference between calling Mary "co-redemptrix" and St. Paul telling us he and Apollos were co-laborers with Christ (1 Cor. 3:5–9) in the salvation of the Corinthians.[346] *All* Christians are "co-redeemers" with Christ inasmuch as all are called to cooperate with God in bringing souls to him through prayer, obedience, suffering, and the labors of the gospel.[347]

If Mary alone is given the *title* co-redemptrix, it is because, in a unique way, she opened the way for God to come into the world and save us. She cooperated with God's grace in the redemption of the whole world.

This teaching is found in some of the very earliest Christian writings we have. St. Irenaeus of Lyons, writing in A.D. 180, is a great example:

> As [Eve], having indeed a husband, Adam, but being nevertheless yet a virgin ... having become disobedient, was made the cause of death, both to herself and to the entire human race [so too] Mary, having a man betrothed [to her], and being nevertheless a virgin, by yielding obedience, became the cause of salvation, both to herself and the whole human race.[348]

Mary's unique cooperation in Jesus' salvific work continued throughout his life. The prophet Simeon tells us that a sword will pierce Mary's soul as her Son is "spoken against" even to the point of being crucified. Why? So that the *thoughts of many hearts would be revealed.*

The Greek text here reads *ek pollon kardion dialogismoi.* The Greek word for "thoughts" is where we get the word *dialogue.* The suffering of Christ on the cross pierces the soul of every man and reveals the innermost "dialogue" of the heart. It is in that "dialogue of the heart" where souls are purified and transformed by grace. Mary's suffering with Christ uniquely participates in both the suffering of Christ and the resulting redemption.

And it is her presence at the crucifixion that allows the cross to become most explicitly the "tree of life," the place where Christians are born. "Woman, behold, your son!" Jesus said to his mother. And to the disciple standing near her, "Behold, your mother!" (John 19:26-27).

229. What is the assumption of Mary?

At the end of her earthly life, God raised Mary to heaven, body and soul. This event, solemnly defined as dogma, is called the *Assumption.*

Meditating at length on the fittingness of this ultimate grace (*Munificentissimus Deus*, 1950), Pope Pius XII "compared the bodily assumption of the loving Mother of God with her other prerogatives and privileges" in the words of St. John Damascene:

> It was fitting that she, who had kept her virginity intact in childbirth, should keep her own body free from all corruption even after death.
>
> It was fitting that she, who had carried the Creator as a child at her breast, should dwell in the divine tabernacles.
>
> It was fitting that the spouse, whom the Father had taken to himself, should live in the divine mansions.
>
> It was fitting that she, who had seen her son upon the cross and who had thereby received into her heart the sword of sorrow which she had escaped in the act of giving birth to him, should look upon him as he sits with the Father.
>
> It was fitting that God's mother should possess what belongs to her son, and that she should be honored by every creature as the mother and as the handmaid of God (21).

The "fittingness" of Mary's assumption has been preached by the Fathers from the earliest days. But however fittingly the Assumption might follow upon these graces, the *cause* of the Assumption is Christ's victory over sin and death, from which all her other graces flow as well.

Although, "according to the general rule, God does not will to grant to the just the full effect of the victory over death until the end of time has come," this does not apply to the New Eve (*Munificentissimus Deus* 4-5). As she was preserved free from original sin by the merits of Christ, so too her bodily assumption is a sign of his "most complete victory over sin and death."

> We must remember especially that, since the second century, the Virgin Mary has been designated by the holy Fathers as the New Eve, who, although subject to the New Adam, is most intimately associated with him in that struggle against the infernal foe which, as foretold in the protoevangelium, would finally result in that most complete victory over the sin and death which are always mentioned together in the writings of the Apostle of the Gentiles. Consequently, just as the glorious resurrection of Christ was an essential part and the final sign of this victory, so that struggle which was common to the Blessed Virgin and her divine son should be brought to a close by the glorification of her virginal

> body, for the same apostle says, "When this mortal thing hath put on immortality, then shall come to pass the saying that is written: Death is swallowed up in victory" (1 Cor. 15:54) (39).

The assumption of Mary body and soul into heaven flows from the death and resurrection of Christ. What he has done in her, he has made known to us, so that, as St. Paul says,

> having the eyes of your hearts enlightened, you may know what is the hope to which he has called you, what are the riches of his glorious inheritance in the saints, and what is *the immeasurable greatness of his power in us who believe*, according to the working of his great might which he accomplished in Christ *when he raised him from the dead and made him sit at his right hand in the heavenly places* (Eph. 1:18-20).

230. How can you say Mary was assumed into heaven when the Bible says the contrary?

For many Christians, the doctrine of the assumption of Mary is more than merely wrong-headed; it is downright blasphemous. And there are two texts of Scripture they commonly use to argue the point:

> For as in Adam all die, so also in Christ shall all be made alive. But each in his own order: Christ the first fruits; then at his coming those who belong to Christ (1 Cor. 15:22–23).

> No one has ascended up to heaven, but he who descended from heaven, the Son of Man (1 John 3:13).

If no one except Christ will be resurrected bodily before the Second Coming, would that not eliminate the possibility of Mary's having been bodily assumed into heaven? And if "no man" has ascended into heaven, wouldn't that include Mary?

Let's take a closer look at these two texts and the implications for the doctrine of the Assumption.

Interpreting John 3:13 as excluding the assumption of Mary is misguided for several reasons.

1) At the time Jesus spoke these words, it was indeed true that "no one has ascended into heaven, but . . . the Son of Man." But that was long before the assumption of Mary.

2) Jesus cannot be saying that no one else will *ever* be taken to heaven. If that is the case, then what is all this Christianity stuff about, anyway?

3) In fact, Mary did not *ascend* to heaven. She was *assumed*. That makes all the difference. Jesus ascended to the Father by his own divine power, just as he rose from the dead by his own power (John 10:18; 20:17). Mary was powerless to raise herself to heaven, just as she was powerless to raise herself from the dead; she had to be *assumed*. The same could be said of all Christians.

4) Here John is demonstrating the divinity of Christ. Historically, we know that he was writing against his archenemy, the heretic Cerinthus, who denied the divinity of Christ. John quotes these words of Jesus to demonstrate that the Son "descended" from heaven while still abiding in heaven, and, as such, is the only path to heaven: "No one has ascended into heaven but he who descended from heaven, the Son of Man who is in heaven" (John 3:14). The Son of Man had already "ascended" into heaven in his human nature, inasmuch as he possessed the beatific vision even while on earth. That is John's theme in the text, not whether someone years after Christ could be assumed into heaven or not.

The argument based on 1 Corinthians 15:22–23 can be resolved with equal facility:

1) We must remember that in Scripture there are sometimes exceptions to general statements that mention "all." For example, consider Matthew 3:5–6, which tells us that "Jerusalem and all Judea and all the region about the Jordan" went out to be baptized by John the Baptist. Luke is even more succinct, speaking of "when all the people were baptized" (3:21). Now, we know that "all" here does not mean "every single person" in a strict sense because Herod, Herodias, and her daughter were surely exceptions to this verse. Moreover, many of the chief priests, scribes, and elders of Jerusalem, notably the Pharisees, are explicitly said not to have been baptized by him (Luke 7:30; 20:5).

2) We have examples of other "assumptions" in Scripture. Both Enoch (see Gen. 5:24) and Elijah were taken up "into heaven" (2 Kings 2:11) in a manner quite out of the ordinary. The "two witnesses" of Revelation 11:3–13 are also assumed into heaven—those who "stand before the Lord of the earth." Why would God be unable to accomplish the same thing for Mary?

> Far from disproving Church teaching about the Assumption, Scripture actually provides a beautiful confirmation of it in the book of Revelation. Among other heavenly visions, John has a vision of the open temple of God (i.e., the glorious mystical body of Christ), within which is seen the "Ark of the Covenant" (11:19). The next verse speaks of this great portent as "a woman, clothed with the sun" who "brought forth a male child, one who is to rule all the nations with a rod of iron" (12:1-5). In this symbolic yet marked way, John tells us that he saw in heaven the glorified body of the mother of Jesus.

Some will object that "the woman" of Revelation 12 is either the Church or, perhaps, ancient Israel. There is truth to both claims, as there are often multiple levels of meaning to biblical texts. Israel is often depicted as the Lord's bride in the Old Testament (see Song of Sol., Jer. 3:1, etc.). And Jesus was "brought forth" in Israel. So there is precedent to refer to Israel as "the woman."

The book of Revelation likewise depicts the New Covenant Church as a "woman"—the "bride of Christ" (see Rev. 21:2). As "the woman" of Revelation 12 is depicted as continuing to beget children to this day "who keep the commandments of God, and have the testimony of Jesus Christ" (12:17), the Church certainly fits this description.

But *on the literal level,* Mary is the obvious fit. "The woman" in Revelation 12 "brought forth" Jesus. There can be no doubt Mary was the one who did this. Though we could discover many spiritual levels of meaning for the flight of the woman in 12:6, Mary and the Holy Family *literally* fled into Egypt, with divine assistance, in Matthew 2:13–15. And "woman" is the title used elsewhere to refer to Mary's role in salvation (Gen. 3:15; Jer. 31:22; John 2:4; 19:26).

Few would dispute that Mary's soul is in heaven. What is unique about the doctrine of the Assumption and the "woman" in Revelation is that, unlike the "souls of those who had been slain" (Rev. 6:9) or "the spirits of just men made perfect" (Heb. 12:23), this "woman" is depicted as having a body with a head and feet. Her maternal body is the "Ark of the Covenant" that John now sees in the glory of heaven. This is how it was understood by the saints and theologians of old:

> Thus, to mention only a few of the texts rather frequently cited in this fashion, some have employed the words of the psalmist: "Arise, O Lord, into your resting place: you and the ark, which you have sanctified" [Ps. 132:8]; and have looked upon the Ark of the Covenant, built of incorruptible wood and placed in the Lord's temple, as a type of the most pure body of the Virgin Mary, preserved and exempt from all the corruption of the tomb and raised up to such glory in heaven (*Munificentissimus Deus* 26).

231. Doesn't the Bible condemn the idea of a queen of heaven?

Catholics honor Mary with the title *Queen of Heaven and Earth*. This dignity gifted to Mary by God is deeply biblical and has been understood in the Church for 2,000 years, but many Protestants stumble over one biblical text from the Old Testament that casts a shadow on this topic. And that text is Jeremiah 7:18:

> Do you not see what they are doing in the streets of Judah and in the streets of Jerusalem? The children gather wood, the fathers kindle fire, and the women knead dough, to make cakes for the queen of heaven; and they pour out drink offerings to other gods, to provoke me to anger.

In *Roman Catholics and Evangelicals—Agreements and Differences*, Norman Geisler and Ralph MacKenzie claim, "To call Mary 'Queen of Heaven,' knowing that this very phrase comes from an old pagan idolatrous cult condemned in the Bible (see Jer. 7:18), only invites the charge of Mariolatry. And Mariolatry is idolatry."[349]

But the truth is, this text has absolutely nothing to do with the Blessed Mother as Queen of Heaven, for at least three reasons:

1) Jeremiah here addresses a *specific pagan cult* that threatened the people of Israel, that of the Mesopotamian goddess Astarte,[350] who is in no way related to Mary.

2) Jeremiah condemned *offering sacrifice* to "the queen of heaven." In Scripture, we have many examples of the proper way we should honor great members of the kingdom of God. We give "double honor" to "elders who rule well" in the Church (1 Tim. 5:17). St. Paul tells us we should "esteem very highly" those who are "over [us] in the Lord" (1 Thess. 5:12–13). We sing praises to great members of the family of God who have gone before us (Ps. 45:17). We bow down to them with reverence (1 Kings 2:19). We carry out the work of the Lord in their names (Matt. 10:40–42, DRV), and more. But there is one thing we ought never to do: *offer sacrifice* to them. Offering sacrifice is tantamount to the adoration that is due God alone. And this is precisely what Jeremiah was condemning. The Catholic Church does not teach—*and has never taught*—that we give Mary the adoration due to God, or that we should offer sacrifice to her.[351]

3) To Geisler and MacKenzie, and to millions of Evangelicals and Fundamentalists, the mere fact that the prophet Jeremiah condemned worshiping a pagan goddess called "queen of heaven" eliminates the *possibility* of Mary being the true Queen of Heaven and Earth. This simply does not follow. The existence of a counterfeit queen does not mean there can't be an authentic one. This reasoning followed to its logical end would lead to abandoning the entire Christian faith! We could not call Jesus *Son of God* because of counterfeit "sons of God" in pagan mythology: Zeus and Hera had Apollo; Isis and Osiris had Horus; and so forth. The fact that there was a false "queen of heaven" worshiped in ancient Mesopotamia does not negate the reality of the true queen who is honored as such in the kingdom of God.

The Catholic Church teaches that Mary is Queen of Heaven and Earth for the simple reason that Scripture reveals her to be the mother of Jesus Christ, who is clearly revealed to be "the King of kings and Lord of lords" (Rev. 19:16).[352]

232. What did the early Church believe about Mary?

The Fathers of the Church—leaders, teachers, and writers during Christianity's first few centuries after the apostles—provide a valuable witness to the Catholic understanding of Mary that is preserved in the Church today.

Mary, Mother of God

The motherhood of Mary is attested to from the earliest hours of the Church.[353] Here are a few examples:

> For *our God*, Jesus Christ, was, according to the appointment of God, conceived in the womb by Mary, of the seed of David, but by the Holy Ghost. He was born and baptized, that by his passion he might purify the water (c. A.D. 107).[354]

> The Virgin Mary . . . being obedient to his word, received from an angel the glad tidings that she was to bear God (A.D. 177).[355]

The fact that God was born of Mary, as these early Fathers clearly state, gave birth to a third-century Coptic hymn still used in the Church today: "Under your mercy, we take refuge, Mother of God, do not reject our supplications in necessity. But deliver us from danger, [O you] alone pure and alone blessed."[356]

The Immaculate Conception

The Fathers from both East and West are unanimous in attributing to Mary the title of *New Eve*.[357] Not all explicitly conclude Mary to be sinless, but it follows nonetheless. If you understand that all Old Testament "types" are inferior to their New Testament fulfillments, to consider the Virgin Mary conceived in sin would make her inferior to the virgin Eve, who did not receive nearly the grace that Mary received.

The Perpetual Virginity

On this point, the Fathers of the Church were also unanimous. An early example can be found in the writings of St. Clement of Alexandria (A.D. 200), who presents Mary as a sort of archetype of the scriptures. Like Mary, the scriptures *give birth* (to the truth) yet *remain virginal*. He similarly viewed Mary as the archetype of the Church, the ever-virginal bride of

Christ, who is "virgin and Mother simultaneously; a virgin undefiled and a mother full of love."[358]

The Assumption

Recently discovered Syriac fragments of written stories about the assumption of Mary have now been dated as early as the *third century*. Although these fragments come from Gnostic works, the volume upon volume of Christian tracts dedicated to combating Gnostic heresies contain not a single condemnation of this particular teaching.[359] On the contrary, we find the early Church both teaching and celebrating it.[360]

For example, a homily of Timothy of Jerusalem (c. 350–390) on the prophet Simeon and the Blessed Virgin Mary asserts Mary to be "immortal to the present time through him who had his abode in her and who assumed and raised her above the higher regions."[361] About the same time, St. Epiphanius (c. 360) wrote that "she is like Elijah, who was virgin from his mother's womb, always remained so, and was taken up, but has not seen death."[362]

Co-redemptrix and Mediatrix

As stated above, the Fathers of the Church are unanimous when it comes to Mary as "the New Eve." The majority of the references to Mary with this title refer explicitly to her unique role in God's plan of salvation. St. Irenaeus is an excellent example of what we find peppered throughout the age of the Fathers:

> Eve . . . having become disobedient, was made the cause of death, both to herself and to the entire human race; so also did Mary . . . by yielding obedience, became the cause of salvation, both to herself and the whole human race.[363]

233. Why do Catholics have devotion to Mary?

Devotion to Mary is not optional for Christians. Rather, as the *Catechism* puts it, this devotion is "intrinsic to Christian worship":

> *All generations will call me blessed*: The Church's devotion to the Blessed Virgin is intrinsic to Christian worship. The Church rightly honors the Blessed Virgin with special devotion. From the most ancient times the Blessed Virgin has been honored with the title

> of "Mother of God," to whose protection the faithful fly in all their dangers and needs (971).

This devotion to the mother of Jesus is rooted in both justice and charity.

First, it is a matter of the Fourth Commandment: "Honor your father and mother." Because parents uniquely cooperate with God in bringing each new human person into the world, children are obliged to honor, respect, and—as long as they are under their authority—obey their parents in the Lord. This obligation is a matter of justice and falls under the virtue of piety.

The devotion we owe to the Blessed Virgin Mary is of a higher order than the honor we give to our parents because Mary's cooperation brings not just biological life, but *eternal life* to "her offspring . . . those who keep the commandments of God and bear testimony to Jesus" (Rev. 12:17).

Such pious affection is spoken of by St. Paul, who instructs us to honor very especially those who are "over us in the Lord" and "to esteem them very highly in love because of their work" (1 Thess. 5:12-13). The fact that Jesus gave his mother to all of us from the cross (John 19:25–26) is a powerful example of just how much he knew that we needed a spiritual mother in our lives.

> With all your heart honor your father, and do not forget the birth pangs of your mother. Remember that through your parents you were born; and what can you give back to them that equals their gift to you? (Sir. 7:27-18).

If nothing else, Christians have a debt of gratitude to Mary for the "birth pangs" she endured in bringing Christ to the world.

But devotion to Mary is not only gratitude for something accomplished for our spiritual benefit long in the past. It is also rooted in the wondrous interaction and profound codependence of the members of the body of Christ, even now, in charity. St. Paul captures this reality concisely and beautifully in the image of "the body":

> The eye cannot say to the hand, "I have no need of you," nor again the head to the feet, "I have no need of you." On the contrary" (1 Cor. 12:21).

To say the members of Christ's body do not need each other for salvation is like saying my finger does not need the rest of my hand for sustenance. God designed the body that way. So it is with the body of Christ.

Finally, in celebrating what the Lord has done, and is doing, in the other members of the body of Christ, we are doing nothing more than celebrating the greatness of God, as Mary said herself:

> My soul magnifies the Lord, and my spirit rejoices in God my Savior, for he has regarded the low estate of his handmaiden. For behold, henceforth all generations will call me blessed; for he who is mighty has done great things for me, and holy is his name (Luke 1:46–49).

Celebrating and remembering those whose spiritual beauty and courage has pleased the Lord and helped to obtain salvation for others is simply a part of what it means to be a member of the believing community.

> I will cause your name to be celebrated in all generations; therefore the peoples will praise you forever and ever (Ps. 45:17).

Or, in the particularly eloquent example of Judith, by whose courageous intervention Israel was saved from its enemy:

> Then Joakim the high priest, and the senate of the people of Israel who lived at Jerusalem, came to witness the good things which the Lord had done for Israel, and to see Judith and to greet her. And when they met her they all blessed her with one accord and said to her, "You are the exaltation of Jerusalem, you are the great glory of Israel, you are the great pride of our nation! You have done all this singlehanded; you have done great good to Israel, and God is well pleased with it. May the Almighty Lord bless you for ever!" And all the people said, "So be it!" (Jth. 15:8-10).

This very special devotion of the faithful for Mary is a share in the great pleasure which the Lord himself takes in honoring and loving her. As such, it "differs essentially from the adoration which is given to the incarnate Word and equally to the Father and the Holy Spirit, and greatly fosters this adoration" (CCC 971).

Ultimately, when we consider that Christ commands us to love one another *as he loved us*, what should that imply when it comes to loving Mary, who is his mother and ours?

234. Why did Jesus have to die on the cross?

Why Jesus died on the cross can be answered in several ways.

From a historical perspective, Jesus died on the cross because he began a popular movement that provoked the jealousy of Jewish authorities, who both envied his influence and believed it might lead to a disastrous war (Matt. 27:18; John 11:47-53). Consequently, they arrested Jesus, handed him over to the Roman governor, and demanded his execution. The governor complied, using crucifixion, which was commonly used for the enemies of the Roman Empire.

Judging from what especially provoked the Jewish leaders to decide his death, one could say that Jesus died on the cross because he "broke the sabbath," because he called God his Father, and because he resurrected his friend Lazarus from the dead (John 5:18; 11:48-53). It is because Jesus wanted to lead us into the eternal Sabbath rest of the sons of God that he accepted to die on the cross.

From a theological perspective, if Jesus died on the cross, it is because *we chose that* for him. His crucifixion is the consequence of our sin and the result of our unwillingness to cooperate with salvation: "He was wounded for our transgressions, he was bruised for our iniquities; upon him was the chastisement that made us whole, and with his stripes we are healed" (Isa. 53:5).

Jesus died on the cross because this is what we chose for him by our sin. This is how far God's respect for our freedom goes. Like the son in the parable of the vineyard, Jesus was sent by the Father, because the fruitfulness in question was that important and it had to be freely given (Matt. 21:33-41). Jesus accepted what this would lead to, even though he could have avoided it had he chosen (Matt. 26:53-54; John 10:17-18).

But why would the Father ever send his Son, knowing that this is how he would be received? How could death on a cross have any place in his loving plan of salvation? Crucifixion was an exceptionally cruel form of execution, and the idea of a crucified Son of God was startling to people in the ancient world. St. Paul described the message of the cross as "a stumbling block to Jews and folly to Gentiles" (1 Cor. 1:23).

Wasn't there a better way?

We gain insight from perhaps the most famous verse in the New Testament: "For God so loved the world that he gave his only Son, that whoever believes in him should not perish but have eternal life" (John 3:16). In a few strokes, this verse encapsulates the basic Christian message. God loves us, and so he used Jesus' death on the cross to save us from eternal death (separation from God, hell) so that we might have eternal life (union with God, heaven).

But why would God choose crucifixion, or any form of execution, to be the means by which he would accomplish our salvation? Some have pointed out that it was prophesied that the Messiah would suffer and thereby save others (Isa. 53), but this doesn't answer the question of why God would deem this an appropriate means in the first place.

From a perspective of divine wisdom, the answer seems to be that God wanted his gift to take the form of sacrificial love. By willingly going to the cross, Jesus sacrifices his own life to save others, and sacrifice was something everybody in the ancient world understood. It was the universal means by which God or the gods were worshiped.

In a sacrifice, people would bring a gift—often an animal—and offer it on an altar. The sacrifice could either be offered as a gesture of apology for having sinned, an act of worship and reverence, or an expression of thanksgiving. Either way, the gift of the sacrifice was meant to cultivate good relations with heaven.

Thus, though the crucifixion of the Son of God might be a surprising way of offering a sacrifice, it was something that, when explained, people could understand: Jesus was presenting himself as a sacrifice on our behalf. Indeed, he was the sacrifice to which all other Jewish sacrifices ultimately pointed, "for it is impossible that the blood of bulls and goats should take away sins" (Heb. 10:4).

In choosing the crucifixion as the means of our salvation, God drew on another theme that had particular meaning for Jews—the theme of Passover. At the founding of their nation, God led them out of slavery in Egypt through the sacrifice of lambs at the time of Passover, when God's wrath passed over the Israelites.

Now Jesus, "the Lamb of God" (John 1:29, 36), was sacrificed at Passover (John 19:14–16), so that God's wrath might pass over us, and we might be led out of enslavement to sin. Thus St. Paul can say that "Christ, our paschal lamb, has been sacrificed" (1 Cor. 5:7).

Could God have chosen another way to bring about the salvation of the world? Yes. He is omnipotent, and he could have redeemed mankind in any way he chose. According to the common theological opinion, he could have simply forgiven our sins and saved us without any earthly sacrifice.[364]

Nevertheless, by choosing this means of accomplishing the redemption of man, God drew on themes that could be understood by men. The impulse to sacrifice is found in cultures all over the world and is innate to human nature, providing a way for people everywhere to understand what Christ did for us. And because the theme of the Passover lamb was of particular meaning to the Jewish people, God accomplished redemption in a way that built on what he had already established among his chosen people.

He also communicated important lessons to us. One is just how serious our sins are, given that the death of the Son of God was set as appropriate atonement for them. Even more fundamentally, though, he showed us just how much he loves us in spite of our sins: "God shows his love for us in that while we were yet sinners Christ died for us" (Rom. 5:8; see CCC 604).

235. How will Christ return, and what will happen when he does?

Jesus concluded his earthly ministry by ascending into heaven as his disciples watched. As they did so, two angels in human form appeared beside them and said, "Men of Galilee, why do you stand looking into heaven? This Jesus, who was taken up from you into heaven, will come *in the same way* as you saw him go into heaven" (Acts 1:11).

The Lord ascended *bodily* into heaven, and he will descend from heaven in the same body. Contrary to some New Age speculation, he will not be born into a new body or descend as a spirit on some new person. Instead, "The Lord himself will descend from heaven with a cry of command, with the archangel's call, and with the sound of the trumpet of God" (1 Thess. 4:16).

When that happens, all of the saved will be caught up to be with him (1 Thess. 4:17). But before the final glorification of the saints, Scripture tells us that three other important things will take place:

- The forces that oppose God and oppress the Church will be definitively defeated.
- The dead will be raised by the command of the Lord.
- The living and the dead will be convoked to the general judgment.

Lest there be any confusion, Paul emphasizes that "We who are alive, who are left until the coming of the Lord, shall not precede those who have fallen asleep . . . [but] the dead in Christ will rise first" (4:15, 17). Those among the dead who are found written in the Lamb's book of life (Rev 20:12–15; 21:27) will receive the gift of immortality. Those among the living who are judged worthy will then also be transformed "in the twinkling of an eye" (1 Cor. 15:51–53; Phil. 3:21; 1 John 3:2).

Speaking of these final events in the history of mankind and of the Church, the *Catechism* tells us:

> Through his Son Jesus Christ, [God] will pronounce the final word on all history. We shall know the ultimate meaning of the whole work of creation and of the entire economy of salvation and understand the marvelous ways by which his Providence led everything toward its final end. The Last Judgment will reveal that God's justice triumphs over all the injustices committed by his creatures and that God's love is stronger than death (1040).

236. Does Scripture tell us when Christ will return?

We often think references to Jesus' coming mean just one thing: the future Second Coming at the end of the world.

On this point, Scripture does *not* tell us when Christ will return. On the contrary, Jesus tells us that "it is not for you to know times and seasons which the Father has fixed by his own authority" (Acts 1:7). And again: "Of that day and hour no one knows, not even the angels of heaven, nor the Son, but the Father only" (Matt. 24:36). Thus, the *Catechism* teaches:

> The Last Judgment will come when Christ returns in glory. Only the Father knows the day and the hour; only he determines the moment of its coming (1040).

However, although we don't know the date of Jesus' definitive Second Coming, there are other comings which he spoke of, and many that have taken place already.

For example, Jesus' prophecy of "coming soon" may have been fulfilled symbolically in the events of A.D. 70. The background needed to understand this reading of the text is found in the Old Testament, where Scripture uses the image of God riding the clouds like a chariot, coming in judgment on those who have done wrong (Ps. 104:3, Isa. 19:1–2, Jer. 4:13–14, Ezek. 1:4, 26–28).

Likewise, when Caiaphas asked him whether he was the Christ, the Son of God, Jesus replied: "I am; and you will see the Son of Man sitting at the right hand of Power, and coming with the clouds of heaven" (Mark 14:62). Jesus was not prophesying that the Second Coming would occur during Caiaphas's lifetime. His statement referred to Daniel 7:13–14, where the Son of Man is brought before God *in heaven* to receive his kingdom. The prophecy thus refers to his Ascension into heaven (Acts 1:9), to receive the kingdom (Acts 7:55–56) where he now reigns (1 Cor. 15:24–26).

Theologians also have explored the idea of an *adventus medius* ("middle advent") of Christ prior to the Second Coming. This is a spiritual "coming" of Christ in which he is preached to the world and to his people in word and sacrament. A beautiful homily by St. Bernard that speaks of this middle coming is read each year during Advent:

> At his first coming the Lord was seen on earth and lived among men, who saw him and hated him. At his last coming *all flesh shall see the salvation of our God*, and *they shall look on him whom they have pierced.* In the middle, the hidden coming, only the chosen see him, and they see him within themselves; and so their souls are saved. The first coming was in flesh and weakness, the middle coming is in spirit and power, and the final coming will be in glory and majesty.[365]

This is the explanation for passages such as when Jesus says, "If a man loves me, he will keep my word, and my Father will love him, and we will come to him and make our home with him" (John 14:23) or "Behold, I stand at the door and knock; if any one hears my voice and opens the door, I will come in to him and eat with him, and he with me" (Rev. 3:20). These refer to spiritual comings of Jesus, not to his Second Coming.

And these comings are happening at this moment.

237. Did the first Christians expect Jesus to return in their lifetimes?

God did not reveal his plan of the ages all at once. As the centuries rolled on, he sent prophets to his people Israel, and they learned more about the shape of his plan. This is a concept that scholars refer to as *progressive revelation*, because the revelation happened in stages.

Jesus also taught his disciples progressively during the years he spent with them. Very quickly, they realized he was the Messiah (John 1:41), but they did not initially understand that his kingdom was "not of this world" (John 18:36). Instead, they expected him to be what most people understood the Messiah to be—a political deliverer who would wage war against Israel's oppressors, kick out the hated Romans, and restore political autonomy to the Jewish people.

They did not expect him to suffer, die on a cross, or rise from the dead. When he told them he would, St. Peter rebuked him and the disciples debated what he meant (Matt. 16:22, Mark 9:10). Even after his resurrection, they still asked him, "Lord, will you at this time restore the kingdom to Israel?" (Acts 1:6).

His reply was "It is not for you to know times or seasons which the Father has fixed by his own authority" (Acts 1:7), and he told them to wait to receive power from the Holy Spirit, after which they would be his witnesses throughout the world. They thus learned that there would be an extended period before the next step in God's plan.

But they didn't know how long this period would last, and—understanding that they were now living in the final age of history—they tended to assume it would not be very long. Many in the early Church expected that Jesus would return in their lifetimes.

We see this in St. Paul's writings when he describes how living and deceased Christians will experience the Second Coming:

> We who are alive, who are left until the coming of the Lord, shall not precede those who have fallen asleep. For the Lord himself will descend from heaven with a cry of command, with the archangel's call, and with the sound of the trumpet of God. And the dead in Christ will rise first; then we who are alive, who are left, shall be caught up together with them in the clouds to meet the Lord in the air (1 Thess. 4:15–17).

Notice that Paul refers to "we who are alive." He envisions himself—and at least some of his readers—as among those who are still alive at the time of the Second Coming, which was a common expectation.

But God's revelation is progressive, and he eventually made it clear that Paul would not live to see the Second Coming. Paul wrote 1 Thessalonians around A.D. 50, early in his literary career, but around A.D. 66 he penned his last letter, and we find him saying:

> I am already on the point of being sacrificed; the time of my departure has come. I have fought the good fight, I have finished the race, I have kept the faith. Henceforth there is laid up for me the crown of righteousness, which the Lord, the righteous judge, will award to me on that Day (2 Tim. 4:6–8).

Similarly, in Peter's last letter we find him cautioning readers against trying to calculate time from God's perspective (2 Pet. 3:8). He also knew his own death was approaching, for he wrote, "I know that the putting off of my body will be soon, as our Lord Jesus Christ showed me. And I will see to it that after my departure you may be able at any time to recall these things" (2 Pet. 1:14–15). He thus received a revelation that he would not live to see Jesus' return.

The disciple who may have received the most insight into how long the Christian age would last was John. When he initially wrote that it was the "last hour," he knew this was hyperbole (exaggeration to make a point), because he didn't literally expect the world to end an hour after he wrote those words. Instead, he meant it was the last hour in terms of God's plan of the ages.

God made it clear to him that the Christian age would go on for an extended period of time. In Revelation 20:1–6, John saw that it would continue for a lengthy era—symbolized as a period of a thousand years—before the final end came.

We thus find passages in the New Testament that reflect the early Christians' initial guess that Jesus would return in their own lifetimes, but we also find passages where—by progressive revelation—God makes it clear to them that this would not be the case.

238. What is the general judgment?

Unlike the particular judgment that each soul will face at the moment of death, the general judgment or "Last Judgment" includes all people, including those who are still alive at the time of the Second Coming. It is a public event that demonstrates God's justice and mercy before all the world. As the *Catechism* says,

> In the presence of Christ, who is Truth itself, the truth of each man's relationship with God will be laid bare. The Last Judgment

> will reveal even to its furthest consequences the good each person has done or failed to do during his earthly life (1039).

Not only will the Last Judgment reveal what each of us has done, but it will reveal all the consequences of our actions in this life. Concerning this momentous event, we have the prophetic testimony of St. John, St. Paul, and Jesus himself:

> The hour is coming when all who are in the tombs will hear my voice and come forth, those who have done good, to the resurrection of life, and those who have done evil, to the resurrection of judgment (John 5:28–29).

> Then I saw a great white throne and him who sat upon it; from his presence earth and sky fled away, and no place was found for them. And I saw the dead, great and small, standing before the throne, and books were opened. Also another book was opened, which is the book of life. And the dead were judged by what was written in the books, by what they had done. And the sea gave up the dead in it, Death and Hades gave up the dead in them, and all were judged by what they had done (Rev. 20:11-13).

And we will experience the results of this judgment in both body and soul, now that the two have been reunited. Those who refuse the gospel of salvation "shall suffer the punishment of eternal destruction and exclusion from the presence of the Lord and from the glory of his might, when he comes on that day to be glorified in his saints" (2 Thess. 1:9). Or in Jesus' own words,

> When the Son of Man comes in his glory, and all the angels with him, then he will sit on his glorious throne. Before him will be gathered all the nations, and he will separate them one from another as a shepherd separates the sheep from the goats, and he will place the sheep at his right hand, but the goats at the left. . . . They [the goats] will go away into eternal punishment, but the righteous [the sheep] into eternal life" (Matt. 25:31–33, 46).

It is worth noting that, in this parable, in contrast to the Protestant idea of salvation by faith alone (*sola fide*), the sheep and goats are not separated by their belief in Christ. Instead, the sheep are those who performed works of mercy for the poor and downtrodden, and the goats are those who did not.

St. Paul likewise said that God would "render to every man according to his works: to those who by patience in well-doing seek for glory and honor and immortality, he will give eternal life; but for those who are factious and do not obey the truth, but obey wickedness, there will be wrath and fury" (Rom. 2:6–8). Finally, James 2:24 bluntly tells us, "A man is justified by works and not by faith alone."

Does this mean that faith is irrelevant in the Final Judgment? Not at all! Ephesians 2:8–9 says, "For by grace you have been saved through faith; and this is not your own doing, it is the gift of God—not because of works, lest any man should boast." Our works do not *earn* eternal life as if it were a wage we were due (CCC 2007). But they do *merit* it if, as children of God through baptism, our works please our Father, who in turn rewards us for performing them.

We must remember that we are only capable of performing the works God prepared for us (Eph. 2:10) because of the unearned gift of grace we first received from him by faith. We are not saved "by faith" or "by works," but, as Paul said, by "faith working through love" (Gal. 5:6).

239. What is death?

The soul is the organizing principle of life that animates the body and makes it living instead of dead. A cloud might dissipate but it doesn't die, because clouds (and other nonliving objects, like rocks) lack souls. Unlike living things, they lack a principle that unifies their parts for the good of the whole. They might dissolve or decay, but they can't die. On the other hand, when the soul is absent from a living body, that body's parts stop coordinating together for the good of the whole. As a result, the living thing, be it a plant, animal, or human, breaks down or "de-composes" into its original parts. This is why death can be broadly defined as the reduction of a living thing to its component parts.

The *Catechism of the Catholic Church* tells us that "In death, the separation of the soul from the body, the human body decays and the soul goes to meet God, while awaiting its reunion with its glorified body" (997). Unlike angels, who exist as pure spirits without bodies (330), humans exist as embodied beings who possess immortal souls. When humans die, they don't become angels. Instead, their disembodied souls continue to exist and await reunification with their bodies.

The *Catechism* tells us, "Even though man's nature is mortal God had destined him not to die. Death was therefore contrary to the plans of God the creator and entered the world as a consequence of sin" (1008). When our first parents sinned in the garden of Eden, they shattered the peaceful harmony and original justice God created. Their disobedience resulted in forsaking the grace God gave them, which would have protected them from suffering and death (400). They not only lost these graces for themselves, but also became unable to pass them to their descendants, who in turn could not pass them on to us.

The *Catechism* calls this *original sin*, or "the transmission of a human nature deprived of original holiness and justice" (404).[366] Original sin is not a fault or crime we committed, because babies have original sin even though they have done nothing wrong (Rom. 9:11). Instead, original sin is an *absence* of God's grace, which all humans inherited through our fallen nature.

God did not create human death nor did he intend for us to die. This came about because of the free choices of our first parents. Fortunately for us, Christ's freely chosen death on the cross redeemed or bought humanity back from being under the power of death. We now have the opportunity to be partakers in the divine nature (2 Pet. 1:4), and death has lost its sting (1 Cor. 15:55). God hasn't changed our fallen, human nature (we still die physical deaths), but he has given us the opportunity to rise from the dead and attain glorious, everlasting life with him. According to the *Catechism*,

> Because of Christ, Christian death has a positive meaning. . . . In death, God calls man to himself. Therefore the Christian can experience a desire for death like St. Paul's: "My desire is to depart and be with Christ." He can transform his own death into an act of obedience and love toward the Father, after the example of Christ (1010–1011).

Prayer for a Happy Death

O God, great and omnipotent
judge of the living and the dead,
we are to appear before you after this short life
to render an account of our works.
Give us the grace to prepare for our last hour

by a devout and holy life, and protect us
against a sudden and unprovided death.
Let us remember our frailty and mortality,
that we may always live in the ways of
your commandments.
Teach us to "watch and pray" (Luke 21:36),
that when your summons comes
for our departure from this world,
we may go forth to meet you,
experience a merciful judgment,
and rejoice in everlasting happiness.

We ask this through Christ our Lord. Amen.

240. How do we know there is an afterlife?

One alternative to the Christian view of death is the atheistic or materialistic view of death. According to this view, just as the information on a computer ceases to exist when the computer is destroyed (provided the information hasn't been backed up anywhere else), the information in our brains that makes us our unique selves ceases to exist when our brains die. Since humans lack the ability to back up their mental experiences, it follows that once the body dies, or even if just a vital part of the brain dies, the person as a whole forever ceases to exist.[367]

But there are several aspects of the human experience that contradict this materialistic view of man and its subsequent denial of the afterlife.

First, if humans have free will and can choose to be moral or immoral, then a person's actions can't merely be the result of chemical reactions in his brain. If they were, then no one could freely choose a course of action any more than a rock at the mercy of gravity and friction can choose which way to roll down a hill. Just as we don't hold landslides or tigers morally responsible for the harm they cause, equally, physical humans would also lack moral responsibility. But humans are morally responsible for their actions (we rightly say that human acts can be good or evil), which means human actions are not purely the result of physical processes.

However, a critic could say that moral reasoning and other distinctly human behaviors like rational thought emerge from the right *mixture* of physical molecules, just as the *Mona Lisa* emerges from the right mixture of paint colors. Tigers and lightning don't have this mixture, but humans do, which is why humans have distinct features like consciousness, the capacity for abstract thought, and moral awareness. An immaterial "soul" then becomes unnecessary to explain these uniquely human behaviors.

The problem with this argument is that uniquely human behaviors aren't only unexplained from a materialist perspective, but also *inexplicable* from that viewpoint, as no physical explanation can ever account for these behaviors.

Humans can both know abstract concepts and communicate them to others through language, something an animal cannot do. This is important because abstract concepts only exist in an immaterial way. They are real, but they cannot be discovered through sensory or other material means. Humans must, therefore, possess an immaterial way of coming to know these real entities—what we call an immaterial soul.

Even atheistic philosophers understand the problem inherent in a physical brain thinking about things that lie beyond the brain's immediate interactions. For example, if our brains were just lumps of matter, then how could anything about frozen Antarctica be inside my brain cells, which have never been there? When my brain is thinking *about* Antarctica, I can examine it with all kinds of instruments, but nothing from the frozen continent will be visible. The atheistic philosopher Alex Rosenberg wrote,

> Consciousness is just another physical process. So, it has as much trouble producing aboutness as any other physical process. . . . Since nothing physical can be about anything . . . the clumps of matter that constitute your conscious thoughts can't be about stuff either.[368]

As a result, Rosenberg rejects the idea that our "selves" really exist and argues that our consciousness, or internal mental life, is just an illusion. But if our self really is "real," then we have good evidence that our mind is not the same thing as our physical brain. We can know that an immaterial principle of being and life—the soul—organizes our physical body and gives rise to our rational abilities.[369]

Because the soul is immaterial, it has no parts. As death involves the reduction of a thing to its component parts, the soul cannot die—it is incorruptible—and so survives the death of the body.

What this life of the soul after death consists of cannot be known by philosophy or science, but there is one who knows and has borne testimony, himself having risen from the dead—Jesus Christ. As St. Paul wrote, "If the dead are not raised, then Christ has not been raised. If Christ has not been raised, your faith is futile and you are still in your sins . . . . But in fact Christ has been raised from the dead, the first fruits of those who have fallen asleep" (1 Cor. 15:16–17, 20).

241. Are souls aware of anything after death?

Another erroneous view of the soul's journey after death is called "soul sleep." According to this view, the postmortem soul is neither aware of being judged nor aware of its existence in heaven, hell, or purgatory. The soul is simply "asleep" and will only awaken at the Final Judgment at the end of the world. Defenders of this view usually cite Scripture verses like Ecclesiastes 9:5 ("For the living know that they will die, but the dead know nothing.") or Daniel 12:2 ("And many of those who sleep in the dust of the earth shall awake, some to everlasting life, and some to shame and everlasting contempt.")

But these passages represent how death *appeared* to the human authors of Scripture at different times in salvation history. Even today the Church speaks of those who have "fallen asleep in Christ" as a reference to the dead, because the dead look like they are asleep. The prophet Daniel is using the same kind of phenomenological language to describe the bodies of the dead being raised to eternal life.

Likewise, the author of Ecclesiastes is expressing the cynical repercussions of a naturalist worldview. He even goes so far as to say of the dead that "the memory of them is lost," which is not true for all dead people. The author's point is that, from the perspective of human reason alone, all looks hopeless, and the dead seem to be gone. But even Ecclesiastes admits that at the end of the world "God will bring every deed into judgment, with every secret thing, whether good or evil" (Eccles. 12:14).

In the perspective of the Old Testament, the dead descended into *sheol*, or the underworld. This was not an unconscious existence, but a realm where the dead were cut off from the living and could be said to "know nothing," although there were special cases in which the dead were aware of the actions of the living—such as when the witch of Endor summoned the soul of the prophet Samuel to converse with Saul (1 Sam. 28:3–19). But now that Christ has opened the gates of heaven for everyone, including those who died before his Resurrection, the afterlife is different (CCC 637, 1026).

Saints in heaven know what is happening on earth and can intercede for us. God can even make it possible for the saints to appear to the living in the form of apparitions (e.g., of the Blessed Virgin Mary).[370] The doctrine of "soul sleep" is incompatible with verses in the New Testament that explicitly describe things like the joys of being with Christ after death (Phil. 1:23), and the souls of martyrs who, at this moment, do not sleep but cry out to God with a loud voice (Rev. 6:9–10).

242. What does resurrection of the body mean?

The fundamental reason for the resurrection is that God created human beings to have both bodies and souls, and we are not complete unless we have both. Death separates the two, for "the body apart from the spirit is dead" (James 2:26). But God will reunite them so that we may physically live again.

At death, we experience what is called the "particular judgment," because it is particular or specific to each one of us. "Each man receives his eternal retribution in his immortal soul at the very moment of his death" (CCC 1022; see Luke 16:19–31).

At the resurrection, another judgment will occur. "The hour is coming when all who are in the tombs will hear [Jesus'] voice and come forth, those who have done good, to the resurrection of life, and those who have done evil, to the resurrection of judgment" (John 5:28–29).

Unlike the particular judgment that each soul will face at the moment of death, the general or "last" judgment will be the time when the eternal destinies of all people will be publicly pronounced and the world as we know it will come to an end. The *Catechism* says, "At the end of time, the kingdom of God will come in its fullness. After the universal judgment, the righteous will reign forever with Christ, glorified in body and soul" (1042).

Before this universal judgment there will be an event called the resurrection of the body, which Christ describes as the time "when all who are in the tombs will hear his voice and come forth, those who have done good, to the resurrection of life, and those who have done evil, to the resurrection of judgment" (John 5:28–29). The souls who are in heaven, hell, and purgatory will be reunited with their bodies and will experience a *bodily* existence in whatever state their soul has been destined for all eternity. This refutes a common misconception that we will exist as immaterial souls in heaven or hell.

However, this does not mean that our risen bodies will have the mortal defects they had in this life. Instead, St. Paul described how at the Last Judgment the bodies of both the living and the dead would be transformed. He said, "We shall not all sleep, but we shall all be changed, in a moment, in the twinkling of an eye, at the last trumpet. For the trumpet will sound, and the dead will be raised imperishable, and we shall be changed" (1 Cor. 15:51–52).

243. Is a "spiritual body" a real body?

The Church in Corinth had questions about the resurrection to come: "How are the dead raised? With what kind of body do they come?" (1 Cor. 15:35). To respond to these questions, Paul uses several analogies. There are many types of bodies, both terrestrial (human, animal, birds, fish) and celestial (the starts, the sun, the moon). As God gives to each the qualities suitable to it, so he will do for the bodies of those risen from the dead (1 Cor. 15:39-41). And just as a seed sown in the ground rises with a body that is both the same and yet somehow different from the one it had, so too the human body buried and risen again "is sown a physical body [but] is raised a spiritual body" (1 Cor. 15:36-37, 42-44).

Far from being a scientific explanation of *how* the dead are raised, Paul's response is an exhortation to trust the risen Lord who has power over all flesh (see John 17:2).

But how should we understand the contrast made between the "physical body" sown in death and the "spiritual body" raised from the dead? If the risen body is "spiritual," does that mean it isn't a real body?

Paul is making two points here:

First, the risen, glorified, body, although *truly corporal*, will not be subject to the *constraints* of the mortal body. The risen body, unlike the physical body, will be *imperishable, glorious, powerful, and spiritual*. The body, which had been buried in corruptibility, dishonor, weakness, and physicality, surrendered to the laws of nature, will be raised victorious over these constraints. Second, Paul's comparison also contrasts the "spiritual body" to the *pursuits* of the carnal body. When we say, for another example, that the Bible is a "spiritual book," or that a certain person is "spiritual," we don't mean that the book or person is incorporeal, or exists only as a kind of vapor. Rather we mean that the book or person has a spiritual *orientation*—not a spiritual constitution or makeup.

St. Augustine, who frequently dueled with Gnostic heretics seeking any text they could find to justify their distaste for matter, wrote, "As the Spirit, when it serves the flesh, is not improperly said to be carnal, so the flesh, when it serves the spirit, will rightly be called spiritual—not because it is changed into spirit, as some suppose who misinterpret the text."[371]

In 1 Corinthians 2:14-15 Paul writes, "But a natural man does not accept the things of the spirit of God, for they are foolishness to him; and he cannot understand them, because they are spiritually appraised. But he who is spiritual [*pneumatikos*] appraises all things, yet he himself is appraised by no one." Clearly, Paul doesn't mean that the ghostly, immaterial man is able to appraise these things but that the man with a spiritual orientation is.

Finally, Paul's belief in a bodily resurrection is evident in his other writings outside of this section in 1 Corinthians. He writes in Philippians 3:21, "He will change our lowly body to conform with his glorified body by the power that enables him also to bring all things into subjection to himself." And in his letter to the Romans, Paul specifically refers to our bodies and what God will do to transform them. In Romans 8:11 he writes, "If the Spirit of the one who raised Jesus from the dead dwells in you, the one who raised Christ from the dead will give life to your mortal bodies also, through his Spirit that dwells in you."

244. Is reincarnation possible?

Reincarnation, which literally means "to be made flesh again," is the belief that after death the soul lives on in another body. The soul might inhabit a similar body (e.g., a human soul enters another human body) or even a radically dissimilar body (e.g., a human soul enters a frog's body). Regardless of what form reincarnation takes, the *Catechism* states,

> Death is the end of man's earthly pilgrimage, of the time of grace and mercy which God offers him so as to work out his earthly life in keeping with the divine plan, and to decide his ultimate destiny. When "the single course of our earthly life" is completed, we shall not return to other earthly lives: "It is appointed for men to die once" (Heb. 9:27). There is no "reincarnation" after death (1013).

In the third century, Origen said reincarnation was "foreign to the Church of God, and not handed down by the apostles, nor anywhere set forth in the Scriptures."[372] There are several arguments that support the Church's rejection of reincarnation. First, in the fourth century St. Ambrose of Milan wrote that it would be impossible that "the soul which rules man should take on itself the nature of a beast so opposed to that of man," or that man, "being capable of reason should be able to pass over to an irrational animal."[373] All the less would it be possible for a soul endowed with only vegetative and sensitive life to effectively assume the operations of a human body.

Second, humans do not behave as if they possessed souls that lived before the birth of their bodies. The third-century ecclesial writer Tertullian put it this way:

> If souls depart at different ages of human life, how is it that they come back again at one uniform age? For all men are imbued with an *infant soul* at their birth. But how happens it that a man who dies in old age returns to life as an infant? . . . I ask, then, how the same souls are resumed, which can offer no proof of their identity, either by their disposition, or habits, or living?[374]

The absence of animals and infants who act like mature adults is evidence against the theory of reincarnation. Of course, a defender of reincarnation could say that although a person's soul inhabits a new body, his memories and personality do not. But this makes reincarnation the practical equivalent of not surviving death. It also raises the question, as St. Irenaeus asked in the second century, "If we don't remember anything before our conception, then how do advocates of reincarnation know we've all been reincarnated?"[375]

Other defenders of reincarnation offer empirical evidence in the form of "past lives" testimony. These testimonies, such as those gathered among children by the late psychiatrist Ian Stevenson, are not convincing. For example, many of the subjects of Stevenson's interviews were children who lived in places like India, where reincarnation is widely accepted. This suggests that their stories were more likely the products of social conditioning than actual memories of past lives.

Moreover, although the children in these studies were not thought to be capable of deceiving interviewers, they were capable of confusing fantasy with reality (e.g., telling stories about imaginary friends or imaginary adventures). In fact, many of the anecdotes Stevenson shares rely on ambiguous details that are better explained by a child's imperfect grasp of reality. Skeptic Robert Carroll offers the following example:

> One case involved an Idaho girl who at age 2 would point to photographs of her sister, dead from a car accident three years

> before she was born, and say "that was me." The believer thinks the two-year-old meant: "I was my sister in a previous life." The skeptic thinks she meant: "That's a picture of me." The skeptic sees the two-year-old as making a mistake. The believer sees her as trying to communicate a message about reincarnation.[376]

There is also a third argument against reincarnation, one that has been called "the population argument." It relies on the claim made by proponents of reincarnation that new souls are never created or destroyed. Instead, souls are only "reborn" into other bodies. But, in Tertullian's words, "If the living come from the dead, just as the dead proceed from the living, then there must always remain unchanged one and the selfsame number of mankind."[377] He noted (and modern science has confirmed) that there has been a "gradual growth of [the human] population." Unless one were to admit the possibility of animal souls assuming human bodies, this growth can only be explained by new souls coming into existence and conflicts with the notion of the perpetual reincarnation of the same human souls into different bodies.

Finally, scientists agree that life on earth began—at the earliest—billions of years ago. This disproves the idea that souls have been reincarnating into physical bodies for all eternity. As the *Catechism* says, "The Church teaches that every spiritual soul is created immediately by God—it is not 'produced' by the parents—and also that it is immortal: it does not perish when it separates from the body at death, and it will be reunited with the body at the final Resurrection" (CCC 366).

245. What is the particular judgment?

After death, a person's soul does not perish, nor does it reincarnate into another body. Instead, the soul waits to be reunited with the body from which it departed. This reunification will occur during the end of the world at the resurrection of the dead. However, before this "general judgment" of all people, every individual soul will face a "particular judgment" after death. The *Catechism* says,

> Each man receives his eternal retribution in his immortal soul at the very moment of his death, in a particular judgment that refers his life to Christ: either entrance into the blessedness of

> heaven—through a purification or immediately—or immediate and everlasting damnation (1022).

In other words, at the moment of death the soul is aware of what happens and goes to heaven or hell. Souls that go to heaven either go there directly, or they are purified before being admitted into heaven. This stands in contrast to the view of some Christians who believe that all Christians immediately go to heaven, or that "to be absent from the body" is necessarily "to be present with the Lord."

But this is a misreading of 2 Corinthians 5:6–9. St. Paul says, "So we are always of good courage; we know that while we are at home in the body we are away from the Lord, for we walk by faith, not by sight. We are of good courage, and we would rather be away from the body and at home with the Lord. So whether we are at home or away, we make it our aim to please him."

Paul is saying that even though our bodies feel like home, we would *rather* dwell in our true home with the Lord. These verses do not teach that when we are not at home in the body (i.e., when we are dead) that we are automatically "at home" with the Lord. It is just an expression of a desire that Christians have and not a reality that all of them will immediately experience, because some believers must be cleansed of their sins before they can dwell with God in heaven.

246. What is heaven?

In some cases, the Bible uses the word *heaven* to refer to the sky, or to the abode of the sun, stars, and moon. This is seen in passages like Psalm 19:1, which says, "The heavens are telling the glory of God." Other times, *heaven* refers to the place where God dwells, as in the Lord's Prayer, where we address "Our Father who art in heaven" (Matt. 6:9). Finally, "heaven" is used to refer to the eternal dwelling place of those who love God. As St. Paul says, "Our commonwealth is in heaven, and from it we await a Savior, the Lord Jesus Christ" (Phil. 3:20).

Many modern people imagine this heaven to be a place in the clouds where saints and angels play harps for all eternity. But although the Bible does use imagery like wedding feasts, the Father's house, or the heavenly Jerusalem, the *Catechism* says, "This mystery of blessed communion with God and all who are in Christ is beyond all understanding and description" (1027). Paul, quoting the promises given to the prophet Isaiah, said, "No eye has seen, nor ear heard, nor the heart of man conceived, what God has prepared for those who love him" (1 Cor. 2:9).

Because of sin and our fallen human natures, we only perceive God indirectly; our relationship with him lacks the intimacy and wonder that it will have with him in heaven. Paul once compared our knowledge of God in this life to our knowledge of ourselves when we see our reflection in a dirty bronze mirror (at this time in history glass mirrors were just beginning to be invented and were not as popular as polished metal). He said, "For now we see in a mirror dimly, but then face to face. Now I know in part; then I shall understand fully, even as I have been fully understood" (1 Cor. 13:12). According to the *Catechism*,

> God cannot be seen as he is, unless he himself opens up his mystery to man's immediate contemplation and gives him the capacity for it. The Church calls this contemplation of God in his heavenly glory "the beatific vision" (1028).

Our inexact knowledge of heaven does not mean that we are ignorant of heaven's general nature. The *Catechism* teaches:

> Communion of life and love with the Trinity, with the Virgin Mary, the angels and all the blessed—is called "heaven." Heaven is the ultimate end and fulfillment of the deepest human longings, the state of supreme, definitive happiness (1024).

> Heaven is the blessed community of all who are perfectly incorporated into Christ (1026).

According to Pope St. John Paul II, "The 'heaven' or 'happiness' in which we will find ourselves is neither an abstraction nor a physical place in the clouds, but a living, personal relationship with the Holy Trinity."[378]

This understanding of heaven answers critics who compare the beatific vision to an eternally long Church service that would be as insufferable as hell. Of course, any earthly activity, be it a Church service, a rock concert, or a day at an amusement park, would be hellish if it were drawn out over an infinite period of time. Heaven won't consist of unending earthly joys, because these finite things can't satisfy our longing for perfect and surpassing happiness. Even sacraments like marriage will not exist in heaven (Mark 12:25), because these earthly realities only serve as signs that guide us to heaven—and signs are no longer needed once one's destination has been reached.

God, infinite being and goodness itself, is the only reality that can provide us with the perfect love and perfect understanding that our hearts desire. In heaven, believers will adore God for all eternity and never reach an end or stagnant plateau of what they adore. Moreover, because God is love and love is self-giving, heaven will be communal in nature. We've already seen how saints and angels in heaven intercede for people on earth, and the *Catechism* informs us that "In the glory of heaven the blessed continue joyfully to fulfill God's will in relation to other men and to all creation. Already they reign with Christ; with him 'they shall reign for ever and ever'" (1029).

247. What is purgatory?

At the moment of death, each soul receives its eternal destiny. For those who die in a state of grace, it is eternal life with God. For those who die in a state of mortal sin, it is eternal life apart from God.

1 John 5:17 says, "All wrongdoing is sin, but there is sin which is not deadly." The Church identifies this "deadly sin" with mortal sin, or freely chosen, gravely evil acts that destroy charity in man's heart and forfeit the hope of eternal life with God (CCC 1855–1859). However, unlike mortal sins, venial sins blemish the soul but do not kill God's grace within it. Even though these sins do not completely separate us from God, Revelation 21:27 says that nothing unclean will enter heaven. This means that our sins, be they mortal or venial, will not be with us in heaven.

What happens to people who die in a state of venial sin rather than a state of mortal sin? Since these people died in a state of grace and friendship with God, there is no possibility they will go to hell. But sin cannot enter into the pure holiness of God's abode in heaven. It logically follows, therefore, that these saved souls will be purged of their sins prior to spending eternity with God in heaven. According to the *Catechism*, "the Church gives the name *purgatory* to this final purification of the elect, which is entirely different from the punishment of the damned" (1031).

Even though the eternal consequences of our sins have been forgiven through Christ's death on the cross, human beings still suffer from the temporal consequences of their sins. For example, God forgave King David for committing the sins of adultery and murder, but he still allowed David to suffer the consequence of committing those sins (2 Sam. 12:7–14). The *Catechism* explains it this way:

> Sin has a *double consequence.* Grave sin deprives us of communion with God, and therefore makes us incapable of eternal life, the privation of which is called the "eternal punishment" of sin.
>
> On the other hand, every sin, even venial, entails an unhealthy attachment to creatures, which must be purified either here on earth, or after death in the state called purgatory. This purification frees one from what is called the "temporal punishment" of sin.
>
> These two punishments must not be conceived of as a kind of vengeance inflicted by God from without, but as following from the very nature of sin (1472).

Purgatory is not an alternative to heaven and hell nor is it a "second chance" to choose God. All souls that go to purgatory belong to those who died in God's friendship. Each of these souls will eventually be united with God in heaven after they have been purified from sin. We don't know exactly what this process of purification entails, but the Church frequently uses the imagery of cleansing fire in order to describe it. We also don't know how long this process takes. For example, Jesus told the thief on the cross, "Today you will be with me in paradise" (Luke 23:43), and Pope Benedict XVI said,

> It is clear that we cannot calculate the "duration" of this transforming burning in terms of the chronological measurements of this world. The transforming "moment" of this encounter eludes earthly time-reckoning—it is the heart's time, it is the time of "passage" to communion with God in the Body of Christ (*Spe Salvi, 47).*

But why didn't God remove both the eternal *and* the temporal effects of our sins? Part of the answer to that question is a mystery, because we can't fully understand why God allows us to suffer in this life. But there are clues that help us understand why God would permit this kind of suffering. The letter to the Hebrews says, "The Lord disciplines him whom he loves, and chastises every son whom he receives.... he disciplines us for our good, that we may share his holiness" (Heb. 12:6, 10).

It is natural for humans to want to make amends for the wrong they have done, but no amount of work on our part can make up for the infinite wrong caused by our sins against an infinitely holy God. Fortunately, God is merciful and allows us to make amends on a small scale, so that we can learn discipline and become holy just as God is holy (1 Pet. 1:15). But we must not allow these images of discipline and growth to mislead us into thinking that purgatory is a place where we "work off our sins" by undergoing arbitrary punishments. Cardinal Joseph Ratzinger (the future Pope Benedict XVI) wrote,

> Purgatory is not some kind of supra-worldly concentration camp where one is forced to undergo punishments in a more or less arbitrary fashion. Rather it is the inwardly necessary process of transformation in which a person becomes capable of Christ, capable of God, and thus capable of unity with the whole communion of saints.[379]

248. What are some common objections to the doctrine of purgatory?

The most common objection to the doctrine of purgatory is that it is unbiblical. It usually proceeds from the critic in the form of a question: "Where is purgatory in the Bible?" Setting aside the fact that this question assumes that all Christian doctrine must be found explicitly in Scripture (an ironically *unbiblical* Protestant belief called *sola scriptura*), there are actually several biblical texts that provide the basis for belief in purgatory.

First, the *Catechism* cites Judas the Maccabee praying for the souls of his slain comrades. He "made atonement for the dead, that they might be delivered from their sin" (2 Macc. 12:46). Since prayers cannot help the damned in hell and are not needed for the saved in heaven, these prayers must have been applied to those being purified of their sins after death. Indeed, the *Catechism* goes on to say, "From the beginning the Church has honored the memory of the dead and offered prayers in suffrage for them, above all the eucharistic sacrifice, so that, thus purified, they may attain the beatific vision of God" (1032). Although Protestants reject the inspiration of deuterocanonical books like 2 Maccabees, they can't deny that it is a historical witness to the ancient Jewish practice of praying for the dead so that their sins could be forgiven in the next life.[380]

The *Catechism* then describes teachings of Christ that fit within this theological context. Quoting St. Gregory the Great, it says, "He who is truth says that whoever utters blasphemy against the Holy Spirit will be pardoned neither in this age nor in the age to come [Matt. 12:32]. From this sentence we understand that certain offenses can be forgiven in this age, but certain others in the age to come" (1031). Since mortal sins cannot be forgiven after death, this implies that venial sins can be forgiven and purged from the believer in the next life before he enters heaven.

In fact, during the portion of the Sermon on the Mount in which Christ discusses entering heaven and hell, he tells a parable about being accused in court. Jesus says that unless you are reconciled with your accuser you will be thrown into prison, and "Truly, I say to you, you will never get out till you have paid the last penny" (Matt. 5:26). Church Fathers and ecclesial writers like Tertullian interpreted this passage as referring to the penance a soul would endure in purgatory before it was "released" and able to enter into the joys of heaven.[381]

Perhaps the most striking text about the purification after death is 1 Corinthians 3:13–15. In this passage, Paul refers to the testing of our works that will take place after death:

> Each man's work will become manifest; for the Day will disclose it, because it will be revealed with fire, and the fire will test what sort of work each one has done. If the work which any man has built on the foundation survives, he will receive a reward. If any man's work is burned up, he will suffer loss, though he himself will be saved, but only as through fire.

These verses unambiguously describe God's judgment after death and how our works will be exposed with fire. The fire may not be literal, because Scripture uses fire in metaphorical ways to describe cleansing and purification (Matt. 3:11–12). But the text does literally say that when inferior works are tested, the man being examined will suffer loss even though he will be saved. What could that loss be, given that he will be saved? The most natural interpretation is that the loss must represent the suffering he will endure after death, as the negative effects of his inferior and wicked works are purged from his soul.[382]

The other common objection to purgatory is the claim that it detracts from Christ's sacrifice on the cross as somehow insufficient to "take away the sins of the world." But far from being insufficient, the Church teaches that

Christ's death on the cross was *supererogatory*. This means that Christ's death merited much more (in fact, infinitely more) grace than was necessary to atone for all of humanity's sins. Far from being something that cleanses sin through our own works, theologians like Pope Benedict XVI have speculated that the cleansing fire of purgatory is none other than Christ himself; thus, purgatory doesn't take away from Christ's work because it *is* Christ's work. He writes,

Some recent theologians are of the opinion that the fire which both burns and saves is Christ himself, the Judge and Savior. The encounter with him is the decisive act of judgment. Before his gaze all falsehood melts away. This encounter with him, as it burns us, transforms and frees us, allows us to become truly ourselves (*Spe Salvi* 47).

249. How do I stay out of purgatory?

Purgatory is not a place to avoid like a tourist trap on the highway. Staying out of purgatory is simply a matter of avoiding the one thing purgatory purifies us of—sin.

Of course, this might be a simple answer to the question, but it is not an easy one. That's because our corrupted human nature gives rise to concupiscence, or an internal inclination to sin that we must constantly battle (CCC 405). That's why the Church urges us to "strive by works of mercy and charity, as well as by prayer and the various practices of penance, to put off completely the 'old man' and to put on the 'new man'" (1473).

As we grow in holiness, we sin less and less, but we will still inevitably sin. Through the sacrament of reconciliation, the loss of communion with God caused by mortal sin is restored, but all sins, mortal and venial, still leave a temporal effect on our souls. They persist in the form of an unhealthy attachment to sin that is not removed by the sacrament of confession alone.

Is there a way to purge the temporal effects of sin from our souls before death and thus remove the need to remain in purgatory after death?

Yes. The Church teaches that the holiness of some can be applied to the benefit of others. For example, Paul said that the Jews of his time were "beloved for the sake of their forefathers" (Rom. 11:28), and God had mercy on the city of Sodom because of Abraham's intercession (Gen. 18). The merits of Christ, which were infinitely more than what was necessary to take away the sin of the world, as well as the merits of the saints in heaven, can be applied to believers on earth and even those in purgatory. The *Catechism* says,

> The "treasury of the Church" is the infinite value, which can never be exhausted, which Christ's merits have before God. They were offered so that the whole of mankind could be set free from sin and attain communion with the Father. . . . . In the treasury, too, are the prayers and good works of all the saints, all those who have followed in the footsteps of Christ the Lord and by his grace have made their lives holy and carried out the mission in the unity of the mystical body (1476–1477).

These merits are applied to those needing purification as an "indulgence." Contrary to popular opinion, indulgences are not special "tickets" one can buy to get into heaven or stay out of hell. Indulgences are instead the Church's way of applying the treasury of merits to individuals in order to "obtain from the Father of mercies the remission of the temporal punishment due for their sins" (CCC 1478). The Church has this authority because Christ told the apostles that they have the ability to forgive sins (John 20:23), and that whatever they bind on earth shall be bound in heaven, and whatever they loose on earth shall be loosed in heaven (Matt. 18:18).

So how do indulgences work? According to the *Catechism*, "An indulgence is partial or plenary according as it removes either part or all of the temporal punishment due to sin" (1471). A partial indulgence, which removes some but not all of the temporal punishments associated with sin, can be obtained by performing with a contrite heart the work to which the indulgence is attached (a list of these works can be found in the "Enchiridion of Indulgences"). A plenary indulgence can be obtained by performing the work while also being in a state of grace, being completely detached from sin, going to confession, receiving the Eucharist, and praying for the intentions of the pope.

What about those who have died and are being purified of their sins? Is there any way to apply the treasury of merits to them? Yes, praying for the dead or gaining an indulgence on their behalf accomplishes this. The *Catechism*, quoting the 1899 Douay-Rheims translation of 2 Maccabees 12:46, says, "'Because it is a holy and a wholesome thought to pray for the dead that they may be loosed from their sins' [the Church] offers her suffrages for them. Our prayer for them is capable not only of helping them, but also of making their intercession for us effective" (958).

250. What is hell?

Many religions teach the existence of a place or state of punishment in the afterlife. The existence of hell is not a pleasant thing to believe in. But then neither is evil.

In Scripture the word *hell* has several different meanings. In the Old Testament it usually referred to *sheol*, or the abode of the dead. The Church teaches that after his crucifixion Christ preached to the spirits in *sheol* (1 Pet. 4:6), an event the Apostle's Creed refers to as Christ's "descent into hell." Regarding this event, the *Catechism* clearly says, "Jesus did not descend into hell to deliver the damned, nor to destroy the hell of damnation, but to free the just who had gone before him" (633).

In the New Testament the word *hell* usually refers to the final, eternal dwelling place for the damned. According to the *Catechism*, "To die in mortal sin without repenting and accepting God's merciful love means remaining separated from him for ever by our own free choice. This state of definitive self-exclusion from communion with God and the blessed is called 'hell'" (CCC 1033).

Scripture uses a variety of images to describe what this awful state is like. For example, Christ spoke of hell being a place of fire (Matt. 5:22), undying worms (Mark 9:48), gnashing of teeth (Matt. 13:42), and an outer darkness (Matt. 22:13). He even compared it to Gehenna (Matt. 23:33), a place where children were offered as fire sacrifices to pagan gods.[383] Since Christ was using earthly images to convey spiritual truths, none of these images, including those of unending fire, should necessarily be taken as literal descriptions of hell.

Pope St. John Paul II said, "The images of hell that Sacred Scripture presents to us must be correctly interpreted. They show the complete frustration and emptiness of life without God. Rather than a place, hell indicates the state of those who freely and definitively separate themselves from God, the source of all life and joy."[384]

Likewise, Pope Benedict XVI said,

> There can be people who have totally destroyed their desire for truth and readiness to love, people for whom everything has become a lie, people who have lived for hatred and have suppressed all love within themselves. This is a terrifying thought, but alarming profiles of this type can be seen in certain figures of our own

> history. In such people all would be beyond remedy and the destruction of good would be irrevocable: this is what we mean by the word *hell* (*Spe Salvi*, 45).

The prospect of hell is terrifying, but it should not lead us to despair. The *Catechism* says, "The affirmations of Sacred Scripture and the teachings of the Church on the subject of hell are a call to the responsibility incumbent upon man to make use of his freedom in view of his eternal destiny" (1036). God's offer of salvation is open to all and we should earnestly seek after it and share it with others. 2 Peter 3:9 says that God is patient with us, "not wishing that any should perish, but that all should reach repentance."

251. Is hell forever?

Contrary to the Catholic teaching of hell as "irrevocable," some argue that hell is not permanent, because the damned will be able to choose God at a later time and thus escape hell. Others say that the damned will be destroyed in hell, and so they won't suffer for all eternity.

This latter view is often called *annihilationism* and the Church soundly rejects it. The *Catechism* says,

> The teaching of the Church affirms the existence of hell and its eternity. Immediately after death the souls of those who die in a state of mortal sin descend into hell, where they suffer the punishments of hell, "eternal fire." The chief punishment of hell is eternal separation from God, in whom alone man can possess the life and happiness for which he was created and for which he longs (1035).

The strongest biblical argument against annihilationism is found in Matthew 25:46, where our Lord says of the damned, "They will go away into eternal punishment, but the righteous into eternal life." Annihilationists say the Greek word rendered "eternal" in this passage, *aionios*, means "age" or "a long period of time" and doesn't necessarily mean "forever." But Matthew always uses this word to mean "eternal." Also, in this context Jesus is making a comparison between the eternal life the righteous will enjoy forever and the eternal punishment the wicked will endure forever.[385] The comparison doesn't make sense if the wicked are destroyed and don't have an everlasting existence like the righteous will.

Others argue that the Greek word rendered "punishment," *kolasin*, is derived from a word that means to "prune" or "cut off." Therefore, hell is just separation from God by being annihilated or destroyed. It is not eternal, conscious punishment.[386] But any Greek dictionary will tell you, *kolasin* just means "punishment" and *kolasin aionion* means "eternal" or "everlasting punishment."

252. How could a loving God send someone to hell?

Many people who object to the doctrine of hell ask, "How could a loving God send someone to hell?" But this question, as honest and important as it is, displays a mistaken view of the relationship between earthly choices and eternal destinies.

First of all, hell is not something God created for the purpose of arbitrarily punishing people. Instead, humans created hell through sinful choices that separated them from God. As the *Catechism* says, "God predestines no one to go to hell; for this, a willful turning away from God (a mortal sin) is necessary, and persistence in it until the end" (1037). Jesus' parable about the Last Judgment makes it clear that, in God's plan, "The eternal fire [was] prepared for the devil and his angels," not for man (Matt. 25:41).

God doesn't wish that "any should perish, but that all should reach repentance" (2 Pet. 3:9). But if humans have free will, then there is the possibility of their rejecting God's love. Those who die having freely separated themselves from God by the way they lived will have their choice respected in the afterlife. God doesn't force himself on them.

If we believed in the afterlife but wanted to throw out the doctrine of hell, we would also have to throw out one of two other beliefs:

- Humans have free will.
- God is love.

Thus you might say that God did not create hell. Rather, sin created hell. As Lewis wrote, "There are only two kinds of people in the end: those who say to God, 'Thy will be done,' and those to whom God says, in the end, 'Thy will be done.' All that are in hell, choose it."[387]

Far from being inconsistent with God's loving nature, hell is a necessary consequence of it. Because God is love, he respects our freedom—*for love is never coercive*. If God forced his love on us, he would not be perfectly loving and thus wouldn't be God.

253. How could a just God send someone to hell?

Another objection to hell is that it's unfair of God to inflict an infinite punishment on someone for having committed a finite crime.

But what do we mean by a "finite" crime deserving only a finite punishment? The length of *time* it took to commit a crime does not indicate what the punishment for the crime should be. After all, a parking violation could happen over a period of hours, whereas a murder could happen in a few seconds. It is the *nature* of the crime and the *intention* of the criminal that are relevant to deciding what the punishment should be.

But are the crimes in this life really so serious that they deserve infinite punishment in the next? Many people are willing to accept that although very awful people like genocidal dictators or sadistic serial killers deserve to go to hell, regular people who commit "everyday" sins do not. However, St. Paul listed several sins that can keep us from entering heaven, including some very common ones. He said, "Neither the immoral, nor idolaters, nor adulterers, nor homosexuals, nor thieves, nor the greedy, nor drunkards, nor revilers, nor robbers will inherit the kingdom of God" (1 Cor. 6:9–10).

When we weigh our sins against our own personal standards, we usually come out on top. But when our sins are weighed against God's perfect holiness, we see how often we cast God aside in favor of evils that seem pleasant in the moment but leave us bitter and ultimately unsatisfied. We also learn how much we need God's grace in order to spend eternity with him and resist the temptations of this life.

Others argue that if God were fair, then hell would be temporary and someone could eventually "work themselves" out of it. But it's possible that one reason that hell is eternal is because the damned continue to reject God. This means that their punishment is everlasting because they make it that way. Moreover, no one can ever work himself out of hell any more than he could work himself into heaven. Salvation is a gift from God that we "work out" in this life (Phil. 2:12) by persevering in faith and working through love until the end of our lives (Matt. 10:22; Gal. 5:6). The Bible makes it clear that the only time we can accept this gift, or this free offer of grace from God, is during our earthly lives. Upon our death, our choices in this life forever seal what our destinies will be in the next life (Heb. 9:27).

254. Is it possible that no one will go to hell?

In 2011, popular Evangelical pastor Rob Bell published a book called *Love Wins: Heaven, Hell, and the Fate of Every Person Who Ever Lived*. Bell argues for a position on hell called *universalism*, or the belief that all human beings will, at some point or another, choose to be with God and that none of them will spend an eternity in hell. His book even landed on the cover of *Time* magazine with the provocative question, "What If There's No Hell?"

The possibility that hell is empty is not a twenty-first century novelty. In the third century, the ecclesial writer Origen argued for *apokatastasis*, or a "restoration" that would unite all things, including unrepentant sinners, to God. This would seem to rule out the possibility that anyone would spend an eternity in hell, though modern commenters are divided over the implications of Origen's theology on this question.[388] According to Bible scholar Richard Bauckham,

> Until the nineteenth century almost all Christian theologians taught the reality of eternal torment in hell. Here and there, outside the theological mainstream, were some who believed that the wicked would be finally annihilated. . . . Even fewer were the advocates of universal salvation . . . though these few included some major theologians of the early church.[389]

This uniformity of thought began to change with the rise of denominations like the Universalist Church of America (which exists today under the name Unitarian Universalism). Even prominent Protestant theologians like Karl Barth expressed sympathy for universalism, which motivated the Catholic theologian Hans Urs von Balthasar to write his book *Dare We Hope "That All Men Be Saved"?*

Von Balthasar does not, as he is sometimes falsely accused of, argue for universalism. Rather, he suggests that hell is a real possibility because we "stand completely and utterly under judgment, and have no right, nor is it possible for us, to peer in advance at the Judge's cards."[390] But if universalism were true, then the "Judge's cards," or our eternal destinies, would not be a mystery because every card would reveal the same outcome—eventual eternal life with God. Von Balthasar did, however, argue for the view that we can, and should, *hope* that no one will go to hell. He writes, "Love hopes all things (1 Cor. 13:7). It cannot do otherwise than to hope for the reconciliation of all men to Christ."[391]

Should we hope that no one goes to hell? Any Christian can affirm von Balthasar's argument in the sense that they should not be indifferent to the plight of the damned, or even rejoice in it. Consider Ezekiel 18:23, where God says, "Have I any pleasure in the death of the wicked and not rather that he should turn from his way and live?" Or God's desire in 1 Timothy 2:4 that all people be saved. But just because we can hope and pray that each individual would turn to God before death (or even at the point of death), it doesn't follow that we can realistically hope that every individual has done or will do this. Hoping for the salvation of *anybody* is not the same thing as hoping for the salvation of *everybody*. Hoping for the latter becomes problematic because Scripture seems to affirm that some people will be damned, and we can't hope for something that God has said will not happen.

For example, in *Crossing the Threshold of Hope*, Pope St. John Paul II said, "In Matthew's Gospel [Jesus] speaks clearly of those who will go to eternal punishment (see Matt. 25:46). Who will these be? The Church has never made any pronouncement."[392] The late pontiff doubted only *who* might end up in hell, not that some people would consign themselves to such an awful fate. Indeed, the *Catechism* says, "Jesus solemnly proclaims that he 'will send his angels, and they will gather . . . all evil doers, and throw them into the furnace of fire'" (1034). This does not seem to be a hypothetical scenario, but rather a foreboding promise to those who persist in practicing evil.

Remember that God can save people who seem to have rejected him because he alone knows the secrets of the heart (Ps. 44:12). This includes God's unique knowledge of last-minute, genuine repentance of sin. That's why the *Catechism* tells us, "In the eucharistic liturgy and in the daily prayers of her faithful, the Church implores the mercy of God, who does not want 'any to perish, but all to come to repentance'" (1037).

255. Are we living in the end times?

The end times. The last days. The end of the world. People have wondered about these for thousands of years.

Some religions have the idea that history is an endless series of cycles, just as day follows night, one year follows another, and generations are born, grow up, and pass from the scene. But the Bible teaches something else. Although there are cycles in the world, they don't endlessly repeat.

Instead, history follows a definite course. It tells a story with a beginning, a middle, and an end. The beginning of the story is creation: "In the beginning God created the heavens and the earth" (Gen. 1:1). After man fell into sin, God began working to redeem him. He made a covenant with the patriarch Abraham, from whom came God's chosen people, Israel. Then, "when the time had fully come, God sent forth his Son" (Gal. 4:4), and Jesus Christ performed the supreme act of redemption by his death on the cross. After rising from the dead, he ascended into heaven and sent the Holy Spirit to empower his followers to spread his message throughout the world.

These events are not part of a cycle that keeps repeating. They are unique parts of God's plan of the ages. And that plan has an end point. God promised that Jesus would *return* and that the *dead would be raised*. Following the *Final Judgment*, there will be "a new heaven and a new earth" (Rev. 21:1), where God will dwell with his people and "wipe away every tear from their eyes, and death shall be no more, neither shall there be mourning nor crying nor pain any more, for the former things have passed away" (Rev. 21:4).

History is thus heading toward its end point, and Christians have always wondered how close they might be to that end. There is even a special branch of theology devoted to the subject: *eschatology* (Greek: *eschatos,* "last," *logos* "teaching"), or the study of the *Last Things.*

Eschatology has two parts. It is called *individual* or *personal* eschatology when it deals with the last things that individual people experience: "the four Last Things" (i.e., death, judgment, hell, and heaven—with purgatory thrown in as a bonus topic).

The other part, which we will deal with here, is called *universal, cosmic,* or *corporate* eschatology, and it deals with the last things the world as a whole will experience.

So, are we living the end times?

This is a natural question to ask in a society that has changed more in the last century than in the many thousand years that preceded it.

Traditional values are under attack. Millions live under totalitarian regimes. The twentieth century saw two world wars that were cataclysmic global conflicts and then endured a decades-long Cold War with the prospect of imminent nuclear annihilation. Today, we live with the threat that new and even more deadly wars could break out, with even more advanced military hardware. We face terrorism, pandemics, and social upheaval, and the uneasy prospect of technology running amok. Some are even contemplating the possibility that, because of artificial intelligence, we may face a "technological singularity" that could fundamentally transform or end the human race.

No wonder people ask if we're living in the end times!

The answer is that *we are*. In his first letter, St. John makes a striking statement: "Children, it is the last hour; and as you have heard that antichrist is coming, so now many antichrists have come; therefore, we know that it is the last hour" (1 John 2:18).

Not only does this passage contain an ominous reference to the Antichrist—even multiple antichrists—it twice repeats the bold declaration that "it is the last hour." So, yes, there is a sense in which we are living in the end times.

But John wrote this in the first century. The "last hour" he speaks of has been going on for almost 2,000 years. So, although it's true that we are living in the end times, this doesn't mean what many suppose. From a biblical perspective, the end times—and even the last hour—cover a much broader sweep of history than we'd initially guess.

To understand this, it's helpful to look at a pair of passages from St. Peter. On the one hand, he tells his readers, "The end of all things is at hand; therefore, keep sane and sober for your prayers" (1 Pet. 4:7). On the other hand, he tells them, "But do not ignore this one fact, beloved, that with the Lord one day is as a thousand years, and a thousand years as one day" (2 Pet. 3:8).

In other words: yes, we are near the end, but God doesn't reckon time the way we do. We can't calculate the time left in human terms.

This provides the key to understanding the sense in which we're living in the end times. The Christian age is the final stage of world history, the last period in God's plan. All the ages that preceded the coming of his son are past, and there will be no future ages before the Second Coming and the consummation of the world. We are thus in the final period—the end times—from God's perspective.

Many have tried to calculate just how close we are to the end, and they have repeatedly set dates for Christ's return or other apocalyptic events.

So far, every one of them has been wrong.

The practice of date-setting has a poor track record, and the Church warns the faithful against it: "The Last Judgment will come when Christ returns in glory. Only the Father knows the day and the hour; only he determines the moment of its coming" (CCC 1040).

Nonetheless, there are certain signs that will precede the Second Coming, including a widespread conversion of the Jewish people (CCC 674) and the final persecution of the Church (675–677).

256. When will the end times take place?

It is universally agreed among Christians that certain events are yet to come. These include the Second Coming of Christ, the final resurrection of the dead, the Last Judgment, and the establishment of the eternal order, with the appearance of what Scripture describes as "a new heaven and a new earth" (Rev. 21:1).

The biggest question upon which Christians disagree is whether, after the Second Coming—but *before* the final resurrection and the other events mentioned—there will be a lengthy period in which Jesus physically reigns on earth, perhaps from the city of Jerusalem.

Revelation 20:1–6 does describe a period of "a thousand years" in which Christ and the saints rule before the final resurrection, but the interpretation of this text is in dispute.

The position that it is an earthly reign, and that it comes after the Second Coming, is historically known as "millenarianism"—from the Latin word *millennium* (*mille* "thousand" + *annus* "year").

Recently, Protestant theologians have introduced a specialized set of terms connected with this view. The belief that the Second Coming will be followed by a millennium in which Christ rules on earth has come to be called *premillennialism* because Christ is said to come back before (*pre-*) the millennium.

An alternative view is known as *postmillennialism*. It holds that there will be a future golden age in which Christ reigns *from heaven*. The Second Coming will then occur after (*post-*) this millennium.

A final position is known as *amillennialism*. This view holds that there will not be a future golden age on earth, either before or after the Second Coming. Instead, Christ is reigning from heaven right now.

The word *amillennialism* suggests that there is no (*a-*) millennium. However, this is a misnomer, since people who hold this viewpoint do acknowledge the heavenly reign of Christ—and the effects it is having on earth here and now through God's action in the world.

Since the Protestant Reformation, all three of these views have had ups and downs. The original Reformers were primarily amillennial. In the nineteenth century, postmillennialism was common. And amid the catastrophic wars of the twentieth century, premillennialism became popular.

Of special note is a Protestant school of thought that arose in the mid-nineteenth century known as *dispensationalism*. This view embraced premillennialism but added a new distinctive teaching: the Rapture.

According to this view, there will be an event *before* the future, earthly millennium in which Christ returns in the sky and "snatches away" his earthly followers, taking them to heaven for a period of time (typically seven years) before the millennium begins. The name *Rapture* is based on the Latin word *rapere* ("to snatch").

Because of this new teaching, scholars sometimes speak of "historic premillennialism"—which does not posit that there will be a Rapture before the millennium—and "dispensational premillennialism," which does.

In the late twentieth century, dispensational premillennialism became very common in Evangelical Protestant circles, being advocated in books and movies like *The Late Great Planet Earth* and *Left Behind*. However, it was less common among other Protestants, and today its popularity has begun to fade.

For its part, the Catholic Church does not use the terminology that has developed in Protestant circles. Church documents still refer to *premillennialism* by its historic name, *millenarianism*.

This view is incompatible with Catholic teaching. According to the *Catechism of the Catholic Church*, "The Church has rejected even modified forms of this falsification of the kingdom to come under the name of millenarianism" (676). The *Catechism* then references a 1944 document that concluded that this view "cannot be taught safely" (Denzinger-Schönmetzer, *Enchiridion Symbolorum* 3839).

The Church has not explicitly rejected the view that there will be a future golden age on earth in which Christ rules from heaven (i.e., postmillennialism), though it has said that God's kingdom will be fulfilled "not by a historic triumph of the Church through a progressive ascendancy, but only by God's victory over the final unleashing of evil" (CCC 677).

Consequently, Catholic thinkers have generally held to what Protestants would call amillennialism—the view that the millennium is happening now, with Christ reigning from heaven, with corresponding positive effects on earth (668–671).

257. What does the Church teach about the end times?

The Catholic Church does not have a detailed set of teachings regarding precisely what will happen in our future nor about exactly how and when the end times prophesized in Scripture will be take place. It largely leaves the interpretation of biblical texts to individual scholars.

However, the Church does have a set of teachings in broad strokes regarding what will happen in the future.

First, the Church rejects the theory that there will be a period before the end of the world in which Christ reigns physically on earth—perhaps from Jerusalem—as taught in millenarianism or premillennialism (CCC 676). Instead, the Church teaches that in the present age, Christ already reigns from heaven (668; see Matt. 28:18; 1 Cor. 15:25; Eph. 1:20–21) and through the Church on earth (CCC 669–670; see Matt. 28:19–20; Eph. 1:22).

This present reign is partial in that not all of Christ's enemies have been defeated. There is still evil in the world, and, as St. Paul tells us, Jesus "must reign until he has put all his enemies under his feet. The last enemy to be destroyed is death" (1 Cor. 15:25–26). Therefore, Christ's kingdom will be fulfilled in a more definitive way in the future (CCC 671).

> According to the Lord, the present time is the time of the Spirit and of witness, but also a time still marked by "distress" and the trial of evil which does not spare the Church [Acts 1:8; 1 Cor. 7:26; Eph. 5:16; 1 Pet. 4:17] and ushers in the struggles of the last days. It is a time of waiting and watching (CCC 672).

How long this time will last is not known.

> Since the Ascension Christ's coming in glory has been imminent, even though "it is not for you to know times or seasons which the Father has fixed by his own authority" [Acts 1:7; see Mark 13:32]. This eschatological coming could be accomplished at any moment, even if both it and the final trial that will precede it are "delayed" (CCC 673).

This imminence does not mean that there will be no signs of the Second Coming. On the contrary, there will be.

One of these signs is a large-scale conversion of the Jewish people. "The glorious Messiah's coming is suspended at every moment of history until his recognition by 'all Israel,' for 'a hardening has come upon part of Israel' in their 'unbelief' toward Jesus" (CCC 674, quoting from Rom. 11:20–26).

Another event that will occur is a great calamity, which the *Catechism* refers to as "the Church's ultimate trial," explaining,

> Before Christ's Second Coming, the Church must pass through a final trial that will shake the faith of many believers. The persecution that accompanies her pilgrimage on earth will unveil the "mystery of iniquity" in the form of a religious deception offering men an apparent solution to their problems at the price of apostasy from the truth. The supreme religious deception is that of the Antichrist, a pseudo-messianism by which man glorifies himself in place of God and of his Messiah come in the flesh (675).

This trial will take a heavy toll on the Church, which "will follow her Lord in his death and resurrection. The kingdom will be fulfilled, then, not by a historic triumph of the Church through a progressive ascendancy, but only by God's victory over the final unleashing of evil, which will cause his bride to come down from heaven [see Rev. 13:8; 20:7–10; 21:2–4]" (CCC 677).

When Christ's final enemy—death—is destroyed, the resurrection of the dead will occur, with every human who has ever lived brought back to life (CCC 988–1004) and convoked to the Final Judgment.

At this point, men will receive their final recompense—either heaven, if they have opened themselves to God's love, or hell, if they have definitively closed themselves off from his offer of mercy and love (CCC 1023–1037).

> After the universal judgment, the righteous will reign for ever with Christ, glorified in body and soul. The universe itself will be renewed (1042).
>
> Sacred Scripture calls this mysterious renewal, which will transform humanity and the world, "new heavens and a new earth" [2 Pet. 3:1; see Rev. 21:1] (1043).
>
> In this new universe, the heavenly Jerusalem, God will have his dwelling among men [see Rev. 21:5]. "He will wipe away every tear from their eyes, and death shall be no more, neither shall there be mourning nor crying nor pain any more, for the former things have passed away [Rev. 21:4] (1044).

Although much about the future remains uncertain, we may be confident that the whole course of history is in God's hands and that he will one day bring it to a grand and glorious conclusion. He will end the tyranny of death and suffering, and fulfill our deepest longings in ways that far exceed anything we can presently imagine.

258. What does the Old Testament say about the end times?

The earlier books of the Old Testament don't have much to say about the end times. However, as God's revelation progressed, he began to disclose more about them.

Passages like Isaiah 7:14 contain predictions of the Messiah, whose coming would inaugurate the final period of world history. The Old Testament also contains veiled prophecies of Christ's death and resurrection.

The expectation of the Messiah was founded on a covenant God made with King David, telling him, "Your house and your kingdom shall be made sure for ever before me; your throne shall be established forever" (2 Sam. 7:16). There might be temporary interruptions in the line of Davidic kings, but the permanent nature of this covenant meant that a son of David would eventually appear and reign as God's anointed king or "Messiah" (Hebrew *mashiyakh*, "anointed one").

Many expected the Messiah to be an ordinary political ruler, but God had something different in mind. Prophecy revealed that—before his glorious reign would begin—the Messiah would experience suffering and death. But people would not understand this:

> Who considered that he was cut off out of the land of the living, stricken for the transgression of my people? And they made his grave with the wicked and with a rich man in his death, although he had done no violence, and there was no deceit in his mouth (Isa. 53:8–9).

Yet he would come back from the dead in triumph, having redeemed people from their sins:

> He shall see the fruit of the travail of his soul and be satisfied; by his knowledge shall the Righteous One, my Servant, make many to be accounted righteous; and he shall bear their iniquities.

> Therefore, I will divide him a portion with the great, and he shall divide the spoil with the strong; because he poured out his soul to death, and was numbered with the transgressors; yet he bore the sin of many, and made intercession for the transgressors (Isa. 53:11–12).

The Old Testament also has prophecies about the messianic or Christian age:

- Ezekiel 36:25–26 predicts that God will "sprinkle clean water upon" his people and give them "a new heart and a new spirit," which corresponds to the sacrament of baptism.
- Jeremiah 31:31 predicts that God will make a New Covenant, which Christ inaugurated.
- Malachi 1:11 prophecies "a pure offering" being made to God everywhere among the Gentiles, prefiguring the Eucharist.
- Isaiah 66:21 says that God will even take some Gentiles to be his priests, pointing to a Christian priesthood that isn't dependent on being a descendant of the tribe of Levi.

When it comes to events at the very end of the Christian age, we learn there will be a time of trouble that will be followed by the resurrection and judgment of the dead. The prophet Daniel is told,

> At that time shall arise Michael, the great prince who has charge of your people. And there shall be a time of trouble, such as never has been since there was a nation till that time; but at that time your people shall be delivered, every one whose name shall be found written in the book. And many of those who sleep in the dust of the earth shall awake, some to everlasting life, and some to shame and everlasting contempt (Dan. 12:1–2).

This time of trouble will be followed by the resurrection of the dead ("many" is another way of saying "all" in Hebrew, so "many who sleep in the dust" means all of the dead).

The resurrection of the dead also appears in other passages, such as when Isaiah says, "Your dead shall live, their bodies shall rise. O dwellers in the dust, awake and sing for joy!" (Isa. 26:19).

When the dead rise, there will be great rejoicing, which Isaiah describes as a feast:

> On this mountain the *Lord* of hosts will make for all peoples a feast of fat things, a feast of choice wines—of fat things full of marrow, of choice wines well refined. And he will destroy on this mountain the covering that is cast over all peoples, the veil that is spread over all nations. He will swallow up death for ever, and the Lord *God* will wipe away tears from all faces (Isa. 25:6–8).

But not all will participate in this joy, because the dead will first be judged. As Daniel was told, some will wake "to everlasting life, and some to shame and everlasting contempt." The righteous thus will be rewarded, and the wicked will bear the consequences of their sins, having excluded themselves from God's joy.

The destruction of death means a fundamental change in the way the world operates, so Isaiah also prophesies that God will produce "a new heavens and a new earth" (Isa. 65:17). This renovated earth will include a new Jerusalem: "Be glad and rejoice forever in that which I create; for behold, I create Jerusalem a rejoicing" (Isa. 65:18).

These themes figure prominently in what the New Testament has to say about the end times.

259. What does Jesus tell us about the end times?

Because the end times stretch from Christ's first coming to his second, everything Jesus says about the Christian age deals with them.

He gave some of his prophecies in the form of parables, such as how his kingdom would grow from a tiny beginning (Matt. 13:31–32) or how it would contain both the good and the bad (Matt. 13:36–43).

However, Jesus also gave prophecies in a more traditional manner, known as the *Olivet Discourse*. This is a speech that he gave on the Mount of Olives, across the Kidron Valley from Jerusalem's temple. It is his longest prophecy, and it's found in Matthew 24–25, Mark 13, and Luke 21.

Shortly before the Crucifixion, Jesus' disciples remarked on how beautiful and impressive in size the Jerusalem temple was. He responded by saying, "Do you see these great buildings? There will not be left here one stone upon another, that will not be thrown down" (Mark 13:1).

The disciples were startled and asked him, "When will this be, and what will be the sign when these things are all to be accomplished?" (Mark 13:4; see Luke 21:7).

Because Jesus responded using apocalyptic language, including cosmic catastrophe language, many assume he was talking about events in our future. Or, alternately, they assume he was predicting the end of the world in his own day.

To understand the Olivet Discourse, we must read it in light of the two questions Jesus is answering: How long will it be until the temple is destroyed? What sign will God give to show this is about to happen?

Answering the first question, Jesus says, "This generation will not pass away before all these things take place" (Mark 13:30)—and it didn't. The temple was destroyed less than forty years after Jesus uttered these words, in A.D. 70, and many people who witnessed the Crucifixion were still alive.

Answering the second question, Jesus says a number of things will happen before the destruction of the temple, and he specifically warns that *not all* of these are signs that the time is imminent:

> When you hear of wars and rumors of wars, do not be alarmed; this must take place, but the end is not yet. For nation will rise against nation, and kingdom against kingdom; there will be earthquakes in various places, there will be famines; this is but the beginning of the sufferings (Mark 13:7–8).

He then names a sign that *does* call for action: "But when you see the desolating sacrilege set up where it ought not to be (let the reader understand), then let those who are in Judea flee to the mountains" (Mark 13:14).

The desolating sacrilege—also called the *abomination of desolation*—was an event predicted and partially fulfilled in the Old Testament. It dealt with pagan forces entering and desecrating the temple (Dan. 11:31; 12:11; 1 Macc. 1:51–61; see Dan. 9:27; Matt. 24:15).

Gentile readers would not be familiar with this, so Luke clarifies in his version of the discourse:

> But when you see Jerusalem surrounded by armies, then know that its desolation has come near. Then let those who are in Judea flee to the mountains, and let those who are inside the city depart, and let not those who are out in the country enter it (Luke 21:20–21).

The approach of pagan armies thus represents the abomination that will cause the desolation of Jerusalem and its temple.

On the literal level, the Olivet Discourse as found in Mark and Luke is about the events leading up to A.D. 70. However,, prophecy can have more than one fulfillment, so it may also point to events that are still in our future.

It's significant that Matthew adds certain parables to the Olivet Discourse (Matt. 24:45–25:46). These clearly deal with the Second Coming, and to set them up, Matthew has included an additional question at the beginning of the discourse: "What will be the sign of your coming and of the close of the age?" (Matt. 24:3).

The natural way to understand the Olivet Discourse is that the common material found in all three of these Gospels has its primary, literal fulfillment in the years leading up to A.D. 70, but may also foreshadow events in our future; *and* that the added material in Matthew deals directly with the Second Coming.

260. Did Jesus predict the end of the world in his own day?

Because of certain statements Jesus made, some have thought he predicted the end of the world in his own day. Even the apostles had to adjust their interpretations!

One such statement was that "This generation will not pass away" before the events of the Olivet Discourse take place (Mark 13:30). However, Jesus wasn't predicting the end of the world when he said this. When read in context, this statement refers to the events leading up to the destruction of the Jerusalem temple in A.D. 70.

Another statement often misunderstood is when Jesus describes the coming events and says, "And then they will see the Son of Man coming in clouds with great power and glory. And then he will send out the angels, and gather his elect from the four winds" (Mark 13:26–27).

Since Jesus will definitively return from heaven at the end of the world (Acts 1:11), many have understood his remarks on this occasion as a reference to the Second Coming. And, because prophecy can have more than one fulfillment, it may point to the Second Coming. However, this wasn't what it referred to in the context of events leading up to the destruction of the temple.

Part of the confusion is caused by the fact that many only study their Bible and don't read the historical sources that reveal what happened when Jesus' words were fulfilled.

The Jewish historian Josephus, who was an eyewitness of the events, reported that God gave great signs in the heavens to show that the temple would soon be destroyed. These included a star that resembled a sword hanging over the city, unexplained light shining around the temple and its altar, chariots and soldiers fighting in the clouds, and heavenly voices saying, "We are departing" from the temple.[393] The same signs are mentioned by the Roman historian Tacitus.[394]

It is quite possible that the sign of Jesus appeared in the clouds to signify judgment. However, it's also possible that this should be understood as a continuation of the common Old Testament image of God riding the clouds like a chariot, coming in judgment on those who have done wrong (Ps. 104:3; Isa. 19:1–2; Jer. 4:13–14; Ezek. 1:4; 26–28). It was even prophesied that the Son of Man would ride on such a cloud and be given dominion by the Lord (Dan. 7:13–14).

In such passages, God did not appear visibly in the clouds but came spiritually as a judge. Jesus' prophecy thus may have been fulfilled symbolically in the events of A.D. 70. And, now that he has been given dominion by the Father, he gathers his elect or chosen people from the four winds through the spread of the gospel. The cessation of worship at the Jewish temple thus corresponds to the dawning of the Christian age.

This also explains a statement that Jesus makes to the high priest Caiaphas. When asked if he is the Christ, the Son of God, Jesus replies: "I am; and you will see the Son of Man sitting at the right hand of Power, and coming with the clouds of heaven" (Mark 14:62).

Jesus is not prophesying that the Second Coming will occur during Caiaphas's lifetime. His statement makes reference to Daniel 7:13–14, where the Son of Man is brought before God *in heaven* to receive his kingdom. The prophecy thus refers to the Ascension (Acts 1:9), when Jesus received his kingdom (Acts 7:55–56), where he now reigns (1 Cor. 15:24–26).

A final statement that should be considered is, "There are some standing here who will not taste death before they see that the kingdom of God has come with power" (Mark 9:1; see Matt. 16:28; Luke 9:27).

This is not about the end of the world, for "the kingdom of God is in the midst of you" (Luke 17:21), and some of Jesus' disciples were about to see it manifested in a powerful way.

In each Synoptic Gospel (Matthew, Mark, and Luke), the Transfiguration *immediately* follows Jesus' announcement (Matt. 17:1–9; Mark 9:2–10; Luke 9:28–36). Jesus takes three of the disciples—Peter, James, and John—up a mountain. His clothing becomes dazzlingly bright; Moses and Elijah appear beside him; everyone is enveloped in a cloud; and God the Father speaks from heaven, identifying Jesus as his Son, his chosen, and declaring, "Hear him!"

This manifestation is the coming of the kingdom "with power" that Jesus referred to, and the text of each Gospel suggests this is the way the Evangelists understood it. Not only does the Transfiguration happen right after the announcement, but each Gospel says it was about a week later (Matt. 17:1; Mark 9:1; Luke 9:28) the slight difference in the number of days may reflect reckoning parts of days as wholes and counting days as beginning at sunset, midnight, or dawn. Peter, James, and John thus were the three who did not taste death before they saw the kingdom coming with power.[395]

261. What does St. Paul say about the end times?

Paul's letters don't deal primarily with prophecy. However, they do contain prophetic passages. He regularly stresses common Christian themes such as the Second Coming of Christ, the Final Judgment, and the salvation and rewarding of the righteous.

In one of his earliest letters—1 Thessalonians—he had to correct his readers' understanding on certain prophetic points. Some Thessalonians apparently thought that those who died before the Second Coming would miss out on the kingdom of God, but Paul assured them this was not the case: "For the Lord himself will descend from heaven with a cry of command, with the archangel's call, and with the sound of the trumpet of God. And the dead in Christ will rise first" (1 Thess. 4:16).

He warned them not to be concerned about when the Second Coming would happen, and said it was not humanly predictable: "But as to the times and the seasons, brethren, you have no need to have anything written to you. For you yourselves know well that the day of the Lord will come like a thief in the night" (1 Thess. 5:1–2).

Some Thessalonians continued to misunderstand these points, even thinking that the day of the Lord may have already come. Paul thus told them that this is not the case and gave a number of signs that will precede the event: "That day will not come, unless the rebellion comes first, and the man of lawlessness is revealed, the son of perdition, who opposes and exalts himself against every so-called god or object of worship, so that he takes his seat in the temple of God, proclaiming himself to be God" (2 Thess. 2:3–4).

Paul states that the coming of the "lawless one" will be accompanied by false signs and wonders that will deceive many (2 Thess. 2:9–12). This apparently plays a role in the "rebellion" (Greek: *apostasia*, "apostasy") that will accompany the man of lawlessness (see 2 Tim. 3:1–9).

He also indicates that something is currently holding back these events (2 Thess. 2:6–7), but eventually, "The lawless one will be revealed, and the Lord Jesus will slay him with the breath of his mouth and destroy him by his appearing and his coming" (2 Thess. 2:8).

Paul also had to correct another group of Christians—this time at Corinth—who were denying that we will be resurrected on the Last Day. His reply was pointed: "If the dead are not raised, then Christ has not been raised. If Christ has not been raised, your faith is futile and you are still in your sins" (1 Cor. 15:16–17). He thus explained to them that the resurrection of Christ was simply the first fruits of the great harvest of resurrection to occur at the Second Coming (vv. 23–26).

The Corinthians were curious about what our resurrected bodies will be like, so Paul compares the difference between our present bodies and our future ones to the difference between a seed and the plant that grows from it. He explains that the resurrection will involve a transformation that will change our current earthly, mortal bodies into glorious, immortal ones (1 Cor. 15:35–44), which will be like Jesus' resurrected body (1 Cor. 15:49)—a theme he also stresses elsewhere (Phil. 3:20–21). For those who are alive at the time of the Second Coming, this transformation will occur "in the twinkling of an eye," without their dying first (1 Cor. 15:51–52).

The resurrection of the dead also will be accompanied by divine judgment, and Paul indicates that the saints (i.e., faithful Christians) will judge the world, including even angels (1 Cor. 6:2–3).

262. Should we expect a Rapture at any moment?

The end-time prophecies contained in Scripture have led Christians in every age to wondered whether they will be the ones to face such tribulations. The historic answer is *yes*. Jesus warned us that we would have to face persecution (John 15:20), and no generation of Christianity has been exempted.

However, in the nineteenth century, dispensationalists began teaching that Christians will not have to face this trial. Instead, before the great tribulation begins, they will be caught up to heaven and spared the reign of the Antichrist and the horrors it contains.

They referred to this event as the *Rapture*, based on the Latin word *rapio* ("to snatch, to carry away"), in reference to an event Paul describes when "we who are alive, who are left, shall be caught up together with them in the clouds to meet the Lord in the air; and so we shall always be with the Lord" (1 Thess. 4:17).

According to the scenario dispensationalists propose, the Rapture is the next event in God's plan and will happen without warning, at any moment. Jesus will descend into the atmosphere and all true Christians will be caught up to be with him in the sky. This will include dead Christians, who will be raised back to life. Jesus will then take his followers back to heaven while the Antichrist reigns and all hell breaks loose on earth. Then, at the end of the great tribulation, Jesus will return to earth, slay the Antichrist, and begin his thousand-year earthly reign.

There are multiple problems with this view. First, as we have seen, the Church rejects the idea of a future earthly millennium, so the overall scenario is based on a false premise.

Furthermore, the dispensationalist view does not fit what St. Paul says. It splits the Second Coming in half, with Jesus first descending to claim his Church and then, years later, returning to deal with the Antichrist. Yet in the relevant passages, Paul speaks only of a single coming.

This is confirmed when he takes up the same subject in his second letter to the Thessalonians, referring to a single event involving "the coming of our Lord Jesus Christ and our assembling to meet him" (2 Thess. 2:1), the same event he had spoken of just prior to this, describing what will take place "when the Lord Jesus is revealed from heaven with his mighty angels . . . when he comes on that day to be glorified in his saints" (1:7, 10).

Paul very clearly explains, however, that this "day of the Lord . . . will not come, unless the rebellion comes first, and the man of lawlessness is revealed, the son of perdition, who opposes and exalts himself against every so-called god or object of worship, so that he takes his seat in the temple of God, proclaiming himself to be God." (2:3-4).

In the end, "The Lord Jesus will slay him with the breath of his mouth and destroy him by his appearing and his coming" (2:8). On the same occasion, "those who do not obey the gospel of our Lord Jesus . . . shall suffer the punishment of eternal destruction and exclusion from the presence of the Lord" (1:9).

The sequence Paul lays out clearly does not involve Christians being caught up to heaven while the Antichrist reigns on earth a thousand years before the Final Judgment. Instead, it involves the Antichrist reigning first *and then* Jesus returning to destroy the Antichrist, raise the dead, accomplish the Final Judgment, and take the faithful to be with him in the heavens.

Thus we shouldn't expect a Rapture to take place at any moment now. We *will* be caught up to be with Jesus—after the reign of the man of lawlessness, not before.

In the meantime, the promise of Jesus—"I will keep you from the hour of trial which is coming on the whole world, to try those who dwell upon the earth" (Rev. 3:10)—should not be interpreted as an exemption from struggles but as a special grace of perseverance in the midst of them: "While I was with them, I kept them in thy name.... I do not pray that thou shouldst take them out of the world, but that thou shouldst keep them from the evil one" (John 16:12, 15).

263. Who (or what) is the Antichrist?

One of the most notorious and misunderstood figures from biblical prophecy is the *Antichrist*. There are only four verses in the Bible that speak about the Antichrist—at least under that name—and they are all in the letters of St. John.

As the name suggests, the Antichrist is someone opposed to (*anti-*) Christ. The coming of the Antichrist is linked to the end times, but John reveals that these began in the first century. He also reveals that there is more than one Antichrist, telling his readers: "As you have heard that Antichrist is coming, so now many Antichrists have come; therefore, we know that it is the last hour" (1 John 2:18).

John identifies these individual antichrists as former members of the Christian community: "They went out from us, but they were not of us; for if they had been of us, they would have continued with us" (v. 19).

Though they claimed to be Christians, in fact they were heretics: "Who is the liar but he who denies that Jesus is the Christ? This is the Antichrist, he who denies the Father and the Son" (v. 22). "For many deceivers have gone out into the world, men who will not acknowledge the coming of Jesus Christ in the flesh; such a one is the deceiver and the Antichrist" (2 John 7).

The individual antichrists—both then and now—are those who deny the truth of Christ incarnate, either by denying that he was born in human flesh (as some early heretics did) or by denying the Christian faith altogether. This movement of antichrists is animated by evil spirits: "Every spirit which does not confess Jesus is not of God. This is the spirit of Antichrist, of which you heard that it was coming, and now it is in the world already" (1 John 4:3).

The portrait of the Antichrist that John gives us is thus of a dark, anti-Christian spiritual movement that has been in the world since the first century. But will this movement culminate with a single person serving as the final villain of world history?

Many have thought that it will, and they have proposed that this villain is discussed under other names elsewhere in Scripture. For example, some have identified him as the "man of lawlessness" or "man of sin" spoken of by St. Paul:

> The day of the Lord . . . will not come, unless the rebellion comes first, and the man of lawlessness is revealed, the son of perdition, who opposes and exalts himself against every so-called god or object of worship, so that he takes his seat in the temple of God, proclaiming himself to be God.

The activity of the lawless one by the activity of Satan will be with all power and with pretended signs and wonders, and with all wicked deception for those who are to perish, because they refused to love the truth and so be saved (2 Thess. 2:3-4, 9-10). Others have identified him as a figure in the book of Revelation that is pictured as a great beast arising from the sea (13:1–18). Throughout history, most commentators have held that there will be a single individual who opposes Christ at the end of the world. However, the *Catechism* is cautious on this question and does not settle it one way or the other.

It links the Antichrist to a movement or ideology of "pseudo-messianism," without precluding that this movement would have a single person serving as its leader:

> Before Christ's Second Coming the Church must pass through a final trial that will shake the faith of many believers. The persecution that accompanies her pilgrimage on earth will unveil the "mystery of iniquity" in the form of a religious deception offering men an apparent solution to their problems at the price of apostasy from the truth. The supreme religious deception is that of the

> Antichrist, a pseudo-messianism by which man glorifies himself in place of God and of his Messiah come in the flesh (CCC 675).

264. Do Israel and the Jewish people have a special role in the end times?

Christian scholars of all persuasions have recognized that God's plan of the ages unfolds in stages. Prior to the coming of Christ, God dealt with the people of Israel in a unique way, taking them as his chosen people among all the peoples of the earth.

With the beginning of the Christian age, God's family expanded to include people from every nation who, like the Jewish people, become children of Abraham by faith (Gal. 3:7; see Rom. 2:25–29). The Church thus became a new chosen people, mirroring what the children of Israel had been (see Exod. 19:6; 1 Pet. 2:9; Rev. 5:9–10).

This raised the question of what role the Jewish people now have in God's plan. After the Reformation, some Protestants proposed that the Israelites no longer had a special role. The Church had completely taken over the promises God had made to Israel, and so Jews no longer had a unique status. They were simply one people among many, with no special destiny. This view is sometimes called "replacement theology," because it holds that the Church has replaced Israel in God's plan.

However, beginning in the nineteenth century, a school of thought arose in Protestant circles known as *dispensationalism*. One of the distinctive teachings of this movement is that Israel very much remains God's chosen people, and it has a unique role that has yet to be fulfilled. According to some dispensationalist authors, the Christian age is simply a "parenthesis" in God's plan, in which he deals with Gentiles, and at the close of this age he will turn back to dealing with Jews.

Dispensationalists commonly hold that the Jewish people still have a God-given right to the promised land, and it was taken as a prophetic sign when the modern nation-state of Israel was founded in 1948. Many dispensationalists expected the Second Coming to occur within a forty-year generation of Israel's founding, though the twentieth century ended without this happening.

They still commonly hold that Jesus will return soon, after which he will reign as a king in Jerusalem for a thousand years. Dispensationalism is thus a form of premillennialism. According to dispensationalists, the Jewish people will have a prominent role in the world during the millennium, there will be a temple in Jerusalem, and—according to many—animal sacrifices will again be offered to God there.

The Catholic Church's position does not go to either the extreme proposed by replacement theology or the one advocated by dispensationalists. Regarding the former, the Church acknowledges that the Jewish people still have a special role in God's plan. As St. Paul says, "I ask, then, has God rejected his people? By no means! . . . As regards election they are beloved for the sake of their forefathers. For the gifts and the call of God are irrevocable" (Rom. 11:1, 28–29; see CCC 839).

On the other hand, the view proposed by dispensationalists is problematic. Although the Church does not have a teaching on whether the Jewish people still have a divine right to the Holy Land—or whether the current state of Israel has any prophetic significance—it rejects the dispensational belief in the millennium as a future, earthly reign of Christ (CCC 676).

Especially problematic is the idea that God's plan includes literal animal sacrifices being offered in a future Jerusalem temple. Christ did away with these by offering himself "once for all" on the cross (Heb. 7:27; 8:13; 9:12, 26; 10:10)!

However, one sign of the end is that there will be a major conversion of the Jewish people to Christ (Rom. 11:11–12, 25), which apparently occurs shortly before the end of the world (Rom. 11:15).

Thus the *Catechism* states:

> The glorious Messiah's coming is suspended at every moment of history until his recognition by "all Israel," for "a hardening has come upon part of Israel" in their "unbelief" toward Jesus. St. Peter says to the Jews of Jerusalem after Pentecost: "Repent therefore, and turn again, that your sins may be blotted out, that times of refreshing may come from the presence of the Lord, and that he may send the Christ appointed for you, Jesus, whom heaven must receive until the time for establishing all that God spoke by the mouth of his holy prophets from of old" [Acts 3:19–21]. St. Paul echoes him: "For if their rejection means the reconciliation of the world, what will their acceptance mean but life from the dead?" [Rom. 11:15] (674).

265. Does the book of Revelation contain coded secrets about the end times?

The final book of the Bible, the book of Revelation, was written by St. John while he was in exile on the island of Patmos (Rev. 1:9). It contains information about our future, but perhaps not as much as many people suppose.

The book was addressed to a group of seven churches in the province of Asia Minor (in modern Turkey) for a specific purpose: "to show to [Christ's] servants what must soon take place" (Rev. 1:1). It thus encourages Christians to hold fast to their faith in the face of persecution and the traumatic events that were to happen in their immediate future.

Today many assume that the events prophesied in Revelation are all still in our future, but it is often an error to suppose that just because a passage is a prophecy it hasn't yet been fulfilled.

However, since prophecies can have multiple fulfillments, even if Revelation may primarily apply to the early Christian age, it can also have secondary fulfillments throughout Church history—including at the end of the world.

266. What light can private revelation shed on the end times?

Although public revelation—found in Scripture and Tradition—ceased with the death of the last apostle, God has nonetheless continued to communicate to various people through what is known as private revelations.

These private revelations may contain messages for a general audience, but they are not binding as matters of faith the way public revelation is. According to the *Catechism*, their role is not to "improve or complete Christ's definitive revelation, but to help live more fully by it in a certain period of history. Guided by the Magisterium of the Church, the *sensus fidelium* [Latin, the "sense of the faithful"] knows how to discern and welcome in these revelations whatever constitutes an authentic call of Christ or his saints to the Church" (67).

Sometimes such private revelations contain predictions about the future. When they do, their purpose is not to satisfy human curiosity but to help people live out their faith—as was the case with the biblical prophets.

Many have sought to develop a picture of the future using information from both public and private revelation. Just as one must handle biblical prophecies with care, so to private revelation.

What should our basic attitude toward it be? Many people received private revelations in the first century, and so the New Testament addresses the question. St. Paul expresses a balanced view that is open but critical, telling his readers: "Do not quench the Spirit, do not despise prophesying, but test everything; hold fast what is good" (1 Thess. 5:19–21).

What mistakes do we need to be on guard against when assessing material from private revelations?

One mistake is simply assuming that a quotation is genuine. Many books and websites copy and paste quotations attributed to apparitions without checking to see if they are accurate. This results in numerous poorly sourced quotations, and sometimes they turn out not to be genuine. For example, Padre Pio is often claimed to have predicted a proposed event known as the "Three Days of Darkness," in which the entire earth will be shrouded in darkness. However, he did not make such predictions, and the quotations attributed to him are inaccurate.

Another mistake is assuming that a quotation is from a private revelation when it isn't. For example, St. Edmund Campion is often claimed to have predicted a proposed event prior to the Second Coming known as the "Illumination of Consciences," in which each person on earth will be given a mystical insight into the state of his soul. However, when the passage is read in its original context, it's clear that Campion was not relating the contents of a private revelation. He was recounting how he once preached a sermon about Judgment Day.

We also should not assume that just because an apparition speaks of the future it is speaking about the end of the world. Like the public revelations received by the biblical prophets, private revelations are meant to help people live "in a certain period of history," and their predictions are most likely about that period.

For instance, although many assumed that the 1917 apparitions of Mary at Fátima, Portugal, were about the end of the world, they actually applied to the twentieth century, and by the year 2000, the future Benedict XVI could say of their predictions: "Insofar as individual events are described, they belong to the past. Those who expected exciting apocalyptic revelations about the end of the world or the future course of history are bound to be disappointed."[396]

Finally, although private revelations can give genuine insights into the future, we must recognize that many of the scenarios proposed by apparition-based books and websites are highly speculative and often do not prove to be true with the passage of time. The falsification rate for scenarios based on sensationalistic interpretations of private revelations is as high as that of scenarios based on sensationalistic interpretations of biblical prophecies. Many authors are simply too willing to embrace shaky speculation and present it as truth.

267. How should we live in light of the end times?

The fact we are in the end times—the final age of human history—has implications for how we live our lives.

Since, from one perspective, the "end times" are synonymous with the whole of the Christian age, the proper way to live in the end times is simply to be Christians! From another perspective, the "end times" are yet to come, and people naturally wonder how close we are to the grand finale of human history. We can say with confidence that we are closer to the end than we used to be, "for salvation is nearer to us now than when we first believed" (Rom. 13:11), but this has been true all through the Christian age. The mere fact that we are closer doesn't mean we are close. The final end could come soon from our perspective—or it might not occur for centuries. According to the *Catechism*,

> Since the Ascension Christ's coming in glory has been imminent, even though 'it is not for you to know times or seasons which the Father has fixed by his own authority' [Acts 1:7]. This eschatological coming could be accomplished at any moment, even if both it and the final trial that will precede it are 'delayed' (673).

Part of the folly of date-setting is the fact that God does not view time as we do. As St. Peter says,

> Do not ignore this one fact, beloved, that with the Lord one day is as a thousand years, and a thousand years as one day. The Lord is not slow about his promise as some count slowness, but is forbearing toward you, not wishing that any should perish, but that all should reach repentance (2 Pet. 3:8–9).

This provides the key to how we should live in the interim: we should *repent*. Peter goes on to say:

> Since all these things are thus to be dissolved, what sort of persons ought you to be in lives of holiness and godliness, waiting for and hastening the coming of the day of God" (2 Pet. 3:11-12).

If God delays the fulfillment of prophecy, it is so that more souls can repent and come to him for salvation. "Or do you presume upon the riches of his kindness and forbearance and patience? Do you not know that God's kindness is meant to lead you to repentance?" (Rom. 2:4).

Scripture emphasizes that the day of the Lord will come "like a thief in the night" (1 Thess. 5:2; see Matt. 24:43; Luke 12:39; 1 Peter 3:10; Rev. 3:3; 16:15), and it emphasizes the need to repent. Thus, St. Paul says,

> You are not in darkness, brethren, for that day to surprise you like a thief. For you are all sons of light and sons of the day; we are not of the night or of darkness. So then let us not sleep, as others do, but let us keep awake and be sober. For those who sleep, sleep at night, and those who get drunk are drunk at night. But, since we belong to the day, let us be sober, and put on the breastplate of faith and love, and for a helmet the hope of salvation (1 Thess. 5:4–8).

Whether we live close to the Second Coming or not, we will all stand before the Lord, and we do not know when this will happen. We must repent and make ourselves ready not only because the Lord could return soon but also because we could die and stand before him in individual judgment at any moment.

The proper response to living in the end times—whether we are close to the final end or not—is not to be preoccupied with precisely *when* the Second Coming will occur or precisely *how* prophecy will be fulfilled. We must leave these matters in God's hands. As Jesus told us, "Seek first his kingdom and his righteousness, and all these things shall be yours as well. Therefore, do not be anxious about tomorrow, for tomorrow will be anxious for itself. Let the day's own trouble be sufficient for the day" (Matt. 6:33–34).

Our present life is one of limitations. We do not know God or his prophecies perfectly, but one day the mystery will be revealed to us, and our task in the meantime is to live lives of love and virtue. "For now we see in a mirror dimly, but then face to face. Now I know in part; then I shall understand fully, even as I have been fully understood. So faith, hope, love abide, these three; but the greatest of these is love" (1 Cor. 13:12–13).

268. Will there be a new earth and a new heaven?

Many people think that after the end of the world, the earth will cease to exist and only heaven and hell will remain. But throughout Scripture we find references to God's promise to create "a new heaven and a new earth." Isaiah says that after making this new heaven and new earth, "the former things shall not be remembered or come into mind" (Isa. 65:17). Peter tells us that at the end of the world, "The heavens will be kindled and dissolved, and the elements will melt with fire! But according to his promise we wait for new heavens and a new earth in which righteousness dwells" (2 Pet. 3:12–13). The most famous description of this new heaven and new earth are found in St. John's vision in Revelation 21:1–5. This is what he saw:

> I saw a new heaven and a new earth; for the first heaven and the first earth had passed away, and the sea was no more. And I saw the holy city, new Jerusalem, coming down out of heaven from God, prepared as a bride adorned for her husband; and I heard a great voice from the throne saying, "Behold, the dwelling of God is with men. He will dwell with them, and they shall be his people, and God himself will be with them; he will wipe away every tear from their eyes, and death shall be no more, neither shall there be mourning nor crying nor pain any more, for the former things have passed away."

Among ancient Jews, the sea was a symbol of chaos (Gen. 1:1), a source of danger (Jon. 1:4), and the home of the apocalyptic beast (Rev. 13:1). The description of a sea-less creation means that God's kingdom will be without the evil and dangers that accompany this life. According to Peter S. Williamson in his commentary on Revelation,

> These words should not be interpreted as a literal description of the new creation, indicating that there will be no large bodies of water in it. The vision of the eschatological temple in Ezekiel 47 tells how the Dead Sea will be renewed by the river flowing from the temple. Neither vision aims at literal description; both communicate truths about the age to come through symbolic descriptions.[397]

Although we may not know exactly how the world will be renewed, we do know that it will be renewed, and that "The creation itself will be set free from its bondage to decay and obtain the glorious liberty of the children of God" (Rom. 8:21). The *Catechism* likewise says, "The visible universe, then, is itself destined to be transformed, so that the world itself, restored to its original state, facing no further obstacles, should be at the service of the just, sharing their glorification in the risen Jesus Christ" (1047).

As we saw in our discussion of heaven, our life with God will not be a disembodied one focused on eternal harp playing high up in the clouds. Instead, heaven and earth will be united and we will have a bodily existence in a perfect earthly realm. Just as Jesus had perfect knowledge of the angelic and the earthly realms as well as God, we too will see God as he is and delight in the glory of the new creation he has made for us.

ENDNOTES

1 Christopher Kaczor, The Seven Big Myths About the Catholic Church.

2 *Summa Theologiae* (ST) II-II Q.4, a.1.

3 "Evidence taken from the proper principles of a thing makes it apparent, whereas evidence taken from divine authority does not make a thing apparent in itself." Ibid.

4 David Hume, *Enquiry Concerning Human Understanding*, 4:1.

5 Ibid., 12:3.

6 Peter Kreeft, *Socratic Logic* (South Bend, IN: St. Augustine's Press, 2005), 78.

7 Pope Benedict XVI, General Audience. March 24, 2010, https://www.vatican.va/content/benedict-xvi/en/audiences/2010/documents/hf_ben-xvi_aud_20100324.html.

8 See section 2:3, ad. 5 in Thomas Aquinas, *Super Boethium De Trinitate*, trans. Rose E. Brennan, S.H.N. (New York: Herder, 1946), St. Isidore Forum, https://isidore.co/aquinas/english/BoethiusDeTr.htm#L22.

9 ST I:1:1.

10 Thomas Nagel, *The Last Word* (Oxford University Press: 1997), 130–131.

11 ST I:1:1.

12 Robert Barron, *Catholicism: A Journey to the Heart of the Faith* (New York: Image Books, 2014), 67–68.

13 The First Vatican Council teaches in canon 5, "If anyone does not confess that the world and all things which are contained in it, both spiritual and material, were produced, according to their whole substance, out of nothing by God; or holds that God did not create by his will free from all necessity, but as necessarily as he necessarily loves himself; or denies that the world was created for the glory of God: let him be anathema."

14 Robert Jastrow, *God and the Astronomers* (Toronto: McCleod, 1992), 107.

15 See, for example, Ronald Aronson, "The New Atheists," *The Nation*, June 25, 2007.

16 E. Larson and L. Witham, "Leading Scientists Still Reject God," *Nature* 394 (1998): 313–314, https://www.nature.com/articles/28481.pdf.

17 National Academy of Sciences (2024), https://www.nasonline.org/membership/. Members belong to one of the following six categories: physical and mathematical sciences, biological sciences, engineering and applied sciences, biomedical sciences, behavioral and social sciences, or applied biological, agricultural, and environmental sciences.

18 "Measures and Size of U.S. S&E Workforce with a Bachelor's Degree or Higher: 2019," Science & Engineering Indicators, National Science Foundation, https://ncses.nsf.gov/pubs/nsb20212/data.

19 Eugenie C. Scott, "Do Scientists Really Reject God?," *Reports of the National Center for Science Education* 18, no. 2 (March-April 1997): 24–25, https://ncse.ngo/do-scientists-really-reject-god.

20 The question used for this survey was identical to the one used in a Gallup survey of the general population, asking whether one agreed that "man evolved over millions of years from less developed forms of life, but God guided the process, including the creation of man." Scott, "Do Scientists Really Reject God?" The original survey was published by E. Larson and L. Witham, "Scientists Are Still Keeping the Faith," *Nature* 386 (1997): 435–436, https://doi.org/10.1038/386435a0.

21 Pew Research Center, "Scientists and Belief," November 5, 2009, http://www.pewforum.org/2009/11/05/scientists-and-belief/.

22 Ibid.

23 Germain Grisez, *Living a Christian Life*, The Way of the Lord Jesus, http://twotlj.org/G-2-1-J.html.

24 Ibid.

25 Ibid.

26 Ibid.

27 Cited in Randy Boyagoda, "Cordially, Richard John Neuhaus," *First Things*, August 2012, 18.

28 *The Baltimore Catechism*, 2:8, http://www.catholicity.com/baltimore-catechism/lesson02.html.

29 Pope John Paul II, General Audience, July 10, 1985, https://www.vatican.va/content/john-paul-ii/it/audiences/1985/documents/hf_jp-ii_aud_19850710.html.

30 A variant of polytheism is *henotheism*, which acknowledges the existence of many gods but deems only one god worthy of worship and obedience.

31 "Their purpose was the persuasion of the masses and general legislative and political expediency. For instance, the myths tell us that these gods

are anthropomorphic or resemble some of the other animals." Aristotle, *Metaphysics* (New York: Penguin Books, 1998), 380.

32 ST I:11:3.

33 Pontifical Council for Culture and the Pontifical Council for Interreligious Dialogue, "Jesus Christ: The Bearer of the Water of Life: A Christian Reflection on the 'New Age,'" *L'Osservatore Romano,* August 13/20, 2003.

34 C.S. Lewis, *Mere Christianity* (New York: Simon and Schuster, 1952), 152.

35 Christian Smith and Melinda Denton, *Soul Searching: The Religious and Spiritual Lives of American Teenagers* (New York: Oxford University Press, 2005), 162–164.

36 ST I:2:1.

37 ST I:2:2.

38 For more information see John Farrell, *The Day Without Yesterday: Lemaître, Einstein, and the Birth of Modern Cosmology* (New York: Thunder's Mouth Press, 2005), 115. Farrell cautiously notes that, "There is some confusion as to the extent of Einstein's enthusiasm for Lemaître's primeval atom theory . . . Encouraging as Einstein was, it's unlikely that he regarded Lemaitre's primeval atom theory as the last word on the subject—and unlikelier still that he would have employed the word 'creation' to describe it."

39 Although the standard model is still the majority view, it is incomplete. Scientists have proposed new mechanisms such as "inflation" to account for irregularities in the standard model, such as the flatness problem or the horizon problem. Scientists also need a quantum theory of gravity to account for the universe's structure at the Big Bang itself, because relativity theory becomes incapable of describing the singularity prior to what is called the Planck time, or 10^{-43} seconds. For a more thorough treatment of this subject see the "Advanced cosmology" appendix in Trent Horn, *Answering Atheism* (El Cajon, CA: Catholic Answers Press, 2013).

40 Lisa Grossman, "Why Physicists Can't Avoid a Creation Event," *New Scientist,* January 11, 2012. In their original paper, Audrey Mithani and Alexander Vilenkin wrote: "Did the universe have a beginning? At this point, it seems that the answer to this question is probably yes." Mithani and Vilenkin, "Did the Universe Have a Beginning?" High Energy Physics—Theory, Cornell University Library, April 20, 2012, http://arxiv.org/abs/1204.4658.

41 Martin Rees, *Just Six Numbers: The Deep Forces That Shape the Universe* (New York: Basic Books, 2000), 10.

42 The phrase was first expressed in book I of the Roman philosopher Titus Lucretius's work *De Rerum Natura.*

43 David Albert, "On the Origin of Everything: 'A Universe from Nothing' by Lawrence M. Krauss," *New York Times Book Review*, March 23, 2012.

44 See Robert J. Spitzer, *New Proofs for the Existence of God: Contributions from Contemporary Physics and Philosophy* (Grand Rapids, MI: Eerdmans, 2010), 27.

45 ST I:2:3.

46 International Theological Commission, *Communion and Stewardship: Human Persons Created in the Image of God, July 23,* 2004, https://www.vatican.va/roman_curia/congregations/cfaith/cti_documents/rc_con_cfaith_doc_20040723_communion-stewardship_en.html.

47 See Francis J. Beckwith, "How to Be an Anti-intelligent Design Advocate," *University of St. Thomas Journal of Law and Public Policy* 4, no. 1 (2010).

48 Some (such as Lawrence Krauss, Quentin Smith, and others) have argued that physics gives examples of particles coming into existence out of nothing and that we therefore have grounds for thinking that the universe came into existence out of nothing. This is misleading and inaccurate. The "nothing" they are referring to is not nothing, but rather, the quantum vacuum which "is not truly empty but instead contains fleeting electromagnetic waves and particles that pop into and out of existence" http://www.aip.org/pnu/1996/split/pnu300-3.htm.

49 Jastrow, *God and the Astronomers*.

50 Arvind Borde, Alan H. Guth, and Alexander Vilenkin, "Inflationary Spacetimes Are Not Past-Complete," General Relativity and Quantum Cosmology, Cornell University Library, January 14, 2003, http://arxiv.org/abs/grqc/0110012.

51 William L. Craig, "What Is the Relation Between Science and Religion," Reasonable Faith, https://www.reasonablefaith.org/writings/popular-writings/science-theology/what-is-the-relation-between-science-and-religion.

52 Michael Ruse, "Evolutionary Theory and Christian Ethics: Are They in Harmony?" *Zygon* 29, no. 1 (1994): 5–24, http://philpapers.org/rec/RUSETA.

53 Michael Ruse, *Darwinism Defended* (London: Addison-Wesley, 1982), 275.

54 Francis J. Beckwith and Gregory Koukl, *Moral Relativism: Feet Firmly Planted in Mid-air* (Grand Rapids: Baker, 1998), 166.

55 ST I:3.

56 St. Anselm, *Anselm of Canterbury: The Major Works*, ed. Brian Davies and G.R. Evans (Oxford: Oxford University Press, 2008), 98.

57 *The Shepherd of Hermas*, 2:1:1.

58 Process theology has its roots in the thinking of Alfred North Whitehead (1861–1947). A brief summary can be found in Alister McGrath, *Christian Theology: An Introduction*, 5th ed. (West Sussex, England: Wiley-Blackwell, 2011), 214–215.

59 Tatian the Syrian, *Address to the Greeks*, 4.

60 ST I:11:3.

61 *Summa Contra Gentiles*, 1:44, 50.

62 *City of God*, 5:10.

63 *Against Heresies*, 2:13:3.

64 Peter J. Kreeft and Ronald K. Tacelli, *Handbook of Catholic Apologetics: Reasoned Answers to Questions of Faith* (San Francisco: Ignatius Press, 2009), 104.

65 C.S. Lewis, *The Problem of Pain* (New York: Macmillan, 1947).

66 *Enchiridion*, xi.

67 ST III:1:3.

68 ST I:48:5.

69 ST I:49:1.

70 ST I:49:2.

71 Paul Brand, Philip Yancey, *In the Likeness of God* (Grand Rapids: Zondervan, 2004), 461–501. See book by same authors, *The Gift of Pain* (1997).

72 Stephen J. Gould, "Impeaching a Self-appointed Judge," *Scientific American* 267, no. 1 (1992): 118–121.

73 Lewis, *Mere Christianity*, 140.

74 See Heb. 11:3, Rev. 19:3.

75 Jasper James Ray, *God Wrote Only One Bible* (Junction City, KS: Eye Opener, 1955), 118.

76 Pontifical Biblical Commission, *The Interpretation of the Bible in the Church* (Washington, DC: USCCB, 1993), 19.

77 "Address of Pope John Paul II to Pontifical Biblical Commission," April 23, 1993, in *The Scripture Documents: An Anthology of Official Catholic Teachings*, ed. Dean P. Bechard (Collegeville, MN: Order of Saint Benedict, 2002), 174.

78 Patrick Madrid, "Sola Scriptura: A Blueprint for Anarchy," in *Not by Scripture Alone: A Catholic Critique of the Protestant Doctrine of Sola Scriptura*, ed. Robert Sungenis (Santa Barbara, CA: Queenship, 1997).

79 Eusebius, *Church History*, 4:23:11.

80 R.C. Sproul, *What Is Reformed Theology? Understanding the Basics* (Grand Rapids, MI: Baker Books, 2005), 54.

81 Douglas Wilson, "A Severed Branch," *Credenda Agenda* 12, no. 1. http://www.credenda.org/archive/issues/12-1thema.php.

82 Bruce Metzger, *Introduction to the Apocrypha* (New York: Oxford University Press, 1957), 171.

83 See, for example, Steve Ray, "The Council That Wasn't," *This Rock Magazine* 15, no. 7 (September 2004).

84 "[Rabbi] Akiba's repudiation shows that there must have existed a wide acceptance of the Deuterocanon as sacred texts (along with the New Testament) among Jewish Christians *in Judea before* AD 132." Gary Michuta, *The Case for the Deuterocanon: Evidence and Arguments* (Livonia, MI: Nikaria Press, 2015) 62. See 55–65 for a full treatment.

85 There were also some Reformers who wanted to remove or relativize books of the New Testament as well. For example, Luther called the letter of James "an epistle of straw" because it contradicted his theology of justification by faith alone (see James 2:24). Happily, they were unable to accomplish any such changes in a widespread way.

86 J.N.D. Kelly, *Early Christian Doctrines* (New York: HarperCollins, 1978), 55.

87 The word *apocrypha comes from the Greek word kryptein (hide or conceal) and, in its original sense in ancient Christian usage, simply designated a text meant to be read in private, rather than in public church settings. In other words, a text that is non-canonical but useful for instruction. This is the sense in which many Protestant Bible translations today include the books they esteem apocrypha as a sort of appendix, considering them a valuable part of Christian heritage even though not canonical Scripture.*

88 "Canon of the Old Testament," in *Catholic Encyclopedia.*

89 For a complete list of Patristic citations and analysis, and a defense of the inspiration of the deuterocanonical books, see Gary Michuta, *The Case for the Deuterocanon: Evidence and Arguments* (Livonia, MI: Nikaria Press, 2015).

90 Pope John Paul II, "Old Testament Essential to Know Jesus," Address to the Pontifical Biblical Commission, *L'Osservatore Romano*, April 23, 1997, 2.

91 David Lamb, *God Behaving Badly: Is the God of the Old Testament Angry, Sexist, and Racist?* (Downers Grove, IL: InterVarsity Press, 2011), 9.

92 Tertullian refers to Marcion as a shipmaster from Pontus (a narrow strip of land on the southern coast of the Black Sea) and says he went "with the two hundred sesterces which he had brought into the church, and, when banished at last to a permanent excommunication, they scattered abroad the poisons of their doctrines." *Prescription Against Heresies*, 30.

93 This idea is rooted in the early heresy of Gnosticism. For a survey of this belief system, see John Arendzen, "Gnosticism," in *The Catholic Encyclopedia*, vol. 6. (New York: Appleton, 1909), 20, www.newadvent.org/cathen/06592a.htm.

94 *General Audience*, August 3, 2011.

95 Yves Congar, O.P., *The Meaning of Tradition* (San Francisco: Ignatius Press, 2004), 22.

96 *Commonitory*, 2:4–5.

97 *The Holy Spirit*, 27:66.

98 *Medicine Chest Against All Heresies*, 61:6.

99 *Homilies on Second Thessalonians.*

100 *Against Heresies*, 1:10:2.

101 Ibid., 3:3:1.

102 *The Fundamental Doctrines*, 1:2.

103 Fragment in Eusebius, *Church History*, 3:39.

104 Ibid., 4:21.

105 *On Baptism, Against the Donatists*, 5:23.

106 Ibid., 5:26.

107 *Responsum ad Dubium* on *Ordinatio Sacerdotalis*, October 28, *1995, https://www.vatican.va/roman_curia/congregations/cfaith/documents/rc_con_cfaith_doc_19951028_dubium-ordinatio-sac_en.html.*

108 For example, converts who had been previously ordained in another Christian community may be accepted to ordination on a case-by-case basis.

109 A helpful summary of dogmatic teachings can be found at https://www.virgosacrata.com/dogmas.html.

110 See John Paul II, *Ordinatio Sacerdotalis* (May 22, 1994) and its official clarification, *Responsum ad Dubium (*October 28, 1995) issued by the Congregation for the Doctrine of the Faith.

111 See, for example, the CDF's treatment of the role of the theologian in *Donum Veritatis*, especially 24–31.

112 *Christus Dominus, Concerning the Discipline to Be Observed with Respect to the Eucharistic Fast, January 6, 1953, https://www.ewtn.com/catholicism/library/concerning-the-discipline-to-be-observed-with-respect-to-the-eucharistic-fast-8946, 13. This was later extended in the 1957 motu proprio Sacram Communionem.*

113 St. Basil the Great, *Moralia, Regula* 80, 22: PG 31, 867. Cited in *Verbum Domini*, September 20, 2010, https://www.vatican.va/content/benedict-xvi/en/apost_exhortations/documents/hf_ben-xvi_exh_20100930_verbum-domini.html, 48.

114 Pontifical Biblical Commission, *The Inspiration and Truth of Sacred Scripture* (Collegeville, MN: Liturgical Press, 2014), 70.

115 For an in-depth treatment of this issue, see *Letter and Spirit, vol. 6: For the Sake of Our Salvation: The Truth and Humility of God's Word*, ed. Scott Hahn and David Scott (Steubenville, OH: Emmaus Road, 2010), especially the entries by Hahn, Pitre, and Fr. Harrison.

116 *Letters*, 82:1:3.

117 General Audience, May 8, 1985, https://www.vatican.va/content/john-paul-ii/it/audiences/1985/documents/hf_jp-ii_aud_19850508.html.

118 *Hard Sayings: A Catholic Approach to Answering Bible Difficulties* by Trent Horn addresses dozens of these alleged contradictions from a Catholic perspective.

119 Justin Martyr, *Dialogue with Trypho*, 65.

120 Karl Keating, *What Catholics Really Believe: Answers to Common Misconceptions About the Faith* (San Francisco: Ignatius Press, 1992), 37–38. Cardinal Ratzinger also said, "It is because faith is not set before us as a complete and finished system that the Bible contains contradictory texts, or at least ones that stand in tension to each other." Joseph Cardinal Ratzinger and Peter Seewald, *God and the World: Believing and Living in Our Time* (San Francisco: Ignatius Press, 2000), 152.

121 Pontifical Biblical Commission, *The Inspiration and Truth of Sacred Scripture*, 120.

122 ST I:1:1

123 ST I:1:9

124 ST I:1:10

125 See Acts 2:42; 15:2.

126 For evidence for the theory of evolution that does not come from authors with an atheistic worldview, see Francis Collins, *The Language of God: A Scientist Presents Evidence for Belief* (New York: Free Press, 2007), and Kenneth Miller, *Finding Darwin's God: A Scientist's Search for Common Ground Between God and Evolution* (New York: Harper Perennial, 2007).

127 *Augustine, The Literal Meaning of Genesis*, 1:14.

128 Ibid., 15:29.

129 *Alister McGrath, The Passionate Intellect: Christian Faith and the Discipleship of the Mind (Downers Grove, IL: InterVarsity Press, 2010), 140.*

130 Pope John Paul II, General Audience, November 7, 1979, https://www.vatican.va/content/john-paul-ii/en/audiences/1979/documents/hf_jp-ii_aud_19791107.html.

131 See canons 1–5 of the First Vatican Council (1870), and Pope Pius XII's encyclical *Humani Generis* (August 12, 1950).

132 *G.K. Lieten and Talinay Strehl, Child Street Life: An Inside View of Hazards and Expectations of Street Children in Peru (New York: Springer, 2015), 22.*

133 Rachelle Gilmour, *Juxtaposition and the Elisha Cycle* (London: Bloomsbury T&T Clark, 2014), 102.

134 ST I–II:94:5.

135 Lawson Younger Jr., *Ancient Conquest Accounts*, 227–228. Cited in Paul Copan and Matt Flanagan, *Did God Really Command Genocide? Coming to Terms with the Justice of God* (Grand Rapids, MI: Baker Books, 2014), 104.

136 Richard Hess, "The Jericho and Ai of the Book of Joshua," in *Critical Issues in Early Israelite History*, ed. Richard Hess et al. (Winona Lake, IN: Eisenbrauns, 2008), 34.

137 "If any one receive into his house a runaway male or female slave of the court, or of a freedman, and does not bring it out at the public proclamation of the major domus, the master of the house shall be put to death." *Law of Hammurabi, 16, trans. L.W. King, The Avalon Project, Yale Law School, avalon.law.yale.edu/ancient/hamframe.asp.*

138 Christopher J.H. Wright, *Old Testament Ethics for the People of God* (Downers Grove, IL: InterVarsity Press, 2004), 292.

139 One example of this is the philosopher Seneca, who, although he discouraged merciless corporal punishment, compared slaves to valuable property like jewels that one must constantly worry about. According to Joshel, "Seneca sees slaves as inferiors who can never rise above the level of humble friends." Sandra R. Joshel, *Slavery in the Roman World* (New York: Cambridge University Press, 2010), 127.

140 See also the Old Testament expression, "the wife he hates," which only refers to a wife in a polygamous relationship who is loved less (Gen. 29:31; Deut. 21:15).

141 Fr. William Most. *The Consciousness of Christ* (Front Royal: Christendom College Press, 1980) 60.

142 Benedict XVI, *Jesus of Nazareth, vol. 1* (San Francisco: Ignatius Press, 2008), 317.

143 Sonja Lyubomirsky, *The How of Happiness: A Scientific Approach to Getting the Life You Want* (New York: Penguin, 2007), 172.

144 *General Audience*, January 29, 1986, https://www.vatican.va/content/john-paul-ii/it/audiences/1986/documents/hf_jp-ii_aud_19860129.html.

145 Mark Giszczak, *Light on the Dark Passages of Scripture* (Huntington, IN: Our Sunday Visitor, 2015), 40.

146 Ibid., 144.

147 See also ST I-II:103:3.

148 *General Audience*, May 8, 1985.

149 *General Audience*, May 8, 1985.

150 *General Audience*, May 8, 1985.

151 Just a few of the many who have made dated predictions for the end of the world are medieval heretic Joachim of Fiore (predicted that the millennium would begin between 1200 and 1260), Anabaptist Thomas Müntzer (predicted that the millennium would begin in 1525), Puritan Cotton Mather (predicted the end of the world in 1697), Baptist William Miller (predicted the Second Coming in 1844), Jehovah's Witness Charles Taze Russell (saw the battle of Armageddon beginning in 1914), Evangelical Hal Linsey (saw the 1980s as "the countdown to Armageddon"), and Protestant Harold Camping (predicted the Rapture in 1994).

152 E.g., Moses Maimonides, *Guide for the Perplexed*, 2:29.

153 General Audience, April 2, 2003; see Benedict XVI, *Lenten Meeting with the Clergy of Rome*, February 22, 2007.

154 The title "Son of Man" (in Hebrew, *ben adam), is repeated almost a hundred times in the Old Testament: ninety-three times in conversation between the Lord and Ezekiel, once in a vision of the prophet Daniel (Dan. 8:17) and once in Psalm 80 in a general way (Ps. 80:17). For Christ to refer to himself as "Son of Man" would naturally infer a parallel between himself and the prophet Ezekiel. However, in the Hebrew and Aramaic, there is an important detail. The formulation that Jesus uses when speaking of himself is not ben adam but kebar enash*, the distinct formulation appearing *only once* in Scripture,

in Daniel 7:13–14. Although this distinction disappears when "Son of Man" is translated into the Greek of the New Testament, the Aramaic New Testament clearly preserves this distinctive formulation of *kebar enash* on the lips of Jesus in every instance. He is claiming not only to be *a "son of man" (ben adam) like other men or even like the prophet Ezekiel, but the "Son of Man"* (*kebar enash*) who enters into the presence of the Ancient One to receive an everlasting dominion, as beheld by the prophet Daniel.

155 *Studies in the Gospel of Mark*, 64–84.

156 *Lives of Illustrious Men*, 9, 18.

157 *Church History*, 3:39:6.

158 Benedict XVI, *Jesus of Nazareth*, vol. 1, 226–227; Richard Bauckham, *Jesus and the Eyewitnesses*, 2nd ed. (Grand Rapids: Eerdmans, 2017).

159 Tacitus, *Annals*, 15:44.

160 1 Clement 5:7b; Eusebius, *Church History* 2:22:1–8.

161 *Lives of Illustrious Men*, 59.

162 *On Modesty*, 20.

163 Eusebius, *Church History*, 6:25:14.

164 *Lives of Illustrious Men*, 2.

165 Josephus, *Antiquities of the Jews*, 20:9:1.

166 See Richard Bauckham, ed., *The Gospels for All Christians* (Grand Rapids: Eerdmans, 1998).

167 See David Trobisch, *Paul's Letter Collection: Tracing the Origins* (Bolivar, MO: Quiet Waters, 2001).

168 *Church History*, 3:25:1–6 with 3:3:5–6.

169 Bruce M. Metzger and Bart D. Ehrman, *The Text of the New Testament: Its Transmission, Corruption, and Restoration* (New York: Oxford University Press, 2005), 29.

170 George W. Houston, *Inside Roman Libraries* (Chapel Hill, NC: The University of North Carolina Press, 2014), 175.

171 F.F. Bruce, *The Books and the Parchments: How We Got Our English Bible* (Grand Rapids, MI: Revell, 1984), 78.

172 Ibid., 126.

173 "When the bishop of Oea (modern Tripoli) introduced Jerome's recent rendering into his community service, Augustine worriedly related, the congregation nearly rioted. (At issue, perhaps, was the identity of the vine under which the prophet Jonah had rested—a 'gourd' so the traditional version, or an 'ivy' so Jerome; *Letter* 75.7, 22; Jonah 4:6.)" Paula Fredriksen, *Augustine and the Jews: A Christian Defense of Jews and Judaism* (New Haven, CT: Yale University Press, 2010), 289.

174 Jimmy Akin, "The Cost of the Gospels and the Synoptic Problem," January 30, 2016, https://jimmyakin.com/2016/01/the-cost-of-the-gospels-and-the-synoptic-problem.html.

175 Matthew Larsen, *Gospels Before the Book* (Oxford: Oxford University Press, 2018).

176 Preserved in Eusebius, *Church History,* 6:14:7.

177 *Contra Faustum XXXIII.6.*

178 See, for example, Bart Ehrman, *Jesus: Apocalyptic Prophet of the New Millennium* (New York: Oxford University Press, 1999), 248–250.

179 Brant Pitre, *The Case for Jesus: The Biblical and Historical Evidence for Christ* (New York: Doubleday, 2016), 17.

180 Martin Hengel, *Studies in the Gospel of Mark* (London: SCM Press, 1985), chap. 3.

181 Preserved in Eusebius, *Church History,* 3:39:15.

182 Preserved in Eusebius, *Church History,* 6:14:6.

183 For a detailed historical, exegetical, and theological analysis of the Johannine authorship and identity question, and its implications for Gospel spirituality, see *Gabriel-Mary Fiore, Spirituality in John's Gospel: Historical Developments and Critical Foundations* (Eugene, OR: Wipf & Stock, 2024).

184 See Bauckham, *Jesus and the Eyewitnesses,* Martin Hengel, *The Johannine Question* (London: SCM Press, 1990); see also Benedict XVI, *Jesus of Nazareth,* vol. 1, chap. 8.

185 See Bauckham, *Jesus and the Eyewitnesses.*

186 See Richard Bauckham, "John for Readers of Mark," in *The Gospels for All Christians* (Grand Rapids: Eerdmans, 1998), Jimmy Akin, "Did John Use Mark as a Template?," November 15, 2014, https://jimmyakin.com/2014/11/did-john-use-mark-as-a-template.html.

187 For an extensive discussion of the synoptic problem, see Jimmy Akin, "The Synoptic Problem," September 27, 2014, JimmyAkin.com/Synoptic.

188 Reginald Fuller, *The New Testament in Current Study* (New York: Scribner, 1962), 74.

189 B.H. Streeter, *The Four Gospels: A Study of Origins* (London: Macmillan, 1930), 183.

190 Preserved in Eusebius, *Church History,* 3:39:16.

191 Chris McKnight, "Matthew, Gospel of, Hebrew Version of," *The Lexham Bible Dictionary* (Bellingham, WA: Lexham Press, 2016).

192 Raymond E. Brown, *An Introduction to the New Testament* (New York: Doubleday, 1997), chaps. 7, 8, 9, and 11.

193 For more discussion, see Jimmy Akin, *The Bible Is a Catholic Book* (San Diego, CA: Catholic Answers Press, 2019), and especially Jimmy Akin, "When Were the Gospels Written?," December 27, 2020. https://jimmyakin.com/2020/12/when-were-the-gospels-written.html.

194 *Church History,* 3:25:5.

195 *See Jerome, Lives of Illustrious Men, 2:11–14.*

196 Bart D. Ehrman and Zlatko Pleše. *The Other Gospels: Accounts of Jesus from Outside the New Testament* (Oxford: Oxford University Press, 2014), 138–139.

197 See Stephen C. Carlson, *The Gospel Hoax: Morton Smith's Invention of Secret Mark* (Waco, TX: Baylor University Press, 2005).

198 See Ariel Sabar, "The Unbelievable Tale of Jesus's Wife," *The Atlantic,* July/August 2016, and Ariel Sabar, "Karen King Responds to 'The Unbelievable Tale of Jesus's Wife,'" *The Atlantic, June 16, 2016, https://www.theatlantic.com/politics/archive/2016/06/karen-king-responds-to-the-unbelievable-tale-of-jesus-wife/487484/.*

199 *Bart Ehrman, Did Jesus Exist? The Historical Argument for Jesus of Nazareth* (New York: HarperOne, 2012), 4.

200 Earl Doherty, *Jesus: Neither God nor Man* (Ottawa: Age of Reason Publications, 2009), 61.

201 See Jimmy Akin, "Jesus Without the Gospels," May 3, 2022, https://jimmyakin.com/2022/05/jesus-without-the-gospels.html.

202 Josephus, *Antiquities of the Jews,* 18:3:3; 20:9:1.

203 See Rick Brannan, *Greek Apocryphal Gospels, Fragments, and Agrapha: Introductions and Translations* (Bellingham, WA: Lexham Press, 2013).

204 Preserved in Irenaeus, *Against Heresies,* 5:33:3.

205 Ibid., 5:33:4.

206 Justin Martyr, *Dialogue with Trypho,* 47.

207 Robert Van Voorst, *Jesus Outside the New Testament: An Introduction to the Ancient Evidence* (Grand Rapids, MI: Eerdmans, 2000), 83.

208 James Dunn, *Christianity in the Making, Volume 01:* Jesus *Remembered* (Grand Rapids, MI: Eerdmans, 2003), 141.

209 Some people claim they are mentioned in passages like 2 John 1:7 which says that there are "many deceivers, who do not acknowledge Jesus Christ as coming in the flesh." But most scholars agree these passages refer to Docetists—heretics who denied that Jesus had a *physical body* (due to their gnostic belief that the body, or anything made of matter, was evil)—not that he ever existed at all.

210 Timothy Freke and Peter Gandy, *The Jesus Mysteries: Was the "Original Jesus" a Pagan God?* (New York: Three Rivers Press, 1999), 134.

211 David Fitzgerald, *Ten Beautiful Lies About Jesus*, http://www.nazarethmyth.info/Fitzgerald2010HM.pdf, 19.

212 Rob Bell, *Velvet Elvis: Repainting the Christian Faith* (New York: HarperOne, 2005), 124–126.

213 For a more comprehensive survey see Craig Blomberg. *The Historical Reliability of the Gospels*. (Downers Grove, IL: IVP Academic, 2007).

214 See also Richard Burridge. *What Are the Gospels? A Comparison with Greco-Roman Biographies* (Grand Rapids, MI: Eerdmans, 2004).

215 William Ramsay, *The Bearing of Recent Discovery on the Trustworthiness of the New Testament* (London: Hodder and Stoughton, 1915), 222.

216 A.N. Sherwin-White. *Roman Society and Roman Law in the New Testament* (Oxford: Clarendon Press, 1963), 188–191.

217 For more information on these topics see Jon Sorensen, "*Horus Manure: Debunking the Jesus/Horus Connection,*" *Catholic Answers Magazine*, November/December 2012, and *"Exploding the Mithras Myth," Catholic Answers Magazine*, May/June 2013.

218 John R. Hinnells, "Reflections on the Bull-Slaying Scene," in *Mithraic Studies,* vol. 2.

219 Some Mithraic scholars believe that adherents of Mithraism may have identified their God with the Roman god Sol, who had a feast day on December 25, but this claim has little evidence to support it.

220 The Mithraic scholar Richard Gordon simply concludes, "There was no death of Mithras." Richard Gordon, *Image and Value in the Greco-Roman World*, Studies in Mithraism and Religious Art, Collected Studies Series, 551 (Variorium, 1996), 96. Edwin Yamauchi also says, "I know of no references to a supposed death and resurrection." Quoted in Lee Strobel, *The Case for the Real Jesus* (Grand Rapids, MI: Zondervan, 2007), 172.

221 T.N.D. Mettinger. *Riddle of Resurrection: "Dying and Rising Gods" in the Ancient Near East*, Coniectanea Biblica, Old Testament, 50 (London: Coronet Books, 2001), 221.

222 For more, see Jimmy Akin, "How the Accounts of Jesus' Childhood Fit Together," https://jimmyakin.com/how-the-accounts-of-jesus-childhood-fit-together.

223 Paul Maier, "Herod and the Infants of Bethlehem," in *Chronos, Kairos, Christos II, ed.* Jerry Vardaman (Macon, GA: Mercer University Press, 1998), 177–178.

224 Macrobius, *Saturnalia*, 2:4:2.

225 Josephus, *Antiquities of the Jews*, 17:6:5–6.

226 "Census," in *Encyclopedia Britannica*, 2016 ed., emphasis added.

227 *The Birth of the Messiah*, 549.

228 Josephus, *Antiquities of the Jews*, 17:8:4; 20:9:5.

229 m. Pesachim, 8:6.

230 According to Sura 4:157 in the Qu'ran, "And [for] their saying, 'Indeed, we have killed the Messiah, Jesus, the son of Mary, the messenger of Allah.' And they did not kill him, nor did they crucify him; but [another] was made to resemble him to them. And indeed, those who differ over it are in doubt about it. They have no knowledge of it except the following of assumption. And they did not kill him, for certain." Since the Qu'ran was written almost six hundred years after Jesus' death, its testimony is simply not helpful in trying to determine from a historical perspective, what happened to Jesus. With regard to the view that the Qu'ran is the word of God and so Muslims should trust it over what the Bible says, see Jacques Jomier, *The Bible and the Qur'an* (San Francisco, CA: Ignatius Press, 2002).

231 John Dominic Crossan, *Jesus: A Revolutionary Biography* (San Francisco, CA: HarperCollins, 2009), 163.

232 William Edwards, Wesley Gabel, and Floyd Hosmer, "On the Physical Death of Jesus Christ," *Journal of the American Medical Association* 255, no. 11 (March 21, 1986): 1457.

233 David Strauss, *The Life of Jesus for the People*, vol. 1 (London: Williams and Norgate, 1879), 412.

234 See Mark 15:43; Matt. 27:57; Luke 23:50; John 19:38.

235 Matthew W. Maslen and Piers D. Mitchell, "Medical Theories on the Cause of Death in Crucifixion," *Journal of the Royal Society of Medicine* 99, no. 4 (April 2006): 185–188.

236 See Gary Habermas and Michael Licona. *The Case for the Resurrection of Jesus* (Grand Rapids, MI: Kregel, 2004), 70.

237 Talmud, Sotah 3:4, 19a, cited in Rachel Keren, "Torah Study," in *Jewish Women: A Comprehensive Historical Encyclopedia, Jewish Women's Archive*, March 20, 2009, http://jwa.org/encyclopedia/article/torah-study, and Talmud Rosh Hashanah, 22a.

238 Josephus, *Antiquities of the Jews*, 4:8:15.

239 For more on how to defend the Resurrection using just the "minimal facts" related to the life of Christ, see Habermas and Licona, *The Case for the Resurrection of Jesus*.

240 For more information, see Jimmy Akin, "How the Resurrection Narratives Fit Together," January 23, 2017, https://jimmyakin.com/2017/01/how-the-resurrection-narratives-fit-together.html.

241 Gerd Ludemann, *What Really Happened to Jesus?* (Louisville, KY: Westminster John Knox Press, 1995), 80.

242 Gary Habermas and J.P. Moreland. *Immortality: The Other Side of Death* (Nashville, TN: Thomas Nelson, 1992), 60.

243 For example, in Acts 2 Peter declares that King David's tomb is still in existence and that David has suffered decay, but that Jesus as the Messiah has not suffered decay because he was resurrected.

244 E. Randolph Richards, *Paul and First-Century Letter Writing: Secretaries, Composition and Collection* (Downers Grove, IL; Leicester, England: InterVarsity Press; Apollos, 2004), 163.

245 Richard Bauckham, *The Climax of Prophecy: Studies on the Book of Revelation* (London; New York: T&T Clark, 1993), xvi.

246 Richard Bauckham, *Jesus and the Eyewitnesses: The Gospels as Eyewitness Testimony* (Grand Rapids, MI; Cambridge, U.K.: Eerdmans, 2006), 85.

247 *Dialogue with Trypho the Jew*, 81:4.

248 Some Church Fathers also attribute some of the Johannine books of the New Testament to him. Jerome reports that many held him to be the author of 2 and 3 John. Eusebius, *Church History*, 3:39:4–6.

249 Bauckham, *Jesus and the Eyewitnesses*, 445–452.

250 Scott Hahn, *The Lamb's Supper* (New York: Doubleday, 1999), 56.

251 David E. Aune, *Revelation 1–5*, Word Biblical Commentary, vol. 52A (Dallas, TX: Word, Incorporated, 1997), lvii.

252 Irenaeus, *Against Heresies,* 5:30:3.

253 Aune, *Revelation 1–5*, Word Biblical Commentary, vol. 52A, 78.

254 Jerome, *Against Jovinian*, 1.26.

255 Scholars are divided about how to count this succession of emperors. See Aune, *Revelation 1–5*, Word Biblical Commentary, vol. 52A, lxi–lxii.

256 Jimmy Akin, "The Structure of Revelation," https://jimmyakin.com/the-structure-of-revelation.

257 For a discussion, see ibid.

258 Steve Gregg, *Revelation, Four Views: A Parallel Commentary* (Nashville, TN: Thomas Nelson, 1997), 181–183.

259 There also are books devoted to analyzing these matters, such as Steve Moyise's *The Old Testament in the Book of Revelation* or G.K. Beale's *John's Use of the Old Testament in Revelation* and his *The Use of Daniel in Jewish Apocalyptic Literature and in the Revelation of St. John.*

260 Gregg, *Revelation, Four Views*, 34.

261 Ibid., 31–32.

262 Ibid., 40.

263 Ibid., 32.

264 Robert H. Mounce, *What Are We Waiting For? A Commentary on Revelation* (Eugene, OR: Wipf & Stock, 2004), 65.

265 For example, in 3:15–16 Christ says that he wishes that the Laodiceans were either hot or cold, but because they are lukewarm, he will spit them out of his mouth. Archaeology has shown that this reflects the situation with the local water supply at the time. "The hot waters of Hierapolis had a medicinal effect, and the cold waters of Colossae were pure, drinkable, and had a life-giving effect. However, there is evidence that Laodicea had access only to warm water, which was not very palatable and caused nausea. Indeed, Laodicea had grown as a town because its position was conducive for commerce, but it was far from good water. When the city tried to pipe water in, it could manage only to obtain tepid, emetic water." G.K. Beale, *The Book of Revelation: A Commentary on the Greek Text*, New International Greek Testament Commentary (Grand Rapids, MI; Carlisle, Cumbria: Eerdmans; Paternoster Press, 1999), 303. Both hot water and

cold water are useful, but lukewarm water is useless and unpleasant—the state that Jesus says characterizes the Laodiceans.

266 Josephus, *The Jewish War, 6:9:4, p. 428; cf. 6:9:3, pp. 421, 425, in The Jewish War: Books 1–7, vol. 3, ed. Jeffrey Henderson et al., trans. H. St. J. Thackeray (Cambridge, MA; London; New York: Harvard University Press; Heinemann; Putnam, 1927–1928).*

267 Josephus, *War*, 7:1:1, p. 3.

268 Benedict XVI, *Jesus of Nazareth: Part Two: Holy Week: From the Entrance into Jerusalem to the Resurrection* (San Francisco: Ignatius Press, 2011), 222, emphasis added.

269 General Audience, August 23, 2006, https://www.vatican.va/content/benedict-xvi/en/audiences/2006/documents/hf_ben-xvi_aud_20060823.html.

270 See Adrienne Mayor, *Gods and Robots: Myths, Machines, and Ancient Dreams of Technology* (Princeton, NJ: Princeton University Press, 2018), chap. 9.

271 "There were many reports in the ancient world of statues turning (Dio Cassius 41.61; 54.7), sweating (Cicero, *De div.* 1.43.98; Plutarch *Cor.* 38.1; *Anton.* 60), weeping (Augustine *Civ. dei* 3.11), or speaking (Dionysius of Halicarnassus *Ant. Rom.* 8.56.2); several similar stories are collected in Plutarch *De pyth. orac.* 397E–398B." David E. Aune, *Revelation 6–16*, in *Word Biblical Commentary, vol. 52B (Dallas, TX: Word, Incorporated, 1998), 762.*

272 Other translations merely say that they "lived and reigned" with Christ during the millennium. The Greek allows either translation.

273 Patrick Lee, "Does God Have Emotions?," in *God Under Fire*, ed. Douglas Huffman and Eric L. Johnson (Grand Rapids, MI: Zondervan, 2002), 229–230.

274 John Chrysostom, *On the Incomprehensibility of God*, 3:3, 722/200, cited in Stephen Benin, *The Footprints of God: Divine Accommodation in Jewish and Christian Thought* (Albany, NY: SUNY Press, 1993), 68.

275 Kreeft, *Socratic Logic*, 173.

276 According to the *Catechism*, "Because it does not divide the divine unity, the real distinction of the persons from one another resides solely in the relationships which relate them to one another . . . Because of that unity the Father is wholly in the Son and wholly in the Holy Spirit; the Son is wholly in the Father and wholly in the Holy Spirit; the Holy Spirit is wholly in the Father and wholly in the Son" (255). For a more in-depth discussion see Joseph Ratzinger, *Introduction to Christianity* (San Francisco: Ignatius Press, 1990), 183; and St. Augustine, *On the Trinity*.

277 The *Catechism* says that "'Father,' 'Son,' and 'Holy Spirit' are not simply names designating modalities of the divine being, for they are really distinct from one another" (254).

278 ST I:27:1.

279 ST I:27:3.

280 ST I:27:4.

281 ST I:28:4.

282 ST I:40:2, citing Boethius, *De Trinitatis*.

283 ST I:29:1.

284 ST I:29:3.

285 Ibid.

286 Although sometimes we use the name *Father* to speak of God in relation to his creatures, in which case it embraces the whole Trinity, Thomas notes: "God is the Father of the Son *from eternity*; while He is the Father of the creature *in time*. Therefore paternity in God is taken in a personal sense as regards the Son, before it is so taken [in a general sense] as regards the creature." ST I:33:3.

287 *Letter to the Ephesians*, 1.

288 ST I:107:3.

289 ST I:52:1.

290 ST I:52:2.

291 ST I:112:3.

292 ST I:108:3

293 ST I:113:4.

294 Fourth Lateran Council, decree 1.

295 *The Shepherd of Hermas*, 2:1:1.

296 St. Theophilus of Antioch, *To Autolycus*, 2:10.

297 David Albert, "A Universe from Nothing," *New York Times*, March 23, 2012, http://www.nytimes.com/2012/03/25/books/review/a-universe-from-nothing-by-lawrence-m-krauss.html?_r=0.

298 Canons on God the Creator of All Things, canon 5.

299 *De Principiis*, 4:16.

300 Joseph Razinger, *In the Beginning* (Grand Rapids, MI: Eerdmans, 1995).

301 Pope Benedict XVI, Meeting of the Holy Father Benedict XVI with the Clergy of the Dioceses of Belluno-Feltre and Treviso, July 24, 2007, http://www.vatican.va/holy_father/benedict_xvi/speeches/2007/july/documents/hf_ben-xvi_spe_20070724_clero-cadore_en.html.

302 Rees, *Just Six Numbers*, 33–34.

303 "Gravity Mysteries: Why Is Gravity Fine-Tuned?," *New Scientist*, June 10, 2009, https://www.newscientist.com/article/mg20227123-000-gravity-mysteries-why-is-gravity-fine-tuned/.

304 Alexander Vilenkin, *Many Worlds in One* (New York: Hill and Wang, 2006), 10.

305 Lisa Dyson, Matthew Kleban, and Leonard Susskind, "Disturbing Implications of a Cosmological Constant," High Energy Physics—Theory, Cornell University Library, November 14, 2002, http://arxiv.org/abs/hep-th/0208013.

306 James Armstrong. *General, Organic, and Biochemistry: An Applied Approach* (Stamford, CT.: Cengage, 2012), 61.

307 ST I:75:1.

308 Catholic philosophers and theologians have traditionally held that the soul of nonhuman animals is like the body of those animals, and so neither it, nor the animal itself, survives death. However, it is possible God could achieve the survival of animals in the next life through some other means, an idea a minority of Catholic thinkers have considered.

309 ST I:75:5.

310 See John Paul II, General Audience, November 14, 1979, https://www.vatican.va/content/john-paul-ii/en/audiences/1979/documents/hf_jp-ii_aud_19791114.html.

311 Darby Proctor et al., "Chimpanzees Play the Ultimatum Game," *PNAS* 110, no. 6 (January 14, 2013): 2070–2075, doi.org/10.1073/pnas.1220806110.

312 Alex Rosenberg. *The Atheist's Guide to Reality* (New York: Norton, 2011).

313 Charles Darwin, *The Life and Letters of Charles Darwin Including an Autobiographical Chapter*, ed. Francis Darwin (New York: Appleton, 1898).

314 ST III:1:1.

315 *Commentary on the Gospel of John*, 14:2.

316 *Against Heresies*, 5:19:1.

317 Peter Kreeft and Ronald Tacelli, *Handbook of Catholic Apologetics* (San Francisco, CA: Ignatius Press, 1994), 159.

318 Ibid., 167.

319 From "The Buddha's Farewell Address" in *The Gospel of Buddha: Compiled from Ancient Records by Paul Carus* (Chicago and London: Open Court, 1915).

320 See Isaiah 5:1–30.

321 Dan Brown, *The Da Vinci Code* (New York: Anchor Books, 2005), 233.

322 Ibid., 264.

323 Romans 1:3 tells us Christ "was descended from David according to the flesh," which would mean Mary would have descended from David. And the fact that Mary and Joseph offered the offering of the poor at the Presentation in Luke 2:24 (see Lev. 12:2–8) indicates Mary to have been poor.

324 According to the second-century document *The Protoevangelium of James*, Mary was between fourteen and seventeen when she conceived Jesus. There is a discrepancy in the manuscripts, with variants reading all four ages.

325 See Eccles. 12:7.

326 Irenaeus, *Against Heresies*, 1.10.

327 Justin Martyr, *Dialogue with Trypho the Jew*, 100.

328 Eric Svendsen, *Evangelical Answers: A Critique of Current Roman Catholic Apologists* (Lindenhurst, NY: Reformation Press, 1999), 137.

329 Rev. S. Shearer, "The 'Brethren of the Lord,'" in *A Catholic Commentary on Sacred Scripture, ed.* Rev. R. Ginns, O.P., and Dom Bernard Orchard, O.S.B. (New York: Thomas Nelson, 1953), 844.

330 Some will claim that Mary is *Miriam* in Greek while her sister is *Maria*. However, in Scripture, the two spellings are actually used interchangeably, as we see in the case of Mary Magdalene in Mark 15:40 (she is called "Maria"); Matt. 27:56 ("Maria"); 27:61 ("Mariam"); and 28:1 ("Mariam"). They are essentially the same name.

331 Svendsen, *Evangelical Answers*, 137. Galatians 1:19 is one among a list of seven texts that Svendsen uses to "prove" Mary gave birth to other children through conjugal relations with St. Joseph.

332 The Greek word *apostolos* means "sent one" or "emissary" (CCC 858). Some will include, for example, Andronicus and Junias as apostles in this sense in Romans 16:7. The text is unclear. It says they were "of note among the apostles," not necessarily that they were apostles. But Barnabas is clearly referred to as an apostle, along with St. Paul in Acts 14:14. Moreover, 1 Corinthians 15:5–7 lists *the Twelve* and *the apostles* as two distinct categories, indicating there were apostles beyond the Twelve. See also 1 Thessalonians 1:1; 2:6.

333 See Faculty of Theology of the University of Navarre, *The Navarre Bible: The Acts of the Apostles* (Dublin: Four Courts Press, 1992), 107.

334 See Acts 8:1.

335 Orchard, *A Catholic Commentary on Sacred Scripture*, 1115. This well-respected biblical scholar agrees that this visit was a visit to "the Twelve" and that among them he saw only Peter and James. St. Jerome, *The Perpetual Virginity of Mary—Against Helvidius*, 15, concurs.

336 In *The Perpetual Virginity of Mary*, 14, St. Jerome adds: "James is called 'the less' (see Mark 15:40) in order to distinguish him from James the Greater, who was the son of Zebedee" among the Twelve. This is more evidence that the James who is called "the brother of the Lord" was one of the twelve apostles.

337 *Commentary on John*, 1:6. See also Eusebius of Caesarea, *Ecclesiastical History*, 2:1:2–5 (A.D. 350); St. Athanasius, *Discourse Against the Arians*, 2:70 (A.D. 356); St. Epiphanius, *Panarion*, 11:5 (A.D. 360); Pope St. Siricius, *Letter to Bishop Anysius* (A.D. 392); St. Ambrose, *Letters*, 11:5 (A.D. 396); St. Augustine, *On Holy Virginity*, 4:4 (A.D. 401), etc.

338 Eric Svendsen, *Evangelical Answers*, 144.

339 Dave Hunt, *A Woman Rides the Beast—The Roman Catholic Church and the Last Days (Eugene, Ore.: Harvest House Publishers, 1994)*, p. 436.

340 *On the Perpetual Virginity of Blessed Mary*, 6.

341 Pope John Paul II, *Redemptoris Mater*, March 25, 1987, https://www.vatican.va/content/john-paul-ii/en/encyclicals/documents/hf_jp-ii_enc_25031987_redemptoris-mater.html, 8, 9; Ginns and Orchard, eds., *A Catholic Commentary on Sacred Scripture*, 748.

342 See John 19:3; Acts 23:26.

343 See Gen. 17:5, 15; 32:28; Exod. 3:14.

344 St. Jerome translated *kekaritomene* into Latin as *gratia plena*, or "full of grace," to get at that sense of Mary being *completed* in grace, which is what the *perfect tense* in Greek tends to indicate.

345 Concerning the enigmatic response of Jesus, see Fr. William Leonard, in *A Catholic Commentary on Sacred Scripture*, 984.

346 "What then is Apollos? What is Paul? Servants through whom you believed, as the Lord assigned to each. I planted, Apollos watered, but God gave the growth. . . . For we are God's *fellow workers*; you are God's field." "Fellow workers" is *sunergoi*, or "co-laborers," in Greek.

347 See James 5:19–20; 1 Tim. 4:16; 1 Cor. 9:22; Rom. 11:14; 1 Cor. 7:16; Col. 1:24; 2 Cor. 1:6; etc.

348 *Against Heresies,* 3:22:4.

349 Norman Geisler and Ralph MacKenzie, *Roman Catholics and Evangelicals—Agreements and Differences* (Grand Rapids, MI: Baker Books, 1995), 322.

350 See Raymond Brown, S.S., Joseph Fitzmeyer, S.J., and Roland E. Murphy, eds., *The Jerome Biblical Commentary* (Englewood Cliffs, NJ: Prentice-Hall, 1968), 310.

351 See CCC 2110–2114, 971; Pope Paul VI, *Lumen Gentium, November 21, 1964, https://www.vatican.va/archive/hist_councils/ii_vatican_council/documents/vat-ii_const_19641121_lumen-gentium_en.html, 66–67.*

352 See Matt. 16:18–19; Luke 22:29–32; 2 Kings 11:1–4; 2 Chron. 15:16; Jer. 13:18; 1 Kings 2:13–23; Luke 1:43; Rev. 12:1–2, 5, etc.

353 See also Origen, *Commentary on Romans,* 1:1:5 (A.D. 246); Alexander of Alexandria, *Letter to Another Bishop Alexander and All Non-Egyptian Bishops,* 12 (A.D. 324); St. Athanasius, *On the Incarnation of the Word of God,* 8 (A.D. 365). St. Epiphanius, *The Man Well-Anchored,* 75 (A.D. 374). St. Gregory Nazianzen, *Letter 101* (A.D. 382), etc.

354 Ignatius of Antioch, *Letter to the Ephesians,* 18:2.

355 *Against Heresies,* 5:19:1, cited in William Jurgens, *The Faith of the Early Fathers,* vol. 1 (Collegeville, MI: Liturgical Press, 1979), 101.

356 *Sub tuum,* cited in Luigi Gambero, *Mary and the Fathers of the Church* (San Francisco, CA: Ignatius Press, 1999), 69–70, 79.

357 See, for example, Justin Martyr, *Dialogue with Trypho the Jew,* 100 (A.D. 150); Tertullian, *On the Flesh of Christ,* 17:5 (A.D. 210); Cyril of Jerusalem, *Catechetical Lectures,* 12:15 (A.D. 350); Epiphanius, *Panarion,* 78:18 (A.D. 360); Ephrem of Syria, *Diatesseron,* 10:13 (A.D. 360); and *Op. syr.* 2:37, quoted in Ludwig Ott, *Fundamentals of Catholic Dogma* (Rockford, IL: TAN Books, 1952), 201; John Chrysostom, *Commentary on Psalms,* 44:7 (A.D. 390).

358 *The Instructor, 1: 6.*

359 Michael O'Carroll, *Theotokos—An Encyclopedia of the Blessed Virgin Mary* (Collegeville, MI: Liturgical Press, 1982), 59.

360 See also Theodosius of Alexandria, *On the Dormition of Mary,* 5 (A.D. 567); St. Gregory of Tours, in Jurgens, *The Faith of the Early Fathers,* vol. 3, 306 (A.D. 590); Theoteknos, bishop of Livias, Homily, "On the Dormition," (A.D. 625); St. Germanus of Constantinople, Homily 1, "On the Most Venerable Dormition of the Holy Mother of God" (A.D. 733); Andrew of Crete, Homily, "On the Dormition

of Our Most Holy Lady, Mother of God" (A.D. 740); John Damascene, Homily 3, "On the Dormition of Our Lady" (A.D. 750).

361 Quoted in O'Carroll, *Theotokos*, 388. The author states that there is disagreement among scholars as to the dating of this homily. "Fr. M. Jugie, A.A., opting for the fourth century against Dom Bernard Capelle, O.S.B., an eminent liturgical historian, who defends the sixth or seventh centuries as the probable time."

362 Epiphanius, *Panarion* 79:5:1. The Church has never defined infallibly whether Mary died or not before being assumed into heaven, though at the level of the Ordinary Magisterium, the Church does teach that Mary died. See, for example, Pope Pius XII, *Munificentissimus Deus*, November 1, 1950, https://www.vatican.va/content/pius-xii/en/apost_constitutions/documents/hf_p-xii_apc_19501101_munificentissimus-deus.html, 17, 20, 21, 29, 35, 39, and 40.

363 Irenaeus, *Against Heresies*, 3:22:4. See O'Carroll's *Theotokos* for more examples of Mary as "the New Eve."

364 See ST III:46:2, reply to obj. 3.

365 See Benedict XVI, *Jesus of Nazareth*, vol. 2, epilogue.

366 The *Catechism* goes on to say, "That is why original sin is called 'sin' only in an analogical sense: it is a sin 'contracted' and not 'committed'—a state and not an act" (404).

367 Advocates of so-called "transhumanism" claim that science will one day enable us to upload consciousness to computers. Even if this were possible, it would only serve to make a copy of an original person who had died, not save the original person. Moreover, there are strong philosophical arguments against the idea that machines could ever be conscious. For more on this issue see Jimmy Akin, "The Threat of Transhumanism," *Catholic Answers Magazine*, November/December 2015.

368 Rosenberg, *The Atheist's Guide to Reality*, 193.

369 In response to these arguments, some critics say the soul cannot exist because science has shown that a person's personality can be affected by injuries to the brain. If a person is a soul, then how could his personality change just because his body is damaged? But, as we've seen, a person is not just a soul. A person is a composite of soul and body and both elements are capable of affecting one another. If the body—in this case, the brain—is damaged, the soul may not be able to manifest itself properly or even at all. Consider a car whose axle is warped so that the car always veers to the left. You might think the person driving the car is a bad driver, but he may simply be unable to compensate for the damage to the vehicle he is driving—just as the soul cannot compensate for the damage to the body it is united to and so cannot display a proper rational function.

370 The Church hasn't definitively taught about how we should interpret experiences of the deceased that are often called "ghost sightings." These could be cases of God allowing the soul of the deceased to communicate with those on earth, or they could be examples of demonic activity. In any case, the Church has definitely taught that it is a grave sin to attempt two-way communication with ghosts or spirits (CCC 2116).

371 *City of God*, 13:20.

372 *Commentary on Matthew*, 13:1.

373 *On Belief in the Resurrection*, 127.

374 *A Treatise on the Soul*, 31.

375 *Against Heresies*, 2:33:1.

376 Robert Todd Carroll, "Ian Stevenson (1918–2007)," The Skeptic's Dictionary, https://skepdic.com/stevenson.html.

377 *A Treatise on the Soul*, 30.

378 General Audience, July 28, 1999, https://www.vatican.va/content/john-paul-ii/en/audiences/1999/documents/hf_jp-ii_aud_28071999.html.

379 Joseph Ratzinger, *Eschatology: Death and Eternal Life*, 2nd ed. (Washington, D.C.: CUA Press, 2007), 230.

380 The Deuterocanon comprises seven books: Tobit, Judith, Wisdom, Sirach, Baruch, 1 and 2 Maccabees, as well as portions of Daniel and Esther that Catholics believe to be inspired Scripture but Protestants do not. For more on this subject see Gary Michuta, *The Case for the Deuterocanon: Evidence and Arguments* (Livonia, MI: Nikaria Press, 2015).

381 See, for example, *Treatise on the Soul*, 58.

382 One could argue that the loss refers to future rewards in heaven, but this interpretation does not take into account the temporal loss associated with the fiery judgment on the Last Day. See John Salza, *The Biblical Basis for Purgatory* (Charlotte, NC: Saint Benedict Press, 2009), 124–132.

383 Gehenna was in the valley of Hinnom, which 2 Kings 23:10 and Jeremiah 7:31–32 refer to as a site of child sacrifice.

384 General Audience, July 28, 1999.

385 Even when Paul talks about the wicked being "destroyed," he clarifies his point saying, "They shall suffer the punishment of eternal destruction and *exclusion* from the presence of the Lord and from the glory of his might" (2 Thess. 1:9).

386 See, for example, "What Did Jesus Teach About Hell?" *Watchtower Online Library*, November 1, 2008, 7–8, wol.jw.org/en/wol/d/r1/lp-e/2008802.

387 C.S. Lewis, *The Great Divorce* (San Francisco, CA: HarperSanFrancisco, 2001).

388 See, for example, Frederick W. Norris's entry on "Apokatastasis" in *The Westminster Handbook to Origen*, ed. John Anthony McGuckin (London: Westminster John Knox Press, 2004).

389 Richard J. Bauckham, "Universalism: A Historical Survey," *Themelios* 4, no. 2 (January 1979): 48.

390 Hans Urs von Balthasar, *Dare We Hope "That All Men Be Saved"?* (San Francisco, CA: Ignatius Press, 1988), 131.

391 Ibid., 213.

392 Pope John Paul II, *Crossing the Threshold of Hope* (New York: Knopf, 1994), 185.

393 *War*, 6:3:5, pp. 288–310.

394 *Histories*, 5:13.

395 Benedict XVI, *Jesus of Nazareth*, vol. 1, chap. 9.

396 Joseph Ratzinger, "Theological Commentary," in Congregation for the Doctrine of the Faith, *The Message of Fatima*, June 26, 2000, https://www.vatican.va/roman_curia/congregations/cfaith/documents/rc_con_cfaith_doc_20000626_message-fatima_en.html.

397 Peter S. Williamson, *Revelation* (Grand Rapids, MI: Baker Academic, 2015), 342.